A~Z
of
Grenada
Heritage

Macmillan Caribbean A–Z Series

A~Z of Grenada Heritage

John Angus Martin

MACMILLAN
CARIBBEAN

Macmillan Education
Between Towns Road, Oxford OX4 3PP
A division of Macmillan Publishers Limited
Companies and representatives throughout the world

www.macmillan-caribbean.com

ISBN: 978-0-333-79252-0

First published 2007

Designed by Richard Jervis
Typeset by Amanda Easter Design Ltd.
Map by Peter Harper
Cover design by Gary Fielder
Cover photographs courtesy of Hulton Getty, PA Photos and the author.

Printed and bound in Thailand

2011 2010 2009 2008 2007
10 9 8 7 6 5 4 3 2 1

Contents

Preface

Tim Tim... Papa welcome. And how are you my children? I am going to tell you a story, a wonderful story, about a beautiful island, about three beautiful islands in the Caribbean Sea. Oh, they have plenty beautiful islands in the Caribbean Sea, but these three, these three are different, these three are special, especially the one they call Grenada.

And why is Grenada so special? Well, that is what this story is about. Now, it's just a story, you hear? So don't go saying how I telling lies. I just telling you what other people tell me. But I don't think big people go' lie just so, so it must be true.[1]

Since achieving independence in 1974 the tiny Caribbean state of Grenada, Carriacou and Petite Martinique has been propelled into the international spotlight by a number of remarkable events, though its romp on the world stage seems in stark contrast to its small size. In March 1979 it became the first state in the English-speaking Caribbean to experience a successful coup d'état. For the next four-and-a-half years, it figured into the affairs of superpowers as Cuba and the Soviet Union became ideological and financial supporters and the United States increasingly became an adversary. US President Reagan, in speeches in March and April 1983, made references to Grenada and the growing Cuban and Soviet influences there and the potential threat to democracy in the region. He insisted that 'It isn't nutmeg that's at stake in the Caribbean and Central America; it is the United States national security', and questioned the possible military uses of the Point Salines International Airport by Cuba and the Soviet Union. In October 1983 the country exploded into world news headlines when its charismatic prime minister, Maurice Bishop, was placed under house arrest and subsequently executed by a faction within his own government. A few days later Grenada was invaded by the US military, and for the first time 'East' met 'West' when Cuban 'soldiers'/militia fought against invading US troops.

Having recovered from the political chaos of the 1970s and 1980s, Grenada suffered a devastating setback in September 2004 when Hurricane Ivan scored a direct hit and left the islands in ruins; in July 2005 Hurricane Emily caused further damage. These events have created immense interest for students of history and politics from around the world as is evident by the numerous books and articles so far written on the Revolution and US military intervention. There is, however, a growing interest in many aspects of Grenada's history and culture, and a book of this nature, incorporating the varied aspects of culture, history, the natural environment and politics, will be a valuable resource to anyone interested in these islands.

The threat of the disappearance of the islands' cultural and natural heritage, as in the cases of Shango and the Grenada dove, respectively, have made it absolutely necessary that we begin to preserve and conserve these unique attributes for future generations. They are a valued inheritance to Grenadians as a source of pride and identity, as well as of potential monetary value if managed appropriately as a heritage tourism product that visitors can appreciate and respect. In this fast evolving world where the global village is quickly becoming a reality, it is difficult to define our own particular community because its uniqueness is disappearing before our eyes. This book is meant only as a first step towards establishing a framework for the preservation of our islands' natural beauty and cultural heritage.

There is so much more about Grenada, Carriacou and Petite Martinique I could have included, but I had to confine myself to the people, events and places that have had the greatest impact on our historical environment. The inclusion of elements of the natural milieu—flora and fauna—was based on criteria of both beauty and frequency of appearance, and in many cases their impact on the economy and the ecology of the islands. Though Grenada shares many of its social and political institutions with the countries of the region, it nonetheless displays marked differences and uniqueness. It exhibits singular characteristics like the Big Drum Dance and the Grenada dove because of its geographical separation.

I have tried to represent culture and history across social class lines, illustrating the evolving nature of the society. I have attempted to capture the overwhelming influences of Africa and Europe, and to a lesser extent those of India and the Americas on Grenadian identity. Entries include the AMERINDIANS who first made these islands their home; ANANSI stories from West Africa that have provided entertainment for generations; prominent leaders like Julien FÉDON, T A MARRYSHOW, Sir Eric GAIRY and Maurice BISHOP; the natural beauty of GRAND ÉTANG NATIONAL PARK and GRANDE ANSE BEACH, which are so inviting to visitors to our shores; the religious celebrations of FISHERMAN'S BIRTHDAY and EASTER; the ceremonies of the BIG DRUM DANCE and SHANGO that beat out the rhythms of Africa; the festivals of CARNIVAL and CARRIACOU REGATTA which unite all in national celebration; the bitter but tangy taste of DAMSEL, the sweet taste of sugar apple, and the red Christmas drink of sorrel, spiced with RUM, that all define us as Caribbean, but more specifically as Grenadians (Carriacouans and Petite Martinicans).

[1] Paul Keens-Douglas, 'The Eighth Day', *Twice Upon a Time: Poetry and Short Stories*. Keensdee, Port-of-Spain, Trinidad, 1989.

A major asset of this book is its arrangement, with entries alphabetically listed as in a dictionary to afford easy access. Words or phrases in upper case/capital letters throughout the book mean that there is an extended entry. To be consistent throughout I have adopted the standard spellings for patwa/Creole words as presented by Richard Allsopp in his monumental work *Dictionary of Caribbean English Usage*. The term Grenada may refer to the major island or the tri-island state; its meaning will be made clear in its context.

This book, it is hoped, will offer a great deal to many people: to Grenadians, at home and abroad, old and young alike, it affords a chance to reminisce, pass on a heritage, or explore a rich legacy; to the researcher it is a source book; to the visitor it is a guidebook to the islands and its people, culture and history; to the historian it offers a diverse, but coherent look at the past; and to the trivia buff it is a treasure trove.

Lastly, I would like to comment on the facts and stories I have assembled here. In the over ten years of research for this book I have stumbled upon facts, figures, folklore and oral history that were often confusing, conflicting and sometimes absurd, yet fascinating. Oral history often conflicted with written history, and folklore and facts were jumbled, making separation often difficult. The reliance on certain secondary sources sometimes, the only sources available, was unavoidable. Yet, through it all, I have made an exhaustive effort to verify all the stories, facts and folklore to the best available knowledge. I hope that when readers detect inconsistencies, they will bring them to my attention so that this book can become a more complete and accurate repository of a people's history, culture and the natural environment.

Acknowledgements

A book of this nature, incorporating so many aspects of a country's history, culture and the natural environment, could not be written without the many historians, travel writers, naturalists, journalists, folklorists, researchers and civil servants who have been profuse in their recording of stories, vital statistics, oddities and insights over the years. This book is a tribute to the many named and nameless individuals.

I am indebted to many people who provided significant contributions to the research, writing and publication of this book. I extend my appreciation to them all. To the memory of my mother, Jean Albertina Martin, I acknowledge the cultural heritage she so joyfully passed on to me, and the ability and desire to remember the past. And to my father, Venis Malcolm Martin, I am indebted for the love of agriculture and the natural environment. I must acknowledge a fellow traveller, my brother Liam, for supporting me in this pursuit, especially through his dialogues and by his example. He has also read the manuscript and I am grateful for his many corrections and suggestions. My sister Janice and her husband Gregory Williams, and brothers Wayne and his wife Judy, and Raphael and his wife Yon Sik have aided this effort in numerous ways. For the love and support of family I am forever grateful. David Lord and Louis Charles aided me tremendously, and Hubert Xavier has 'Certainly' been a friend. Andrew Neckles and Patrick James have been friends for as long as I can remember and help keep the memories of Grenada alive. Dr James D Pitt and Jean Pitt have aided me on my many visits to Grenada, always ready to offer a place of refuge. Thanks to John Mark King for sharing the privileges of American University, and Robert Bartholomai for always willing to oblige a favour. Dr Haile Larebo, Dr Suzanne Sinke, Dr Steve Marks, Dr J C O Nyankori, Anita Knight, Celia and William Medford, the late Willie Weeks, Roland Lewis, Shaine St. Bernard, Robert Claussen, Rafael Sanchez-Sola, Monica Martin, Robert Pierre, Thelma Philips, the late Dr Alister Hughes, Joslyn Nicholson, Marylyn Winsborrow, Haroun Hallack, Melanie Hill, Nellie Payne, Sir Reginald and Lady Palmer, Kent and Brenda Joseph, Beverley Steele, Jean Fisher, Michael Jessamy and Valentine Joseph provided useful suggestions, stories, support and assistance.

I would like to thank the Grenada National Library, Grenada National Museum, Marryshow Memorial Library, Grenada, the LDS Family History Library, and the Beinecke Lesser Antilles Collection at Hamilton College, New York for the use of their collections, and the Spiceislander Talkshop for its lively discussions on Grenadian history and culture. I owe a great debt of gratitude to Abdul and Ruth Kanu who read an early draft of the manuscript and suggested valuable corrections. Sophie Lemesre and Jean-Marc David shared their French language and culture that I might more fully understand my own heritage. I would like to add a special thank you to Janice Thacker, Victoria Hamilton, Tracy James and Betty Carson, the many reference librarians, the staff of Acquisitions/Receiving, especially Wilma Burkett, all of Clemson University, South Carolina. Also, thank you to the staff of the Cushing Memorial Library, Texas A&M University, and the many friends and supporters at the Peace Corps. I also acknowledge Dr Thomas Lacher, Jr and Dr Kandice Karl for their inspiration and vote of confidence. Of the numerous others who contributed in various ways, I would like to specially acknowledge the Kennedy family, especially Connie and Neil, and welcome them into my Grenadian family. Through it all Elizabeth, a wellspring of love and understanding, has been by my side to give of her undying support of love and words. And at the end of it all we celebrated the birth of our son, Yeredh Liam Martin.

About the Author

JOHN ANGUS MARTIN was born and grew up in St. George's, Grenada, where he attended the J W Fletcher Memorial School and Presentation Brothers' College before emigrating to Brooklyn, New York with his family in 1978. He graduated in 1986 with a BSc in Biological Sciences from the State University of New York at Stony Brook, Long Island. He spent the next three years as a Peace Corps volunteer in Sierra Leone, West Africa, teaching at an agricultural institute and as an agricultural extension agent to subsistence farmers in rural villages. He has travelled widely in west and east Africa for work and as a visitor. He holds master's degrees in History and Agricultural and Applied Economics from Clemson University, South Carolina. He currently works as a Country Desk Officer in the Africa Region of the US Peace Corps. He returns to Grenada often to carry out research on the country's history and culture. This is his first book.

PETITE MARTINIQUE
CARRIACOU
Hillsborough
LEVERA I. (Sugar loaf)
GREEN I.
SANDY I.
Levera Bay
Sauteurs
Levera Pond
La Fortune
Grenada Bay
Duquesne Bay
Morne Fendue
Chantimelle
Union
Samaritan
Mt Rich Estate
La Taste
St Mark's Mts.
ST. PATRICK
Lake Antoine
St Patrick R.
Tivoli
La Poterie
ST. MARK
Conference
Mt St. Catherine 2,757 ft (840 m)
Pearls Airport (disused)
Gouyave
North
ST. ANDREW
Paradise
Great River Bay
ST. JOHN
Telescope
Telescope Point
Great R.
Palmiste
Windsor
Grenville
Mt Gregory 2,240 ft (683 m)
Belvidere
L'Esterre
Grenville Bay
Grand Bay
La Digue
Grand Roy
Soubise
Birch Grove
MARQUIS I.
Marigot
St James
Bellevue
Concord Falls
Concord
Mt Qua Qua
St Andrew's Bay
Fédon's Camp 2,509 ft (765 m)
Halifax Harbour
Grand Etang Lake
Mt Lebanon 2,347 ft (715 m)
ST. GEORGE
Brizan
Gt. Bacolet Bay
Willis
Mt Sinai 2,308 ft (703 m)
Happy Hill
Crochu
Beausejour
Molinière
La Tante R.
Crochu Harbour
ST. DAVID
Grand Mal
Grand Mal Bay
Fontenoy
St David's
Tempe
Perdmontemps
St George's
St Paul's
Corinth
Richmond Hill
Grande Anse Bay
Westerhall
Quarantine Point
Woburn
Morne Rouge Bay
Canoe Bay
Point Salines International Airport
ADAM I.
HOG I.
Egmont Harbour
CALIVIGNY I.
Black Bay
Prickly Bay
GLOVER I.
Scale
0 1 2 3 km
0 1 2 3 miles
Parish boundary
National capital
Major town
Large village
Place of interest
Body of water

List of Abbreviations

AC	(Interim) Advisory Council
AHS	(St. George's) Anglican High School
AS	Associated Statehood
b.	born (date of birth)
BCE	Before Common Era (syn. with Before Christian Era)
BWI	British West Indies
c.	circa; about, approximately
C&PM	Carriacou and Petite Martinique
CBE	Commander of the Order of the British Empire
CC	Crown Colony
CE	Common Era (syn. with Anno Domini)
CHS	Carriacou Historical Society
CM	Chief Minister
CMG	Commander of the Order of St. Michael and St. George
Co.	Company
d.	died (date of death)
EC	Eastern Caribbean
Eng.	English (language)
est.	established
f.	founded
Fr.	French (language)
Fr. Cr.	French Creole (language)
FWI	Federation of the West Indies
GBSS	Grenada Boys Secondary School
G'da	Grenada
GDF	Grenada Defence Force
GDP	Gross Domestic Product
GG	Governor General
GHS	Grenada Historical Society
GLL	Grenada Literary League
GMMWU	Grenada Manual and Mental Workers' Union (later GMMIWU)
GMMIWU	Grenada Manual, Maritime and Intellectual Workers' Union (formerly GMMWU)
GNP	Grenada National Party
GNT	Grenada National Trust
GOG	Government of Grenada
Gov./gov.	Governor
Govt.	government
GSC	Grenada Supreme Court
GSF	Grenada Sugar Factory
GULP	Grenada United Labour Party
Hin.	Hindi (language)
HS	High School
Is.	Island
Is. Car.	Island Carib (language)
JEWEL	Joint Effort for Welfare, Education and Liberation
Lt. Gov.	Lieutenant Governor
MBE	Member of the Order of the British Empire
MBPM	Maurice Bishop Patriotic Movement
MCC	(T A) Marryshow Community College
MPs	Members of Parliament
NDC	National Democratic Congress
NJM	New Jewel Movement
NNP	New National Party
NP	National Park
OAS	Organization of American States
OBE	Officer of the Order of the British Empire
OECS	Organisation of Eastern Caribbean States
OM	Order of Merit
OREL	Organisation for Revolutionary Education and Liberation
ORS	Old Representative System
PA	People's Alliance
PB	Political Bureau (of the NJM)
PBC	Presentation Brothers' College
Pg.	Portuguese (language)
PM	Prime Minister
PRA	People's Revolutionary Army
PRG	People's Revolutionary Government
PSIA	Point Salines International Airport
RC	Roman Catholic (religion)
RGA	Representative Government Association
RMC	Revolutionary Military Council
SGU	St. George's University
sp./spp.	species
Sp./Am. Sp.	Spanish/American Spanish (language)
St.	Saint/Street
SWWU	Seaman and Waterfront Workers' Union
syn.	synonymous (with)/synonym
TAWU	Technical and Allied Workers' Union
UK	United Kingdom
UN	United Nations
US	United States (of America)
UWI	University of the West Indies
Var.	variety, cultivar (plants)
WIC	West India Company (French)
Yor.	Yoruba (language)

Measurements/Symbols

ft	foot/feet	ha	hectare
g	gram	kg	kilogram
m	metre/million	km	kilometre
oz	ounce (s)		
/	and/or	?</<	possibly/derived from

Dedication

To my mother and father for a Grenadian heritage
Through which flows the majesty of the Thames
The strength of the Niger
The natural beauty of the Highlands
The elegance of the Seine
And the creation of a new world.

Also to Rex, Janice, Gail, Wayne,
Raphael, Liam, Elizabeth,
And my son, Yeredh.

A

ADAMS, Ferguson (c. 1890-1983) 'Sugar Adams' was probably the most legendary Big Drum Dance performer and 'certainly one of the greatest musicians that the Caribbean has produced.' At the age of 12 years he learned to play the drum, and thereafter excelled on the cot/cut drum, the lead drum in the Big Drum ensemble. With the Mt. Royal drummers he achieved his greatest fame in the 1950s and 1960s. Though he is remembered most for his drumming, Adams was an accomplished dancer and singer. In 1975 he and other BIG DRUM DANCE performers were honoured at the American Museum of Natural History, USA. He has been described as being 'one of the most knowledgeable old heads on the Big Drum' and 'probably the best known Carriacouan to folklorists and anthropologists'. Together with his common-law wife Mary FORTUNE, they were known as 'Carriacou's premier musical couple'. Recordings featuring Adams' drumming include *Carriacou Calaloo*, *Saraca* and *Tombstone Feast*.[51, 85, 153, 302, 349]

Adams playing the cot drum

ADVISORY COUNCIL The Advisory Council (AC) was established on 15 November 1983 as an interim/caretaker government after the US-led military INTERVENTION three weeks earlier. Its primary objectives were the restoration of public services and economic institutions, and the preparations for parliamentary elections. With Governor General SCOON in his constitutional role as (the representative of the) HEAD OF STATE, the nine-member AC (made up of technocrats with diverse political views), chaired by Nicholas BRATHWAITE (who took over when Sir Alister McIntyre did not assume the chairmanship position due to illness), was on par with a constitutional representative government, possessing executive and legislative powers. It was confronted with a number of pressing problems; paramount among these was national security. It also had to contend with the popular view that its decisions were sanctioned, if not dictated by the US military command. The AC's major policy objective was the dismantling of PRG state-run enterprises through privatisation and closures and removing any and all vestiges of Socialism, orchestrating a clear ideological change. Though there were apprehensions about holding early elections, many believed that needed foreign investment would be withheld until a stable government was in place. Thus the AC began the formidable task of voter registration and election preparations. On 27 November 1984 the AC was dissolved effective 4 December 1984, clearing the way for ELECTIONS on 3 December. Though the AC was marginally successful overall, its notable achievements included creating a period of calm and security, the opening of the PSIA, successful elections and the restoration of parliamentary democracy, especially in only a year.[100, 111, 306]

AFRICAN HERITAGE Of Grenada's present population roughly 82 per cent are of African ancestry, with another 12 percent exhibiting partial descent. African slaves were first brought to Grenada after the mid-1500s by Island CARIBS who captured them from the Spanish and continued their enslavement. In the early 1650s the French brought slaves to Grenada, but it was not until the 1660s that appreciable numbers of African slaves arrived, thereby establishing chattel SLAVERY. The first census in 1669 listed a slave population of 222 (45 per cent of the population), and by 1690 the African slaves and their descendants had surpassed the whites, dominating the population thereafter.

Though the total number of Africans brought to the islands is not known, one estimate places the number around 124,621 for the period 1650 to 1867. Among these various Africans were AKAN and YORUBA peoples. Between 1836 and 1865, just over 3,200 Africans entered Grenada as LIBERATED AFRICANS or as part of the process of INDENTURED IMMIGRATION. By 1881 there were only 807 African-born residents, gradually decreasing to 36 by 1924, and disappearing by the 1930s. Yet, elements of African cultures have persisted in Grenada despite slavery, colonialism and concerted efforts by the white PLANTOCRACY and established churches to destroy them. Many aspects of Grenada's Creole culture have been infused with a rich diversity of Africanisms. Though greatly altered by time, place and history, these African survivals have persisted in the religious belief of SHANGO, the sorcerous practice of OBEAH, foods like CONKIE and COU-COU, ANANSI STORIES, BIG DRUM DANCE, CALYPSO, LANGUAGE, PARENTS' PLATE, SUPERSTITIONS like DWENN and MAMA-GLO, and various other folk traditions. A number of African plants and animals, including the watermelon, ackee, sesame, okra, AFRICAN TULIP TREE, KOLA NUT, MONA MONKEY and the mabouya lizard were brought to Grenada, altering the natural environment as the descendants of the African slaves have transformed the social milieu. Since the 1970s and the emergence of BLACK POWER and RASTAFARIANISM, Grenadians have begun to embrace their African heritage after centuries of denigration.

AFRICAN TULIP TREE (*Spathodea campanulata*) is native to West Africa and was brought to the Caribbean by the early 1800s. It can be found across the island, most noticeably when it produces an abundant display of its spectacular red tulip-shaped blossoms several times during the year, hence another of its names flame-of-the-forest. The tree grows to about 50 ft (14 m), producing large brown boat-shaped seed pods. Fountain tree, another common name, is derived from the flower buds' ability to retain water that spurts out when squeezed, creating a fountain-like effect. Its FRENCH CREOLE name bâton-de-sorcié (<Fr. Cr.: 'witch stick') originates in the folk belief in the tree's association with witchcraft or OBEAH.

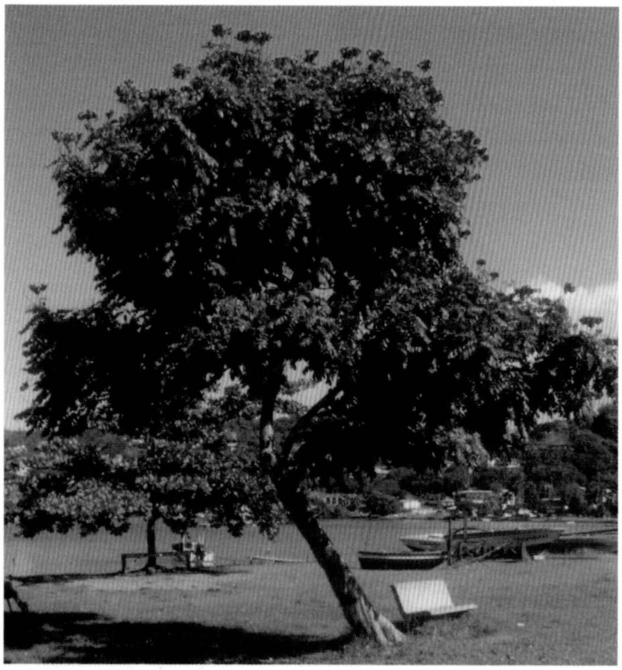

African Tulip Tree in bloom

AGOUTI (*Dasyprocta aguti*) is presently extinct in Grenada as a result of predation by man and possibly the MONGOOSE. It was probably introduced by AMERINDIANS hundreds of years ago as part of their 'live food' since it is easily tamed. This solitary rodent, once confined to the forests of Grand Étang and Mt. St. Catherine, lives on seeds, berries, leaves and roots. The agouti (<Guarani *acuti*) is known for its speed and endurance as affirmed by the popular saying 'fas' like agouti'. It has a short naked tail, coarse black hair, small ears, and hoof-like claws. Adults measure between15-24 inches (40-60 cm) and weigh 4.5-11 lb (2-5 kg). Some have expressed interest in seeing this once indigenous rodent reintroduced, among them naturalists and hunters, the latter desiring it as a game species.

AGRICULTURE Endowed with no exploitable mineral resources (though the hope of finding deposits of crude oil are ever present), commercial agriculture has been the strength of Grenada's economy for most of its modern history. The islands' settlement by the French and British established plantation agriculture, which has dominated the economy beginning with TOBACCO and followed consecutively by INDIGO, SUGAR CANE, COTTON, COCOA and COFFEE. The demise of many of these crops led to the establishment of new ones, particularly spices like NUTMEG and CINNAMON, and still later BANANA. Following EMANCIPATION former slaves gradually gained access to land, some through LAND SETTLEMENTS, and created a well developed landed peasantry predominantly engaged in subsistence agriculture. They produce much of the islands' food crops, including 'provisions' like BREADFRUIT, YAMS, CASSAVA, and SWEET POTATO, and fruits like MANGO, AVOCADO, PLUMS, GOLDEN APPLES and ANNONA. Many of these fruits and vegetables are important to the informal intra-islands trade known as TRAFFICKING.

Adverse effects in the agricultural sector and the development of other industries, particularly TOURISM, have led to the decline in importance of agriculture; its share of the GDP, recording 25 per cent in 1984, declined to 8.5

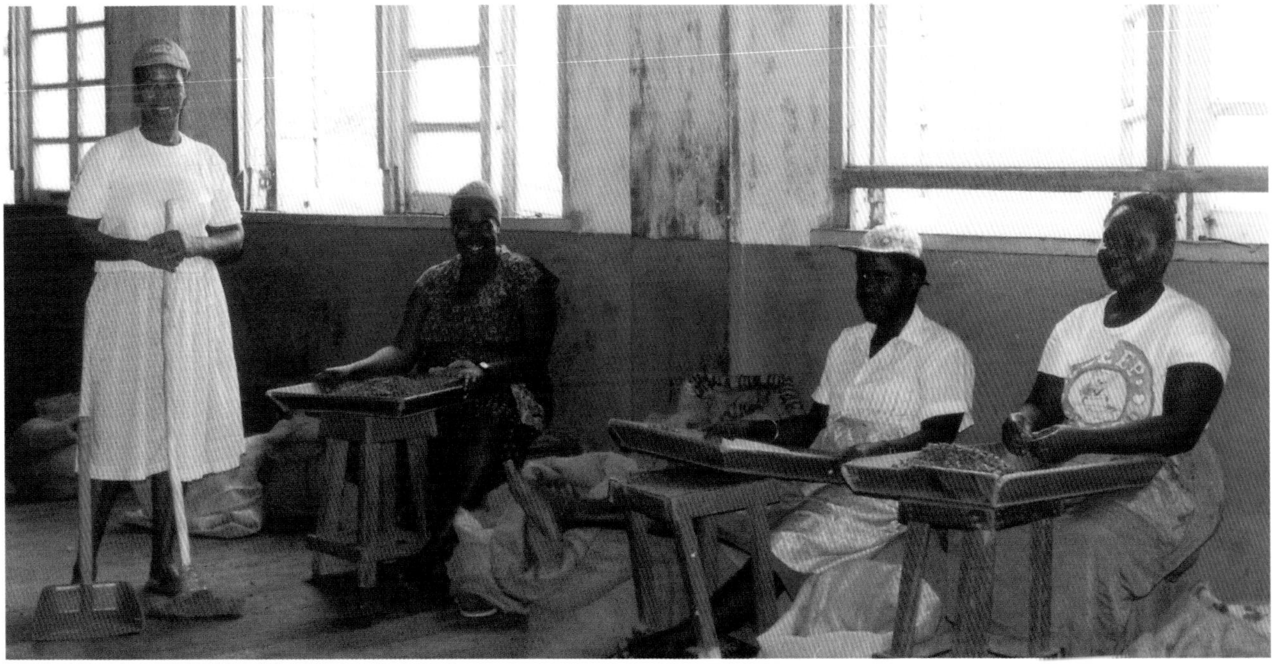

Agricultural workers sorting mace at the Gouyave Nutmeg Processing Plant

per cent by 2004, and continues to decline. Agriculture presently accounts for just under 45 per cent of exports and 17 per cent of employment, having experienced tremendous setbacks; it accounted for 90 per cent of exports in 1984. Agriculture remains one of Grenada's most valuable resources, but is confronted with a number of problems, including underdeveloped infrastructure and markets, low productivity, high production costs, scarcity of labour, and periodic damages from natural disasters like HURRICANES as was the case in 2004 when HURRICANE IVAN devastated the sector. Hundreds of hectares of cultivable land remain under-utilised while unemployment is a problem, especially among the young who perceive employment in the sector as unattractive. Acreage classified as agricultural lands have declined from 71 to 41 percent between 1961 and 1995, illustrating the decreasing importance of the sector. C&PM have had a similar agricultural history, but due to a drier CLIMATE have relied on cotton, LIMES and groundnuts as cash crops, and CORN and PIGEON PEAS as food crops. Livestock and FISHERIES are presently important to both. In Grenada fisheries rank second to crops in importance, with smaller contributions from the livestock and forestry sub-sectors.[14, 27, 29, 35, 153, 333]

AJOUPA/'JOUPA Historically represented as a shed, thatched hut, or 'lean-to', this is usually a temporary and hastily erected wall-less structure. Over the years the name has been applied to various structures with tapia (mud) walls and thatched roof and with walls made of wood and roofed with corrugated iron or 'galvanise'. The ajoupa (< Is.Car. *ajouppa*: 'shed') is usually located in the backyard or on a farm and used to shelter from rain while gardening or as a farm kitchen/storeroom. It also refers to 'a broken down old house', or is a reference to a modest house as in the saying, 'All I want is a little 'joupa, a good woman, and two children to make me happy.'

AKAN people, belonging primarily to present-day Ghana, have left an indelible cultural imprint on Grenadian society as a result of African slavery. The Akan comprise various but linguistically related peoples who are known by their tribal names, the most significant being the Asante/Ashante/Ashanti, Fante and Akuapem. The most noticeable cultural survival is the folkloric character of Anansi portrayed in ANANSI STORIES. At least four personal names have survived as family names: Quashie, Cudjoe, Cuffie and Quamina, all corresponding to the Akan (Twi) male day-names Kwesi/kwashi: 'Sunday,' Kojo: 'Monday,' Kofi: 'Friday' and Kwami: 'Saturday,' respectively. Up until the early 1900s Quashie was used as a derogatory name for the stereotypical unsophisticated black, like Sambo was in the US. Twi words like mumu (*e-mumu*: 'deaf and dumb'), cocobay (*kokobé*: 'leprosy,' i.e. skin disease), and asham (*o-siám*: 'parched, ground and sweetened corn') have also survived, as have PROVERBS & SAYINGS, SUPERSTITIONS, riddles and idiomatic expressions long since incorporated into the islands' rich Creole culture. Traditions like breaking an egg for good luck, MAROON, 'wet the ground' or pouring libations to the ancestors, and sacrificing chickens are common to the Akan as they once were to many Grenadians. Ancestral reverence for the Koromanti/Coromanti tribe or nation, considered the first nation, remains a significant part of the BIG DRUM DANCE. It is the opening Nation Dance of any ceremony when Cromanti CUDJOE, an 'ancestor' of that nation, is summoned to 'wake up.' Coromanti, regarded as a tribal name, was the generic name applied to slaves taken from the former Gold Coast region and historically referred to a British slave port located east of the infamous Elmina slave castle in present-day Ghana at Cormantin. Satire, especially political satire essential to CALYPSO and extempore, can be found in traditional Asante society like the *Apo* rites 'where ridicule of authority was especially sanctioned and encouraged for a limited period'. The impact and survival of Akan culture in Grenada may have been due to the power of and fear for their practice of OBEAH and their forceful presence. Quobna CUGOANO was one of the thousands of Akans brought to Grenada as slaves.[154, 228]

ALL SAINTS'/SOULS' DAYS Annual Christian festivals held on the first and second of November to honour the Christian saints and celebrate the souls of the departed. All Saints' Day is a national ceremony at which many celebrate requiem masses at the RC and Anglican churches, where candles are blessed and the names of the deceased read. Following mass are candlelight processions to cemeteries across the islands. Throughout the evening cemeteries are transformed by light and chatter as relatives and friends of the dead gather to remember them by burning candles. In CARRIACOU many still practise the African ancestral rituals of 'wetting the ground' or pouring libations on graves and asking the ancestors for their protection, and celebrating the BIG DRUM DANCE. Children carry packets of asham—sweetened, parched, ground corn—to the cemetery, and are known to offer each other a taste, hoping to cause coughing fits. On All Souls' Day candles are lit on the steps of homes in the hope that the deceased will 'find their way home.'

ALLSPICE (*Pimenta dioica* syn. *P. officinalis*) is an evergreen tree native to the region and grows to 23-32 ft (7-10 m). Its name is derived from its reputed mixed aromatic flavours of CLOVE, CINNAMON and NUTMEG, reflecting its complex aroma. The globular fruit is picked before ripening and dried in the sun until the small kidney-shaped berries turn reddish brown. The pungent berries are used to flavour confectionery, foods, meat products, and as an ingredient in curry powder. Extracts from both the leaf and berry are used in flavouring essence and perfume. Its antiseptic and anaesthetic qualities have led to its uses in dentistry and as a carminative in FOLK MEDICINE. Berries are harvested from July to August. Other common names include pimento (<Sp. *pimiento*: 'pepper') and Jamaican pepper. It is related to BAYLEAF.

Allspice and other spices have earned Grenada the name 'Isle of Spice'

ALMOND (*Terminalia catappa*) A seashore shade tree introduced from SE Asia at the end of the 1700s and bears no relation to the commercial almond (*Prunus dulcis*). The tropical or Malabar almond is valued as an ornamental, but it is also an important component of the remaining scattered littoral woodland. It grows to over 60 ft (18 m), with large leaves that provide shade when planted in front yards. Inside the soft edible yellow-green skin of the fruit is a thick corky shell, within which is a small oblong seed. The light brown, mildly flavoured kernel is rarely made use of due to the difficulty in removing it, except by children who extract it by breaking open the fibrous shell. The almond fruits between July and December, and is found on many BEACHES where it provides shade and helps control beach erosion. It is also known as West Indian almond.

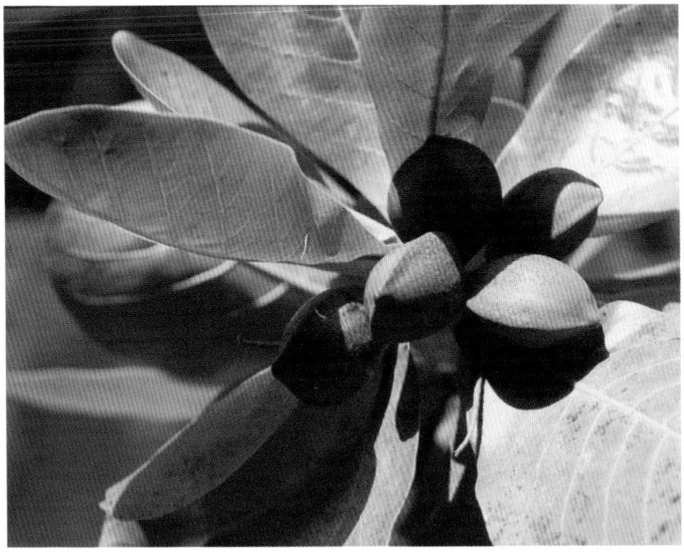

Almond tree with unripe fruits

ALMSHOUSES Public almshouses were created by the 1860 Poor House Act due to the increasing numbers of the criminally and mentally insane, destitute and invalid. Prior to this date almshouses were funded by private voluntary contributions. The abandonment of the RICHMOND HILL FORTS in 1854 made available space that the colonial government 'converted' for civilian uses. The housing of these public institutions in the old forts and surrounding facilities led to the area being called 'Institution Hill'. The public 'Poor House' was situated in the old military barracks at Fort Matthew in 1861. In 1933 its name was changed to the House of Refuge and in 1954 to the Richmond Home for the Elderly. It is the only facility for indigent incurables in the islands and houses about 100 chronically ill, elderly handicapped and psychiatric patients who need constant medical care.

The first Lunatic Asylum (est. 1850) was located on the CARENAGE, and in 1855 was removed to Richmond Hill. In 1880 the Central Lunatic Asylum was removed to Fort Matthew and for the next century it functioned as the Richmond Hill Mental Hospital, but was variously referred to as the 'Crazy/Mad House'. In 1983 US military planes, during the INTERVENTION, 'accidentally' bombed the compound, causing the deaths of 16 patients. In May 1987 it was removed to Mt. Gay to a new 80-bed facility, the Mt. Gay Hospital. The Dorothy Hopkin Centre, established in 1963 as the Kennedy Home, provides for the care of the physically and mentally handicapped. It was located just beneath Fort Matthew, but in 1997 moved into its new facilities at Tempe, St. George.[55, 356]

AMERINDIANS The word Amerindian (<American indian) is used to group the indigenous peoples of the Americas, among them meso-indians (popularly, but incorrectly referred to as Ciboney), Island Arawaks/Tainos, Island Caribs and Galibis who inhabited the Caribbean islands. A growing body of archaeological, linguistic, historical and ethnographic evidence has shed light on the so-called pre-history of the region. Yet that period remains no less daunting than the fervently debated post-1492 era of European colonisation and destruction of the region's Amerindian peoples. Much remains shrouded in an on-going debate that is likely to continue for quite some time.

Human habitation of the Caribbean islands dates to at least 3000 BCE, but the earliest occupation of Grenada was probably about 2000 BCE. No evidence has been unearthed to identify who exactly they were, but they may have been meso-indians of the Archaic or Stone Age. Though evidence of their occupation of the Caribbean has been found in other islands, no scholarly archaeological evidence has been found in Grenada because attempts to date have concentrated on ceramic cultures. 'Stone celts and axes' collected by amateur archaeologist Leon Wilder, according to Cody, 'could possibly reflect an Archaic occupation of the island. Unfortunately, the artefacts lack provenience.' Relying on the sea for fish and the land for food gathering, these hunter-gatherers possessed no knowledge of pottery or crop cultivation. This pre-ceramic people were stone and shell workers, fashioning their tools from flint, marine shell and rock. They are believed to have lived in small familial bands and resided in caves like the one at Black Bay, St. John.

Analyses of ceramics or pottery styles excavated from Grenada suggest that three distinct periods or cultures existed; the large quantities found also suggest that population densities may have been higher than some of Grenada's northern neighbours. Though there is still much debate on who are the groups represented, the archaeological nomenclature defines the various periods as Cedrosan Saladoid (c.100 BCE-650 CE), Troumassan Troumassoid (c.650-1100 CE), and Suazan Troumassoid (c.1100-1450 CE). The Cedrosan culture developed from the Saladoid who, it is believed, were pushed out from the mainland by the expanding Barrancoid peoples and arrived in the Caribbean from Venezuela around the first century current era. Evidence of the Cedrosan Saladoid culture has been unearthed at the Pearls Amerindian site (a large trading and manufacturing centre for beads and jewellery), Black Point, Point Salines and SEAMOON, St. Andrew. A second phase is evident in the changing ceramics after 650 CE, and manifests itself in the Troumassan Troumassoid subseries, of which the Calivigny series (see CALIVIGNY ISLAND) is now identified as a complex. It is associated with the group popularly identified as Island Arawaks. They were slash-and-burn cultivators of CASSAVA, SWEET POTATO, CORN and vegetables, and supplemented their diet with CRABS, SEA EGGS, SEA TURTLES, LAMBIE and fin fishes. The Calivigny culture may have depended more on the sea and practised a 'mixed economy,' more so than the earlier Cedrosan Saladoid. The Troumassan Troumassiod (<Troumassee, St. Lucia) did not possess knowledge of metallurgy, fashioning their tools from bone, wood, stone and shell. Their 'art'/religious paintings or PETROGLYPHS can still be seen stencilled on rocks throughout Grenada.

Amerindian family, c. 1780

The Suazan Troumassoid period (<Savannah Suazey, St. Patrick) was thought to represent the people commonly identified as Island CARIBS and was associated with the migration of Cariban speakers from the Guianas. Others have argued that the Island Caribs may be purely a 'local development', and related to the Taino with whom they shared language roots. The Suazan Troumassoid is no longer associated with the Island Caribs, and ceramics tentively identified with them (Cayo found in St.Vincent) have not been unearthed in Grenada, despite the fact that they persisted in Grenada into the eighteenth century. The Galibis, who arrived in Grenada from the Guianas in the seventeenth century, may have left little or no material evidence to support the historical data, which asserts that they lived with the Island Caribs and fought alongside them against European invaders. Despite the debate, Roget suggests that 'Grenada and its dependencies, Île de Ronde and Île de Caille, and above all Carriacou, constitute in a way the archaeological memory of the Lesser Antilles,' as these various Amerindian groups, in their travels from South America through the Caribbean, must have used Grenada as the entrance, transit point and trading centre. A selection of pre-Columbian artefacts can be seen at the CARRIACOU MUSEUM and the GRENADA NATIONAL MUSEUM.[44, 59, 60, 155, 292]

ANANSI/'NANSI STORIES are children's folk tales told throughout the English-speaking Caribbean, with Anansi (or Anancy) the Spider or Compè Zayen (<Fr.Cr. *compère*: 'brother' + *(le)s—araignés*: 'spiders') the primary folk hero/antihero. These stories take their subject matter from everyday life experiences and are narrated by elders to children usually under moonlit skies at festivals; they were also once popular at funerary wakes. The influences of West Africa, where the spider trickster tales are common, are quite evident. The AKAN influences are especially noticeable in names of characters like Anansi (<Twi *anànse*: 'spider'), his son Tacooma (<Twi *ntikûma*: one of Anansi's sons), and Assonoo (<Twi *e-sóno*: 'elephant'), which were brought to the islands by African slaves. Among the Asante, Kwaku Anansi is an important mythological figure and is popular in folktales.

The practised storyteller has songs and a repertoire of voices and sounds to portray the many animal characters. He begins the evening with the greetings 'Tim, Tim?' (<?Fr. *Tiens*! *Tiens*!: 'Hello! Look!') or 'Cric?,' and the audience responds in unison 'Papa Welcome!'/'Bwa Seche' (<Fr. 'dry wood') or 'Crac,' respectively. The storytelling format is typically West African, but since FRENCH CREOLE was the language of the slaves and peasantry, the characters have titles like compè, and names such as Tig (<Fr. *tig(re)*: 'tiger'). Numerous characters enliven the tales as Anansi the trickster spins his web of deception over his foes, who include man, Compè Tig, Compè Macoucou, Assonoo, Mongoose, Dog and Snake. Often he gets caught in his own schemes.

Though entertaining, Anansi stories and their rebel hero came to represent resistance for the enslaved and colonised peoples in the region. To 'tell 'nansi story' is to tell an untruth or an unbelievable story, while the usual retort to a ridiculous tale is 'You telling 'nansi story!' To 'play Anansi' is to play tricks on someone. Almost every community had a storyteller, some so well known and liked that they were in demand at festive events. The advent of television and electronic games have displaced storytelling and few pass on the art form.[114, 313]

ANGEL HARPS Steel Orchestra is the oldest existing steelband in Grenada, dating to 1965. It began with the mergers of the Teenville (led by Charles Moses) and Troubadours (led by George Croney), and grew with the addition of the Harp Tones (led by Maudsley Parkes) and Panasonic (led by Father Emmanuel, winner of the 1972 panorama) STEELBANDS. 'The Wharf Band' or 'Harps', as it is popularly known, was first housed on the CARENAGE or Wharf in the former Coals Market (as was the Hell's Cats Steel Orchestra, Grenada's first steelband). It moved to TANTEEN in 1973 where it has been ever since. Among its many accolades is the record of having won the national panorama competition more times than any other band, a total of 11 times between 1969 and 2005. Angel Harps has produced four recordings to date, and is regarded as the 'institution of pan' in Grenada, with its long history of beautiful pan music. See www.ncbangelharps.com.

ANGLICAN HIGH SCHOOL The AHS was founded as the Church of England High School (CEHS) in September 1916 by Archdeacon Walton. It was preceded by the privately funded St. George's Girls' HS (1891-1911)/Victoria Girls' HS (1912-1915), which closed due to low attendance. The CEHS was established, like its predecessors, to cater to girls of the Anglican faith. It proved far more successful and grew in the next few years, aided by government and private scholarships and donations. It was first housed at 'Bachelor's Hall', Simmonds Alley, before moving to 'Lamollie House', the present site of Barclays BANK. Estelle Garaway was the first headmistress (1916-1939), and M A 'MAB' Bertrand, who was senior assistant (1916-1939), succeeded Garraway (1939-1954).

The CEHS is credited with the introduction and establishment of NETBALL in the 1920s and the first Girl Guides in 1925. In 1946, under its new name, the AHS moved to the 'Tanteen Huts', the newly vacated military barracks that also housed the GBSS. In 1952 it relocated a few hundred yards away to its present location, following the construction of new buildings. In 1972 a fire, believed 'set by political activists', destroyed 'Top School' - since rebuilt. It has a student body of over 700 students. Noted graduates include the 1970 MISS WORLD and Celia Clyne-Edwards, the first woman to win the ISLAND SCHOLARSHIP. AHS was heavily damaged by HURRICANE IVAN.

Angel Harps Steel Orchestra

ANGLICANISM or the Church of England came to Grenada with the first wave of British inhabitants who arrived following the French ceding of the islands to Britain in 1763. For the next 16 years four Anglican clerics officiated in Grenada, but legislation instituting Anglicanism was not passed until 1784. For its first fifty years disorganisation and absenteeism characterised the Anglican Church throughout the Caribbean, having, according to Ragatz, 'failed sadly both as a religious and a cultural force due to the combination of inferior representatives and the general indifference on the part of the planter class.' Though the initial period of British occupation (1763-1779) was marked by limited religious tolerance, religious persecution and intolerance came to monopolise the first eighty years of the British-French/Anglican-RC relationship. The British, after 1783, began a systematic persecution of Catholics, which fuelled FÉDON'S REBELLION.

The arrival in 1824 of Bishop Coleridge, the first Bishop of the Diocese of Barbados with jurisdiction over Grenada, brought many changes. In 1825 the two parishes were increased to four, and a concerted effort to convert the slaves to Anglicanism was begun. Also, churches and chapels were constructed throughout the islands, beginning in 1826 with the ST. GEORGE'S ANGLICAN CHURCH. Being a beneficiary of the slave-holding PLANTOCRACY, its role in the anti-slavery movement was negligible (some clergy even owned slaves). It did, however, play a prominent part in the establishment of EDUCATION, beginning in 1824. The Anglican Church administers 15 primary schools and three secondary schools throughout the country. In 1874 the Anglican Church was disestablished by law and lost the status of a state religion. In 1877 Grenada was incorporated into the new Diocese of the Windward Islands, following Barbados' separation from the Government of the WINDWARD ISLANDS. The Bishop is resident in St. Vincent (first appointed in 1927), and an archdeacon resident in Grenada.

The Anglican faithful, predominantly descendants of Africans, presently constitute 14 per cent of the population, but a small number are the descendants of the elite class that once dominated its initial membership. In the late 1800s the faithful comprised over 30 per cent of the population, but as the whites and elite families emigrated, their numbers declined. Of the churches and chapels distributed over 16 PARISHES across the islands, the original parish churches have celebrated over 100-year anniversaries and are valued for their architectural and historical significance. Baptismal, marriage and burial records, dating from the 1700s, are extensive. Slave baptisms, dating to at least the 1810s, are also preserved.[89]

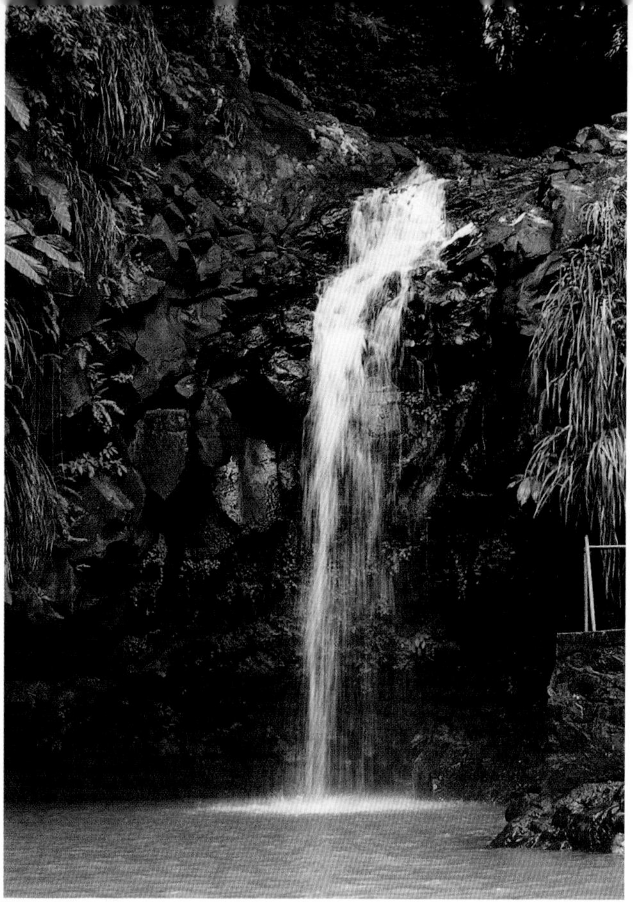

Annandale waterfall

ANNANDALE WATERFALL is situated outside the village of Willis (about 10 miles/16 km north of St. George's), along the central range of hills on the headwaters of the Beauséjour River. This small, yet picturesque waterfall derived its name from the surrounding Annandale estate which dates to the 1820s and was established by William Johnstone of Annandale, Scotland who consolidated the estate from smaller properties. The fall is approximately 30 ft (9 m) high, with the natural pool about 15 ft (4.6 m) deep; it is surrounded by dense tropical forest. Annandale, because of its accessibility, was one of the first natural areas in the islands to be made a visitor attraction and has been beautifully preserved as such. It is surrounded by flower, spice and herb gardens. It is an ideal site for swimming, picnicking and hiking. A small vendors' market provides visitors with samples of local arts and crafts, and spices.

ANNONA A genus native to tropical America and the Caribbean and including a number of trees noted for their delicious fruits. Popular in Grenada are the sugar apple (*A. squamosa*), soursop (*A. muricata*) and custard apple (*A. reticulata*). The sugar apple is a small deciduous tree that grows to almost 20 ft (6 m) and produces a sweet custard-like fruit eaten fresh or made into a drink. Its creamy white flesh is broken into segments, each enclosing a black seed. The soursop is an evergreen tree that grows to over 20 ft (6 m), and produces large green fruits weighing as much

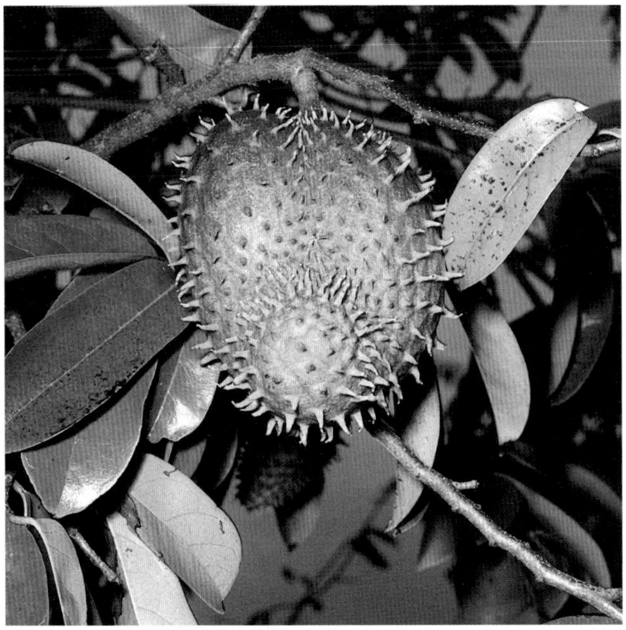

Soursop fruit

as 6 lb (2.7 kg). The outer skin is covered with fleshy spines. The white pulp has a pleasant custard-like flavour, especially when made into a drink, in flavouring ice-cream and 'snow-ice', or made into 'babalé', a local drink used as an APHRODISIAC. Fruits are available from June to September. The roots, fruits and leaves are prescribed by FOLK MEDICINE to cure roundworms, 'cooling of the blood', and insomnia, respectively. The answer to the riddle, 'green as grass, not grass; white as milk, not milk; black as pot, not pot,' is soursop, with reference to its skin, flesh and seeds.

The custard apple or tjè bèf (<Fr.Cr. *coeur boeuf*: 'cow's/bullock's heart' because of its shape) grows to 25 ft (7 m) and produces a smooth round fruit that turns brown or red when ripe. Its reddish-yellow pulp is sweet and custard-like. It bears between July and September. These fruits are important in the TRAFFICKING trade to TRINIDAD.

ANTOINE (fl. 1650s) was a village headman or Island Carib 'chief' at the time of the French settlement in Grenada. In June 1650, following the initial Amerindian-French conflict and the French ambush of the Island CARIBS at LEAPERS' HILL, he was entreated by the French colonists to seek peace, since it was 'the ones from Martinique' who had done the dastardly deed. It is almost certain that a number of places in the NE of Grenada—River Antoine (*Rivière Antoine*), Lake Antoine (*Étang Antoine*), Antoine Bay (*Anse d'Antoine*) and Black Rock (formerly *Islet d'Antoine*)—were named after 'Captain' Antoine. The general area that bears his name today was the place of his *cabet* or village in the 1650s.[8, 155]

APHRODISIACS Every culture has devised an abundance of exotic teas, potions and tonics reputed to possess the ability to enhance sexual performance and desire. The word aphrodisiac itself is derived from the name of the Greek goddess of sexual love and fertility, Aphrodite. Legend claims she arose from the sea foam created by the Greek god Uranus' severed genitals. Hence the association with sexuality and sea products, including fish broth, SEA EGG, oysters and sea or Irish moss, a species of red algae (*Gracilaria* spp.) dried and blended with milk into a local drink. FOLK MEDICINE further ascribes to a number of herbs, tree barks, roots and animal products aphrodisiac properties. The more popular among these are TANNIA log, babalé (?<Fr.Cr.<Fr. *bébé*: 'baby' + *lait*: 'milk'), a milky-white drink made from soursop, and bobanday or bwa-bandé (<Fr. *bois*: 'wood' + *bandér*: 'to have an erection'), a drink made from the bark and roots of the tree *Chione venosa,* not *Richeria grandis* as is often stated. Bobanday, also known as bwa-dome (<Fr. Cr. *bois* + *d'homme*: 'tree of man'), has been rumoured to cause priapism if 'too much' is taken, requiring ice to relieve the often painful and prolonged erection, or even hospitalisation. Pieces of bark and root and 'other ingredients' are added to rum to create a 'potent drink'.

Bobanday's physiological effects, if any at all, have not been scientifically confirmed, but many who have used it swear by it. It is also claimed that 'stinging red ants', boiled with their nest, make a 'good' aphrodisiac. All of these supposedly potent concoctions are usually said to be 'good for the waist', a reference to the male's sexual prowess. These remedies have gained prominence as sexual stimulants due to sympathetic magic, and chemical analysis of most reveal extracts which have no known physiological effects.

APPRENTICESHIP In August 1833 the British Parliament passed the Imperial Act of EMANCIPATION, bringing an end to SLAVERY within the BWI; the Grenada legislature passed its version on 11 March 1834. It took effect on 1 August 1834, with the implementation of a compulsory apprenticeship of slaves to their former owners; field slaves for the next six years and four years for all other slaves. For three-quarters of the week ex-slaves over the age of six years were required to work for their former owners without pay, but given adequate rations. For the remainder of the week they tended personal KITCHEN GARDENS from which they sold the produce, or hired out for wages. Children under six years of age were completely free, but their dependence on the estates for their rations forced most into similar situations as the apprenticed. Apprenticeship was meant to allow estate owners adequate time to adjust to the drastic changes due to the end of slavery, and help promote industry through wage employment for the slaves to prepare them for freedom.

The four years of the Apprenticeship system were not as smooth a transition from slavery as envisioned. Estate owners used legal and coercive means to extract as much labour as possible from apprentices with as little remuneration as possible. Apprentices protested as best they could, but the preponderance of laws against them made their many actions futile, even dangerous. Though special magistrates were employed to safeguard the rights of the apprentices, estate owners/managers abused these rights, oftentimes with impunity. By 1838 opposition to Apprenticeship was widespread, especially as a result of the impending freedom of non-agricultural apprentices in August 1838. On 25 May 1838 the Grenada Legislature voted to end the Apprenticeship system two years prematurely for field workers, demonstrating its perceived failure. Finally, on 31 July 1838, all forced servitude within the BWI came to an end. The over 18,000 men, women and children who were apprenticed were finally free, but they continued dependence on wage labour on the estates meant their exploitation for another century.[35, 79, 218, 219, 333]

APRIL FOOLS' DAY The first day of April when tricks and practical jokes are played on 'unsuspecting' individuals. It is believed that this celebration originated in France after 1582 when the Gregorian replaced the Julian Calendar, and New Year's Day moved from 25 March (the feast of the Annunciation which began eight days of celebration that culminated on 1 April) to 1 January (the British did not adopt the Gregorian calendar until 1752). People who were unaware of the change were called 'April fools' and pranksters continued to make mock New Year's Day calls on them. In Grenada, the day, also known as Tamfool Day (<Eng. tomfool: 'foolish, silly'), is celebrated with jokes and tricks played on the unsuspecting. One popular trick is termed 'send the fool further on'. The 'April fool,' unaware of the trick, is sent on frivolous errands with a message that informs the receiver to continue the 'fool's errand' until someone takes pity on the victim. Children especially enjoy 'tamfooling' each other, with the unfortunate victim of such pranks derisively called 'tamfool puppydog'. The day is also known as All Fools' Day.

ARCHITECTURAL HERITAGE The town of St. George's has been described by travellers since time immemorial as the most beautiful in the English-speaking Caribbean. This blend of historic architecture, dating back centuries, illustrates major influences by the British and, less so, by the French. Travel writer Patrick Leigh Fermor remarks that 'there must be something in the atmosphere of Grenada that prevents an architect from going wrong.' Grenada's historical architecture spans a wide range of structures—military, religious, industrial, commercial, public and domestic buildings. Though it was probably minimal, several ST. GEORGE'S FIRES in the 1700s

Eighteenth-century stone and brick building with tile roofs, Monckton Street, St. George's

destroyed a century of French architectural influence, except FORT GEORGE and a few other structures. Following the fire of 1775 the island received its first 'building code' when an act, 'for rendering St. George Town more safe and healthy...' was passed.

Today, many of the brick buildings constructed since still stand, covered with the red tiles that distinguish this town from most others in the Caribbean. Specific French architectural flavours can be detected in many of the older buildings, with their fish-scale tile roofs, dormer-windows, porches, shutters and iron balconies. Many of these buildings are in the Caribbean Georgian style, with a few showing British aristocratic influences exemplified by SEDAN PORCHES as seen on CHURCH STREET. The commercial architecture of St. George's is the most striking, showing predominantly British influences in the warehouses and buildings along the CARENAGE, MARKET SQUARE and MELVILLE STREET.

Though most of the architecture that once dominated sugar estates has all but disappeared, RIVER ANTOINE still utilises much of the old technology and equipment to produce RUM. The remains of abandoned aqueducts, LIMEKILNS and SUGAR MILLS litter the landscape. The construction of over ten churches between 1825 and 1850 ushered in what has been termed 'the church building era'.

The mix of French and British styles in domestic houses, the dominant vernacular styles for centuries, has of late given way to American and other influences. The majority of new buildings are constructed with cement, the most widespread building material in the islands' modern economy. These structures have replaced the ubiquitous vernacular wooden FRAME HOUSES and the wattle and daub structures, which were the predominant dwellings of the slaves and the peasantry until the early 1900s. There has been a concerted effort to preserve and restore Grenada's architectural heritage, though many of the old buildings are degraded or were destroyed to make way for new buildings. The GRENADA NATIONAL TRUST, Grenada Historical Society, Willie Redhead Foundation, and the Grenada Civic Awareness Organisation have sought to enhance places in St. George's of interest to the growing TOURISM industry, which will aid the preservation of this historic 'city on the hill'. A number of the older buildings in St. George's are identified with plaques that provide some interpretative information about the structures. Carriacou's historical architecture, except for a number of ruins dating to the French, sugar and cotton works and GREAT HOUSES from the British era, is sparse. Some of the islands' historical buildings and the unique fish-scale tile roofs, especially in St. George's, were either destroyed or severely damaged by HURRICANE IVAN, altering the beauty and history of the town.[41, 127, 129]

ARMADILLO (*Dasypus novemcinctus hoplites*) is a burrowing toothless mammal, with an armour-like covering of bony plates. It is of South American origin (like its local name tatu/tatoo <Guarani), and was most likely brought to the island by AMERINDIANS, establishing its northernmost range. It measures about 3 ft (0.9 m). Its full name is nine-banded armadillo (<Am.Sp.: 'little armed one') because of the nine movable bands in its armour. Peculiar to it is the birth of exactly four young having the identical sex in each litter due to their development from a single fertilised egg. Predominantly nocturnal, it is found almost exclusively in the Grand Étang Forest Reserve and GRAND ÉTANG NATIONAL PARK where it feeds on insects, small animals, decaying flesh and vegetables. In the 1800s it was referred to as 'haginamah' (<hog-in-armour) because of its likeness to the hog/pig in taste. It is a game species and can be legally hunted between September and March. Its present status is listed as 'rare', with remaining populations threatened. It appears on Grenada's INDEPENDENCE coat of arms. The armadillo is not present on Carriacou.

ARTS The dramatic and performing arts in the early colonial period, like in many of the Caribbean islands, were restricted to shows or acts staged by travelling troupes and individuals. Early performers included jugglers, rope-dancers, prize fighters, and 'players of interludes'. Up until the early 1900s travelling shows, among them minstrel shows, circuses, singers, and novelty acts were common. As early as 1828 a group of 'coloured amateurs in Grenada staged a Shakespearian tragedy' and various local groups began staging concerts, dances, and dramatic performances. By the 1920s concerts, foreign plays, musicals and operettas were staged at the local theatres. The opening of the UWI Extra-Mural Department in the early 1950s fuelled drama and local theatre. Among the early participants were F M COARD, actor, and Wilfred REDHEAD and Thelma Phillip, playwrights. Beginning in the 1950s the BEE WEE BALLET and the Divi Divi Dance Group (est. 1964) began performing dances and songs from Grenada's FOLK CULTURE, influenced by the islands' AFRICAN HERITAGE.

The early dramatic arts were staged at YORK HOUSE beginning in the late 1800s, the Anglican Church Hall between 1910 and 1930, Wesley Hall, CINEMAS like the Empire Theatre after the 1930s, the Deluxe Theatre in Grenville, and school halls. The Marryshow Folk Theatre (constructed 1982) and the Grenada Trade Center are the primary venues for the performing arts. During the GULP reign there was a revival of FOLK DANCES, especially the lancers, and folk culture in general. The PEOPLE'S REVOLUTIONARY GOVERNMENT encouraged the dramatic and performing arts and incorporated culture within the REVOLUTION. The National Performing Company was formed and toured the US and UK as 'Fruits of the Revolution'. There is at present a NATIONAL FOLK GROUP. The annual CARNIVAL is by far the islands' most creative and popular performing arts. Performing art groups include the Spice Island Youth Quake (f. 1980), the Theatre of Unique Music and Dramatic Arts (f. 1993), the Tivoli Drummers (f. 1995) and the Heritage Theatre Company (f. 1989).[330, 331]

ARUBA & CURAÇAO These Dutch-controlled islands attracted hundreds of migrant workers from Grenada between the 1940s and 1950s to their oil refining industry. Migration climaxed in the 1940s due to the expanding industry after World War II, peaking by 1949. Though male labour migrants were by far the majority, women also travelled to Aruba, seeking employment as domestic servants and nurses. The majority of Grenadians went to Aruba, working for the Largo Oil and Transport Co. at San Nicholas, which employed over 7,000 workers. Carriacouans made up a large segment of the Grenadian migrants. Workers in the oil refineries sought sponsorship for relatives and friends back home who joined the growing migrant communities. Remittances to relatives in Grenada aided the local economy and enabled individuals to purchase land, construct houses and establish businesses upon their return home. By the 1950s large numbers of foreign workers were laid off due to mechanisation and the 'indigenisation' of labour, with Grenadians 'repatriated in droves'. Many Grenadians, among them politicians Ben JONES, Herbert BLAIZE and Eric GAIRY, and businessman Rupert Bishop, worked in Aruba, and writer Merle Collins and former PM Maurice BISHOP were born there to Grenadian parents. Collins, in her novel *Angel*, captures aspects of life of the Grenadian worker in Aruba in the 1950s.[13]

ASSOCIATED STATEHOOD In January 1967 the British government announced that on 3 March 1967 Grenada would achieve internal self-rule. Associated Statehood with the UK, created by the 1967 West Indies Act, was seen as the only alternative in light of the fact that the other options—independence or Caribbean federation—were viewed as unacceptable or impractical. The failures of FEDERATION, Little Eight and UNITARY STATE had forced the British government to grant more autonomy to its smaller territories in the Caribbean. This was also aided by the world-wide decolonisation taking place and

First day cover commemorating the inauguration of Associated Statehood

widespread support for self-determination, regardless of the size of the territory. This resulted in a new constitution that granted full internal self-government, leaving the UK with the responsibilities of defence and external affairs. Eric GAIRY, then opposition leader, resigned from the Grenada Legislature in protest, insisting on a referendum on the new constitution by holding general ELECTIONS.

The Associated Statehood constitution instituted a bicameral PARLIAMENT with a nine-member nominated Senate and a ten-member elected House of Representatives. The GOVERNOR was 'relieved of any political or legal responsibility for the actual business of government,' assuming the position of a figurehead. Herbert BLAIZE, then chief minister, became the first premier. The islands received their first national flag, the Statehood flag—blue, gold and green horizontal stripes, with a nutmeg sprig in a central oval. The attainment of Associated Statehood and the appointment of a black, Grenadian-born woman, Dr Hilda BYNOE, as governor in 1969 signalled the changing politics in the region. Though he became premier that same year, Eric Gairy continued to criticise Associated Statehood, characterising it as 'quite meaningless... a farce and a mockery', and worked towards its termination. Associated Statehood ended with INDEPENDENCE in 1974.[343]

AUGUSTINE was a slave who, in 1767, gained his freedom through the legislature, 'notwithstanding the dissent of the owner of the said Slave'. He, like PAULINE, was among a few slaves who gained freedom by legislative acts because they had captured MAROONS or foiled escape plans of slaves. Governor Melville, confronted with the growing threat by the maroons in the 1760s, was convinced that Augustine was 'very helpful by his activity, care, and ability, in seizing and destroying many runaway slaves [and was] capable of further great utility.' He was permitted 'to enjoy the Liberties and Privileges allowed to Free Negroes,' but became embroiled in the ongoing controversy between the governor, the PLANTOCRACY and the legislature over the governor's administration of the colony. The Grenadian plantocracy protested against Melville's action, accusing him of supporting a slave who was 'publicly accused of having Committed a Rape on a white woman, and having murdered Mr. Vandell, and of other Atrocious Crimes.' Gov. Melville reportedly harboured Augustine at his home for several months until served with a warrant by the grand jury for his arrest 'for the aforesaid crimes', but Augustine had already made 'his escape' to the disappointment of the grand jury. Thereafter he disappears from the historical record.

Avocado fruit

AVOCADO (*Persea americana*, syn. *P. gratissima*) is also referred to as 'pear' due to its similar appearance to the temperate fruit of the same name. The avocado (<Mex. Sp. *aguacate*, <Nahuatl *ahuacatly*: 'testicle' for the shape of the fruit) was brought to Jamaica from Central America by Spanish explorers around 1650 and thereafter spread throughout the region. This evergreen tree attains a height of 65 ft (20 m). The avocado, also known as zabòca (<Fr. Cr. <Fr. *(le)s—avocats*: 'avocados'), has a thick and warty skin, hence another name alligator pear. The flesh is light yellow and soft when ripe, surrounding a large, oval-shaped seed. Its buttery characteristics have meant its use as a spread when mashed, and earned it the name butter pear. It is commonly used in salads and makes a popular dip, guacamole, but can be eaten as a vegetable.

With its high oil, calorie and protein contents, and being rich in a number of vitamins, the avocado has the highest energy value of any vegetable. The leaves are made into a tea and used as a folk remedy to treat hypertension. The grated seed is mixed with clay and vinegar and applied to strained muscles and swollen glands. Oil, extracted from both the seed and the pulp, is used in the medical and pharmaceutical industries. Fruits are harvested from July to November.

B

BACCOO A folk spirit that many believe possesses supernatural powers and lives in a bottle. Its master uses these powers to acquire wealth or bring about harm, even death to an adversary. It arrived in Grenada via Guyana from Surinam (<Saramaccan *bakulu*: 'dwarf-spirit; elf'), but its origin is African (<Kikongo *mbaka*: 'bewitched dwarf or animal'). If neglected by its master, this temperamental spirit can create numerous disturbances in its owner's life and bring about his/her social and financial ruin, even death. A baccoo is usually discovered following the death of its owner, and the intervention of a priest is necessary to capture it. Some believe that the beating of a drum can compel the partly human baccoo to dance in a trance-like state right back into its bottle that is then discarded. Strange occurrences in the home – scattered food, lighted stoves, wrecked furniture – are often explained by the belief that someone has 'sen' a baccoo' to cause trouble. It is quite similar to the poltergeist in Western European folklore. A person of small stature, usually a man and often unattractive, is derisively referred to as a baccoo.

BACKRA AND BÉKÉ Terms used by the slaves and peasants to refer to Europeans/whites, or anyone of a light or fair-skinned complexion who could be associated with whites. Backra is a term of West African origin, from the Efik (Nigeria) *mbakara*: 'whiteman'. It was also applied to objects identifiable with European culture such as the Bible: 'Backra Book', or a doctor: 'backra doctor'. During SLAVERY the term referred to the master/plantation owner or white overseer, with the meaning of 'sir' or 'boss', and the equivalent of 'massa'. The term backra was most recently used to describe the mixed-race residents of MADAM PIERRE, Petite Martinique and in association with the small white community at MT. MORITZ, whose residents were contemptuously teased 'poor backra' and 'backra Johnny', as in the song: 'cricket gill and dry bonavis (bean)/ good enough for poor backra.'

Béké (<Ijo *beké*: 'European', and <Nembe *beke*: 'yellow in colour') referred to 'white Creoles' and was common in the French Antilles, hence its survival in Grenada. It was also associated with poor whites, hence the term poor béké, or béké-nèg (<Fr.Cr. béké: 'white person' + <Fr. nègre: 'black person', meaning 'white trash'). It later became associated with an individual of white and black parentage, or a 'fair-skinned' or 'red-skin' person, especially an individual with red hair and fair skin colour. Béké-nèg (<Fr.Cr.: 'red-nigger') was also used derisively for a mixed-race person who was seen as 'playing white' or uppity, or an albino. Backra and béké are sometimes used interchangeably.

BAILLIE, James (1737-1793) was one of many Scots who immigrated to Grenada after the French ceded the islands to the British in 1763. He was the most successful of three brothers who were involved in trade and plantations in the BWI. He arrived in the BWI in 1755 and resided in Grenada between 1765 and 1771, owning estates and served as a member of the General Assembly. He belonged to the influential Scottish community, which dominated the government and businesses in the late 1700s. As a business partner in Baillie and Hamilton (c. 1783), and [Duncan] Campbell, Baillie and Co. (c. 1784-1787), he was one of several slave factors or agents in the islands, responsible for the selling of thousands of African slaves in the region. According to Baillie, testifying in 1790 before the British Parliament on whether or not the British should end its Atlantic SLAVE TRADE, he 'was in the habits of selling considerable numbers of slaves in every year' while resident in the West Indies. As a Member of the British Parliament he was an ardent supporter of slavery and defended the cause of the West Indian slave-owning plantocracy. He became so wealthy from his dealings with the slave trade and plantations that in 1784 he commissioned Thomas Gainsborough to paint a portrait of 'The Baillie Family'. The family name survives in the village name Baillies Bacolet, ST. DAVID which is derived from a large estate owned by James' son, Alexander (1777-1853), a magistrate in Grenada for many years.[159]

Portrait of the Baillie Family by Thomas Gainsborough, c. 1784

BAMBOO (*Bambusa vulgaris*) is probably the most versatile tropical plant after the COCONUT. It was brought from SE Asia to the French Antilles in the mid-1700s to build 'small aqueducts and drains', as well as for erosion control on steep and denuded slopes. Its availability and low cost have led to its extensive utilisation as a building material, in musical instruments like the TAMBOO-BAMBOO, domestic utensils like the 'yard broom' and drinking cup and spoon, industrial utensils such as the gaulette or COCOA knife pole, baskets, and a variety of local crafts. Up until the 1950s fish-pots or traps made of bamboo were quite common. Bamboo uses today are confined to temporary huts or tents for outdoor activities, fences, scaffolding, and the local crafts industry. The traditional celebration of Guy Fawkes Day included the bursting of bamboo knots as 'bamboo bombs'. A member of the grass family, the hollow-stemmed bamboo grows in clumps from an underground rhizome to 35-50 ft (10-16 m). The creaking sounds heard in a 'bamboo stool' are said to be those of evil spirits which reside there. FOLK MEDICINE prescribes a brew of bamboo leaves as a cure for female infertility.

Banana plant with fruits and flowers

BANANA/PLANTAIN/BLUGGO (*Musa* spp.) are native to the Malay Peninsula and in 1516 varieties were brought to Hispaniola from the Canary Islands by the Spanish. Varieties were brought to Grenada by the Island CARIBS before European SETTLEMENT. Locally, banana (*M. acuminate*) is known as fig (<Fr.Cr. *fig(ue) du pays*: 'native or local fig' hence fig-tree, fig-leaf, fig-skin and ripe fig), but bears no relation to the sweet fig (*Ficus* sp.) which probably gave it its name. It grows to 10-20 ft (3-6 m) from an underground corm and produces a 'stem' with about 150 seedless fruits or 'fingers' on about 10-20 bunches or 'hands'. Each plant produces fruit only once and dies, but is replaced by a new shoot or sucker.

Intensive banana (<Pg.Sp. <Wollof/Fulani) cultivation dates back to the French who cultivated it as a food crop. In 1923 the idea of establishing a banana export industry was examined, and local entrepreneurs formed a number of companies 'to plant and deal in bananas.' Yet it was not until 1934, following an agreement to sell bananas to the Canadian Buying Company, that production steadily increased. The crop was given a major boost in 1953 when Geest, a British company, became the sole marketing agent. In 1954 bananas accounted for just over two per cent of exports, but HURRICANE JANET devastated the crop. Cultivation quickly recovered and expanded. By 1962 bananas accounted for 20 per cent of exports, climaxing at 39 per cent by 1968, and ranked as one of the islands' three main exports until 1993 when exports began to decline. Exports practically ceased by 1997 as a result of export bans due to low quality. Though exports resumed in 1999, Grenada and the other Windward Islands lost their preferential status in the EU in 2006 as a result of an unfavourable ruling by the World Trade Organization.

The Grenada Banana Cooperative Society (f. 1954) was the umbrella body that organised banana farmers and managed production and export until it closed in 2003 as part of the GOG's attempt to modernise the sector. In September 2004 HURRICANE IVAN devastated the small banana crop, and though it can be easily replanted, its economic importance remains minor. Popular varieties include the sweet silk/rock fig and red fig, and the commercial varieties lacattan and cavendish. Scientists believe that the banana is in danger of being wiped out by diseases due to its low resistance because it reproduces vegetatively, not genetically. Bananas can be cooked as a vegetable when green, 'green fig', a widespread practice throughout the world; when deep-fried, they are eaten as chips. Unlike the sweet breakfast bananas, the plantain (*M. paradisiaca*) and bluggo (*M. balbisiana*) are starchier and always cooked before consumption. They can be cooked as vegetables either green or ripe, the ripe plantain being especially tasty when fried. The juice from plantain leaves is prescribed by FOLK MEDICINE for earaches and nosebleeds.

Bluggo, plantain and green bananas were staples of the slaves' and peasants' diets, and are presently major items in the TRAFFICKING trade. For many years these 'provisions' were held in low esteem, consumed predominantly by peasants and poor urban residents. They can, however, be found on menus at hotels and restaurants across the islands in various exotic dishes. Banana is probably the number one fruit consumed world-wide. Relatives of the banana include the pretty flowers of heliconias or balisiers like wild plantain (*Heliconia bihai*), lobster-claws (*H. caribaea*) and parrot's plantain (*H. psittacorum*), the exquisitely beautiful bird-of-paradise (*Strelitzia reginae*), and the large fan-shaped travellers' tree/palm (*Ravenala madagascariensis*).[35, 300, 341]

BANKS The first commercial bank to operate in Grenada was Barclays Bank, incorporated in 1836 by Royal Charter as the Colonial Bank and catering specifically to the BWI. The original branch was opened on MELVILLE STREET, St. George's, in 1837 and introduced the first standardised British CURRENCY. It is the oldest financial institution in Grenada and has branches across the country, including a branch in GRENVILLE (opened by 1879) and in CARRIACOU (opened 1968). Barclays moved to CHURCH STREET by 1889, and moved into a new building at the corner of Church and Halifax Streets, in the 1960s. In 2002 Barclays Bank and the Canada Imperial Bank of Commerce (est. 1963 in Grenada) combined their Caribbean operations into the First Caribbean International Bank. It is one of five major banking institutions operating in Grenada, including the Grenada Cooperative Bank or 'Penny Bank' (est. 1932), the Bank of Nova Scotia (est. 1963), the Grenada Bank of Commerce (which took over from the Royal Bank of Canada (1913-83), the Republic Bank (Grenada) which began as the National Commercial Bank (est. 1979), and Capital One International (est. 1997).

BASSETERRE & CAPESTERRE In settling Grenada in 1649, the French occupied the western part of the island, which they called the Basseterre (<Fr.: 'low land', but used by sailors to mean 'protected', as the leeward side of the islands are less affected by the trade winds and provide safe anchorage for ships and protection from storms). It is very mountainous and afforded settlements only along a thin coastal belt. Since the sea was the primary connection between these settlements, the many small bays provided easy access and anchorage. In the southern extreme of the Basseterre were salt ponds that proved invaluable to the early settlers. The Capesterre or Cabesterre (<Fr. Cr. *Cap Esterre*: 'headland', or *Caput Terre*: 'first land sighted on arriving in the east' from Europe) comprised the eastern and northern regions, separated from the Basseterre by a central range of hills running north to south. As a result of the CARIB-French conflicts the Island Caribs were displaced from the Capesterre by 1700, though a small group continued to occupy settlements there into the mid-1700s. By 1687 the primary settlement in the Basseterre was made the principal district and parish, with the town at the Ville du FORT ROYAL. The British officially renamed it ST. GEORGE in 1764 when they occupied the islands.

BATHWAY BEACH, St. Patrick Situated on the NE coast of the island in the Grenada Bay, it has become a popular picnicking area, commanding a scenic view of the coast and Green and Sandy Islands. Unlike the BEACHES on the leeward coast, Bathway experiences rough seas because of its exposure to the Atlantic Ocean, despite protection from a fringing CORAL REEF located a few feet from the shore that creates a 'crystal clear pool perfect for diving and snorkelling'. Bedford Point, just north of Bathway Beach and the NE extreme of the island, once housed a fort. A redoubt of six guns, it was built by the British in the 1770s, but had been

Bathway Beach and offshore reef

established by the French as a fortified point/battery since the early 1700s. It is now in ruins. The name Bathway Beach dates to the mid to late 1800s, replacing the French name Anse Grenade. The beach is part of the LEVERA NATIONAL PARK. The area once called Bedford Bay is presently Levera Bay.

BATS There are eleven species of bats in the islands, primarily continental in origin: the greater fishing bat (*Noctilio leporinus mastivus*), Seba's short-tailed bat (*Carollia perspicillata perspicillata*), greater fruit-eating bat (*Artibeus lituratus palmarum*), lesser grey fruit-eating bat (*Artibeus glaucus bogotensis*), Jamaican fruit-eating bat (*Artibeus jamaicencis grenadensis*), black myotis bat (*Myotis nigricans nigricans*), lesser dog-like bat (*Peropteryx macrotis phaea*), Geoffroy's tailless bat (*Anoura geoffroyi geoffroyi*), Miller's long-tongued bat (*Glossophaga longirostris rostrata*), and Davy's naked-back bat (*Pteronotus davyi davyi*). Except for the greater fishing bat, all bats are primarily insectivorous. The fishing bat hunts at night when it alights over bodies of water, scooping up small fish with its long legs and talon-like claws. Though not the most common and widespread (this title is held by the Jamaican fruit and Miller's long-tongued bats), Pallas' mastiff bat (*Molossus molossus*) is more conspicuous because it nests in the roofs of houses where it becomes a nuisance, creating noise and structural damage. These winged nocturnal mammals also make their nests in caves, trees and buildings. Some species form colonies of thousands of bats and are quite noticeable in the early evening as they begin their nightly search for food.

The vampire bat is absent from Grenada, but its 'blood-sucking' habit and potential to carry diseases have earned all bats an unfavourable reputation. The status of most of the bat populations in Grenada remains fairly good if the 'current ecological situation prevails.' At least four species are known to be historically rare while the others are quite abundant. Yet the disappearance of at least seven species of bats in the Antillean region and the continued destruction of habitat leave one to question the future of these nocturnal creatures and the important roles they play as seed dispersers, pollinators and insect predators.[120]

BATTLE HILL, St. Andrew A popular religious centre that developed in the 1900s, it has become a place where Roman Catholics gather on special occasions for pilgrimages and worship. Its strategic location overlooking the St. Andrew's and Grenville Bays made Battle Hill a heavily contested position during FÉDON'S REBELLION and earned it its name. Battle Hill, relinquishing its former claim to fame (though ruins of fortifications still remain), is dominated by the National Shrine of Our Lady of Fatima, which welcomes pilgrims from across the islands. The six annual pilgrimages, commemorating the anniversaries of Mary's apparitions at Fatima, Portugal, begin at the old ST. ANDREW'S RC CHURCH, Grenville, and end at the shrine, about 2 miles (3.2 km) away.

BAY GARDENS, St. Paul's Situated 3 miles (4.8 km) from ST. GEORGE'S, on the slopes of Morne Delice. It is home to thousands of specimens of tropical plants, both indigenous and introduced. Among these are PALMS, spices, ferns, ornamentals and agricultural crops. The privately owned Bay Gardens, its name derived from the bay-leaf trees at its entrance, is the initiative of Keith St. Bernard. In 1974, on the site of an old sugar estate (concrete remains of its sugar mill are still evident), he began a living museum of Grenada's botanical history. Bay Gardens exhibits lath houses, fishponds, nutmeg shell-covered trails, and numerous plants that are ideally laid out within the confined 3 acre (1.2 ha) space. The garden affords easy access to the islands' botanical beauty and history, with much more to offer than the almost non-existent BOTANICAL GARDENS.

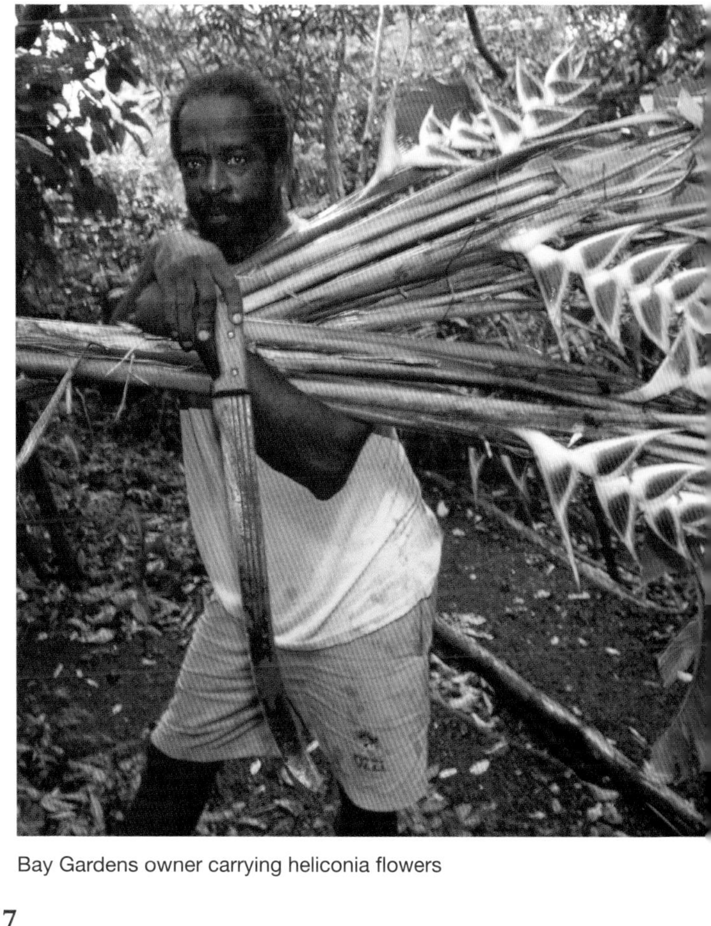

Bay Gardens owner carrying heliconia flowers

BAY LEAF (*Pimenta racemosa*) is an indigenous evergreen tree and should not be confused with the temperate bay laurel (*Laurus nobilis*) after which it was named. It grows to 35 ft (10 m), with large glossy leaves for which it is valued. When crushed the leaves exude a strong, pleasant odour and are used either fresh or dried to season meat dishes, soups and desserts. The leaves are used to produce bay oil, an ingredient in cosmetics, and bay rum, which is used in the preparation of toiletries. FOLK MEDICINE prescribes the leaves as a tea to treat fevers and a refresher in baths. The tea was once popular at funerary wakes. Also known as wild cinnamon and bwa-den (<Fr.Cr. bois d'Inde: 'tree of India', i.e. the West Indies). It is related to ALLSPICE.

BAY TOWN was the general name for the western part of ST. GEORGE'S Town after the late 1700s, remaining in use into the mid-1900s. The Bay referred to the fact that the town looked out over the St. George's Bay (formerly La Grand Bay). It ran from SENDALL TUNNEL, where fishing boats and schooners once docked, and along Bruce St. (built in 1895 to connect Melville St. to the Sendall Tunnel and named after Gov. Charles Bruce, 1893-97) and MELVILLE STREET (<Gov. Melville). It enclosed the central area of the town, including the MARKET SQUARE, ESPLANADE and the business establishments. It faced the outer harbour, with the CARENAGE the other major part of St. George's. The other main streets overlooking the bay include Gore St. (<Lt. Gov. Francis Gore, 1765), Grenville St. (<George Grenville, British PM, 1763-1765), Halifax St. (<Lord Halifax), Hillsborough St. (<Earl of Hillsborough, secretary of the colonies, 1768-1772), Granby St. (<Marquis de Granby, secretary of state, 1763-65), the once cobbled Market Hill or Constitution Hill (formerly part of Granby St.), Maloney St. (<Gov. Alfred Maloney, 1897-1900), St. John and St. Juille (or rather Saint-Jule after the French surname) Streets. The French established this entire area by the early 1700s, but none of their names survives, except Grand Étang Road, connecting the town to the General HOSPITAL. The general area is popularly known as 'The Market' or 'Town'.

BEACHES The islands of Grenada, C&PM are home to over 45 white and black (volcanic origin) sandy beaches. GRANDE ANSE BEACH is by far the most magnificent, but the many smaller beaches that dot the islands' coasts are beautiful. Along the eastern coastline of Grenada are beaches that can experience rough seas due to the effects of the Atlantic Ocean, while on the west and SW coasts the sea is much calmer. Most of the beaches are ornamented with PALMS, SEA GRAPE, ALMOND, COCONUT, manchineel, and other seashore vegetation, which prevent sand erosion and provide shade to sunbathers. Quite a number of the smaller beaches remain unspoiled, and their protection and management are environmental concerns.

Within the past decades beaches have become economically important because of their aesthetics and value to the TOURISM industry. Yet that has not meant their immediate and absolute protection. Many beaches

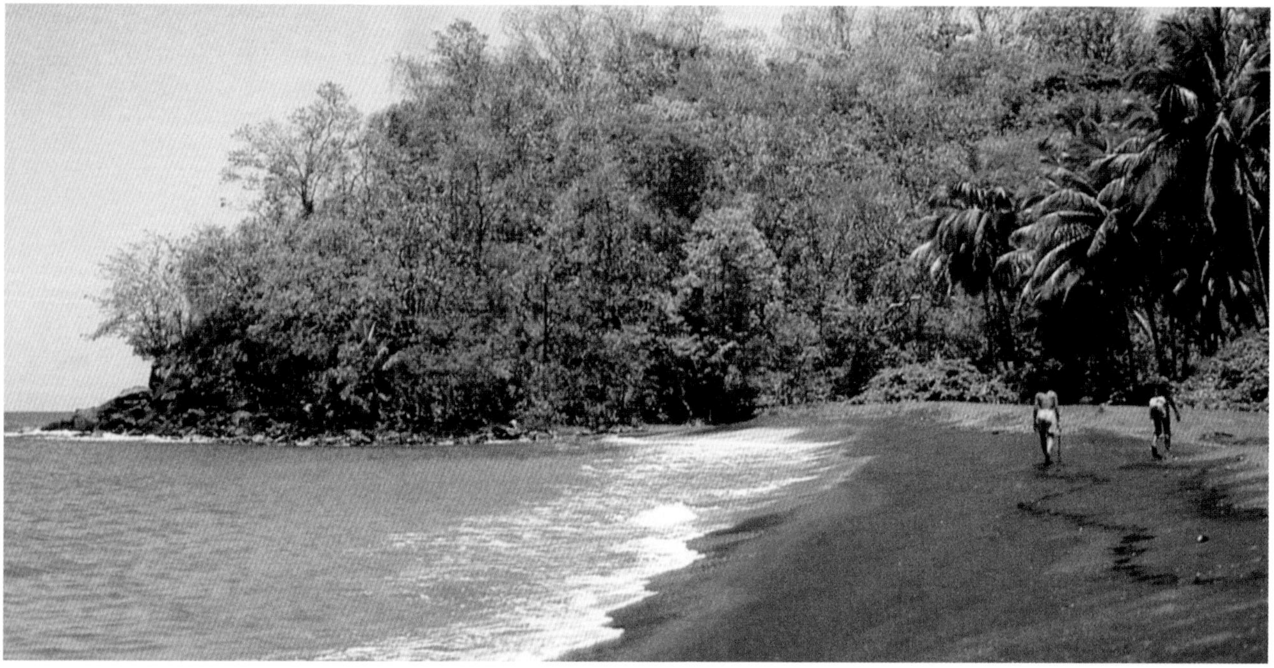

Black Bay, St John

have undergone erosion, leaving some almost devoid of the sand that make them attractive. Some of the erosion—caused by natural disasters—is natural and therefore unavoidable (but nonetheless manageable). But human action, in the form of sand mining, vegetation removal, coastal development and CORAL REEF damage, has led to increased and detrimental beach erosion. Laws so far have done little to protect the beaches, though the GOG has been monitoring beaches since 1985. The most glaring example of beach destruction began in 1927 when some of the trees were removed from the beach that extended from the Queen's Park Bridge to the Cherry Hill bluff so that four US Army amphibian planes could land there. Over the years it lost its sand, which has since been replaced with gravel and boulders. A number of other beaches across the islands are gradually following the same course. The GRENADA GRENADINES are home to some of Grenada's finest beaches, especially SANDY ISLAND.[50]

BEAUSÉJOUR, St. George, was established as a French settlement in October 1649. It was the first expansion of the original settlement meant to relieve the cramped conditions at PORT LOUIS in the LAGOON. Literally translated from the French, *beau séjour* means 'beautiful place'. The settlement witnessed numerous attacks by the Island CARIBS in the first fifty years of occupation, and was destroyed by them a number of times. By 1669 the small settlement developed into a separate district, the Quartier du Beauséjour, bordered to the south by the St. John's River, and by the Beauséjour River to the north. Situated at the mouth of the Beauséjour River on the western coast along the main road between Happy Hill and Brizan (<Fr. *brisant*: 'shoal, breakers'), the Beauséjour settlement gave its name to the 700 acre (284 ha) sugar estate, which has been owned by many notable Grenadians. Its old water wheel powered the generator for an ice factory in the mid-1900s. Beauséjour Point once housed a military battery used for the defence of the landing area. The Beauséjour River watershed, originating at the Grand Étang Lake and draining into Beauséjour Bay, is the second largest in Grenada after the GREAT RIVER. The area housed a radio transmitter that became the scene of a fierce battle to take and destroy it during the US INTERVENTION in 1983.

BEE WEE BALLET was established in 1955 from the Drama Group founded in 1950 by Christine Sturgeon of the UWI Extra-Mural Department. It quickly expanded to include dance and song, hence the Grenada Dancers and Players designation it temporarily adopted. Early prominent members included Allistair Bain (Grenadian dramatist and writer living in the UK), Thelma 'Aunty Tek' Phillips (dramatist and storyteller), Monica Hercules, Ann Peters and Bert Marryshow. It is considered Grenada's first folk dance company, having spent considerable time exploring the FOLK DANCES of the islands. By 1958, following its performance at the Federal Arts Festival in Trinidad to inaugurate FEDERATION, the Bee Wee Ballet garnered high praise. Yet, it soon lost some of its most talented members, especially its leader Bain, who migrated to the UK. The group nonetheless continued to progress under the leadership of Phillips, performing at national celebrations to commemorate events like ASSOCIATED STATEHOOD, EXPO '69, and INDEPENDENCE. As the first folk dance group, it became the prototype for the many subsequent performing ARTS groups that have developed since. In 1972 the junior members of the company were formed into the Tamarind Dance Company, and the senior members formed the Veni Vwai la Grenade Dance Company in 1975.

BELL, Sir Henry Hesketh (1864-1952) A career colonial civil servant who worked in the Treasury Department, Grenada, between 1883 and 1890. He is better known as the administrator of Dominica who in 1902 lobbied the Colonial Office to create the Carib Reserve in order to preserve what remained of Carib culture in the Caribbean. In 1889 he published the first of a number of books, *Obeah: Witchcraft in the West Indies*. According to Steele, *Obeah* is 'a biased but nonetheless absolutely fascinating commentary on Grenada'. Bell, fascinated with the local culture, provides a descriptive study of the rural peasantry in the late nineteenth century, especially their cultural expressions. The book's historical significance cannot be overstated, providing a glimpse of African cultural survivals like SHANGO and OBEAH. In the book's final chapter Bell rebuts the negative views of the Caribbean that famed English historian James Froude expresses in his 1888 book *The English in the West Indies*.[18]

BELMAR, Innocent (1936-1978) was a controversial police officer and political figure. He joined the police force in 1956 and in 17 years had worked through its ranks. As assistant superintendent of police he served as the officer of the Eastern Police Station at Grenville, St. Andrew. Nicknamed the 'Sheriff', Belmar was implicated in a number of violent acts against Premier Gairy's opposition in the early 1970s. The most celebrated of these were the beating and arrest of the 'NJM six' on BLOODY SUNDAY, and the wounding by gunshot of two known NEW JEWEL MOVEMENT supporters.

But Belmar's power was soon curtailed when in 1975 the DUFFUS COMMISSION published its report on police brutality in Grenada, recommending his dismissal from the POLICE FORCE and preclusion from holding future public office. PM GAIRY insisted that Belmar was 'the best policeman Grenada has seen and known for a long time,' refusing to take any action against him. Belmar, however, resigned from the Police Force.

In the 1976 parliamentary ELECTIONS he was easily elected to the House of Representatives as a GULP candidate. He served as a special advisor to the PM before being appointed Minister of Agriculture on 3 January 1978. On that same day he was shot at the Bamboo Bar, Birchgrove and died the following day, a casualty of the political VIOLENCE which had engulfed the island and in which he was a participant. Kennedy Budhlall and Lauriston Wilson, rumoured members of a clandestine anti-Gairy group operating in the countryside, were accused of his murder. Many rumours surrounded the incident, with the opposition even suggesting that PM Gairy was somehow involved in Belmar's death, even though the NJM had viewed Belmar as a real threat to their goal of gaining political power. Budhlall and Wilson were defended by Maurice BISHOP and subsequently acquitted. The case remains unsolved, though rumours and accusations continue to suggest that Gairy's political opposition was responsible for killing 'the most feared Gairyite in the State'.[94]

BELVIDERE ESTATE, St. John A COFFEE and COCOA estate owned by Julien FÉDON between 1791 and 1796. It served as the secret meeting place and headquarters of the insurgents before and during FÉDON'S REBELLION. As a result it was named Camp de la Liberté: 'Camp of Liberty'. Surrounded by mountains and located just north of centre of the island, it was ideal as the headquarters of the rebels. After the insurrection was quelled the government seized and sold the estate. A 1797 report claimed that Fédon had never paid 'any part of the purchase money'. Belvidere, a common French and British PLACE NAME, is from the Italian meaning 'fair view/beautiful to see'. The Duncan family owned it for over a hundred years, beginning with Thomas Duncan in the early 1800s (Duncan Town, GOUYAVE, is named after the family). The 900 acre (365 ha) estate was described in 1890 as 'one of the finest cocoa and spice plantation[s] in Grenada'. By the 1920s NUTMEG cultivation had proved successful and it became known as 'the largest economically and scientifically planned nutmeg estate in the world', helping to make Grenada the second largest producer of that spice. It later produced a number of other cash crops, including BANANA. Not to be confused with the village/estate of the same name in CARRIACOU.[174]

BENJAMIN, Robert was a revenue officer in the Treasury Department, Gouyave who on 19 October 1907 attacked the colonial treasurer, Norman Lockhart. F M COARD suggests that Benjamin had 'felt that a mean advantage was being taken of him' by Lockhart and refused to comply with an order given him. Benjamin is believed to be one of the first 'black-skinned' persons hired into the racially biased colonial civil service. With a gun he carried because of the large sums of money he handled, Benjamin shot Lockhart, wounding him in the arm and stabbing him in the chest; McKie, the chief clerk, received a non-fatal gunshot wound when he came to Lockhart's assistance. Benjamin was tried and sentenced to 12 years hard labour, following which spectators began to throw stones at the court house, leading to a riot by many residents of the town who felt Benjamin was unjustly treated.

BIANCA C An Italian passenger luxury liner that caught fire in the outer harbour on Sunday 22 October 1961 shortly before departing for Europe. An explosion in the engine room engulfed the entire ship with flames, forcing its passengers and crew to abandon ship. The quick response by the people of St. George's was instrumental in the rescue of the over 300 passengers and 200 crew; only one crew member died and eight people were injured. The people of St. George's housed the passengers, mostly Italians and Venezuelans, until they left the island a few days later. The remnant of the smouldering ship was removed to avoid its obstruction of the harbour entrance, but prematurely sank 1.5 miles (2.4 km) off Long/Quarantine Point. In appreciation of the hospitality and heroism of the people of Grenada, the Costa family presented them with the CHRIST OF THE DEEP statue that now stands on the CARENAGE.

Today, decades after this tragedy, the *Bianca C* has been brought to life from its watery grave. Dubbed the 'Titanic of the Caribbean' because it is the largest and most spectacular wreck (550 ft or 183 m) discovered to date, it has become an underwater museum. Situated some 150 ft (48 m) below sea level, its rusted hulk has become a man-made reef and home to numerous marine organisms. Artefacts have been illegally recovered from the wreck, and to prevent further pillaging, it has been proposed to designate the *Bianca C* a maritime national park. Its massive remains attract experienced divers who are captivated by this modern wreck.[232]

BIG DRUM DANCE A Carriacouan cultural expression dating to the 1700s which celebrates the ancestors of particular African nations or tribes brought to the island, hence another of its names African Nation Dance. This ancestor worship was established in Grenada and Carriacou during SLAVERY, and though rooted in West African culture, incorporated numerous French and British Caribbean cultural influences over the years, creating a unique Creole fusion. It was common in Grenada until the 1940s, and is still visible in villages like RIVER SALLEE, or as staged performances by FOLK DANCE groups. Elements can be traced directly to at least nine West African societies such as the AKAN (Cromanti) who, as slaves, brought with them the beliefs in ancestral spirits. The dances and music of the Akan incorporated other African ethnic influences, among them the Arada, Igbo, Congo, Mandingo, Chamba, Banda and Temne.

Big Drum is a combination of drums, songs and dances, each playing a specific role in the ceremony. There are three drums (the lead cot drum and two bula drums) at a Big Drum celebration, with the 'oldhoe' (an implement used for cultivating the soil), and the chac-chac (a CALABASH sealed with CORN seeds) providing the additional textures of percussion. The songs are performed in the traditional African call (statement) and response (chorus) fashion, with the singer or chantwèl leading the chorus. There are as many as 25 dances that fall into three primary categories: African nations' dances, old Creole dances, and new Creole/frivolous dances. The Big Drum has become a central part of most Carriacouan ceremonies—marriage, baptism, business opening, schooner launching, MAROON, and religious celebrations to honour the ancestors.

Noted Big Drum performers include(d) musicians Caddy Lazarus John, Felix 'Titus' Lambert, Daniel Aikens, Canute CALISTE and the legendary Ferguson ADAMS; singers Mary FORTUNE, Lucian Duncan and Jemina Joseph; and dancers Collie Lendore, Lucian Duncan, and Estimie Andrews. Winston Fleary and Christine David have been instrumental in the promotion of the Big Drum Dance in and out of the islands. The Carriacou Cultural Organisation and the Carriacou Big Drum Nation Dance Co. of New York have helped to promote the Big Drum Dance through their many staged performances. Audio recordings include Andrew Pearse's in 1952 and Donald Hill's in 1970, as well as the readily available Alan Lomax recordings of 1962 that provide a unique introduction to Carriacou culture.[51, 85, 227, 228, 302, 349]

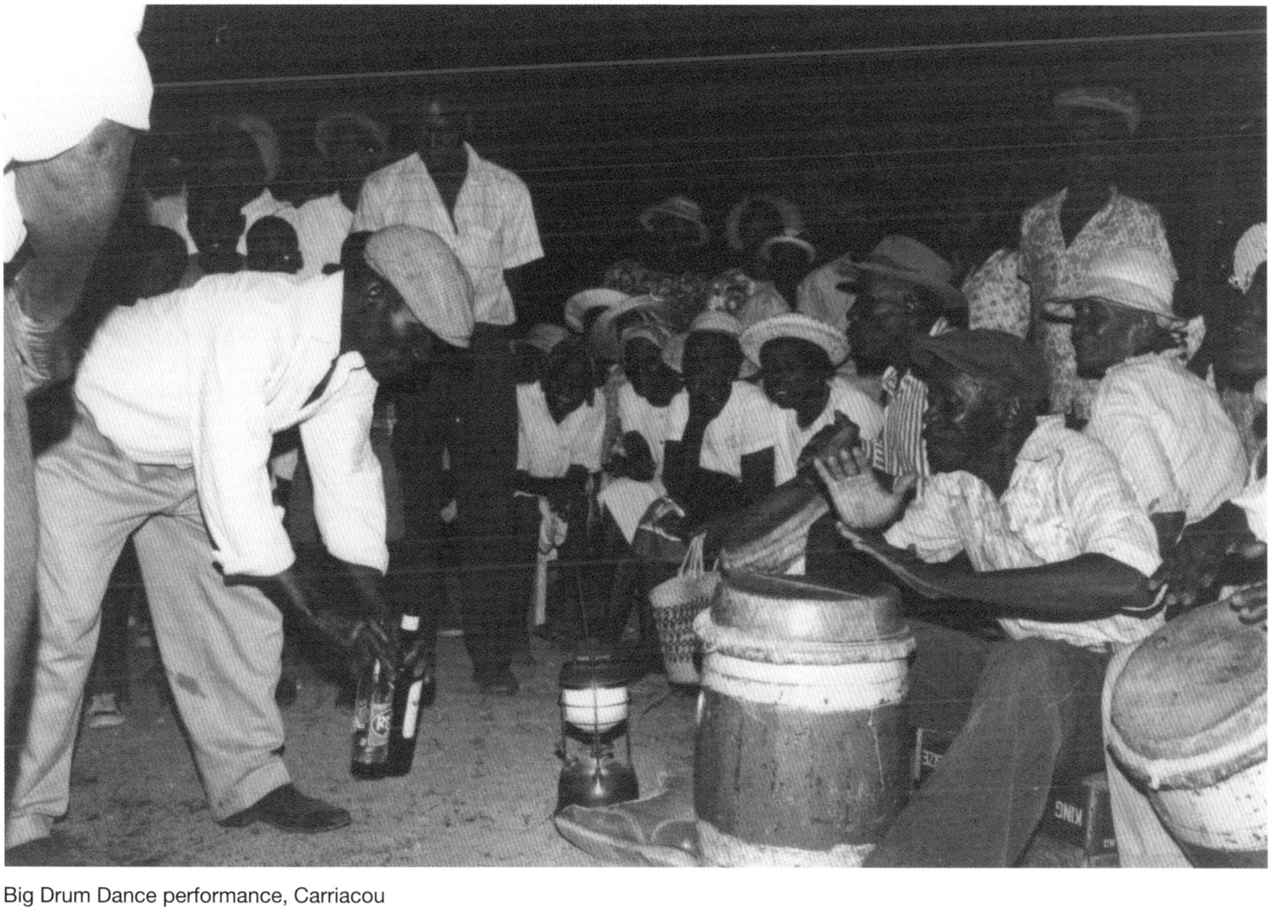

Big Drum Dance performance, Carriacou

BIRDS There are over 150 species of birds that can be seen on the islands, some quite common, many migrants, others rare, and even a few fortuitous visitors. Grenada is situated only 100 miles (160 km) from South America, and its avifauna 'is primarily West Indian with a strong South American element.' Though humans have altered the natural environment tremendously over the years, most of the original avifauna survives. Except possibly for a Grenada parrot (*Amazona* sp.) and parakeet (*Forpus* sp.), which historical evidence places in Grenada in the seventeenth century, there is no recorded evidence of bird extinction in the islands. Today, however, more than 16 species are threatened, and many others endangered. Among the residents are two in particular, the GRENADA DOVE and HOOK-BILLED KITE, both endemic and endangered.

Among the over 35 resident species can be found a number of regional endemic species. Grenada is home to five species of doves and three species of HUMMINGBIRDS. One of the largest birds is the migrant peregrine falcon or chicken hawk (*Falco peregrinus*) which, due to legal hunting, is endangered. There are a number of resident sea birds, found predominantly in the GRENADA GRENADINES. Over fifty species are North American migrants wintering in Grenada. Most of these can be found in the MANGROVES surrounding LEVERA POND, LAKE ANTOINE, Grand Étang Lake, the many cays along the SE coast, the Grand Étang Forest Reserve and the Grenada Grenadines. CARRIACOU and the Grenadines are home to over thirty resident birds, including eight waterfowls and about 15 seabirds. Approximately 35 migrants, predominantly water birds, visit annually.

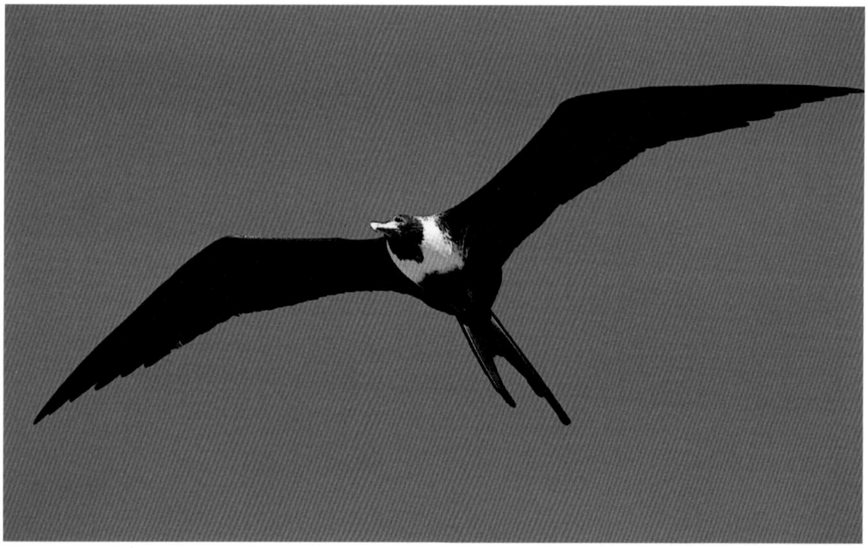

The magnificent frigate bird (Fregata magnificens)

Attempts to protect the islands' avifauna date to 1891 when the legislature passed the Birds and Fish Protection Ordinance 'for the protection of certain birds and fishes'. The legislation was enhanced in 1928, 1957 and 1964, but lack of implementation has rendered only minor protection to birds. With such limited action previously taken towards the CONSERVATION of the islands' avifauna, it is not surprising that a number of species are endangered. The decline in bird species and populations has been due to natural disturbances, predation by man, the introduction of FAUNA like the MONGOOSE, and the destruction of habitats for TOURISM and AGRICULTURE.[90, 104]

BIRTH To mark the beginning of life folk culture has created a number of rituals and traditions that begin even before conception, since certain measures may have to be taken to ensure a successful pregnancy. Even further back still, there are portions and rituals to 'catch' a desirable mate. Though many of these are no longer adhered to, they are nonetheless observed, in part because of habit, especially in rural villages. But once a woman becomes pregnant, the rituals and rites of birth begin. She is forbidden to look at disgusting or unattractive things so as not to adversely affect the unborn child's physical appearance. This probably derives from African beliefs like those of the Asante, among whom the practice of possessing an Akau-mmu or fertility doll provides the ideal model of a child.

Diet during pregnancy is very important because certain foods can aid pregnancy and delivery, or the absence of certain foods can result in deformities like birthmarks. Before the widespread availability of nurses, doctors and maternity wards at HOSPITALS, village midwives were responsible for the delivery process and every village or community had a woman experienced in delivering babies. Nurses, or rarely doctors, were called in if the delivery proved problematic. Once the baby was born its 'nabel string' or umbilical cord and afterbirth were buried under the house or a tree to 'ground the child' or give him/her 'roots'. The child and mother remained in the house for at least eight days, with a celebration held on the eighth day to mark the birth of the child and give it a name. (Because many children died within the first few days after birth, especially during SLAVERY, the survival of a child beyond eight days was a good sign that it might survive much longer.)

Babies usually receive a silver coin for good luck among their many gifts. To protect the child from malevolent spirits, especially MALJOE, JUMBIE BEADS and other folk remedies are employed. Baptism is the final stage to cement the child in this world, and as the child grows, many other SUPERSTITIONS and rituals protect it. A baby who dies before christening becomes a DWENN, while a woman who dies in childbirth is called a MAMA-MALADIE.[85, 153]

BISHOP, Maurice Rupert (1944-1983) became the PM of Grenada after the successful overthrow of the GULP government in March 1979. He was born on 29 May 1944 in ARUBA to Maria Alimenta *nee* LA GRENADE and Rupert Bishop. In 1950 the family returned to Grenada. Maurice left Grenada in 1963 to study law at Gray's Inn, London University, after graduating from the PBC. Completing his legal studies in 1969, he returned to Grenada in 1970 and began a private law practice. Between 1970 and 1973 he was involved in a number of political organisations. The last of these groups, the Movement for the Assemblies for the People, merged with JEWEL in March 1973 to form the NEW JEWEL MOVEMENT. Throughout the 1970s Bishop, by spearheading the NJM's efforts against the GULP, was harassed by the Gairy government, arrested and even brutalised. But this victimisation served only to complement an already charismatic personality.

PM Bishop and Foreign Minister Unison Whiteman

In 1976 he became the leader of the parliamentary opposition's coalition party, the PEOPLE'S ALLIANCE. In 1979 the NJM seized power in a 'bloodless' coup, and Bishop became PM, heading the PEOPLE'S REVOLUTIONARY GOVERNMENT. He enjoyed broad support, both locally and internationally. But after four-and-a-half years as PM, the Central Committee of the party decided that Bishop should share political power with his deputy, Bernard COARD. When he refused, he was accused of 'one-manism' and creating a cult of personality. He was placed under house arrest, but was released by a crowd of his supporters on BLOODY WEDNESDAY. On that same day he was executed by the PEOPLE'S REVOLUTIONARY ARMY. His body, along with those of his colleagues and supporters, was burned in a pit at Camp Fédon and never recovered.

In 1994 the highway leading to the POINT SALINES INTERNATIONAL AIRPORT was named in Bishop's memory, but his supporters agitate for the airport, the PRG's enduring legacy, to be renamed in his memory. Bishop, though still a controversial figure, is hailed by many as a revolutionary and patriot. He is regarded as a martyr for his leadership of an initially progressive and popular REVOLUTION, who subsequently died for that revolution. But widespread political victimisation, unlawful detention, deprivation of civil rights, and political VIOLENCE against the opposition during his reign will forever tarnish his legacy. Thorndike, however, believes that a positive consequence of the revolution was the emergence of 'an extraordinary leader' in Bishop, adding, 'In time, he may perhaps be recognized as the most politically significant personality which the West Indies has ever produced.' Many of his speeches have been published, but a complete biography remains to be written.[19, 20, 21, 117, 147, 243]

BISHOP'S COLLEGE was the first secondary school in Carriacou when it opened in February 1964 (the Hillsborough Secondary School was opened in 1971 as a junior secondary school, but has since been made a senior school). Bishop's College was opened under the auspices of the Anglican Church as a co-educational institution, with grant-in-aid from the GOG. Before 1964 secondary EDUCATION was only available in Grenada, which created a financial burden for the parents of C&PM wishing to send their children to secondary schools. In 1972 a new building adjacent to the Botanical Gardens was completed. Recently a new four-classroom block was added to cater to the growing enrolment, averaging between 150 and 200.

BLACK POWER In the late 1960s mass protests emerged throughout the region, and in 1970 almost brought down the government of PM Eric Williams in Trinidad. Premier GAIRY, fearing that similar protests could develop in Grenada, responded with the passing of the Emergency Powers Act, which gave the police increased powers of arrest, and his now famous radio broadcast on the Black Power movement on 3 May 1970. The premier was responding to the unrest in Trinidad and the possible implications for his government in Grenada. Premier Gairy found it puzzling that Grenadians should be demanding 'Black Power' when he had already won it for them in 1951, a reference to SKYRED. In his radio broadcast, Gairy dismissed the protesters as 'malcontents influenced by nationals returning home', insisting that there was no situation which warranted 'Black Power' since power was 'in the hands of the black[s]. Our Governor is black, our Premier is black, our Chief Justice is black, and our Bishop [of the Catholic Church] is black... If Grenada wants any power at all today it is certainly not "Black Power".' Gairy vowed not to 'sit by and allow individuals or groups of individuals to agitate or incite, to promulgate or promote any racial disharmony in this "Isle of Spice"—the Caribbean Garden of Eden.' Vowing that 'law and order will always reign supreme in this great little state of ours,' Premier Gairy wasted no time in establishing a body of POLICE AIDES to counter the perceived Black Power threat.

In late 1970 anti-government protests began with demonstrations by nurses at the General HOSPITAL. Individuals and groups who termed themselves 'black power' joined the protest, and on 15 December demonstrators occupied the Ministry of Health building, but were dispersed by the police using tear gas. The 22 people arrested were later acquitted. The rallying cry of the movement, 'power to the people', became the slogan of the anti-Gairy protests that challenged the GULP's political dominance throughout the 1970s. One lasting consequence of the movement was the political VIOLENCE that became part of the political dialogue in the 1970s and after.[94, 176, 201]

BLAIZE, Herbert Augustus (1918-1989) was the political leader of the GRENADA NATIONAL PARTY (1956-1984) and NEW NATIONAL PARTY (1984-1989), and served as chief minister (1960-1961, 1962-1967), premier (1967) and PM (1984-1989). He was born in CARRIACOU, the son of Mary *nee* Ackee and James Blaize. He attended the GBSS and worked as a civil servant before migrating to ARUBA in 1945. He returned to Carriacou in 1952 and two years later made an unsuccessful bid for the legislature. In 1956 he joined the GNP and won a seat in Legislative Council elections, winning every election he contested thereafter. The GNP formed a coalition in the legislature with Blaize as the leader. In 1960, following constitutional changes and the establishment of ministerial government, he became CM, but his party lost the 1961 elections. The Grenada constitution was suspended in 1962 as a result of SQUANDERMANIA, and in elections later that year, Blaize was again elected and became CM.

After ASSOCIATED STATEHOOD was granted in 1967 he became the first premier. He offered to step down as party leader after the GNP lost the 1967 elections, but remained because no one came forward. Blaize's leadership of the party achieved a new low when the GNP suffered a resounding defeat in the 1972 elections, winning two of 15 seats. A result of the poor showing was a struggle for the leadership of the party between himself and Wellington Friday, but Friday later resigned. In 1976 Blaize participated in the PEOPLE'S ALLIANCE. Following the Grenada REVOLUTION in 1979 he was forced to abandon politics. In 1983, following the US-led military INTERVENTION, he was 'picked' as the most likely choice to lead Grenada

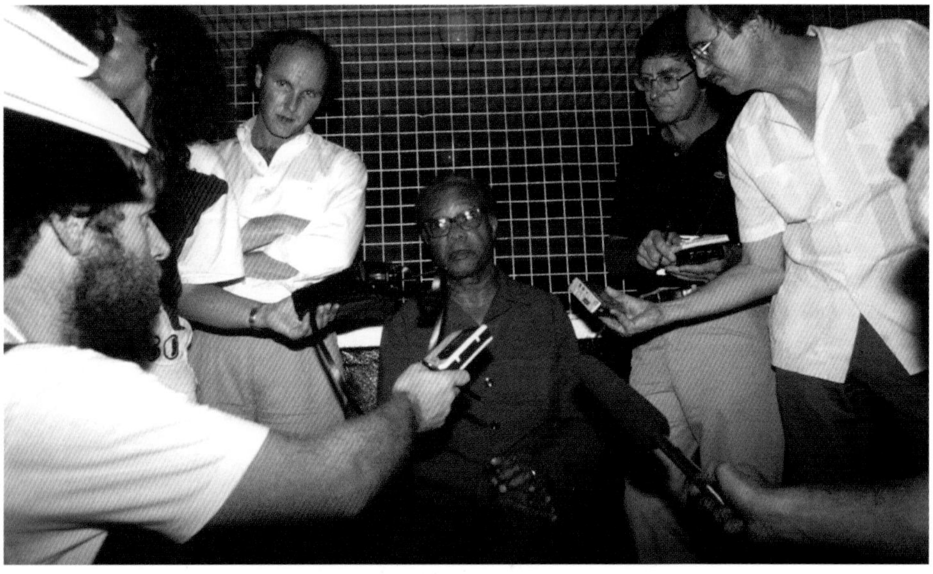

Prime Minister Blaize at press conference

'back to the fold'. In August 1984 he became leader of the NNP coalition and PM following the NNP's resounding victory at the polls.

His government was confronted with a number of political and economic problems, which soon led to internal party conflicts that practically destroyed his government. After five turbulent years as PM, Blaize died of cancer in December 1989 while in office. Though involved in politics for over three decades and was the 'longest serving legislator', his political contributions are a source of constant debate. In 1994 Tyrrel Street, St. George's, was renamed in his memory.[243]

BLOOD/BLACK PUDDING is a large sausage locally made with animal blood and bread crumbs and encased in pig's intestines or tripe. Though it is common to England and northern France, its introduction into Grenada may be as a result of the islands' SCOTTISH HERITAGE. The blood and bread are mixed with a variety of spices that give the dish its particularly spicy flavour. The ingredients are packed into the tripe and boiled. The pudding, sold by STREET VENDORS, is usually eaten with bread after being cut into small slices and deep-fried.

BLOODY MONDAY On 21 January 1974 Premier GAIRY sent his POLICE AIDES to 'harass' demonstrators at Otway House (the SWWU Headquarters) on the CARENAGE who were demanding, among other things, an end to police brutality and the illegal harassment by his paramilitary forces. For the previous few months, following a number of confrontations between Premier Gairy and his opposition, the island had become politically divided. The events that culminated in Bloody Monday were set in motion when the COMMITTEE OF 22 threatened Gairy's government with a nation-wide labour strike if he did not comply with their demands to disband his Police Aides and bring to justice those responsible for the events of BLOODY SUNDAY.

After initially agreeing to the Committee's recommendations and establishing a Commission of Inquiry, Premier Gairy reneged on the remaining conditions and the Committee of 22 resumed its nation-wide labour strike on 1 January 1974. The strike resulted in the complete shut down of the country, including businesses and the central port, leaving the Gairy government few alternatives. Casualties of the conflict included Gov. BYNOE, who resigned (but, according to Premier Gairy, she was dismissed for insubordination), Rupert Bishop, who was killed, and many others who were injured. The secret police, after violently confronting the demonstrators, reportedly continued the destruction by looting many of the groceries and general stores in St. George's, an accusation the GULP government has always denied. This was viewed by Gairy's opposition as retaliation against the businesses that took part in the strike against his government. Subsequently, the people joined them in looting and temporarily destroyed some of Grenada's prominent businesses.

The labour strike continued for two more months, but the opposition failed to force the resignation of Premier Gairy and forestall INDEPENDENCE. The turbulent events of Bloody Sunday and Bloody Monday, representing the climax of the early political VIOLENCE in Grenada, brought Premier Gairy's penchant for circumventing the constitution and laws to the notice of the world. The DUFFUS COMMISSION rendered a severe indictment against the GULP government with its investigation, concluding that '...the cause of the riot on the Carenage on Monday, January 21, 1974 was the gross negligence of Mr. Gairy in dispatching his police aides'.[35, 94, 333, 363]

BLOODY SUNDAY On 18 November 1973 Maurice BISHOP, Hudson Austin, Unison Whiteman, Selwyn Strachan, Simon Daniel and Kendrick Radix were attacked by members of the MONGOOSE GANG and arrested in Grenville, St. Andrew, by Assistant Superintendent of Police BELMAR. They were there to meet with businessmen in connection with a planned island-wide labour strike should Premier GAIRY not resign following a 4 November 'People's Indictment' which called for the resignation of his 'corrupt government'. In response to the 'People's Indictment', Premier Gairy vowed to 'bring the NJM rebels to their senses and wake them up from their dreams in a very short time for fifty-four reasons including treason and sedition.' After the beating by members of the Mongoose Gang and POLICE AIDES, the six were incarcerated without medical attention, and denied bail and legal advice. They were charged with the possession of a firearm and ammunition, which Gairy's supporters charged were to be used to seize control of the Grenville Police Station and the eventual violent overthrow of the government. The DUFFUS COMMISSION later ruled that the firearm and ammunition charges were fabricated. Bishop, upon release, had to be flown to Barbados for surgery as a result of injuries sustained in the beating.

The violent events of Bloody Sunday sparked off reactions from a large segment of the Grenadian population which was now convinced of Premier Gairy's willingness to subvert the constitutional rights of citizens in order to suppress the growing and vocal (some might add seditious) opposition to his rule. The COMMITTEE OF 22 attempted to broker an end to the violence by forcing Premier Gairy to disband the Mongoose Gang and bring to justice those responsible for the beatings under threat of a nation-wide labour strike. Bloody Sunday had the added effect of creating martyrs of the NEW JEWEL MOVEMENT leaders, but would ultimately culminate in BLOODY MONDAY two months later.[35, 94, 333, 363]

BLOODY WEDNESDAY On the morning of 19 October 1983 the mood in the country was tense, but no one could have foreseen the bloody conclusion to the day. The Central Committee had placed PM BISHOP under house arrest because he had refused to comply with its majority decision that he share power with his deputy Bernard COARD. Attempts to resolve this volatile issue, both domestically and internationally, produced a 'proposal' that would have reinstated Bishop as PM pending his approval, but the inevitable events of Bloody Wednesday annulled the possibility of a peaceful resolution. In a massive demonstration led by Unison Whiteman and Norris Bain, between seven and eight thousand of Bishop's supporters marched to his residence and released him from house arrest. The armed forces stationed at Bishop's residence did not confront the demonstrators and these moved on to FORT GEORGE where the army headquarters was 'taken over'.

IN EVERLASTING MEMORY OF
PRIME MINISTER MAURICE BISHOP
FITZROY BAIN
NORRIS BAIN
EVELYN BULLEN
JACQUELINE CREFT
KEITH HAYLING
EVELYN MAITLAND
UNISON WHITEMAN
ANDY SEBASTIAN ALEXANDER
SIMON ALEXANDER
GEMMA BELMAR
ERIC DUMONT
AVIS FERGUSON
VINCE NOEL
ALLEYNE ROMAIN
NELSON STEELE
KILLED AT THIS FORT, OCT. 19, 1983
THEY HAVE GONE TO JOIN THE STARS
AND WILL FOREVER SHINE IN GLORY
ERECTED 19TH OCTOBER, 1993
WITH THE CO-OPERATION OF THE GOVERNMENT OF GRENADA
BY THE MAURICE BISHOP AND MARTYRS FOUNDATION

Plaque at Fort George commemorating those killed there on 19 October 1983

The situation in the country was very tense as PM Bishop tried desperately to regain control of the government by calling on his opposition to surrender. In a reckless move to regain control of its headquarters and bring about the surrender of PM Bishop, the PEOPLE'S REVOLUTIONARY ARMY ordered the fort stormed. In the ensuing gun battle a number of people were killed and scores injured. The captured PM, three cabinet members and key supporters were subsequently executed in the fort's central courtyard, though the PRA claimed they were killed during the exchange of gunfire. The PRA listed 24 officially dead, and over 100 injured in the panic that followed.

The PRA immediately imposed martial law, with a 24-hour shoot-on-sight curfew. General Austin announced that a 16-member REVOLUTIONARY MILITARY COUNCIL now ruled the country. The events of that day resulted in the US-led military INTERVENTION six days later. In 1993 a controversial plaque was erected on the hallowed site in memory of the people who were killed on Fort George that infamous October day, but supporters have been lobbying to have 19 October declared a national holiday (25 October, the day the US began its military intervention, is celebrated as Thanksgiving Day, a national holiday). Even after the trial of the GRENADA 17, apologies by those convicted, and years of exhaustive analysis, the demise of the Grenada Revolution is still shrouded in controversy, leaving many important questions still unanswered. It remains one of the most tragic and bloody events in Grenada's recent history.[2, 35, 298, 303, 333, 344, 363]

BOAT BUILDING communities have thrived on Grenada, Petite Martinique and Carriacou, with the latter island possessing by far the oldest, most famous and respected community of all. Carriacou's SCOTTISH HERITAGE dates to the 1760s, and it is believed that the need for trading vessels to and from the UK led to the establishment of boat building on the island, since ships built in England deteriorated quickly in the tropics. In the late 1830s a number of Scot shipwrights arrived in CARRIACOU. Little is known of them except that many of the recent boat builders of Carriacou have Scottish surnames like Steille, MacLaren, McLawrence and McFarlane (many have also retained European physical features, notwithstanding over a century of intermarriage with the black population). The first boat of consequence registered from Carriacou, a sloop, dates to 1840 and may establish the industry's beginning. Yet, it appears that small sailing crafts regularly travelled between Carriacou and the other islands, 'trafficking' in agricultural produce, soon after EMANCIPATION. Schooners (two-masted) were not registered, and possibly not built until the 1870s, and not in appreciable numbers until the early 1900s.

Of the early shipwrights, John Rock (1866-1942), a Barbadian who migrated to Carriacou in the 1880s, is the most memorable. He is credited with the introduction of the overhanging or counter stern that allowed greater stability and displacement of the boat in the water. The importance of the industry to inter-island trade and the FISHERIES industry cannot be overestimated, and it is essential to TRAFFICKING. In Carriacou, boats at differing stages of construction can be seen in backyards and along BEACHES as shipwrights go about the task of constructing all manner of fishing and cargo vessels, utilising traditional methods and techniques.

The ceremony to launch a boat is as important as the building of the boat itself. This ritual consists of the blessing of the boat, animal sacrifices, pouring of libations to the ancestors for good luck, a BIG DRUM DANCE and feasting. Today, as on other islands, the boat building industry has not fared well due to its inability to compete with more efficient steel-hulled ships. Boat building has always been fuelled by the need to transport produce, especially from Carriacou to other islands. The collapse of Carriacou's export agriculture, particularly COTTON and LIMES, signalled the demise of the industry. Imported steel-hulled ships have responded to the island's new status as a visitor attraction and the need to transport people thither. Yet, boat building continues as an art form, illustrating a rich aspect of the history and culture of the people of the GRENADA GRENADINES. The annual CARRIACOU REGATTA is nothing less than a celebration of the skill of the great boat builders and mariners of C&PM.[85, 266, 271]

Boat building, Carriacou

BONFIRE RIOTS On 4 November 1885 police constables patrolling the town of ST. GEORGE'S to discourage the lighting of bonfires and discharging fireworks were pelted by the 'poorer residents' of the town when they tried to extinguish the lighted barrels. This conflict resulted from the newly passed Bonfire Act, forbidding the traditional lighting of bonfires as part of the annual Guy Fawkes Day celebrations. Local merchants, aware of past disasters and fearful of the damage uncontrolled fires could cause, had petitioned the legislature to pass the law. On 5 November one hundred 'respectable' citizens were made special constables and prepared to control the 'rowdies' should they attempt to break the law again. It was believed that opponents of CROWN COLONY status roused the people, possibly activists like W G DONOVAN who wanted to create widespread opposition to Gov. Walter Sendall (1885-1889). On the night of 5 November the police were again pelted with rocks and areas of the town thrown into darkness after street lamps were broken. The governor blamed the police for the rioting because of their 'rough handling of the delicate situation'. To discourage the rioters some 400 special constables patrolled the town the following night.[35, 288, 333]

BOTANICAL GARDENS In mid-1886 St. George's was chosen as the site for a new Botanical Station. It was one of the many ideas of Gov. Walter Sendall who envisioned the station as a research facility to improve methods of AGRICULTURE through the introduction and cultivation of medicinal, ornamental and economically beneficial plants. A year later the Botanical Station was opened to the public in TANTEEN. At its inception it housed a nursery to propagate economically valuable plants, and for many years thereafter served as a field experimental and demonstration area. Today it functions mainly as a central location to view some of the trees, shrubs and ornamentals on the island. Though a number of interesting trees still remain, its neglect and dwindling size have left it little more than a passing attraction. In 1968 the GULP government opened a National Zoo to the rear of the gardens. Functioning mainly as a local attraction, it became a venue for relaxation and adventure, especially for children. By the early 1980s the zoo was neglected and allowed to decline. The empty and decaying cages were finally destroyed to make room for government office buildings. The government buildings there, especially the recently constructed government office complex, have consigned the area to little more than a FLOWER GARDEN. In 1994 a CENOTAPH was constructed in honour of Grenada's veterans. The small Botanical Gardens in HILLSBOROUGH, Carriacou, dates to the late 1800s and has a beautiful collection of plants.

BOUGAINVILLEA (*Bougainvillea spectabilis/glabra*) has been the national flower of Grenada since the islands' achieved INDEPENDENCE in 1974. It is a native plant of Brazil, brought to France in 1768 by the French explorer Louis-Antoine de Bougainville, after whom it is named. It blossoms year-round, but is abundant from November to June when the vibrant and ubiquitous red variety can be seen growing on vines, hedges and trellises. Three bracts ('flowers') or modified leaves surround an inconspicuous white flower. Thorns along the stem protect its small, dark green leaves. As a hedge plant, it is sheared to provide an ideal privacy screen. Other common colours include mauve, light orange, pink, purple and white.

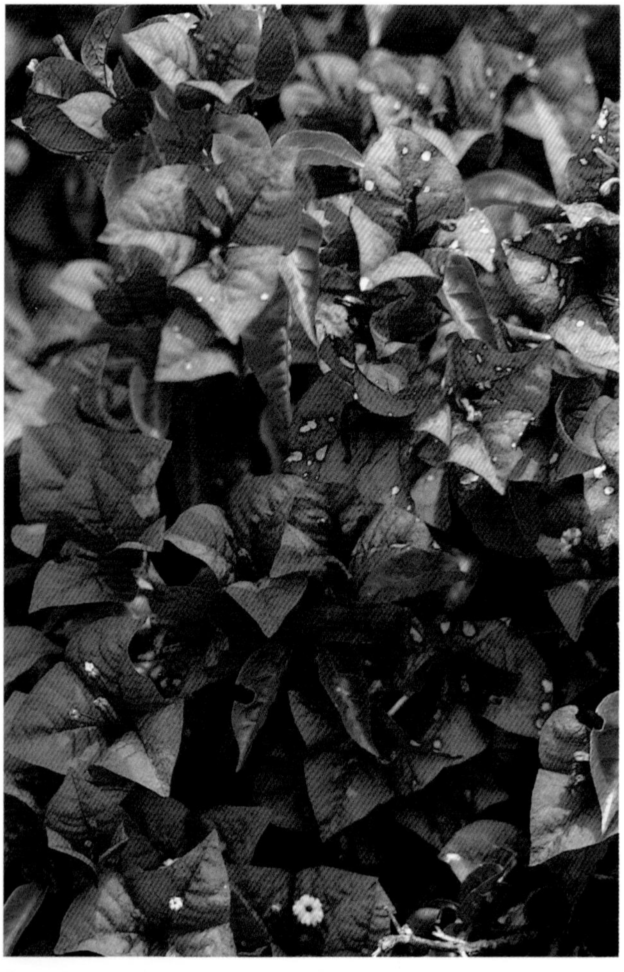

Bougainvillea, Grenada's national flower

BOULAM FEVER From its 'diagnosis' in February 1793 by Dr Colin CHISHOLM, Boulam fever became embroiled in controversy until the 1850s, and remains to this day a medical enigma. Chisholm believed that Boulam or blackwater fever was a 'foreign plague, contagious and utterly unknown'. This was reflected in the name, for the disease was believed brought to Grenada aboard the ship HANKEY from the West African island of Boulam/Bulama. In 1791 *The Hankey* was one of three ships that sailed from England with 'stores and adventurers for the projected colony at Boullam', off the coast of Guinea-Bissau, and became the grave of most of the 260 colonists, most of whom succumbed to 'the malignant fever'. Unable to return to England, the ship, its small crew deathly ill, sailed for the West Indies and arrived in Grenadian waters in February 1793. Sailing into the CARENAGE a few days later, *The Hankey*, according to Chisholm, introduced 'a disease before, I believe, unknown in this country'. This supposedly infectious disease, 'unequalled in its destructive nature', took the lives of over 250 people in the first three months. Though Chisholm had requested the establishment of quarantine facilities, none were set up and the disease soon spread beyond St. George's. Interestingly, the virulence of the disease soon slowed to the point where Chisholm himself described its progression as 'so trifling'. Long at issue is the 'contagious' nature of this disease, since many believed that the symptoms resembled YELLOW FEVER, which was non-contagious and already present in Grenada.

It is presently difficult to determine if Boulam fever was in fact a new disease, but the inconsistencies of this disease with the known symptoms of yellow fever, especially in its first few months, leave open the question of whether it was unknown. Yet, the fact that Grenada was possibly the origin of the yellow fever epidemic that swept the Caribbean, as well as New York and Philadelphia in the mid-1790s, begs the conclusion that Chisholm simply misdiagnosed yellow fever, malaria or typhus fever, or a combination of the three. Boulam fever and its subsequent debate seemed less an issue of a misdiagnosed disease than a reflection on the state of medicine and science in the late eighteenth century.[55]

BRATHWAITE, Sir Nicholas Alexander (b. 1925) is a former educator and politician who served as PM. He was born in Mt. Pleasant, CARRIACOU, the son of Sophia and Charles Brathwaite. He attended the GBSS, Teachers' Training College, Trinidad, and obtained a B.Ed from the UWI. He worked in the oil refinery in Curaçao, and upon returning to Grenada, served as a secondary school teacher, principal of the Grenada

Teachers' College, and chief education officer. Working in Guyana as the regional director of the Commonwealth Youth Programme, he was sent to Grenada as an adviser to the GOVERNOR GENERAL following the US-led military INTERVENTION. He subsequently chaired the ADVISORY COUNCIL. In 1989 he was elected chairman of the NATIONAL DEMOCRATIC CONGRESS and following elections in March 1990, representing C&PM, became PM. His term in office was shaped by the worsening economy, particularly the growing fiscal deficit and cash flow problems. He will probably be remembered most for his pardoning of the 14 who were sentenced to die as a result of the trial of the GRENADA 17. In July 1994 he resigned as chairman of the NDC, and stepped down as PM in February 1995 in favour of George BRIZAN. Brathwaite had earlier described his role as PM as 'thankless', though his leadership was instrumental in creating a stable political environment. A member of the Privy Council since 1991, he was knighted in 1994.[308, 333]

BREADFRUIT (*Artocarpus altilis*) was brought to Jamaica and St. Vincent from Tahiti by Captain Bligh in 1793 and spread throughout the region. An attempt four years earlier had resulted in the infamous 'mutiny on the *Bounty*', the subject of two Hollywood films. The breadfruit (var. *non-seminifera*) had come highly recommended as a possible staple for the slaves, but its introduction was not initially successful. It was only after EMANCIPATION that it became a mainstay of the peasants' diet. The breadfruit or 'cow' (<Fr.Cr. *bèf* <Fr. *bœuf*: 'cow', but used as 'huge' in reference to its size) is an evergreen tree that grows to 70 ft (20 m). The breadfruit is a combination of multiple fruits that coalesce from numerous flowers. It is seedless and large, the size of a small soccer ball (10 inches or 25 cm in diameter), and weighs up to 25 lb (55 kg). Its creamy white or yellowish flesh has a rather pungent odour.

Though a fruit, it is consumed primarily as a vegetable, roasted, baked, fried or boiled. It is a main ingredient in one of the islands' most popular dishes, OIL DOWN. Fruits are harvested from June to December and February to March. The breadnut, a seeded variety (*seminifera*) of the breadfruit, has a chestnut flavour when boiled or roasted, hence another name, chataign (<Fr.Cr. 'chestnut'). The 'nuts' or seeds, about 30-50 in each fruit, are imbedded in a mass of yellow flesh that is removed before cooking. The outer skin of the fruit is covered with fleshy spines. The 'monkey apple' or jack fruit (*A. heterophyllus*) is not popular in Grenada. The saying, 'to have more guts than breadfruit' means to be bold, almost unflatteringly so, but to 'swallow breadfruit' is to become pregnant.[146b, 312]

Breadfruits

BREAKING THE BARREL is a ritual common in C&PM and performed at wakes, prayer meetings, and the TOMBSTONE FEAST for a dead mariner. It is one of the many elements of SCOTTISH HERITAGE still evident in the islands. Mourners, imitating sailors (a captain and his crew), dance around a rum barrel turning a makeshift windlass and beating the barrel as they banter and sing sea shanties. The ritual climaxes with the breaking or smashing of the barrel. In Grenada it was known as 'fishermen's wake songs'.[153, 302]

BRESSON, Bénigne (fl. 1650s) A Dominican priest who resided in Grenada between 1656 and 1659, having replaced the first priest, Abbot Desmieres (1651-1656). Bresson left Grenada for Guadeloupe because of disagreements with the then owner of the island FAUDOAS DE CÉRILLAC. A number of researchers strongly believe that Bresson is the anonymous author of the seventeenth-century French manuscript *Historie de l'isle de Grenade en Amérique, 1649-59.* The manuscript was first quoted in the 1870s by French historian Pierre Margry, but was not published until 1975.

The manuscript recounts in great detail the first ten years of the French occupation of Grenada and the subjugation of the Island CARIBS. It depicts the settlement of what became known as PORT LOUIS and the early trials of the colonists, which according to Jacques P Roget, were most likely recreated by Bresson from records kept by Dominique de la Belarde, notary and registrar of the island. It also disputes a number of important points of the historically accepted account by J-B DU TERTRE concerning the arrival date of the French colonists and the events of the Carib-French conflicts. Roget argues that this document appears 'more accurate' than du Tertre's, adding that 'when Father du Tertre states that possession of Grenada had been taken in June 1650, apparently he is only trying to hide the illegality of his friend du Parquet's act.' And as the anonymous author states, du Parquet took Grenada 'by force, with no previous authorization from the gentlemen of the Compagnie [des Isles d'Amérique]' in March 1649. The anonymous author in his history makes references to two other manuscripts written by him, one about the island's FAUNA and FLORA, and the second relating to the Island Caribs. Neither has surfaced to date and are feared lost.[8, 95]

BRIDGES & ROADS The over fifty rivers and streams criss-crossing the island of Grenada have resulted in the construction of bridges and causeways to assist efficient island-wide travel. Though the French constructed a number of wooden bridges along the coastal *Chemin Royal* or King's Road, they relied extensively on the sea for transportation across Grenada. The British, though also relying on the sea for island-wide travel until around the early 1900s, built many bridges, beginning in the early 1800s. The British were responsible for extending and paving (with macadam) the road network, especially the interior roads across Grenada; the steep and winding road through Grand Étang was an engineering feat when it was begun in 1774. Carriacou already had an extensive system of roads dating to the French.

Until the advent of MOTOR VEHICLES in the early 1900s, roads remained primarily dirt or surfaced with gravel. Over the years many of the old bridges in Grenada have been rebuilt after storms destroyed the original structures, but a few of these unique bridges can still be found. These include the old iron bridge at Nonpareil, ST. MARK. No longer in use, this small and rather quaint

Paradise Bridge, Paradise, St. Andrew

metal truss bridge spans the Little Crayfish River and dates to the early 1800s. Another is the Paradise Bridge, built in 1813 across the GREAT RIVER at Paradise, St. Andrew. This triple span bridge was constructed of solid stone and stands over 30ft (9 m).

One of the most famous bridges on the island is the Queen's Park or Green Bridge. This simple metal truss bridge, built 1942, has withstood many storms and floods, including HURRICANE JANET. It most probably derives its name from the administrator at the time of its construction, George Green, but its colour has also been green. The bridge spans the mouth of the St. John's River at the entrance to the sea, at what is called the bouchourie (<Fr. *embouchure*: '(river) mouth'). It replaced the previous cement structure that was destroyed in 1938 by a severe rainstorm. Some of the present bridges are too narrow to allow two-way traffic and are being rebuilt.

BRITISH WEST INDIES REGIMENT (1915-1919) was established at the outbreak of World War I to allow West Indians in the British colonies to defend the British Empire following their request to serve and the Colonial Office's rejection of non-whites fighting alongside whites in the British Army. Some of the 15,600 men served in the Egyptian-Palestine campaign, East Africa and Mesopotamia, but the majority served as labour details in France. Of the 1,256 casualties, 1,071 died as a result of diseases. T A MARRYSHOW was among those who supported the BWIR and encouraged Grenadians to enlist because he believed that their participation in war would give the West Indian greater credibility in his fight for self-determination.

Grenadian volunteers numbered 445, four of whom were officers. Of those who served 32 died and 20 returned invalid. A few received honours and awards for a variety of services. In April 1919 the men of the Grenada contingent returned home after the dissolution of the BWIR. CENOTAPHS have been erected to honour the memory of those who died during the war.[36, 138, 333]

BRIZAN, George Ignatius (b. 1943) An educator, historian and former PM. He was educated at the PBC, Grenada and the University of Calgary and Carleton University, Canada. A secondary school lecturer, he served as the acting principal of the Institute of Further Education and chief education officer. He was associated with the NEW JEWEL MOVEMENT and GRENADA NATIONAL PARTY, but formed his own party, the National Democratic Party, to contend the 1984 ELECTIONS. He subsequently joined the NNP coalition and was one of 14 NEW NATIONAL PARTY members elected to parliament and later appointed a minister of government. In 1987 he resigned his cabinet position and formed the NATIONAL DEMOCRATIC CONGRESS, becoming a minister of government following the NDC victory in 1990. In 1994 he won the leadership of the NDC, and in February 1995 was sworn in as PM, serving until elections in June. In 1995 the NDC failed to capture a majority in elections, and he became opposition leader. In the run-up to the 1999 elections Brizan, due to ill health, surrendered political leadership of the party. The NDC failed to win any seats and Brizan, losing his constituency for the first time, retired from active politics. He is the author of a number of pamphlets, books and a history of the islands, *Grenada: Island of Conflict*.[34, 35, 36, 37]

BROADCASTING The radio was introduced to Grenada by the 1920s, but it remained inaccessible for most of the population until the 1950s. In 1950 Frank Hughes started the islands' first commercial broadcasting station, Radio Lektro.

The Windward Island Broadcasting Service (WIBS), located at Morne Rouge, St. George, began broadcasting via short-wave between the islands in 1954 as the radio service for the government of the WINDWARD ISLANDS. The arrangement between the islands fell apart in 1971, and the following year Radio Grenada was created as part of the Grenada Broadcasting Service. Between 1972 and 1979 Radio Grenada, known disparagingly as 'Radio Lionel', was part of the propaganda machinery of PM Gairy. On the morning of MARCH 13, 1979 it was seized by the NEW JEWEL MOVEMENT as part of its coup and renamed Radio Free Grenada. It soon became the propaganda machine of the PEOPLE'S REVOLUTIONARY GOVERNMENT, and was bombed by the US military during its 1983 INTERVENTION, with the destruction of irreplaceable historical documents, musical recordings and audio tapes. In early 1984 Radio Grenada returned to the airwaves from its new location at San Souci, St. George.

Though the GULP and PRG monopolised the local airwaves, Grenadians have always relied on the many radio stations in the region for news and entertainment. In 1988 the domestic broadcasting monopoly ended when Stanley Charles opened the controversial Radio LaBaye in GRENVILLE. In late 1989 Young Sound FM began operating from MUNICH, and Spice Capital Radio emerged in 1991. There are at least eight radio stations in the islands.

With the advent of television in the region in the 1970s, the few TV owners received a limited service from Trinidad. In 1974 businessman Joseph Pitt began a very limited and unpredictable service under the name Grenada Television; he also received a monopoly on TV imports, which he lost as a result of the PRG coming to power in 1979. By June 1980 the PRG had acquired the television station, renaming it Television Free Grenada. The Grenada Broadcasting Act (1990) incorporated the public radio and TV stations as part of the Grenada Broadcasting Corporation. Though operated as a statutory body since 1991, majority shares were sold to Ken Gordon and the Grenada Broadcasting Network in 1997. At present there are at least four television stations operating in the islands, including cable television programming from the US.

BUSES Board buses were once the common mode of public transportation throughout the islands, beginning in the 1920s; before then island-wide public transport was by mail buses or boats. In 1934 there were 33 board buses, increasing to 47 by 1939. Starting with the chassis of an Austin, Morris or Bedford truck, the skill and art of board bus building transformed this skeleton into a work of art. A wooden superstructure was built onto the back of the truck to house the 'loads' and the approximately forty passengers on benches. There was even a 'Most Beautiful Bus' competition in the 1970s to acknowledge the skill and creativity of the designers and builders. The advent of the minibus in the early 1970s, with Maitland's *One More* and McBert's *Control*, displaced board buses within the decade, leaving only a handful of board buses on the roads today.

The efficiency in speed and size of the minibuses, though lacking the charm and beauty of the board buses, makes them more ideal for Grenada's narrow, steep roads and passengers who desire quick service across the islands. Each bus has a name that expresses the philosophy of the driver, for example *Have Faith*, *Live and Let Live*, and *Easy Going*. Others are more personal, with nicknames like *Monkey Toe* and *Papa Seato*, while some advertise their qualities of *Comfort*, *Reliance* and *Unique Service*. There are hundreds of busses providing service across the islands.

BUTLER, TUBAL URIAH 'BUZZ' (1897-1977) was born on 21 January 1897 in St. George's, Grenada to working-class parents and went on to become, in the 1930s, one of the leading trade unionists in the Caribbean. He served with the BRITISH WEST INDIES REGIMENT in Egypt, and was among the few to experience combat. He returned to Grenada in 1919 and formed the Grenada Union of Returned Soldiers (GURS) to lobby for pensions and employment opportunities for veterans. In 1920 rising food prices sparked off protests by the GURS, which culminated in disturbances. In 1921 Butler emigrated to TRINIDAD and found work in the oil refining industry. In the 1930s he emerged as a labour leader when he led a hunger march from the oil fields to the capital. He served two years in prison for his leadership of the 1937 oil field labour strike that resulted in a bloody confrontation with the police. The strike echoed throughout the BWI as similar riots erupted across the region.

Butler participated in electoral politics for a number of years, but soon faded from prominence. He will be remembered most for the leadership role he played in 1937 in promoting the working class of the Caribbean as a major political force. Butler is a national hero in Trinidad and Tobago. During the Grenada REVOLUTION he was hailed as a national hero, with BUTLER HOUSE and Camp Butler named in his memory.[35, 175]

BUTLER HOUSE was situated on the eastern hill overlooking the entrance to the ST. GEORGE'S HARBOUR on the site of Moncton's (Hill) Redoubt. The building first housed the Santa Maria Hotel (1949-1962), which opened in March 1949 as Grenada's first luxury hotel. It was later managed as the Islander Hotel (1962-1970) before becoming the property of the GULP government, and later housed the Berean Bible School. In 1979 it became the offices of the PM and was named Butler House after T U BUTLER. During the 1983 US-led military INTERVENTION the compound was destroyed. The US military nonetheless recovered PEOPLE'S REVOLUTIONARY GOVERNMENT documents that became the basis for many of the books and articles written on the Grenada REVOLUTION. The building's charred remains, long a reminder of the failure of the revolution, were demolished in December 2006 to make way for a 120-room hotel.

BYNOE, Dame Hilda Louisa (b. 1921) is a medical doctor who became the first native-born governor of Grenada. She was born in St. David's to Louisa *nee* LaTouche and T J GIBBS. A graduate of the SJC, Bynoe obtained a medical degree from the Royal Free Hospital Medical School, UK, in 1951. She practised medicine in London before returning to the Caribbean in 1953. At the time of her appointment as governor in 1968, she had served in the colonial medical service in the region, and in private practice in Trinidad. The attainment of ASSOCIATED STATEHOOD and the appointment of a black, Grenadian-born woman as GOVERNOR signalled the changing politics in the region. During the civil unrest in 1974, she resigned on 13 January, though Premier Gairy claimed he dismissed her for 'insubordination'.

Dame Hilda, who left Grenada in January 1974, presently resides in TRINIDAD where she had a private medical practice until her retirement in 1989. She is the author of *I Woke at Dawn*, a collection of vignettes, short stories and poems of her life. Dame Hilda sits on the Academic Board of St. George's University. [46]

Dame Hilda Bynoe, the first Grenadian on a postage stamp, 1968

CACQUERAY DE VALMENIÈRE, Louis de (1628-1682) was the governor of Grenada following the sudden death of Gov. Le Comte in 1654. His appointment by DU PARQUET led to a political struggle between himself and Captain Le Fort, major of the MILITIA and second to Le Comte who felt that he should have been appointed governor. Le Fort and Le Marquis, his second, refused to accept de Valmenière's authority, and together with a number of supporters, fortified themselves at the BEAUSÉJOUR settlement. De Valmenière, with the help of hired soldiers, attacked the settlement, killing a number of colonists and capturing Le Fort and Le Marquis. Le Fort committed suicide while imprisoned and Le Marquis was banished from the island. In July 1658 he handed over governance of the island to François DU BU, the representative of FAUDROS DE CÉRILLAC, Grenada's new owner. Though no longer governor, he remained on the island. His abduction of a slave belonging to the Island Carib Captain DUBUISSON, and subsequent denial created contention between the Island CARIBS and the French and almost destroyed the fragile peace in 1658. De Valmenière left Grenada in 1659 and returned to Martinique.[8, 95]

CALABASH (*Crescentia cujete*) is a small spreading tree native to tropical America and the Caribbean that grows to 25 ft (8 m). The flowers bloom at night and are pollinated by BATS. Its large green spherical fruits are harvested for use as domestic utensils and in the manufacture of local crafts. When cut, the two hemispheres are called calabashes (<Fr. *calebasse* <Sp. <Arabic). If left whole to make a chac-chac or rattle, the fruit is called a boli (<Mende 'bowl'). The calabash and boli were used extensively during SLAVERY and after as kitchen utensils such as bowls and water dippers. The pulp is used in FOLK MEDICINE as a cure for a number of ailments. Unlike true gourds, the calabash is a member of the bigonia family. The saying to 'not talk in boli' means to speak freely and bluntly, and having 'more guts than boli' implies boldness and bravado.

Calabash fruit

CAILLE ISLAND 12 16N 62 34W is located 3.5 miles (5.6 km) north of Grenada in the Grenadines, formed as recently as 1,000 years ago by volcanic eruptions. It rises to 275 feet (91.4 m) and has a surface area of almost 400 acres (161 ha), two-thirds of which is covered with tropical vegetation. Its name is derived from the French name for the island, Île des Cailles ('Island of Quails', for the bird). As early as the late 1800s Caille Island reportedly 'served as a whaling station from which northern whalers... launched their expeditions and converted the precious blubber into oil.' In the early 1900s local whalers, with small 'open boats' and six-man crews, scoured the southern Caribbean for humpback whales and porpoises between January and May. The exhaustion of the whale population by the mid-1920s led to the cessation of whaling operations. Place names along the eastern and southern coast like Whale Lookout, Whale Bay, Whaler's Peak, and Whaler's Cave attest to this aspect of the island's history. The stone ruins on its shore are the remains of the old whaling station. Caille Island was one of many islands in the Grenadines used as food gathering sites by AMERINDIANS. As a result a number of shell middens are located on its shores. There are a few modern houses located in the south. The island is privately owned.[110, 336]

CALISTE, Emmanuel (1914-2005) 'Canute/Papa CC' was a Carriacouan folk artist popularly known for his simple style in capturing, through paintings, the cultural and natural beauty of his rural island community. Caliste maintained that a childhood encounter with a mermaid, at the age of nine years, was responsible for his artistic talents, but it was not until he received art supplies from

Canute Caliste

the sisters at the Madonna House in Carriacou that he seriously started painting. He painted in the naïve style infused with intense colours, straight lines, the almost 'childlike' appearance of his portrayals, and a general inattention to the accuracy of human anatomy and nature. A collection of his paintings is featured in a children's book *The Mermaid Wakes: Paintings of a Caribbean Isle* (with a tale by Lora Berg). The book inspired the 1991 off-Broadway play of the same name. His paintings have been exhibited and sold throughout the Americas and Europe. He was also a boat builder, and an accomplished QUADRILLE dance musician, playing the fiddle, guitar and quattro. Recordings featuring Caliste's music include *Carriacou Calaloo*.[47, 51, 156b]

CALIVIGNY ISLAND 12 00N 61 44W is located off the southern coast of Grenada at Calivigny Point, 0.62 mile (1 km) SE of Hog Island. Its name dates back to the French period as Caliveni. The 60 acre (25 ha) island is privately owned and historically used as a stock farm. Archaeological excavations by the Bullens in 1963 revealed possibly the first traces in Grenada of a second cultural occupation by AMERINDIANS known popularly as Island Arawaks. The pottery excavated from Calivigny Island has been defined as a complex within the Troumassan Troumassoid subseries. The beach is popular with snorkellers.[42, 44]

CALYPSO is a musical form popular throughout the English-speaking Caribbean and synonymous with CARNIVAL. Like a number of other islands, Grenada developed its particular form of popular music that was a precursor to the modern calypso as a result of its AFRICAN HERITAGE, FRENCH HERITAGE, FOLK CULTURE, FOLK MUSIC, FOLK DANCES and history of SLAVERY and colonialism. Though TRINIDAD is today regarded as its home and foremost in its development, it was French Grenadians and their slaves, migrating there since the 1760s who contributed much to Trinidad's popular culture, particularly carnival; the continuous cultural exchanges between them have enriched both.

Like other Caribbean cultural expressions, calypso is synergistic, owing much to traditional African customs of satire and ridicule, the work songs of the slaves and peasants, and French culture. By the early 1900s folk expressions like bélé, lavwé (<Fr.Cr. <Fr. *la voix*: 'the voice', i.e. 'loud mouth'; or *la vrai/la varite*: 'the truth'), KALENDA and other folk elements common at village festivals and religious celebrations had merged to create a popular mode of expression celebrated by STRING BANDS. Singers or chantwèls headed these groups, producing their brand of mépris (<Fr. *mépris*: 'contempt') or mavé-lang (<Fr. *mauvais*: 'bad' + *langue*: 'tongue', i.e. 'malicious gossip'), and picong (<Am.Sp. *picón*: 'mocking'<Sp. *picar*: 'to prick, peck'), as they sang and competed against each other.

By the 1930s musical groups became synonymous with their lead singers who often engaged in verbal contests with each other to determine the 'king' of calypso; among these was Papa Edmund (d. 1990) of St. Andrew, who was one of the early pioneers. The 1950s witnessed the final transformation when many of these singers adopted the popular Trinidadian style, and in 1958 the opening of the first 'calypso tent' in the Drill Yard, St. George's, by Lord MELODY and Quo Vadis ushered in modern calypso. Among the early calypsonians were Bomber (Clifton Ryan who won the calypso king title in Grenada between 1940-47 and went on to win the 1964 title in Trinidad), Wadally, Invader, Scaramouche and Lord Roamer (Wilfred Henry), some of whom went on to Trinidad to compete in a more dynamic environment. Though calypso king or monarch competitions date to 1958, it was not until 1970 when it was staged at the Dimanche Gras show for the first time that calypso took on its present popularity.

Having developed over the years, calypso is a simple song that has as its base social commentary, the popular voice of protest. Calypso's roots are often satirical and allusive, commenting on ills within society, gossip, celebrities and celebrations. It is also dynamic, reflecting changes within society, and has also evolved significantly from its early days of predominantly social commentary and satire to a more celebratory, popular form called soca that began in the 1970s. Though calypso and soca are criticised by some as promoting vulgarity and profanity, the lyrics are often disguised as euphemisms or double entendre. In the last decade Grenadian calypso has become vibrant, as calypsonians like Ajamu, Black Wizard and Talpree have demonstrated. Edson Mitchell, aka King Ajamu, is Grenada's most prominent award-winning calypsonian. He is considered 'easily the best calypsonian in Grenada and some critics say, one of the best in the business today.' He has won the calypso monarch title seven times between 1987 and 2004. Ajamu has produced at least ten albums, including PARANG and reggae compositions. Elwin McQuilkin, aka Black Wizard, is another of the islands' top calypsonians noted for his politically conscious lyrics. He captured the road-march title in 1988 and the calypso monarch title in 1994, 2002 and 2003. He has produced at least six calypso albums and a number of parang songs. Talpree (Wilt Cambridge) represents the younger

Calypsonian King Ajamu performing on stage

generation of calypsonians with his creative blend of soca and JAB JAB rhythms, exemplifed by his massive 1999 hit 'Old Woman Alone'; he won the road march title in 2000 and 2001 and soca monarch title in 2003. Though female calypsonians have been competing since 1972 with Lady Beginner (Doris Alexander), only two women have won the calypso monarch title (Lady Cinty, 1983 and Akima Paul, 2001) to date.

Prior to 1970 the modern calypso movement was centred in St. George's, but since the 1980s it has been dominated by individuals from the other parishes. Calypsonians have traditionally sung under pseudonyms that are often fanciful like the Mighty PAPITETTE, or disparaging like Flying Turkey (Cecil Belfon) or Mighty Unlucky. The word calypso, in use since the 1890s, is popularly believed to be a corruption of cariso or kaiso (<Efik *ka isu*: 'go on'; and/or Ibidio *kaa iso*: 'continue, go on'), a once common expression among the slaves and peasants when encouraging an entertainer or contestant. Yet carrousseau (<Fr.Cr. 'convivial party'), because of its French Caribbean association, is another possibility.[230, 308]

CAMPBELL, Alexander (1739-1795) was a proprietor and elected member of the General Assembly who between 1776 and 1785 served as the colonial agent for the islands and represented their financial interests in Great Britain. He arrived in Grenada in 1763 after purchasing a number of COFFEE and sugar estates; he had previously resided in Virginia and North Carolina (1753-59) and Antigua (1759-62). He was one of a number of members of his family who owned businesses and estates throughout the region and North America. In 1765 he brought a lawsuit against the British Crown following its imposition of the four-and-a-half per cent export duty tax on the merchants of the Ceded Islands. In a landmark decision that was ten years in the making, Campbell won and the tax was repealed. A fellow Scot and close friend of Lt. Gov. HOME, he was with him when FÉDON'S REBELLION broke out, and on 3 March 1795 he was captured at GOUYAVE, St. John, along with Home. Julien FÉDON, knowing Campbell to be wealthy, approached him for a loan to finance the rebellion. Dr HAY, a fellow captive, saw this as an opportunity to arrange a ransom for at least Campbell and Home. Campbell, however, rejected the idea 'as pregnant with most imminent danger, and therefore ought not to be adopted.' A month later Campbell was among the 47 British hostages executed by the rebels. See also Quobna CUGOANO.[159, 272]

CARAILA (*Momordica* spp.) is a small annual herbaceous vine native to the Old World, possibly Africa or India. It was brought to Brazil during the SLAVE TRADE, thereafter spreading throughout the Americas. The popular varieties are *M. charantia*, which is used by EAST INDIANS to make a curry dish, and *M. balsamina*, whose pulp-covered seeds are eaten by children as a fruit. Caraila (<Hin. *karelaa*: 'bitter gourd') leaves are used in FOLK MEDICINE to treat intestinal worms, as a poultice, a tea to treat diabetes and cold, and a 'cooling' when applied in a bath. The crushed seeds yield oil used as a purgative. Caraila has been used to treat menstrual problems, and in C&PM the roots and fruits were reportedly used 'as an effective method of birth control through early abortion'. Other names include Coolie PAWPAW from its similarity with the papaya, and bitter gourd. Research into the medicinal properties of caraila is ongoing, but is showing promise especially in treating stomach problems.

CARENAGE, St. George's The area historically defined as running from the Fire Station (formerly the Rum Bond/Burns Point) to the Port Authority. The remaining arc carried a number of names including Hankeys, Hubbards, and the Treasury Wharves because docking facilities were located in front of these businesses before the construction of the ST. GEORGE'S HARBOUR in 1939. The Carenage (<Fr. *carénage*: 'careening') is part of the eroded and filled-in crater of an extinct volcano. On 18 November 1867 a dramatic rise in sea level resulted in 'damage to buildings and boats' caused by a small tsunami after an earthquake in St.Thomas. Other volcanic activities in the region in 1902 and 1929 resulted in sea level rises, and storm surges caused extensive damage in 1955 and 1999.

Over the years it has seen numerous changes, evident in the many illustrations and photographs taken of this natural beauty; it is the one sight on the island visitors have captured as representative of Grenada. On any given day ships, water taxis, sloops, schooners, yachts and fishing boats can be seen either loading passengers or provisions for their journeys. On other days huge luxury liners unload thousands of visitors to the island. 'Carenage Town' or 'Over Town' witnessed early development

View of the Carenage

beginning with the French, but was overshadowed by BAY TOWN, with its many businesses and the central MARKET SQUARE. The old warehouses, with their red brick walls and tile roofs, stand as a testament to the islands' colonial ARCHITECTURAL HERITAGE. The historical authenticity of the Carenage has contributed to St. George's Town being considered the best and most beautiful example of Caribbean Georgian architecture in the region, and 'possessing an inviting Mediterranean flair'.

CARIBBEAN REGIMENT A contingent of volunteers from the BWI, commissioned in 1944 to fight on the side of the British and her allies in World War II. It comprised the Southern Caribbean (Barbados, Guyana, Trinidad and Tobago and the Windward Islands) and Northern Caribbean (Bahamas, Belize, Jamaica and the Leeward Islands) Forces. Volunteers were being trained in Egypt in 1945 when the war ended. At least 139 Grenadians volunteered for service with the Grenada Detachment of the Windward Islands Garrison and served in Grenada and in several islands in the Caribbean. Soldiers serving in Grenada were stationed at the TANTEEN Barracks, and gun emplacements were located at Ross Point and Richmond Hill. A number of Grenadians also volunteered in Trinidad, Canada and the UK. The force was disbanded in 1946 following the Allied victory over Germany and Japan. The names of the three soldiers who died in World War II as part of the British Royal Air Force are engraved on a CENOTAPH located in the BOTANICAL GARDENS.[36, 333]

CARIBS/ISLAND CARIBS The name given to a 'group' of AMERINDIANS who inhabited the Lesser Antilles around the time Europeans first arrived in the Americas. Though it has been over 500 years since the Island Caribs (<Taino (Arawak) 'caniba' or 'cariba') encountered European invaders on their shores, almost every aspect of their origin, culture and occupation of the Lesser Antilles remain shrouded in an ongoing debate. The centre of the debate is on their origin, which has led to models that fit into either the 'Carib invasion' or the 'Arawakan continuity' models. The most commonly held theory of origin is that they were recently migrated Cariban speakers from South America who captured the islands from the Island Arawaks. Another model asserts that they were Arawakan speakers (as is now widely accepted, even though the men spoke a Cariban pidgin) who were long-time residents of the Windward Islands and culturally distinct from mainland populations. A recent model suggests that the people whom history identifies as Caribs were in fact a heterogeneous mix 'composed of multiple ethnic groups with more than one contributing ancestor'. It further contends that they were neither unitary nor 'arrived at the same time or in the same place.'

In the case of Grenada, they were in fact two groups of Amerindians, one group the French called Caraïbe, and the other Galibis. The Island Caribs, however, are recorded as identifying themselves as Kalinago (<Cariban: 'brave warrior,' or 'bitter manioc people') which has aligned them to Cariban ethnic groups in northern South America. They were said by Columbus and generations of Europeans who ventured into the Caribbean thereafter, to be habitual cannibals. Many scholars dispute this, but believe they most likely practised some form of 'ritual cannibalism'. Others contend that this undeserved branding by Europeans justified the Caribs' subsequent enslavement and virtual extermination.

Between 1498 and the mid-1600s, the Island Caribs on Grenada encountered Spanish slave raiders, colonisers, and traders from the Greater Antilles, TRINIDAD, Margarita and South America. These encounters intensified after

Depiction of an Island Carib couple

1511 when the Spanish Crown granted its colonists in the region sanction to wage war on the Island Caribs and enslave them. Thereafter open hostility reigned. The Spanish slave raiders attacked Carib settlements and they in turn disrupted Spanish trade and shipping in the region. The Island Caribs captured African slaves and Europeans from Spanish settlements, and kept them as slaves. In 1561 at least thirty Spaniards, mainly women and children, were held in Grenada following a shipwreck. The Spanish at Margarita tried unsuccessfully to rescue them.

By the early 1600s the island had acquired an unfavourable reputation among Europeans, Thévet describing it as unapproachable. Attacks and counterattacks continued between the Island Caribs and Spanish, the latter gradually losing control of the region to the northern Europeans who came to trade for TOBACCO and timber, and ultimately established SETTLEMENTS. The establishment of the French in Grenada in March 1649 progressed amicably for the first seven months, but once the Island Caribs recognised that the French were there to stay, they reacted swiftly Thus began the conflicts between the French and the Island Caribs The Grenadian conflicts were usually tied to events and the larger conflict in the region between Amerindians and Europeans. In November 1649 a force of about 500 Island Caribs from Grenada and St. Vincent attacked the remote settlement at BEAUSÉJOUR. Though the French were warned of the attack, the tiny palisade fort barely resisted the prolonged siege, with only eight of the over twenty colonists surviving. The attacks and counterattacks continued for a year, forcing the French to seek refuge in fortified houses.

In March 1650 the French exacted their revenge, ambushing and killing many at what became known as LEAPERS' HILL. Guerrilla attacks against the French colonists continued despite a peace, and in April-June 1654, the Island Caribs began a second offensive against the remote settlement of Beauséjour, destroying it. A month later the French launched an offensive against the Island Caribs in the Cabesterre and killed about eighty of them, destroying houses, provision grounds and canoes. Attacks and counterattacks continued until December 1657 when the French sued for peace. Inevitably, the Island Caribs of Grenada were totally subdued by 1659, though their presence in the region would threaten the French for another four decades. By the beginning of the 1700s the French had totally displaced the Island Caribs in Grenada.

The Island Caribs were expert hunters and fishermen, exploiting the abundance of fish and small game animals on the islands. They cultivated CASSAVA, SWEET POTATO, CORN, tobacco and beans in small plots next to their houses. The Island Caribs of the Windward Islands were loosely unified and on numerous occasions assisted each other in battles against Europeans. In Grenada, the Island Carib population in the early 1600s may have been less than 1,000, scattered in villages on the NW and NE; the Galibis occupied villages in the SE.

A number of Island Carib words have survived in the Grenadian vocabulary (through the French), including AJOUPA, boucan ('a wooden cot or grill'), MANICOU, MOROCOY, and boutou ('war club'). Evidence of their habitation in Grenada has been recorded on French censuses between 1678 and 1735, and reported by travellers to Grenada like J-B LABAT in 1700. Grenada served as an important transit point for various traders from the islands and the continent. Grenada's present 'Amerindian' population of 62, less than one per cent of the population, is most likely not descended from native Island Caribs, though some claim partial descent. The Caribbean Sea has been named after the Island Caribs who fiercely defended their way of life against European colonialism and policies of genocide, today representing a fitting memorial to their resistance.[8, 25, 91, 95, 155, 239]

CARNIVAL The roots of Grenadian carnival are tangled in French masquerade balls dating to the 1700s, numerous West African cultural dances and musical forms, rowdy British Christmas and New Year celebrations, the canboulay celebrations of the slaves, and influences from TRINIDAD. Pre-1838 carnival was the domain of the French elite and FREE COLOUREDS, even though slaves participated as musicians or secondary entertainment. After SLAVERY carnival celebrations became heavily influenced by African cultural survivals as the former slaves began to participate in the activities. It became more rowdy and competitive as the ex-slaves dominated it, forcing the elite to abandon the street celebrations altogether. Groups of people paraded through the streets of the major towns displaying an amalgam of African, French and British costumes, dancing to music made by pounding on drums, bottles, tins (cans) and chac-chac (maracas). Most groups represented villages or localities, with a strong sense of rivalry, each trying to eclipse the others with their costumes, merrymaking and fighting prowess. Much of the early masquerades like KALENDA, shortknee and PAYWO revolved around confrontations between rival groups. Up until the 1970s street fighting between rival bands was common, some resulting in bloody confrontations that required the police to intervene.

Traditional carnival was celebrated the three days prior to Ash Wednesday. It began with canboulay (<Fr.Cr. *cannes brûlées*: 'cane burning') on Sunday night when

Pretty mas': King of the band

people gathered around bonfires to watch stick-fighting. It was a rowdy affair, and violence often erupted as the supporters of the contestants clashed. Others staged fetes and 'cook out', celebrating till 'foreday' morning. On Monday masquerades or simply old mas' like JAB-JAB, long-mouth, pizané and jamette paraded through the streets until the late afternoon. On Tuesday the pretty mas' like paywo, maypole, WILD INDIAN, SHORTKNEE, MOKO-JUMBIE and TAMBOO-BAMBOO took to the streets in their splendour. Many of these mas' came from the outlying districts.

The two days of street celebrations prior to Lent represented a kind of social liberation that the RC Church sanctioned. By the 1950s local celebrations began to adopt characteristics of Trinidad's carnival as Grenadians returning from that country brought with them the new additions. By 1970 it had become a mirror image, with Grenada staging queen shows, STEELBAND contests, calypso monarch competitions, and large mas' bands, replacing many traditional mas', but retaining some that have survived to the present.

Today, carnival is the islands' largest celebration and begins right after one carnival ends with the planning for the next. Events begin months before with CALYPSO 'tents' and the preparations of the lavish costumes for carnival Monday and Tuesday. The events 'heat up' the weeks before the street celebrations, incorporating the August EMANCIPATION holiday with activities in GRENVILLE Town and the CARRIACOU REGATTA. Following Dimanche Gras, Sunday night, the activities proceed to JOUVAY morning when people take to the streets portraying traditional old mas'. The afternoon celebrations begin with the costumed bands parading through the streets and at the Pageant to be judged. Recently, Monday Night Mas, supported by local businesses, has been added. On carnival Tuesday, the bands again take to the streets for the final judging to determine, among other things, the 'band of the year'. As darkness approaches, the spectators join in the 'jump up' or 'last lap' celebrations of the carnival festivities.

Carriacou carnival is still celebrated per the Church calendar, on the Monday and Tuesday proceeding Ash

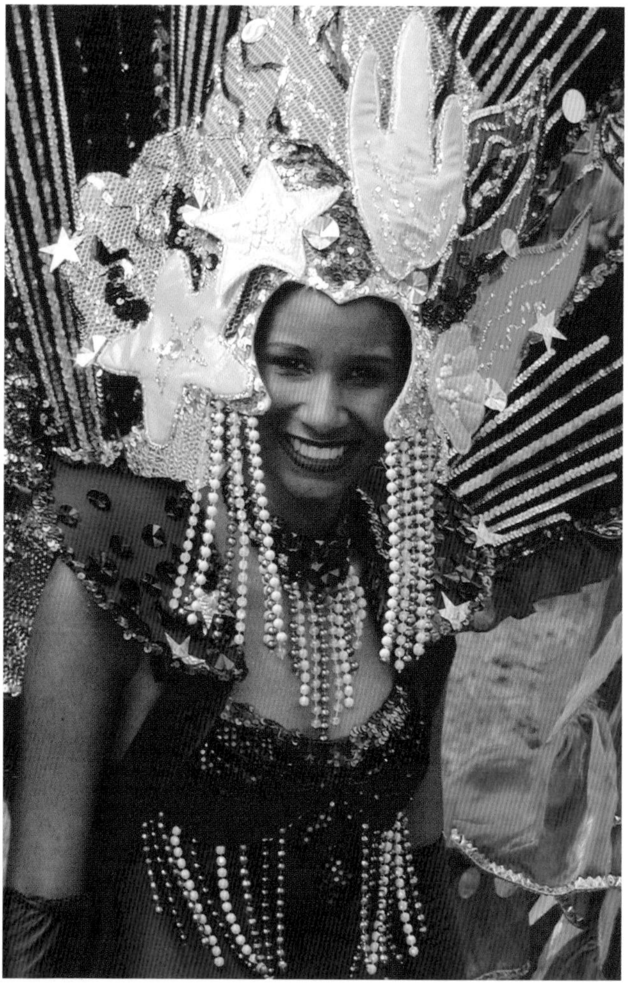

Carnival: pretty mas'

Wednesday. Grenada, due to a number of political events, no longer celebrates carnival at that time, but in August since 1981, becoming independent of Trinidad's celebrations.[255]

CARRIACOU 12 29N 61 27W is an island in the GRENADA GRENADINES, some 23 miles (37 km) north of Grenada. It is Grenada's largest DEPENDENCY, with an area of 13 sq miles (34 sq km) and measures 7 miles (11.3 km) and 3 miles (4.8 km) at its extremes. The word Carriacou is the anglicised spelling of the Island CARIB name for the island *Cárou-cárou*: 'land of reefs, or surrounded by reefs'. The people are referred to as Carriacouans, or more commonly as Kayacs. It has an indented coastline and a rugged interior that rises in the north and south, connected by a broken ridge that reaches 700 ft (227 m). In 1656 J-B DU TERTRE observed, 'Kayrioüacou is a beautiful and good land, with the advantage of having a very good harbour, and is capable of supporting a colony.'

Even though it had been used for hunting and fishing since at least the 1650s, it was probably not officially settled until the early eighteenth century. According to the Abbé Raynal, it was 'the only one of the [Grenadines] which the French have occupied, was at first frequented by turtle fishermen, who, in the intervals of leisure afforded them by their occupation, attempted some kind of [agri]culture.'

The 1750 census gives a detailed picture of the 199 residents (92 slaves, 92 whites and 15 free coloureds/blacks). In 1774 a visitor described the island as 'one of the fairest and finest spots in this part of America [Caribbean], enjoying a climate equally wholesome and pleasant, a soil wonderfully fertile, abounding with valuable timber, as well as fine fruit trees.' By 1776 the population had grown significantly, rising to 3,239 of which the majority, 3,153 were slaves who laboured on fifty estates producing predominantly COTTON. Just prior to EMANCIPATION in 1834 the population was 3,274 (2,800 slaves, 432 free coloureds/blacks, and 42 whites).

The collapse of the sugar industry by the 1850s and the slump in cotton production by the late 1800s devastated the island's economy. Once described as 'the abode of a wealthy and flourishing community of sugar and cotton planters', the island witnessed the almost total abandonment of its estate agriculture. In 1897 a visitor lamented that he 'landed at a little decaying island called Carriacou, where all the people were wretchedly poor. It is all owned by a few absentee proprietors in England and the people cannot get land of their own or rent any except by the year at exorbitant terms.' He suggests 'the experiment of land nationalisation without compensation might well be inaugurated in Carriacou.' Beginning in 1903 the government bought a number of these abandoned estates and sold them cheaply under its LAND SETTLEMENT.

Since 1700 the island has experienced tremendous changes as traditional estate agriculture and present 'over-development' have resulted in the degradation of the natural environment. In 1891 a visitor observed, 'There are no large indigenous trees in the island so that timber is pretty expensive and most of the people are poor. The roads are good and as no rain has fallen for a long time there is a drought in the land,' which made it necessary to import water from Grenada. Over 80 per cent of the island is devoid of natural vegetation (in 1776 only 880 acres (357 ha) were in forest, decreasing to 335 acres (136 ha) by 1990). The 80 miles (129 km) of roads that criss-cross the island date to the French who established the extensive road network to transport crops to the island's many bays for export. BOAT BUILDING, a century-old craft, is still practised by skilled boat builders in villages like WINDWARD and HARVEY VALE.

The population of about 5,000, who make their homes predominantly in coastal villages, exhibit a distinct gender and age bias towards women and older individuals. This is due to the limited resources of such a small island, leaving a large number of men employed as mariners and an out-migration pattern which has forced many males to travel abroad to find employment since the mid-1800s. The island's economy is based on maritime trading, subsistence agriculture with dependence on CORN, PIGEON PEAS and ground provisions, FISHERIES, and remittances from relatives abroad. Carriacou is noted for its annual CARRIACOU REGATTA in August and its BIG DRUM DANCE.

The island is accessible from Grenada by sea and air. Direct flights to the Lauristan Airport, constructed in 1968 and upgraded in 1994 with a 2,500-ft (800-m) runway, are regular. Politically, the island, as a dependency of Grenada, was governed directly by the central government in Grenada until 1904. In the latter year it was established as a separate district under a district commissioner who reported to the colonial secretary. He acted as the magistrate, nominated town wardens and represented C&PM in the Grenada Legislature, even after the limited franchise in 1925. In 1947 the administrator became a district officer with limited executive powers. In 1967 Carriacou was placed under a permanent secretary, with an administrative officer directly in charge of the dependency. In 1997 the NEW NATIONAL PARTY government appointed a Minister for Carriacou Affairs to be resident on the island as opposed to on Grenada.

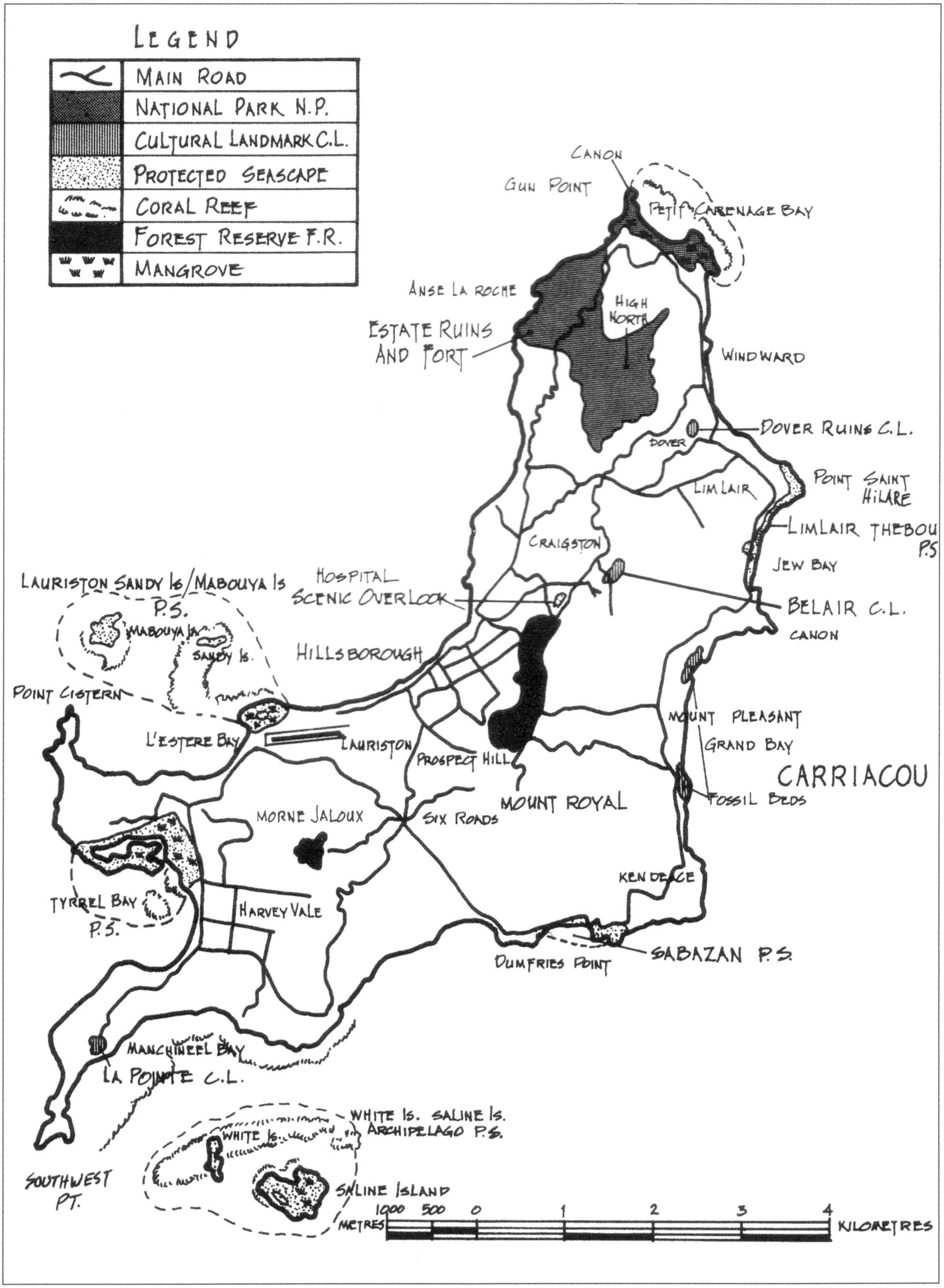

Map of Carriacou and surrounding islands, showing natural and cultural features

Water scarcity has been and continues to be a problem as the prevalence of cisterns in every home indicate. In 1999 a desalination plant was installed at Seaview to help relieve some of the water shortage. Though they were long in coming, Carriacou has many of the modern facilities and services available in Grenada. These include the PRINCESS ROYAL HOSPITAL and a number of Visiting (Health) Stations, five primary and two secondary schools, ELECTRICITY, TELECOMMUNICATIONS, HOTELS, banks, a radio station, post office and other government services. Beginning in the 1760s, many Scots arrived in Carriacou and have left a lasting SCOTISH HERITAGE.[31, 33, 89, 91, 153, 193, 195, 286, 319, 321]

CARRIACOU AUTONOMY As dependencies of Grenada the relationship between the islands of the tri-island state has been anything but equal, particularly when Grenada was a colony and C&PM were double dependencies. Relations have been strained on a number of occasions, leading to political and economic neglect by the central government. Thus Carriacou's secession from Grenada has been a recurrent theme in their historical relationship. During the political unrest in the mid-1970s, the Carriacou Constituency Committee was very anti-GULP and even threatened secession. According to Thorndike, the overwhelming Grenada National Party victories in Carriacou were 'less to support Blaize's policies than to oppose Grenada and [the] GULP for its own sake, and to gain autonomy'. That historical neglect has resulted in C&PM's economic development beyond Grenada's reach, as unauthorized importation of merchandise or 'smuggling' became an important aspect of their economy. Historical attempts to curtail the activity are legendary, as are the 'smugglers' (traders purchasing duty-free merchandise in the French islands and St. Maarten for resale in the southern Caribbean, primarily liquor, cigarettes and electrical goods). In 1991, the GOG confiscated 'smuggled' merchandise from one of the island's businessmen, with the intention of forcing non-compliant businesses in Carriacou to abandon their 'illegal' activities and pay import duties. Some residents of Carriacou protested the GOG's crackdown as an attack on their economic livelihood and questioned their partnership with Grenada. The situation grew worse when in 1996 the GOG authorized the construction of the COAST GUARD BASE on Petite Martinique without much consultation with the residents. This perception of disrespect has created a fierce nationalism, notwithstanding the fact that two of the country's recent PMs were from Carriacou. Though there is a minister for C&PM Affairs resident in Carriacou who represents the dependencies in the GOG, there are a number of constitutional options available, including limited political autonomy guaranteed by the INDEPENDENCE Constitution. The plea by Carriacouan calypsonian Sugar Patch to 'Put we name on the passport cover' is a heartfelt desire by Carriacouans to be respected as an integral member of the tri-island state.[347]

CARRIACOU CULTURE The geographic isolation of C&PM has resulted in their unique social development, with 'extreme demographic peculiarities'. Carriacou, with its 'cultural and social homogeneity', according to M G SMITH, 'provides an instructive comparison with other Creole societies' in the Caribbean. Though politically and economically attached to Grenada since their settlement, C&PM exhibit marked differences. Smith attributes these differences not only to geographic isolation, but also to Carriacou's social homogeneity. This was due to the abandonment of the peasantry by the PLANTOCRACY following the demise of estate agriculture by the late 1800s, producing, according to Smith, a 'classless society'; many scholars disagree with Smith's analysis. Its culture is a synergism of African, French and British influences, preserving many Creole folk expressions since lost throughout the region.

Of Carriacou's cultural distinctiveness the most celebrated aspect is the BIG DRUM DANCE. Other unique cultural characteristics are its 'kinship and community organization', illustrated by 'peculiar modes of mating' and a 'well-developed lineage system'. Yet others include the TOMBSTONE FEAST, MAROON, dancing of the FLAGS & CAKES, BREAKING THE BARREL, and DADA/SHANGO HAIR. Like many developing societies, foreign influences in the form of popular music, dance and cinema have been gradually eroding traditional culture. This has been especially true of the Caribbean islands due to their proximity to the US. Yet for most of the 20th century Carriacou was able to retain elements of its traditional culture, even though MIGRATION has been the one defining characteristic of its population.

Since the 1950s a number of scholars have studied Carriacou's culture, dissecting its religious practices, LANGUAGE and family structure. Much of their work has been recorded and published in books and scholarly articles. Though audio recordings of the island's cultural expressions have been produced since the 1950s, the 1962 field recordings by American musicologist Alan Lomax are the most accessible.[51, 153, 207, 225, 302, 321, 324, 349]

CARRIACOU MUSEUM has had a turbulent history like that of the people it represents. Since its inception in 1976 by members of the Carriacou Historical Society, it has been housed in four different locations. Its second location on the waterfront was formerly a coffin shop. The rear of this building and a large portion of the AMERINDIAN collection were lost when a strong ground-swell destroyed the structure in 1984. The museum was then housed in a tiny room in the former police station until 1986 when it was relocated to its present site, a renovated nineteenth-century COTTON ginnery that had ceased to function as such. The simple two-storey building, located on Paterson St. (<FB Paterson, legislator, 1931-51, 1954-57) is comprised of a lower floor of stone and an upper floor of wood. The museum's collection, much of which is on loan from private individuals, covers the diverse history of the island—Amerindian, French, British and African/black. The pottery of the Amerindians, depicting cooking utensils, tools and religious artefacts, is well represented, many items collected from archaeological sites like Sabazan and Great Bay. A number of bottles, utensils, earthenware jars, a chamber pot and old coins represent the European material impact. The African collection depicts, among others, the drums and chac-chac (percussion gourds) used in the BIG DRUM DANCE for which Carriacou is famous. The collection has been termed 'a living museum', and represents the achievement of a small group of concerned individuals towards the preservation of the past of this unique island.

CARRIACOU REGATTA In 1965 Jamaican-born American yachtsman Linton Rigg (1894-1976) organised the first Carriacou Regatta with a yacht race from St. George's to HILLSBOROUGH, and various work boat races; Rigg had retired to the island in 1960 and owned the Mermaid Tavern, a guesthouse, and the legendary *Mermaid* schooner. Though he initiated a lasting tradition, boat racing was not foreign to Carriacou or to locals like Bernard McLawrence who organised races on a number of occasions. Schooners, sloops and open boats, as well as yachts from the southern Caribbean and even North America, take part in the racing events. There are also donkey or juba, road, bicycle and swimming races, model boats, calypso and beauty contests, and various other activities. Over the last forty years the event has grown to become the largest festival in Carriacou. It takes place on the first weekend in August each year, incorporating the 'Emancipation' holidays. The regatta has evolved into a celebration of dance, games like tug-of-war and GREASY POLE, and music, as visitors from the nearby islands flock to Carriacou. The event also exhibits the things Carriacou is famous for—BOAT BUILDING, BIG DRUM DANCE, Black Wine and Jack Iron (rum). There is a growing concern that the decline in the boat building industry in general, and the absence of participants in the boat races may result in the end of the Carriacou Regatta, which Rigg had hoped would rejuvenate the declining boatbuilding industry. The Regatta is run by the Carriacou Regatta Committee and supported by the GOG. See www.carriacouregatta.com.

Carriacou Museum on Paterson Street, Hillsborough

CASHEW (*Anacardium occidentale*) is an evergreen tree native to tropical America and the Caribbean that produces the cashew nut of commerce. The tree grows to 40 ft (12 m), producing bright yellow to red 'apples', the fleshy flower stalk or receptacle consumed locally as either fruit, or made into wine and preserve. The nut or true fruit grows attached to the pear-shaped receptacle, and after picking is dried and roasted. It is eaten as a nut, or used in a variety of food dishes and confectionery. Substances in the shell can cause dermatitis and blistering, but an oil distilled from the shell is used in the commercial manufacture of various products. An ink can be extracted from its bark. Cashew (<Fr. *acajou*, <Tupi *acajú*) fruits between May and August.

CASSAVA (*Manihot esculenta*, syn. *M. utilissima*) was most likely introduced to Grenada from South America, brought by AMERINDIANS for whom it was a major food item. In the 1600s and 1700s cassava (<Am.Sp. *cazabe*, <Arawak *caçábi*) was an essential part of the diets of European settlers and slaves. This perennial plant grows to over 15 ft (5 m), but is usually harvested while still a shrub. There are two common varieties, locally referred to as 'bitter' and 'sweet', based on their toxicity (prussic acid), which is significant enough in the bitter variety to warrant a process of juice extraction (by a basket press) before consumption. Each plant produces between 5-10 tubers.

The starchy root is used as a vegetable when roasted or boiled, or made into a coarse flour or meal farine (<Fr. *farine*: 'flour'), used as a cereal and thickening agent. A starch is made from the juice of the grated tubers, as is casareep (<Arawak *kashiripo*), a black thick syrup used to preserve meat. It is the essential ingredient in the local dish 'pepper-pot'. Though cassava was a staple of the Amerindians, slaves and peasants, it does not contribute much to the present local diet, except in the form of cassava bread and farine. It is also known as manioc.

CATHOLIC CHURCH SCHISM Beginning in 1829 Roman Catholics suffered 'a troublesome schism' between Father Anthony O'Hannan, and the RC Church and civil authorities. Before the ten-year-long religious squabble ended, it involved the Grenada Legislature and courts, the Bishop of the Archdiocese of Trinidad, the Colonial Office, the British Privy Council, the Pope in Rome, the threat of a slave revolt, and divided the local RC community. The feud began following O'Hannan's reneging on his planned resignation and departure from Grenada. His licence to officiate in the colony was immediately cancelled by the governor, but O'Hannan had influential supporters. As the conflict escalated a number of government officials fell victim to the feud and lost or were forced to resign their jobs. O'Hannan had set up his own chapel and school on LUCAS STREET in the building known today as the La Chapelle, and for six months administered to his followers. O'Hannan, because of his influence over the slaves and FREE COLOUREDS, was a threat to the PLANTOCRACY who regarded his position as 'dangerous'. But the freeing of the slaves and O'Hannan's influence over them proved to be his advantage. In 1835 a number of proprietors wrote to the Colonial Office acknowledging their indebtedness to O'Hannan for preventing disturbances among the slaves following EMANCIPATION, an event which he was rumoured to have taken credit for. The final reconciliation did not take place until O'Hannan returned from Rome to apologise for his 'scandalous attitude towards ecclesiastical authority'.[89]

CATHOLICISM As a result of the French SETTLEMENT in 1649 Roman Catholicism became the *de facto* religion of Grenada. The first chapel, constructed in 1649 at PORT LOUIS, was 'made of only pitchforks and reeds', and a second built at BEAUSÉJOUR in 1656. The early French missionaries included a secular priest Desmieres (1651-1656), and Dominicans Alleaume (1653) and Bénigne BRESSON; at least two Capuchins served the colonists between 1659 and 1664. In 1677 the Dominicans were ordered out of the colony by the governor, but returned in the 1720s. The Franciscan Capuchins were the official clergy until 1901 when the Dominicans took over; secular clergy operated throughout, as well as a small number of Jesuits in the early 1700s.

The 1685 Code Noir or Black Code stipulated that all slaves be baptised and given instructions in the Catholic faith and forbade them the practice of their animist religions. The slaves, however, secretly found spiritual accommodations within RC theology, with its elaborate rituals, numerous saints and festivals that blended so nicely with their animist beliefs and rituals.

The first hundred years of the RC Church witnessed its establishment throughout Grenada, especially after the founding of the six parishes by 1741 and the construction of churches and chapels across the island. Beginning in 1763, the French Catholics and their Protestant compatriots clashed over religious and cultural differences. After 1783 the feuds worsened as the Protestants tried to rid the islands of Catholic/French influences. Catholics were restricted in their worship and all churches and lands were confiscated by the Protestant-dominated legislature for the use of the Anglicans. Catholics, in order to hold public office, were obliged to renounce their faith by swearing to the 'Test'. The feuds climaxed in FÉDON'S REBELLION.

After many years of religious prosecution by the Protestants and the exodus of many French, Catholics were granted religious freedom in 1842. Like the Anglicans, the Catholics sanctioned SLAVERY, and their clergy owned domestic and field slaves.

The RC Church has played an instrumental role in the establishment of public EDUCATION since

EMANCIPATION, and presently administers some 26 primary schools and five secondary schools across the islands. In February 1956 the RC Church was constituted a separate diocese, the Diocese of St. George's, which comprises Grenada, C&PM, with a bishop resident in Grenada. It was formerly part of the Archdiocese of Port-of-Spain, Trinidad (est. 1850) and the Prefecture of the West Indies (est. 1820). In November 1974 it became part of the Province of Castries. Catholic adherents constitute the largest religious denomination: 63 per cent in 1851, 56 per cent in 1881, 60 per cent in 1921, and 54 per cent in 2001. A number of Grenada's festivals are of RC origin, among them ALL SAINTS' DAY, FISHERMAN'S BIRTHDAY and Corpus Christi. The RC Church has about twenty clergy who administer 59 churches and chapels in 21 parishes across Grenada, C&PM.[89, 260]

CENOTAPHS To honour Grenadians who died during the world wars, the Commonwealth War Graves Commission erected a memorial on the ESPLANADE. The monolith, officially consecrated by the Duke of Edinburgh in 1966, listed the names of the 32 men who died in World War I as part of the BRITISH WEST INDIES REGIMENT. In 1968 Premier GAIRY removed it to the centrally located MARKET SQUARE that accommodates many public events. In so doing it replaced the Wallace Fountain. Yet the unsightly state of the Market Square and of the monument itself led to the erection of a new monument in a Memorial Park at the BOTANICAL GARDENS in 1994 (the original monument still stands in the Market Square). The names of three Grenadians who died in World War II as part of the British Royal Air Force were added in 1994. The new memorial is a plaque, beneath a white cross, inscribed with the names of those who died. Armistice Day (11 November was formerly a public holiday) is celebrated with a parade and the wearing of red poppies. Interest in the annual event has been declining as the few remaining veterans migrate or have died. There are no memorials to the Grenadians who died during the 1983 US-led military INTERVENTION, but at least two to the US soldiers who died during the invasion.[36]

Cenotaph, Botanical Gardens, St. George's

CENTIPEDE & MILLIPEDE Known locally as 'santopee', the centipede (*Scolopendra subspinipes*) is a rapidly moving arthropod that lives under stones, tree barks and decaying leaves. A carnivore, it is considered 'a useful scavenger' because it preys on millipedes and crickets. Its elongated body, measuring anywhere from 4-8 inches (10-20 cm), is highly segmented, with a pair of legs attached to each part. The centipede (<Fr. *cent*: '100' + *pied*: 'foot') has 21-23 pairs of legs, not 100. It is possibly Grenada's most 'poisonous and dangerous' animal. A bite from its jaw-like venomous claws usually causes great discomfort and results in the inflammation of the affected area. Gardeners were known to roast and eat a centipede, repeating the phrase 'by St. Peter, by St. Paul', the belief being that in doing so they would gain the ability to see the centipede before it bit them. Chickens or 'yard fowls' prey upon them.

The millipede (*Anadenobolus* spp.) is another arthropod commonly seen throughout the islands. They are neither fast moving nor dangerous, though when molested they release a toxic mist harmful to the human skin. Unlike the centipede, the millipede has two pairs of legs attached to each body segment, except the first five segments that have only one pair each. There are over ten species, measuring between 1-6 inches (2.5-15 cm) and can be found in the soil, under leaves and rotting trees, roaming the

Curled millipede

forest floor and climbing trees, consuming decaying plant material. Of the many species the most common is the 'congoree' (*A. arboreus*), though the name can be applied to various types as well. It measures about 5 inches (12.7 cm) and is more rounded and darker than the centipede. To protect itself it frequently rolls into a ball.

CENTRAL SCHOOLS were established in St. George's by the Grenada Benevolent Society in 1824. The goal was to provide 'a plain education to all poor children, instructing them in their moral and religious duties and on the principles of the established Church of England.' The schools received funding from subscriptions to the Society, which was formed by FREE COLOUREDS, under the auspices of the Anglican Church and the Society for the Education of the Poor. The Central School was the first public school; a handful of private and denominational schools also provided EDUCATION. Though it began as co-educational, it later separated into single-gender schools.

In July 1825 the two schools enrolled 74 males and 21 females, of whom the majority, 69, were free coloureds, 23 were free blacks and three were whites. Over 70 per cent of the student body was from St. George's, illustrating the difficulty for the children from the outer districts in attending school. Though it was against its rules, a small number of slaves were admitted after 1826, with the aim that they would in turn educate more slaves on the estates. The schools' enrolment peaked in 1832 at 210 students, consisting of free blacks and coloureds. Though it was the highest funded and largest of the early public schools, the emergence of denominational schools throughout the islands in the post-EMANCIPATION period soon overshadowed the Central Schools.[35]

CHADEAU, Jacques (d. 1808) was a former slave and rebel captain during FÉDON'S REBELLION who evaded capture for twelve years. He became legendary after the rebellion when he was captured by the LOYAL BLACK RANGERS near Mt. Qua Qua in May 1808. The story goes that Chadeau's involvement in a love triangle led to his capture following the disclosure of his whereabouts by the disgruntled woman. He was later executed and his body left hanging on the gallows at Cherry Hill (St. Eloy Point) as a caution to would be traitors. There is another local legend that claims he was locked in a cage on Cherry Hill where food was placed out of his reach, eventually dying of starvation.

CHERRY (*Malpighia glabra/emarginata* syn. *M. punicifolia*) is a small bushy tree native to tropical America, and grows to 7-18 ft (2-5 m). It produces a three-lobed bright red to yellow fruit when ripe, usually around July and August. These fruits can be sweet or rather tart, and are eaten fresh or made into jam or preserve. Green, it is a rich source of vitamin C. Its leaves are used in FOLK MEDICINE to treat dysentery and liver disorders. Its name is derived from the temperate cherry, with which it has no taxonomic relationship. Other names are acerola and West Indian and Barbados cherry.

CHILD WELFARE LEAGUE Established in 1924 by Lady James, wife of Gov. Seton James (1924-1930), the CWL's goal was to aid mothers by educating them in the proper rearing of their infants, teach proper hygiene, and improve overall child welfare and mortality. It was a volunteer organisation aided by donations and a small government grant. In 1924 it opened a crèche to care for the babies of working mothers, and a weekly clinic for infants in St. George's. It was run by mainly middle-class women volunteers and the Girl Guides, an organisation also started by Lady James. The CWL was also instrumental in the establishment in 1927 of a nurse-midwife service at the newly constructed Visiting (Health) Stations across the islands that were for many years the only permanent medical personnel in rural areas.

In 1927, under its new name Maternity and Child Welfare League (MCWL), it organised the first of its popular baby shows, staging competitions among babies for prizes. In 1929 the show was extended to all the PARISHES, but it was a disaster the following year when mothers rioted because they believed the competition was unfair (the show was revived in 1938 and ran into the 1950s). The MCWL was reorganised in 1940, with new emphasis on training mothers to properly feed and care for their babies. By the 1950s, with the extension of public health facilities across the islands and the availability of medical personnel, the MCWL's volunteer work came to an end. It has been credited with the introduction of the cloth nappy or diaper, the establishment of proper infant feeding, the distribution of subsidised milk, and the improvement in the overall welfare of children from the lower classes. During the period of its operation, child mortality rates fell from 132 per 1,000 births in 1920 to 47 per 1,000 in 1954. One of its foremost volunteers was S J MAHY.[55]

CHISHOLM, Dr Colin (c. 1747-1825) was a Scottish physician, and surgeon to the Ordnance Medical Department in Grenada (1783-1798). A British Army surgeon in the American War of Independence, he was among the new immigrants to Grenada following the British regaining the islands in 1783. Through his writings has emerged an extensive picture of Grenada in the 1780s and 1790s, along with an excellent description of DISEASES afflicting the inhabitants and the methods used to treat them. In 1793, with the outbreak of what appeared to him as a previously unknown disease in Grenada, Chisholm and the island appeared in books and medical journals in Great Britain and the US. His belief that BOULAM FEVER was a new and contagious disease sparked off an acrimonious debate between himself, supporters, and detractors after the publication of his treatise in 1795. He is the author of various books on tropical medicine, but the treatise on Boulam fever led to a controversy that occupied much of his later life.[55]

CHOLERA had been detected in Grenada for many years, but in 1854 it reached epidemic proportions and resulted in the deaths of at least 4,000 people. It is an acute bacterial infection of the small intestines resulting in severe diarrhoea, with rapid loss of body fluids and salts, and can lead to death. On 24 June cases of Asiatic cholera were detected among soldiers garrisoned at FORT GEORGE. Their removal to the military hospital was not prompt enough to contain the spread to ST. GEORGE'S Town. As was foreseen, the disease was deadly because of the unsanitary conditions in the town. As the days went by the number of fatalities increased. With the lack of adequate medical services, the disease spread unimpeded throughout the island and to the Grenadines, exacting a heavy toll.

A major effort to contain the disease failed due to the shortage of medical supplies and personnel, some of whom were requested from neighbouring islands. The military barracks at Fort George (later the General HOSPITAL) was temporarily converted to a quarantine facility in an attempt to contain the disease. From June to September cholera raged throughout the islands, ravaging the population and killing at least 11 per cent, many from St. Patrick (1,250). The cholera epidemic struck many islands in the West Indies leaving 20,000 dead in Barbados and 30,000 in Jamaica. It prompted the Grenada government to pass legislation providing each parish with medical personnel and to improve sanitary conditions in the towns.[55, 333]

CHRIST OF THE DEEP A replica of an underwater statue of Jesus Christ off San Fruttuoso Bay, Genoa, Italy for the protection of those at sea. It was a gift to the people of Grenada by the Costa Shipping Line (CSL) of Genoa for their help in rescuing the passengers of the BIANCA C. The 8.5 ft (2.8m) four-ton bronze statue was the second casting of Guido Galletti's 1954 *Il Cristo Degli Abissi*. The CSL agreed to pay the cost of erecting the statue, provided that it overlooked the sunken ship. The two sites chosen—the eastern entrance to the harbour beneath BUTLER HOUSE and on the ESPLANADE—both met that condition, but the City Council and the ship's agent in Grenada disagreed on which was the appropriate site. The City Council had the statue erected at the eastern entrance to the

Christ of the Deep statue on the Carenage, St. George's

CARENAGE in March 1963, but the CSL did not pay the cost because its agent refused to concede to the City Council's choice. In 1989 the statue was removed from its original site and placed at the centre of the Carenage where it now stands on the Pedestrian Plaza. With outstretched arms, it stands as a blessing to mariners leaving the port, but no longer overlooking the remains of the *Bianca C.*

CHRISTOPHE, Henri (1767-1820) was a former slave who rose to prominence during the Haitian Revolution, crowning himself king of northern Haiti in 1811. Though debate surrounds his birth, it is widely held that he was born in Grenada on 6 October 1767 on the Sans Souci estate, ST. ANDREW, a small COFFEE estate then owned by Alexander Cockburn. The story then becomes uncertain, but at the age of 12 he reportedly left Grenada for St. Domingue with a French naval officer who was part of the Comte d'Estaing's invading force in July 1779. Local mythology adds that he was engaged as a slave on the construction of the RICHMOND HILL FORTS when he escaped. As a young boy he is said to have fought in Savannah, Georgia with Comte d'Estaing in support of American independence.

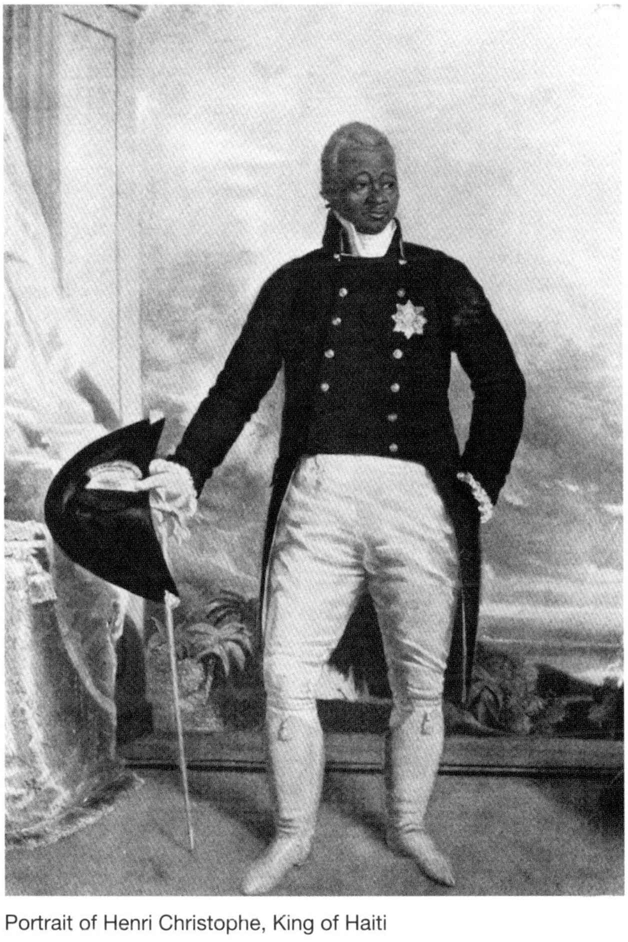

Portrait of Henri Christophe, King of Haiti

A 'hotel' owner/manager, Christophe joined the Haitian slave revolt and in 1793 became a lieutenant of Toussaint Louverture. He quickly rose to fame as a leader, and following Toussaint's capture in 1802, was one of the Haitian leaders who continued the fight, achieving independence in 1804. As the leader of northern Haiti, he established a hereditary nobility, crowning himself King Henry I. His massive, baroque-style palace, Sans Souci, is believed named after his birthplace. A mutiny among his troops and a subsequent paralytic stroke in 1820 plunged the country into civil war. He later took his life, rumoured to have shot himself in the heart with a silver bullet.[62]

CHURCH OF CHRIST THE KING, Carriacou Erected c. 1856 as the Anglican parish church, this small church is located on Second Avenue in HILLSBOROUGH; its most distinguishing features are the prominent buttresses and its entrance. The GREAT HOUSE at Beauséjour estate serves as the Rectory. The structure was badly damaged as a result of HURRICANE JANET in 1955. ANGLICANISM did not become established in CARRIACOU until the late 1790s under the Rev. William Nash. He must have been popular among the slaves because the planters in 1806 accused him of inciting them to revolt with his religious teachings. An investigation later ruled the accusation unfounded. In 1807 the island was created a separate benefice or parish. Parish records date to 1842. There is a beautiful flower garden on the compound.

CHURCH STREET is a major and picturesque street in St. George's Town. It runs from the junction of Young and Halifax Streets and becomes Cemetery Hill or Hospital Hill Road where it meets Williamson Road and the ST. GEORGE'S CEMETERY. It runs the length of the ridge that separates the CARENAGE from BAY TOWN. It derives its name from the two churches located there, ST. GEORGE'S RC CHURCH and ST. GEORGE'S ANGLICAN CHURCH. The PRESBYTERIAN CHURCH, though appearing to be located at the far end of Church Street, is in fact on the Grand Étang Road. In 1765 the name Church St. was restricted to present-day Simmon Alley directly behind the Anglican Church and connected Scott St. to Hospital St. Church Street's 'Old World charm' is still evident in its narrow street and the many Caribbean Georgian buildings that illustrate the islands' ARCHITECTURAL HISTORY. These interesting buildings and styles include SEDAN PORCHES, YORK HOUSE, Anglican Church Hall, the present and former VICARIATE, and the former

Church Street, St. George's

Wesleyan Mission House. Church Street is also home to two secondary schools, SJC and PBC, and two primary schools. It has been described as 'a street of charm and antiquity' where many established Grenadian families once lived. Many of the former residences have been turned into offices, particularly legal offices. Present-day Church Street was formerly known as Hospital Street (plus Government Street) until the early 1900s because it led to the French HOSPITAL. Under the French it was known as Grand Étang Road, which began at FORT GEORGE and connected to the main road along the west coast and across the centre of the island.[282]

CINEMAS The Grenada Electric Theatre Co., opened in 1919, was Grenada's first cinema. It functioned as a music and concert hall, and the islands' first commercial theatre. Since electricity had not yet been installed in St. George's, it utilised a 'noisy delco' to generate its power and 'provided the chief source of night entertainment for the town.' It went out of business in the late 1920s when Millicent DOUGLAS opened the Gaiety Theatre, itself displaced by the opening of the Empire Theatre in 1935 on the CARENAGE on the site of the Electric Theatre. Its opening changed the face of entertainment in Grenada. Empire grew to become both a popular cinema and concert hall, hosting numerous local and foreign shows. Empire, like Regal, had a capacity of between 650 and 700 seats divided into 'Pit', 'House' and 'Balcony'. Following its closure in 1991, the Empire building housed a retail business until its demolition in 2006.

W E Julien opened the Regal Cinema, under the name Reno, in 1960. These two cinemas were the centres of entertainment in St. George's for many years, with residents from the rural districts travelling many miles to see movies and local performing and dramatic ARTS (there have been cinemas in GRENVILLE since the 1920s). The closure of Empire left Regal as the only cinema in St. George's until it too closed in 2000. Regal was later bought by the GOG and transformed into a cultural centre, but in 2002 reopened as the Reno cinema. The Drive-In Cinema, opened in 1970 and closed in 1985, was the islands' only drive-in cinema and was located at Frequente, St. George. The Deluxe Cinema in GRENVILLE, St. Andrew, dates to the 1940s, and has been the primary entertainment centre in Grenville. In June 2003 TripleReels Cineplex, with three screens, opened at the Excel Plaza in Grand Anse; after closing it was reopened in 2006 as the Movie Palace.

CINNAMON (*Cinnamomum verum,* syn. C. *zeylanicum*) is native to the Indian subcontinent, and Rear Admiral Rodney reportedly brought the first seedlings to the region, having captured them from a French ship transporting them to St. Domingue (Haiti) in 1782. It may have been introduced earlier, but cultivation either proved unsuccessful or was neglected due to the profitability of SUGAR CANE. This evergreen tree grows to 25-50 ft (8-17 m), but is pruned to produce many branches that are harvested every two years. The outer skin of the bark is scraped then pounded to loosen it from the branch, and then carefully peeled off. The curled pieces are then dried in the sun. The small rolled pieces of bark, the cinnamon of commerce, are either used whole or ground as flavouring in a variety of foods. Its sharp aroma adds a sweet flavour to cakes, cookies, puddings, bread, liqueur, perfumes and drugs.

The use of cinnamon dates back thousands of years to the Egyptians who used it in the embalming of their dead and in the practice of witchcraft, and still further back among the East Indians. Cinnamon exhibits a number of medicinal properties, among them its antiseptic and antimycotic abilities that are utilised in FOLK MEDICINE and the

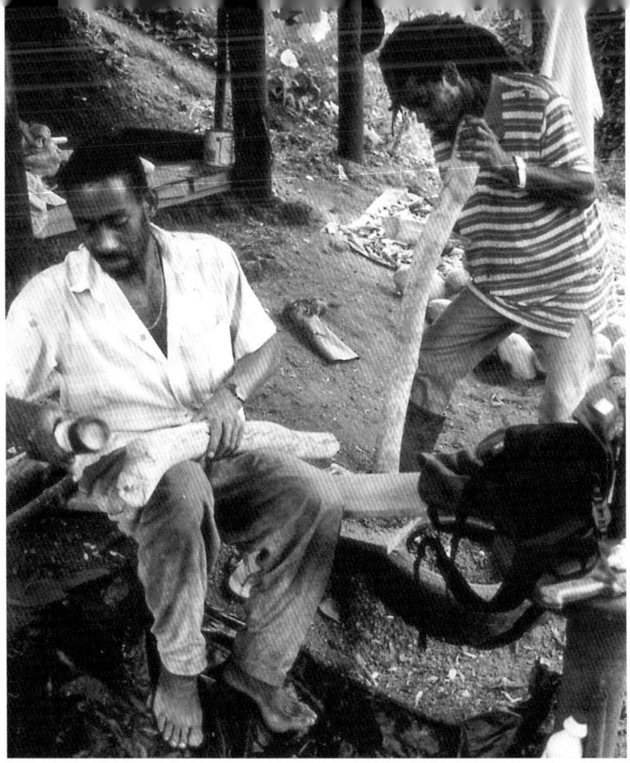

Removing cinnamon bark from the branch

pharmaceutical industry. A small quantity is exported, but most is packaged for the local TOURISM industry. It is locally referred to as 'spice'.

CLANCY The pseudonym of Elmer Eugene Zeek (1930-1993), an American race-horse trainer, who was on the run from the US law for allegedly cashing about US$1.1m in illegal cheques in Philadelphia; the Internal Revenue Service was also investigating him for non-payment of taxes. In January 1974 he surfaced in Grenada, a welcomed guest of Premier GAIRY. Accompanying him were Richard Palletto, wanted for questioning by police for the murder of Mafia crime boss Joey Gallo, and jockey Karl Korte, who said he was 'forced' into exile because of his knowledge of Palletto's Mafia involvement. Palletto and Zeek became known locally as the Clancy Brothers, having adopted the names of Frank and John Clancy respectively. In 1976 PM Gairy refused the US's request to extradite Zeek to face charges of 'wire fraud', insisting that he was a naturalised citizen. When Desmond Christian, attorney general and director of prosecutions, tried to prosecute Clancy against PM Gairy's wishes, he found himself out of a job and debarred from entering Grenada as he was Guyanese.

The Clancy Brothers operated a boat-charter business, a duty-free shop and a discotheque, which became popular as the 'Love Boat' or simply 'Clancy's' or Clancy Island. In 1977 Palletto drowned in a pool under questionable circumstances. Between 1974 and 1979 Zeek was a Grenadian fixture because of his financial largesse and close association with Gairy. He also ran the restaurant at the Drive-In Cinema, introducing American-style pizza. In March 1979, with the PEOPLE'S REVOLUTIONARY GOVERNMENT taking power and Zeek facing possible extradition or worse, he sailed away from Grenada. In a deal with the US government, he pleaded guilty and served two years in jail.[53]

CLIMATE Situated at the southern end of the Caribbean archipelago, Grenada is just above 12 degrees N and located within the northern tropics. It has two seasons, the rainy season from June to December, and the dry season from January to May. August is the hottest and February the coolest month. At the turn of the twentieth century Grenada was already 'regarded as one of the healthiest and most desirable spots in the West Indies.' The early French settlers, however, characterised it as 'the grave of the West Indies' because of DISEASES like MALARIA and other 'fevers'. BELL argues that it was not the result of 'this fatal climate', as was the common eulogy to the many dead Europeans, 'but to their careless habits, grossly immoral conduct and hard rumdrinking'. Most of the year the hilly interior is cool, with the NE trades blowing refreshingly throughout the island, especially in the dry season. The average temperature ranges between 70-90°F, with a low of 65°F at night in the interior.

Grenada has three primary climatic zones: the tropical wet interior above 475 ft (152 m), the tropical wet and dry coastal zone below 475 ft, and the 'hot' steppe zone of the SW. With plenty of rainfall, 60-140 inches (150-350 cm) over much of the island, the vegetation is lush throughout the rainy season, especially in the hills of Grand Étang and Mt. St. Catherine. Grenada is considered 'outside' the HURRICANE belt, but has been visited by rainstorms and three severe hurricanes in recent memory. Its agreeable climate has made it dependent on its soils, and AGRICULTURE remains one of the primary economic activities. The southern coast is drier, with plenty of sunshine along the BEACHES, which explains why the TOURISM industry has made this area its home. For C&PM the lack of rainfall and the absence of permanent RIVERS & STREAMS result in them being much drier year-round.

CLOVE (*Syzygium aromaticum*) is a tropical evergreen tree native to the Spice Islands of Indonesia. Until the latter half of the eighteenth century when the French broke the Dutch monopoly by smuggling cloves to the Indian Ocean islands and the Americas, it was exclusively grown in the Spice Islands. Historically, clove was an essential commodity in the spice trade between Europe and the

Far East. Its strong aroma and pungent taste makes it an ingredient in foods like meat and bakery products, and was even used as a breath freshener in China centuries ago. The tree grows to 25-40 ft (8-12 m) and begins flowering in its fifth year, with small reddish brown flowers. From January to May, the immature flower buds are picked and dried in the sun. Its pungent flavour in whole or ground form is added as a flavouring to meat dishes, cakes, puddings and local beverages like sea moss. The strong flavour of cloves is primarily due to eugenol, an aromatic oil used in the manufacture of germicides, perfumes, mouthwash, vanillin, sweeteners and intensifiers because of its antiseptic and digestive properties. A clove bud, pinched between the teeth, is a folk remedy for toothaches. Grenada is a minor producer of cloves, exporting a small quantity and selling the rest through its local TOURISM trade.

COALPOT Once used throughout the islands as a cooking stove, a coalpot utilises charcoal as its fuel, locally produced from the underground burning of wood in a 'coal pit'. It was common in outdoor kitchens up until the 1970s, and is responsible for many popular 'one pot' dishes like OIL DOWN because it could cook only one pot at a time. The coalpot (<Dutch *koolpot*: <kool 'charcoal' + pot), should not to be confused with a Dutch oven or Dutch pot, but it constituted part of the box oven where a galvanised-lined box was placed over a coalpot and used as an oven. According to Allsopp, it is the English homophone of the Dutch who introduced 'these portable field "cookers"' in the seventeenth century, replacing the three-stone fire. The shape is like a large flattened goblet or wineglass, and made of cast iron. With the availability of petroleum fuels, the coalpot has become a thing of the past, except among the poorest families or for traditional roasting or barbecuing. They can still be found in use by STREET VENDORS.

COARD, Bernard Winston (b. 1944) is a former deputy PM and a controversial political figure. He was born on 10 August 1944, the son of Flora *nee* Fleming and F M COARD. He attended the GBSS and later studied economics and political science in the US and UK. He returned to the Caribbean and lectured at the Jamaica and Trinidad branches of the UWI. He attended the 1973 Grenada Constitutional Conference in London to voice opposition to Premier Gairy's plans for INDEPENDENCE. In 1976 he contested and won the general ELECTIONS as a NEW JEWEL MOVEMENT candidate for the PEOPLE'S ALLIANCE, becoming a Member of PARLIAMENT. After MARCH 13, 1979 he was appointed minister of Finance and deputy PM in the PEOPLE'S REVOLUTIONARY GOVERNMENT.

As the party ideologue, he commanded strong support among its staunch members, contending with PM Bishop's immense popularity among the people. Coard's leadership and organisation of the Ministry of Finance further earned him respect and praise within the PRG. As the revolution progressed, a rivalry seemed to have developed between Coard and BISHOP. In 1982 Coard resigned from the Central Committee and the Political Bureau due to what he termed 'differences in organizational style and leadership' with Bishop. In 1983 his supporters within the party advocated power sharing between himself and Bishop. Bishop's rejection of the idea, combined with economic stresses and political trepidation by Coard, Bishop, and their immediate supporters, smouldering within a conspiratorial atmosphere, culminated in a coup that resulted in Bishop's assassination and the destruction of the revolution.

Coard was captured during the US-led military INTERVENTION and sentenced to die following the trial of the GRENADA 17. His sentence was later commuted to life imprisonment. In 1996 he and the other inmates accepted 'moral' responsibility for the disastrous events of October 1983, but not criminal responsibility. He is the author of a number of books and pamphlets. His wife, Phyllis Coard, who served as deputy minister for Women's Affairs in the PRG, was sentenced to life imprisonment for her role in the deaths of Bishop and his supporters, but was conditionally released in 2000 to seek medical treatment for a life-threatening illness.[118, 147, 303]

COARD, Fredrick McDermott 'Mackie' (1893-1978) was a career civil servant and the author of *Bitter Sweet and Spice: These Things I Remember*, which tells the story of his growing-up in colonial Grenada. He was born on 8 January 1893 in St. George's, the son of Mary *nee* Agassiz and Christopher Coard. Though his formal education was limited, he nonetheless attained the highest positions within the civil service then opened to Grenadians. After primary school, he entered the Grenada civil service as an apprentice in the Government Printery. After forty-odd years as a public servant he had held numerous positions, including revenue officer, district overseer of CARRIACOU, acting colonial treasurer, and ex-officio member of both the Executive and Legislative Councils. He was a member of the GRENADA LITERARY LEAGUE and served as its president. He served as president of the Civil Service Association, co-founded the Grenada Credit Union Movement, and founded the Grenada

Pensioners' Association. His autobiography is one of the first by a Grenadian and chronicles the experiences of a civil servant, providing a vivid portrayal of his struggles against entrenched prejudices and favouritism. He was also an avid cricketer who played on many local teams and the National Cricket Team. He was the father of former Deputy PM Bernard COARD.[57]

COAST GUARD BASE In early 1996 the GOG granted the US military permission to construct a coast guard base/police station on PETITE MARTINIQUE like it had done in 1984 with the construction of the main Coast Guard Base at True Blue. Its stated purpose was to intercept illegal drugs transhipped through the region and to stop contraband merchandise entering Grenada. The US$¼m project brought protest from home and abroad, once it was disclosed, along with many rumours and misconceptions. The GOG had not consulted the islanders, and once the story broke provided little information to counter the rumours. Many viewed the impending base as economically and socially detrimental to the island community. The proposed base threatened the traditional 'smuggling' or 'bobol trade' that Petite Martinicans have participated in for generations, and some claimed their economic survival to be at stake. Others erroneously believed that the facility would be used to train US military personnel, whose presence on the small island would introduce 'corrupting influences'. Some called for the immediate cancellation of the project. The proposed site, historically used as an all-purpose recreational venue because it is the only flat area on the island, created the most controversy.

In the end, the site of the base was moved some distance away. The base, begun in April 1997, was completed that June and handed over to the GOG and officially opened on 17 June 1997. Repairs to the water treatment facility, the levelling of the playing field, construction of a basketball court, and repairs to the medical clinic and primary school helped pacify most of the residents. The facility is solely operated by the POLICE FORCE/Coast Guard.[74]

COCOA (*Theobroma cacao*) was introduced into Grenada in the late 1600s, becoming established by 1700, and a trade item in the 1710s. The 1718 census recorded its cultivation, but c. 1724 many fields were destroyed by 'blast', either disease, hurricane or drought. In 1742 a more sturdy variety was introduced from Cayenne, resulting in its re-establishment. By 1762 cocoa had become a significant secondary crop, produced predominantly in the hilly

Broken cocoa pod showing attached beans

districts of St. John and St. Mark by middling farmers. In 1771 Grenada was supplying 75 per cent of Caribbean exports to Britain. Exports thereafter fluctuated, but by the 1860s, with the collapse of the sugar industry, cocoa became the primary export crop. Cocoa's expansion was facilitated by the MÉTAYER labour regime, cocoa's relative low production costs, the availability of land in the interior, and the willingness of the peasantry to embrace its cultivation. Other developments like the invention of the cocoa press in Europe in 1828, created greater demand on the world market. In the late 1800s cocoa became known as the 'golden bean' because of the wealth it brought many large farmers. In the 1890s cocoa accounted for, on average, 80 per cent of exports, and in 1895 Grenada supplied 11 per cent of the world market.

By the 1920s the cocoa boom had ended, with exports accounting for less than two per cent of the world market. Today, Grenada produces less than one per cent of the world's crop. Like all other agricultural commodities, the cocoa industry has experienced a number of production and marketing difficulties, but the attack by the pink MEALYBUG in the 1990s and HURRICANE IVAN in 2004 were devastating, further weakening the already declining sector. Most of the trees are very old and replacement planting is inadequate. In 1998 the industry witnessed its lowest production level since 1869, and a report characterised the industry as financially non-viable.

This evergreen tree is native to Central America and can grow to 20-45 ft (6-14 m). From October to January, and again from April to June, fruits are harvested. The 20-60 cocoa seeds or beans, once removed from the pod, are placed in a wooden box in the boucan (<Is.Ca. 'a wooden cot or grill') or cocoa-house and covered to allow fermentation or 'sweating', giving the beans their distinct flavour. They are then dried on large trays in the sun. Following drying and 'shinning', the brown beans are exported, where they are processed into cocoa butter, chocolate and cocoa powder. A small amount of beans is processed into cocoa balls to make local 'cocoa tea'. The Grenada Cocoa Association (est. 1964) has a monopoly of the island's production, with authority to set prices, collect, store, process, and export cocoa. The Grenada Chocolate Company, begun in 1999, is a small private company that produces a number of products from organically grown cocoa.[35, 103, 221]

Coconut trees along the beach

COCONUT (*Cocos nucifera*) is native to SE Asia, its pan-tropical dispersal believed to have been by man rather than by its ability to survive sea-borne voyages. Synonymous with the tropics, it is seen mostly on BEACHES and coastal regions where this stately member of the PALM family grows to 80 ft (25 m), dominating the skyline. The coconut produces year-round, with graps (<Fr. *grappe*: 'bunch') or clusters of huge green to yellowing-brown fruits drooping from the crown. The thick-shelled nut or kernel inside the fibre-like husk contains a liquid endosperm or sterile 'coconut water', drunk as a refreshing juice or added to alcoholic beverages. The soft white pulp, called the 'jelly', can be eaten fresh. When mature, the jelly condenses and is usually grated, yielding 'coconut milk/cream', an addition to local dishes like OIL DOWN and TANNIA log. Grated, it is also used to make coconut and chip-chip sugarcakes, 'rocks' or coconut buns, and various other confectioneries. The coconut's primary economic use is in the manufacture of edible oil processed from the copra (<Hin. *khopra*), the dried meat or kernel of the coconut.

Beginning around 1912 coconut cultivation was pursued in earnest, and its husbandry was advocated to replace the MANGROVES after they were filled in. Production remained small-scale until the mid-1900s when a number of large estates, especially in the SE, undertook its cultivation. A soap factory operated between 1909 and 1916, and the Tempe Manufacturing Co., Ltd. (1941-1982) processed copra into laundry soap, crude and edible oils, and coconut meal for animal feed. In the early 1970s the industry was at its peak, but by the late 1970s disease caused production to decline.

The coconut is probably the most versatile and useful tropical tree, providing food, drink, fuel and oil from its fruits and fibre, and timber and thatch from its trunk and fronds, respectively. The fronds are made into cocoyea (<Fr.Cr. *coco*: 'coconut', + (suffix) *ier*: 'tree') brooms, hand-woven hats and bags, and the midribs are used to make kite frames; the fibre from the husk were used to make mattresses and scrub brushes. Though it has the potential to yield various raw materials for local industries, its exploitation remains limited. The answer to the riddle, 'Ah go and call the doctor, doctor reach before me?' is coconut because the fruits are expelled from the tree by the picker and fall to the ground before s/he climbs down from the tree.

COFFEE (*Coffea arabica* & *C. canephore*) Though not important as a cash crop today, coffee was one of the first crops cultivated in Grenada, following its introduction into the French Antilles around 1722. Its production was recorded on censuses beginning in 1731 and it soon became the major crop after sugar. In 1763 when the British took over there were 208 coffee estates. Though SUGAR CANE cultivation expanded and SUGAR production dominated the economy, coffee production had doubled by 1764, with continual increases throughout the next decade. By 1775 exports had begun to rival sugar, with Grenada the leading coffee producer (82 per cent) in the BWI. In 1779 production plummeted to less than two per cent of the previous year's. The financial crisis in Britain caused lenders to refuse new credit and called in loans that left the islands devastated where a culture of credit had become the norm of the estate economy. Coffee planters were heavily in debt to some £2m, and forfeited coffee estates were sold for one-sixth and one-tenth of their value. French planters, the main producers of coffee, left Grenada in droves, taking with them their slaves and leaving behind unrecoverable debts. Coffee recovered somewhat in the late 1700s, but by 1800 was still a minor crop. After 1834 it became insignificant as a cash crop.

A small tree that needs regular pruning to be kept a shrub, coffee produces red cherry-like berries that are dried, roasted and ground, producing the coffee of international commerce. In 1980 the PEOPLE'S REVOLUTIONARY GOVERNMENT opened the Spice Island Coffee Processing Plant, which depended almost exclusively on imported beans from TRINIDAD. The PRG had hoped to encourage local production and resuscitate the dormant industry, but the plant was closed in 1983.[35, 126, 221]

COMISSIONG, Dr Leonard Merrydale (1910-1980) came of a long established Grenadian family. He was the son of Florence and J G M Comissiong, and attended the GBSS (he is the author of the school's song, '*Non Palma Sine Labore*') where he excelled both in academic work and sports. In 1929 he was awarded the ISLAND SCHOLARSHIP to study medicine. He returned to the Caribbean in 1934 and served as District Medical Officer of Grenada (1936-1939) and Carriacou (1939-1946). A small book of 'patriotic verse', describing the terrible medical conditions in the islands, was published in 1947 and related to his two years at the ALMSHOUSES. He held a number of medical positions in the Caribbean, before returning to Grenada following his retirement in 1968. He served as health advisor to the GOG, and his final position as Chief Medical Officer of Grenada (1978-1980). He was instrumental (with Dr Frank Alexis) in the formulation of the PEOPLE'S REVOLUTIONARY GOVERNMENT's health plan. In 1940 he was nominated to the Executive Council. Among his commendations is the CBE in 1974. He is the author of medical papers and two books of poems on his 'beloved' Grenada, *Whither Grenada* and *Poems of Life*.[69, 70]

COMMITTEE OF 22 A 'non-political' coalition of groups including labour unions and the Conference of Churches in Grenada. Its formation on 19 November 1973 was 'to assuage public anxieties' following what many considered the breakdown of law and order in the wake of the BLOODY SUNDAY incident, for which it held the GULP government responsible. The Committee petitioned Premier GAIRY to disband his MONGOOSE GANG and POLICE AIDES, release the imprisoned NEW JEWEL MOVEMENT leaders, arrest the parties responsible for the bloody attack, and establish a Commission of Enquiry to examine the charges of human rights violations. In return, the Committee suspended an island-wide labour strike already in its first week. Though Premier Gairy described the Committee members as 'mere political diehards' whom he had constantly beaten at the polls, he was nonetheless forced into accepting their demands due to the ongoing INDEPENDENCE talks with the British government.

With little progress made by the GOG, except the appointment of a Commission of Enquiry, the Committee, in December, voted to continue its strike on 1 January 1974. For three weeks thereafter the country fell deeper and deeper into chaos as more and more workers struck, with schools eventually joining in the daily demonstrations against the government. The crowds grew larger and larger, threatening Premier Gairy's authority as he vowed to 'cut them down to size.' On 21 January the confrontation culminated in BLOODY MONDAY. The Committee did succeed in forcing the GULP government to establish the DUFFUS COMMISSION.[94, 176, 201, 333]

CONCORD FALLS A series of three waterfalls within the Concord valley along the Black Bay River. To get to the first fall, Gué (<Fr. 'ford'), the only one accessible by road, requires a scenic drive of some 3 miles (4.4-km) in from the coast along a winding road. About 50 ft (15 m) high, Gué is the second highest of the three, cascading down a huge rock into a small basin surrounded by lush vegetation. During the rainy season the river cascades down at two places. Changing rooms, washrooms, and other facilities are available. The second fall, Au coin (<Fr. 'on the corner'), is about a 0.6-mile (1 km) hike

Gué, the first and most accessible of the three Concord Falls

up the river, and is only 5ft (1.5 m) high. An hour's hike into the interior will reveal the last of the three falls, Fontainbleau, which cascades 70 ft (20 m) into a huge blue basin. Concord Falls is part of the NATIONAL PARK SYSTEM, connected to Grand Étang Lake over trails that provide a rather taxing hike through Grenada's rain forest.

CONKIE A bread or pudding made from either corn-meal flour, plantain and pumpkin, and less often from SWEET POTATO or CASSAVA. The somewhat starchy flour or paste from these is sweetened with sugar and raisins, spiced, then wrapped in singed BANANA leaves and steamed until cooked. Conkie (<Twi *nkankye*: 'cake') was introduced to the region by AKAN slaves from West Africa, as its Twi-derived name attests. It is popular around Guy Fawkes Day celebrations in November. It is known as dunkanoo in Jamaica.

CONSERVATION Grenada has seen human habitation for at least 2,000 years, intensified since 1649 following European colonisation. The natural environment has been altered significantly with the destruction of natural habitats, predominantly for estate AGRICULTURE and the uncontrolled introduction of FAUNA and FLORA. In the last century, the increasing human population has meant greater demands on the natural environment, resulting in the extinction of a number of wildlife species, including the AGOUTI, MOROCOY, BIRDS and possibly two species of SNAKES. Only recently has there been a growing awareness with regard to the impact of human actions on the natural environment as the number of endangered terrestrial and marine species increases. In 1988, with technical co-operation from the OAS, the GOG developed a *Plan and Policy for a System of National Parks and Protected Areas in Grenada and Carriacou* in an effort to slow the uncontrolled exploitation of its natural and cultural resources. These ambitious plans were the first in the islands' history and represented a major effort towards the conservation of the natural environment.

Yet the idea of wildlife conservation was not brought to the general public until 1991, when the GRENADA DOVE was named the national bird, and the inauguration of an unprecedented public campaign to save this endangered species. Recognition of the benefits of protected areas, especially for the TOURISM industry, has produced a number of efforts on the part of the GOG, non-governmental groups and private individuals to become active crusaders for the environment and wildlife. The dangers to the environment are many, from the over-exploitation of SEA TURTLES, LAMBIE and ARMADILLO, to the destruction of habitats like MANGROVES, resulting in the extinction of snakes, FROGS and birds. The illegal and legal removal of sand from BEACHES has left many once beautiful beaches threatened, and contributed to the destabilisation of the coast and the marine environment. The release of raw sewage into the sea, a common practice since the building of a water-carriage sewerage system in 1939, adversely impacts CORAL REEFS and can have devastating effects on marine fisheries, upon which many depend for their livelihoods. Natural disasters like HURRICANES have destroyed habitats and wildlife as was the case with HURRICANE JANET and HURRICANE IVAN.

Bumper sticker as part of efforts to 'Save the Grenada Dove'

The conservation laws of Grenada, though dating as far back as the 1890s, are at best outdated and do not reflect the growing need to protect endangered species and habitats. Some laws have offered protection to threatened species during closed seasons, but few of these have been enforced, thus providing little reprieve for Grenada's wildlife especially since Hurricane Ivan. There is a need for an in-depth study of Grenada's wildlife, habitat protection, new legislation that reflects viable conservation objectives, and a concerted attempt at enforcing these laws. The preservation of the islands' wildlife, seascapes, natural landscapes, and historical and cultural sites is a national obligation and must begin now so that the next generation will have a treasured inheritance.[45, 50, 140,146b]

CONSTITUTIONAL HISTORY In 1674 Grenada became a French colony after 25 years of proprietary rule. Administration of Grenada fell under the ÎLES DU VENT, and as such it had a constitution similar, yet much more restrictive, to the one it would later have as a British CROWN COLONY. It formulated no laws of its own, but implemented the laws sent from France via Martinique. In 1763 Grenada was ceded to the British following its capture the previous year and became part of the GOVERNMENT OF GRENADA. The British Crown granted a representative constitution under the OLD REPRESENTATIVE SYSTEM that same year. After 110 years of dubious representation it was dissolved and succeeded by Crown Colony rule. In 1886 a semi-representative LOCAL GOVERNMENT was introduced, but affected only a small portion of the population. Protest by a number of individuals, predominantly members of the landed and professional elite, brought to the forefront the growing dissatisfaction with the Crown Colony system. The early 1900s witnessed renewed protests, especially after the establishment of the WEST INDIAN newspaper and the formation of the REPRESENTATIVE GOVERNMENT ASSOCIATION. A partially elected legislature was granted in 1925, and a growing regional pressure for federation and a broader representation between the 1930s and 1950s led to the gradual transfer of power to elected members of the legislature.

The year 1951, regarded as a 'political milestone in the Windward Islands', saw the abandonment of Crown Colony status and the granting of universal adult suffrage, without qualifications. The Committee System was introduced in 1955 and led the way for the Ministerial System in 1960. Both had progressively granted more control of the administration of the colony to the elected members of the legislature, but the suspension of the constitution in 1962, due to SQUANDERMANIA, temporarily delayed the process. The failure of FEDERATION and the UNITARY STATE project led to the granting of full representative government under ASSOCIATED STATEHOOD in 1968, and in 1974 Grenada was granted INDEPENDENCE. When the NEW JEWEL MOVEMENT took power in 1979 the constitution was suspended and replaced by People's Laws. By 1983 the PRG's Constitutional Committee had formulated a draft constitution, but it was never implemented as a result of the US-led military INTERVENTION. Between 1983 and 1991 the Independence Constitution was restored. Though there have been a number of constitutional reviews, no changes to the Grenada Constitution have been made to date despite controversial constitutional issues that have arisen.[3, 35, 72, 139, 179, 333]

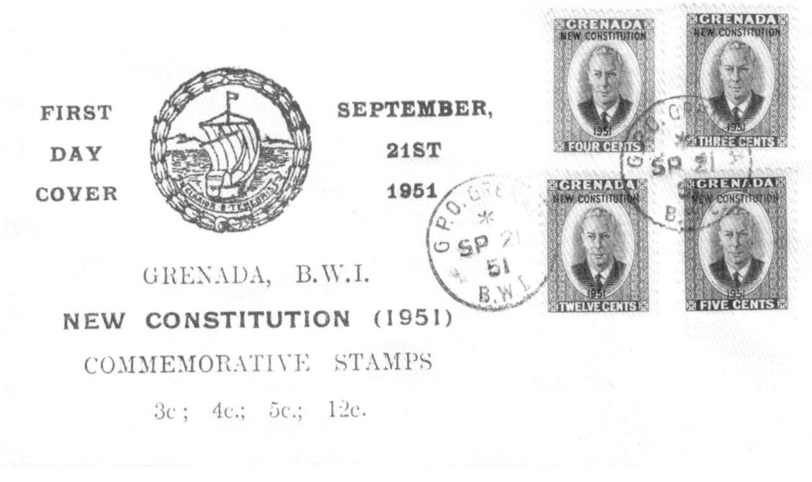

Celebrating Grenada's 1951 Constitution and the inauguration of adult suffrage

CORAL REEFS Grenada, C&PM are surrounded by coral reefs that are home to an array of marine life forms including corals, anemones, molluscs, sponges, sea cucumbers, fin fishes and algae. One of the most fascinating characteristics of coral reefs is the symbiotic or mutual relationship between the coral, comprised of tiny invertebrate marine organisms (class Anthozoa), and one-celled algae called zooxanthellae. The energy produced by the algae through photosynthesis is used by the coral animals or polyps to extract carbon dioxide from sea water to secrete their hard stony skeletons. Coral communities form colonies upon the sea floor where, under conditions of clear, well circulating, gentle water flow, they can deposit skeletons of calcium carbonate. Over geological time this secretion can create extensive masses forming reefs, atolls like SANDY ISLAND, and islands like Barbados.

The most common type of coral reef around Grenada is the fringing reef. These reefs sustain an unimaginable array of marine life forms that play an integral role in the stabilisation of the coasts and serve as nurseries for hundreds of tropical fin fishes and organisms like the SEA EGG. Due to their fragility, coral reefs have been threatened by sedimentation, coastal development for TOURISM (even though they are attractions for visitors), sand mining for construction, wave surge caused by tropical rain storms like HURRICANE LENNY, diseases, over-fishing, and freshwater runoff from floods. They are constantly in danger of being irreversibly damaged because of the increasing release of highly toxic pollutants like human sewage, fertilisers and pesticides into the sea. The uncontrolled harvesting of various corals for sale to visitors is also a significant threat to reefs. Grenada's north, east and southern coasts possess the majority of the reefs that occur around the island. Some of these reefs include Grande Anse, Grand Mal and Molinière Reefs; the latter is considered the island's 'best reef' and has been slated for conservation as a marine reserve. The islands of the GRENADA GRENADINES possess some of the more spectacular coral reefs. The region has witnessed die offs of corals in the 1980s and 1990s, threatening the fragile marine ecosystem.[50, 140]

CORN (*Zea mays*) is a cereal of the grass family native to Central America, but has become common throughout the tropics and temperate regions where it is a major food for humans and animals. Though corn is cultivated in Grenada as part of its subsistence AGRICULTURE, it is the staple food crop in Carriacou and has been traditionally mixed-cropped with PIGEON PEAS. The crop was so important to Carriacou that low harvests due to drought resulted in threats of famine on a number of occasions, including 1836, 1873 and 1959. The availability of imported rice and flour has led to a decline in the production of corn since the 1960s.

The grain is borne on cobs and picked at differing stages of maturity depending on its intended use. The cobs are picked fresh and young for boiling and roasting. During the 'roasting season' children play a guessing game, known as 'ship sail' in C&PM, to determine the number of kernels someone has in their hands by saying 'Chip-chip sailor, how many men on deck?' or 'Ship sail, sail fast, how many men on deck?' If the challenger guesses right then s/he gets the kernels, but an incorrect guess means that s/he has to give that person the number of the guess.

When fully mature, corn is picked and further dried in the sun, then ground into a flour (corn meal) that is variously made into COU-COU, CONKIE, porridge and dumplings. Asham (<Twi *o-siam*: 'parched and ground corn') is a confectionery relished mainly by children around ALL SAINTS' DAY when each child carries little bags to the cemetery. It is made from parched, finely ground corn mixed with sugar. Corn is planted at the beginning of the rainy season and usually harvested from September to January. The seedless cob was once used as fuel and as a scrubbing brush while the corn straw was used to stuff mattresses. Other names include maize, Indian corn and field corn.

COTTON (*Gossypium hirsutum*) was one of the first crops cultivated in Grenada by the French, beginning in the late 1600s. The Caribbean tree cotton, Marie-Galante variety, is native to the region, and its cultivation dates back to the AMERINDIANS. Carriacou, Petite Martinique, RONDE ISLAND, and the SW of Grenada were the primary growing areas. Between 1700 and 1762 production was small, but by 1764 the islands were producing the largest quantity of seed cotton among the Ceded Islands. Production climaxed in the mid-1790s, leading Ragatz to comment: 'Grenada was producing cotton on a scale undreamed of in any of the colonies settled by Englishmen.' In the early 1800s production gradually declined in Grenada. Carriacou, however, continued to produce cotton throughout the 1800s and for much of the 1900s, with production increasing in the first half of the 1900s.

The cotton plant cultivated in the Grenadines was a perennial, drought-resistant shrub that produced a coarse lint. Its production, exclusively by peasants and often inter-cropped with corn, was quite successful because it was not a demanding crop. In 1944 the government opened a central gin at HILLSBOROUGH, with the lint exported to Trinidad, and the seed to St.Vincent for processing into edible oil and meal. By the 1950s production had declined, replaced mainly by LIMES. By 1982 its cultivation in Carriacou as a cash crop had ceased. Sea Island cotton(*G. barbadense*) cultivation proved less successful.[35, 221]

COTTON BAILEY TRAGEDY On the morning of 16 January 1991 a twenty-ton boulder dislodged from its moorings above the road and landed on a passing BUS carrying nine people, crushing them to death. The majority of the passengers were children on their way to school. The steep slopes of the western coast have always been a constant threat to passers-by since it was not uncommon for rocks to become dislodged and slide down the hills. There had been incidents when individuals were injured by falling rocks, but nothing on a scale that prepared anyone for the tragedy at Cotton Bailey, ST. JOHN. A memorial to the victims was dedicated near the site of the tragedy, a constant reminder of the unpredictability of the natural environment. An inquest later ruled that the GOG was responsible for the accident and recommended compensation for the families of the victims.[257]

COU-COU A local dish made from boiled cornmeal flour, flavoured with COCONUT milk and seasoned. It is still prepared and consumed much as it was when the slaves brought the recipe with them from West Africa where it is a common food under various names. One has to 'turn cou-cou' with a cou-cou stick so that it does not stick to the pot. Cou-cou (?<Twi *nkuku*: 'a species of yam', used to make cou-cou, a 'cooking pot', or a 'cook') is eaten with calalu and a fish entrée that add flavour and taste to a rather bland dish. Leftover cou-cou is usually deep-fried for the next meal. It can also be made from a number of provisions like YAM and BREADFRUIT. In C&PM cou-cou pwa (<Fr. *pois*: 'pea') was once a popular dish made from PIGEON PEAS and cornmeal.

CRABS The islands support a number of marine and terrestrial species of crabs along their BEACHES and MANGROVES. The most conspicuous is the land or blue crab (*Cardisoma guanhumi*) which is caught by 'torching' when hunters, armed with a bottle torch or massanto, go out at night to catch crabs that are out feeding. It is consumed in a number of dishes including 'crab back' and the popular soup dish 'crab and calalu'. The red or jumbie crab (*Gecarinus lateralis*) is found the furthest inland, while the ghost crab (*Ocypode quadrata*) can be seen on beaches dashing in and out of holes, disappearing within the waves. The hermit (*Coenobita clypeatus*) or soldier crab (also known as toolooloo <Fr. Cr. *tourlourou*: 'common soldier, private' because of its red markings, <Is. Car. *itorourou*) constantly seeks the discarded shells of molluscs as it grows. The mangrove crab (*Artus pisonii*) lives and mates in the mangroves across the islands.

Crabs for sale

The manicou crab (*Guinotia dentata*) is found near RIVERS & STREAMS, occasionally under water where it can remain for long periods. This edible fresh-water crab is yellow and brown. Peculiar to it is the ability of the female to carry its fertilised eggs attached to its abdomen beneath a flap, and the complete development of the eggs to juvenile crabs while attached, hence the name MANICOU crab. The serries or sally lightfoot crab (*Grapsus grapus*) is a tiny land crab that spends considerable time close to the sea. It is brown coloured and speckled, with an almost circular shell. Seen on rocks near the sea, these swift crabs disappear at the slightest disturbance, hence the local name, scuttle. There are a number of marine crabs including the red sea crab and the Caribbean king crab or spiny crab. The term man-crab, as in the saying 'Two man-crab can't live in the same hole,' refers to males, usually both headstrong and unable to agree on anything. A promiscuous woman or man is also described derogatorily as a 'crab', but this last meaning may come from the venereal disease crab louse, which sexually loose men and women are apt to 'catch'.

CRAIGSTON is an estate located in NW Carriacou, along the coast. The estate and surrounding village take their name from the Urquarts of Craigston Castle, Aberdeen, Scotland, who owned the estate between 1769 and 1840. COTTON was the major crop produced between 1769 and the 1810s, after which a small quantity of SUGAR and RUM was produced on the 316 acre (128 ha) estate. In 1806 the estate was at the centre of a rumoured 'slave uprising' when a number of slaves refused to obey the manager. They sought the help of Rev. Nash, the Anglican rector, to intercede on their behalf, but he was accused of inciting them to revolt. The slaves were later punished and the ringleaders sold in Trinidad.

The original GREAT HOUSE dates to 1777, with many additions and alterations over the years. HURRICANE JANET destroyed the main part of the house in 1955, and in 1975 a new one was rebuilt on the old foundations. Since 1928 the proprietary Kent family has owned the estate, which produced LIMES and cotton until 1981. The estate presently breeds pedigree cattle and sheep. Its influence on the island's agricultural history is evident with the introduction, around 1917, of the Craigston System, a variant of the MÉTAYER. The village of Craigston developed on the borders of the estate.[319]

CRAPPO (*Bufo marinus*) Though it is locally called a FROG, the crappo (taxonomically) is a large toad, also known as the cane or giant toad. It was introduced from South America in 1835 as a pest management measure in SUGAR CANE fields. The crappo (<Fr. *crapaud*: 'toad') survives mainly on insects, many of which cause considerable damage to crops; it has also been known to eat small BIRDS and reptiles. It releases a milky secretion, bufotalin, from glands behind the eyes as a defence. Though poisonous if swallowed by a small child or animal, there have been deliberate attempts by individuals to 'lick' toads to get a 'high'; its ancient use as a drug dates back to the Chinese. The crappo is an amphibian and needs water to reproduce. Once common throughout the island, it is presently restricted to forested areas and its status listed as 'rare'. A familiar proverb, 'What is fun for school children is death for crappo,' is frequently used by older folks to express to children the need to be considerate of others: a not uncommon pastime of children was to throw stones at frogs and toads. Another popular proverb, 'Crappo smoke your pipe,' expresses the certainty of extremely straightened circumstances (especially if current errors or problems are left unchecked).

CRIBO (*Clelia clelia*) is a large native serpent once found in forested areas, especially close to streams. It is black with yellow on the tail and underside, and looks like a giant eel. Though it has a reputation for being violent, it is non-venomous and will not attack unless molested. There is some debate about the cribo's classification: Greer lists it as a single-island endemic sub-species (*C. c. groomei*), and Groome suggests that it may be a valid species because it exhibits some differences from the mainland species, like being diurnal while the latter is nocturnal. Others disagree, insisting that the Grenada cribo is not significantly different enough from the mainland species to be classified as a sub-species, nor a species. It consumes rodents and the MONGOOSE, with which it can be frequently seen in mortal combat, and for that reason the 'planters [in the 1800s] protect[ed] them as much as we can, as they wage continual war on our worst enemies, the rats.' According to local SUPERSTITION, it wears a 'crown of diamonds' on its pointed head. When the cribo goes to the river to 'bathe' it removes its crown and many dream of finding the abandoned riches or magic talisman, but people are warned that the cribo would never abandon the search for its crown. Though prominent in the folk culture, the cribo's status is listed as 'uncertain, possibly extinct,' with no sightings recorded in decades. Its disappearance may be due to the use of toxic pesticides or predation by the mongoose, or both. The local name cribo is common to a number of colubrids of Central and South America belonging to *Drymarchon* spp.[131]

CRICKET is probably the most popular team sport played throughout the English-speaking Caribbean. Though it shares the spotlight with FOOTBALL, it holds a special place in the social life of the islands. It is an outdoor game played under intricate rules, lasting from one to five days. It was introduced by the British around the mid-1800s, developing into a recreational sport among Grenada's elite and British colonial civil servants in the late 1800s, and a national sport by the early 1900s. The children's game of bat and ball is very popular, and for many future cricketers provides the initial love of the game. Around the 1860s cricket took hold in parts of

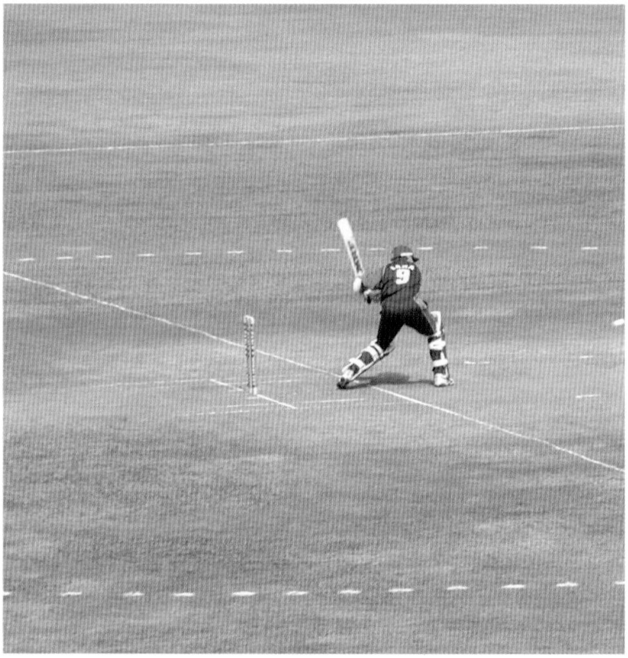

WI cricketer Brian Lara at National Stadium

Grenada, particularly St. George's, and to a lesser extent St. Mark and St. John's parishes. One of the earliest recorded games took place in GOUYAVE between Victoria and St. George's in 1865. Sports clubs, but more so cricket clubs, sprang up along the west coast and represented parishes, towns or villages. Among these clubs were foremost the Grenada Cricket Club (est. 1890), St. Mark's Royal Cricket Club and the Wanderers Cricket Club. Teams regularly engaged each other or visiting teams of British sailors, and clubs from Trinidad and St.Vincent. In 1909 the Cork Cup Tournament brought together the members of the Windward Islands and helped advance the game during the early decades of the 1900s. It ended in 1955, but was replaced by a number of other competitions.

Grenada participates through the Windward Islands or Combined Islands teams in competitions in the Caribbean like the Shell Cup. Inter-secondary school competition dates to 1952, though the GBSS has participated in competition with clubs since the 1890s because it was the only secondary school until the 1940s. The 1950s marked a turning point for cricket, with the appearance of international matches at the QUEEN'S PARK. It also signalled the demise of the elite's control of the game.

In 1993 Junior Murray became the first Grenadian cricketer to represent the West Indies in test cricket as a wicket-keeper/batsman, becoming the islands' most treasured sports personality. Murray has since been followed by leg-spinner Rawle Lewis in 1996 and opening batsman Devon Smith in 2003. The construction of the NATIONAL STADIUM and the opening of the Cricket Academy at ST. GEORGE'S UNIVERSITY are expected to make Grenada a centre for cricket in the region.[367]

CROWN COLONY In December 1877 the British Parliament imposed Crown Colony (CC) government in Grenada and most of the BWI. The previous year the local legislature had surrendered the administration of the colony to the British Crown. Of the three legislators who voted against the measure, Dr William WELLS objected on the grounds that CC 'sets aside the undoubted right of the people to have a voice in the making of the laws by which they are ruled, and particularly in the imposing of taxes.' The imposition of CC brought to a close 112 years of the OLD REPRESENTATIVE SYSTEM and was seen as a backward step in the islands' CONSTITUTIONAL HISTORY. The British government believed that CC would safeguard the political freedoms of the poor from the dominance of the plantocracy, as was evident in the ORS. The PLANTOCRACY, which supported CC, saw it as a safeguard against the dominance of the peasantry should they be granted political representation.

In the end CC resulted in the dictatorship of the GOVERNOR and his appointed Executive and Legislative Councils, which comprised members of the plantocracy. It soon became evident, even to some who had supported CC, that citizens were without a voice in the governance of their political and economic affairs. By 1880 a considerable opposition developed and openly protested CC. These included T E Passe, William DONOVAN, and H B Beckwith who had been a staunch supporter.

The appointment of Walter Sendall as governor in 1885 quelled some of the dissatisfactions with the CC system as he made a concerted effort to improve social and economic institutions with such measures as the introduction of LOCAL GOVERNMENT, revamping EDUCATION, and extending health facilities and basic infrastructure. Agitation nonetheless continued, and in 1925 the REPRESENTATIVE GOVERNMENT ASSOCIATION was able to effect representative changes in the CC Constitution. Between the 1930s and the 1950s attacks on CC throughout the region led to changes that in 1951 brought about the demise of what the Moyne Commission referred to as a 'benevolent despotism', resulting in universal adult suffrage.[35, 98, 333]

CUDJOE According to Carriacou legend, Cromanti Cudjoe, celebrated in the BIG DRUM DANCE, was a Jamaica MAROON who had led the fight against the British in the first maroon war in the 1730s. Though there is no evidence that Captain Cudjoe left Jamaica, the story is that he somehow ended up in Grenada. During FÉDON'S REBELLION he was reportedly a lieutenant of Julien FÉDON. Following the crushing of the rebellion by the British in 1796, Cudjoe escaped to SAUTEURS, and from there swam 23 miles (37 km) to Carriacou. His eldest son is said to have died at Sauteurs. Cromanti Cudjoe, disguised as a woman, hid among the slaves who gave him food and shelter. He is said to have travelled from estate to estate, instigating resistance among the slaves against the British, even though Carriacou was unaffected by the 15-month rebellion that devastated Grenada. There is an actual headstone to a well-known 'Cudjoe' who died in 1823 in the HARVEY VALE area (there is also a headstone to his wife Zarraba). Over the years Cromanti Cudjoe, an acclaimed drummer, has attained mythical status as one of Carriacou's ancestral spirits. A designated song is sung, along with the opening Big Drum Dance, to invoke this revered ancestral spirit. Hill speculates that it were slaves brought to Grenada from Jamaica, and not Captain Cudjoe himself, who 'sang praises of "Cudjoe" and "Nani"' and created the legend of Cromanti Cudjoe. Cudjoe (<Twi (AKAN) male 'day name' Kedjo: Monday), a common family name exclusive to Carriacou, is one of the few West African names that survived SLAVERY and colonialism.[51, 154]

CUGOANO, Quobna Ottobah (c.1757-c.1803) was a slave, author and abolitionist. At the age of 13 years he was captured in Ajumako (presently Ghana) and brought to Grenada as a slave. He spent less than a year on a sugar estate working with a 'slave-gang'. He described his confinement as 'Being in this dreadful captivity and horrible slavery, without any hope of deliverance... beholding the most dreadful scenes of misery and cruelty, and seeing my miserable companions often cruelly lashed, and as it were cut to pieces, for the most trifling faults; this made me often tremble and weep.' He later became the personal servant of Alexander CAMPBELL, and travelled with him to England at the end of 1772, giving 'Thanks be to God, I was delivered from Grenada, and that horrid brutal slavery'. Under what circumstances Cugoano gained his freedom is not clear, but he was encouraged by 'some good people to get myself baptised, that I might not be carried away and sold again'. On 20 August 1773 he was baptised at St. James' Church, Piccadilly, London and changed his name to John Stuart; this act did not guarantee emancipation as was widely believed. He worked as a domestic for royal painter Richard Cosway. He became a vocal abolitionist and in 1787 published *Thoughts and Sentiments on the Evil and Wicked Traffic of the Slavery and Commerce of the Human Species*. The tract is primarily a condemnation of SLAVERY, the first anti-slavery text written in English by an African. He was a friend of another former slave and author Olaudah Equiano, both belonging to an anti-slavery organization, 'Sons of Africa'. Cugoano was also involved with noted abolitionist Granville Sharp and the Sierra Leone Company, encouraging the return of slaves to Africa.[264]

CURRENCY & COINAGE Before EMANCIPATION most economic transactions throughout the region were made with the exchange of agricultural products, predominantly SUGAR, but various coins also circulated. French colonial coinage circulated in Grenada beginning around 1670, and after 1731 specific coinage was issued for the ÎLES DU VENT. After 1738 the 'stampee' or 'black dog', French coinage over-stamped with a 'C' for colonies, was in circulation. For the first few decades of British rule coins of various European countries circulated in Grenada since it was illegal to export British currency. After 1787 Spanish silver dollars were cut into pieces or bits, and counter-stamped with a 'G' as official currency. In 1822 'Anchor Coinage' began circulating in the BWI, but was partially replaced by British coins in 1825. In 1841 the sterling currency was adopted as the local currency, replacing the previous two-and-a-half to one exchange rate.

In 1951 the British Caribbean Territories issued the first local currency, replacing the historical British pound, shilling and pence currency. All coins and paper currencies bear the likeness of Queen Elizabeth II, HEAD OF STATE for the majority of the members of the Eastern Caribbean Central Bank (est. 1983). The EC dollar is the basis of financial transactions among its members, with a fixed exchange rate of EC$2.70 to US$1.00 since July 1976. Denominations are coins 1, 2, 5, 10, 25, 50 and 100 cents, and paper 5, 10, 20, 50 and 100 dollars.

Currency used in Grenada

D

DADA/SHANGO HAIR is the soft, curly hair of some children and is believed by the folk of CARRIACOU to be abnormal because it stays curled despite combing, hence the elaborate ceremony to remove it. The hair-cutting ceremony is carried out when the child is between two-and-a-half to three years of age so as 'to protect the child, who will otherwise be "troubled and afraid"'. The ceremony includes the sacrificing of animals, pouring of libations to the ancestors, and the cooking of elaborate meals for the saraka/salaca and PARENTS' PLATE. The godfather of the child cuts the 'abnormal' hair and pays the child with a silver coin for the severed hair. The drumming and singing of the BIG DRUM DANCE accompanies the ceremony. This practice may be related to the SUPERSTITION where the cutting of a child's hair before proper speech development is believed to cause a permanent speech disability. The ceremony is rare and has not been observed in many years. The Carriacou ceremony is derived from the West African practice known as dada (<Yor. for the name of a child with curly hair/god of babies and gardens) and is almost identical to ceremonies among various tribes in Sierra Leone. Dada hair also refers to matted hair as that of the followers of RASTAFARIANISM.[85, 321]

DAMSEL (*Phyllanthus acidus*, syn. *P. distischus*) This tree is native to Madagascar and India, even though another of its regional names, Otaheite goosberry, connects it with Tahiti from where it was introduced into the Caribbean in 1793 by Captain Bligh of 'Mutiny on the Bounty' fame. It grows to 30 ft (9 m) and produces an astounding number of small green fruits directly on the trunk and branches. The ribbed fruits are acidic and pale yellow to light pink when ripe. Children eat them, but their major uses are to make damsel wine and stew or compote. Its name damsel is probably derived from the diminutive for dame (damsel <Fr. *demoiselle*: 'young girl') because of the fruits' small size or a corruption of damson. It is also called West Indian gooseberry.

DASHEEN (*Colocasia esculenta*, var. *esculenta*) is an underground 'tuber' or corm, locally referred to as a ground provision, like so many of the vegetables that are either underground roots or tubers. It is a perennial herbaceous plant native to SE Asia, and produces a rosette of cormels surrounding a large central corm. The corm is boiled as a vegetable, or eaten roasted, baked or fried. Young dasheen leaves are stewed, occasionally with okra, as spinach, and locally referred to as calalu (<Malinke *kalalu*: 'many things'; Mandingo *colilu*: 'an edible herb resembling spinach'). It is found in popular dishes like 'crab

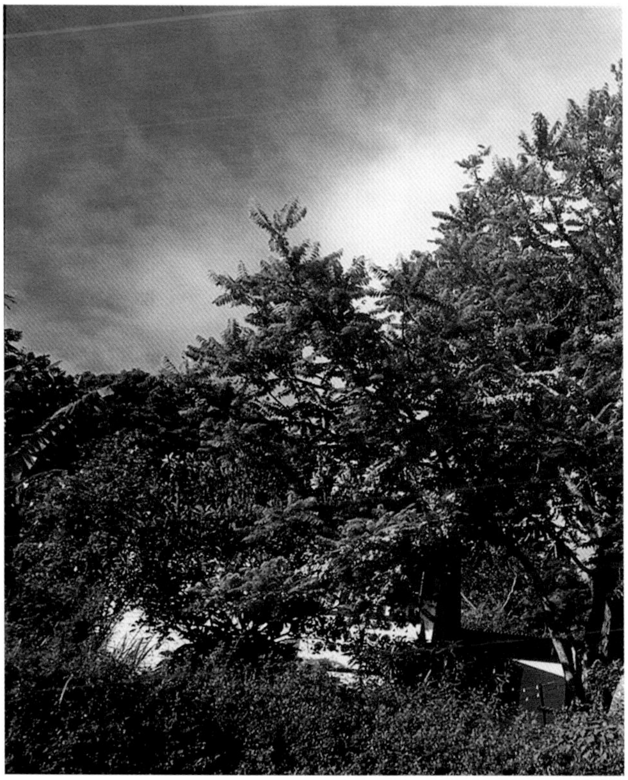

Damsel tree with fruits

Dasheen leaves or calalu

and calalu' and 'calalu soup'. The term calalu also refers to a confusion or mix-up, as in the dish. 'Calalu culture' describes Caribbean Creole society with its mixture of different cultures. During SLAVERY dasheen (<Fr. *de Chine*: 'of China') was part of the slaves' diet, and continues to be part of the diet of many Grenadians. Cultivated near small streams and outlet drains, the corms are harvested from January to April while the leaves are picked year-round. Dasheen leaves should not be confused with zepina (<Fr.Cr. z'épina(rd) <Fr. *(de)s—épinards*: 'spinach') which is sometimes referred to as calalu, but is in fact *Amaranthus* spp. The eddoe (*C. esculenta*, var. *antiquorum*) is a variety of dasheen that produces a rosette of 16-20 cormels surrounding a small central corm. Its leaves are rarely consumed. Eddoe (<Fante *edwo*: 'yam'; Ibibio *edomo*: 'potato yam'). Dasheen is also known as coco yam.

DEATH To mark the end of life various rituals have been used to solemnise this occasion, especially among rural folk. Most of these ceremonies or major parts of them have long since disappeared, except in the rural villages where they are still performed and preserved by oral tradition. As soon as someone expires, the news spreads throughout the community. Decades ago, but until recently in CARRIACOU, it was the village crier who communicated the news to everyone. Many SUPERSTITIONS surround death and funerals, and these are taken seriously by a large number of people. Until the mid-1900s most dead remained in the community until burial, and the deceased's house acted as the funeral parlour. The dead were washed, placed in coffins made by local carpenters and left in the house to await burial. Often they were buried right next to their homes, especially in rural communities, causing the legislature to pass laws to force burial in cemeteries.

Before interment, usually the first night after death, relatives and friends hold a wake to celebrate the life of the deceased. Throughout the night, mourners participate in various activities, including card playing, ANANSI STORIES, bongo FOLK DANCES (no longer practised) and prayers. There is also food and drink, including BAY LEAF tea, COFFEE and strong RUM. Most funeral ceremonies take place at churches in the late afternoon. From the church the funeral cortege proceeds to the cemetery for burial. To complete the mourning process relatives can choose to celebrate either the 'third night', 'nine-night', or 'forty night', or a number of these, depending on resources. These comprise prayer meetings

Roman Catholic cemetery at Sauteurs

where food and drinks are served, and in C&PM the PARENTS' PLATE is observed. Most people celebrate the 'nine night', and though it is usually celebrated as one event nine nights after death, it could also culminate nine nights of activities that are performed to ensure the final peace of the deceased's spirit. In C&PM the TOMBSTONE FEAST completes the rituals associated with death. Each year the deceased are remembered on ALL SAINTS' DAY.[85, 302, 323, 349]

DEGALE, Sir Leo Victor (1921-1986) was Grenada's first GOVERNOR GENERAL following the attainment of INDEPENDENCE in 1974. He replaced Gov. BYNOE as the representative of the British HEAD OF STATE. Sir Leo was the son of Marie and George V DeGale of the influential proprietary family. He went to Canada after graduating from the GBSS and later served in World War II. He qualified as an accountant and returned to Grenada in 1945, co-founding an accounting firm. He was very active in the public service, and served on the boards of many clubs and societies. On a number of occasions he served as the acting governor. There was much controversy surrounding the issue of independence and DeGale's acceptance of the GG position under PM GAIRY. After four years of service, following rumoured disagreements with the PM, he demitted office on 30 September 1978 and was replaced by Paul SCOON. Sir Leo emigrated in 1980 to the UK, where he died.

DEPENDENCIES Along with Grenada, some thirty islands, islets and rocks constitute the state of Grenada, the majority belonging to the GRENADA GRENADINES. Immediately off the NE coast of Grenada are Green Island (formerly Islet du Milieu: 'Middle Islet', 22 acres or 9 ha), (Islet de) Levera or Sugar Loaf Island (17 acres/7 ha), and Sandy Island (formerly Islet Haut: 'Upper Islet', 17 acres/7 ha). Off Grenada's east coast are Black Rock (formerly Islet d'Antoine), Pearls Rock (formerly Islet de la Conférence, 2.50 acres/1 ha), Telescope Rock (formerly La Baye, 5 acres/2 ha), Marquis (7.5 acres/3 ha), and Bacolet or Hope Islands. Off Grenada's SE coast are (Islet Jacques) Adam, GLOVER ISLAND, CALIVIGNY ISLAND and Hog Island (formerly Islet à Cachon: 'Hog Islet', 50 acres/20 ha). In the Grenadines, just north of Grenada are London Bridge (formerly La Pierre Percée: 'stone opening', a reference to the hole through it forming a 'bridge'), Three Sisters (formerly Les Rochers: 'The Rocks', 5 acres/2 ha), RONDE ISLAND, Les Tantes (historically Islet de la Tante for the larger islet, 44 acres/18 ha; and the other 35 acres/14 ha), Bird (formerly Mouchicarri <Fr *mouchoir carré*: 'square handkerchief'), Diamond Rock, Kick-em-Jenny or Gwizô (formerly Les Grison, 50 acres/20 ha), and CAILLE Islands. Off Carriacou's south coast are Bonaparte (2.5 acres/1 ha) and Rose (2.5 acres/1 ha) Rocks, Frigate (74 acres/30 ha), Large (12.5 acres/5 ha), Saline, Mushroom (2.5 acres/1 ha) and White Islands. Off Carriacou's west coast are Jack-A-Dan or Jack Adam, Mabouya (15 acres/6 ha) and SANDY

Dependencies

ISLAND (the latter two formerly known as Les Deux Freres: 'Two Brothers'). And off Carriacou's NE coast are PETITE MARTINIQUE and Petite Tobago (74 acres/30 ha). Some of these islands are privately owned, and a few, including Green, Levera and Sandy Islands are protected as part of the NATIONAL PARK SYSTEM. Many are home to wildlife populations of BIRDS, LIZARDS and MOROCOY, and their CONSERVATION will protect key habitats and ecosystems from human development.

DEVAS, Raymund (1887-1975) was for many decades a resident RC parish priest in Grenada and Carriacou, beginning in 1923. An amateur historian and ornithologist, he devoted much of his spare time to research on the islands' history and BIRDS. In his over forty years of residence in the islands, he wrote four books, including one of the first scholarly histories, *History of the Island of Grenada*. His history of CATHOLICISM in Grenada, *Conception Island*, is an impressive work. His first book, *Up Hill and Down Dale in Grenada*, is a personal tour of Grenada's natural beauty. Because he lived in Grenada for so many years, he thought of himself as a 'Grenadian' and has left a body of work that attests to his love and appreciation for his adopted country.[88, 89, 90, 91]

DISEASES Throughout its history, Grenada has been subjected to many of the world's diseases, made worse by its tropical CLIMATE and limited access to medical resources. The islands' history is spotted with epidemics of BOULAM FEVER, CHOLERA, YELLOW FEVER, MALARIA, YAWS, and the presence of tuberculosis, Guinea worms, elephantiasis, rabies, chigger, leprosy, small pox, dengue fever, typhoid or enteric fever, and numerous other 'fevers'. These earned Grenada the name 'grave of the West Indies' by French colonist who cited disease as the main hindrance to its economic growth in the seventeenth and eighteenth centuries. In the late 1700s there was an increase in private medical practitioners, many 'self-styled doctors' who had little, if any, medical training. This led to the first medical law in 1770, making it illegal to practise without a licence.

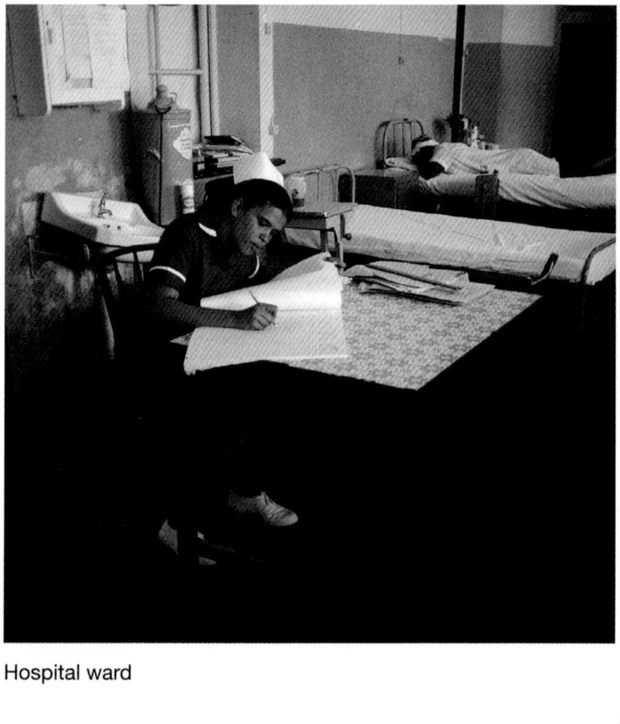

Hospital ward

The islands' medical history is still evident in the ruins of the many isolation hospitals like QUARANTINE STATION, the Leprosy Settlement at Morne Rouge (1928-1957), and the Typhoid and Isolation Hospital at Cherry Hill. The 'Rat Gangs' in the 1930s and the 'Mongoose Gangs' in the 1950s and 1960s led to the control of the rat and MONGOOSE populations, vectors of many diseases. Many of the tropical diseases which still plague developing countries have been brought under control in Grenada due to eradication and inoculation schemes between the 1920s and 1970s, and the establishment of public health measures and primary health care facilities throughout the islands. Today Grenada attracts visitors to its shores who come to enjoy the salubrious climate, unaware of the islands' historical reputation.[55]

DONOVAN, William Galway (1856-1929) was a journalist and political activist who is remembered most for his ardent support of representative government and West Indian federation. Nicknamed the 'Lion' because of his 'prickly red hair', he was the son of Irish and black parents. He was considered the 'foremost intellectual rebel of his time' and beginning in 1877 took up the challenges that consumed his adult life: representative government and federation. He was a vociferous critic of CROWN COLONY (CC) status, which he described as 'simply odious'. Between 1883 and 1920 Donovan edited and published a number of NEWSPAPERS, including the *Grenada People* and *The Federalist*, in which he regularly attacked CC; he was imprisoned for six months in 1884 for 'accusing an expatriate judge of incompetence'. He was a radical member of the REPRESENTATIVE GOVERNMENT ASSOCIATION, fighting for the restoration of representative government and an extension of the franchise for Grenadians. In recognition of his many contributions, the Grenada legislature voted him a pension in 1927, though he never served in that body. T A MARRYSHOW, however, cast the only dissenting vote. A dispute between the two following Donovan's refusal to sell Marryshow his newspaper press, led Donovan to

WG Donovan

call him 'an ungrateful son'. Upon Donovan's death in 1929 Marryshow delivered the eulogy, and in 1958, after the creation of FEDERATION, Marryshow headed a delegation that laid a wreath at Donovan's grave in recognition of his lifelong struggle for federation. He is recognised as the grandfather of West Indian federation. A contemporary believed that Donovan was 'an achiever of great and permanent results under conditions that would have daunted less resolute and more mercenary souls into discouragement and despair'.[35, 81, 310,333]

Dougaldston worker demonstrates 'dancing cocoa' to visitors

DOUGALDSTON, St. John One of the oldest functioning estates, dating to the mid-1700s. Investment by absentee owners like Lord Dundas led to its establishment as a prosperous SUGAR estate, its legacy visible in a decaying water wheel and aqueduct that operated into the late 1800s. The over 740 acre (300 ha) estate produces NUTMEG, COCOA and BANANA, but its production priority is spices, and many can be seen in some form of cultivation and/or processing. A number of innovations have occurred here, including the invention of a cocoa-bean polisher in the 1930s, and the distilling of nutmeg oil in the 1940s and 1950s. The old wooden GREAT HOUSE stands as a testament to the estate's grandeur, and the boucan and drying trays form a page out of the islands' agricultural history. The name is from the Scottish place name Douglaston, the 'd' added because of a transcription error; it dates to the 1760s when the estate was owned by John Graham who was from Douglaston, Scotland.

DOUGLAS, Millicent (fl. 1920s-50s) was one of the first notable women who participated in public life and government. She was the daughter of prominent proprietor H M E Douglas. She went to England to study and later visited West Africa, but returned to Grenada in the 1920s and became involved in many social and commercial activities. She is considered the first to advocate for the rights of women. She established the Gaiety Theatre, opposite the ESPLANADE, in the mid-1920s, which showed foreign films and staged performing and dramatic ARTS. She also ran the Eastern Theatre in GRENVILLE. Douglas was awarded the MBE, and in 1933 was nominated to the St. George's District Board, the first woman to serve in LOCAL GOVERNMENT. In 1939 she moved to Nigeria to write for the *Lagos Pilot* newspaper begun by Nnamdi Azikine, that country's future president. She returned to Grenada but left in 1957 on a trip to West Africa with her niece HV Keens-Douglas. The following year she became a Baha'I, and together with her niece and Julian Edwards, she travelled throughout Liberia spreading the Baha'I faith. She died in West Africa.

DU BU(C), François (1620-1659) commanded FAUDOAS DE CÉRILLAC's expedition to take possession of Grenada from DU PARQUET, arriving there in July 1658 as the new governor. He soon created distrust among the colonists following initial attempts to intimidate them. He circulated 'talks of a possible conspiracy', stemming from the Island CARIB-French conflicts in Martinique, which became a 'convenient excuse to exile [from Grenada] anyone he didn't like.'

He was accused by some of the colonists of tyrannical rule, immoral and illegal activities, and total disregard for the colonists' well being. His 'brutal manners' forced many settlers to leave the island, but a small group, on 28 October 1659, arrested and had him 'put in irons.' Though the intent was to banish him, a trial found him guilty of crimes against the colonists and he was condemned to death. Du Bu, claiming noble birth, demanded to be beheaded, but was instead shot.[8, 95]

DUBUISSON An Island Carib 'chief' who in December 1657, following the second Carib-French conflict, approached the French settlers to negotiate a peace. After verbal agreements with the Island Caribs in Martinique, Dominica and St. Vincent, the French accepted. In April 1658 the 'peace' was threatened because of Dubuisson's anger over the abduction of his African slave by Gov. CACQUERAY DEVALMINIÈRE in May 1657, and the governor's subsequent refusal to return her. De Valminière argued that the slave was a refugee, fleeing from the Island Caribs because she was mistreated, and 'being Christians they couldn't live like Christians among people who are living like animals.' De Valminière nonetheless 'compensated' Dubuisson for the slave without acknowledging that he had abducted her, continuing the mistrust between the two groups. The peace was temporarily broken in 1659 as a result of events in Martinique and the wider Lesser Antilles when Indian Warner attacked French settlements in Grenada. Dubuisson's end is unknown.[8]

DUFFUS COMMISSION This body was established on 6 December 1973 by Gov. BYNOE as a result of the COMMITTEE OF 22 demanding that the GULP government investigate the events that led to a perceived state of lawlessness at the end of 1973. Premier GAIRY agreed because of the INDEPENDENCE issue being debated in the British Parliament and to avoid the threatened island-wide labour strike that would have crippled his government. The commission comprised Sir Herbert Duffus, former Jamaican chief justice, Aubrey Fraser, Legal Department head at UWI, and Samuel Carter, Jamaica's RC Archbishop. They were tasked with investigating reports of police brutality, the beating of the 'NJM six' on BLOODY SUNDAY, and whether the police and courts had violated the constitutional rights of citizens. Initially charged with examining events from October 1972 to November 1973, the Commission extended its investigation to include the civil unrest of January 1974 and BLOODY MONDAY.

The Commission sat for six months and heard evidence from private citizens, police officers and government officials. In May 1975 it issued its report, recommending the immediate disbanding of the MONGOOSE GANG and POLICE AIDES, reorganisation of the POLICE FORCE, dismissal of Innocent BELMAR, investigation of a number of civil servants, and the speedy processing of criminal charges stemming from violent incidents during the period examined. The GULP government responded with a white paper declaring that Premier Gairy had (partially) accepted five of the eight recommendations, rejecting outright the convening of a commission to determine compensation for victims of the January 1974 rioting and looting, and dismissing the others. The Duffus Report dealt a political blow to the GULP, and Premier Gairy always regarded it as a personal attack on his government. In 1984 he gloated that he was vindicated by the recent political events in Grenada, resulting in the US INTERVENTION. He believed that 'Duffus would be very much embarrassed if you were to talk to him now on the question of his report, because all that we are saying is that those people were communists and Duffus and other people are trying to dress them in the habiliment of angels and saints.[35, 94, 201, 333]

DUMOULIN, François Louis (1753-1834) was born in Vevey, Switzerland and at the age of twenty began travelling throughout the Caribbean. Between 1773 and 1782 he resided in Grenada under both French and British administrations. He was one of a small number of Swiss immigrants living and working in Grenada following the British gaining control of the islands. Many of them managed or owned ESTATES, as was the case with Dumoulin who owned a 120 acre (48 ha) COFFEE estate in Requin, ST. DAVID. During the FRENCH INTERREGNUM, he acted as the secretary to the French intendant, Jacques Lequoy. With the British regaining the islands he returned to Switzerland.

As a painter and writer Dumoulin has left one of the few artistic impressions of the island during the 1700s. Among his paintings is the French capture of Grenada in 1779. The memoir of his travels and residence in Grenada provides a cursory glimpse of life on the island in the late eighteenth century.[238]

DUNFERMLINE, St. Andrew A rum distillery located just outside GRENVILLE, one of only two estates that utilised centuries-old technologies like the water wheel to process RUM into the twentieth century. James Seaton, the Earl of Dunfermline (Scotland) owned the 480 acre (194

Painting by Dumoulin while resident In Grenada

ha) estate in 1824, hence its name. In 1929 George Seton-Browne (member of the legislature, 1901-1913) owned the estate, which was later purchased by the proprietary DeGale family. The estate also cultivated NUTMEG and COCOA. A stone on one of the buildings records 1797 as the date of establishment, but the sugar estate dates to the mid 1700s under the French. The estate distilled various types of white rum, including *Dunfermline Rum* and *Spicy Jack*. Main streets in GRENVILLE are named after both James Seaton and George Seton-Brown.[166]

DU PARQUET, Jacques Dyle (1606-1658) was the governor of Martinique (1637-1658) who outfitted the successful French SETTLEMENT of Grenada in March 1649. Du Parquet arrived in the Caribbean in 1634 and 'became one of the leading figures in the early history of the French West Indies.' Though the Grenada settlement was established in 1649, du Parquet did not purchase the islands until September 1650 from the bankrupt Compagnie des Isles d'Amérique. In August 1651 he was made governor general of his territories by the French king, and he guided the subjugation of the Island CARIBS. According to DU TERTRE, 'that colony has drained the greatest part of du Parquet's wealth,' and together with St. Lucia 'were the two leeches that exhausted the best part of his wealth' because of the Island Carib-French conflicts. Du Parquet, suffering from worsening health, sold Grenada to FAUDOAS DE CÉRILLAC in 1657.[8, 95, 178]

DUQUESNE An Island Carib village 'chief' who resided in Grenada at the time of the initial French SETTLEMENT. He lived on the NW coast near to the places that bear his name today: Duquesne Bay, Duquesne River, and Duquesne village. At the start of the Carib-French conflict in November 1649, 'Captain' Duquesne warned the French colonists at BEAUSÉJOUR of the planned attack by the Island CARIBS. The 500-strong force attacked Fort du Marquis, killing the majority of the French after a prolonged siege. In retaliation the French attacked Duquesne's village and destroyed houses and gardens; the village had been evacuated. Duquesne appears in a tale of love, deceit and murder involving his son, daughter and the Island Carib 'traitor' Thomas. Thomas, rejected by Duquesne's daughter, killed her brother, and ran away to Martinique to escape retaliation. There, Thomas informed Gov. DU PARQUET that he could 'deliver' the Island Caribs in Grenada. With Thomas' help, the French ambushed many at what became known as LEAPERS' HILL.[8, 155]

DUTCH ATTACK, 1675 During the Third Dutch War (1672-1678), Jan Erasmus Reining, a Dutch privateer, attacked the major French settlement in Grenada. He arrived in the region in 1673 with Commander Jacob Binckes, both operating under the sanction of the Dutch West India Company with the intention of attacking French colonies and causing as much destruction as possible. In December 1674 he raided slaves from four estates along the coast. On 28 March 1675, together with Privateer Jurriaen Aernouts and about 100 privateers, Reining attacked the Ville du FORT ROYAL and took control of the small fort, which was not well protected. A French man-of-war 'sent post haste by [GG] de Baas slipped into the harbour behind the privateers and an infantry landing party quickly rounded up about 80 free booters' and forced the others to take refuge in the fort. Besieged and famished, they surrendered and were taken to Martinique as prisoners of war. They were forced to work on plantations, but in June 1675 Reining, Aernouts, and six companions managed to escape in a dugout canoe 'by drugging the guards with wine.' They were subsequently captured by the Spanish at Venezuela on their way to Curaçao, but escaped the following year to rejoin the Dutch in the war against the French. Reining was known to the French as Ramus.

DU TERTRE, Jean-Baptiste (1610-1687) was a French Dominican priest who visited Grenada in October 1656 to arrange for the purchase of the islands for FAUDOAS DE CÉRILLAC. In a letter to de Cérillac he outlined the advantages of the islands, providing one of the few descriptions of the settlement at PORT LOUIS. He is considered the 'Herodotus of the Antilles' following the publication of his monumental memoir, *Histoire générale des Antilles*, which documents the establishment

Slaves carrying out various tasks on a plantation

of the French in the region, complete with descriptions of the natural environment, and Island CARIB culture in the first half of the 1600s. For centuries his narrative on Grenada represented the sole contemporary source regarding the settlement of the French there, but the 1975 publication of an anonymous seventeenth-century French manuscript, *Histoire de l'isle de Grenade en Amérique, 1649-59* (see BRESSON) calls into question some of his facts. There appear to be some discrepancies concerning du Parquet's settlement of Grenada in March 1649 (du Tertre records June 1650), and the events surrounding the subjugation of the Island Caribs. Roget adds that du Tertre 'is generally a scrupulous historian but he is quite short on the subject of the establishment of the French on the island of Grenada.[8, 95]

DWENN/DUENNE The spirit of a child who dies before being baptised and as such wanders in the forest forever, in limbo. Its origin is probably African, bearing remarkable resemblance to the Asante *mmoatia* ('little folk/animals'), but incorporating RC beliefs. Like the dwenn, the *mmoatia* is short in stature, with feet pointing backwards, and causes all kinds of mischief. The dwenn (?<Fr. Cr.<Sp. duende: 'goblin, mischievous child, elf', or <Kalabari: 'spirit of the dead') lives in the forest, but ventures into the villages and lures children, who are out playing, into the thick woods where they become scared and lost. To prevent this, it is advisable not to call children's names after dark. The dwenn is commonly portrayed as a faceless, sexless child, with a mouth and a mushroom-like hat, sometimes covering long plaits of hair. One of its common tricks is to lie by the roadside and pretend to cry, in the hope that a passer-by will take it home. Being carried, the dwenn grows larger and larger, finally demanding in a manly voice to its host to 'put me down where you get me!' Terrified, the host deposits the dwenn at the roadside and runs away. It is mischievous, and not disposed to cause harm. They are said to congregate in groups to perform their tricks.

E

EAST INDIANS As a direct result of the migration of East Indians under the system of INDENTURED IMMIGRATION, about 3,200 came to Grenada to work as agricultural labourers. Fewer than 400 returned to India, some emigrated to TRINIDAD and Guyana, but over half stayed. Many remained settled in the rural PARISHES not far from the sugar and cocoa estates where their ancestors laboured in villages like SAMARITAN and Diego Piece, St. Patrick; Forde, Cumma (?< Hin. Kumar, a personal name), Clozier and Florida, St. John; and St. James and Belmont, St. Andrew. Unlike Trinidad and Guyana, with larger East Indian populations, the small number in Grenada has been absorbed into the larger Creole society, resulting in the loss of much of their culture. In 1871 there were 1,344 East Indian-born residents in Grenada, declining to 181 by 1921, and within the next three decades the population became almost exclusively native-born. At the Indian Arrival Day celebrations on 1 May 1957, Indo-Grenadians gathered 'to honour the surviving ex-indentured immigrants.' The Indo-Grenadian population has never risen above five per cent of the total population, recording 2,500 (three per cent) in 2001.

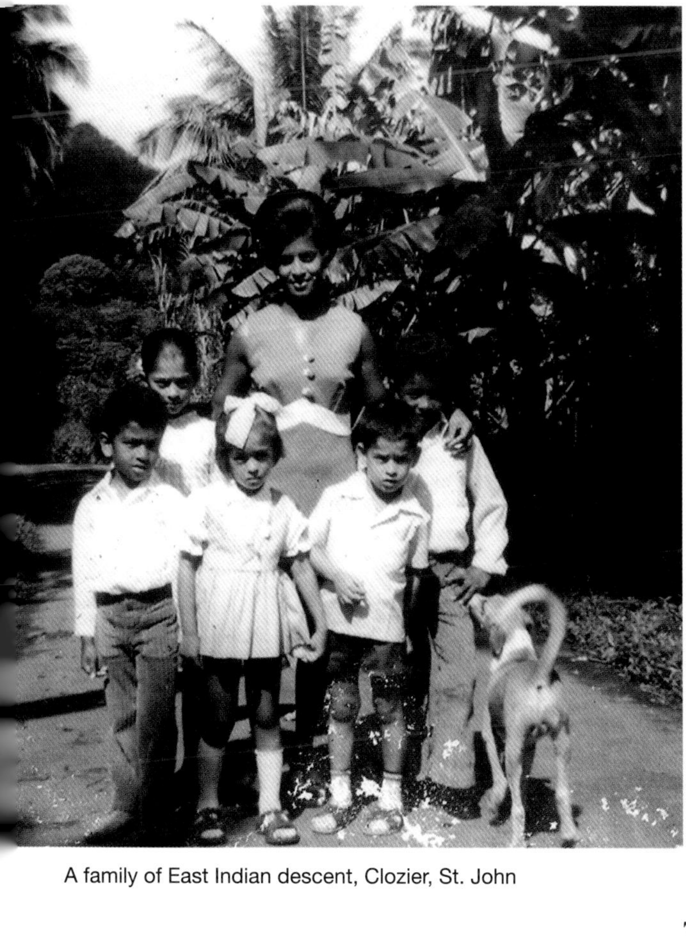

A family of East Indian descent, Clozier, St. John

Some aspects of East Indian culture have survived, especially in the few villages where their numbers have been relatively large. Noticeable East Indian survivals, possibly influenced more through contact with Trinidad, are mainly foods like channa (<Hin. *chanaa*: 'grain, chick pea'), the rice dish pelau, bhaji (<Hin. *bhaajii*: 'vegetable leaves') or spinach, achar (<Hin. *achaar*:'pickles') or pickled mango, the curry dish roti (<Hin. *rotii*: 'bread'), and a few words like jagabat (<Hin. *dagabaj*: 'bad woman or one of questionable character') and dougla (<Hin. *dogalaa*: 'hybrid, mongrel'), the offspring of Indian and black. Despite their small numbers, Indo-Grenadians are very noticeable across Grenada, owning successful businesses and ESTATES (some of the Indian entrepreneurs in St. George's are recent immigrants from India and the Indian Diaspora). Prominent Indo-Grenadians were/are Norbert Nyack (d. 1969), RM Bhola (1922-2002), LL Ramdhanny, Dr. RR Japal, LJ Ramdhanny and Kenny Lalsingh. East Indian family names like Bhola, Japal, Laldee, Nyack, Ragbersingh and Ramdhanny are quite common. 35, 211, 329, 333

EASTER A Christian religious observance of abstinence and ritual cleansing to mark the death and resurrection of Jesus Christ following the 40 days of Lent. The central celebrations are the observations of Good Friday and Easter Sunday. There is a folk ritual that single women observe on Good Friday. The 'first' egg laid on this day is broken and the albumen poured into a glass of water lying out in the sun. This is all done at the ominous hour of 12 noon. The dispersed egg white forms a number of images in the water that are interpreted as predictions of the future. A 'ship' or 'plane' means that the individual will travel, a 'ring' or a 'church' is an indication of marriage, while a 'coffin' is a portent of death. The tradition of beating the coquete or effigy of Judas Iscariot is no longer observed. The Easter holidays are also associated with boating and YACHTING activities, including the PETITE MARTINIQUE Regatta and the now discontinued Easter Water Parade (1977-1978). Easter is synonymous with KITE FLYING and hot cross buns.

EDUCATION The idea of educating slaves was seen as incongruent with both SLAVERY and estate agriculture that had as their objective the continued exploitation of a chattel labour force. Slave owners objected to any form of education for slaves because they believed it would alter their submissiveness and encourage dissent. The idea of educating slaves surfaced the decade preceding EMANCIPATION because it was widely held that education was a 'civilising agency' and would help integrate the slaves into society. In 1823 there were eleven private schools in the islands, all catering exclusively to the free population. A year later the Grenada Benevolent Society established CENTRAL SCHOOLS.

Since the churches saw religious education as essential to the moral and social advancement of the former slaves, they were at the forefront of educational development. In 1838 there were twelve primary schools, the majority operated by the Anglican Church and catering to a paltry ten per cent of the eligible children. The government viewed the obstacles to improved education as the RC religion and the FRENCH CREOLE spoken by the majority of the children, too few clergy, and the discord among the four major religious denominations. The latter problem dominated the education debate throughout the 1800s. The latter half of the 1800s witnessed the development of primary and secondary education, but the main problem was school attendance, which remained low due to widespread child labour. In 1875 the government established the grant-in-aid system for all schools. In 1900 there were forty primary schools, almost half administered by the Catholic Church, and two secondary schools in St. George's. Schools were still plagued by low attendance, and in 1920 the Compulsory Education Ordinance made it mandatory for children between the ages of six and 14 years to attend primary school.

By the 1930s education had made some progress, but the 1940s brought major changes, including the extension of primary education, the provision of trained teachers, and vocational training. Secondary education was established in the rural districts in the 1940s, and in 1963 the Teachers Training College was opened in St. George's. The period from the 1960s to the 1980s witnessed continued expansion of both primary and secondary education. There are about 76 primary schools with approximately 20,000 students and 880 teachers, and 22 secondary schools, with about 7,370 students and 380 teachers. Adult literacy is at a high of 98 percent. The MARRYSHOW COMMUNITY COLLEGE has consolidated post-secondary education throughout the islands, further aiding the development of technical and vocational training. There are schools providing special education, including the deaf and the mentally retarded. There are a number of skills training centres across the islands, and the UWI School of Continuing Education at Marryshow House provides some post-secondary education. The ST. GEORGE'S UNIVERSITY, which began as a US proprietary medical school in 1977, has become a centre of learning in Grenada. [35, 89, 333]

ELECTIONS The first general election was held in 1951 following the introduction of universal adult suffrage that same year; it replaced the restrictive systems that existed under CROWN COLONY and the OLD REPRESENTATIVE SYSTEM. Since 1951 Grenada has held 13 general elections: 10 October 1951, 21 September 1954, 24 September 1957, 27 March 1961, 12 September 1962, 25 August 1967, 28 February 1972, 7 December 1976, 3 December 1984, 13 March 1990, 21 June 1995, 18 January 1999 and 27 November 2003. The GULP under Eric GAIRY won elections in 1951 (with 7 seats), 1954 (7), 1961 (8), 1967 (7), 1972 (13, later 14), and 1976 (9). The GRENADA NATIONAL PARTY under Herbert BLAIZE formed a coalition government in 1957 (4) and won in 1962 (6). The NEW NATIONAL PARTY under Herbert Blaize won in 1984 (14), and under Dr Keith MITCHELL in 1995 (8), 1999 (15) and 2003 (8). The NATIONAL DEMOCRATIC CONGRESS under Nicholas BRATHWAITE formed a coalition government in 1990 (10). Since 1951 there has been active voter participation, ranging from a low of 56 per cent (1961) to a high of 84 per cent (1972).

Though elections are scheduled every five years (three years prior to 1957), they can be called at any time if the ruling party fails to win a parliamentary majority, or loses it, fails a no-confidence vote, or at the discretion of the PM (due to high popularity and confident of victory). In 1951 there were eight constituencies—Town of St. George, Parish of St. George (in 1961 it split into two, St. George N and S, and in 1972 these split into four, St. George NW, NE, SE, and SW), St. John and St. Mark (split into the two respective constituencies based on PARISH boundaries in 1961), St. Andrew N and S (in 1972 they split into four, St. Andrew NE, NW, SE, and SW), St. Patrick (in 1972 it split into St. Patrick's E and W), St. David, and C&PM—having increased to 10 in 1961, and to 15 in 1972. [35, 97, 98, 99, 100, 111, 233, 254]

ELECTRICITY In 1895 the Annandale and Souliere Rivers were assessed as to whether they could provide the town of St. George's with hydroelectricity, but it wasn't until 1925 that electricity arrived in Grenada when electric lights were installed at the HOSPITAL with funding from the British Red Cross Society. On 14 February 1928 St. George's was electrified for the first time, with regular service beginning in December, and expanding thereafter. The GOG funded the electrification of the town, and the Public Works Department managed the two diesel generators at the Power Station at Burns Point on the CARENAGE. Between 1934 and 1937 two new generators were installed to supply increasing demand. Electric streetlights were soon installed, replacing the kerosene Tilly lamps that had operated since 1882. In 1935 electric power was extended to Springs and Belmont, and two years later to Woodlands and Grande Anse, St. George. In 1961 the Power Station was moved to the Queen's Park, and expanded its generating capacity. In January 1961 the Grenada Electricity Services Ltd. (GRENLEC) was incorporated, with the British and Grenada governments as shareholders. Between 1961 and 1965 electricity reached beyond St. George as St. David, GRENVILLE, Gouyave, Victoria and finally SAUTEURS were lighted. Hillsborough, Carriacou received electricity in 1960 and a power station was built in 1963 at Beausejour, gradually extending electricity across the island. Petite Martinique received electricity in the early 1980s following the installation of an engine. Kerosene lamps and candles, however, remained the primary means to light most homes.

In 1982 the GOG became the sole owner of GRENLEC, but it was made a public company in 1993 and in 1994 WRB Enterprises of Miami, US, bought controlling interests of 50 per cent shares. Prior to 1960 consumers remained in the hundreds, predominantly in St. George's, but increased gradually. Between 1983 and 2003 consumers increased from 9,549 to 40,012, with installed capacity growing from 8,355 kW to 40,000 kW. Commercial consumption quadrupled in the same period and continues to rise steadily. At least 99 per cent of the POPULATION has access to electricity, which in the past few years has been regular and uninterrupted. C&PM, whose electricity services became part of GRENLEC in 1993, have their own power generating stations that were built in 2000. HURRICANE IVAN in 2004 devastated Grenada's electricity network, requiring months to repair the damages to downed poles and wires as many parts of the island were without electricity.

EMANCIPATION The British Parliament in July 1833 passed the Imperial Act of Emancipation, 'freeing' all slaves in its colonies. Though SLAVERY ended over a century and half ago, there are ongoing debates on the causes of and reasons for emancipation, the slaves' role in their emancipation, and slavery's lingering effects. Though economics contributed significantly to the end of slavery, the vociferous British anti-slavery movement was instrumental in forcing the British government to abolish the SLAVE TRADE and subsequently slavery. By 1824, with the passage of Canning's Resolution and the adoption of a number of Amelioration Proposals, the British Parliament began preparations to end slavery in its colonies.

After some ten years of generally unsuccessful amelioration, the British Parliament in 1833 voted to end slavery. Members of the PLANTOCRACY protested against the proposed loss of their slave labour force, but with compensation provided by the British Parliament, and the establishment of APPRENTICESHIP, they grudgingly accepted that the system they had profited from was no longer acceptable. On 31 July 1834 over 23,600 slaves were freed, with plantation owners compensated for their loss of property to the sum of £616,255 (equivalent to £37.5m in today's money). The idea of compensation for the slaves for their many years of labour and undue hardships was never discussed, the feeling being that their freedom was compensation enough. This has led, however, to the present debate over reparations by some of the descendants of the slaves, while others have demanded apologies from governments and institutions that benefited from the slave trade and African slavery.

The act took effect on 1 August 1834 and instituted a system of compulsory Apprenticeship. 'Complete' freedom was not achieved until 1838. Emancipation holiday on 1 August is still celebrated, but with little reference to slavery and emancipation. Unlike a number of the other islands, there are no monuments or memorials to the ending of slavery.[35, 79, 81b, 333]

ENGLISH HERITAGE In 1974 the British government relinquished all remaining sovereignty over Grenada. It bade a lacklustre farewell to over 200 years of colonial rule and left behind a legacy of social, political and economic institutions. This legacy, however, is fraught with the pain and suffering of SLAVERY and historical oppression shaped by colonialism. It nonetheless forms, together with AFRICAN HERITAGE and FRENCH HERITAGE, the basis of Grenada's Creole identity. At the core of Grenadian society—institutions of government, EDUCATION, criminal justice, LANGUAGE and sports—are British institutions, albeit altered, which have shaped the way Grenadians

British telephone boxes, remnants of the islands' English heritage

think and act. The British colonial legacy has bequeathed ANGLICANISM, PLACE NAMES, a JUDICIAL SYSTEM, including the Privy Council, and the holidays of Boxing Day and Guy Fawkes Day, which are still celebrated. Grenada is a member of the Commonwealth of Nations, with the British monarch, Queen Elizabeth II, the HEAD OF STATE. Grenadians annually receive historical British honours from the Queen. The islands' continued associations with aspects of their colonial past are constantly debated.

ESPLANADE A promenade in St. George's Town overlooking the outer harbour. After 1917 it took on the appearance it would have for the rest of the century when its 'ramshackle barrack-type buildings' were torn down,

Cruise ships docked at the new cruise ship port

and a seawall constructed, creating a promenade. It was situated on MELVILLE STREET, from the SENDALL TUNNEL to the boundary of Hillsborough Street. The bay before the tunnel was once used as the dock for fishing boats bringing their catch to market. The Esplanade was the historical site of the annual lighting of the Christmas tree and STEELBAND and DJ concerts or 'blocos'. At the far end of the Esplanade sits the newly reconstructed Melville House, home of the National Insurance Scheme. The Pitch Pine Bar and the many small tourist shops were probably the area's most distinguishing feature. Over the years the Esplanade has lost its beauty as the trees were replaced with buildings. In 2000 the buildings were levelled for the construction of the Melville Street Cruise Terminal/Port and the Esplanade Shopping Mall which opened in December 2004 and beautifully transformed the area.

ESTATES are large areas of tropical commercial farm cultivated with crops meant primarily for export. Beginning in the 1600s they came to represent an economic farming system that spawned and bolstered the institution of SLAVERY in the region. For much of its history, the estate has been at the centre of the economic and social life in the Caribbean islands. A historical estate comprised the GREAT HOUSE, slave quarters, and fields which covered acres of SUGAR CANE, COTTON, or a number of other crops which happened to be of economic value at any given time. The estate system of cash crop cultivation was established by the French beginning in 1649. The sizes of estates were not static, increasing in size from the late 1600s until EMANCIPATION, and gradually decreasing thereafter. Under the French the estates were small and crop cultivation was relatively diversified. The British occupation after 1763 saw an increase in the size of estates due to the high investment needed for sugar production, making larger estates more economical and forcing small coffee and cocoa farmers out. The sugar estate achieved its climax in the late 1700s and the early 1800s. It was replaced by cocoa estates in the mid-1800s, which climaxed between 1870 and 1919. The NUTMEG estate achieved its climax in the mid-1900s. The collapse of the sugar industry by the 1880s led to the disintegration of many large estates into either smaller estates or 'acre plots', which were sold to the peasantry. In 1946 estates comprised over 45 per cent of all cultivated land, and were owned by 103 proprietors. In 1972 the large proprietors had decreased to 50, but they owned 53 per cent of the land.

As the sole employer of unskilled labour during slavery and after, a dependent relationship developed between estate owner and labourer. It was not until the disturbances known as SKYRED in 1951 that the dependency of the peasantry was broken. Yet, estate agriculture had already begun to experience a number of problems by the early 1900s, among them labour desertion, absentee ownership, commodity price instability, and adverse government policies which eventually led to its demise and dethronement as the backbone of the economy.

A number of estates still dominate cash crop production, but subsistence farmers play an important role. A small number of estates have been preserved, leaving intact their historical appearance, specifically the great houses and the sugar refining machinery, which today offer a view

A cocoa-drying house on an estate in Grenada, 1857

into a distant past. Many estates bear the personal names of their former owners, while others carried fanciful or euphemistic names; many of these estate names have become the names of villages that developed on their borders, or altogether engulfed them.

The island of CARRIACOU, experiencing the total collapse of the sugar industry by the mid-1800s, saw the abandonment of its estates by the PLANTOCRACY. Most of the estates remained owned by absentee planters until the early 1900s when the government purchased a few and distributed plots to peasants under its LAND SETTLEMENT. Carriacou, as a result, developed a predominantly peasant agriculture devoid of the dependent planter-peasant relationship common to Grenada.[30, 35]

EXPO '69 Between 5-30 April 1969 Grenada hosted a regional Caribbean Free Trade Association (CARIFTA) Exposition, an idea conceived by Premier Gairy after Grenada's participation in the Worlds' Fair and Exposition in Montreal, Canada in 1967. After convincing the other CARIFTA members, Premier Gairy billed it as 'a showcase of Caribbean progress and togetherness', and as a way to publicise the regional CARIFTA. It also provided publicity and attracted visitors to the islands, expanding the emerging TOURISM industry. The site of the Expo was the undeveloped promontory of True Blue situated on the SE coast. The festival comprised pavilions by each participating nation, exhibiting agricultural, manufactured and cultural displays and events. Premier GAIRY hoped it 'would help in cementing a true spirit of West Indianism'. The three-week-long event propelled Grenada into the limelight of Caribbean affairs, but its extravagance left a US$1.1m debt. Among the costly items were 30 Carifta Cottages intended for the many guests, but incomplete at the time of the event. Expo '69 did succeed in placing Grenada on the international tourism map, and exhibiting Grenadian visual and performing ARTS and culture. It was the first international exposition of its kind in the region.

Depiction of the True Blue site

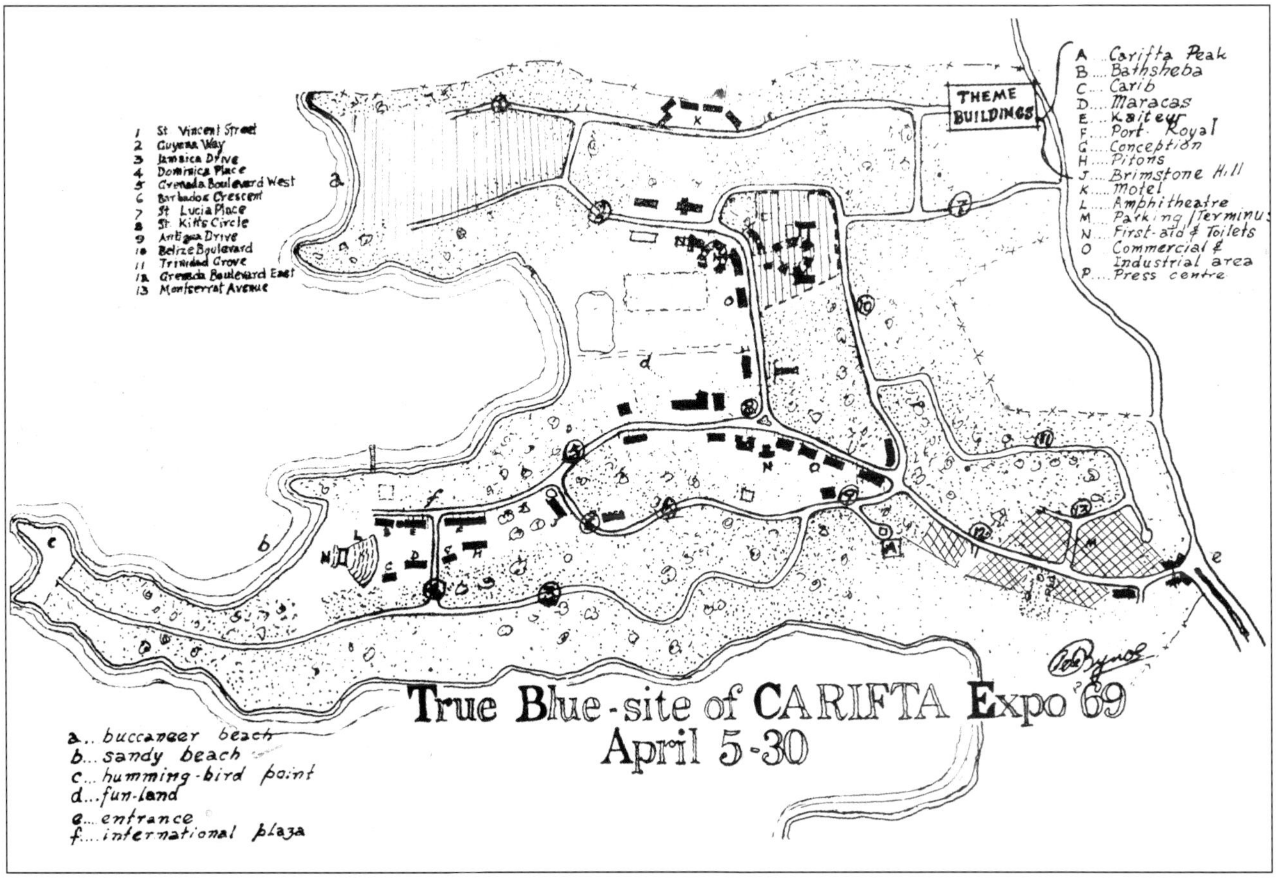

FAUDOAS DE CÉRILLAC, Jean de (1600-1679) was the proprietor of Grenada between 1657 and 1664 after purchasing it from DU PARQUET for 90,000 *livres* (about £3,600). In 1655 he approached Father DU TERTRE for assistance in purchasing a colony in the Americas and du Tertre recommended Grenada, travelling there in 1656 and sealing the deal with du Parquet in October 1656.De Cérillac planned to sail from France to take possession of Grenada in October 1657, but difficulties delayed him. A second attempt in December 1657 ran into a storm that left twenty dead. He decided not to continue the trip, but instead sent François DU BU and eighty men to take possession. A third attempt in April 1658 also failed. Between 1660 and 1662 de Cérillac resided in Grenada, arriving to quell the insurrection against du Bu. Before he left he installed his sons Jean de Faudoas as governor, and Pierre as the major. In 1664 the WEST INDIA COMPANY took over Grenada, forcing de Cérillac to sell it for 100,000 *livres* (about £4,000). De Cérillac's plans to develop the colony proved a failure and left Grenada in a worse state than when he bought it seven years earlier.[8, 95, 199]

FAUNA/WILDLIFE Grenada is home to a variety of animal species that are generally small and less exotic than other islands like Trinidad only 90 miles (145 km) away. Grenada's fauna, especially the herpetological fauna, exhibit predominantly South American influences. Among the fauna are amphibians—CRAPPO and FROGS; reptiles—LIZARDS, SNAKES, SEA TURTLES, MOROCOY; BIRDS; and mammals—MANICOU, ARMADILLO, MONGOOSE and BATS. The MONA MONKEY, a West African import, is Grenada's largest terrestrial wildlife. A number of species are believed to have become extinct in recent years, including the AGOUTI and two species of snakes. The loss of habitat due to AGRICULTURE, TOURISM development, increasing human population, and legal/illegal hunting for food/recreation have threatened many wildlife species, which have had little protection from CONSERVATION laws.[50]

FEDERATION The idea of federation among the BWI gained momentum in the late 1800s and early 1900s among a number of West Indians, including W G DONOVAN and T A MARRYSHOW who are known as the grandfather and father of federation, respectively. The idea of federation was at least 200 years old, with quite a number of attempts by the British colonial government to create such a union among various groups of colonies. Campaigning for both representative government and federation of the West Indies, Marryshow believed that federation would ensure the future success of West Indian self-government. The British Colonial Office had traditionally pursued federation as a means of creating a centralised administration and control of these geographically diverse territories as it did with the GOVERNMENT OF GRENADA. In 1869 it proposed the union of Grenada, Tobago and Trinidad, and federation between the Windward Islands and Barbados in 1875 that led to the Confederation Riots in the latter country. In 1931 the British tried unsuccessfully to establish a union between its two smaller groupings of the Windward and Leeward Islands.

Following a number of conferences over an eleven-year period in the 1940s and 1950s, the structure of the Federation of the West Indies was finally agreed upon. Grantley Adams of Barbados was elected PM and Port-of-Spain, Trinidad, was named the capital. Marryshow had proposed Grenada as the capital but the Grenada government declined. The islands forming the new federated country were Anguilla, Antigua and Barbuda, Barbados, Dominica, Grenada, Jamaica, Montserrat, St. Kitts-Nevis, St. Lucia, St. Vincent, and Trinidad & Tobago. From its inception the Federation was confronted with a number of problems, the least of which was its lack of centralised political power. Dr Alban Radix, Deputy Speaker of the House, and T J GIBBS represented Grenada in the 45-member House of Representatives. Of the 19-member Senate, T A Marryshow and J B Renwick represented Grenada; following Marryshow's death in 1958 A Norris Hughes replaced him. With independence movements gaining momentum within the British Empire, the larger islands of the Federation, i.e. Jamaica and Trinidad, opted out of the union in pursuit of self-government, terminating Federation after only four years, and bringing to an end the dream of Caribbean unity. See also UNITARY STATE.

FÉDON, Julien (1752?-1796?) was the leader of a popular eighteenth-century revolt against the British, and is today regarded as a national hero. Though it is popularly held that he was born in Grenada, he may have been born in Martinique and immigrated to Grenada with his family in the 1750s. He was the son and one of eight children of Pierre Fédon, a French jeweller who arrived in Martinique in 1749 from Bordeaux, France, and Brigitte, a free black from Martinique. In 1780 he married Marie Rose Cavelan, a free coloured from a prominent Martinican family also resident in Grenada. They had at

Michael Donelan's impression of Julien Fédon

least two children, both girls. Julien and his wife owned Lancer, a small estate and slaves in St. Mark, but in 1791 they purchased the 450 acre (182 ha) BELVIDERE estate, a large estate in St. John worked by 100 slaves. His brother Jean owned a 138 acre (56 ha) coffee estate.

Fédon was a FREE COLOURED living in a British colony that regarded him as a third-class citizen and had since 1763 persecuted its French inhabitants. Yet his only known political association was a pledge of loyalty, together with other free coloureds, to the British in 1790 in the wake of widespread civil unrest in the region. It is believed that Fédon and a number of other free coloureds seriously began planning the revolt in 1794, maybe as early as mid-1793, and by 1795 Fédon emerged as their leader. On the night of 2 March 1795 Fédon led a group of insurgents in a bloody attack against the British inhabitants, beginning FÉDON'S REBELLION. Throughout the often-chaotic insurrection, Fédon was able to maintain the dominance of his forces, most of which comprised thousands of freed slaves, and controlled most of the island. Yet, he was unable to force the beleaguered British in St. George's to surrender, or carry out an attack against them after 13 months of fighting. His leadership of the revolt also alienated his French supporters in Guadeloupe. They soon lost confidence in him, replacing him as the commander of French forces in Grenada by October 1795.

In June 1796 General Abercromby, arriving with a large military force, executed the final offensive against the rebels. His offer of £500 bounty for Fédon 'dead or alive', went uncollected because Fédon was never captured nor his body recovered after the rebellion was crushed. Many myths surround his life and death, but it is widely suspected that he drowned while trying to escape by boat to Trinidad, since he was never heard of again.

During the Grenada REVOLUTION the image of Fédon underwent a transformation when he was hailed as a national hero, replacing the image of a brigand with which the British and generations of Grenadians depicted him. Though many view Fédon as the leader of Grenada's only slave revolt, it seems an interesting title for a slave owner whose revolutionary objectives were the replacement of the British government with the French and greater civil rights for free coloureds, though the revolt did accomplish the temporary freedom of the slaves.[76, 78, 174]

FÉDON'S CAMP/MORNE FÉDON is situated in St. John just north of Mt. Qua Qua, at a height of 2,509 ft (765 m). Located just north of the centre of Grenada, it commands a view of many parts of the island and the coasts. Fédon's Camp derived its name, sometime in the mid-1800s, from its use during FÉDON'S REBELLION as the main fortified camp of Julien FÉDON and his insurgents. Morne Fédon had two separate fortified camps and was defended by large cannons protecting its almost inaccessible approaches. The lower camp was known as *Camp de la liberté*. The upper camp was called Qua-Qua or Quaco, or the *Camp de la mort* following the executions of 47 British hostages in April 1795. A lookout called Vigie (<Fr.: 'look-out post') also occupied the mountaintop. Morne Fédon, formerly the Montagne du Vauclin under the French, has become a historical site as it was the place of the executions and burial of numerous British hostages and the scene of some of the bloodiest fighting which ended the revolt. At the summit of one of the spurs sits a pillar on which is engraved, 'Site of Fédon's Camp, 1795.'

FÉDON'S REBELLION (2/3 March 1795-19 June 1796) The 1790s in the Caribbean in general, and Grenada in particular, were reverberating from the French and Haitian Revolutions and the cry of 'Liberté, égalité, fraternité!' The French population in Grenada, whites and especially free coloureds, had many grievances against the British, having suffered religious, social and political persecution for the past dozen years. Even though the situation in Grenada was tense and some of the British residents had noticed unusual activities among the French inhabitants, especially the free coloureds, the attack on the night of 2/3 March 1795 by Julien FÉDON and his followers surprised many. Fédon and his forces, with the rebel cry of '*Liberté, égalité ou la mort!*,' surrounded the town of MARQUIS (then called Grenville), capturing and putting to death eleven of the British inhabitants. Simultaneously in GOUYAVE, another group of insurgents captured over forty British residents, including Dr John HAY and Rev. Francis McMahon, who were taken to BELVIDERE where they were held captive. Lt. Gov. HOME and Alexander CAMPBELL were captured at Gouyave later that day.

Beginning on the 3 March the ranks of the rebels began to increase as French planters, free coloureds/blacks, and slaves flocked to the military camp at Belvidere, probably due to a combination of fear of the rebels and a desire to be free of the British. The president of the General Council called on the insurrectionists to surrender, promising a pardon and amnesty to all except those who participated in the massacre at Grenville. The Grenada government requested assistance to put down the revolt, but help was slow in coming; revolts, influenced by the French, erupted in a number of British-occupied territories. The MILITIA and fewer than 200 regular troops prepared to defend St. George's if attacked. On 8 April the long awaited assault on the rebel camps commenced, but proved unsuccessful. In what appeared to the British as utter barbarity, Fédon ordered the execution of 47 of his hostages, carrying out his threat to kill his prisoners if attacked. The government changed strategy by establishing coastal posts to intercept incoming supplies for the insurgents and arming slaves under the LOYAL BLACK RANGERS. For the remainder of the year there were a number of sporadic attacks by both sides as the insurrection dragged on.

By early 1796 the rebels controlled most of the island, but in March the British, with reinforcements, captured the strategic sites of Post Royal and PILOT HILL, cutting off the rebels' primary external supplies of weapons and food. On 19 June General Abercromby arrived with reinforcements, and rebel positions were attacked and successfully captured. The insurgents, suffering heavy losses, fled to their mountain stronghold at FÉDON'S CAMP and awaited the final assault and defeat. It took the British 16 regular military units, inclusive of hired troops, 15 months, and the loss of hundreds of soldiers from YELLOW FEVER and hostilities before the rebellion of its New Subjects and their slaves was quelled. Some fifty rebels were captured, tried and found guilty of high treason, and 14 'noted brigands' were publicly executed 'on a large gibbet in the Market place in St. George's'. In a final act of vengeance the heads of the rebels were reportedly severed from their bodies and publicly displayed. Rebels not jailed or executed, together with their families, were deported to Honduras.

Fédon's Rebellion brought ruin to the island's economy, its AGRICULTURE devastated by fires and plunder. Some 7,000 slaves lost their lives and hundreds of British soldiers were killed or died from DISEASES. Financial losses amounted to a low estimate of £2.5m and a high of £4.5m from the death of slaves, destruction of crops and estate machinery. Fédon's Rebellion, quite violently, brought about 'an end of French power and influence in Grenada', paving the way for the emergence of 'a new Grenada with a distinct British colonial stamp'. Fédon's Rebellion is regarded by many as a slave revolt despite the fact that its initial objectives had nothing to do with freeing the slaves (though it temporarily achieved that), but rather the replacement of the British government with the French and increased civil rights for free coloureds. Also known as the Brigands' War.[12, 35, 76, 91, 174, 333]

FISHERIES Grenada's marine resources are a means of livelihood for fishermen (and their families) who venture out in small boats and trawlers each day in search of fish. Some 2,000 full- and part-time fishermen catch approximately 2,000 metric tons of fish annually. Fishing communities, involved in both line and seine fishing, are scattered across the islands, with important ones concentrated near the major towns. It is common to see fishermen pulling or 'hauling nets' at many of the islands' BEACHES, or small fishing boats docked on many of those same beaches. Over the past two decades ocean long-line fishing, introduced in the 1950s, has become common. It has replaced other traditional practices like seine and bottom hand lines, and now accounts for approximately half of all fish landings. During the 'low season' from July to December and the 'high season' from November to June, fishermen catch a variety of fishes, including yellow (*Thunnus albacares*) and black fin tuna (*T. altantivus*), dorado or dolphin fish (*Coryphaena hippurus*), blue marlin (*Makaira nigrican*), and cavalli (*Caranx hippos*). Divers also catch SEA EGG, LAMBIE, SEA TURTLES and lobsters, which together with a large portion of the fish landings, are exported within the Caribbean and to Canada.

Present annual exports, mainly from the artisanal sector, are around 17 per cent of total export earnings. Attempts to organise the fisheries sector date to the 1950s, with emphasis on increasing catch size through technological improvements like the motorisation of boats, cold storage facilities, loans to increase craft ownership by fishermen, and the establishment of co-operatives. Projects like the

National Fisheries Corporation and the Artisanal Fishing Development Project have tried to develop the fishing industry, principally by organising co-operatives and providing needed financial and technical resources. They have met with some success, but fishing communities remain relatively poor.

The sector is confronted with a number of problems, some unexpected as in the case of the 1999 fish kill which resulted in thousands of dead reef and near-shore fishes washing up on some of the beaches. The fish kill, caused either by bacterium or toxic marine algae, was the worst experienced in Grenada and threatened the local fisheries industry. Two months later wave surge from HURRICANE LENNY destroyed many fishing boats along the west coast and HURRICANE IVAN dealt a severe blow. An annual Billfish Tournament, organised since 1964 and held each January, attracts anglers from the Caribbean and North America.[50, 102, 208, 209, 251, 262]

Dancing the flags at a wedding ceremony in Carriacou

FISHERMAN'S BIRTHDAY is a Roman Catholic festival celebrated on 29 June each year as the feast of St. Peter and St. Paul. In the town of GOUYAVE, one of the largest fishing communities in the islands, festivities are the 'grandest' and are attended by visitors from all across Grenada. Under the French the parish was dedicated to St. Pierre, the patron saint of fishermen. After church services in each parish and the blessing of fishermen's boats and nets, there are boat races, eating, drinking and merrymaking for the remainder of the day; the merrymaking dates to the mid-1960s. In Gouyave an awards ceremony celebrates the achievements of fishermen and women, including 'fisherman of the year' and the 'largest catch'. The Mabouya Fisherman's Museum provides an exhibition of the social life of the fishing communities in Grenada. Feasts are also celebrated in the major towns and C&PM.

FLAGS & CAKES In C&PM there are two rituals that accompany a traditional wedding ceremony. Though rarely seen today, 'Fighting the Flags' and 'Dancing the Cakes' were once quite common. These two rituals are meant to demonstrate the union of marriage, but also to confirm the man as the head of the household. The two families meet before the ceremony, usually at the bride's house where the reception is to take place. The unfurled flags are emblazoned with messages such as 'True Love Never Ends', 'Unity is Strength', and 'Love is the Answer'. After the African-derived custom of pouring libations by the bride's father, 'expert' flag bearers, in a ring surrounded by singers and other spectators, do 'battle' in mock duels that will always result in the groom's flag 'defeating' the bride's, or rather, her submission. During the dancing the groom's flag should always be kept above that of the bride's.

Dancing the Cakes means exactly that, the dancing of the wedding cakes, but substitutes are often used. Here women, representing each party, carry bride and groom's cakes on their heads or in their arms and engage in a provocative dance with sexual overtones. If a cake should fall it is a bad omen, signifying that the marriage will not last. Again, the groom's cake is kept above that of the bride's, illustrating his perceived sexual prowess. The flags will hang over the bride's house until the thanksgiving ceremony known as 'return thanks' two weeks later. This precedes the religious ceremony and reception. These rituals are derived from West African customs.[153, 321]

FLAMBOYANT (*Delonix regia*) is a magnificent tree native to Madagascar and grows to 40-50 ft (12-15 m). It can be seen throughout the islands, especially from May through August when it is in bloom. Its dense scarlet-orange or yellow (rarer) flowers create an unrivalled bloom that truly justifies its name flamboyant (<Fr. 'flaming'). Children, in mock fencing duels, use the unopened flower buds in cokyoco fights as each individual wields an antenna-like stamen in battle against his opponent's. The tree loses its leaves in the dry season and the long brown seed pods hang from the bare branches. These seed pods or chac-chacs, double as a rattle and percussion instrument, nicknamed 'mountain piano'. The seeds within the pods are used in the manufacture of local crafts. The flamboyant is an ideal shade tree with its umbrella-like crown. The flamboyant or cokyoco is Carriacou's national flower. Its

name poinciana is derived from de Poincy, seventeenth-century governor general of the French Antilles. Cokyoko, also known as cock-and-hen in the region, is probably derived from the sound of a rooster crowing after threading or copulating with a hen to signify 'victory'.

Flamboyant tree in bloom

FLETCHER, Joseph Wiltshire (1894-1972) was involved in the field of EDUCATION for most of his life, and is considered one of the islands' respected educators. He began his career as a pupil teacher, serving as an assistant teacher at the St. David's RC School before volunteering for the BRITISH WEST INDIES REGIMENT in 1915. He served in the Fifth Reserve Battalion in Egypt and Palestine during World War I, and received the Pilgrims Cross of Honour in 1918. Returning to Grenada in 1919, Fletcher became the head teacher at the St. George's Senior RC Boys' School and held that administrative position until his retirement in 1955. As headmaster, he administered the development of the school, guided by the belief that 'education built character.' The school was renamed the Fletcher Memorial RC Boys' School in memory of the man who had elevated its standards to make it one of the best. Fletcher was also an elected member of the St. George's District Board, commissioner of the Boy SCOUTS, president of the GRENADA UNION OF TEACHERS, and served in a number of religious organisations. He was awarded both the OBE and MBE.

FLORA Grenada's oceanic origin and small size have produced poor biological diversity and endemism when compared to oceanic islands like Dominica and continental islands like Trinidad. The sea and wind most probably carried many plants that eventually adapted themselves to the islands' ecology. The early AMERINDIANS brought a few economic plants like the CASSAVA with them from South America, and the Island CARIBS cultivated early Spanish introductions to the region. The islands are home to about 1,000 vascular plant species, including 450 flowering plants, 151 ferns and 120 tree species, both native and introduced.

The occupation of Grenada by the French and British resulted in the introduction of flora, mainly agricultural crops and ornamentals, which inevitably resulted in the displacement of indigenous species. Of Grenada's plants only four are believed to be single-island endemics: the Grenada gouti tree (*Maytenus grenadensis*), the Grenadian towel plant (*Rhytidophyllum caribacum*), *Lonchacarpus broadwayi* and *Cyathea elliotii*; the latter two are probably extinct or mistakenly recorded for Grenada. See the field guide *Caribbean Spice Island Plants* for extensive treatment of the islands flora'.[143, 146b, 160]

Grand Etang fern covering the steep hills at Grand Étang

FLOWER GARDENS Most striking to visitors to Grenada is the profusion of flowers that adorns almost every home, especially in the countryside. Like the British who bequeathed their obsession with gardening, Grenadians are preoccupied with having a beautiful flower garden. It can occupy a small space at the front or a large area around the house. Ornamentals can be seen growing in small patches beside the house or in old pots and pans along outdoor steps. Trees and shrubs are not only grown for their beauty, but provide privacy from prying eyes in the form of hedges and privacy screens. Some of the common garden flowers include buttercup (*Allamanda cathartica*), ixora (*Ixora coccinea*), croton (*Cordiaeum variegatum*), BOUGAINVILLEA, HIBISCUS, POINSETTIA, and FRANGIPANI, many of which can be seen covered with BIRDS and numerous insects when in bloom. Within the last number of years American-style lawns have replaced traditional flower gardens, especially in the middle-class neighbourhoods, but beautiful gardens can still be found throughout the countryside. Gardens open to the public include Joydon in St. Paul's, Laura Herb and Spice Garden in St. David, St. Rose Nursery and Garden in St. George's, and the BAY GARDENS.

FOLK CULTURE constitutes the popular expressions of the predominantly rural peasantry and urban poor, which traditionally have been viewed as being in opposition to the established culture of the middle class and elite. It has a distinct LANGUAGE or dialect, FOLK DANCES, FOLK MEDICINE, PROVERBS & SAYINGS, RELIGION and SUPERSTITIONS. Though influenced by European cultures, it is steeped in the survival of various cultural expressions of West Africa brought to the islands generations ago by slaves and indentured immigrants. Folk culture creates security and identity, and is preserved through oral tradition. FOLK MUSIC, folk tales and dance, once popular throughout the country, can only be found in the remote corners of the islands, preserved by a declining, ageing generation and a younger generation who are trained to perform them. Traditional children's GAMES have given way to imports. The islands' rich and diverse cultural heritage is quickly losing ground to the more popular 'American pop culture'. In Carriacou, the BIG DRUM DANCE, KALENDA, ANANSI STORIES, WILD INDIAN mas' and other traditions survive, yet for how much longer? Groups like the NATIONAL FOLK GROUP have contributed significantly to the preservation of the islands' folk culture. Yet, it is very difficult to preserve a cultural heritage when so many people emigrate and become exposed to cultures they find more appealing.[85, 153, 323]

FOLK DANCES Though not common today, some of the islands' traditional folk dances have been superficially preserved by groups like the NATIONAL FOLK GROUP which continue to perform the bélé, lancers, quadrille, bongo, maypole and BIG DRUM DANCE. Before the 1930s and the popularity of non-Caribbean cultures, dances throughout Grenada were celebrated with tradition, costume and pageantry. African cultures, fusing European and African dances, created a Creole synergism that can only be described as Grenadian (and Caribbean). These dances survived among the folk, constantly undergoing changes in style and execution.

One of the oldest of these dances is the quadrille. Introduced by the French around 1736, it was popular among the elite who taught it to the slaves in order to replace African dances that they felt were either vulgar or uncivilised. The quadrille, a modified square dance, is a set of five dances for four couples. In CARRIACOU the lancers, introduced around 1830 by the British, is referred to as QUADRILLE. Another of the dances which survived until recently is the bèlè or belair. It is an impassioned dance, combining stylised foot movements to the beat of drums. It is danced by a group of women who dictate the tempo of the drums by their movements. It survives as staged performances. The bongo is of African origin (<Congo *mgombo*: 'drum'), and was a popular dance at funerary wakes. It is performed by men who compete against each other. Cheered on by drummers and the audience's singing, a dancer enters the circle and sets the pace for a challenger whose sole intent is to outperform him. Performers literally 'dance till they drop,' as the dances become more difficult and the pace quickens, with the one left standing the champion.

Maypole was a popular folk dance once common throughout Grenada and Carriacou. The British brought it to the islands, but its present form bears little relation to the northern European celebration commemorating ancient spring rites and fertility. Both males and females usually perform it. A rarely seen tradition today is the fancy headgear, 'supposed to represent a stylised ship,' which was once common. Eight dancers, each holding a multi-coloured ribbon attached to the top of a pole, weave in and out of each other, plaiting the ribbons in a circular pattern along the pole to create designs like a 'spider's web', 'ladder' or 'basket'. Folk music and songs can accompany the dancers. This dance was also once popular at CARNIVAL. The maypole is still danced in Grenada, its 'stronghold' in Windsor Forest, St. David. It also continues to be part of the May Day festivities in Carriacou. The KALENDA, a lesser-known dance because it has all but disappeared, is a duelling dance associated with stick-fighting. The heel-and-toe remains a popular dance among older Grenadians, but folk dances like the piké, a French-derived Creole dance, are long since lost. There are a number of dances associated with folk religions like SHANGO and BIG DRUM DANCE. As the modern music of CALYPSO and reggae predominate, folk dances have declined, replaced by the ubiquitous wining and other fleeting dances which are themselves threatened by American dances and music. Notable folk dance personalities included Pansy Rowley, Crofton McGuire, Thelma 'Aunty Tek' Phillip and Gloria Payne. [85, 331]

FOLK MEDICINE combines traditional pharmacopoeia from African, AMERINDIAN, EAST INDIAN and European herbal knowledge, creating a medico-religious practice that was an essential part of the lives of many Grenadians. Its association with religious practices dates back centuries to the slaves who brought with them their knowledge of folk remedies and beliefs. The power of roots, leaves and seeds serves the various functions of medicine and magic. Traditional healing involves potions and ointments from wild and cultivated plants that are used to cure physical ailments, or illnesses supposedly caused by evil persons or spirits. Folk medicine was used to treat dreaded DISEASES like MALARIA, YAWS and syphilis. Certain remedies were used as charms or amulets to ward off evils like MALJOE, while bush bathes washed away evil or bad luck. Though many of the prescribed folk cures achieved successful or positive results, others were little more than placebos with no known physiological effects.

The recent availability of primary health care and increased formal education have resulted in reduced reliance on traditional medicines except in the most remote areas, or when associated with folk religions. Where traditional medicine is still used, it is taken in conjunction with western medicine. The taking of folk remedies as medicine should be approached with due caution or with the assistance of someone knowledgeable about local plants. Folk remedies are prescribed from these common plants: ALLSPICE, BAY LEAF, CARAILA, GINGER, LEMON GRASS, PAWPAW, black sage/bwa bouc (*Cordia curassavica*) to treat colds, coughs and diarrhoea, santa Maria/wild sage (*Lippia alba*) for colds and coughs, chado(n) beni (*Eryngium foetidum*) for gripe and belly aches, and aloes (*Aloe vera*) for skin and hair care. [146b, 156, 236]

FOLK MUSIC is the popular music of the Grenadian rural and urban folk, often associated with everyday activities of work (work songs), rituals and play (pass play). It is an amalgam of West African, French and British musical forms, with influences from Latin America and other Caribbean islands. These songs are varied because they are passed on through oral tradition, altered by each singer or group. The African slaves, with their drums, flute, chac-chac (maracas) and other instruments, took every available opportunity to sing (in the call and response fashion) and dance, even though they were prohibited from celebrating many of their cultural expressions. African forms, influenced by the French and English LANGUAGE and culture, created a rich folk heritage. Over the last 350 years these diverse groups have forged a unique Grenadian FOLK CULTURE and music.

It was not until after EMANCIPATION and the freeing of the slaves that folk music flourished, despite the colonial government placing restrictions on drum beating and certain celebrations. Some common musical forms, many no longer extant, include work songs, lavwé (<Fr. Cr.<Fr. *la voix*: 'voice', = 'loud singing'), cantiques (French hymns sung at wakes, prayer meetings and Christmas) in C&PM, and songs to accompany FOLK DANCES like the maypole, bélé, KALENDA and bongo. There are songs for weddings, funerals and wakes, children's GAMES and festivals, sea shanties or chanteys especially in CARRIACOU, and religious meetings like SHANGO and BIG DRUM DANCE. The STRING BANDS and QUADRILLE bands were the musical accompaniment at dances and fetes, but the development of modern

Norris Welsh playing the cocoa lute/mouth bow, a one-string instrument, 1962

CALYPSO music by the 1950s and its huge acceptance inadvertently displaced them. The availability of recording technology and imported musical forms have displaced traditional folk music and its musicians.

Some of the folk songs can still be heard in their original FRENCH CREOLE on occasions like the pre-carnival celebrations at GRENVILLE, St. Andrew, or performed by the NATIONAL FOLK GROUP. The once common cocoa-lute, a string instrument shaped like a bow and played by holding one end in the mouth and plucking the string, has all but disappeared. Like the cocoa-lute, children's songs have also disappeared from most communities as television has replaced nocturnal entertainment. The erosion of folk culture has been due to the islands' migratory population and foreign influences that appear more culturally appealing and enduring.[51, 132, 205, 230, 234]

FOOTBALL/SOCCER is a popular team sport played in the islands. Though CRICKET has a longer and popular history, the ease of playing football makes it more ubiquitous. The game 'originated' in England by 1863 when certain rules were set and most likely arrived in the islands soon thereafter. By the 1890s clubs and teams began to appear in St. George, St. Mark and St. John's PARISHES, with one of the earliest organised games taking place at the QUEEN'S PARK on Whit Monday in 1907. Throughout the year, but especially from June to December, games are played on any field across the islands, and engaged in by both adults and children. Organized league soccer has been popular for many years, with clubs representing towns and villages across the islands. Some of the popular football clubs include Hurricanes, (Queen's Park) Rangers, Carenage, Honved and the GBSS. There is much rivalry and often fierce competition between the various clubs/teams (as many as 30) which compete in the Premier, First Division and Second Division Leagues organised by the Grenada Football Association (f. 1924).

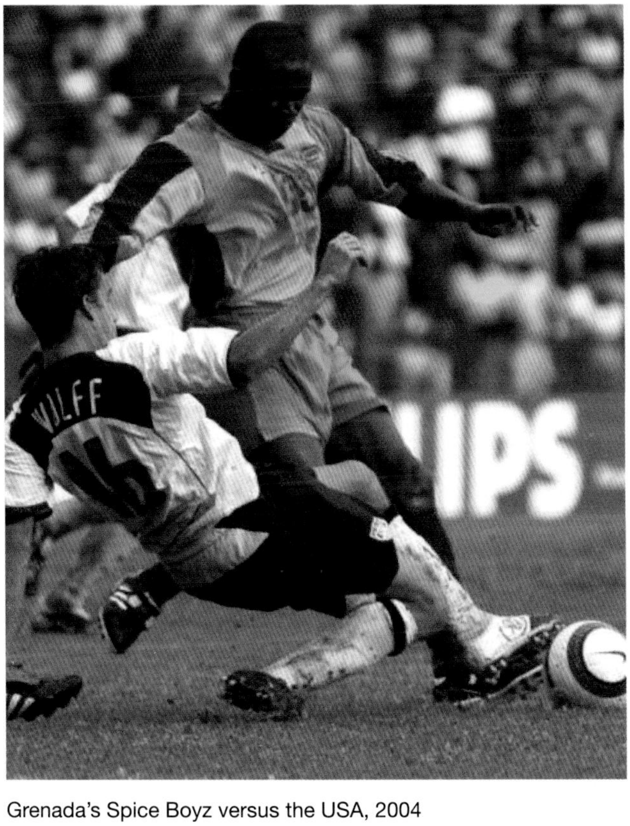

Grenada's Spice Boyz versus the USA, 2004

The Hurricanes (f. 1958) of VICTORIA is one of the most distinguished teams, winning the National Championship more than any other team. The national soccer team competes throughout the region, especially in the Windward Islands Football Championships and the Caribbean Shell Cup. Over the past few years women's soccer has become popular, breaking the monopoly of this traditional male-dominated sport.

FORT GEORGE was first begun as Fort Royal under the French and dates to the seventeenth century. It was designed in 1666 by François Blondel and constructed the next year with stone rather than 'earth and fascines' as Blondel recommended; it commanded the maritime approaches to the ST. GEORGE'S HARBOUR and shipping at the Ville du FORT ROYAL. In 1675 the fort was briefly captured following a DUTCH ATTACK. The small fort was remodelled between 1706 and 1710, as part of a plan to make Grenada an entreport for the Asiento to supply slaves to the Spanish between 1701 and 1713; it was based on a new design by Jean de Giou de Caylus, but incorporated the earlier structure. It has been described as 'the finest original example of a Vauban-style, bastion-trace fort in the Western Hemisphere'. Two huge bastion traces, exceeding 70 ft (21 m), were added onto the landward side, to protect it from the higher ground commanding Fort Royal. It has an extensive system of underground bunkers and tunnels and a large cistern for water. About ten guns, dating from the 1800s, are mounted on cast-iron carriages to envoke memories of their historical use.

Fort Royal was renamed Fort George by the British in 1763 when the islands were ceded to them. The original military barracks on Young Street was built around 1704, soldiers being previously housed within Fort Royal. The French built artillery barracks within the fort around 1710 and the British added another around 1800. These old buildings, together with the two-story Police Administration Building, constructed in 1920, are the primary buildings within the fort. A new military hospital was completed in 1779, replacing the dilapidated structure within the fort. Between 1796 and 1798, and 1819 the British built two new military barracks below the fort at Pointe de Cabrits/Goat Point (presently the HOSPITAL).

In 1854 Fort George became the headquarters of the POLICE FORCE and functioned in that capacity until 1979 when it became the headquarters of the PEOPLE'S REVOLUTIONARY ARMY. It was renamed Fort Rupert between 1979 and 1983 in memory of Rupert Bishop, father of PM Maurice BISHOP. On BLOODY WEDNESDAY at least 24 people were killed there, among them Bishop and four members of his cabinet. They were executed in the central courtyard where a controversial plaque, erected in October 1993, now honours those killed. Though the police headquarters has again been housed in the fort since 1984, there is public access to the compound.[177, 369]

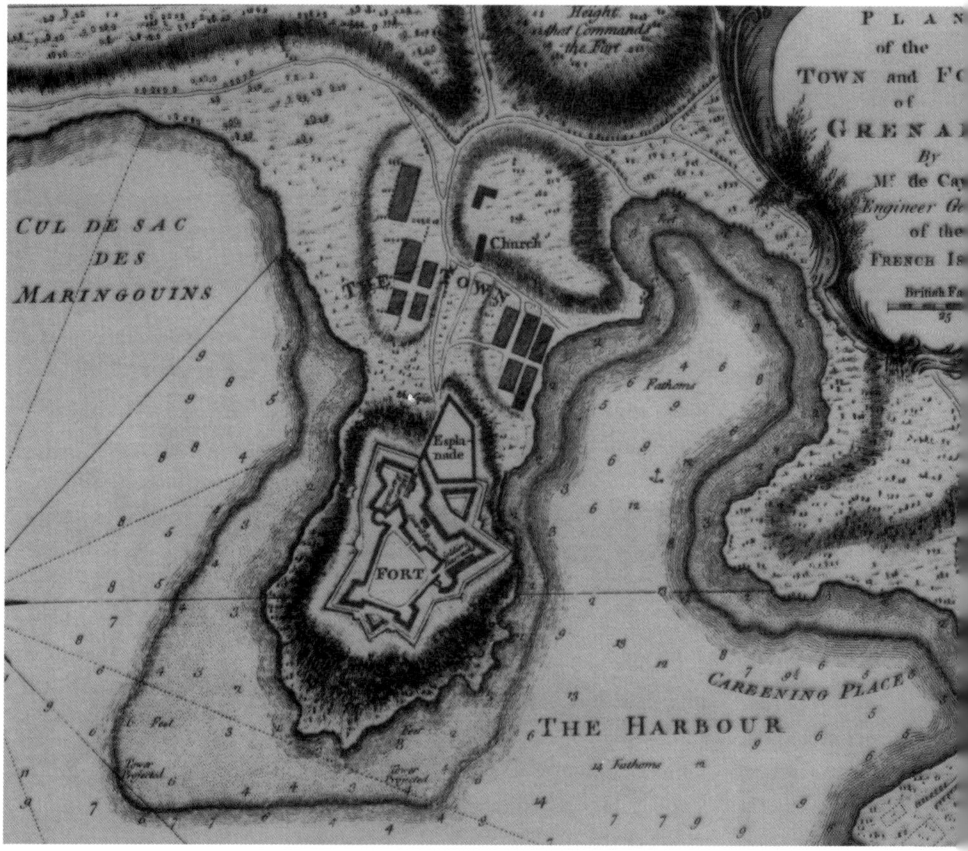

Plan of Fort Royal/Fort George, 1705

FORT ROYAL was the major town that developed in Grenada under the French. The original settlement of PORT LOUIS had proved inadequate within a few years, and the French colonists soon expanded from the LAGOON across the CARENAGE. In 1667 a small fort, Fort Royal was built on the eastern promontory overlooking the Carenage and central port, and the town that developed in the open bay was called the Ville du Fort Royal. It was established by 1700, its central square occupied by the Place d'Armes. A larger fort was constructed in the early 1700s, enclosing the old Fort Royal (now FORT GEORGE). La Ville du Fort Royal became the centre of economic, political and social activities on the island. Following the capture of Grenada by the British in 1762, the name of the town was changed to ST. GEORGE'S, but reference to its French name continued for some time thereafter.

FORTS The conflicts of occupation in the Lesser Antilles between the Island CARIBS and Europeans in the mid-1600s, and colonial wars among the various European powers thereafter made security and strong defences primary concerns. The first forts built in Grenada were palisade forts, constructed of pointed stakes stuck in the ground, forming a fence and surrounding the main settlements. Cannons, dispersed throughout the periphery, were usually enough to protect the French from the Island Caribs. An example was Fort l'Annunciation, the first fort built in Grenada to protect PORT LOUIS. There was paranoia among the planters who constantly requested the colonial government to construct towering forts and fortified points, the purpose of which was doubtful since many forts could only delay invasions while defenders hoped for reinforcements or the retreat of the enemy. Each town was an extension of the fort, as was the case with St. George's where the town or Ville du FORT ROYAL was named after its protecting fort.

An examination of some PLACE NAMES, for instance Fort Jeudy (<Fr. *Jeudi*: 'Tuesday', built 1651) and Soubise, illustrates the importance of these settlements as defence sites. The town of ST. GEORGE'S, the major French settlement, was littered with forts and batteries, some leaving hardly a trace of their earlier existence. By 1741 there were 15 forts and batteries manned by the MILITIA. These increased under the British until the 1790s with the

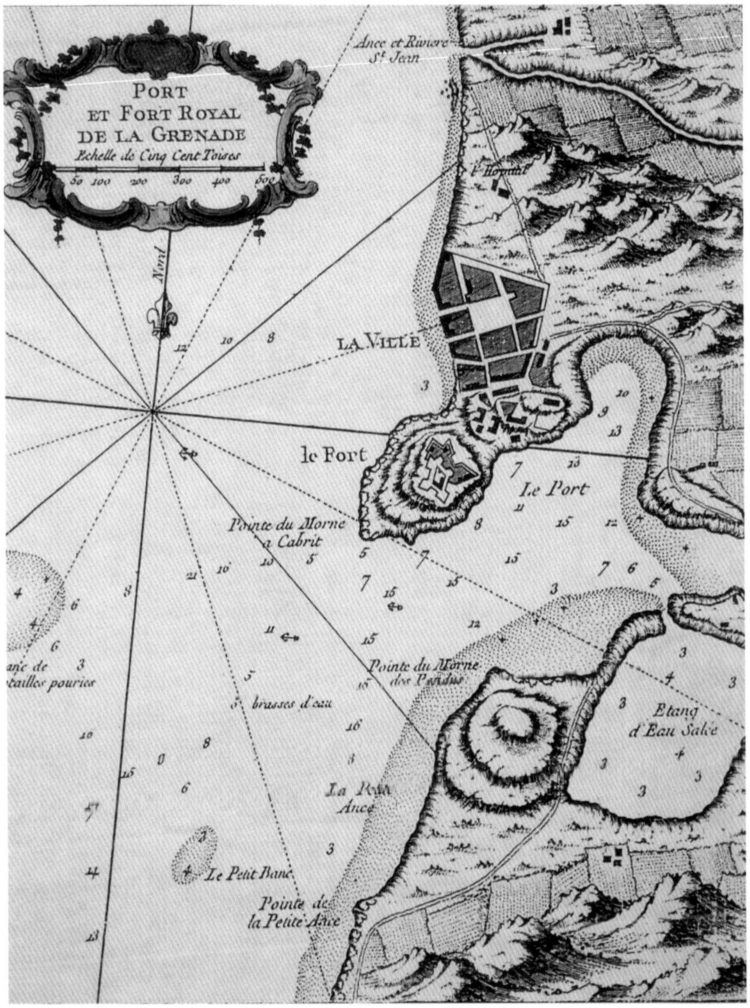

Port and town of Fort Royal by Bellin, c. 1758

construction of the RICHMOND HILL FORTS. There are over thirty military sites identified by the GRENADA NATIONAL TRUST, including BEDFORD POINT, Monckton's (Hill) Redoubt, FORT GEORGE, and the HOSPITAL HILL REDOUBTS. Throughout the island, especially on coastal sites, small forts or batteries were installed and equipped to discourage attacks by privateers and, rarely, invaders.

The island of CARRIACOU, being smaller, possessed only one permanent fort, but there were 16 batteries around the coast in the late 1700s. On Fort Hill, about 200 ft (61 m) above HILLSBOROUGH, 'has been constructed a small octagon (fortification).' A blockhouse was built in 1806 by the estate owners as a result of the threat caused by the SLAVES at CRAIGSTON and the potential for revolt caused supposedly by the teachings of Rev. Nash. The removal in 1813 of the sick soldiers, victims of MALARIA, left the island without a garrison thereafter. Armaments were comprised primarily of 18-, 9- and 6-pounder CANNONS and 10-inch mortars.

Grenada's system of forts represents a potential dividend as historic attractions if properly preserved. This prospect has not escaped the GOG and individuals interested in promoting TOURISM. Though most of the forts are in varying states of neglect and some entirely destroyed, a few have been preserved and are ideal visitor attractions.[41, 177]

FORTUNE, Mary 'May' (d. 1973) was a well-known Big Drum singer, 'one of the most accomplished singers of her generation and the primary instructor of the next generation of Big Drum vocalists'. She and her common-law husband Ferguson ADAMS were known as 'Carriacou's premier musical couple'. Like Adams, she was very knowledgeable about CARRIACOU CULTURE in general and the BIG DRUM DANCE in particular, knowledge which she gladly shared with many scholars. A contemporary commenting on Fortune's dancing: 'When May dance, that May used to dance! I don't know if you ever see those turkey cocks when they kawé. When she turn that way, oh, she used to be graceful'. Audio recordings featuring Fortune include *Carriacou Calaloo*, *Saraca*, & *Tombstone Feast*.[51, 302, 349]

May Fortune

FRAME/BOARD HOUSES are the common domestic buildings of the labouring classes. They replaced the houses of the early French settlers, rudely constructed domiciles of thatch and wood, and the wattle and daub houses (tapia) which were the dominant dwellings of the slaves and peasantry up until the beginning of the twentieth century. The wattle and daub house was constructed of sticks or BAMBOO, woven into a frame and filled in with mud for the walls, and roofed with thatch. These houses were 'rapidly disappearing' by the 1880s. Frame houses became popular in the late 1800s and by the mid-1900s had become the typical house-type of the rural peasantry and urban labourers (in 1931, 85 per cent of houses were built of wood). These cabin-type houses were almost always raised to avoid flooding, built upon masonry piers or sitting precariously on tall stilts or boulders. The front had a door almost to its centre and at

Frame house

least two windows on either side, sometimes embellished by heavy wooden shutters or 'jalousies' to protect from heavy rains or storms. Within, partitions separated the major rooms, leaving the area directly beneath the hip or gabled roof open to aid air circulation, but not privacy.

Furnishings were basic. Most frame houses are simple one-, two- or three-room rectangular buildings, each reflecting the poverty or wealth of their owners; some could be rather crowded depending on the size of the family. An extra room was often added onto the back as money became available. Quite a few often contained decorative fretwork, dormer windows, open verandas, Demerara windows and transoms. Usually out back, not far from the house, were the kitchen or shed with its COALPOT and brick oven, and pit (latrine) that enjoyed widespread use until the 1960s. Over the years the frame house has changed, its shingled roof replaced by corrugated iron (galvanise), wooden louvered windows replaced with glass, and the wooden frame becoming stuccoed, with the kitchen and toilet moving indoors. Few truly traditional frame houses remain, even in the rural areas where bricks and cement have replaced wood as the common building material. Also known as chattel houses because they could be moved when needed. Many of the islands' board houses were either damaged or destroyed by HURRICANE IVAN.[82, 127, 129]

FRANCIS, Simon Augustin 'Bigs' (1887-1957) was a proprietor, businessman, financier, and racehorse enthusiast. An ex-policeman, Francis immigrated to the US in 1917. In the 1920s Francis, better known as Panama Francis 'because he wore only Panama hats and because he had lived and worked in Panama,' resided in Harlem where he worked as a 'banker' in the illegal 'numbers' game. He was known as 'one of the most fearless bankers in the business because he accepted large plays of one, two and three dollars when most numbers barons preferred the smaller nickel and dime games.' The *Amsterdam News*, in a story titled 'Panama Francis is Set for Life', reported gleefully that he fled the US in 1932 with one million US dollars 'to escape arrest for income tax evasion' and possible imprisonment for his illegal activities. When he surfaced in Grenada in 1932, he reportedly had 'money to burn, which some say, came locked up in a big "Pierce Arrow", the biggest car then seen in Grenada.' A prominent businessman, he was a principal shareholder in a number of businesses, including the GRENADA SUGAR FACTORY and the Telescope Racetrack, Everybody's Stores, and the Antilles Hotel (formerly the HOME HOTEL). M G SMITH described Francis as 'a very wealthy and unusual black Grenadian' in 1950s Grenada.

He was a well-known gambler and established the Diamond Club in 1953 'so he could gamble in it with his associates, who were drawn from widely differing status levels.' He figured prominently in HORSE RACING activities across the islands and the southern Caribbean, owning, training and racing horses. Francis was proprietor of many estates, some reportedly gained as gambling debts. In 1941 he was 'reputed to be the wealthiest man in Grenada.' Francis or 'Bigs,' as he was popularly known, has became part of local mythology and attained a somewhat heroic status in 1940s and 1950s Grenada as he did in Harlem in the 1920s and 1930s.

FRANCO, Aaron (1628-aft. 1670) was one of a few Jews resident in Grenada in the late 1600s and may have been the first to establish a sugar estate in the islands. He was one of the many Jews who had settled in the French Antilles following their expulsion from Brazil by the Portuguese in the 1650s, along with the Dutch. They contributed both capital and expertise to the establishment of sugar production in Martinique and Guadeloupe. Franco most likely arrived in Grenada between 1664 and 1669 from Martinique. On the 1669 Grenada census he is listed as holding a contract with the French WEST INDIA COMPANY, the then administrator of Grenada, which wanted to establish sugar production in order to transform the island's economy. Franco resided in the Quartier de la Grande Anse and owned three INDENTURED SERVANTS, 13 male slaves, six oxen and four cows. The ownership of slaves and oxen probably meant that if he was producing sugar, he most likely had a cattle mill for grinding the SUGAR CANE. In 1675 sugar was listed as an export, and by 1683 four estates were producing sugar.

FRANGIPANI (*Plumeria* spp.) is native to Central America and grows to over 15 ft (4.6 m). It loses its leaves in the dry season, while the flowers begin to bloom before the long dark green leaves reappear. From March to September the waxy, sweet-scented red, pink, white and yellow flowers adorn the many trees across the islands. The most common species grown in FLOWER GARDENS is *P. rubra*, with white and pink flowers clustered at the tips of its branches.

The frangipani is host to the hawk moth caterpillar or the frangipani caterpillar (*Pseudosphinx tetrio*), which feeds on its milky, poisonous sap. The caterpillar's striking black, yellow and orange stripes discourage any potential predators. It later falls to the ground and burrows into the soil where it pupates. A large silver-grey hawk moth emerges from the ground. Two chemicals extracted from the plant have been successful against the poliovirus and pathogenic fungi. Their use as marine anti-fouling agents against algae and barnacles has proved successful.

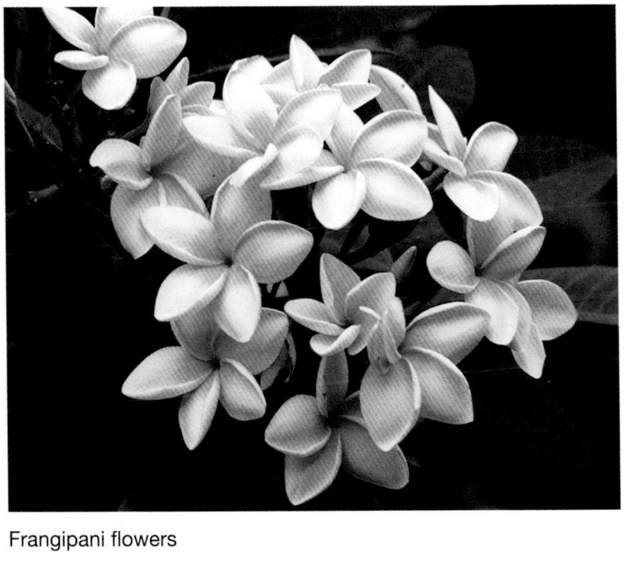

Frangipani flowers

FREE COLOUREDS In seventeenth-century Grenada (and the Caribbean) slave society began to exhibit another degree of complexity with the emergence of a group of individuals who were metaphorically 'neither black nor white', and 'neither slave nor free'. This group comprised individuals of mixed racial ancestry, usually black and white. They were termed 'coloured', or designated by the more derogatory term mulatto (<Am. Sp. 'young mule'; or Sp. <Arabic *muwallad*: 'person of mixed race'). The term coloured is used here to group only individuals of mixed racial ancestry. For these, recognising their peculiar ethnicity, developed an intermediate social order within Grenadian slave society and subsequently played a defining role throughout the archipelago. As had occurred in other islands following the establishment of SLAVERY, Grenada, by the 1680s, witnessed the emergence of a sizeable group of mixed-race individuals. They, because of their own white ancestry, saw themselves as somehow entitled to the status of whites. This ancestral claim to whiteness would give the mixed race an obvious advantage over the blacks, which their future economic and social prominence would bear out. This pride in race would not come to the blacks for another hundred years, but when it did it would mean the political displacement of the mixed race.

The census of 1687 listed 31 free 'mulattoes'. By 1700 that number was 53 'Free Coloureds', increasing to hundreds in 1755. Social and economic restrictions on the free coloureds grew as their population increased. Whites, especially poor whites, believed that free coloureds posed a threat to slave society. In the late 1700s the free coloureds constituted a distinct group, closely allied with members of the free black population, but nonetheless exhibiting phenotypic characteristics that singled them out. Though it had been recognised earlier, it was not until the late 1700s that the PLANTOCRACY began viewing the enslavement of mixed-raced individuals as wrong because of their shared white heritage, leading to the manumission of many free coloureds by their fathers.

Although free coloureds were freed persons, possessing some basic civil rights, they could not participate in either local or legislative elections and were not equal to whites in regard to the law, or social status. Even in the eyes of the established churches they were seen as second-class citizens and forced to accept segregated seating during regular church functions, well into the 1800s. This social separation did little to discourage many of the free coloureds who shared similar interests with whites and developed comparable social institutions that in turn excluded some free blacks. Society became segregated, based on the hierarchy of wealth and skin colour, with whites at the top and slaves at the bottom, the intermediary strata filled by poor whites, coloureds of varying shades of brown, and free blacks. The free coloured-slave relationship could best be described as ambiguous, with many free coloureds (especially individuals who owned property), supporting the white plantocracy on the issue of slavery. A sizeable group owned estates and slaves, justifying slave ownership as a way to financial and social advancement. A fear of the white ruling class was that free coloureds would conspire with free blacks and slaves to challenge their minority rule. The whites, despite creating numerous restrictions to free coloureds' advancement, did work against any 'racial' solidarity by 'tempering the enforcement of segregation laws and by granting exceptions and favours.'

The free coloureds made their most ardent bid for equality when they staged a bloody revolt, FÉDON'S REBELLION, against the British in 1795. As leaders of the revolt in which slaves took part, they received some of the harshest punishments, including death. Their defeat inevitably led to their persecution and population decline for quite some time. It took many years before the free coloureds assumed their pre-rebellion numbers and status. In the 1810s free coloureds began to officially protest their unequal treatment and to petition for equality. In 1823 they received the franchise but were not allowed to stand for elections to the legislature. In 1832 they were granted civil and political rights and responsibilities as white citizens when they were allowed to give evidence in all court cases, elect their own representatives to the House of Assembly, and become members of grand juries. In the 1837 elections three free coloureds were elected to the legislature for the first time.

The EMANCIPATION of the slaves in 1838 altered the social and political dynamics of Grenadian society, but historical social conditions prevailed. The social, political and economic advantages gained by the former free coloured community over the majority ex-slaves placed them in a position to fill the social and political vacuum left by the white plantocracy. It was this stratum that made up the elite of all institutions on the island until the 1950s and the rise of the peasantry (there were many phenotypic blacks who were members of the elite). Unlike the US, where the term coloured has become associated exclusively with anyone possessing African ancestry, it is still used in Grenada to refer to individuals of white and black parentage.[78, 216]

FRENCH CASHEW (*Syzygium malaccensis*, syn. *Eugenia malaccensis*) is native to Malaysia, hence another name: Malay apple. It is found throughout the Caribbean under the name of rose apple. The cashew or kushu tree grows to 65 ft (20 m). Its bright red stamens turn the tree into a scarlet haze during flowering between April and May. As the flowers fall to the ground a mat of soft red stamens litters beneath the tree. It produces a slightly astringent oblong fruit, either entirely crimson pink, or crimson pink with white stripes. Its high water content makes it rather refreshing. Its flesh is white and rose-scented, covering a large seed. Fruits are generally eaten fresh, but can be made into preserve, pies and wine. The pomme rose or plum rose (*S. jambos*, syn. *E. jambos*) produces a small rose-scented pale yellow fruit that is eaten fresh or made into preserve. The name cashew is derived from its resemblance to the CASHEW nut. The French cashew is also known as pomerac (< pomme: 'apple'+ Malacca, a reference to Malacca, Malasia where the fruit originated). It was possibly brought to the island by the French, hence its name.

FRENCH CREOLE/PATWA A French-based dialect spoken in various forms in the French and former French Caribbean. Grenadians, primarily in the countryside and certain villages in CARRIACOU, spoke a French Creole up until the 1950s. In 1889 BELL labelled patwa (<Fr. *patois*: 'provincial dialect') as 'a most barbarous lingo, and is formed of a jumble of French most vilely corrupted, mixed up with a few words of broken English.' The strong influence of patwa among the slave population made British cultural impact minimal for many years. It was variously cited as the prime hindrance to EDUCATION 'making inroads among Grenada's peasant population,' and the 1875 Education Ordinance 'insisted on efforts to discourage patois in schools.'

Yet, it was French patwa that enabled the strong survival of CATHOLICISM, even after many years of persecution by the Anglicans. As formal education spread throughout the islands and the older generations died, so did the French Creole that can only be heard on rare occasions, spoken by a few older Grenadians or 'for poetic or ritual emphasis'. Numerous French Creole phrases and words have become a part of Grenadians' everyday idiom. Though there have been attempts to produce a dictionary of Grenadian speech, no publication has yet appeared to date. It is often reported that French patois is still spoken, but that is incorrect; it is quite rare.[5, 64, 190, 192]

FRENCH HERITAGE The French settled Grenada in 1649 and occupied the islands for over a century afterwards. During that period French language, culture, religion and political institutions became entrenched among the slaves, free blacks and FREE COLOUREDS. British occupation of Grenada, which lasted for just over 200 years, was unable to uproot many French influences, even though the former had succeeded in forcing the emigration of the French PLANTOCRACY. The French legacy is most evident in PLACE NAMES, festivals and celebrations like CARNIVAL, ALL SAINTS' DAY and FISHERMAN'S BIRTHDAY, and in the FOLK CULTURE and various SUPERSTITIONS.

Many Grenadians, in their local speech add 'we' after a sentence, unaware that the word is from the French *oui*: 'yes', or sometimes both are used as in the case 'yes we'! A substantial number of words and phrases used in the everyday Grenadian LANGUAGE are directly derived from French or FRENCH CREOLE. Today, French influences are most noticeable in the large number of Grenadians who practise the Roman Catholic religion, itself dating to the establishment of CATHOLICISM in the seventeenth century.

Unlike St. Lucia and Dominica, which retained a prominent French influence, Grenada, confronted with religious and cultural conflicts between the French and British, experienced an exodus of French Grenadians between 1763 and 1800, primarily to TRINIDAD. Numerous French family names like Antoine, Baptiste, LaBarrie, LaTouche, Pierre and Toussaint, are quite common.[221]

FRENCH INTERREGNUM As a result of French support for the North American colonies fighting for independence from the British, war again broke out between the French and the British in 1779. The French fleet in the Caribbean, intended to attack Barbados, but due to some difficulty encountered from adverse winds, attacked Grenada. The small British force, comprising some 300 MILITIA and 160 regulars, had prior knowledge of the impending attack and made necessary preparations to defend the island. With a fleet of 25 ships, 12 frigates and over 5,500 soldiers and seamen, the Comte d'Estaing anchored off Molinière Bay, about 1 mile (1.5 km) to the north of ST. GEORGE'S and took control of the surrounding area on 2 July. With the British refusing to surrender, French forces began an assault on the Hospital Hill Redoubts, the British stronghold. The superior French force, though suffering 'heavy losses', eventually forced the British to retreat to FORT GEORGE, which then came under bombardment from French frigates in the St. George's Bay. The British left behind cannons and mortar at Hospital Hill that the French later used for their bombardment of Fort George. With the captured British cannons pounding Fort George, the British, under Gov. MACARTNEY, accepted an unconditional surrender on 5 July, thereby returning the islands to French rule.

The French captured some thirty merchant ships and 'carried off immense booty from the town of St. George's.' (In October 1779, *La Prise de la Grenade*, a comedy based on the French capture of Grenada, was performed in Paris, France.) On 6 July a British fleet under the command of Admiral John Byran engaged d'Estaing and his superior forces in an attempt to retake Grenada. After hours of exchanges between the two forces, the British retreated, their fleet badly damaged. According to Jamieson, Grenada was the most valuable colony after Jamaica and its loss to the French had been 'the most serious blow to Britain since the American rebellion had been transformed into a global war'

On 19 September 1779 an ordinance reinstated French laws in Grenada and the Grenadines. Two months earlier the Comte d'Estaing had appointed the Comte de Durat as governor. One of the governor's first acts was the elimination of all debts owed to British creditors by residents of the island. The rule by the French during the four-and-a-half years of their occupation was described by the British as being 'in the most despotic manner... and that the British colonists were sorely oppressed.' One of

French capture of the Hospital Hill Redoubts, July 1779

the most contentious issues was French 'conservatorship' of British absentee-owned estates, the revenues of which were deposited into the state treasury. Appeals to the French Crown led to its abolition and the restoration of the estates to their original owners, but the damage had already been done. In September 1783 the Treaty of Versailles returned Grenada to the British who immediately began the systemic persecution of the French.[35, 91, 177, 240, 333]

FRIENDLY SOCIETIES were voluntary organisations established to provide mutual assistance to their members, predominantly peasants in the countryside and urban labourers. The St. George's Friendly Society, a middle-class organisation associated with the Anglican Church, was the first such body (f. 1849). Seven years later the St. George's Benevolent Society, a RC friendly society, was established. In 1868 the legislature passed the 'St. George's Friendly Society Incorporation Act', incorporating that society. With the Grenada government providing little or no social services to the majority of its citizens, the advent of friendly societies in the mid- to late nineteenth century proved opportune. Families and communities saw the need to make provisions in the event of financial need occasioned by sickness or death, beyond what was provided for with the informal YORUBA-derived SUSU.

At their first peak in the 1920s, there were some 66 societies with over 12,000 members. Recovering from a lull in the early 1940s, friendly societies were revived by 1948. In that year there were 99 societies registered, with 20,000 members (27 per cent of the population). Grenada was second only to Barbados in the percentage of its citizenry assisted by these self-help organisations. The societies functioned through the monthly contributions of their memberships and assisted members experiencing financial need. By the late 1960s, friendly societies had declined dramatically due to their inability to meet the increasing needs of their members, and were burdened with management failures. The establishment of insurance plans, labour unions, and the Credit Union Movement (est. 1946) by the 1960s only quickened the demise of friendly societies, which disappeared by the early 1970s.[113]

FROGS There are three species of frogs in Grenada, excluding the CRAPPO, which is taxonomically a toad. These are the introduced whistling or piping frog (*Eleutherodactylus johnstonei*), the native highland piping frog (*E. urichi*), and the native Garman's woodland frog (*Leptodactylus validus*). The mating call of the male whistling and piping frogs, synonymous with the noises of the tropical night, can be heard during the rainy season. They are mostly nocturnal and feed on insects. Unlike many amphibians, the whistling frog does not need water to reproduce, laying its eggs beneath moist leaves and stones, an adaptation to the forest. It is abundant in Grenada. The highland piping frog is common to forested areas; it is darker than the whistling frog, slight build and has longer toes. The woodland frog is larger than the others; its population is small and fragmented. The introduction of the edible mountain chicken (*L. fallax*) from Dominica proved unsuccessful because of the predatory crappo.[122]

GAIRY, Sir Eric Matthew (1922-1997) 'Uncle Gairy' dominated Grenadian politics for almost three decades, serving as a legislator (1951-1979), chief minister (1961-1962), premier (1967-1974) and prime minister (1974-1979). He was born on 18 February 1922 in Moyah, St. Andrew to Theresa and Douglas Gairy. After a primary school education, he emigrated to TRINIDAD in 1941 and two years later to ARUBA in search of employment. In 1949 he returned to Grenada reportedly deported because of labour union activities, and within a few months founded the GMMIWU, a labour union representing agricultural labourers. The next year Gairy achieved national and regional prominence following a number of labour stoppages culminating in SKYRED. Taking advantage of his popularity, he formed the GULP in 1951, and was elected to parliament in every election he contested between 1951 and 1976. In 1957, however, he was disenfranchised for five years for disrupting a rival's political meeting. In 1962, as a result of SQUANDERMANIA, he was removed from office on charges of financial improprieties in his government. In 1967 he returned to power, and until 1979, he ruled Grenada with an increasing disregard for its constitution and laws.

Prime Minister Gairy

He often publicly displayed his mystical beliefs, claiming that he was chosen by God to rule Grenada, and expressed an obsession with Unidentified Flying Objects. He became known as 'the little man from the east [parish]', a Biblical reference he took quite literally by 'attempting to walk on water'. On a trip to the US, his government was overthrown by the NEW JEWEL MOVEMENT on MARCH 13, 1979. The PRG unsuccessfully appealed to the US government for his extradition. He spent the next five years in exile, but quickly returned in 1984 after the US-led military INTERVENTION. Gairy revived the GULP, but he did not participate in the 1984 ELECTIONS. In 1990 and 1995 he unsuccessfully contested elections, which signalled the end of his political career.

At the 1996 INDEPENDENCE celebrations, Sir Eric was hailed as the 'Father of the Nation' in recognition of possibly his most lasting achievement. Ageing and almost blind, he suffered a stroke in 1996, and died on 23 August 1997; He was given a state funeral. In death, as in life, Sir Eric remains a controversial figure. His political malfeasance, attracting much notoriety during his reign, has diminished in the eyes of many Grenadians, especially in light of the REVOLUTION, BLOODY WEDNESDAY and the US invasion. His ultimate legacy remains to be written, but his over thirty-year political career was renowned for its financial extravagance, police brutality, victimisation, and political intrigue. Yet the memory of the revolution he orchestrated in 1951 looms large in many people's minds, and places him in the company of other Caribbean political leaders. His wife, Lady Cynthia (b. 1923), is a former social worker, politician, parliamentarian and minister of government between 1967 and 1979, and presently resides in the US.[35, 94, 117, 202, 243, 318, 333]

GAMES & TOYS Over the years Grenadian children have created or modified many games and toys for their entertainment. Though some reflect African cultural survivals, most are influenced by European cultures. While seasonal games like bat and ball, MARBLES and KITE FLYING are popular, folk games were once the most widespread year-round. Among these games are pound-stone, the ball game of round doves, jacks, pick-ups, hopscotch and moral. Some of the most common games are ring games or pass-plays, where songs and hand clapping combine to create rhythmic exchanges. These 'songs and dialogue games' are learned in school or in the community, and were played by boys and girls daily, especially on moonlit nights. They provide entertainment, but also teach social interactions and community inclusion.

Rhyming is a verbal game, especially among boys competing to determine the most versatile with words. Rhymes could be innocent, but the boys with their irreverent repertoire are always the champions. Riddles often began with the phrases 'Tim Tim?' or 'A riddle a riddle a ree', and though usually innocent they often developed into a foul contest between skilled riddlers. Oncc popular home-made toys included (cone-shaped wooden) spinning tops, rollers (the rim or tyres of bicycles, motor bikes, cars and trucks), slingshots, and zwill or spinning cutter (the flattened cover of a can or crown cork). The emergence and popularity of video games and television have displaced many of the traditional games and toys, which are presently confined to the countryside among some poorer children.[206]

GBSS The acronym for the Grenada Boys' Secondary School, and the name by which it is popularly known. The failures of the government-sponsored secondary school for boys (opened in 1858, closed in 1863, reopened in 1865, closed in 1873, reopened in 1874, and finally closed in 1878) resulted in the establishment of a privately funded boys' school in 1885 in 'Mrs. Gray's premises in Hospital Street'. With few government and school scholarships and the high costs of attending, the St. George's Grammar School educated the sons of wealthy landowners, professionals, merchants and civil servants.

After much advocacy in favour of government control, the Grammar School, renamed Grenada Boys' School, came under the administration of the government and moved into new quarters on MELVILLE STREET (the present police barracks) in 1911. It registered only 38 pupils in 1911, but increased to 72 in 1912, and 82 in 1913, growing sharply thereafter, especially with the addition of boarding facilities. In 1915 it became the Grenada Boys' Grammar School, and in 1946 was transferred to TANTEEN in the newly vacated military barracks, ten years after the site was designated for the school. A number of new buildings have been added over the years, but the barrack-type classrooms have defined the campus for thousands of students.

Until 1947, with the opening of ST. ANDREW'S ANGLICAN SECONDARY SCHOOL and PBC, the GBSS was the only secondary school for boys, with many of the islands' young men passing through its halls before leaving for Trinidad, the UK and North America. Among its noted graduates are Lord David PITT, Bernard COARD, PAPITETTE Redhead, Herbert BLAIZE, Wilfred REDHEAD, and Sir Leo DEGALE, to name but a few. The GBSS remains one of the foremost secondary schools in the country, demonstrating its excellence in both academic and sporting activities. Devastating fires in 1993 and 2005 destroyed buildings and valuable records.[80]

GEOLOGY Grenada, C&PM share a similar volcanic origin with many of the other oceanic islands in the Lesser Antilles, and may be as old as fifty million years; they are the remnants of a larger island, the Grenada Bank. Grenada's volcanic origin is demonstrated by its rocks, soils, black sandy BEACHES, HOT SPRINGS and extinct crater lakes. Some forty craters are known to exist, including Grand Étang Lake, LAKE ANTOINE and LEVERA POND. The CARENAGE, Grenada's deep-water harbour, and the QUEEN'S PARK are the eroded craters of extinct volcanoes. The islands of Grenada, C&PM are rugged and very hilly. Grenada rises to a height of 2,757 ft (840 m) at its highest point, Mt. St. Catherine. A central north-south ridge dominates the island, with peaks interspersed along its length and dissected by numerous RIVERS & STREAMS. Seventy-seven per cent of the island has a slope greater than twenty degrees and only six per cent has a slope under five degrees; for Carriacou 54 percent has a slope greater than 20 percent. The western coast rises precipitously from the sea, its roads cut from the steep slopes that dominate the coast. The eastern region of the island rises much less steeply.

The difference in topography accounted (and still accounts) for the predominance of tree crops in the western region, while much of the eastern and northern regions were covered by SUGAR CANE in the 1700s and 1800s. The NW extreme, predominantly Mt. Alexander, St. Patrick, and parts of CARRIACOU are capped with coral limestone. The PARISHES of St. George, St. Andrew and St. Patrick exhibit a more diverse topographic regime than the others, and therefore allow greater agricultural diversity. Since the 1700s there have been recordings of earthquake shocks, some of which have caused minor damage to infrastructure, especially BRIDGES & ROADS. Recent volcanic activity is restricted to the submarine volcano at KICK-EM-JENNY.[11, 140, 143]

GIBBS, Thomas Joseph (1887-1977) 'Uncle Joe' was an educator, legislator and acting governor of Grenada. He was born in St. David and began his teaching career as a pupil teacher following school-leaving examinations. He subsequently worked his way to the top of the system when in 1913 he became the school's head teacher, working in that capacity until his retirement in 1943. A proprietor, Gibbs 'emerged as one of Grenada's most respected black land-owners,' and in

1947 was an unsuccessful candidate to the legislature. A founding member of the GULP, he ran as a candidate representing St. David beginning in 1951, and won every election he contested. He served on both the Legislative (1951-1958) and Executive (1954-1958) Councils. After 1955 and the establishment of the Committee System, he served as Minister of Communication and Works. He was one of two Grenadian representatives to the lower House of Parliament of the West Indies FEDERATION (1958-1962), having won election to that body.

From 1967 to 1969 Gibbs served as the president of the Grenada Senate. He was the first Grenadian of African ancestry to act as GOVERNOR, and his daughter Hilda BYNOE, became the first Grenadian-born governor. He was involved in many community activities, including LOCAL GOVERNMENT, and sporting activities like CRICKET and HORSE RACING. He was one of the organisers of the St. David's Race Club, which held meetings at LASAGESSE.[213]

GINGER (*Zingiber officinale*) is a herbaceous perennial that produces rhizomes, which when dried, cracked or ground, produce the ginger of commerce, a common spice used to flavour food dishes and confectionery. It is the primary ingredient in ginger wine and the popular non-alcoholic drink ginger beer. Having its origin in China and India, where it has been in use for thousands of years, the ginger plant was introduced to Europe by Arab spice traders and became a valuable spice. Introduced into the Caribbean, it was cultivated in Grenada from the late 1600s. The crop, available year-round, is the primary ingredient in the once popular fontay (?<Fr. *fondante*). Grenada's own production is small and used locally. FOLK MEDICINE prescribes hot ginger tea for the treatment of flatulence. Its carminative and antacid properties have led to its use in laxatives. The ginger lily or red ginger (*Alpinia purpurata*), a relative of ginger, produces brightly coloured and attractive 'flowers'.

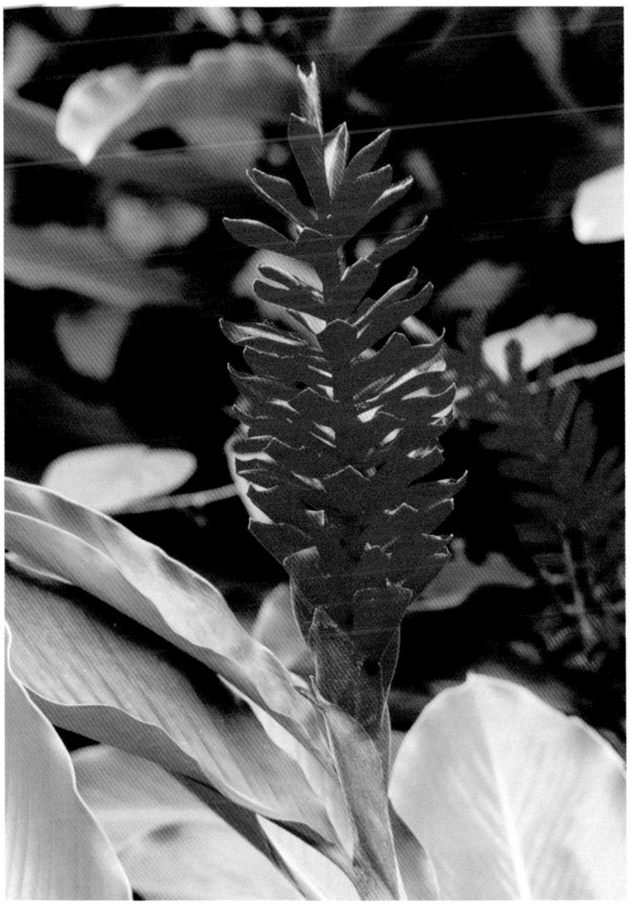

Ginger lily/Red ginger

GLOVER ISLAND 11N 61W is a small island (10 acres/4 ha) off the rugged SE coast of Grenada. Local whaling operations date to at least the 1700s, and American whalers operated in Grenadian waters and employed Grenadians as early as 1857. Around 1920 C V C Horn, a local banker, bought Glover Island and together with Ernest Greaves, they began whaling operations from its shores. Greaves was one of the last whalers in Barbados and brought two whaleboats with him to start the Grenada operations. They operated between 1920 and 1923 when Horn, hoping to modernise the industry, invited Norwegians who began whaling in 1923, and subsequently established large-scale whaling operations after the visit of noted explorer and whaler Otto Sverdrup in 1924. A whaling station was established on Glover Island as a processing site for whale oil. The Norwegians brought modern steel whaling ships, replacing the artisanal operations. In the three years the Norwegians operated there (1924-1926) they caught at least 220 whales, the majority humpbacks (*Megaptera novaeangliae*). The processed whale oil was exported, while most of the meat was sold and consumed locally. The residual flesh and bones were pulverised for fertiliser. The final structures on Glover Island were completed at the end of 1925.

After the season in 1926, however, whaling operations ceased because of the precipitious decline in the whale population and the 'the installation of ramps on factory ships [that] made land stations like Glover redundant.' The whaling station was dismantled in 1929 and some whaling equipment is displayed at the GRENADA NATIONAL MUSEUM. The island's less frequently used name, Ramier Island (<Fr. Île des Ramiers) originates from the presence of the ramier or red-necked pigeon (*Columba squamosa*), which can be found in the island's drier lowland habitat.[294]

GMMIWU The acronym for the Grenada Mental, Maritime and Intellectual Workers' Union, which began as the Grenada Manual and Mental Workers' Union (GMMWU). Its founder and president-general Eric GAIRY officially registered it as a union in 1950, seeking to act as the representative of agricultural labourers. In that same year Gairy staged the first of many successful labour strikes, demanding wage increases for workers at the GRENADA SUGAR FACTORY. In February 1951 members of the GMMWU staged a mass demonstration in St. George's, demanding recognition as the bargaining body for agricultural workers. Gairy's arrest and incarceration initiated a wave of violent protest that became popularly known as SKYRED.

The GMMWU succeeded in its demands and soon became one of the largest unions in the islands' history. Gairy's concurrent foray into politics resulted in the decline of the union, but it experienced a minor resurgence in the 1960s while Gairy was out of political power. Yet its popularity had begun to wane following the emergence of unions in the late 1950s and 1960s representing the growing and influential urban labour force. In 1972 it changed its name to the GMMIWU, but failed to recapture its popularity. Between 1979 and 1983 the union languished due to its disbandment by the PEOPLE'S REVOLUTIONARY GOVERNMENT. Gairy revived it in the 1980s and tried, unsuccessfully, to regain the union's pre-eminence in labour relations.

The GMMIWU's early confrontation with the government had a lasting impact on labour politics, especially the laws implemented to curb industrial action, and in 1951 it brought about nothing less than a revolution. By the 1970s it had lost its place in labour relations, but like the GULP, it has continued in a much reduced capacity.[35, 176, 243, 333]

GOD-HORSE/WALKING-STICK (*Diapherodes gigantea*, syn. *D. gigas*) is one of the longest insects in the world. This wingless insect has a body of elongated segments, measuring about 8 inches (20 cm). Its stick-like form and green or brown colour make it difficult to detect, being well camouflaged in trees and bushes. It feeds on the leaves of the MANGO and GUAVA trees, hence one of its local names: guava-lobster. It has the ability to partially regenerate body parts through molting. Much SUPERSTITION surrounds the god-horse, as its name suggests, and many fear it as a harbinger of misfortune. According to folklore God rides around on a walking stick. It is also known as the devil's horse.

GOLDEN APPLE/POMME-SITÉ (*Spondias dulcis*, syn. *S. cytherea*) is a large tree that grows to 60 ft (18 m). It is native to the South Pacific and was among the plants brought to the Caribbean by Captain Bligh in 1793. The golden apple, common throughout the island, is often seen in backyards or along roadsides. The globular green fruit has a fragrant smell as it ripens to a dull yellow, hence its name. The acidulous fruit surrounds a spiky seed and care should be taken when eating. The fruits can either be eaten green in a pickle, as a fresh fruit when ripe, or used to make jam and wine. They are available from September to January. It is a major fresh-fruit export. The pomme-sité (<Fr. *pomme*: 'apple' (+ de: 'of') + *cythère*: 'Cythera', a Peloponnesian island sacred to Venus; the name is a reference to the golden apple of Greek mythology) is a relative of the red and yellow PLUMS, and is also known as June plum.

GOUYAVE is situated on the NW of the island, 12 miles (19 km) north of St. George's along the Western Main Road. It is the chief town and main commercial centre in the district of ST. JOHN. Lying between Millet and Gouyave Bays, it is the third largest town in the islands. Though Palmiste was suggested as the site for the parish centre, the town or Bourg de l'Ance Goyave was established at Gouyave (<Fr. *goyave*, <Arawakan *guayavá*: 'guava') around 1734; in the early 1800s the spelling changed to Gouyave. The town, or more accurately hamlet, consisted of a chapel and catered to a small and dispersed population. In 1763 the British renamed it Charlotte Town (<Charlotte Sophia, the wife of the then reigning British monarch, King George III), but it has borne both French and British names since. Recent maps have either both names listed, or just Gouyave, with only few Grenadians ever using the British name.

In the late 1800s it saw sporadic improvements, including the opening of the St. John's District Hospital (1878-1891) operating primarily as a YAWS treatment facility. It was not until the early 1900s that social amenities became established; a Visiting (Health) Centre was built in the mid-1920s, but replaced in 1947 by a Health Centre. Diseases like MALARIA presented special problems for the town due to the many MANGROVES and swamps where mosquitoes breed. In 1910 concrete outlet drains were built to allow the continuous flow of water into the sea. In 1905 a waterworks was constructed, and in 1919 a government-owned dispensary opened. By the 1920s public pit latrines were prevalent, the town receiving its first water-carriage latrines in 1952, and ELECTRICITY in 1965.

View of Gouyave town

In the early 1900s Gouyave was second only to St. George's for its social and economic activities. Among its most prominent businesses were McIntyre Brothers, a general store and later automobile dealership and garage/gas station which opened in 1900. Gouyave boasted prominent citizens, among them the Hughes, DeFreitas, Branch and McIntyre families who maintained a vibrant social atmosphere with many clubs, sporting events and celebrations.

GRENVILLE's ascendancy in the 1950s saw Gouyave's decline as the second most important town. Many of its 2,500 residents find employment in FISHERIES and AGRICULTURE. The fishermen of The L'Ance are noted for their fishing skills. In Gouyave is located one of the three processing plants for NUTMEG and mace where every aspect of the curing, sorting and packaging of this ubiquitous spice can be seen. Its primary thoroughfares include Depradine (<Jean de Pradines, a French planter of the 1700s and subdivided into Lower, Central and Upper Depradine Streets), Edward, St. Francis and St. Dominic Streets. Two church steeples dominate its skyline, with the copper spire of the Old RC Church most prominent. The town has two primary and two secondary schools. Its primary recreational ground is the Cutbert Peter's Park. It is popularly known as the 'town that never sleeps'.[121, 208, 209]

GOVERNMENT HOUSE has been the official residence of the British-appointed GOVERNORS since the 1780s, and GOVERNORS GENERAL since independence. Before then the governor resided in ST. GEORGE'S Town, but a fire destroyed the building in 1772; between 1772 and the 1780s the governor's residence was on the site of present-day Knox House, in the shadow of FORT GEORGE. Sometime after 1784 the governor's residence was removed to its present location on Upper Lucas Street, 1 mile (1.6 km) from St. George's. Situated on 20 acres (8 ha), it is secluded behind trees, privacy fences and walls, with its entrance guarded by a pith-helmeted sentry.

The brick and sandstone building dates to the late 1700s, but underwent major renovations and additions over the years. It was renovated between 1802 and 1807, but many of its original Caribbean Georgian architectural features were preserved. Between 1887 and 1888 it was again extensively remodelled, with its most prominent addition a two-storey gallery in the Italianate style. Arches and intricate masonry highlight the gallery. A two-level annex was added in 1902, and a verandah over the arched entrance built in the mid-1920s. FLOWER GARDENS and tennis courts surround the unusually large building.

Government House, c. 1900

Over 200 years as the residence of the governor, Government House has hosted a queen, presidents, prime ministers, heads of state, and distinguished personalities who have graced its halls and ballroom for state ceremonies and charitable events. There is an old tale illustrating the secrecy and power of the governor's residence. It was said that TOWER HOUSE had 100 windows, as many as Government House, but only 99 could be opened at any one time. Government House was the only building on the island that could have all 100 windows opened at any given time. It was badly damaged by HURRICANE IVAN, requiring extensive rebuilding.

GOVERNMENT OF GRENADA On 10 February 1763 France and Great Britain signed the Treaty of Paris, ending the Seven Years' War (1756-1763) which had resulted in the British capture of Grenada in 1762. The newly won Caribbean territories became known as the Ceded Islands and were incorporated in 1763 as the Government of Grenada of the Southern Caribbean Islands, Grenada being the most developed of the four islands and the seat of government. Residents of the British colonies of the Leeward Islands and Barbados began immigrating to Grenada even before the signing of the Peace of Paris. The British wasted no time taking over the island from the French, who emigrated in large numbers. Sugar production burgeoned and led to a doubling of the slave population. Grenada recorded extensive economic growth under initial British occupation; in 1773 its total exports amounted to eight times that of Canada and in 1775 exports were valued second only to those of Jamaica within the BWI.

Yet there were economic problems in the mid-1770s, especially for COFFEE growers. Under the British the islands witnessed a number of conflicts that tore at the fabric of society. The British and French residents clashed over cultural and political issues; paramount among these were political representation and religious freedom. The British subjects themselves battled with Gov. Melville (1764-1771) over political power and the establishment of the legislature. Gov. MACARTNEY, upon his arrival in 1776, expressed his dismay at the situation he met, describing the inhabitants as 'a strange and discordant mass of heterogeneous animals... easily irritated to do mischief, and but seldom to be roused to do good.' Macartney believed that these divisions 'in a great degree, had destroyed its [the islands'] credit, diminished its resources, and impeded its general welfare.' In 1771 Dominica separated from the Government, and St. Vincent in 1776. The British government was replaced by the FRENCH INTERREGNUM following the capture of the islands by the French in July 1779.[126, 273]

Bust of Governor Walter J Sendall

GOVERNORS Between 1649 and 1762, the governors of Grenada represented private owners, the French WEST INDIA COMPANY, or the ÎLES DU VENT. As a French colony, a total of 23 governors served Grenada and the Grenadines. Under the British, who occupied Grenada between 1763 and 1974 (excluding 1779-1783), over 100 governors, lieutenant governors, presidents of the General Council and administrators oversaw the government. The governor was the executive authority of the state, and his duty was the implementation of the Colonial Office's policies. As the representative of the British Crown, the governor almost always found himself in opposition to the local legislators. Under the CROWN COLONY system the governor's authority was practically absolute. After 1967 and the establishment of ASSOCIATED STATEHOOD, the governor's position became purely symbolic. Between 1762 and 1833 governors served in Grenada, but were replaced by lieutenant governors between 1833 and 1885, with the governor resident in Barbados. In 1885 (and until 1960) the governor of the WINDWARD ISLANDS was stationed in Grenada and an administrator was in charge of the immediate affairs of the islands' governance. In 1967 a governor was again resident in Grenada only to be replaced by GOVERNORS GENERAL following INDEPENDENCE in 1974.[9, 149]

GOVERNORS GENERAL The 1973 Independence Constitution grants executive authority of Grenada to the British monarch, whose authority is exercised by an appointed governor general (who is nominated by the Grenadian PM). The governor general (GG) replaced the GOVERNOR following the attainment of INDEPENDENCE in 1974. The GG, as the representative of the HEAD OF STATE, sits at the head of the PARLIAMENT. His/her duties include the 'selection' of the PM, the appointments of the ministers of government and the Senate, the leader of the opposition, permanent secretaries, and other important government positions, all on the advice of the PM. The GG is also charged with the summoning and dissolution of the Parliament, again on advice.

The functions of the GG are strictly symbolic, and some continue to argue that the position represents a colonial anachronism. Its relevance is constantly debated, while some individuals and groups have even suggested that the position be terminated altogether, as was done in Dominica when it became a republic. Though the GG is a titular ruler, s/he is not without power, as political events in October 1983 proved, especially since the GG was acknowledged by some foreign governments as the only constitutional authority in Grenada. In 1996 Opposition Leader BRIZAN openly challenged the appointment of the new GG, Sir Daniel WILLIAMS, on the issue of his political impartiality. Individuals who were apolitical, or at least had a history of no open political alignments, have traditionally held the office of GG. In protest the NATIONAL DEMOCRATIC CONGRESS boycotted the swearing-in ceremony, to the dismay of some who viewed its actions as an 'insult to Her Majesty'. GGs to date have been Sir Leo DEGALE (1974-1978), Sir Paul SCOON (1978-1990), Sir R O PALMER (1990-1996), and Sir Daniel WILLIAMS (1996-).[3, 4]

GRAND ÉTANG NATIONAL PARK was officially established in 1992 and comprises just under 2,500 acres (1,000 ha). It is located within the south-central ridge that cuts the island almost vertically. It encompasses the ranges of Mt. Granby, Mt. Qua Qua and FÉDON'S CAMP. Within these hills can be found old crater basins, the largest and most conspicuous of which is the Grand Étang Lake, located just inside the parish of St. Andrew. Its name is derived from the French meaning 'Great Pond', while the British added the redundant 'Lake'. This filled-in explosion crater of an extinct volcano forms an almost perfectly circular fresh-water lake 1,742 ft (531 m) above sea level. The lake, a fascination for centuries, is the central attraction of the Grand Étang NP. Also in the park can be

Grand Étang Lake

found Honeymoon Fall, a 45 ft (13.7 m) high waterfall, and HOT SPRINGS. The management plan for the park includes habitat CONSERVATION, environmental education and research, and low-density TOURISM, predominantly hiking. There are a number of delineated trails linking important mountain sites within this historic area that was the scene of fighting during FÉDON'S REBELLION.

The park is the islands' primary eco-tourism centre and provides challenging and scenic hiking. The Grand Étang Forestry Centre is operated as a visitor centre for the park, providing interpretation of the islands' FAUNA, FLORA and cultural activities to aid visitors. The Forest Reserve, on the eastern boarder of the NP, is a 3,800 acre (1,540 ha) protected tropical forest. In 1906 the Grand Étang Reserve Ordinance earmarked the area bordering the lake as a forest reserve 'for the conservation and promotion of rainfall and water-supply in the island of Grenada'. Its status as a reserve has provided protection for many threatened and endangered wildlife species, including the ARMADILLO and MONA MONKEY.[50, 106, 140]

GRANDE ANSE BEACH A crescent-shaped 2 mile (3 km) long white sandy beach along the SW coast of Grenada, about 3 miles (5 km) from ST. GEORGE'S Town. The phrase (La) Grande Anse is from the French: 'Great Bay/Cove'; the British added the redundant 'Beach'. Considered one of the most beautiful BEACHES in the Caribbean, it is at the heart of Grenada's TOURISM industry, with HOTELS and resorts scattered along its length. Its calm clear turquoise water gently bathes the length of white sand, interspersed with COCONUT palms, SEA GRAPES, ALMONDS and manchineel trees which provide shade, scenery and erosion control.

The popularity of Grande Anse Beach as a bathing venue developed quite slowly because it was 'notorious for malaria'. In 1918 the area surrounding the beach and village was drained and as stated then, 'this could enhance the value of the beach as a pleasure resort and would generally benefit the whole island by encouraging tourists and pleasure seekers.' As early as 1916 the Grenada government constructed a bathing house, charging a fee for use. But it did not become an important attraction until the 1930s with the establishment of the GRENADA AQUATIC CLUB. In 1948 the two main wastewater outflows to the sea that cut across the beach were covered with huge seaheads, thus disguising them.

In the 1950s HOTELS like the Silver Sands and Spice Island Inn were constructed along the beach, and by the late 1960s Grande Anse Beach was known to travellers around the world. Continued use and misuse over the years have taken their toll as beach erosion has led to the destruction of many trees that once lined the shore and protected the CORAL REEFS. There have been recent

Grande Anse Beach

efforts to establish procedures for controlling runoff, sewage and pollutants that were allowed to flow into the sea, and preserve this natural beauty for both Grenadians and visitors.[50, 140, 161]

GREASY/HAM-POLE was once a popular activity at festivals, entertaining the audience as the participants slipped and slid their way up a greased inclined telephone pole in pursuit of a prize hanging at the other end. The long pole was usually baited with cured hams or bottles of liquor to entice participants to attempt the difficult climb. Because the climb could be dangerous the pole was horizontally suspended over the sea so the participants could fall into the water uninjured. Only a few skilled individuals who scampered up the pole and lunged at the swaying prize were successful. Greasy-pole was once a popular event at Boxing Day (day after Christmas) celebrations and can still be seen at the CARRIACOU REGATTA. The greasy pole was introduced from Europe, where it is a popular event at regattas and among fishing communities.

A contestant climbs the greasy pole in quest of the prize, Carriacou Regatta

GREAT/ESTATE HOUSES St. George's Town is by far the most interesting and architecturally unique site in the islands, yet there is a rich and varied display of great houses and ruins throughout Grenada and its sister islands. Though they are far less grand than the plantation houses of either Barbados or Jamaica, they nonetheless represent an integral part of the islands' ARCHITECTURAL HERITAGE. Great houses were neither extensive nor elaborate because many estate owners either owned comfortable town houses in St. George's or were absentee planters living in Europe. The French chateau-type houses, built between the early 1700s and 1762, were rather modest structures. These are known through ruins in both Grenada and CARRIACOU. The SUGAR boom of the late 1700s produced the second and most pronounced phase of great house construction, with a number of examples still evident today. Examples include Mt. Nesbit, Snell Hall, Woodford, and DOUGALDSTON.

Samaritan Great/Estate House

The last and enduring phase of great house construction was financed by the COCOA boom of the late 1800s and early 1900s, with many of these stone structures still in excellent condition.

The great house, the centre of the ESTATE, was the residence of the estate owner/manager and his family. Influenced by a number of architectural styles, the great houses could best be described as Creole, with their blend of French, British and Caribbean features. Interiors were plain, with a minimum of furniture. Many of the specialised decorative features that adorned great houses were imported from Europe. Examples of these are still evident at old estates like the massive wrought-iron gates at the entrance to Snell Hall estate, St. Patrick.

The decline of estate AGRICULTURE in the 1900s resulted in the neglect and destruction of many of the great houses. The GRENADA NATIONAL TRUST lists some 52 great houses across the islands, many in disrepair and suffering from neglect. The preservation of some of these great houses could be accomplished through renovation and possible uses like museums, hotels and guest houses. Examples of great houses can be seen at Morne Fendue, Mt. Horne, Loretto and Beauséjour estates.

GREAT RIVER, St. Andrew's Grenada's longest river has many tributaries originating in the central highlands of the GRAND ÉTANG NATIONAL PARK and MT. ST. CATHERINE NATIONAL PARK and draining into the Great River Bay on the eastern coast. Its name dates back to the French Grande Rivière, not to be confused with the earlier named Grande Rivière (du Beauséjour) that is located on the western side of the island. It is the major watershed on the island and is situated in the parish of St. Andrew. Spanning the Great River at certain points are BRIDGES & ROADS, among them the Paradise Bridge, which are necessary for MOTOR VEHICLES travelling across the island. Like the many RIVERS & STREAMS, the Great River was important as a source of waterpower to turn the many SUGAR MILLS in the 18th to 20th centuries. Also known as the Great (St. Andrew's) River.

GRENADA ('DISCOVERY' OF) Like many of the islands of the Caribbean, Grenada was reportedly 'sighted' by Columbus on 13/14 August 1498. It was his third voyage to the Americas and he allegedly named the island (la) Concepción. Neither Columbus nor any of his crew landed on Grenada, just discernible, if at all, by its mountainous peaks in the distance. Whether Grenada was in fact the island Columbus sighted and named 'la Concepción', as is generally accepted, is still a point of debate since some believe that the name accepted for Tobago, Assumption, was in fact Grenada. In his journal Columbus simply noted that two islands north of Trinidad were sighted which he named 'Assumption' and 'Concepción', the former accepted for Tobago some 80 miles (129 km) SE of Grenada.[91, 239]

Spanish ships approaching Island Carib canoes along Grenada's north coast, 1613/14

GRENADA (NAMES) 12 07N 61 40W The name Grenada (pronounced Gre-nay-dah, and not Gran-a-da) was rendered after 1763 following the British gaining control of the islands from the French. Yet it was only a slight change from what the French had called it, (la) Grenade. The French themselves had altered the Spanish name (la) Granada when they occupied the island in 1649. So it was the Spanish, in the early 1520s, who bestowed on Grenada its name. The Spanish called the many small islands to the north of Grenada Los Granadillos ('little Grenadas'), known today as the Grenadines. The most likely of the many speculations as to the origin of the name is that it was either a Spanish map-maker or sailors who called the island Granada after Granada, Spain. Speculation has added that they must have thought the hills resembled those of their home country that belies the Mediterranean Sea.

The name Grenada is often confused with Granada, as many foreigners pronounce it as such and assume because of its Spanish namesake that the people of Grenada speak Spanish. As a matter of fact, the Spanish never colonised Grenada. Another theory argued that the island has the shape of a grenadier's hat. The people are called Grenadians (pronounced Gre-nay-dians).

Between 1500 and 1522 Grenada was known as Mayo, a name supposedly given by the Italian explorer Amerigo Vespucci who, together with Spanish explorers Alonso de Ojeda and map-maker Juan de la Cosa, travelled through the West Indies in 1499. The Spanish Cédula of 23 December 1511 'On the subject of the Caribs' listed both 'Mayo' and 'Concepción'. Grenada probably appears as 'Isla do Mayo' on de Reinel's map, as 'de Maxo' on Fréducci d'Ancône's map, and in 1520 as 'y de Mayo' in the Atlas zur Entdeckung. Yet, on all of these maps it is located about 10 degrees north latitude in the same position as Madelena Island and not the 12 degrees north where it is in fact located. The origin of Mayo has remained unclear, yet its association with the month of May (<Sp. *mayo*: 'May'), and one of the Cape Verde Islands, Maio, has not escaped researchers. Mayo never caught on in use and was soon replaced by (la) Granada.

It is also accepted that Columbus, in 1498, named Grenada la Concepción, following his 'discovery' of Grenada. The Island Caribs called the island Camàhogne, according to French Dominican priest Father Raymond Breton who resided among the Island Caribs of Dominica for many years. The name is listed in Breton's *Dictionnaire Français-Caraibe* (Leipzig: BG Teubner, 1900), but its meaning remains obscure. A map of the Eastern Caribbean, 'Le Monde Caraïbe et les Occupants des Îles au XVII', by Breton shows the islands with both Island Carib and European names; Grenada is listed as 'Camáogne—Grenade, Français.' The people of Carriacou refer to Grenada as the 'mainland', being the larger island in the group.[91, 239]

GRENADA 17 Following the US-led military INTERVENTION in October 1983, 20 individuals were charged with the BLOODY WEDNESDAY murders of PM BISHOP, Cabinet members Unison Whiteman, Norris Bain and Jacqueline Creft, trade unionists Fitzroy Bain and Vincent Noel, businessmen Keith Hayling, Evelyn Maitland and Evelyn Bullen, and Avis Fergusson and Gemma Belmar. Of the original 20 accused, Ian St. Bernard was acquitted in the preliminary inquiry, and Fabian Gabriel, after being pardoned, became the state's primary witness.

From the beginning the trial presented a number of problems, the least of which was whether the accused could get a fair jury trial. Added to that was the fact that the US military had already condemned the defendants as 'communist', a convictable crime in light of the recent political developments. The trial began in November 1984, but adjourned following repeated postponements by the detainees and their lawyers. The trial resumed in April 1986 following the ruling that the GSC was legal based on the 'doctrine of state necessity' and could hear the trial. The 18 accused included Bernard and Phyllis Coard (she was conditionally released from jail in 2000 to seek medical care for a life-threatening illness and has remained free since), Hudson Austin, Selwyn Strachan, Liam James, Ewart Layne, and Callistus Bernard. Throughout the trial the accused made every attempt to disrupt the proceedings, which they termed a kangaroo trial.

In December 1986 the trial ended with the sentencing of 14 of the accused to death. Raeburn Nelson was found not guilty while Andy Mitchell, Cosmos Richardson and Vincent Joseph received long sentences (an appeal by them in 2002 granted their release because of unusually long sentences for their crimes, which was subsequently blocked on appeal but released in December 2006 for good behaviour). The Court of Appeal upheld all 14 death convictions in July 1991, but PM BRATHWAITE, just days prior to the planned August 1991 executions, commuted the sentences to life imprisonment.

Though it has been many years since the verdict, some consider the trial still open. Supporters of the prisoners, who consider them political prisoners, continue to insist that their incarceration is illegal and unfair. In 1996 the prisoners, in a statement to the press, accepted moral, but not criminal responsibility for the events of October 1983 and apologized to the Grenadian people. Since then the case has been back and forth in the courts due to numerous appeals by the accused and counter appeals by the GOG. In 2003 an OECS High Court judge ruled that the sentencing of 14 of the accused, who had appealed since 2002, was illegal and unconstitutional, but a further appeal by the GOG resulted in a stay of execution; the subsequent ruling in January 2004 upheld the convictions. In 2006 the Truth and Reconciliation Commission (est. 2000 to examine the events of 1983) recommended a new trial for the Grenada 17. The 14 serving life sentences are awaiting an appeal to the Privy Council which, in a separate appeal, ruled that the remaining three have to serve out their sentences. The name 'Grenada 17' is derived from the original 17 who were found guilty in the deaths of PM Bishop and his supporters.[6, 22, 111, 118, 119, 363]

GRENADA AQUATIC CLUB was established as a seaside recreational facility on Grande Anse Beach in the early 1930s by John Branch. Following the abandonment of the whaling station at GLOVER ISLAND, Branch bought the old barrack building and floated it to GRANDE ANSE BEACH where he established the Grenada Aquatic Club. It was an exclusive club, catering to the middle class and elite, and provided changing rooms, bar, entertainment and amusement to its members. Under Henry Hall its name changed to the Morne Rouge Beach Club because of its location at the southern end of Grande Anse Beach in the area known as Morne Rouge. Until the early 1960s and the appearance of HOTELS, it was the primary recreational facility along the beach. It later became known as the Africa Club in the 1970s, but burned down in 1977. The area was recently occupied by the Cot Bam Restaurant and Bar. The International Club, also known as Silversands (and later the site of the first hotel on Grande Anse Beach, Silver Sands Hotel) was another early beach club at the opposite end of the beach.

GRENADA ARTS COUNCIL The GAC was established in 1964 after a successful art exhibition. Its organisers formed themselves into a body to promote local art, and under the directorship of Margaret Blundell, resident tutor of the UWI Extra-Mural Department, it identified aspiring artists and provided them with a forum to exhibit and market their artistic creations. Some of these young artists went on to careers in the arts. GAC has been responsible for 'bringing out' many closet artists who would not have dreamed of showing their work

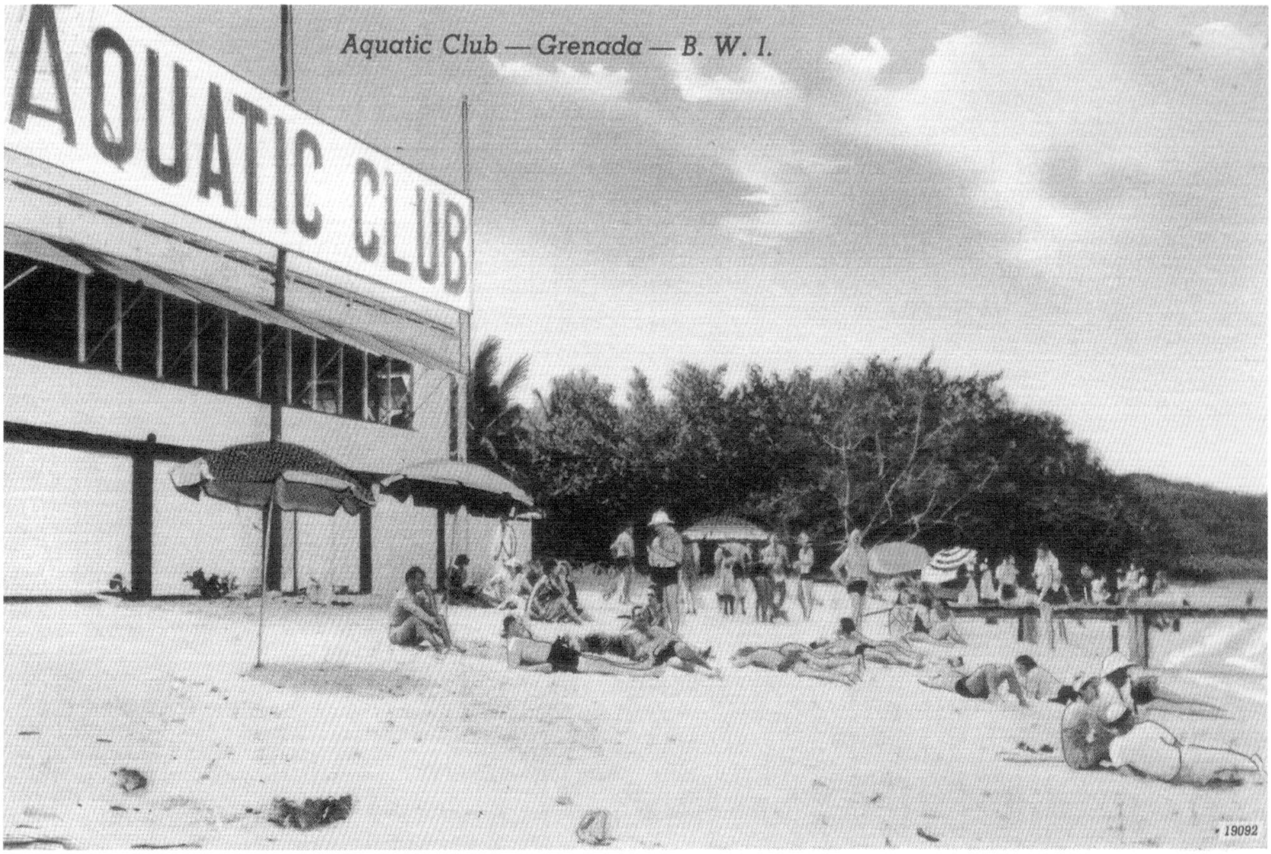

Grenada Aquatic Club

in public. Over the last three decades the Arts Council, together with the YWCA Art Club, Jim Rudin's Yellow Poui Art Gallery (est. 1968), and a number of boutiques like Tikal, have continuously supported and promoted appreciation for the arts in Grenada. Each year GAC hosts an annual visual arts exhibition where awards are given to artists to encourage their work and provide them with public exposure.[212]

GRENADA DEFENCE FORCE The GDF was established in 1973 as a supplement to the POLICE FORCE to aid Premier GAIRY counter 'subversive activities' by the political opposition against his autocratic rule. It was locally referred to as the 'Green Beasts' or '(I)Guanas' because of its members' dark green uniforms and ferocity. The group of men consisted predominantly of uneducated recruits, many of whom had criminal records; after 1974 some were former members of the disbanded POLICE AIDES and MONGOOSE GANG. A few members of the GDF were reportedly trained in Chile under the notorious Pinochet military regime. It is believed that the force numbered at least 200 men and as many as 320.

The GDF was used to suppress and harass opponents, especially NEW JEWEL MOVEMENT members. Under Gairy's personal command, the GDF usurped many of the duties of the police and further undermined its authority. Many did not like the GDF, whose tactics of harassment elicited little respect, but it was nonetheless feared. On the morning of MARCH 13, 1979 armed members of the NJM attacked the GDF Headquarters at True Blue. After setting fire to the entire military complex, the soldiers were forced to surrender. The force was disbanded by People's Law No. 32 effective 13 March 1979.

GRENADA/WHISTLING DOVE (*Leptotila wellsi*) was first described in 1884, its scientific name a tribute to John Wells, a local bird enthusiast who observed it in the 1800s. Though Blockstein insists that the Grenada dove is a single-island endemic species because of its distinct song and plumage, it was classified in 1983 as a subspecies of the grey-fronted dove (*L. rufaxilla*). The Grenada dove, measuring approximately 1 ft (30 cm), makes its home in the dry woodland of the southern region of Grenada and in the area of Perseverance, HALIFAX HARBOUR. Thought to be extinct as a result of HURRICANE JANET, it was 'rediscovered' in 1961. Its numbers have historically been low and the species is uncommon. A study in 1987 by Blockstein revealed the startling fact that only about 105 individuals may be alive. The demise of the Grenada dove is due to the destruction of its habitat for agriculture and TOURISM, and possibly to MONGOOSE predation.

By 1989/90 the number of birds had dwindled to an estimated 75-80, the majority of which were concentrated in the Mt. Hartman area in the SW. In an attempt to save the species from extinction, the GOG and organisations like the RARE Center for Tropical Conservation initiated a programme 'promoting love for the Grenada dove.' Their goal was to increase national awareness about the Grenada dove by first designating it the national bird in 1991, featuring it on a postage stamp in 1992, and executing an island-wide education campaign to make Grenadians and visitors aware of the dove and its plight. Though the GOG has established sanctuaries in both regions, its survival is in doubt.[23, 24, 45, 295]

Grenada Dove

GRENADA GRENADINES 12 30N 61 30W are situated in the Grenadine archipelago consisting of over 125 small islands, islets and rocks belonging to both Grenada and St. Vincent. The chain of islands, with a total area of about 34 sq miles (88 sq km), was once entirely owned and administered by Grenada, hence its original name Granadillos (<Am.Sp. *Granada* + *illos*: 'little Grenadas'). The group of islands was first settled by the French in the late 1600s, the last islands to be colonised by Europeans, most likely due to their small size, arid landscape, and the absence of yearlong RIVERS & STREAMS. Of the total, only 24 are habitable, of which ten are permanently occupied. CARRIACOU, PETITE MARTINIQUE, RONDE and some thirty small islets, are DEPENDENCIES of Grenada. In 1791 the Grenadines were officially partitioned (the partition had been in force since 1783 when Edward

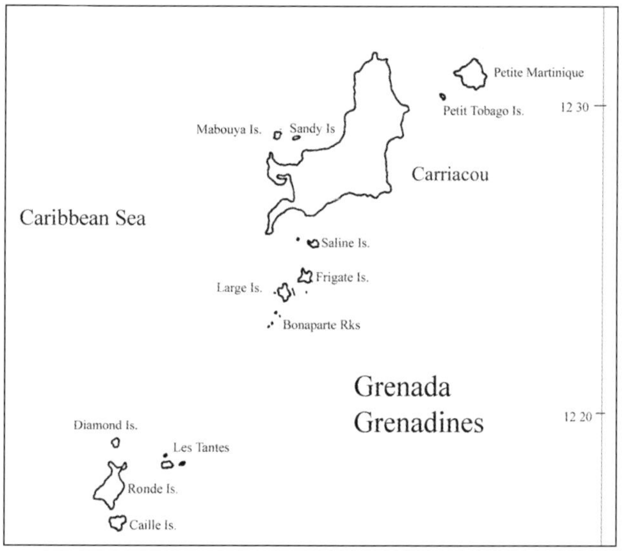

Map of the Grenada Grenadines

Matthew was appointed 'Governor-in-Chief in and over our Island of Grenada, and the Islands commonly called the Grenadines to the southward of the Island of Carriacou, and including that Island and lying between the same, and the said Island of Grenada').

The islands are arid, with an average annual rainfall of about 35-55 inches (89-140 cm), creating serious water shortages for much of the year. An important feature of almost every home is the cistern that collects and stores available rainwater. A consequence of the fragile environment is widespread deforestation brought about by overgrazing by animals and the removal of trees for building construction and BOAT BUILDING, until recently the islands' most noted industry. The economic activities of most of the islanders revolve around FISHERIES and inter-island trade. Though the islands have been administratively isolated for the past 200 years, they display a distinct Grenadine quality as opposed to a Grenadian character. Patricia Schultz lists the Grenadines in her book *1,000 Places to See Before You Die.*[195]

GRENADA LITERARY LEAGUE The GLL was established in 1911 through the merger of the St. George's (f. 1906) and St. Paul's Literary Leagues under the auspices of the Methodist Church. Thereafter leagues were formed in every town and some villages across the islands. The GLL's objective was to create an organisation that would contribute to the educational and cultural advancement of young men; women were later admitted. Among its founding members was T A MARRYSHOW, who inspired many young Grenadians through his work with the GLL and in the LEGISLATURE. The GLL has been described by many of its 'graduates' as a university for Grenada's young, ambitious individuals who did not have the opportunity to attend secondary school and/or university. Notable members included F M COARD, 'CFP' RENWICK, Wilfred REDHEAD, and Louise ROWLEY.

It was a debating and literary society, its members competing in reading, spelling, recitation, debates, and letter and essay writing. It took people who were academically/professionally deficient and produced persons of calibre worthy to be political figures, competent civil servants and journalists. Many went on to be magistrates, writers and lawyers. The GLL became a model in the southern Caribbean, with groups formed even in Trinidad. It was the breeding ground for Grenada's most educated men (and later women), but by the 1960s had lost its place in the islands' changing social and political environment.[57, 213]

GRENADA NATIONAL MUSEUM Established in 1976 by a group of private citizens and expatriates, the GNM became a major achievement in the islands' attempt to preserve its cultural heritage. The museum is housed in one of Grenada's oldest buildings, constructed in the early 1700s by the French. It functioned as the military barracks for the early French soldiers, the Common Gaol between 1763 and 1904, and the storeroom for one of the islands' most popular hotels, the HOME HOTEL. The tiny cells that once housed soldiers and prisoners alike are clearly visible today. Though the building has seen a number of renovations it still possesses some of the original French flavour most conspicuously in its cast-iron balcony and fish-scale tile roof. The historical significance of the building makes it appropriate to house the museum.

Grenada National Museum

The museum houses a varied collection of objects illustrating Grenada's history and culture, including an assortment of pre-Columbian artefacts, excavated from various sites in Grenada and the surrounding islands, representing the material culture of the AMERINDIANS who inhabited the islands. Displayed also are machinery once used in the manufacture of SUGAR and RUM, whaling equipment from the whaling station at GLOVER ISLAND, the supposed bathtub of the French Empress Josephine, a gun collection, historical pictures and documents, MAPS and a bird collection by Raymund DEVAS. Many of the displays are on loan from private collections.

Some financial support comes from the Ministry of Education, but operating funds come from entrance and member fees. In August 1996 the GNM became a non-profit corporation, gaining legal authority to 'own property, accept gifts and to negotiate on its own behalf.' Following the GNM's establishment the Grenada Historical Society (GHS) was founded to provide administrative direction and promote its development. It also promotes the awareness of history, culture and heritage by popularising the GNM. Wilfred REDHEAD, who served as the president of the society, was a founding member and played a tremendous role in its establishment. The GHS, with its association to the GNM, has continued to lobby for the preservation and conservation of the islands' historical and cultural monuments.

GRENADA NATIONAL PARTY The GNP was founded in 1955 as an opposition to the GULP and its political dominance. It represented predominantly urban, middle-class and propertied social groups. Its most instrumental founder was Dr John Watts, who served as political leader between 1955 and 1961. Like the GULP and its association with Eric GAIRY, the GNP became synonymous with Herbert BLAIZE. According to its manifesto, it was a 'nationalist' and 'democratic socialist' party, though its policies were largely pro-business. It lacked broad-based political support, but gained a majority in the Legislative Council in 1957 after orchestrating a coalition with members of the People's Democratic Movement and independents. It lost the March 1961 ELECTIONS, winning only two seats. The party won its first election in 1962 as a result of SQUANDERMANIA and the GNP's campaign for a UNITARY STATE with Trinidad. After losing the 1967 elections, the GNP never regained political power. In February 1972 it suffered a resounding defeat, winning only two of the 13 constituencies. After both the 1967 and 1972 elections, Blaize was criticised for his lacklustre leadership of the party, but no one came forward to replace him, even though he offered to step down. The Duffus Commission Report in 1975 described the GNP as 'not a significant entity in the political life of Grenada', especially after Blaize's 'ill health has precluded effective participation' in PARLIAMENT.

In 1976 the GNP was one of the three parties in the PEOPLE'S ALLIANCE coalition. The suspension of the constitution in 1979 and the dissolution of the parliamentary system forced the GNP to cease political activities. Following the US-led military INTERVENTION in 1983, Blaize quickly re-established the GNP and was the preferred political choice of the US government. The GNP became a major player in the NEW NATIONAL PARTY coalition, with Blaize as the leader.

The GNP, in its 31-year history, was the breeding ground for a number of Grenadian politicians because it represented the most consistent opposition to Gairy and the GULP up until the early 1970s.[35, 176, 201, 243, 333]

GRENADA NATIONAL TRUST The GNT was founded in 1967 by a group of notable Grenadians and friends of Grenada, including J R Groom, Ripley Bullen, Raymund DEVAS, Alister HUGHES, Dr John Watts and Betty Meggers. Its objective is the promotion of TOURISM through preservation of places of historic and architectural interest, and the CONSERVATION of the natural environment. One of its foremost activities was the encouragement of archaeological research in Grenada. In 1969 the GNT hosted the Third International Congress for the Study of Pre-Columbian Cultures of the Lesser Antilles.

GRENADA SUGAR FACTORY The GSF was established in 1934 by local interests, among them S A FRANCIS, at one time the largest shareholder. It is located in the Woodlands valley, St. George, and was intended to revive the local sugar industry by producing SUGAR, molasses and RUM for the domestic market. About half of its SUGAR CANE is produced on its estates or by small farmers, with the remainder imported as syrup. In 1951 it began manufacturing clear sugar, but that proved uneconomical. Since 1983 only rum has been manufactured because of the low volume of sugar cane produced and the low price for sugar on the international market. The GSF distils, bottles and blends at least eight types of rum under the Clarke's Court (<Francis Gadnay Clarke who owned Woodlands estate in the 1770s) label—most notably Pure White and Rum Punch; it had formerly marketed under the names 'Tradewinds' and 'Redneck'. It also produces mentholated spirits. It maintains a hospitality

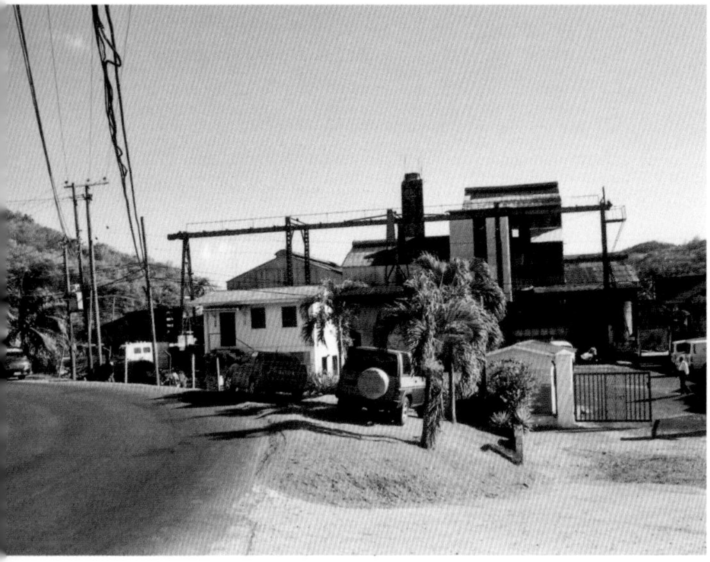

Granada Sugar Factory

centre and operates tours for visitors. Between 1979 and 2000 it was majority government-owned, but an 80 per cent share has been sold to private interests. See www.clarkescourtrum.com

GRENADA SUPREME COURT The GSC was established by People's Law No.4 on 28 March 1979, following Grenada's withdrawal from the region-wide court system. It consisted of a High Court and Court of Appeal, with Archibald NEDD the chief justice. Though the judges on the GSC were independent and free to make decisions based solely on 'juristic considerations', they were constrained by the laws formulated by the PEOPLE'S REVOLUTIONARY GOVERNMENT, especially in cases involving political detention and the rights of habeas corpus. Most apparent of all was the PRG's disregard for some court decisions, particularly the acquittal of political detainees who remained detained long after they were acquitted or served their time. Thus the authority of the GSC was continually undermined by the PRG.

The ADVISORY COUNCIL, coming to power following the US-led military INTERVENTION, did not end the controversial GSC. The People's Laws under the GSC favoured the GOG in its case against the GRENADA 17. The GSC became a constitutional issue when the defence lawyers for the accused argued that the GSC was unconstitutional. In the end the GSC Court of Appeal agreed that it was unconstitutional, but under the 'doctrine of state necessity' it was legal and the trial proceeded. In 1991 Grenada rejoined the OECS Supreme Court, finally bringing the GSC to an end and returning confidence to the islands' legal system.[353]

GRENADA UNION OF TEACHERS The GUT was founded in June 1913 as the Elementary Teachers' Association to organise the growing number of teachers in the islands' expanding educational system; it changed its name in 1917. Its principal founders were W H Jacobs, J S Allamby and N J Nurse. Though it is the oldest labour union, it was not until 1960 that it registered as a union, with a membership of 400. Until then its role as the representative body of teachers was aided by the various religious denominations, especially the Catholic Church, which were constantly at odds with the colonial government over EDUCATION. Teachers, unlike agricultural workers, were a privileged group because of the importance and emphasis placed on the development of education. As such, they benefited from the various attempts to improve education since their role was viewed as vital. A number of ordinances over the years granted teachers regular salary increases, better working conditions and pensions. Since the 1960s the GUT has played a major role in the LABOUR MOVEMENT. In 2000 it confronted the GOG over pay increases. Negotiations finally produced a settlement, but not before the nation's teachers went on strike. The GUT is represented on the Board of Education, the Public Service Commission, and a number of other public bodies. Membership is around 1,500.

GRENVILLE/LABAYE 12 07N 61 37W is the second most important town and port in Grenada, situated in St. Andrew's parish and popularly referred to as 'Rainbow City'. It is the only major town founded by the British, its name derived from George Grenville, a member of the influential British family and prime minister (1763-65). The name was first attached to Grand MARQUIS, the former French town 3 miles (5 km) to the south that was destroyed during FÉDON'S REBELLION. Grenville, situated within Grenville Bay on the east coast, was named LaBaye (<Fr.: *la baie*: 'the bay') by the French, and LaBaye remains in use today as the town's secondary name. Sometime after 1796 and the abandonment of Grand Marquis, LaBaye was renamed Grenville.

The town, located inside a spacious harbour, is almost completely barred by a belt of fringing CORAL REEFS that make vessel entry difficult, even dangerous, hence the former port's pilot facility at PILOT HILL. In 1887 a fire destroyed parts of the town, but spared the new court house and other government buildings erected three years earlier. In 1902 Grenville was still viewed as 'a blot on Grenada as far as sanitary matters are concerned... [and] owing to its unhealthiness there is hardly a well-to-do

Grou-grou Palm

person resident in it... During heavy rains most of the streets are flooded.' It therefore developed mainly as a business community.

The town of Grenville has a number of buildings of architectural interest, including the courthouse (built 1884), both the RC and Anglican churches, and the enclosed market which was completed in 1928 on a former swamp and garbage landfill. In 1896 a waterworks was constructed to supply the town, but not until 1953 did the town receive water-carriage latrines; public pit latrines were installed beginning in the 1910s. The PRINCESS ALICE HOSPITAL replaced the St. Andrew's District Hospital (1878-1948) in 1948. In 1962 ELECTRICITY was installed. The harbour is equipped with a cement jetty capable of docking many vessels that ply between the islands (see TRAFFICKING). Each year, since 1986, Grenville hosts a popular three-day pre-CARNIVAL celebration, the Rainbow City Festival of the Arts.

GROU-GROU (*Acrocomia aculeata*) is a wild prickled palm found growing in hilly areas. It is native to tropical America and grows to 35 ft (10 m), with its entire trunk and fronds covered with 4 in (10 cm) long black spines. The trunk is slightly elongated at the top or middle in older plants, with bunches of fruits drooping from the crown. The gooey, doughy flesh of the fruit is eaten exclusively by children. The hard nut yields edible oil which was used as a local remedy for rheumatism. The black shell surrounding the seed was fashioned into 'grou-grou rings', a once common activity among children. The round seed was grated down on two sides then polished, producing a hand-crafted piece of jewellery. To be 'hard like grou-grou' is to be very stubborn. A grou-grou (<Am. Sp. <Carib: *grugru* for the plant) patch or cluster of trees is believed to be the devil's second favourite place of residence; the SILK COTTON tree is the first. The larva that feeds on the pit of the tree was once eaten as a delicacy.

GUAVA (*Psidium guayava*) is native to tropical America and was probably introduced to Grenada by AMERINDIANS. Its name is derived from the Spanish *guayaba* (<Arawakan *guayava* for the fruit). The low-growing tree has a smooth bark once the outer skin flakes off, leaving a solid wood that was commonly used by children to make spinning tops. It grows to 10-25 ft (3-8 m) and produces a globular to pear-shaped fruit. The green fruit turns a yellow-orange when ripe, at which time it is eaten as a fresh fruit, made

into jam, juice, wine, (guava) jelly, and guava cheese (a paste or sweetmeat). Fruits vary in size, shape and colour, with the flesh of the ripe fruit white, pink or yellow and imbedded with numerous tiny seeds that are also eaten. The acidic, aromatically flavoured pulp is 4-5 times richer in Vitamin C than fresh orange juice. It is in season from May to October. The saying 'to have guava-days' is to experience 'hard' or difficult times. The guava lobster is a GOD-HORSE.

GUINEP/CHENIP/SKINOP (*Melicoccus bijugatus*) is a large native Caribbean evergreen tree that grows to 50 ft (15 m). It produces a round green fruit (like a small lime) that is only eaten fresh. The green skin is easily broken, exposing a cream-coloured, gelatinous flesh that can be sweet, yet astringent. The roasted seed has a chestnut-like flavour. From July to October the fruits are usually sold by STREET VENDORS and are popular among children. Caution should be heeded when giving guinep (<Am.Sp. *quenepa* <Arawakan *kenepa*) to small children who may be unaware that because of its slipperiness, the seed can easily be swallowed; parents usually break the seed to prevent swallowing. Fruits yield a blue-black dye if processed and was used by the Island CARIBS to tattoo designs on their bodies. It is known in Barbados as ackee.

GULP The acronym for the Grenada United Labour Party, which began as the Grenada People's Party in March 1950. It was the political arm of the widely popular labour union GMMIWU, both founded by Eric GAIRY. The history of the GULP is the history of Gairy's domineering personality and his stormy and controversial political career. The GULP represented mainly rural agricultural workers, the majority of whom were poor and had little or no political representation to date. In its first ELECTIONS in 1951 it won six of the eight contested seats in the Legislative Council. It became the first political party to present a comprehensive slate of candidates organised under a leader and a platform. Yet Gairy's autocratic style stifled individual expression within the party, forcing independent-minded members out. As Gairy himself observed, recognising his charisma among his supporters, 'Grenadians would vote for a CRAPPO if I say so.'

In 1954 the GULP formed the majority in the Legislative Council, but won only two seats in 1957. In 1961 it won eight of the ten seats, and Gairy, being disenfranchised, appointed himself 'advisor to government'. It was joked that the legislature met and made decisions at Gairy's residence instead of at YORK HOUSE. Gairy later returned to the legislature after winning a by-election when a GULP member of Parliament resigned his seat. In June 1962 the legislature was dissolved following the suspension of the constitution as a result of SQUANDERMANIA. The GULP lost the 1962 general elections mainly due to its lack of support for a UNITARY STATE proposal with Trinidad. It won seven of the ten seats in the 1967 elections, and in the 1972 elections won 13 of the 15 seats.

Yet the 1970s proved to be a trying period for the GULP, confronted with growing opposition to its rule, especially from the NEW JEWEL MOVEMENT and labour unions. In 1976 it won nine of the 15 seats, defeating the PEOPLE'S ALLIANCE in an election the opposition charged was not free and fair. It was the first time since the early 1960s that it was confronted with significant opposition. With continuous electoral victories between 1967 and 1976, the GULP dominated the PARLIAMENT and Grenadian politics until 1979 when it was overthrown by the NJM in a coup.

In 1984, following the US-led military INTERVENTION, the GULP was revived, but won only one seat in the December 1984 elections. In 1990 the GULP lost what many considered its best chance when it won only four of 15 seats. It won two seats in the 1995 elections, and failed to win any in 1999 or 2003. After half a century of political involvement, the GULP may have lost its traditional constituencies and its role in Grenadian politics, especially since its popular founder and leader died without an heir apparent. The GULP holds the distinction of being the oldest political party in Grenada and the first to be led by a woman, Gloria Payne-Banfield (since 2002).[35, 99, 176, 243, 333]

H

HALIFAX HARBOUR A small sheltered cove situated along the western coast of Grenada between Brizan and Grand Roy. The French called it Petit Havre (<Fr. 'small haven'). In the 1700s and 1800s it was used as a port by ships loading and unloading merchandise, most legal but some illegal. It was believed to be the entry point of the SUGAR ANT infestation of the 1770s. Halifax Harbour offers a safe anchorage that is taken advantage of by yachts cruising around the island. An open rubbish dump, located nearby, washed into the nearby bay, and it is feared that pollutants have caused the death of fish and disturbed the natural balance of this once beautiful bay. A number of groups called for the removal of the dump, which was subsequently moved further inland. Halifax Harbour most probably derived its name from the second Earl of Halifax, or the city in West Yorkshire, England.[295]

HANKEY A British family with estates and businesses in Grenada for over two centuries. John Hankey (1741-92), a London merchant and attorney, was a member of the Hankey family that owned Hankey & Co. (est. 1685), a banking firm which later became part of Consolidated Bank in 1863 and National Westminister in 1995. Together with Peter Simond, he purchased a number of estates in Grenada in the 1760s and operated the trading firm of Simond, Hankey & Son; the family may have traded in Grenada since around 1720. In 1793, *The Hankey*, the family's flagship, was blamed for introducing BOULAM FEVER from West Africa into Grenada. Thomson Hankey (1805-93), the grandson of John Hankey, was a British politician and political economist who served as the colonial agent for Grenada between 1849 and 1850.

By the early 1800s Thomson Hankey & Co. acquired many debtor estates in the course of supplying agricultural produce, but liquidated its many sugar estates by the mid-1900s, concentrating on its retail business in lumber, automobiles, insurance, etc., and exported agricultural produce. In 1946 the firm was incorporated, and five years later reorganised under the name Hankey's Ltd. The company was dissolved in 1964, with the Grenville, St. Andrew branch continuing into the 1970s and owned by the Nyack family. The area in front of the company on the Carenage (now the Food Fair) was known as Hankey's Wharf where ships loaded and unloaded merchandise. Thomson Hankey & Co., considered London's oldest trading company, became part of Lion Foods, Ltd., a food and spice manufacturer. Hankey's was the oldest of the HISTORICAL BUSINESSES to operate in Grenada.

HARMFUL PLANTS There are a number of plants that can cause great discomfort, to say the least, if one comes in contact with them, or consumes parts of the tree or fruit. Cow-itch (*Mucuna pruriens*) is a creeping plant found in thick bush and unnoticeable to the untutored eye, with regrettable results. Also known as pwa-gaté (<Fr.Cr.<Fr. *pois*:'pea-(pod)' + *gratter*:'scratch'), it is benign when green,

Halifax Harbour

Cow-itch pods or pwa-gaté

but when dry the brown pod is covered with numerous tiny hairs that once in contact with the skin become an intense irritant. The common treatment is rubbing dry dust on the afflicted area. FOLK MEDICINE prescribes cow-itch (<Old Eng. *cowage/cowhage*<Hin. *kawach*) hairs mixed with molasses as a cure for intestinal worms, and the root as a remedy for CHOLERA. The broad leaves of the stinging or devil nettle (*Laportea aestuans*), common in gardens and roadside bushes, cause skin inflammation. The zouti (*Tragia volubilis*) is a vine with small green leaves and stems containing tiny stinging hairs. Contact with any part of the zouti (<Fr. *(de)s-orties*: 'nettles') can irritate the skin, resulting in the swelling of the affected area.

There are numerous other plants, especially prickled weeds like the sensitive plant (*Mimosa pudica*), which can cause minor discomfort when in contact with the skin. A number of other plants, including many popular flowers, should be enjoyed for their beauty and little else. Consumption of any plant species other than food crops, especially for medicinal purposes, should be avoided unless recommended by someone with extensive knowledge of folk medicine and the local FLORA.[146b]

HARVEST & BAZAAR are annual social events organised by Christian Churches for the purpose of raising needed funds. The harvest is believed to be an old pagan festival, and as the name suggests, the first fruits of the annual harvest were used as a sacrifice. The event, now incorporated into the local church calendars, is usually held around EASTER. It developed in the early 1800s as a harvest thanksgiving, especially among Catholics who depended upon financial contributions from churchgoers, the majority of whom were peasants. Church faithful were expected to give of their crops that were in turn sold to the public.

The bazaar, on the other hand, is more widespread among the various denominations. Congregants donate crafts and food items like cakes, preserves and pies that are then sold to those who attend the bazaar. Sometimes an entrance fee is charged as well. Bazaars are usually held in the larger towns because they attract the wealthier members of the community. A tea party usually accompanies the harvest and bazaar. Profits from these events are used to sponsor a specific project like the purchase of a piano or to make repairs to the church.

HARVEY VALE is the second largest settlement on the island of Carriacou after HILLSBOROUGH. It is situated at the southern extreme at TYRREL BAY. As late as 1784 it was known by its French name Grand Carenage (or Great Carenage Bay). Its sheltered bay and beach have been home to many sloops, schooners and sailing boats throughout the island's history. The remnants of an old SUGAR MILL attest to the historical use of the area for sugar producing in the late 1700s and early 1800s. The estate, which later became the town, was then owned by John Dallas, a proprietor remembered as a 'cruel master', who 'the day he die a cannon go [off] on [the] hill cause he was too bad.' His massive tombstone can still be seen at the Harvey Vale Cemetery. The government acquired the 330 acre (134 ha) estate in 1892 and in 1904 divided 250 acres (102 ha) into 79 allotments for the peasantry as part of its LAND SETTLEMENT. In 1928 a Visiting (Health) Centre was opened in the town.

Within the last three decades it has seen many improvements, with the arrival of social and infrastructural amenities like schools, telecommunications and ELECTRICITY. Harvey Vale, with its picturesque bay, holds potential for TOURISM. At present a number of restaurants dot the cove. The village developed as a BOAT BUILDING centre and boasted of its skill in producing well-crafted schooners that still ply the waters of the Eastern Caribbean.[324]

HAY, Dr John (1746-1803) A Scottish medical doctor resident in St. John's parish, who was among the British hostages taken at the beginning of FÉDON'S REBELLION. He was captured on the morning of 3 March 1795 at GOUYAVE, St. John, and taken to the rebels' camp at BELVIDERE. Hay was one of three individuals whose lives were spared when the hostages were executed on 8 April 1795. Though Hay himself was not sure why Julien FÉDON spared his life, it was claimed that he had cured Fédon of 'a dangerous fit of sickness'. Fédon, when asked why Hay should be spared, replied that 'I have my reason for it, which I shall communicate to you at another time.'

Though spared, his ordeal did not end. Together with William Kerr (son-in-law of Chevalier De Suze, an aide to Fédon) and Rev. Francis Macmahon (Anglican rector of St. Patrick), Hay was sent as a prisoner to the French Republicans in Guadeloupe. After a few months in Guadeloupe, on occasions meeting with Victor Hugues, Commissioner of the French forces in the Windward Islands, Hay arrived in British-occupied Martinique following a prisoner exchange. He returned to Grenada in August 1795 and participated in efforts to defeat the rebels as captain of the St. John's MILITIA. In 1823 an account of his ordeal, *A Narrative of the Insurrection in the Island of Grenada Which Took Place in 1795*, was published, providing probably the most detailed, but biased, eyewitness account of Fédon and the chaotic rebellion he commanded. A memorial plaque to Hay hangs in the ST. JOHN'S ANGLICAN CHURCH.[35, 333]

HEAD OF STATE Queen Elizabeth II is the present head of state of GRENADA. Her official title is 'Elizabeth II, by the Grace of God, Queen of the United Kingdom of Great Britain and Northern Ireland and of Grenada and Her other Realms and Territories, Head of the Commonwealth.' In 1952 Queen Elizabeth II became the head of the Commonwealth of Nations and the symbolic head of state of many of its member states, including Grenada. The Grenada Constitution recognises her symbolic authority, with an appointed representative in Grenada, the GOVERNOR GENERAL. Over the years the symbolic authority of the head of state has been questioned, with some calling for its termination. Its opponents have called it anachronistic and of no value to Grenada and its citizens.

Queen Elizabeth II has visited Grenada on two occasions, in 1966 and 1985. In October 1985 she made history by becoming the first British monarch to deliver a Throne Speech, as is one of her duties. Twentieth-first June, Queen's Birthday (made a bank holiday in 1887 to commemorate the fiftieth anniversary of the ascension of Queen Victoria), was observed until the mid-1970s.

HIBISCUS (*Hibiscus* spp.) genus has a number of species that are important food crops or beautiful flowers adorning flower gardens. The most important is okro or okra (*Abelmoschus esculentus* syn. *H. esculentus*), which despite its beautiful yellow flower, is grown as a vegetable. The okro (<Igbo *okworo*, for the fruit) was brought to the islands from West Africa during SLAVERY. The green pods are stewed as a vegetable in many local dishes like 'calalu', or made into okro soup, while the young leaves are used as spinach in C&PM. Its slippery consistency once meant its prescription for pregnant women 'to aid in a quick delivery.'

Sorrel or roselle (*H. sabdariffa*) is native to tropical Africa, and was brought to Brazil in the seventeenth century from where it spread to the Caribbean. This annual grows to 10 ft (3 m) and is cultivated for its red and white swollen calyces or sepals, which are sun-dried, then boiled with spices to make a sweet, dark red aromatic drink at Christmas time. The sepals can also be used to make wine or jam (its leaves are used as spinach in West Africa and the drink is called bissap in Senegal).

The ubiquitous hibiscus flowers are native to Asia, but have become one of the most common ornamentals in FLOWER GARDENS

Queen Elizabeth II's visit to Grenada, 1985, with Govenor General Scoon and his wife

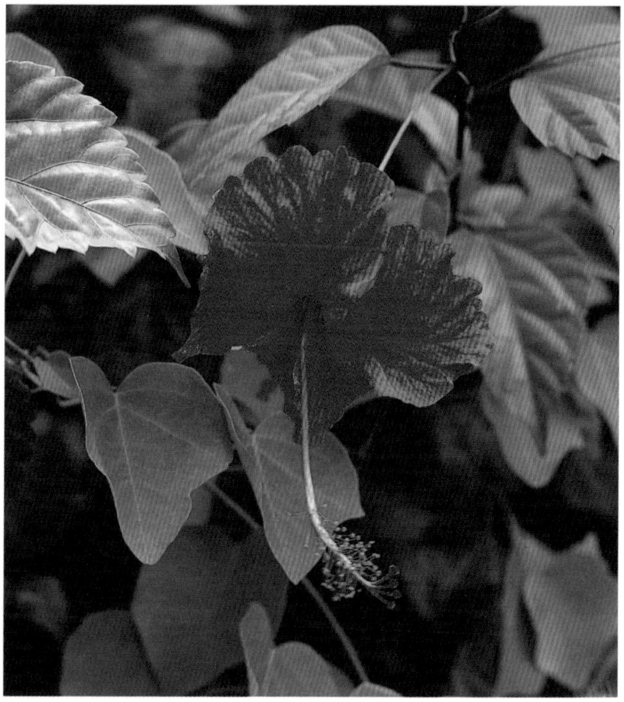

Hibiscus flower

and along roadsides. Its members include shrubs and small trees that grow to 20 ft (6 m). The most common species is the Chinese hibiscus (*H. rosa-sinensis*), with a bright red flower. Other common species include the coral or fringed hibiscus (*H. schizopetalus*), with its lacy pink petals and serrated light-green leaves, and the mahoe or sea hibiscus (*H. titiaceus*), a shrub that produces a large bright yellow flower. Many species, spanning the rainbow of colours and shapes, are grown as ornamentals or hedges. The genus was affected by the pink or hibiscus MEALYBUG infestation, but has since recovered.[146b]

HIGH NORTH NATIONAL PARK is the national park of Carriacou, situated in the northern part of the island's central ridge, occupying some 682 acres (276 ha) of mostly 'undisturbed' vegetation. High North and the surrounding area are the most biologically diverse region in the entire Grenadines. It includes a dry thorn scrub deciduous forest, a mangrove-mud flat ecosystem at Petit Carenage Bay, seascapes, and High North Peak or Bellevue North at 975 ft (297 m), the island's highest point. The historical heritage of the park, such as the French-built ESTATE HOUSE ruins, adds to the area's attractiveness. The scenic beach at L'Anse la Roche (<Fr. *anse*: 'cove' + *roche*: 'rock'; Rocky Cove for the large rocks that stick out of the water just off the beach) further enhances the area, and has led to the recommendation that the region be made a biosphere reserve. A primary goal for the CONSERVATION of High North is to protect the LIZARDS, MOROCOY, MANICOU, SEA TURTLES and BIRDS. The development of High North NP for recreational activities, primarily hiking trails, will aid the growing TOURISM industry, specifically eco-tourism.[140, 301]

HILLSBOROUGH 12 29N 61 28W is the largest town and main commercial centre in Carriacou. It is situated on the leeward side of the island in the Hillsborough Bay (formerly Grande Anse). French colonists from Grenada probably settled the area in the late seventeenth or early eighteenth century. Though not possessing the most advantageous natural harbour, Hillsborough nonetheless became the major port and administrative centre. In 1813 the island was described as 'a healthy residence, except in marshy situations, one of the worst of which has been unfortunately chosen for the settlement of the Town of Hillsbro... It is almost directly in front of a swamp which extends on each side of the town.' Over the last century its population has fluctuated: 344 in 1891, 302 in 1901, 262 in 1921, 276 in 1946, and 600 in 1991. Its possible namesake is Sir Wills Hill, the Earl of Hillsborough and secretary of the colonies.

Hillsborough town

Hillsborough, described as 'overgrown with bush, and surrounded by swamps,' began its development as a modern town after 1903 following the government's purchase of the 708 acre (287 ha) Beauséjour estate for allotment to peasants as part of its LAND SETTLEMENT. Mosquitoes and MALARIA were serious problems in the town, and around 1913 the government initiated a common biological control then practised in the region, introducing the guppy fish or millions to consume mosquito larvae. Yet it was not until 1927 that the drainage problem was addressed, and it would be years before the mosquito and malaria problems abated.

The present street plan of Hillsborough dates to 1886 when the boundaries were set. Running parallel to the bay is Main Street, the primary thoroughfare through the tiny coastal town, where government administrative buildings and commercial banks, the CARRIACOU MUSEUM and the open-air Market Square can be found. Overlooking Hillsborough, on Fort Hill, sit the ruins of an old abandoned fort, its cannons on the hilltop next to the PRINCESS ROYAL HOSPITAL; there is also a Health Centre. The town is equipped with ELECTRICITY and TELECOMMUNICATIONS. Cultural and sporting activities take place at the Tennis Court. There are two secondary schools and one primary school in the town.

HISTORICAL BUSINESSES Some of the islands' oldest businesses have their origins in the early 1800s, though one, HANKEY'S Ltd., had a much longer history. Jonas Browne & Hubbard, Ltd is Grenada's oldest existing business. It began as A. Hubbard & Co. in 1810, founded by an American, Alexander Hubbard. In 1873 Charles Macaulay Browne, son of Jonas Browne, married the daughter of Charles Simmons (member of the Legislature, 1862-77) and took over the company from Simmons upon his death in 1881. In 1947 A. Hubbard & Co., Grenada and Jonas Browne & Sons, England were amalgamated, and in 1972 became locally known as Jonas Browne & Hubbard (Grenada) Ltd. By the 1970s it had become one of the leading businesses in the islands, owning the first modern supermarket, the Food Fair (est. 1964 after taking over the property from Hankey's Ltd.). In 1971 it opened the Grande Anse Shopping Centre, the first shopping centre of its kind in the islands.

George F. Huggins & Co. was not established in Grenada until 1921 after buying Martin Dean & Co., which dates to at least 1889. In 1974 it bought the Everybody's Stores that began operations in 1849 as Ferdinand Marrast & Co., a general merchant store, and renamed it 'Buy Rite'. It was a popular symbol in the island with its motto 'Everybody's for Everything'. It was situated on Halifax Street next to the MARKET SQUARE and housed in the same building since at least 1889. In 1904 it was incorporated as The Stores (G'da) Ltd., changing its name to 'Everybody's Stores' in 1934 when SA FRANCIS bought it. During civil unrest in January 1974, it was looted. In 1998 its name was changed from Buy Rite to Foodland.

Of the older businesses established by locals WE Julien and Co., McIntyre Brothers, LA Purcell and the GSF are the most prominent. Established in 1900 by EF and DW McIntyre, McIntyre Brothers was a general store and later automobile dealership and garage/gas station. WE Julien (1896-1974), a World War I veteran, established a store in 1924 and incorporated it in 1937, becoming a leading trade, and general and commission merchant. LA Purcell was established in 1938 as general and commission merchants. Other historical businesses include Gerald Smith (est. 1928) in St. George's and RM Bhola (est. 1946) in Grenville. Establishments selling drugs have been around for a long time, but it was not until the late 1800s that reputable pharmacies came into being with HB Beckwith's and Powell's. Of the existing drugstores Mitchell's Pharmacy, established around 1910, is the oldest, followed by Gittens' Pharmacy.

HOME, Ninian (1732-1795) was Grenada's lieutenant governor who was captured and executed by the rebels during FÉDON'S REBELLION. He had resided in Grenada since arriving from Scotland in 1762. In 1771 he was appointed judge of the Court of Common Pleas and assistant justice of the Supreme Court in 1784. Before being appointed lieutenant governor in 1792, he was speaker of the General Assembly; it was quite unusual for a long-time resident like Home to be appointed lieutenant governor, but influential family like his brother George Home and friends like Alexander CAMPBELL lobbied the Colonial Office on his behalf. During the Anglo-French conflict, Home led verbal attacks against the French RC inhabitants, continuing his campaign against them after becoming lieutenant governor. He unsuccessfully attempted to curtail the emigration of French FREE COLOUREDS into Grenada in the mid-1790s, his actions further alienating the French and creating conditions that led to Fédon's Rebellion.

While at his estate at Paraclete, St. Andrew, he learned of the rebel sacking of Grenville (Grand MARQUIS). On his seaward route to St. George's from SAUTEURS to take command of the situation, Home was captured at GOUYAVE when he came ashore on 3 March 1795. Accounts show that Home was resigned to his impending death at the hands of the rebels, and on 8 April 1795, along with 46 other British hostages, he was executed. Though he had lived in Grenada for close to thirty years, Home had hoped to return to his native Scotland where his estate at Paxton awaited him (his wife Penelope Payne died in 1794 and was buried at Paraclete). The Grenada Legislature in 1799 dedicated a marble monument at the ST. GEORGE'S ANGLICAN CHURCH to the late lieutenant governor.[272]

HOME HOTEL was opened around 1895 and for many years was considered the islands' best hotel. It was situated on Young Street, St. George's, in the building now occupied by the GRENADA NATIONAL MUSEUM, and located only 150 ft (45 m) from the CARENAGE. On average it was able to accommodate about thirty guests, some of whom were permanent residents such as retired planters and widowers. In the 1920s it was known as the Gordon Hotel and in the 1930s as Hotel St. George and Steele's Place. In 1939 'CFP' RENWICK purchased the hotel and reopened it as the Antilles Hotel in 1940. Following Renwick's death, S A FRANCIS acquired it and continued to run it as the Antilles Hotel. After almost seventy years, it closed in 1960, as the islands' luxury HOTEL industry was emerging.

HOOK-BILLED KITE (*Chrondrohierax uncinatus mirus*) is less known and beloved than the GRENADA DOVE, but its numbers are small, with extinction a strong possibility if immediate CONSERVATION measures are not taken to protect it. Measuring about 16 inches (41 cm) and weighing about 10 oz (275 g), it is the smallest of the hawks, but its deeply hooked bill makes it distinct. The last count placed the total between 15-30 individuals, possibly too small for breeding purposes in the wild. There is some taxonomic controversy surrounding its classification as a single-island endemic species. Some authorities list it as a sub-species of its South American relative, *Chrondrohierax uncinatus*, which is widespread in the Americas yet less common within the Caribbean. The hook-billed kite, like the Grenada dove, makes its home in the dry scrub woodland of the SW where it feeds on tree snails, small mammals, reptiles and FROGS. The destruction of the hook-billed kite's habitat is the prime cause of its demise. Also known as the mountain hawk. In 2006 the GOG and RARE launched a campaign to 'keep the kite in flight.[23, 345]

HORSE RACING dates to the late 1700s and the arrival of the British as a sport for the islands' elite, particularly planters. In 1830 a new racecourse was opened at Grande Anse and hosted a number of annual meetings; it was described as 'oblong and offers a pretty gallop... There is a splendid and commodious building erected on the course as a grand stand.' It operated until the early 1900s when activities gradually moved to the QUEEN'S PARK, St. George, and the Telescope pasture, St. Andrew. Horse racing soon became established at the Queen's Park, reaching its climax in the first three decades of the 1900s. Grenada became well known throughout the southern Caribbean as home to some of the most prominent and award-winning horses. Horses were locally bred, and the top contenders in Grenada went on to compete in TRINIDAD, Guyana, Barbados and even Venezuela. There were several big meetings each year, coinciding with the holidays of EASTER, Whit Monday, August, Christmas and New Year when 'bus loads' of Grenadians came out to partake of the festivities, including gambling.

Horse racing clubs included the St. George's (f. 1895) and St. Andrew's (f. 1897) Race Clubs. Both were 'practically moribund [by the 1940s], and have merely drifted away since the lamented death of Grenada's most famous turfite, HA Berkeley.' (There were also minor clubs in St. Patrick and St. David.) The decline of the clubs was a reflection of horse racing in Grenada, which was 'well on the way to practical extinction, the reason being a dearth of turfites.' The old PLANTOCRACY, which had supported horse racing, was declining and few Grenadians were coming forward to replace them. To revive the fading sport, the two main clubs merged into the Grenada Turf Club in 1940. Horse racing barely survived into the 1960s, held together by enthusiasts like R M Bhola and Norbert Nyack (who helped revive the sport in St. Andrew in the 1950s), Sir William Branch, Joshua Thorne, Dennis Noel, Reggie Evans, Briggs LaMotte and Anthony Romain. Around 1968 the Grenada Turf Club folded and the remaining turfites formed the Grenada Racing Co.

The approaching end of horse racing could not be avoided and the early 1970s witnessed its last hurrah. The last big event in St. George's was the Governor General's Cup in 1974, and two years later Seamoon, St. Andrew, witnessed its final event. The changing social dynamics in Grenada and the decreasing numbers and influence of the elite who had financially and socially supported horse racing, played a major role in its ultimate demise. Sports like golf and lawn tennis became popular among the elite at private clubs.

HOSPITAL HILL REDOUBTS A series of three batteries or redoubts built by the British in the 1760s, though the French, since the 1730s, had maintained the area overlooking the (French) Colony HOSPITAL and QUEEN'S PARK as a military battery. It derives its name from the French name for the hill, Morne de l'Hôpital. Its other name, Fort William Henry, is after Prince William Henry, later King William IV (1830-1837), who visited Grenada in 1787 while an officer in the British Navy. Its higher elevation (400ft/122 m) and commanding view of Fort Royal led J-B LABAT in 1700 to conclude that a fort should be built there. The three redoubts, called 'east', 'centre', and 'west', were situated along the ridge, surrounded by 'a large perimeter wall that ran along the northern face of the hill.' It was the major defence of the British in July 1779 when the French attacked. The French successfully captured the series of redoubts by attacking from inland along the St. Paul's/Richmond Hill ridge. Turning the guns of Fort William against FORT GEORGE, the French forced the British to surrender.

A number of tunnels extended beneath the series of redoubts, believed to have been used as 'listening tunnels' to warn of an enemy's approach. The fortifications had suffered much damage to their battlements in 1779 and by the mid-1800s were abandoned, having previously been deserted once the RICHMOND HILL FORTS were completed in the 1790s. Of little architectural significance, there has been no attempt to restore or preserve these sites, which are now in disrepair and overgrown.[177]

HOSPITALS The French established the first hospital about March 1736 on Hospital or Cemetery Hill, overlooking MELVILLE STREET. In 1742 it came under the administration of the Religieux Hospitaliers de St. Jean de Dieu, who traditionally cared for the sick. In 1760 the French colonial government took control of it following problems with the Brothers and placed it under the administration of a local surgeon. At the end of 1762, during British rule, an appointed Board of Trustees took over and admitted only military personnel until 1765. In 1778 the Colony Hospital Act was passed in an attempt to improve both its financial and medical management under a Charitable Corporation. By the early 1800s it was abandoned, having fallen into disrepair due to insufficient operating funds. It was replaced by a number of dilapidated and unsanitary temporary facilities between the 1820s and 1850s, and permanently replaced in 1859 by the Colony Hospital.

The new hospital's main wards were housed in the old military barracks of FORT GEORGE, which were converted in 1859 after minimal reconstruction when the military garrison withdrew. The majority of its first patients were paupers, but the facilities gradually grew to broaden its access to the larger population. Its deplorable state resulted in thorough renovation and reopening in 1897. Its most noticeable addition was the central staircase, quite in evidence today. By the end of the 1890s the hospital had the only water-borne sanitation system in the islands.

New hospital buildings

Over the years it has expanded to its present state and houses the General Hospital for the State of GRENADA, with mortuary (added 1898), operating room, dispensary and nurses' quarters (1901), analytical laboratory (1905), children's (1931) and private wards. The 240-bed facility has seen many improvements, but Clyde believes that 'the overall cramped situation and improvised lay-out of the General Hospital have not been amenable to significant modernization.' The pressing need to upgrade Grenada's medical facilities to a level capable of providing adequate care for the islands' sick and emergency treatment (to avoid the expense and risk of sending patients to other islands for emergency treatment) has resulted in a new $30m state-of-the-art 198-bed facility that opened in 2003 with further enhancements and expansion completed in 2007.

The islands are divided into eleven medical districts, each with a district medical officer. There are about 28 medical stations and six health centres providing primary medical services throughout the islands. PRINCESS ALICE HOSPITAL in St. Andrew and PRINCESS ROYAL HOSPITAL in Carriacou provide more extensive care for residents in the countryside and the GRENADA GRENADINES, respectively. A number of ALMSHOUSES provide care to the mentally and physically handicapped, and destitute. There are a number of private medical facilities scattered across Grenada.[55]

HOT SPRINGS There are at least seven primary areas in Grenada where either hot or cold springs can be found, located predominantly in the northern region along the central mountain range. These springs are the remaining indications of small-scale geothermicity. A survey of the island completed by the British in the early 1800s commented on the hot springs and added that their 'sulfurous and mineral waters might prove of great service in many disorders if their qualities and virtues were sufficiently known.' Springs can be found at Hermitage Estate ('mephitic spring') and Clabony, St. Andrew, Tufton Hall, St. Mark, Annandale, St. George, and RIVER SALLEE, St. Patrick. The hot springs at River Sallee, described as 'the most interesting of the mineral springs', illustrate the significance of these natural formations. The six springs occupy about a 0.25 acre (0.1 ha) area and are scattered around the Chambord estate. Though situated 1 mile (1.6 km) from the sea, these springs are highly saline, with temperatures as high as 95°F. Orange-yellow deposits from the springs denote the presence of sulphur. The saline nature of the springs led the French to name the nearby river Rivière Salée.

Much SUPERSTITION surrounds these geological phenomena, once known as djabouillant (<Fr.Cr. 'little devil' <Fr. *diable*: 'devil'), with reference to the believed powers of the springs. SPIRITUAL BAPTISTS and SHANGO worshippers make pilgrimages to the revered sites to perform rituals within the 'sacred' waters and honour the river goddess MAMA GLO. Many believe that their acidic and saline characteristics are a cure for some ailments, and were used by YAWS sufferers in the 1800s as a curative.

HOTELS Taverns, coffeehouses, guest houses and other boarding accommodation date back to the French period and the early 1700s. FREE COLOUREDS and blacks were commonly noted as tavern keepers (as well as running brothels and gaming houses). The authorities disliked this because they believed that these taverns were used to harbour escaped slaves. One of the earliest hotels/guest houses of good repute was the St. George's Hotel located on Hospital Street (presently CHURCH STREET) and operated from the 1820s to 1890s (the Victoria and Jubilee Hotels also operated in the late 1800s). Yet it was not until the end of the 1800s, as was evident with the founding

All-inclusive La Source Resort with Pink Gin Beach in the foreground

Silver Sands Hotel

of the ST. GEORGE'S MEN'S CLUB, that hotels began to appear across the island. Around 1895 the HOME HOTEL opened, becoming the primary hotel on the island until the mid-1900s. Hotels, boarding houses and guest houses became prevalent in the late 1800s and early 1900s all over St. George's and even in the outer parishes, where establishments like the Nest in GRENVILLE and the Gouyave Hotel opened. Others were the St. George's Hotel (later the Douglas Hotel, 1800s to 1940s), the Ice House Hotel, and the Hotel St. James.

These were augmented by government rest houses, including QUARANTINE STATION and Grand Étang Lake House in Grenada, and the Top Hill Rest House in Carriacou, which could be rented by visitors. In 1948 the first 'luxury' hotel, Santa Maria (del Conception) Hotel, was constructed on the site of Monckton's Hill Redoubts. Though the economic potential of GRANDE ANSE BEACH and the surrounding areas as tourist resorts had been realised since the early 1930s, construction along the beach did not begin until the late 1950s with the building in 1959 of the Silver Sands Hotel (since demolished). In 1958 there were 130 hotel beds, increasing to 630 by 1967 and catering to over 20,000 visitors.

The 1960s and 1970s witnessed the expansion of the TOURISM industry and with it the construction of many hotels, primarily along the southern coast. Following the US-led military INTERVENTION and the completion of the POINT SALINES INTERNATIONAL AIRPORT, the tourism sector experienced an upsurge in visitors, resulting in a construction boom in the late 1980s. Large seaside resorts, occupying acres of beach-front property and sporting tennis courts, conference rooms, swimming pools, and gyms, have permeated the Grande Anse, Point Salines and True Blue areas. These include Grenada's largest hotels, Rex Grenadian (212 rooms), Grenada Renaissance Resort (186 rooms) and La Source (100), which provide an assortment of accommodation to visitors. With fewer than two thousand hotel rooms (development plans place the upper limit at 2,500 rooms), the islands are still well equipped to handle large numbers of overnight visitors. Many hotels experienced damages due to HURRICANE IVAN, some requiring extensive repairs.

HUGHES, Dr Alister Earl (1919-2005) was a journalist, broadcaster, local historian, amateur archaeologist and travel writer. He came from a long-established family, the son of A. Norris Hughes and Annie H Bain. He attended the Grammar School (later the GBSS) and worked in a variety of jobs before becoming involved in journalism in the late 1960s. In the 1950s and 1960s he served on the St. George's District Board and City Council, and as general secretary of the GNP between 1957 and 1967. He reported on events in Grenada and the Caribbean for news agencies throughout the Americas and Europe. From 1973 to 1994 Hughes and his wife Cynthia published the *Grenada Newsletter,* which reported on economic and political developments in Grenada. Throughout recent political events he was a reliable voice reporting on events in Grenada. His 21 January 1974 recording of the MONGOOSE GANG's violent confrontation with demonstrators at Otway House, St. George's, relayed to the Grenadian populace and the world the confusion, horror and fear of the experience of BLOODY MONDAY. In October 1983, preceding the US-led military INTERVENTION, he was arrested by the RMC as a 'counter revolutionary' when he reported the events that led to BLOODY WEDNESDAY. He received a number of commendations for his reporting, including the 1984 Maria Moors Cabot Prize from Colombia University for 'distinguished journalistic service', and in 1990 an honorary Doctor of Laws from the UWI for his contribution to Caribbean journalism. He was involved in many community activities, especially the preservation and conservation of Grenada's culture, architecture and the natural environment through membership in the GNT, of which he was a founding member. An amateur archaeologist, he was instrumental in the early studies done throughout the islands in the 1960s and 1970s.[164, 165, 166, 167, 168, 169]

HUMMINGBIRDS are small, brightly coloured birds capable of flying backwards as they hover in mid-air, probing flowers with their long beak to retrieve nectar. Their name is derived from the pronounced humming sound they produce while hovering in mid-air. The hummingbird is also known as a doctor bird, possibly from the AMERINDIANS who believed that the hummingbird, readily seen feeding and nesting on the TOBACCO plant, was responsible for bringing tobacco to their ancestors. Hummingbirds are native to tropical and sub-tropical America. These colourful birds, many of which take their common names from precious gems, are widespread throughout the Caribbean.

Grenada is home to three nesting species of hummingbirds, yet vagrant species are sighted from time to time. The rufous-breasted hermit or the brown doctor bird (*Glaucis hirsuta*) is found only in Grenada and TRINIDAD & Tobago in the Caribbean. It is very rarely seen, except in forested areas like the Grand Étang Forest Reserve, CONCORD FALLS and ANNANDALE WATERFALL. The green-throated Carib or emerald-throated hummingbird (*Sericotes/Eulampis holosericus*) is covered with a metallic green all over except for a violet-blue breast and tail. The length of the curved beak aids in identifying the sex (longer beak for females) since both male and female are similar in colour. It is seen throughout the island. The Antillean-crested hummingbird, crested hummer, colibri (name said to be of Carib origin) or the little doctor bird (*Orthorhyncus cristatus*), is the smallest of the three BIRDS and of all the birds on the islands. The brightly coloured metallic green and blue crest, which gives the species its name, is more pronounced in the male. Both sexes are covered with a bright green above and a grey underside. This tiny hummingbird is common throughout the island.[354]

Rufus-breasted Hermit hummingbird

HURRICANE IVAN proved that September is truly a month to 'remember' as far as HURRICANES in Grenada go. On 7 September 2004 Grenada received a direct hit from Hurricane Ivan, a strong category three hurricane that left the island totally devastated. For those who remembered HURRICANE JANET as the worst to hit Grenada in recent history, that memory was brought to life, and all agree that Ivan surpassed it by far in its destruction. The relatively small death toll of 28 people, compared to the 120 who died as a result of Janet in 1955, was probably due to the improved construction of houses and communications. As the hurricane approached, the country appeared unprepared for what was to unfold. For eight hours the islands were pounded with 120 mph (193 kph) winds that left most trees leafless and bent, and numerous buildings levelled; between 80 to 90 per cent of the standing buildings lost their roofs or received heavy damage. The 10 nautical miles-wide eye of the hurricane passed over ST. GEORGE'S and devastated the capital. Approximately 60,000 people were left homeless and without food as shell-shocked Grenadians tried to cope with the catastrophic disaster that befell them. To compound the situation a state of lawlessness broke out the day after the hurricane, with widespread looting and violence that took days to be brought under control.

Most of the island's infrastructure was damaged or altogether destroyed, including TELECOMMUNICATIONS, ELECTRICITY, schools, churches, the NATIONAL STADIUM, roads and the water supply system. The islands' economy was devastated, with AGRICULTURE and TOURISM both affected as tree crops like NUTMEG and COCOA were destroyed and HOTELS damaged. It was the worst hurricane Grenada has experienced in recent history and the worst the English-speaking Caribbean has witnessed in over a decade. Hurricane Ivan caused damage in Barbados, St. Lucia, St. Vincent and the Grenadines, and went on to ravage parts of Jamaica, the

View of damage caused by Hurricane Ivan

Cayman Islands and the south-eastern US. In its wake it left over 70 people dead, from Alabama to Venezuela. Ivan is also known locally as 'Ivan the Terrible', and 'Roofus' for the countless roofs it destroyed. The total estimated damage in Grenada was just under US$1 billion, and it will be many years before the islands' infrastructure is completely rebuilt. Though numerous governments and international organisations responded immediately with relief, the UN reported in mid-2005 that the devastation wrought by Ivan was one of the ten underreported stories of 2005. Ivan was followed ten months later on 14 July 2005 by Hurricane Emily which did extensive damage (totalling US$110m) to the northern part of the island and left one person dead.[244, 245, 368]

HURRICANE JANET Until HURRICANE IVAN in 2004 Hurricane Janet was the worst hurricane to visit the islands in recent memory, leaving them desolate following its attack on 22-23 September 1955. Since Grenada is not frequently affected by HURRICANES, Grenadians did not heed the warning of an impending category three hurricane very seriously. They began praying for the people of Barbados, which Janet had devastated, and St. Vincent, where the eye was expected to pass. From 6:30 P.M. when the 160-mph (260-kph) winds began howling to 3:00 A.M. the next morning, the people were in a state of fear as the hurricane ran its course. The eye passed over northern Grenada and CARRIACOU, leaving many dead and the islands devastated.

In its wake Janet left 120 people dead (of whom 27 were in Carriacou) and thousands homeless, hundreds of acres of denuded forest, and the almost total destruction of the islands' agricultural economy, communication system, water supply and ELECTRICITY. COCOA and NUTMEG trees were severely affected and farmers were forced to diversify by expanding BANANA production. The already decaying ST. GEORGE'S HARBOUR sank and with it millions of dollars worth of merchandise. Many BRIDGES throughout Grenada were destroyed and landslides threatened residents in the mountainous interior. The Carriacou District Hospital, schools and many private houses were destroyed. The torrential downpour flooded RIVERS & STREAMS, carrying everything in its path to the sea. The La Fortune River, St. Patrick, swept away a house and with it eleven people who had sought refuge there.

Under a state of emergency foreign governments and organisations responded to avert the outbreak of DISEASES. Food, blankets, clothes, tents and medicines were sent in from the Caribbean, US, Canada, UK and many other countries. Small wooden houses, later referred to as 'Janet houses', were brought in from Surinam to temporarily house the homeless. Even sailors and soldiers arrived to help with the rebuilding. Bizarrely, Janet left behind swarms of bedbugs, affectionately called Jessica, which tormented the population for years thereafter. Anyone who lived through Janet will always remember the devastation it wreaked, both personally and nationally.

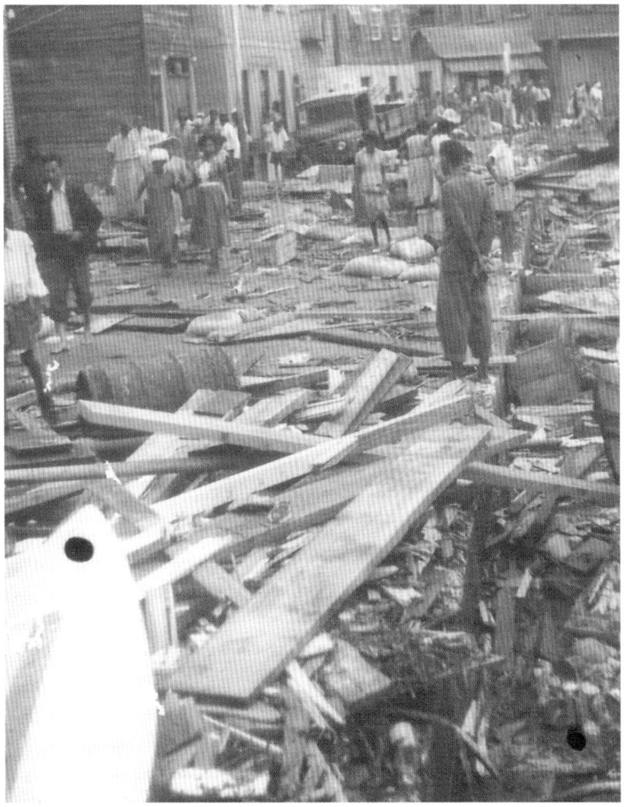

Debris on the Carenage left by Hurricane Janet

Numerous seemingly incredible tales about the hurricane abound, illustrating the violence and severity of this storm. Hurricane Janet left about 681 people dead throughout the region, from Barbados to Belize, including eight storm chasers who were monitoring the storm by aircraft.[333]

HURRICANE LENNY Though the eye of Hurricane Lenny struck hundreds of miles away in the Leeward Islands, violent wave surges associated with it devastated the islands' windward coasts. For approximately three days, 17-19 November 1999, the western coastlines were pounded with 15 ft (4 m) and higher waves. The islands suffered an estimated US$100m in damages to residential and commercial buildings, fishing boats, beach-front property, sea defences, and especially roads. Sections of the 27.5 mile (44 km) Western Main Road connecting St. George's to the towns of GOUYAVE, VICTORIA and SAUTEURS, were destroyed, disrupting normal vehicular traffic. The CARENAGE, St. George's, was especially hard hit, with at least two businesses destroyed and extensive flooding to many others. At least four people were seriously injured, while about a dozen families were left homeless when their houses were washed away or flooded. CARRIACOU experienced flooding and its main road along the west coast was destroyed. The main jetty in PETITE MARTINIQUE was damaged, disrupting the primary means of transportation to and from the island. Fishermen were especially affected when boats were swept out to sea and lost, or destroyed; seines were also damaged. BEACHES, essential to the islands' TOURISM industry, were heavily damaged. Many, including GRANDE ANSE BEACH, witnessed the uprooting of trees, which may in turn worsen beach erosion and damage the health of CORAL REEFS. One consequence of Hurricane Lenny was the apparent lack of disaster preparedness by the National Emergency Relief Organization, charged with providing disaster relief.

HURRICANES A little rhyme that every Grenadian learns goes something like this, 'June, too soon/July, stand by/August, a must/September, remember/October, all over!' (As the attacks by Hurricanes Janet and Ivan in September and storm surge from Lenny in November indicate, the rhyme might be a bit off.) During the rainy season the Caribbean is prone to tropical storms called hurricanes (<Am.Sp. *huracán*; <Is.Car. for the god of the same name). These violent cyclones with sustained winds of 100 mph (164 kph) or higher, are accompanied by torrential downpours and severe thunderstorms. Grenada, though situated 'outside' the hurricane zone or belt, has been visited on quite a few occasions by severe storms (1731, 1768, 1817, 1831, 1832, 1877, 1921, 1963 and 1979) and by at least four hurricanes, the 'Great Hurricane' of October 1780 (three separate storms which attacked the southern Caribbean), HURRICANE JANET, HURRICANE LENNY, HURRICANE IVAN and Hurricane Emily. Both Hurricanes Janet and Ivan rank in the ten most intense Atlantic hurricanes ever (tenth and ninth out of ten respectively). Grenada's export crops are prone to damage from occasional storms and devastation at the hands of severe hurricanes. Any adverse weather can have a detrimental effect on the islands' agricultural and TOURISM economy, as is the case throughout the region.[244, 245, 333, 368]

HUTCHINSON, Leslie Arthur Julien 'Hutch' (1900-1969) was a popular pianist and cabaret singer, and million-selling record artist who was at the peak of a long career in the 1930s and 1940s. He was the first child of George and Marianne Hutchinson of GOUYAVE, St. John. At eight years he began taking piano lessons and later substituted for his father, playing the piano at Sunday mass at the ST. JOHN'S ANGLICAN CHURCH. After leaving the GBSS in 1915, he briefly worked as a government clerk.

In 1916, along with his brother Leon, he left Grenada to continue his studies at Meharry Medical College, leading to a degree in medicine. Hutch abandoned his studies after only six months and ended up in Harlem where he began his musical career, 'and gradually he developed his own style-a skilful mix of technique, tact and velvet-voiced charm.' In 1924 Hutch moved to Paris and it was there that his club act took off. In 1927 he moved to London and made a big name for himself in revue, variety and radio in the carefree London of the 1930s.

At the height of his career he made a secret trip to Grenada in 1937, avoiding all attempts to celebrate the success of a local who had made it big. Grenadians followed Hutch's career, with T A MARRYSHOW seeing him perform in London and writing about him in the WEST INDIAN newspaper. A favourite of the British royal family, he is often linked with Lady Mountbatten, as many suspected that they had a love affair, one of many that established Hutch as a lady's man and philanderer. He is probably Grenada's most celebrated musician, though unknown to most Grenadians.[26]

ÎLES DU VENT Following the dissolution of the bankrupt French WEST INDIA COMPANY in 1674, the islands of the French Antilles came under the control of the French Crown. The islands inherited French social, economical and political institutions. Administration was by the governor general in Martinique, represented in Grenada by a military governor whose duties were to enforce commercial trade restrictions and develop French overseas trade. Much like a CROWN COLONY, Grenada was administered by a governor, whose authority was tempered by an administrator responsible for the judicial and financial regulation of the colony. Grenada experienced marginal economic development due predominantly to restrictions on trade, especially with the Dutch, continued Island CARIB attacks from St. Vincent and Dominica, and colonial conflicts.

All of this occurred despite Jean-Baptiste Colbert's (French minister of finance, 1661-1683) desire to develop Grenada as a trading centre with the Spanish. J-B LABAT, commenting on his brief visit in September 1700, stressed that 'The English are much better at putting any advantages they have to the best of use, and if Grenada belonged to them it would long ago have changed in appearance and have become a rich and powerful colony. Instead of which we have not put to use a single advantage, as we could have done and for so many years now the country has been unexploited, sparsely inhabited, lacking amenities as well as trade, remaining poor... in a word, the island is much the same as it was when DU PARQUET bought it from the savages.' Between 1667 and 1696 various officials proposed that Grenada be given to the British in exchange for the French gaining complete control of St. Christopher, yet it remained French. The extension of the fortifications between 1705 and 1710 was to establish Grenada as the entrepot for the Compagnie de l'Asiento to supply slaves to the Spanish and may have had a positive effect on the islands' subsequent development.

Between 1674 and 1714 the increase in population was moderate (from about 500 to 2,000), a sure sign that the islands were in a state of economic malaise. Following the restructuring of the government of the French Caribbean colonies in 1714, Grenada experienced greater economic and social development through trade with the Dutch in Tobago, the French in Martinique and the Spanish Main. The intensification of AGRICULTURE and the increase in slave labour resulted in dramatic changes by the mid-1700s, especially with the era of peace in the region between 1714 and 1744. INDIGO production had grown steadily and by 1722, when it achieved its climax, there were 159 estates. SUGAR CANE production, beginning in the 1660s, witnessed gradual growth, with 15 estates by 1722, growing to over eighty by the 1750s. Other crops like COCOA and COFFEE assumed importance in the growing and diversified economy. By 1753 the island had developed an extensive agricultural base, and had established a thriving plantation economy based on SLAVERY, leading one commentator to conclude that 'Grenada became a mature plantation society more rapidly than any other French colony'. The Îles du Vent were captured by the British during the Seven Years War (1756-1763), and the 1763 Treaty of Paris granted Grenada to the British.[35, 89, 91, 221, 333]

12 sol coin used in the Îles du Vent in the 18th century

INDENTURED IMMIGRATION Like many of the other islands in the region at the end of SLAVERY, Grenada initiated indentured immigration schemes following the success of similar schemes in TRINIDAD and Guyana. The refusal of many of the former slaves to work for wages on sugar estates created a panic among planters who blamed the reluctant labour force for the continued depression in the SUGAR industry. There was debate on the schemes' moral position, with some characterising them as 'slavery under a new guise'. Yet, between 1839 and 1893, some 5,500 indentured labourers entered Grenada from West Africa, India, Malta and Madeira. In 1839 Grenada received the first of many groups of indentured immigrants, 164 Maltese who were distributed to sugar estates along the east coast. It was also hoped that the Maltese 'would have a civilizing effect on the ex-slaves' and increase the small white population. In 1841, however, estate proprietors dissolved their contracts because they had proved a total failure. The majority emigrated to Trinidad, with the few remaining in Grenada finding employment as porters and petty traders.

Between 1846 and 1847, 601 migrants from Madeira arrived, and they too proved unsuccessful at agricultural work and soon abandoned their assigned estates for more desirable employment. Many subsequently migrated to Trinidad, but a small number remained, their descendants identifiable by Portuguese names like Franco, De Souza and Da Silva. Following these failures and the previous success of the LIBERATED AFRICANS, a scheme for the importation of Africans was initiated. Between 1849 and 1865, 1,542 Africans arrived as indentured labourers. They initially proved successful, but the majority did not re-indenture, becoming 'squatters or independent settlers'. Repatriation was sporadic, resulting in the permanent settlement of most of the African immigrants in Grenada and Trinidad. Some established exclusive African settlements in villages like MUNICH, Concord and LaMode.

The last of the indentured immigrants arrived between 1857 and 1893, mainly from Calcutta and Madras, India. The 3,205 EAST INDIANS worked on sugar and COCOA estates, predominantly in St. Andrew, St. John and St. Patrick. Though some re-indentured following their first period, others abandoned the estates at the earliest possible moment, many to farm on their own or work for wages. Of the Indians who came only 380 returned to India. At the celebration of the one hundredth anniversary of their arrival a small number of East Indian-born immigrants were on hand for the celebrations. Of the indentured labourers only a few were sent to C&PM. The small number of indentured immigrants brought to Grenada proved unable to stop the decline in the local sugar industry even though some estates may have benefited. The descendants of many of the indentured labourers are still distinguishable either by names, and/or physical characteristics.[35, 55, 211, 329, 333]

INDENTURED SERVANTS or *engagés* (<Fr. *engagér*: 'to hire') began arriving in Grenada in the 1650s. In 1656 J-B DU TERTRE recorded 'twenty or twenty-five men engaged for three years' and belonging to DU PARQUET. They left behind poverty in France for the dream of economic success in the Antilles. Though the majority were voluntarily indentured, others were kidnapped, especially children or the unsuspecting. They were under contract, saleable from one master to another, for three years. The majority were men whose lives were often difficult, sometimes harsh, and some died before the end of their contracts. It was often reported that they were treated 'worse than slaves'. Those who survived indenture became freeholders, farming small plots of land. In 1669 there were 55 *engagés* in Grenada, and for the balance of French occupation their annual total remained below seventy. In 1755 there were 19, among the last to serve in the islands. The 1762 British capture of Grenada ended the practice. The total number brought to Grenada probably amounted to a few hundred, possibly 1,000 for the entire French period.[221]

INDEPENDENCE On 7 February 1974 GRENADA became a sovereign nation, ending over 200 years of British colonial rule. It was, for some years thereafter, the smallest independent nation in the Western Hemisphere and the first of the six members of the Associated States to gain independence. Yet, independence was not easily achieved. Premier GAIRY had expressed interest in attaining independence since the late 1960s. According to the ASSOCIATED STATEHOOD Constitution, Grenada could either request independence or have it conferred by the British Parliament; Gairy desired the

First Day cover of postage stamps celebrating Grenadian Independence

latter. In 1970 the British government agreed to consider the issue if the GULP won an ELECTION where independence was the primary issue. The 1972 GULP manifesto included a reference to independence, and when it was overwhelmingly elected accepted that as a mandate from the people to go ahead with independence talks. In October 1972 preliminary talks began in London where it was agreed that a Constitutional Conference would be held in May 1973.

Though initially supportive of independence, Opposition Leader Blaize later mounted opposition to it. To show that the GULP did not have a mandate, the GRENADA NATIONAL PARTY gathered signatures, which it claimed represented 46 per cent of the electorate. Gairy dismissed the calls for a referendum and the signatures, insisting that he had already had a mandate. As the Constitutional Conference was debated in London political opposition mounted at home, culminating in BLOODY SUNDAY and BLOODY MONDAY. A number of opposition groups including the NEW JEWEL MOVEMENT, GNP, labour unions and churches protested against the independence talks on the grounds that Gairy's past abuses of power and political corruption made him unfit to be the leader of an independent Grenada.

In the end the British government, desiring to rid itself of an economic and political burden, decided in December 1973 to confer independence despite the civil unrest in Grenada. Under a state of emergency, Grenada bade a muted farewell to British rule, with only the incoming Governor General De Gale representing the UK (see BRITISH HERITAGE). At independence in 1974 PM Gairy declared that 'We are completely free, liberated, [and] independent. In spite of a wicked, malicious, obstructive, destructive minority of noise-making self-publicists, God has heard our prayers. God has been merciful. God has triumphed'. Independence Day is celebrated as a public holiday. Sir Eric is hailed as the 'Father of the Nation' for his unwavering efforts to attain Grenadian independence.[35, 71, 201]

INDIGO (*Indigofero tinctoria*) is a native plant of India, and through an intricate process yields a blue water-soluble dye used in the dyeing of cotton fabric. After three months in the field, leaf cuttings are taken and packed into large water-filled vats or *tempoires* to steep. It was the first estate crop grown on a large scale, beginning as early as the 1650s. In 1687 there were 21 indigo estates, increasing to 159 by 1722. As the cultivation of SUGAR CANE and COFFEE increased, indigo cultivation decreased, and

Indigo plantation and works

by 1742 no estate was exclusively producing it. Yet it was the cultivation of indigo, like tobacco in Barbados, which laid the foundation for estate AGRICULTURE and large-scale SUGAR production in Grenada. Production continued under the British, but after 1808 decreased and disappeared altogether. According to Bryan Edwards, the decline in the production of indigo by the late 1700s was due largely to the death of slaves from 'vapours, ravages of the worm and the burdens of the duties imposed by the government'. A very small quantity was produced in CARRIACOU.[221]

INTERVENTION On the morning of 25 October 1983 hundreds of US troops began military operations in Grenada, with the objectives of securing foreign nationals (including US students attending ST. GEORGE'S UNIVERSITY), returning the island to democracy, and eliminating all Cuban involvement on the islands. The events of BLOODY WEDNESDAY led the members of the OECS to intervene. Article Eight of the 1981 OECS Treaty, to which the PEOPLE'S REVOLUTIONARY GOVERNMENT was a signatory, provided for member countries to come to the defence of each other in the event of external aggression. Though the charter provided no legal grounds for the intervention into the internal affairs of its members, OECS signatories nonetheless used this pretext to intervene militarily. Lacking the resources, they, together with Barbados and Jamaica, requested military assistance from the US government. Constitutional legitimacy was provided by a letter (later rumoured to have been backdated) from Governor General SCOON, requesting that the US and OECS intervene militarily.

A number of Caribbean countries, including Trinidad, Guyana and the Bahamas, opposed the military action. 'Urgent Fury', though hastily planned, was billed as a 'surgical precision' operation aimed at wresting the island from the grasp of 'communist thugs'. Caribbean supporters formed the Caribbean Peacekeeping Force (CPF), numbering 400-450 paramilitary and policemen as part of the Caribbean Multinational Force of which the US was by far the largest participant.

The major operations were staged at the site of the new runway at Point Salines, PEARLS AIRPORT, GOVERNMENT HOUSE to rescue the governor general, and the RICHMOND HILL PRISONS. On the first day US forces engaged Cubans and Grenadians, especially at the airstrip at Point Salines, capturing it as well as Grand Mal, St. George, and Pearls, St. Andrew. US forces had suffered humiliating setbacks at the prison and BEAUSÉJOUR, and had failed to rescue the GOVERNOR GENERAL. By 31 October US forces had secured Grenada; C&PM were secured on 2 November without any fighting. Most US forces were quickly replaced by the CPF, which was given the task of restoring and securing order. Of the Cubans who participated in the fighting 24 were killed and 59 wounded; 634 were taken prisoner and later repatriated. Though disagreement surrounded the exact number of US casualties, 19 were reported as having lost their lives in the taking of Grenada (monuments to them are located on the SGU campus and PSIA) and 152 were reported wounded. Some of the soldiers died as a result of friendly fire and accidents.

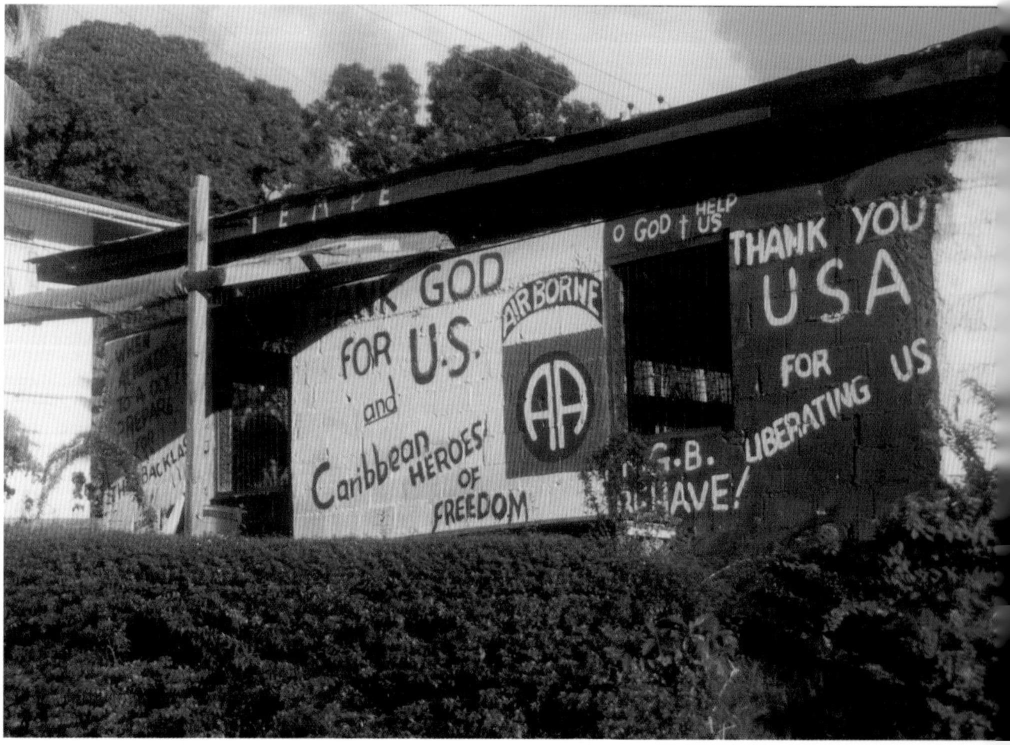

Pro-intervention grafitti

Over 30,000 medals were awarded to soldiers who participated directly or indirectly in the ten-day operations that cost the US government US$75.5m. Another US$1.5m was paid to Grenadian claimants for damages resulting from the military action. It was not clear how many Grenadians were involved in the fighting, but it is believed that of the 3,200-7,500 soldiers and MILITIA, at least 700 participated. Forty-five died, 24 civilians and 21 soldiers (among the civilians were 16 mental patients who died when the Mental Hospital was mistakenly bombed by the US), and 350 civilians wounded.

Twenty-fifth October has since been celebrated as Thanksgiving Day, a public holiday. The invasion sparked a great deal of protest and debate around the world, resulting in a tremendous amount of commentary on the revolution, invasion, and the apparent attempt by the US military to control the media coverage during the invasion. Grenada became the first in a series of invasions by the US that culminated in the invasion of Iraq two decades later. A consequence of the US invasion, according to Gordon Lewis, was Grenada's final break with the UK, as illustrated by the different receptions given to US President Reagan and Queen Elizabeth II when they visited; the British government had condemned the US invasion as illegal. Other names by which this event is known are Operation Urgent Fury, Rescue Mission and US Invasion.[2, 35, 111, 146, 306, 333, 363]

ISAAC, Dr Julius (b. 1928) is a lawyer and former chief justice of the Federal Court of Canada, that country's second highest court. Born in Grenada, he attended the GBSS and in 1950 left to study in Canada. He earned a BA in Arts in 1955 from St. Michael's College and an LLB in 1958 from the University of Toronto. He was admitted to the Ontario Bar in 1960 and began practicing law. Between 1969 and 1970 he returned to Grenada and served as senior magistrate, and chaired a number of boards. Returning to Canada in 1970 due to the uncertain political climate in Grenada, Isaac subsequently joined the Federal Department of Justice. In 1989 he was appointed judge on the Supreme Court of Ontario, and in 1991 chief justice of the Federal Court of Canada. He became the first black to hold that position in the history of Canada. Controversy surrounded Isaac's tenure, overshadowing his contributions to that body. In September 1999 Isaac retired as chief justice. His 2003 report of the enquiry into the deaths of 27 Jamaicans by security forces in 2001 was very controversial. He was awarded the 1992 Commemorative Medal of Canada, an honorary doctor of civil law from the University of Windsor, the Silver Jubilee Award of Grenada and the Order of Canada, that country's highest honour for lifetime achievement.

ISLAND IN THE SUN A 1957 Twentieth Century Fox film, based on the book of the same name by Alec Waugh, who had made two visits to Grenada, and filmed in Grenada (and Barbados) between October and November 1956. It starred James Mason, Dorothy Dandridge, Harry Belafonte, and Joan Fontaine. The film's theme centred on racial tensions, illustrating historical prejudices in the Caribbean. Many scenes such as CARNIVAL had to be staged for the production. The cast of the film was housed at the Santa Maria Hotel, the islands' only 'luxury' hotel. When the film opened in the US it created controversy because it broke long-held American racial taboos. Dandridge became the first black woman to be held in the arms of a white man on the American screen, and the relationship between Joan Fontain's character, a white woman, and Belafonte's, a 'coloured man', had romantic undertones. The exposure may have helped Grenada by displaying its natural and cultural beauty and subsequently giving birth to the TOURISM industry.

ISLAND QUEEN On 5 August 1944 the schooner *Island Queen* left Grenada with 67 passengers and crew for St. Vincent 75 miles (121 km) to the north, but never reached its destination. Its disappearance has remained a mystery, since neither wreckage nor bodies were ever found. The *Providence Mark*, a schooner travelling to St. Vincent that left Grenada shortly after the *Island Queen*, reported nothing unusual during its nocturnal journey. The US Navy searched the area for two weeks without finding any evidence as to the ship's disappearance, and on 29 August officially declared it lost. Many speculations abounded, including the ridiculous, yet popular theory that Adolf Hitler, aboard a German submarine, intercepted

Poster for *Island in the Sun*

it en route to exile and abducted the passengers as slaves. Another theory alleged that the Grenadian-built boat with its German engine was mistakenly identified by a British submarine as German, and that the submarine destroyed it and covered up the blunder.

The most plausible theory at the time, considering that World War II was in progress, supposed that the schooner was sunk by a German U-boat, but the one such vessel operating in the region never claimed its destruction. The official inquiry concluded that the *Island Queen* had caught fire and burned. Considering that mines were laid throughout the region, it was plausible that it struck a drifting mine and was destroyed. The fate of the *Island Queen*, its passengers and crew, remain to this day a mystery. The *Island Queen* was locally designed and built by George Ogilvie and owned by Chykra Salhab, a Lebanese resident in Grenada for many years.[332, 333]

ISLAND SCHOLARSHIP From 1916 the Grenada Scholarship, an annual endowment, was awarded to exceptional students to study at any institution of higher learning in the British Empire. The individuals were chosen from the successful candidates of the London Matriculation (the High School Certificate after 1946, and the GCE Advanced level after 1964). In 1924 it was suspended but resumed in 1926 on a biennial basis. The Island Scholar came to represent excellence in academic achievement and the scheme enabled many underprivileged individuals to pursue higher education. The majority of the award winners went to the UK to study a number of professions, among them AGRICULTURE, engineering, medicine and law, the latter two by far the most popular because of their historical prestige. The scholarship either created or enlarged prominent medical and legal families, some of whom still practise these professions today. Of the scholarship winners, many returned to practice, entering the colonial civil service and working throughout the BWI; others remained abroad. Louise ROWLEY, though achieving great results in 1929, was not awarded a scholarship because it was only awarded to men. It was not until the 1950s that it was open to women, and not until 1974 that a woman, Celia Clyne-Edwards of the ANGLICAN HIGH SCHOOL, won the coveted award. The scholarship, presently sponsored by the GOG, is awarded annually to the individual who attains the best passes in the GCE 'A' Level. Scholarship winners included Dr Leonard Comissiong, Sir Archibald Nedd, Lord David Pitt, Sir Sydney Gun-Munro, former govenor general of St.Vincent and Akima Paul, calypso monarch.

J

JAB-JAB Groups of men and women, blackened and shining in the pre-dawn light, rush through the streets beating drums and bottles singing an old FRENCH CREOLE song: 'Ou lay ou lambé, jab-jab. Ou lay ou la, jab-jab. Gi' jab a coppa. To pay a passage. To go back to hell. Ou lay ou lambé.Ou lay ou la.' The streets clear to allow them easy passage for no one wishes to be daubed black The glistening black of their skin contrasts with the red of their mouths, with blood-like liquid oozing from their lips. Their grotesque appearance is further exaggerated by the chamber pots on their heads and bulls' horns protruding, clanging claws, Dracula-type fangs, tail and pitch fork, bringing the apparition of the devil to life. 'Cow chains', SNAKES, FROGS and serpents adorn their bodies, creating an atmosphere that can be utterly frightening and repulsive to the uninitiated.

Exactly where the masquerade originated is not clear, but its present characteristics combine West African and European influences. The word jab-jab is a reiteration of the French *diable*:'devil'. The traditional jab-jab comprised small groups, unlike the large bands that roam the streets today. Long ago, the jab-jab mas' was accompanied by imps, usually small boys, who either held the chain that restrained the group, or pounded on bottles and cans and sang the jab-jab song. The imps were the servants and messengers of hell. The objective of the jab-jab has remained the same: to create fear, and early bands accosted spectators to exact a payment so they could 'return to hell'; in 1911 'they had to be stopped [because] they got into the habit of running amuck and spoiling spectators' clothes'. The traditional attire of crocus or sugar bags has given way to short pants or only underwear, the latter barely noticeable because it is smeared in black. An older form of jab jab, jab mollasie (daubed in 'red mud' or molasses), can still be seen.

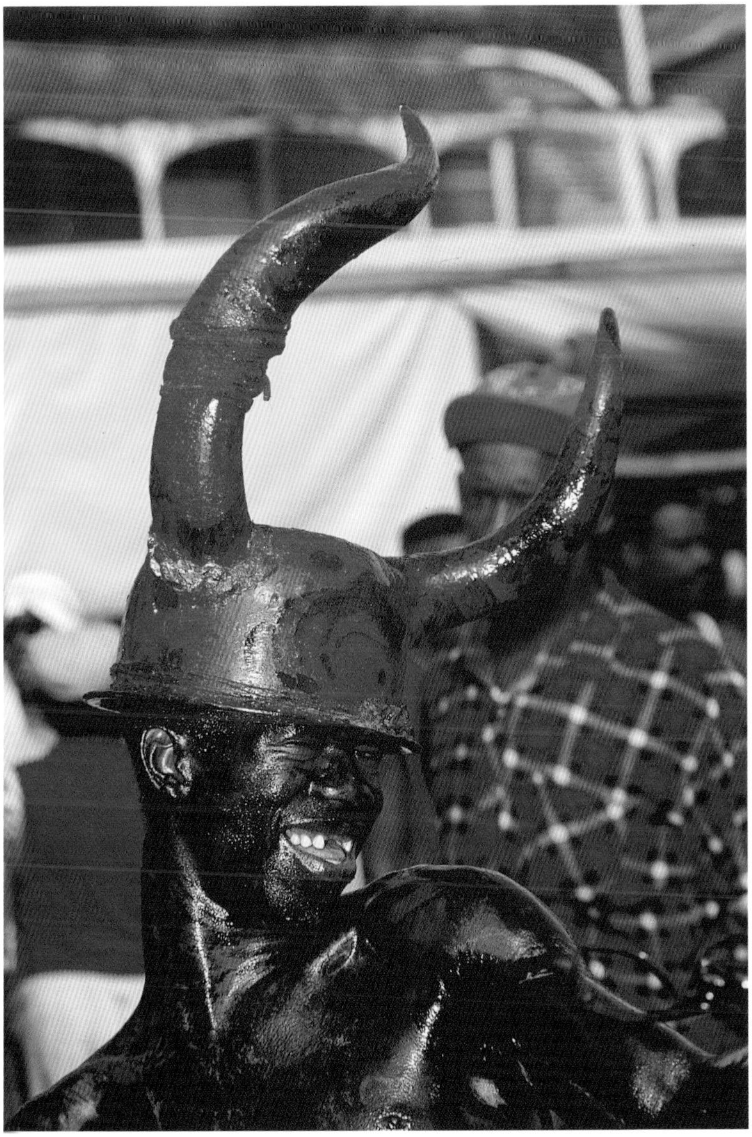

Jab-Jab masquerade

Over the years there have been calls to reign in or altogether ban jab-jab because of the aggressive behaviour and defacement of property caused by some individuals and groups. Previous attempts to ban jab-jab have failed, and it would be sad if the misbehaviour of some of the revellers leads to the end of this most exciting and historical masquerade of JOUVAY whose absence could render the festivities boring and predictable. In TRINIDAD the 'jab-jab' is a clown/court jester while the 'jab molassie' is the 'devil mas'.

JACKS/JACKFISH The name for several finfishes, especially various carangids like the bigeye scad (*Sela crumenophthalus*) that are very popular and eaten in a variety of local dishes because of their 'good flavour and firm white flesh'. These silvery-grey fish are caught primarily by nets (seine) cast within a few hundred yards of the shore and hauled by fishermen on the western coast of Grenada and in the Grenadines, especially the fishing villages of GOUYAVE and VICTORIA. The fish range in size from 3-12 inches (8-30 cm), with the smaller ones fried, and the larger ones stuffed and baked. Jacks broth is a popular dish, claimed by some to be an APHRODISIAC because of the belief in the virility-inducing properties of the fish-head and as 'waters for the waist'. Its name is always plural. Its popularity has even led to a place name, Jacks Alley in St. George's, where the old fish market was on the CARENAGE.

JONES, Ben Joseph (1924-2005) was a lawyer and prominent Grenadian politician who served as deputy PM (1984-89) and PM (December 1989-March 1990). Together with many Grenadians, he spent nine years working in ARUBA before migrating to the UK to study law. In 1962 he was called to the British Bar. He first contested ELECTIONS in 1967 as a candidate for the GNP, but was not successful until 1984 when he was elected as a member of the NNP. Previously he had served as a magistrate and GNP Senator (1972-79). In the Blaize cabinet he served in a number of ministries and as attorney general. A long-time friend of Blaize, Jones was one of the few NNP members to remain loyal to him, and following PM Blaize's death in 1989 Jones became PM and leader of the newly formed TNP. In general elections in 1990 The National Party won only two seats, which were pivotal in the formation of the next government since no party had won a majority. Jones eventually formed a 'coalition' with the NDC and became Minister of Agriculture. In January 1991 he resigned from the BRATHWAITE government, taking his seat as a member of the opposition. In the 1995 general elections Jones was unsuccessful in his bid to win a seat in PARLIAMENT, leaving politics and returning to his law practice; he subsequently retired due to ill health. In 1994 Albert Street, GRENVILLE was renamed in his honour.

JOOK is derived from the Fulani *jukka*: 'to poke', and/ or Hausa *duka*: 'to have intercourse with a woman', its many meanings a combination of the two. It is prefixed to many words: jooking or scrubbing board, a thick slab of wood with one side corrugated and used in laundering or 'scrubbing clothes' (to emphasise the addition of stimulus or power of stimulation), jook up (to poke or prick as in 'he jook up the thing'), jook down (to pick fruits as in 'jook down the mango'), jook out (to poke as in 'you want to jook out me eye'). A doctor can 'jook you' with a needle or administer an injection, 'a pika (<Fr. *piquant*: 'sharp') can jook you,' someone can 'jook you' with a knife or stick, and a man can 'jook a woman,' implying rough sex. The PROVERB 'remember, if you climb pika tree, pika go jook you' is a warning to those who may not be aware of the consequences of their actions.

JOUVAY (J'ouvert) is a French Creole phrase derived from the French *le jour est ouvert*: 'the beginning of the day'. It is the first part of the two-day street celebrations of CARNIVAL. Many years ago the blast of a cannon from FORT GEORGE signalled the beginning of jouvay, but now people usually begin to gather around the MARKET SQUARE around 3:00 A.M., many coming straight from the Dimanche Gras show. At around 5:00 A.M. the streets begin to fill with spectators and 'ol' mas' bands that will perform through the streets, dressed in an assortment of home-made costumes. Ridiculously dressed and often satirical, these characters refer to social, political and international incidents that occurred during the past year. Masquerades are usually caricatures of politicians and political scandal, social gossip, and humorous sexual innuendoes disguised in outlandish dress, or suggestive statements attached to the masquerade. Two popular traditional mas' were the 'long-mouth' or 'dog mas', which wore unsightly faces of animals moulded from paper or mud, and the 'pissenlit' (piss-in-the-bed), which dressed in sleeping attire and imitated the once common scene of the nocturnal emptying of the chamber pot in the gutter or sea before the installation of the sewer system. Long ago, the ol' mas' of jouvay lasted the entire Monday, with Tuesday reserved for 'pretty' or 'fancy' mas'.

Jouvay abounds with wit and humour as the participants shuffle through the streets to the rhythm of the STEELBANDS and DJ sets playing the latest CALYPSOS. The single most spectacular event of the celebrations is JAB-JAB. Jouvay is 'jump up' for everyone since there is no prerequisite of a costume to share in the festivities. By 8:00 A.M. the crowds begin to dwindle as people depart to prepare for the afternoon celebrations, when the pretty mas' take to the streets.

JUDICIAL SYSTEM Grenada, because of its colonial legacy, has inherited the British legal system, complete with black robes, white wigs and the British Privy Council; these vestiges of the islands' BRITISH HERITAGE are constantly being debated. Though there are vestiges of French inheritance laws, the legal system is based on British common and statute laws. After 1763 the British colonial government established the Court of King's Bench and the Grand Sessions of the Peace which dealt with criminal jurisdiction; the two were combined in 1800 to form the Supreme Court of Judicature. The Court of Common Pleas (est. 1791) dealt with civil jurisdiction. The judiciary, up until the 1820s, administered justice for and by the white minority. It kept FREE COLOUREDS and free blacks in check since their access to the courts was minimal. Though various laws applied specifically to slaves, they were, for much of the period of SLAVERY, at the mercy of their owners and overseers. Slaves were not allowed to give evidence in court until 1828, the same year that freeborn coloureds/blacks were allowed to sit on juries, subject of course to property qualifications. In 1832 all free blacks and coloureds were granted the right to sit on juries. It was not until 1937 that women were allowed to sit on juries.

In 1859, following the establishment of the Government of the WINDWARD ISLANDS, a joint Appeals Court was instituted for its members, and in 1919 the West Indies Court of Appeal was set up for the BWI. In 1940 the Grenada Supreme Court was dissolved following the creation of the Supreme Court of the Windward and Leeward Islands, and in 1967 the West Indies Associated States Supreme Court was constituted. The present judicial system of Grenada, like that of the OECS members, is under the OECS Supreme Court, comprising the High Court of Justice and the Court of Appeals, an itinerant court that sits in each member state. The PEOPLE'S REVOLUTIONARY GOVERNMENT established the GRENADA SUPREME COURT in 1979 following its withdrawal from the OECS Supreme Court. Grenada was not readmitted until the end of the trial of the GRENADA 17 in 1991. Each of the seven districts in Grenada has a Magistrate Court, with two in St. George's, which preside over summary jurisdiction. The INDEPENDENCE Constitution grants a final appeal to the Privy Council, which can issue a pardon or commute a sentence, but its continuance is constantly debated. In 2005 the Caribbean Court of Justice was inagurated and will take over the role of the Privy Council when it becomes fully functional. Grenada's prime ministers are members of the Privy Council.[4, 35, 179, 353]

JUMBIE The spirit or ghost of a deceased person believed capable of influencing the living. Its origin is West African, common among a number of tribes with its meaning of 'God' (Kikongo *nsambi*) or 'Devil' (Kota *ndsumbi*). It is commonly believed by the folk that the spirit of the dead, in human form but nonetheless invisible to most people, will 'roam around,' especially within the first forty days after death, hence the old ceremony of a 'forty-day' to pray for the soul of the deceased. Like the Haitian zombie, the spirit can be found roaming around at night and is responsible for many people being afraid to pass near cemeteries, or 'battening down' their houses at night to make sure jumbies do not 'blow on them' and make them ill. People often 'see' or 'hear' the jumbie of deceased relatives and friends. Since the motive of the jumbie is not readily evident, a number of SUPERSTITIONS surround the blocking of their spirits from entry into one's home, especially after dark, although jumbies can roam during the day. There are good jumbies that bring good luck, and bad jumbies that bring bad luck. It was once customary to give children 'jumbie names' or 'home names' after dead relatives. A common African practice, they supposedly provided protection to children since they are especially vulnerable to evil. The term jumbie has been applied to a number of feared or unpleasant objects, including the jumbie bird or corbeau, JUMBIE BEAD, JUMBIE UMBRELLA, MOKO JUMBIE and jumbie or SILK COTTON tree. It is known as duppy in many other countries in the region.

JUMBIE BEAD/CRAB EYE is the red and black seed of the crab eye plant (*Abrus precatorius*), a woody vine found throughout Grenada. The colourful glossy seed—red with a black spot—contains the chemical abrin, considered one of the most toxic plant extracts. Though the seeds are poisonous, the leaves are boiled and drunk as

Jumbie beads

a tea for the relief of the common cold and flu. The seeds are used to decorate local crafts and jewellery. The roots are prescribed by FOLK MEDICINE for the treatment of nervous conditions. Its name, jumbie bead, is derived from its use as a talisman to protect against evil spirits or JUMBIES and MALJOE (when a child is born a string of these beads was placed on its wrist to ward off evil spirits). In 1922 a visitor observed 'Many of the children wore strings of glass beads, castor-oil beans, or scarlet Jumby seeds round the neck to protect them from fevers and all manner of ills.' Others claim that if the beads are kept in the home the seeds can bring misfortune. Jumbie or Jumby bead is also known locally as gwenn-lé-gliz (<Fr.Cr. *graine*: 'grain', *l'eglise*: 'church', i.e. pray beads). The larger red glossy seed of the red-eye tree or the red sandalwood tree (*Adenanthera pavonina*) is also called jumbie bead. It is used to decorate crafts and beadwork, but when crushed is used to treat boils. Both plants are legumes.

JUMBIE UMBRELLA The local term for mushrooms in general, but may have originally applied to a specific type of fungus. The term JUMBIE is of West African origin and its application in this instance may be directly related to African folk beliefs. There may also be some European influences springing from the superstitious belief that rings of mushrooms were left by dancing fairies during the night. The unusual growing habits of mushrooms that 'appear' overnight in a variety of formations, and their poisonous nature, have definitely not endeared them to superstitious folk. Wild mushrooms are not consumed in the islands.

JUNE 19 At the Heroes'/Butler-Strachan Day political rally at the QUEEN'S PARK on 19 June 1980, a bomb exploded beneath the platform on which sat PEOPLE'S REVOLUTIONARY GOVERNMENT members and dignitaries. If it was intended to harm the PRG leadership, the bomb's positioning was flawed, or the reinforced concrete platform deflected the blast. Though rumours and circumstantial evidence point an accusing finger at the PRG itself, no definitive evidence has ever been uncovered to link it with the planting of the bomb. The bomb blast took the lives of three young women and injured about 100 people, 22 seriously. The PRG charged that the bombing was the work of 'imperialism and its local agents'. It accused former associates and initiated an immediate search for the suspects.

Within hours of the bombing Strachan Phillip, a Sandhurst Military Academy-trained officer and former sergeant in the PEOPLE'S REVOLUTIONARY ARMY, was killed in an exchange of gunfire with PRA personnel. Some of the suspects eluded capture for weeks, but by early July at least five people were arrested and charged with the bombing. Among them were the Budhlall brothers (formerly associated with the NEW JEWEL MOVEMENT and PRA), Grace Augustine (who supposedly planted the bomb), and Layne Phillip. In October 1982 the trial began and after two weeks, four defendants—Russel and Kenneth Budhlall, Augustine and Phillip—were sentenced to death for the murder of the three young women. As a result of the bombing, the PRG issued PEOPLE'S LAW No. 46, which made it easier to convict people accused of terrorist acts. Following the October 1983 US INTERVENTION, the convicts were released from prison and pardoned.[101]

Jumbie Umbrella/fungi

K

KAIROÜANE An AMERINDIAN leader on Camàhogne (see GRENADA (NAMES)) when the French made their appearance in March 1649. Though referred to as the 'captain of all the Careibes on the island', he was in fact a Galibis (Cariban speaker from South America), one of many on the island. As the 'chief', Kairoüane 'welcomed' DU PARQUET and the colonists to 'trade', allowing them to 'settle' on the land they had cleared. The French, in an attempt to procure a peaceful settlement, presented the Amerindians with an assortment of 'gifts'—cloth, axes, knives, glass beads, mirrors and two bottles of brandy. Kairoüane personally received 'a beautiful red coat strewn with silver, and a grey hat trimmed with a bunch of white and red feathers.' These exchanges have been erroneously accepted by many as a transfer of ownership of the island which it most definitely was not since the Amerindians brought food to trade for these goods. It appears that Kairoüane lost his authority once the Island CARIBS, including those on St. Vincent, realised that the French had no intentions of leaving, blaming him for allowing the French to settle. Fearing reprisals, he went into hiding and is not mentioned further in the historical account.[8, 95, 155]

KALENDA/STICK-FIGHTING was once a common sport at celebrations such as wakes and CARNIVAL. It is a martial art with origins in West Africa where it was a popular contest in many ethnic communities and part of festivals like the *Agemo* among the YORUBA. BELL claims that 'calenda' was a favourite dance, 'supposed to have been introduced from Arda, a country on the coast of Guinea.' Contestants or stickmen (<Fr.Cr. batonniers <Fr. *bâtonner*: 'to beat with a stick') normally belonged to groups or localities, with contests involving a high degree of rivalry.

Kalenda/stick-fighting dance, La Floretta, Grenada, 1962

Each contestant has a stick just over 3 ft (1 m) long, and squares off against another, usually paired according to skill. Battles can be very dangerous depending on the skill of the players. The movements are sometimes stylised and calculated. The end of the contest is brought about when one of the players is knocked to the ground or draws blood. Contestants have been known to die, as was the case in February 1900 when stickman Hankey was 'killed by a blow received by playing at "sticks" during carnival.' The fight is traditionally accompanied by praise singing and drumming.

The sport disappeared from Grenada sometime in the 1960s but is still practised in Carriacou, especially by the PAYWO during CARNIVAL. This event was banned on many occasions by the authorities because of its bloody nature, but the rivalry between villages and communities kept it alive. The battles of the Banroys and Heroes of Carriacou are legendary. The EAST INDIANS once practised a type of stick-fighting, their stick being a bit longer, and fighters danced to the beat of the Indian tabla drum. Kalenda (<Fr.Cr. calentura: 'fever, heat'), as Bell describes it, was also a FOLK DANCE with 'figures and postures [that] were very improper'. Don Hill sees the CALYPSO tent as the successor to the kalenda ring, as contestants square off against each other using their skill with words to defeat opponents.[331]

KATA/CATA A carrying pad for the head, traditionally made of dry BANANA leaves or a small piece of cloth or rag. It fits on the top of the head for protection and to comfortably balance heavy loads. The kata (<Congo *nkata*: 'a pad for the shoulder or head'; Twi ŋ*kata*: 'a covering') is usually worn by women to transport agricultural produce or heavy loads. The practice of carrying loads on the head among Grenadians is an African tradition brought to the region during SLAVERY. Local SUPERSTITION believes that if the kata is placed under the seat of a suitor, his love will forever be yours and he may even fall so deeply in love that he becomes *bazodi* (<Fr. *abasourdir*: 'to daze, stun').

KICK-EM-JENNY 12 20N 61 35W is an active submarine volcano 5 miles (8 km) north of Grenada on the western edge of the Grenada Bank, and 3.1 miles (5 km) west of RONDE ISLAND. It should not be confused with Diamond Rock, which is also known as Kick-em-

Jenny. Kick-em-Jenny (?<Fr.Cr. *Quai Que Gêne*: 'quay of difficulty' which describes the rough seas that boats normally experience in the vicinity) is the only active sub-marine volcanoe in the Lesser Antillean arc. Hydro-thermal turbulence is frequently experienced, but in January 1939, its first eruption, it sent a 'black column of volcanic ash and steam' 886 ft (270 m) 'out of the boiling sea.' Since then it has produced at least twelve mild eruptions, the last one in December 2001, with intense yet mild earthquake activity for a six-hour period.

In 2003 the volcano's dome was estimated to be 591-623 ft (180-190 m) below the sea's surface, and contrary to earlier reports, has not grown since 1966. Its believed rate of growth had caused fears that it could soon break the surface and possibly produce tidal waves which might have devastating effects in the southern Caribbean, but recent observations have displaced those fears far into the future. A monitoring system, with stations on Mt. St. Catherine in Grenada and Three Sisters in the Grenadines, collects data on the volcano's activity and is administered by the Seismic Research Unit of the UWI. Ships are banned from a 1 mile (1.6 km) radius in the event of an unexpected eruption. In carrying out a study of Kick-em-Jenny in 2003 scientists discovered an inactive volcano only three kilometres away from it, dubbing it Kick-em-Jack.[315, 326, 355]

KITCHEN GARDENS/PROVISION GROUNDS constitute a primary component of subsistence agriculture in Grenada, C&PM. Both are responsible for a substantial portion of the local diet. The major differences between the two are size/location, and diversity of plants/animals.

Kitchen gardens are located around the house (hence backyard or dooryard gardens), occupying a few boxes or pans to a few hundred square yards. Provision grounds, on the other hand, range in the thousands of square yards to several acres, and are usually located some distance from the residence. The plants in a kitchen garden typically include temperate vegetables—tomato, bean, lettuce, beet, carrot and cabbage; seasonings—chive, thyme, and peppers; tropical vegetables/crops—BANANA, CORN, PIGEON PEAS, calalu, okro, pumpkin, and cucumber; fruits—PAWPAW; and ground provisions—DASHEEN, TANIA, eddoe, YAM, and SWEET POTATO; animals are generally restricted to chickens or 'yard fowls', but goats, sheep or even a pig or two are not uncommon.

Provision grounds can include the things cultivated in the kitchen garden except the smaller vegetables, which require more attention and protection from stealing, but will also include larger plants like BREADFRUIT, cassava, and a variety of fruit trees—CASHEW, MANGO, ANNONA and GOLDEN APPLE, and citrus—LIMES, oranges and lemons. Tree crops like the COCONUT, AVOCADO, and cash crops like COCOA and NUTMEG can also be found in provision gardens, but rarely in kitchen gardens.

The size and diversity of plants are affected by region—rural or urban, or north, south, east and west, and physical characteristics like topography and CLIMATE. The

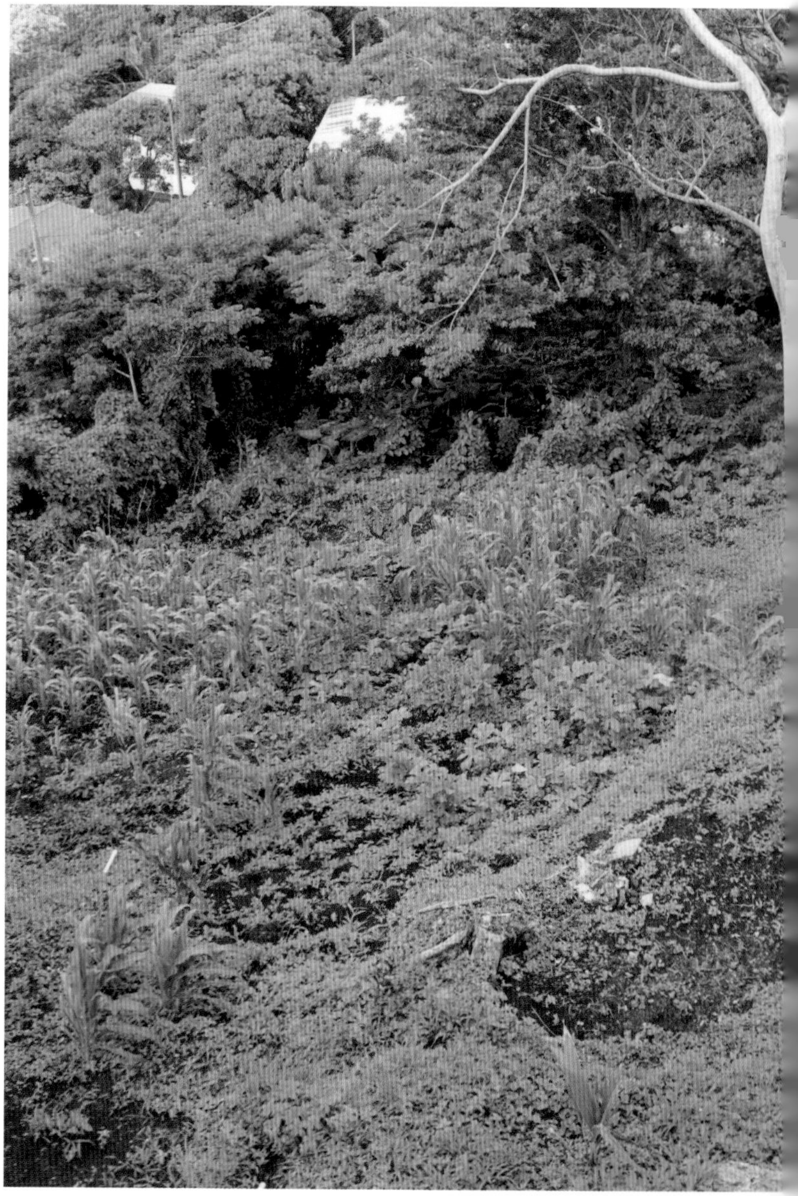

Kitchen garden

arrangement of plants is scattered and may appear jumbled, but nonetheless maximises the benefits of inter-cropping.

The history of kitchen gardens and provision grounds dates to plantation SLAVERY and the mandatory production of food by slaves. This had been guaranteed by legislation since the French, who gave the slaves scheduled time off to tend their garden plots. Personal food production was important to the slave who sold the excess at Sunday markets. By EMANCIPATION the practice had became entrenched in subsistence agriculture and survives today almost as it was practised in the nineteenth century. For the peasantry it contributed to its self-sufficiency. Yet as supermarkets and the Marketing Board provide more and more of these products and the social structure changes, self-sufficiency in vegetable production is declining.[27, 29, 220]

KITE FLYING Easter, because of the prevailing trade winds, is traditionally kite-flying season in the islands. Everywhere colourful kites are noticeable, bobbing through the sky as children run through the streets with long strings trailing behind the kites. Kites are made from a variety of materials and designs that give them their names—bamboo, flex (from COCONUT branches), diamond, moon, man and box kites. Good Friday and Easter Monday are the major kite-flying days when everyone with a kite climbs up hills, rocks, or to any high place so that his/her kite will get a lift from the breeze. Popular venues for kite flying include the ST. GEORGE'S CEMETERY and Fort Jeudy. To revive kite flying and promote TOURISM, the GOG and other organisations sponsor a kite-flying contest at Fort Jeudy, Westerhall, on Easter Monday.

KOLA/COLA NUT (*Cola nitida/acuminata*) was brought to the Caribbean by slaves from its native West Africa. Its continued importance is of a spiritual nature, with links to SHANGO and SPIRITUAL BAPTISTS' rituals. According to an 1889 report, 'great attention is paid to the kola nut an African fruit said to contain a large proportion of caffeine. The tree grows in all parts of the Island and was introduced by the African slave who used it as a specific against intoxication.' By the early 1900s it was exported. The slender tree grows to 70 ft (20 m) and produces a brown seed the size of a chestnut. The seeds of the kola nut contain alkaloids and have been used as a mild stimulant to allay hunger among West African peoples for centuries.

Its spiritual value is derived from the YORUBA, among others, who upon arrival in Grenada secretly continued its use in the practice of their religion. Among Shango and Spiritual Baptist adherents, it is used in divination rituals and offerings. The kola nut is quite bitter due to its tannin content, but is used as a folk remedy for heart problems and was once added to flavour 'local cocoa tea'. Because of its caffeine content the kola nut is used in medicines and was widely used in the manufacture of carbonated drinks, hence the well-known Coca-Cola.

LABAT, Jean-Baptiste (1663-1738) was a French Dominican missionary and plantation owner who lived on Guadeloupe between 1693 and 1706, and travelled throughout the Eastern Caribbean, visiting Grenada in September 1700 for one week. The memoir of his travels is chronicled in the *Voyages aux Isles de l'Amérique, 1693-1705.* It contains one of the first accounts of the French settlement on Grenada and has been extensively quoted since its publication. Labat presents a brief description of the struggling colony, including his views on the FORTS in Grenada, especially the defences of St. George's which he concluded were inadequate. He criticises the 51-year-old colony, characterising it as severely underdeveloped, and adds that had it been in the hands of the British it would have progressed more quickly (see ÎLES DU VENT). His memoir has two important MAPS, one of the settlement of La Ville du FORT ROYAL showing the original settlement of PORT LOUIS, and a plan of Fort Royal (see FORT GEORGE) with an outline of the original 1667 Fort Royal.[91, 197]

LE R.P.J.B. LABAT, JACOBIN
MORT A PARIS LE 6 JANVIER 1738
Ecrivain curieux des païs et des moeurs,
Il orne ses Ecrits des graces de son stile ;
Corrige en amusant, l'homme de ses erreurs,
Et sait mêler par tout, l'agréable et l'utile.
Jean-Baptiste Labat

LABOUR MOVEMENT By Caribbean standards, the Grenadian labour movement was slow to develop. The labour riots and protests throughout the Caribbean in the 1930s did not affect Grenada, though the rudiments of its trade union movement can be traced to the founding of the Grenada Workers' Union (GWU) in 1929 and the Grenada Workingman's Association (GWA) in 1930. Even further back, beginning in the late 1800s, a number of organisations like FRIENDLY SOCIETIES, the GRENADA UNION OF TEACHERS, and the Grenada Union of Returned Soldiers (f. 1919) characterised themselves as unions. But as Emmanuel observes, 'The year 1946 can be regarded as the year of the birth of trade unionism in Grenada because it was then that the first agreement on wages and conditions of work between employers and trade unions was made.' The unions of the 1940s and before have been criticised as weak because they sought a non-confrontational co-operative relationship with employers and failed to appeal to the mass of workers. They were, however, important building blocks leading to the emergence of the GMMIWU in 1950, which signalled a radical change. The 1950s also witnessed the establishment of no fewer than ten labour unions, among them the SEAMAN AND WATERFRONT WORKERS' UNION and the TECHNICAL AND ALLIED WORKERS' UNION, which attracted the growing urban labour force.

This trend continued in the 1960s and 1970s, despite the GULP government's concerted efforts to restrict the unions' growth and activities. The coming to power of the PEOPLE'S REVOLUTIONARY GOVERNMENT in 1979 ushered in a new era for trade unionism, as it attempted to align labour unions with the government and to gain the support of the labouring classes. Though the relationship was not always amicable, the PRG had succeeded in creating a more co-operative labour environment.

Post-PRG governments witnessed a return to the traditionally antagonistic government-labour relationship, especially under NEW NATIONAL PARTY governments. In 1983 the PRG established the National Insurance Scheme to provide retirement benefits for workers, and following layoffs due to HURRICANE

IVAN some workers were paid unemployment benefits. In 1999 the NNP government passed a Labour Code, stipulating basic wage rates and working conditions for all workers. There are presently about nine major unions on the islands, the most influential are SWWU, TAWU, GUT and the Grenada Public Workers' Union. Labour unions have a combined membership of 20-25 per cent (about 10,000) of the total labour force, and have had and continue to have a major role in the political process. The Grenada Trades Union Council (f. 1955) is the umbrella body for eight of the most important unions, with an appointed senator representing labour in PARLIAMENT. May Day or 1st May is celebrated annually in Grenada, as it is around the world, as Labour Day, with a parade and other celebrations recognising the role of workers.[35, 98, 171, 333, 344]

LAGOON, St. George's A body of water that the French called Étang d'Eau Salée: 'Salt Water Pond' (LABAT referred to it as Étang du Vieux Bourg: 'Pond of the Old Town'). It had once been separated from the CARENAGE by a sandbar on which was situated the first successful European SETTLEMENT founded by the French in 1649 and later called PORT LOUIS. The sandbar gradually sank as a result of geological activity and possible fluctuating sea levels. The idea of opening the Lagoon to regular shipping dates to 1656, when J-B DU TERTRE suggested that it might be 'possible to cut through the neck of land separating the harbour from the lagoon and open up additional anchoring space.'

Yet it was not until 1960 that a channel was cut through the reef to allow the entry of large yachts into the Lagoon. Additional dredging was completed in 1980 and again in 1998 to widen its entrance and allow the entry of larger boats, as well as extend berthing facilities for schooners. Between 1926 and 1933 the swamps surrounding the Lagoon were reclaimed, creating the Mang or Lagoon Road by 1947. It remained unpaved for many years, but once paved in the 1980s became the popular thoroughfare to Grande Anse and the southern region. The area surrounding the Lagoon, formerly the Mang (<Fr. *manglier* <Am.Sp. <Arawakan for the tree), has seen extensive development as part of the extension of St. George's Town. The Lagoon is home to the Grenada Yacht Club (f. 1954) and the Grenada Yacht Services, and the primary YACHTING centre in St. George's.

LA GRENADE FAMILY Louis La Grenade, Sr. (1733-1808) was the patriarch of one of Grenada's oldest families, which can trace its lineage back 250 years. He was a FREE COLOURED who during the British-French conflicts renounced his RC faith to become a British naturalised citizen. This entitled him to privileges that soon became exclusive to Protestants, even though he was still regarded as a third-class citizen because of his mixed heritage. In 1776 he unsuccessfully petitioned the Assembly to allow 'me and my Heirs male to enjoy every Privilege as a free White Person.' He was a successful entrepreneur and planter, owning estates across Grenada, and by the 1790s was probably the most prominent free coloured. Unlike most free coloureds, he fought with the British during FÉDON'S REBELLION, captaining a militia company. His marble mausoleum at Morne Jaloux, St. George, is a historical monument.

Louis La Grenade, Jr. inherited much of his father's property and with it an established reputation. In 1833 he was appointed aide-de-camp to Gov. Smith, and in 1837 became one of the first free coloureds elected to the legislature. The La Grenades remain a prominent Grenadian family of which its most recent and notable

View of the Lagoon

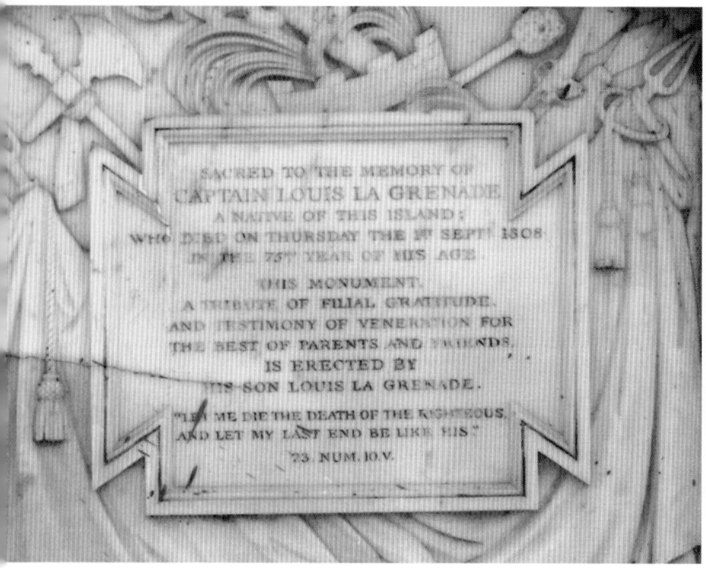

Inscription on Louis La Grenade's tomb

member was Maurice BISHOP. The family tradition continues in the De La Grenade Industries, established in 1966 as a cottage industry. It expanded over the years and in 1992 opened a modern factory, producing a number of products including the renowned, prize-winning La Grenade Liqueur, Morne Délice Nutmeg Syrup, and La Grenade Rum Punch. (See www.delagrenade.com).

LAJABLESS The folk spirit of a woman who, many believe, strolls late at night and lures unsuspecting men to their deaths. Like most folk spirits, her characteristics vary depending on the teller of the tale, but she usually appears as a beautiful woman who attracts men with her sweet smelling perfume. Dressed in a long, black skirt, she walks on the grass or soil so as to muffle the clip-clop of a cloven hoof, while with a large floppy hat she covers the skeletal appearance of her face. Usually found along deserted roads in the dead of night, this enchantress leads her gullible victims to a mysterious death. It is said that men who were not able to escape from her spell have been found dead, every bone in their bodies broken and no sign of violence having occurred. Some just go stark raving mad. The lajabless (<Fr.Cr.<Fr. *la diablesse*: 'she-devil') is believed to be the spirit of a spinster who died a virgin, hence her desire to attract men and bring about their deaths. However, from our modern perspective, she seems more of a deterrent to wayward husbands. In the stories told of encounters with her, men claim to have been saved by lighting a cigarette since she is afraid of fire and smoke. A crucifix supposedly repels her, while salt will cause her to melt away.

LAKE ANTOINE An extinct volcanic crater situated on the NE coast in St. Andrew. A cone-shaped volcano, it collapsed in upon itself and filled in with water. It is larger and possibly older than Grand Étang Lake, occupying 16 acres (6.5 ha). Unlike Grand Étang Lake, it is no more than 20 ft (6 m) above sea level and abuts the seashore. A variety of waterfowls and other BIRDS can be seen in the immediate vicinity of the lake, making the area ideal for bird watching. The 84 acre (34 ha) area surrounding the lake is privately owned and the GOG hopes that a management plan, developed in tandem with its owner to include wildlife CONSERVATION and recreational uses, will protect the area. Lake Antoine probably derived its name from 'Captain' ANTOINE, an Island Carib 'chief' resident in the area in the 1650s. The Antoine River, just south of the lake, is part of the Tivoli watershed and not connected to the lake.

Lake Antoine

LAMBIE/QUEEN CONCH (*Strombus gigas*) is a popular seafood eaten for thousands of years and dating to the early AMERINDIANS. Between the seventeenth and nineteenth centuries, pulverised lambie shells, after heating in LIME KILNS, were used to make mortar for building purposes and as a purifying agent in the processing of SUGAR. It is collected by diving fishermen who specialise in its capture during open season from January to May. The lambie (<Fr. *lambi* <Is.Car. for the mollusc) is removed from the shell and tenderised by pounding before being stewed, soused or deep-fried. Its taste and texture are similar to that of squid or octopus.

Its beautiful shell is sold as an artefact either natural or polished. The blowing of the lambie shell, which sounds much like a fog horn, is still done by fishermen and fishmongers to signal to prospective customers that they have returned from the sea with a 'catch of fish'. This tradition possibly began with a 1766 law that required fishermen, before the sale of any fish, to blow the shell as a 'Five minutes previous Notice to the Inhabitants of the said Town'. Its standing as a delicacy has led to over-fishing, especially in shallow waters close to shore. The lambie is listed as 'endangered'. The blowing of the lambi shell has become a symbol of resistence because of its association with the MAROONS.

L'ANCE AUX ÉPINES 12 00N 61 45.7W is situated on a peninsula in the SE of Grenada. Its name is from the French, meaning 'thorny cove', possibly because of the historical abundance of acacia trees (*Acacia* spp.) in the area. In the 1700s and 1800s it was part of the Grande Anse estate, producing COTTON and SUGAR. In 1889 it was listed as a stock farm, and in 1957 was still rearing cattle and sheep on the flat dry scrubland when Gordon Brathwaite bought the estate. He later pioneered the area's development, making it one of Grenada's trendiest residential districts. Its characteristic flatness, low rainfall, privacy and superb small BEACHES have made L'Ance Aux Épines (pronounced lance-ah-peen) an exclusive residential community, with many grand and expensive residences occupied by local professionals, businesspersons and retirees from North America and Europe. Due to the area's status as a YACHTING centre, Prickly Bay is an official port of entry. It boasts a small marina located at Spice Island Shipyard and another at the Moorings, Secret Harbour. There are also a number of hotels and restaurants in the area catering to the TOURISM industry, including the Moorish-style Azzurra Castle, and the Calabash Hotel, one of the first in the area which dates to the 1960s.

LAND SETTLEMENT/DEVELOPMENT Peasant ownership of agricultural lands, especially in Grenada, steadily increased after the 1850s, yet land tenure remained acutely skewed. Carriacou exemplified the woeful state of land tenure, with many of its estates abandoned by absentee planters, and peasants with little access to arable land. The 1897 Royal Commission recommended the distribution of idle lands to aid rural development, and between 1903 and 1921 the Carriacou Land Settlement Scheme divided a number of estates, and sold holdings to people. By 1911 some 8,349 peasants across Grenada owned on average 10 acres (4 ha) or less, which they planted with cash crops, KITCHEN GARDENS and spices. In 1911 three estates in Grenada were allotted to farmers. By 1930 about 15,000 peasants owned less than 10 acres of land each, the majority owning less than five.

Political upheavals in the Caribbean in the 1930s led to a concerted effort by the colonial government to redistribute land, with the goal of alleviating the islands' social and economic inequalities. Between 1933 and 1968, the scheme distributed hundreds of acres to as many as one thousand farmers. Though some people gained access to land cheaply, the schemes may have failed in not providing greater access to more peasants. The Land for the Landless scheme, under the GULP government, was billed as a land reform and redistribution scheme and operated between 1969 and 1979. During that period the GULP had either purchased, or more commonly appropriated, about 24 ESTATES, comprising some 3,201 acres (1,295 ha) intended for redistribution. The Land Settlement Development Act, intended to make acquiring unproductive estates easier and more accessible to small farmers, ultimately gave Premier Gairy the power to acquire estates at will, and operate a well-intentioned policy on patronage. Though the scheme had sought to increase the availability of arable land to the rural poor, less than 20 percent was redistributed. It is believed that it contributed to decreases in production of the islands' export crops and became another tool by which the GULP government intimidated its opposition, continuing the exploitation of the peasantry, and hastening the economic ruin of the estate system which had been the backbone of the islands' agricultural economy. The PEOPLE'S REVOLUTIONARY GOVERNMENT, though altering the approach to land acquisition through its controversial Land Development and Utilization Law (1980), continued acquiring 'idle' properties, which by October 1983 accounted for 20 per cent of the arable land in Grenada (a large percentage was inherited from the GULP government). The PRG did not redistribute land since its goal was collectivization into state farms that were administered by worker cooperatives. Following the US-led military INTERVENTION many of the contested estates were returned to their owners or purchased by the GOG.[30, 35, 267, 324]

LANGUAGE With the name of the country sounding Spanish and many PLACE NAMES French, it is no wonder that foreigners often ask, 'What language do you speak in Grenada?' Most people from Grenada and the Grenadines speak Grenadian Standard English (GSE) as well as a 'Caribbean Atlantic Creole (English-lexicon).' The latter is also called dialect, patwa (patois) or English pidgin, and is the primary form of communication in Grenada. It is, of course, the legacy of the islands' last and longest-lived colonial rulers—the British.

Dialect is spoken predominantly by the majority of Afro-Grenadians, though most Grenadians can converse in it. One's social status, educational level attained, and the person to whom one is speaking will determine the type of idiom used. The transition from dialect to GSE is an easy one for most people, though there are some—due mainly to a low level of formal education—for whom it is not. Grenadian dialect, like the many Caribbean Creoles, reflects the many stages of contact between Europeans and black Africans. The Portuguese, who were among the first to take part in the SLAVE TRADE, left their linguistic footprints. Words like pickney (<Portuguese *pequenio*: 'little boy') and caca (<Portuguese *cagar*: 'to defecate') are common to both West Africa and the Caribbean. The French, the first European colonisers of Grenada, would make an even more fundamental contribution to the islands' linguistic form. In addition to the numerous words, phrases and place names, much of the underlying linguistic structure reveals a French or Latin influence (see FRENCH CREOLE).

Grenadian dialect is, of course, an English form, but even here the influence is quite eclectic: Scottish, Irish and lower-class British forms. Its lexicon includes archaic words from the English language (cutlass <Eng. 'sword worn by sailors'), and English words with modified meanings (for example 'foot' which refers to the entire limb from the hip to the toes and not just the portion from the ankles down). The long duration of the Slave Trade also ensured a constant infusion of African words, phrases and speech patterns (see AFRICAN HERITAGE).

Dialect's modification of Standard English is greater than that of its American and Australian siblings because it affects not only vowels but also consonants. Those peculiarities of the English tongue, the dental fricatives, th/ and th(, are replaced by 't' or 'd' as in 'dis' for 'this' and 'tanks' for 'thanks'. The 'd' in the double consonant 'nd' is dropped when it occurs at the end of words, as in 'sen' for 'send' and 'len' for 'lend'. Similarly, the 't' in the double consonant 'st' as in 'las' for 'last'. The 'r' sound that follows a vowel is also not pronounced, the vowel simply stressed as in 'hahd' for 'hard'. Words are often compounded and duplicated for emphasis. Many of these modifications may be seen in the dialect sentence: 'De win blowin hahd hahd ova de fiel./ The wind is blowing very hard over the field.'

Many Grenadians, because of historical biases, hold dialect in low esteem. It was seen as humorous and ridiculed as 'play talking', hence some of the appeal of dialect poetry and plays. Grenadians speak at least three dialects that are comprehensible to every Grenadian, though the dialect of the urban elite is widely accepted for obvious reasons. Residents from the countryside are often called 'country booky' because of their strong accents and the absence of GSE pronunciation and grammar in their speech. The people of C&PM, due to their geographical, social and political isolation, speak a dialect slightly different from either of those of Grenada.

Under the colonial educational system the emphasis was on urging children to alter their speech pattern to speak 'properly' as opposed to 'bad' or 'broken' English. If EDUCATION was viewed as the key to open doors, speaking properly gained you welcome and acceptance. Some critics of the present system contend that dialect is the first language for many Grenadians and should be taught as such in schools, with Standard English being made the second language. Such nationalist-minded critics have begun to support measures that would put in place a Caribbean culture with its own 'native' or 'nation' languages. Others still have argued that dialect has become a part of the culture, and that our identity as Grenadians and Carriacouans hinges upon it. The status quo has not changed, but there is now accommodation within the system, especially with the accepted teaching of literary works by Caribbean dialect poets and novelists within the formal school curricula. Dialect may have become fashionable, but its place in the school curriculum is still debated.

There have been a number of individual attempts to study, record and collect the islands' fast disappearing dialects by individuals like Claude Francis and Alister Hughes, but an extensive dictionary has yet to be published. Ronald Kephart has studied the dialect of Carriacou and is widely published on the topic. The dialect of Grenada is beautifully captured in the poetry of Paul Keens-Douglas. Merle Collins' novel *Angel* also captures the melodious voice of the rural peasantry and illustrates the diverse influences on the Grenadian language.[5, 164, 188, 189, 190, 191, 192]

LASAGESSE, St. David has been included in the GOG plan for CONSERVATION because of the area's natural and cultural significance. Abutting the LaSagesse River is a unique natural area occupied by a mangrove estuary, salt pond, littoral woodland, dry thorn scrub cactus woodland, offshore CORAL REEFS, BEACHES, and a wildlife habitat for some of the island's migrating BIRDS. Its designation for protection can lead to the development of the area as a managed natural resource, providing nature trails, bird watching and hiking as opposed to the indiscriminate expansion of the growing TOURISM sector. Not far from the natural area are the remains of the old French settlement at Megrin, with the ruins of a church and other structures. The LaSagesse GREAT HOUSE, once owned by Lord Brownlow, equerry to the Duke of Windsor, is presently the LaSagesse Nature Centre. The former LaSagesse Rum Distillery, with its decaying water wheel and crumbling aqueduct system, further enhances the cultural history of the area. It was reopened as the LaSagesse Natural Works Establishment, providing a venue to sell local CRAFTS and spices and an entertainment centre for local artists.

LAURENT, Sir Pierre-François (d. 1784) A French Grenadian, who, because of his allegiance to the British between 1763 and 1779, was called a 'collaborator' by his French compatriots. Following the French ceding of the islands to the British in 1763 Laurent converted to Protestantism and in 1768 received '[t]he honour of knighthood which His Majesty has been graciously pleased to bestow on' him. In 1776, even after swearing allegiance to the British and anglicising his name to Peter Francis Laurent, Protestants objected to his appointment as assistant judge. When the French regained power in 1779 he 'reversed' his faith and was appointed an honorary member of the Supreme Court. His appointment was opposed by the president of the court, who felt that 'the laws and constitution of the colonies exclude him for more than one reason from any form of public office or duty.'

Laurent's inappropriateness may have stemmed more from the fact that he was married to 'a certain Miss St. Bernard, a woman who was known to be [free] coloured,' and Laurent himself was previously accused of being mixed race. Despite his association with the French during their brief occupation of the islands, he was appointed to the General Council in 1784, but Protestants again protested against his appointment. He was burned in effigy by a mob, forcing him to 'discontinue his attendance' in the legislature. He was a wealthy proprietor, owning COFFEE and SUGAR estates.

LA VALETTE, Jean-Pierre (?1775-1795) was one of the prominent leaders of FÉDON'S REBELLION. La Valette (or La Vallée) was a FREE COLOURED who, according to Dr John HAY, was 'a native of the island' and was employed as a tailor in the town of SAUTEURS, St. Patrick. In early 1795, together with Charles NOGUES, he travelled to Guadeloupe to meet with Victor Hugues, the French Republican leader. There he received a commission as captain in the French Republican Army and arms and ammunition to undertake the revolt in Grenada. At the start of the rebellion he commanded a detachment of rebels and slaves from Sauteurs and joined Julien FÉDON in the attack on GRENVILLE, St. Andrew, on the night of 2 March 1795. La Valette is said to have shot and killed the Catholic priest, Father Peissonier, without provocation. He had accused Peissonier of being an aristocrat because he offered a coat to a scantily clad British hostage of the rebels. Hay describes him as 'A young man of about twenty, dressed in nankeen [a buff-coloured, durable cotton cloth], with gold epaulets, of good appearance, but violent beyond description in his manner; threatening death to every Englishman.' Within a week of the revolt La Valette came to a brutal end when he was hacked to death with a cutlass by a 'coloured captain named Ragon while interceding to save another's life.'

LEAPERS' HILL/CARIBS' LEAP The events that led to the 'leap' off the hill at SAUTEURS are shrouded in a tale of war, colonisation, love, revenge, greed, deceit and genocide, and subject to centuries of mythology. The story begins with the Island Carib Thomas, who having been rejected by Chief DUQUESNE's daughter, killed her brother and ran away to Martinique. While in Martinique, Thomas informed Gov. DU PARQUET that he could 'deliver' the Island Caribs of Grenada because he knew of their secret meeting place. On 30 May 1650 a force of sixty men, under the cover of darkness, surprised the Island Caribs in their *cabet* or 'long house', situated on a hill overlooking the sea, and began a bloody slaughter. As many as forty Island Caribs may have plunged several hundred feet to their deaths. Rather than offer an inglorious surrender to the French, the Island Caribs committed an act that has left them a legacy remembered today as a symbol of resistance to European domination. The hill from which they leapt bore the French name Le Morne des Sauteurs: 'Hill of Leapers', and was later affixed to the town that developed around the small bay.

A number of writers seem to think that this bloody attack against the Island Caribs represented the annihilation of their population in Grenada, but they survived into the

Leapers' Hill/Caribs' Leap from Sauteurs Bay

mid-1700s in much reduced circumstances. Symbolically, though, the Leapers' Hill incident was the turning point in the Island Carib struggle against the French in the latter's favour. The site attracts visitors who are probably awed by this ultimate act of self-sacrifice, but the outcome nonetheless evokes sadness and anger. The only monument remains the solitary hill.[8, 91, 95, 197]

LEBANESE/SYRIAN COMMUNITY Grenada's Middle Eastern-derived community dates to the first half of the 1900s. They were the last major group in a stream of immigrants beginning after the abolition of SLAVERY. Mainly Christians, they fled economic hardships and religious persecution in Lebanon and Syria under the Muslim Turks. Like in many of the other islands, they constitute a small community, numbering less than one per cent of the Grenadian population, and are mainly involved in entrepreneurial activities. Many began as hucksters and small retailers, selling various kinds of wares like cloth, household items and food, and within a few years had become successful in retail businesses. The 1921 census recorded only six 'Syrians' in Grenada, but a dozen or so may have permanently settled until the mid-1930s when their migration slowed.

The Grenadian community has grown over the years through additions from within the region. The 1991 census recorded only 43 individuals who defined themselves as 'Syrian/Lebanese'. Among the early families in Grenada were the Fakhres and Salhabs. George Joseph, who arrived in 1935, was typical of the community. An entrepreneur, he was instrumental in the formation of a number of commercial and industrial businesses in the 1940s and held managerial positions in many. Another notable member of the community was Moses Nahous, entrepreneur, political backer and appointed senator (1972-1976). Common Lebanese/Syrian family names include Aboud, Fakhre, Hadeed and Nahous. The community is known locally as 'Frenchi', the name of one of their businesses.

LEMON GRASS (*Cymbopagon citratus*) is a member of the grass family and possesses a pungent citrus smell, hence its name. It is commonly used in folk remedies as a tea to treat flu and colds, and as a 'cooling' agent in baths. Lemon grass is also used to season foods, adding its aromatic flavour to many local dishes. Citrol, an essential oil in its leaves, is used to flavour soft drinks or soups, and add scent to insect repellents, and eau de cologne. The fibrous root system of the plant is an excellent soil conditioner and erosion control. It is also called fever grass due to its use as a treatment for fevers.

LEVERA NATIONAL PARK was established in 1992 and comprises 450 acres (182 ha). 'The area's natural systems, its contributions to a diversity of ecosystems and the marginal agricultural capability of the area make it a prime area for conservation.' It was officially opened in 1994, following the construction (funded by the European Development Fund) of access roads, hiking trails, a fresh water pond, bird sanctuary, bird-walk bridge that extends into the mangroves, and a visitors' centre which, it is hoped, will make the area a centre for eco-tourism and conservation education. Levera Pond, covering over 22 acres (9 ha), occupies a central part of the park, though not readily visible except at the point where it enters the sea at Levera Bay. It is enclosed on the SW by Levera Hill which rises to 850 ft (259 m).

A number of migratory birds, particularly water fowls, make it their winter home. The park also comprises extensive MANGROVES surrounding the pond, three offshore islands—Sugar Loaf or Levera, Green and Sandy Islands, volcanic hills and Levera and Bathway BEACHES. The marine environment between the mainland and offshore islands is a protected seascape within which CORAL REEFS and sea grass beds provide shelter for lobsters and fin fishes. The protected beaches provide breeding grounds for the two species of SEA TURTLES that nest in Grenada. The mangroves are the largest on the islands, and provide habitat for many aquatic, land and wildlife species, including land CRABS, and are possibly the northernmost roosting site of the scarlet ibis (*Eudocimus ruber*). The park is administered as a national conservation and recreational area, and sustainable management can make this site 'a prime conservation and recreation centre within the Caribbean'. Levera (?<'Le Verard,' an Island Carib.)[106, 140]

LIBERATED AFRICANS/EMANCIPADOS were slaves captured by the British Navy on the high seas following the British Parliament's decision to discontinue its Atlantic SLAVE TRADE in 1808. Between 1819 and 1888 the British Navy patrolled the Atlantic Ocean in an attempt to halt the abduction and transportation of Africans to the Americas, especially Cuba and Brazil, by Spanish and Portuguese slavers. (Between 1808 and 1867

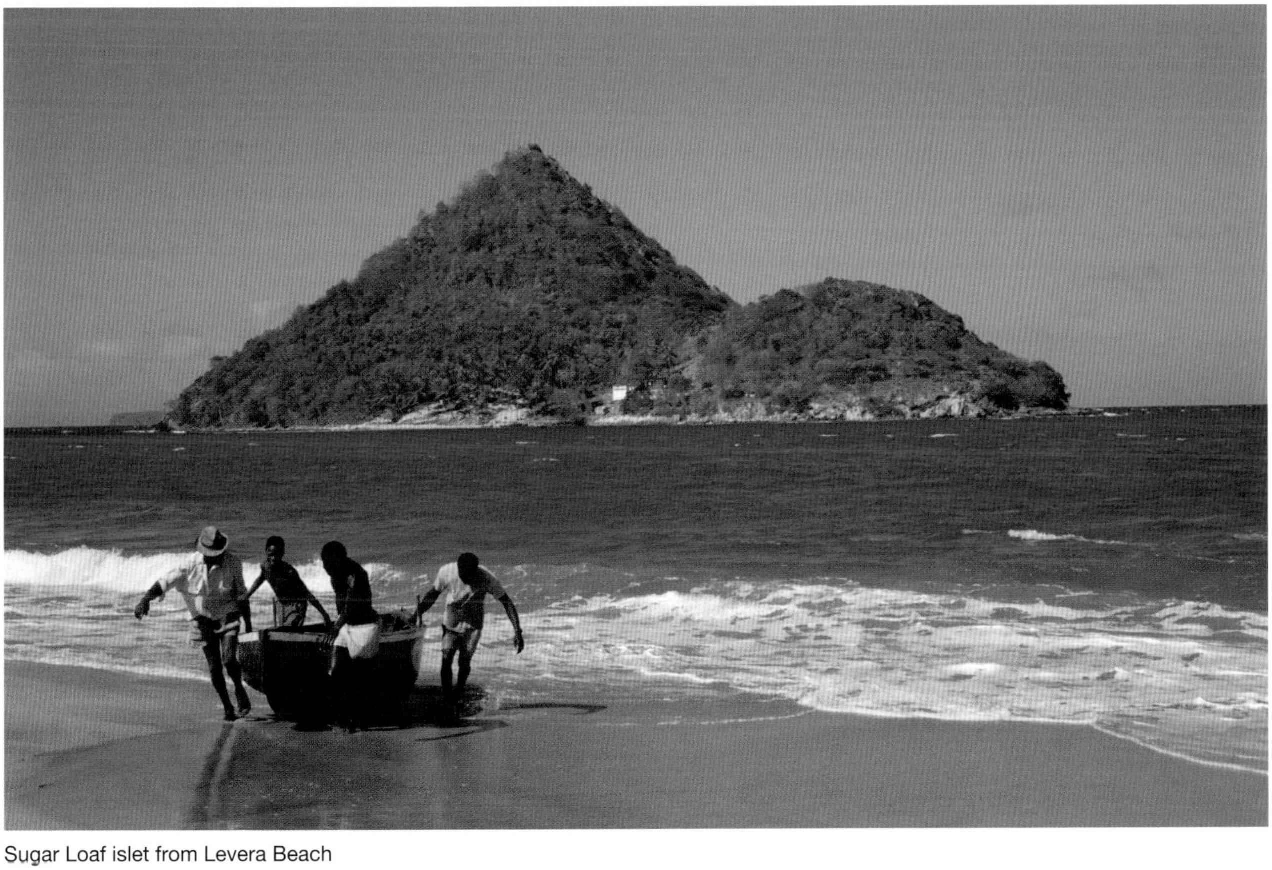

Sugar Loaf islet from Levera Beach

the British government spent £40m on suppressing the slave trade, and between 1820 and 1870 captured about 1,600 slavers and freed 150,000 slaves.) The British Navy, after capturing slave ships on the high seas, resettled the Africans in Sierra Leone and St. Helena. Some of the liberated Africans were part of the indentured immigration schemes to the BWI in the mid-1800s.

Prior to 1836 a small number of illegally imported slaves were regarded as liberated Africans and considered the property of the government. Three slave ships were captured off the coast of Grenada in 1836 and another in 1837. The 1,530 emancipados became the 'property' of the British colonial government. In order to 'integrate them into society' they were indentured for one year to ESTATES in Grenada and given similar treatment to the apprentices. The success of this group led to the importation of over 1,500 Africans under INDENTURED IMMIGRATION. The settlement of the liberated Africans following their indentures in rural villages such as RIVER SALLEE and MUNICH contributed to the strong retention of African cultural expressions like SHANGO and OBEAH.[35, 333]

LIBRARY The Public Library was opened in 1846, but was not established by law until 1851, the same year it received its first librarian. In 1888 it was reorganised and expanded. Before being relocated in 1892 to a 'newly erected and handsome building' on the CARENAGE, the Public Library was housed downstairs of the Supreme Court Registry, and above the General Post Office on the Carenage. It is housed in a handsome, yet simple building that was beautifully restored in 1987 at which time the entire building was made available to the library. The library's collection has seen some development, but there is much room for improvement. The library houses a small West Indian collection and the 'National Archives', which consists of historical documents, including NEWSPAPERS and local and government publications. Before the opening of branch libraries across the islands, a bookmobile visited the outer PARISHES and continues to visit rural villages. The Grenada National Library is named in memory of Sheila Agnes Buckmire (1930-85), who served the library as junior, senior and chief librarian between 1947 and 1985.

Grenada National Library

LIGAROU/LOUGAWOU The most infamous of the folk spirits, rumoured by many to perform unspeakable evils. The ligarou takes two forms: one as the male counterpart of the SUKUYANT, in which it can remove its skin, change into a ball of fire, and enters people's houses and suck their blood; the other is that of a shape shifter. Many believe that living men engage in the practice of turning themselves into animals and inanimate objects—dog, horse, donkey, 'fowl cock', even a cake—in order to practise evil. A popular tale is often told of an individual who turned himself into a cake and was 'kick'-up' by American sailors when they heard it speak. Almost every community has tales of at least one individual who 'sucks blood.'

The ability of the ligarou (<Fr.Cr.<Fr. *loup-garou*: 'werewolf') to transform itself is gained through 'making a deal with the devil,' or 'selling its soul to the devil' for material gain. Individuals make contact with the devil by reading 'special' books on witchcraft and OBEAH. The devil grants whatever their wish might be, but demands a price, the most common being a sacrificial child. Once a deal is made it cannot be broken, otherwise the devil will bring about the economic and social demise of his protégé, even his death. People who suddenly become wealthy are said to be 'dealing' with the devil, and rumours circulate as to the mysterious lifestyle they have adopted. If they should suddenly lose their wealth it would be seen as losing favour with the devil. The ligarou combines both African and French beliefs. Stories are still told of Vung, supposedly a well-known ligarou in St. George's.

LIGHTHOUSE The treacherous rocks of the rugged southern coasts are dangerous to incoming ships, as the wreck of the SS ORINICO in 1900 proved. In 1904 C M Brown donated 'a white light of the forth order' in memory of his father Jonas Browne (of Jonas Browne and Hubbards, Ltd.). It was located on the Point Salines peninsula on a small hill 140 ft (42 m) above the sea. Visibility ranged from a high of 12 miles (19.3 km). A new light was added in 1932 and the lighthouse was built in 1934; it was the only one of its kind in the islands. Its

Lighthouse, Point Salines

oil lamp flashed every 15 seconds and was visible for 20 miles (32 km). The construction of the POINT SALINES INTERNATIONAL AIRPORT resulted in the dismantling of the lighthouse in 1981, as the promontory on which it stood was levelled. Through the efforts of the Grenada Historical Society the lighthouse tower has been preserved in a smaller version of the original lighthouse at the airport, and the lamp is on display at the GRENADA NATIONAL MUSEUM.

LIMEKILNS can be seen along the coasts where these huge towers seem out of place, having no relevance to the present. They were used to manufacture white lime or quicklime (calcium oxide), which was then used to make mortar/plaster and to remove impurities in the processing of SUGAR and RUM. In the absence of cement many of the older buildings were constructed with mortar made in these kilns. They were similar to windmill towers except that the limekiln was a simple circular unlined brick structure. The top was left open and connected to a ramp facilitating back loading of the limestone. The abundance of coral from marine organisms like the LAMBIE made

Limekiln, Sauteurs Bay

it the most likely source of limestone in Grenada, hence the location of the kilns near the sea. Excellent examples can be seen on the western side of Sauteurs Bay, Grenada, and on Saline Island off the southern coast of Carriacou. Lime Kiln Bay, Carriacou, probably derives its name from a limekiln in the area. At least four limekilns have been identified by the GRENADA NATIONAL TRUST and designated for protection as part of the islands' cultural heritage.

LIMES (*Citrus aurantifolia*) were a major crop cultivated in Carriacou until the early 1980s. Tom Archer of CRAIGSTON estate engaged in lime production and by 1908 had established orchards there, thereafter spreading throughout the island, with lime oil, concentrate and juice exported in appreciable quantities. Partial processing was carried out on four estates, primarily the factories at Craigston and Dumfries. In 1937 the Grenada Lime Factory controlled 'practically all the island's lime production'; it closed in 1961 but reopened in 1964. In 1970 production increased, but thereafter gradually declined. By 1981 the industry had died, due directly to a five-year drought and the loss of its export market when the Dominican firm which purchased its lime juice found cheaper raw material sources. Machinery once used in the processing of limes—troughs, boilers, and settling tanks—can still be seen at Dumfries and Craigston estates.

LIMING This term refers in general to informal hanging out, loitering, 'scoping out' people, or congregating to drink and/or converse, often making comments about passers-by. Though the activity is engaged in predominantly by men, school-age boys and girls also participate in some form of it, as do women whose meeting to 'gossip' has often been characterised by themselves as liming. Boys and young men often gather, usually after school, to lime girls. Young men may also gather at a 'bloco', dance or party to do likewise, which includes watching females and making comments about them in the course of general conversation. For older men, among them married men, it means something slightly different. Though older men often gather to lime females, they can be found at rum shops liming and drinking. There, informal groups, generally comprising men who consider themselves 'partners' or drinking buddies, gather to drink alcoholic beverages and play an assortment of games like draughts, dominoes and cards. In the rural villages the rum shop or other centrally located business is usually the place of choice. In the towns there are more places to choose from, and the liming spot can vary from the street corner to someone's house, shop, disco or RUM SHOP. Almost any event—funeral, wedding, wake, party, and christening—will have limers, generally uninvited and inquisitive persons who just want to see what is going on.

Though liming is unorganised, a group can decide to meet in order to 'make a lime' or 'bus a lime'. This can be a moving or stationary lime depending on whether or not the limers have a specific destination in mind. Though liming still has a negative connotation, especially among the elderly, it has become more acceptable, losing its association with lazy idlers or drivéing (Fr.Cr. <Fr. (nautical) *dériver*: 'to drift'). The place name The Limes, Grande Anse, probably originates from its association as a place to lime. The term lime originated during World War II in TRINIDAD, where it was applied to the 'white American sailors from the naval base who hung around bawdy-house areas in groups.'

LITERARY TRADITION Grenada's literary tradition is a late twentieth-century development. The islands have produced a number of notable political figures, but literary writers, especially pre-1960s, are few. Thomas E Passe, the supposed author of the anonymous *An Epic on the Miserable State of Grenada, BWI*, is probably the beginning of that tradition in 1883. The epic poem is an attack on the British colonial government and CROWN COLONY system. In the early 1900s T A MARRYSHOW, in The WEST INDIAN newspaper, published a number of poems under the pseudonym Max T Golden. In 1947 Dr L M COMISSIONG published a collection of poetry. It is interesting that all three had political motivations.

Merle Collins, Grenada's foremost novelist

Beginning in the 1960s a number of writers emerged, including playwright Wilfred REDHEAD, short story writer F M COARD, dialect poet and short story writer Paul Keens-Douglas, and children's writer Ricardo Keens-Douglas. The Grenada REVOLUTION unleashed what is probably the most significant literary episode in the islands' history, giving birth to writers like poet and playwright Christopher DeRiggs, playwright Francis Peters, short story writer Jacob Ross and Dr Merle Collins, Grenada's foremost poet and novelist. Other Grenadian writers include UK-based novelist Jean Buffong, UK-based poet and novelist Jacob Ross, short story writer and former governor Dame Hilda BYNOE, poet/historian Omowale Franklyn, novelist Clyde Belfon, poet Brian Marryshow, and novelist Maurice Patterson.

LITTLE, Louise Helen (1900-1991) was born in La Digue, St. Andrew, the daughter of mixed unmarried parents (her white Grenadian father was named Norton, whose name she used until she married; and Lillian Langdon, her mother). Though Malcolm X, in his autobiography, makes the claim that Lillian was raped by Norton, relatives in Grenada indicated that the relationship was consensual. Louise grew up with her grandparents, Mary Jane and Jupiter Langdon, and aunt Gertrude, following the death of her mother. In 1917 she emigrated to Montreal, Canada, to join her uncle. There she met Earl Little in 1918 at a UNIA meeting sponsored by Marcus Garvey. In 1919 they were married and moved to the US. The Little family continued its association with the UNIA. Malcolm Little (1925-1968), later black nationalist Malcolm X, was the fourth of seven children. In 1931 Earl Little was mysteriously murdered. The pressure of having to support seven children on her own took its toll on Louise Little who was committed to an insane asylum in 1939, the children becoming wards of the state. In 1964 she was released from confinement and lived the remaining years of her life in almost total obscurity. Carew feels that the 'biographers of Malcolm... have never portrayed his Grenadian mother... as the remarkable woman that she was.' In 1993 Wilfred Little, the eldest son of Louise and Malcolm X's brother, visited Grenada and expressed the wish that 'Perhaps someday her remains can finally be laid to rest at La Digue, where she was born and where she grew up.[49]

LIZARDS There are ten species of lizards on the islands, most believed to have arrived in Grenada and the Grenadines on sea-borne driftwood. The green iguana or 'guana (*Iguana iguana*) is the largest, measuring as much as 3 ft (1 m), including its tail. When young it has a bright reddish colour that varies from a dark green to a drab brown upon maturity. It has a crest of spines running all the way down from the head to its taail. The herbivorous

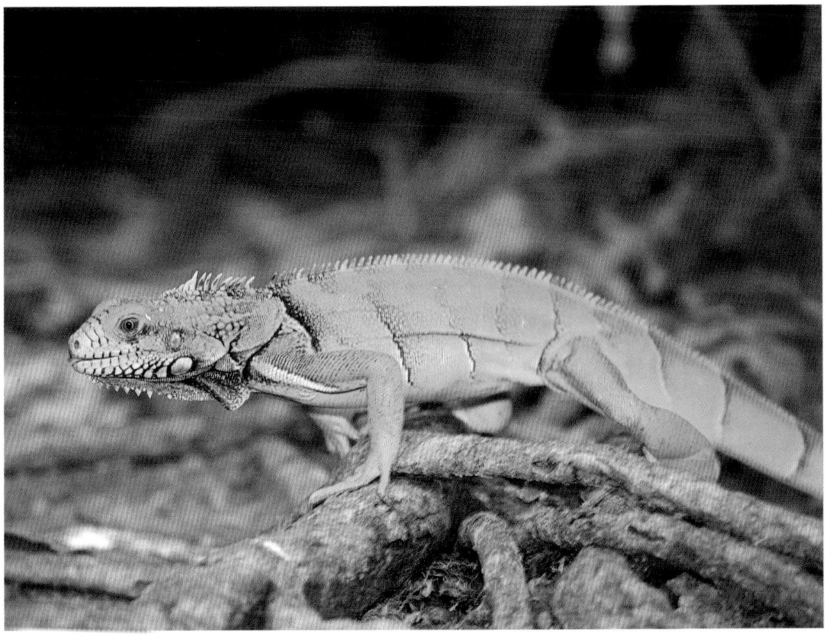

Iguana or 'guana'

iguana (<Arawakan *iuana*) lives mostly in trees, where it feeds on flowers. In the 1870s a visitor observed that, 'Grenada is celebrated as being home to great numbers of these reptiles,' but its present status is listed as 'threatened', most probably due to its consumption as a delicacy.

The zagada or Garman's ground lizard (*Ameiva ameiva*) is also large, but smaller than the iguana. The male is blue and the female is brown with brownish yellow stripes along the sides. This cold-blooded reptile spends prolonged periods in the sun, hence the reference to it as 'sun lizard', and is also known as the 'watching lizard' (<Fr.Cr. zagada, <Fr. *lézard gardant*: 'watching lizard'); there is a related expression, 'Ah watching you like lizard.' Zagada also refers to an obeah person, a connection 'developed from the superstitious fear attached to the insidious-looking zagada [lizard].' The ground lizard does not climb trees and is devoid of a dewlap or throat flap that distinguishes it from the green lizards.

Allen's ground lizard (*Bachia heteropus alleni*) has very short legs and may appear more like a tiny snake. Unlike the slow moving zagada, it is fast and elusive, but is not common. The green lizard or Grenada bush anole (*Anolis aeneus*) is the most common throughout the islands. Also known as the zandoli (<Fr. *(le)s-anolis*, <Is.Car. *anaoli*), it is about 8 inches (20 cm), with a variety of colours including grey, green, brown and mottled. It has the ability to change colours, an important characteristic for camouflage and temperature regulation, but this feature has also led to its capture and sale as a chameleon. The male exhibits a distinctive yellow, red or white dewlap that it uses in courtship and to establish its territory to other males. It also has the ability to regenerate parts of its body, specifically its tail, which breaks off when attacked, attracting the attention of the predator. When scared, it scampers into its hole, resulting in the PROVERB, 'zandolie fin' yu hole,' a polite way of telling someone to mind their own business, or find their place. Fried anole is prescribed by FOLK MEDICINE as a cure for 'pressing' or asthma.

The cocoloba (<Sp. coco: 'head/nut', + loba: 'ridges,' for the crest along the head) or Grenada tree anole/lizard (*Anolis richardi*) is larger than the green lizard, and possesses an olive-green or chocolate-brown colour. There is a crest running along the head and neck, hence the name, crested anole; it is quite common. The house gecko or wood slave (*Thecadactylus rapicauda*) is found in houses, and is usually seen at night when it ventures out in search of insects. Many fear that if it attaches itself to human skin it can cause death if not removed within 24 hours with a hot iron. The Island CARIBS called it mabouya ('evil spirit'), but somehow the latter name was transferred to the common gecko (*Hemidactylus mabouya*), which was probably introduced from Africa during the SLAVE TRADE. It bears a resemblance to the house gecko, but is found outdoors.

The slipperyback skink (*Mabouya mabouya*) is not common in Grenada. Its shiny coppery body is covered with four brown stripes that run from its head to tail. Other lizards present in Grenada are the possible native *Gymnophthalmus underwoodi* and the introduced *Anolis sagei*. Many of the islands and rocks of the Grenadines support populations of lizards that are threatened on Grenada. The status of many of the lizards is uncertain as predation, possibly by the MONGOOSE and most definitely by the growing human population, has reduced their numbers throughout the islands.[73, 122, 143, 327]

LOCAL GOVERNMENT began in 1886 with the establishment of Parochial Boards under the administration of Gov. Sendall (1880-1885). It was instituted to placate the growing vocal opponents to the CROWN COLONY system. There were a total of seven local boards, one for each of the six PARISHES and one for Carriacou and PETITE MARTINIQUE. The propertied elite elected half the boards and the other half was appointed by the GOVERNOR every two years. Electors had to be over

21 years, resident two years in the colony, pay rates over £10, rent over £20, and have an annual income over £40 currency, or be a professional. Certain powers, formerly the domain of the central government, were transferred to the Parochial Boards, including the control and management of the respective towns, levying and disbursement of local taxes, and the maintenance of BRIDGES & ROADS, and sanitation. In 1891 the boards became totally elective, and in 1900 the parish was made the unit of local administration, only to revert to the semi-elective system under the new name of Town Boards. In 1905 the district system was introduced to Grenada, with extensive control and authority over municipal administration. During this period the boards exerted their greatest influence, only to lose most of that authority by 1933 when water and sanitation were placed under centrally appointed boards.

For their 83 years of existence, district boards were the political and social domain of the middle class, since membership was severely limited, and exhibited a definite class bias. Universal adult suffrage in 1951 did not extend to the District Boards and they exerted little influence in the peasant communities. Throughout the 1950s and 1960s the boards remained dominated by the middle class and provided political support to the GRENADA NATIONAL PARTY. In 1969 Premier GAIRY dissolved local government, having been unable to exert any influence over it. The GULP government claimed that a new system, with entirely elected boards, was to be established, but it never was.

Under the PEOPLE'S REVOLUTIONARY GOVERNMENT local government through People's Assemblies was established to allow citizens a 'voice in government' and to influence policies. This socialist participatory form of government, through parish and zonal councils, gave communities and individuals a 'say' in their government, but their influence on the central government appears to have been negligible. Though touted by the PRG as 'people's democracy', zonal and parish councils experienced tremendous shortcomings, and by mid-1982 began to decline, ending in 1983 following the US INTERVENTION. In 1986, under pressure for grassroots political participation and after the recommendations of the Constitution Review Commission in 1985, the NEW NATIONAL PARTY government passed legislation reinstating local government. Singham, however, argues that local government in Grenada is 'a constitutional anachronism', and can be 'considered non-functional at best and more realistically as farcical.' For C&PM, it is possible that local government, similar to Nevis, can aid their economic and political development, but the burdens of a local bureaucracy may make it superfluous.[35, 72, 318, 333]

LOVE LEAF (*Bryophyllum pinnatum*) is known variously as zeb-mal-tet (<Fr.Cr. *(de)s—herbe(s)*: 'herb' + *mal tête*: 'bad head'), leaf-of-life, never die, wonder-of-the-world and sweetheart bush, illustrating its many uses. This small succulent plant can be found growing along roadsides and in bushes where it produces bell-shaped red and green flowers on a tall flower stalk. The plant's ability to generate a new plant on the margin of its leaf, even detached from the plant, has led many children to use it as a love 'potion'. The name of the person you love is written on a leaf and hidden away; if little seedlings grow, then that person will become your sweetheart because 'your love has grown.' The leaf can sprout new plantlets even when placed inside a book. FOLK MEDICINE prescribes the crushed leaves as a cure for boils, bruises, cuts and stings; an extract is also taken to assist urination. For SPIRITUAL BAPTISTS, entry into the spirit world is aided by the leaves that are placed over the eyes to block out the 'carnal world'.

LOYAL BLACK RANGERS The initial success of FÉDON'S REBELLION and the execution of 47 British residents in April 1795 brought to the forefront the government's ineffectiveness in dealing with the insurgents. Britain's occupation with war in Europe and high mortality, due primarily to YELLOW FEVER among the British troops in the Caribbean, forced the British colonial government to organise an 'auxiliary force of soldiers less susceptible to the climate'. The British government requested the Grenada Legislature to provide for its defence by raising a corps of black troops. Though the arming of slaves was a common practice in emergencies it did not augur well in light of the slave revolt in Haiti and the fear of armed slave rebellion.

Yet in May 1795, Brigadier General Nicholls, the new commander of British forces in Grenada, established a corps of soldiers with the arming of 'trusted' slaves. The first 300 slaves constituted five companies, each under the command of a white lieutenant. By August the number had risen to 620. The Rangers, due to their higher resistance to DISEASES and familiarity with the territory, were better equipped to battle the insurrectionists in areas inhospitable or unfamiliar to British troops. They provided invaluable support to fatigued and unseasoned British troops and were instrumental in the final capture of the rebels. Ashby adds that the 'Rangers—perhaps fearful of being returned to slavery—assiduously tracked down "brigands" throughout the island for years afterwards,' displacing the fear that armed slaves represented a threat to the institution of SLAVERY. Before EMANCIPATION the Rangers were used to capture MAROONS. They were disbanded in the 1820s.

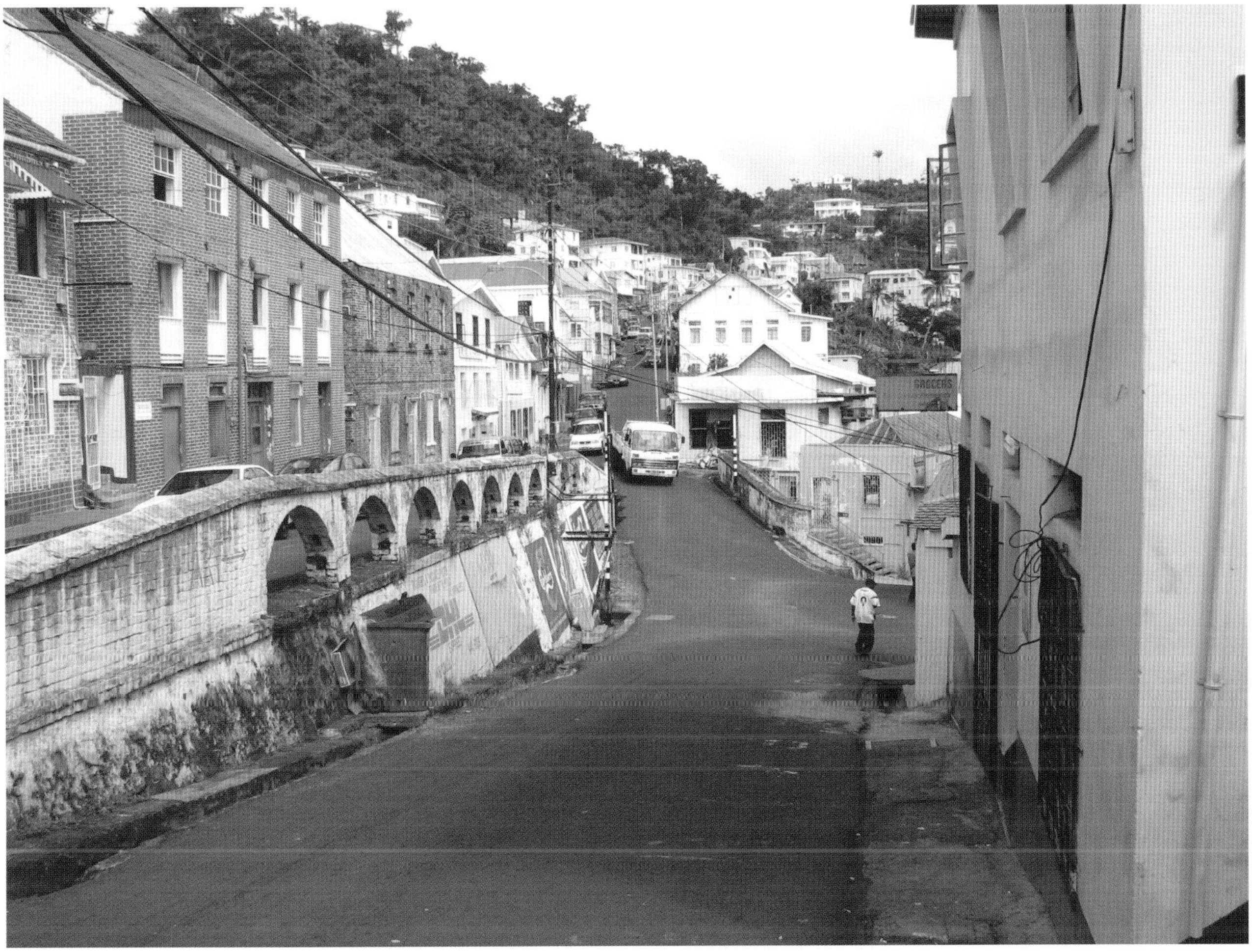

Lucas Street, St. George's

LUCAS STREET A major motorway, business and residential street in St. George's, running from the top of Market Hill to the roundabout at the junction of White Gun/Lowthers Lane and Tempe Roads where it is called Upper Lucas Street. It takes its name from William Lucas, prominent resident, legislator, and president of the General Council (1785-1787). The name probably dates to the late 1700s, following the purchase of William Lucas' Mt. George estate to construct the RICHMOND HILL FORTS after 1783. It is one of the longest streets running in and out of the city, as well as one of the oldest, dating to the French who called it Mont Sarat; (it remains the unofficial name for Lucas Street). The French name Montserrat is still evident in the cobbled alleyway that joins Lucas and Green Streets. Along Lucas Street are a number of buildings of architectural and historical interest, including the former Wesleyan Mission House, La Chapelle (the chapel and free school of renegade priest Father O'Hannan), Wesley Hall, GOVERNMENT HOUSE and Mt. Helicon Great House. The police box, though no longer in use since the installation of a traffic light, reminds of bygone days when policemen directed traffic.

MACARTNEY, Lord George (1737-1806) served as the governor of the GOVERNMENT OF GRENADA, and is probably the best known of the British GOVERNORS to have served in Grenada. Due to financial problems he accepted the position, arriving in the colony in 1776 and hoping he would be able to save enough money to pay off his debts. He found the population divided by religion and culture, describing them—French, British and Scottish—as 'a strange discordant mass of heterogeneous animals... easily irritated to do mischief and but seldom to be roused to do good.'

The War of American Independence brought conflict to the region and it was feared that a French attack was imminent, so Macartney revived the lapsed MILITIA. With FORT GEORGE found inadequate, the HOSPITAL HILL REDOUBTS were readied as the primary defences. On 2 June 1779 the expected French fleet landed off Grenada and ordered the British to surrender. Macartney, with his small force, was said to have put up 'a gallant defence', but had to accept an unconditional surrender on 4 June (see FRENCH INTERREGNUM). He and eight British subjects were taken as prisoners of war to France, but were exchanged in 1780. Needless to say, he returned to England almost penniless.[91, 126 290]

Lord George Macartney and his close friend Sir George Leonard Staunton, both of whom were captured in Grenada in 1779 by the French and taken to France as prisoners of war

MACES Staffs, commonly used as symbols of parliamentary democracy and jurisdiction. Grenada has two maces, one for each of the Houses of PARLIAMENT. The Mace of the House of Representatives represents the authority of the Speaker of the House. The solid silver mace, with a crown and Maltese Cross, dates to 1781 and the islands' General Assembly under the OLD REPRESENTATIVE SYSTEM. Between 1876 and 1925, when representative government was suspended under CROWN COLONY administration, it supposedly 'disappeared' from public view, only to 'reappear' in 1931. Three years later it was refurbished with a coating of gold. Between 1979 and 1983 it was reportedly hidden from the PEOPLE'S REVOLUTIONARY GOVERNMENT for fear of it being destroyed. It resurfaced in 1984 following the restoration of parliamentary democracy. The mace bears the islands' first coat of arms, depicting a scene of slaves at work on a SUGAR MILL, with the motto *Hae Tibi Erunt Artes*: 'These Will Be Thine Arts.' The mace, weighting 44 lb (20 kg) and measuring 4.5 ft (1.4 m), is believed to be one of the largest in the world.

The Mace of the Senate was fashioned in 1967 to inaugurate Grenada's first Senate following the establishment of parliamentary government under ASSOCIATED STATEHOOD. It is 3 ft (1 m) long and weighs 28 lb (13 kg), bearing the motto *Clarior e tenebris*: 'From Darkness Light.' It is the islands' second coat of arms and depicts Columbus' ship, the *Santa Maria (de Guia)*, 'approaching' Grenada in 1498. The hallmark silver mace is a crown orb and cross. On the mace are a reed pattern and motifs symbolising the islands' main agricultural exports—COCOA, NUTMEG and BANANA—and a palm-fringed beach representing TOURISM.

MADAME PIERRE The largest of the seven villages on the island of PETITE MARTINIQUE, with 38 per cent of the island's over 800 inhabitants. It is situated in the north of the island, and its name is supposedly derived from that of the wife of a Frenchman who once owned the island. Many of its residents are referred to as BACKRA or red-skinned complexion because of their mixed racial ancestry. The predominance of mixed-race individuals in the village is, according to legend, the result of the mixing of Africans and Irish. At the end of SLAVERY when the whites decided to leave, 'two young Irish girls, one by the name of "Queenan" and the other "Margaret," refused to return to Ireland' and remained on the island. The 'white' or red-skinned people of Madame Pierre are supposedly the descendants of those two Irish girls. C&PM have a history of French and Scottish mixing with Africans since slavery, producing generations of mixed-raced families. The people of Madame Pierre have historically been described as French, as many of their family names will attest. Today the historical racial/social tensions between the 'White Town' (of Madame Pierre) and the 'Black Town' (of Paradise) have disappeared.

MAHY, Sara Jane (1881-1969) was one of the few women involved in public life in the islands, beginning in the early 1900s. She was educated at ST. JOSEPH'S CONVENT, and like other women of her era was involved in social work. In the 1920s she was instrumental in the work of the CHILD WELFARE LEAGUE. In 1939 she was awarded the MBE for her social work, and involvement in a number of religious and educational organisations; she served on the Grenada Tourist Committee, the Charity Advisory Board, the Hospital Board, the Board of Secondary Education, and the Poor Relief Committee. In 1946 she was elected to the St. George's District Board, becoming one of the first women to hold elective office under LOCAL GOVERNMENT.

MALARIA Beginning with the colonisation of the islands in the mid-1600s and until 1960 malaria, known variously as the ague, remittents, contagious distemper and intermittent fever, plagued the islands. It was a problem for the early French colonists who regarded Grenada as the 'grave of the West Indies' because of the 'fevers' that debilitated those it did not kill. The disease subsequently known as malaria was believed to be caused by miasmata or rotting vegetation, then plentiful in wetlands and MANGROVES. In the rainy season malaria became prevalent as mosquitoes bred profusely. Traditional cures included FOLK MEDICINES, RUM (more to numb the pain than to treat the symptoms), bleeding using leeches, and the cinchona bark, which later proved the most effective treatment against the disease.

In the belief that the wetlands were the immediate cause of the fevers, many were drained and filled in. Later oil was sprayed on stagnant pools of water, and tiny fish, known as guppies or millions, were introduced into bodies of water to consume mosquito larvae. While diseases like YELLOW FEVER and YAWS were brought under control or eliminated, malaria remained a major problem into the mid-1900s. Beginning in the 1920s concerted efforts to eradicate malaria, with the later help of the Rockefeller Institute and the UN, led to the last recorded case in 1959 with the aid of the environmentally destructive insecticide DDT.[55]

MALDJO/GRUDGE EYE A sickness or bad luck supposedly caused by unintentional envy, manifested by praising, looking enviously, staring or gazing at a person, or coveting someone's property. It is not a curse! The origin of the term maldjo is either from the French (*mal d'yeux*: 'evil from the eyes'), or the Spanish (*mal de ojo*: 'evil of the eye'). The Middle-Eastern belief is pervasive, having spread through Europe and from there to the Caribbean and elsewhere. Those most vulnerable are children and babies, who, if praised or envied by childless women, can be made to 'dry up' as a result of vomiting or diarrhoea. This can immediately be cured if the person who unintentionally 'put maldjo', 'pinches' the child to 'take off the eye,' or the mother 'spits on the child' to make him/her dirty, thus unattractive and undeserving of praise. The early meaning in the French Caribbean may have also implied a physical contact, as in 1657 in Martinique when 'a married Frenchwoman was accused of causing a child to wither away under her touch.'

For protection babies wear a small bag containing INDIGO blue or 'maldjo blue', garlic, incense and burnt copper, an amulet, a red string on their clothes, or a string of JUMBIE BEADS around their necks. Some leaves are also used as balm on parts of the body to 'cut the eye,' or 'cut maldjo.' The mildly toxic grudge-pea (*Canavalia ensiformis*) is planted around the house to 'cut envy' and to prevent people from stealing; the unripe seeds are toxic, but upon heating are edible. To cure maldjo FOLK MEDICINE prescribes various teas, baths in holy water, 'smoking' or passing the child over a lighted COALPOT into which are placed a silver bracelet, an onion and garlic. Presently, only a few people probably believe in maldjo, though suspicion is widespread. It should not be confused with 'bad eye' or 'cut eye', which is a gesture of disapproval or anger.

MAMA-GLO/MAMA-DLO The goddess of rivers and lakes who, many believe, can be found combing her long black hair atop river stones where she often sits singing softly to herself. The term mama-glo is derived from the French *maman de l'eau*: 'water mother', but is a derivative of the *mami-wata*, a river goddess/spirit found throughout West Africa. The spirit has been variously described as a beautiful young woman, a mermaid, or an unattractive old woman who can be generous, yet deadly if ignored or disobeyed. She has a human head, but her lower half can be either that of a fish (like a mermaid), or a large snake, which she can use to strangle her victims. The mamaglo has been blamed for the disappearance by drowning of individuals, usually men who may have spurned her love. It is believed that she will force anyone who looks at her to perform menial tasks like scratching her back or collecting fallen leaves. She can become very angry if her requests are refused. As the 'mother of the water', SHANGO believers and certain SPIRITUAL BAPTIST sects regard her with reverence and make offerings to her at lakes and HOT SPRINGS. Also known as mermaid or merrymaid.

MAMA-MALADIE is the angry spirit or ghost of a woman who has died in childbirth, the baby remaining undelivered. For nine nights her presence is known by the voice of a crying child in the night, which is the mother mourning for her lost child. She waits for unsuspecting mothers to open their doors to allow the 'crying child' into their homes, and with the 'child' comes many dreadful diseases—curses from the angry spirit. It is also said that anyone who opens his/her door or looks outside at that moment will disappear. To counter the evil spirit, one usually utters FRENCH CREOLE curses that cause her to disappear. Until the completion of the 'nine day', or prayer meeting meant to help her soul find peace and rest, the tormented wandering spirit of the mama-maladie (<Fr.Cr. <Fr. *maman*: 'mother' + *maladie*: 'sickness', i.e. 'woman who brings sickness') is said to travel continuously from the graveside to her former home.

MAMMEE-APPLE/ZABWICO (*Mammea americana*) A large evergreen tree native to tropical America and the Caribbean, growing to 50 ft (15 m). It is covered with lush dense foliage, and its fragrant white flowers are distilled with spirits of wine to make the Martinican liqueur, crème de Créole. The brownish yellow fruit is 4-9 inches (10-23 cm) in diameter and weighs about 3 lb (1.4 kg). It is edible after the removal of the thick brown skin and a bitter covering. An orange-yellow flesh covers one to four large black-brown seeds. The fruit can be eaten raw or stewed as a dessert. The grated seed, infused in RUM or COCONUT oil, is used to treat lice infestation. Fruits can be harvested from June to September. Zabwico (<Fr. *(le)s—abricot*: 'apricots') is its FRENCH CREOLE name. The Island CARIBS believed the mammee-apple (<Amerindian *mammee* for the fruit + apple) tree to be possessed by a tree spirit.

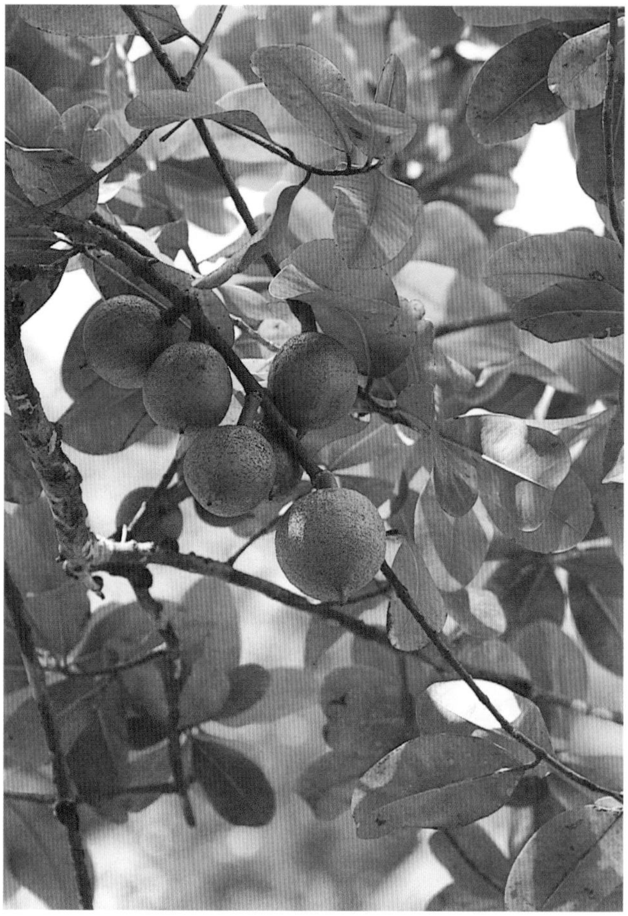

Mammee-apple fruits

MANGO (*Mangifera mammee*) A native plant of India and SE Asia, producing probably the most popular fruit in the islands. The Portuguese most likely introduced it into the hemisphere around 1700, but Admiral Rodney is credited with bringing plants in 1782 following the capture of a French ship carrying seedlings to St. Domingue (Haiti). Sometime in the eighteenth century it first arrived and spread throughout the islands. This evergreen spreading tree can grow to over 50 ft (15 m), providing welcomed shade in many front and backyards. Many varieties of mangoes are grown, with their particular texture, size and taste. Some varieties, like the 'Calivigny', are more fibrous than others. The grafted 'Julie' is prized as a breakfast fruit because of its fine-textured and virtually fibre-free flesh. The sweet, orange-yellow flesh of the mango, while surrounding a large seed, is itself covered by a thick green skin when immature, and yellow or pink when ripe.

There are numerous varieties of mango, including popular ones like 'Julie', 'Ceylon', 'mango long', 'mango bef', 'starch mango', 'water mango', and 'Calivigny'. The green, unripe fruit is used to make mango chutney, while the mature fruit is eaten fresh, or made into jam, preserve

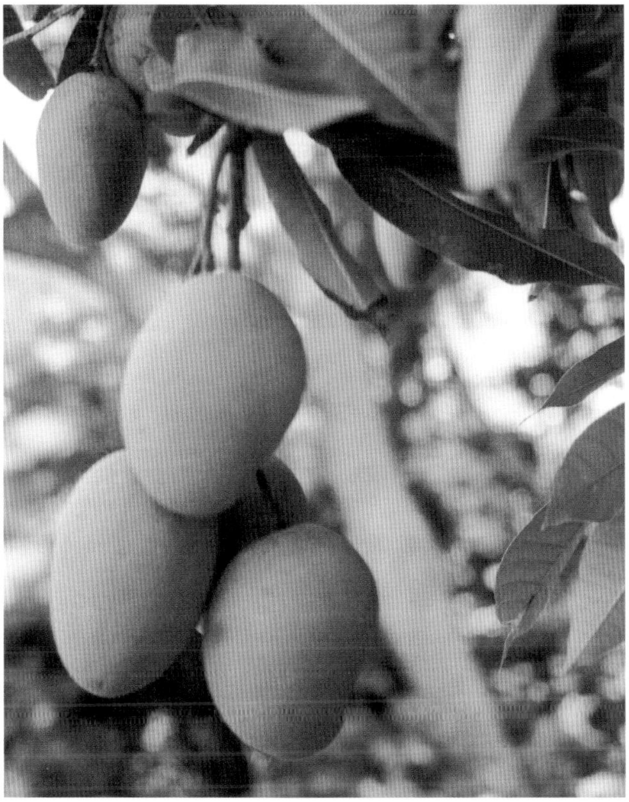

One of the many varieties of mangoes found in Grenada

and desserts. 'Mango season' is from April to September, but certain varieties will produce a second or third crop depending on the weather. Mangoes are among the fresh fruits exported. For some the green fruits, skin and sap, due to a resin, can cause an allergic reaction similar to that of poison ivy. The dried mango seed, with a string through a hole in the centre, was used to make a toy called a seesaw or rah-rah.

MANGROVES & SWAMPS are scattered throughout the islands of Grenada and Carriacou, especially where RIVERS & STREAMS meet the sea. There are almost 500 acres (190 ha) of mangroves in Grenada, less than one per cent of the total land area, and 100 acres (40 ha) in Carriacou, again just under one per cent. These include LASAGESSE, Conference Bay, the bays along the SE coast, and the most extensive mangroves at LEVERA POND in Grenada, and Petit Carenage Bay, TYRREL BAY, and Lauriston in Carriacou. Mangroves, because of their wet environment and ideal breeding conditions for insects, received an unfortunate reputation; it was believed that their 'noxious vapours provoked malarial fevers.'

The destruction of mangroves became a development priority beginning in the 1700s (it was not until 1897 that the mosquito deservedly received the credit for DISEASES like MALARIA andYELLOW FEVER, but that discovery only escalated the destruction of swamps). Mangroves covered a relatively large portion of the islands' coastline, but over the years some have been drained to make way for predominantly economic activity (mangrove swamps originally covered some 2 sq miles (5.3 sq km) or 1.7 per cent of Grenada's surface area). The prime example is the area known today as TANTEEN, St. George's, which was drained from the 1920s, creating the Tanteen Playing Ground. Though the Grenada Legislature in 1893 passed the 'Mangroves Protection Ordinance to prevent the cutting down of mangrove trees and bushes-prejudicial to the public health,' mangroves continued to decrease in the attempt to rid the islands of malaria.

Mangroves are valuable natural ecosystems, teeming with plants, including the common black, red, white, and button mangrove trees, mangrove fern, CRABS, BIRDS like the mangrove cuckoo, and the mangrove oysters of Tyrrel Bay. This very complex ecosystem, long prized for coastal development, has assumed new importance as its contributions to coastal stability, CORAL REEFS and FISHERIES have been recognised. Mangroves and swamps were heavily damaged by HURRICANE IVAN.[55]

MANICOU There are two marsupial rodents in Grenada, the manicou gwo-zyé or greater Chapman's murine opossum (*Marmosa robinsoni*), and the large opossum or lesser Chapman's murine opossum (*Didelphis marsupialis insularis*). AMERINDIANS probably brought the large opossum to Grenada as part of their 'live food'. The manicou, despite its foul smell, is hunted for its meat, and as a result its numbers have gradually declined. It has nonetheless been blamed for the disappearance of poultry

Young manicou

and BIRDS. The manicou gwo-zyé is a small nocturnal rodent about the size of a rat. It is reddish brown in colour, with large eyes, hence the suffix gwo-zyé (<Fr. Cr. gros-yeux <Fr. 'large eyes'), and a prehensile tail used for climbing and by females for carrying their young. A marsupial, the female possesses a pouch used to house its young that are born 'premature' after a 9/10-day gestation period. Many of the young usually die as they travel to the pouch and the mother's nipples to feed until maturity. The manicou (<Is.Car. *maniku*) gwo-zyé lives in the forest and consumes fruits and insects. Its status is listed as 'rare'. It is related to the American tree-living opossum. A manicou-man, like the young manicou that clings to its mother, is an effeminate man or mama's boy. The saying, 'Manicou know which tree to climb,' is illustrative of its sure-footedness, but it is really a warning to those who would underestimate others or situations.

MAPS Grenada first appeared as Mayo on the earliest map depicting the West Indies (Juan de la Cosa's 1500 CE world map), and subsequently on a number of maps until around 1523; some also believe that Ascension on Cosa's map represents Grenada. The name Concepción, given by Columbus, never appeared on any known map. The name Granada first appeared in the 1523 (Spanish) Turin Atlas and persisted. In 1665 Father Raymond Breton produced a map of the 'Carib World', with Grenada listed as Camàhogne, its Island CARIB name.

In 1667 François Blondel, who also designed the small seventeenth-century fort at the Ville du FORT ROYAL, produced a map titled 'l'Île de la Grenade', most probably the first map of Grenada (south was oriented to the north, and up until the 1750s Grenada appeared inverted on maps of the French Antilles). The somewhat distorted map shows the coastal settlements of the French and AMERINDIANS. Around the same period a map of PORT LOUIS was also produced, showing the new fort, batteries and settlements. Most of the coastal PLACE NAMES, designated in the first twenty years of French settlement, remain in some form today. The later map of the new fort by de Caylus, the French engineer-general of the American colonies and published in 1722 in J-B Labat's *Nouveau Voyage*, is popularly known. It detailed the fort overlooking the town and identified the CARENAGE, LAGOON and the original French settlement at Port Louis.

The Bellin map of 1758, possibly a result of the first detailed French survey, is a relief map and shows the parish demarcations, mountains, rivers, churches and major place names; it is the most common map of Grenada of the French period. The Thomas Jefferys map of 1775, based on the 1763 survey by Jean-Baptiste Pinel, the French Royal land surveyor, is the most detailed. This very accurate map shows the entire island divided into estates, coastal roads and major towns. In 1780 Lt. Daniel Patterson, assistant to the quarter-master-general, produced 'A new plan of the island of Grenada' based on the 1763 survey by Pinel, but 'with the addition of English names, alterations of property and other improvements to the present time.' In 1801 (revised in 1899 by W J Lawrence) Gavin Smith, a British land surveyor resident in Grenada since the 1780s, produced a detailed map of the island with names of estates and proprietors corrected to 1824, types of crops grown, and the size of each estate. (It was purchased by the GOG for £750 and is the only major original map to be found in the islands.)

In 1859 the British colonial government produced the Admiralty Chart that has been the basis for official maps produced since. The earliest complete and detailed map of Carriacou is the Walter Fenner map based on a 1784 survey. This relief map shows estates, place names, some of the surrounding islands and CORAL REEFS. Copies of a number of these and other antique prints can be found at the GRENADA NATIONAL MUSEUM.[9,91,350]

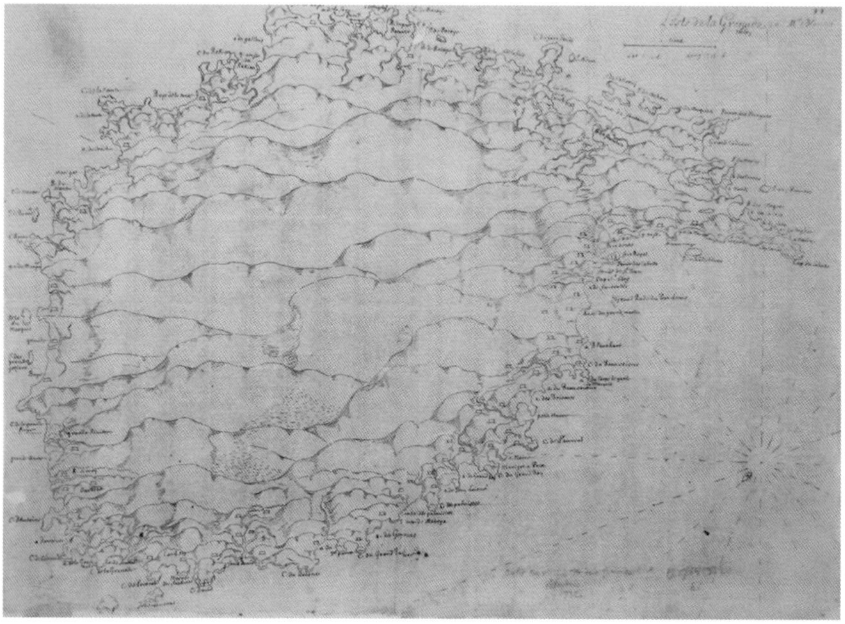

1667 map of Grenada, one of the first, if not the first, map of the island

MARBLES/PITCH A children's game in which a marble is propelled from the players' thumbs towards another player's marble or marbles in a circle, with the intention of knocking either. It was once a popular game played predominantly by boys. You could either play for 'keeps' or for fun. The game begins by 'bouncing', or dropping a marble from the air directly above a line, with the one nearest to the line determining the sequence of players. Each player, based on his rank, 'rolls up' with his favourite marble or taw. If his marble rolled into the ring, 'he fat' (?<Fr. *faite*: 'done'), and has to wait another turn. Players would then 'pitch' at each other or at the ring, and a successful hit or 'prees' (<Fr. *prise*: 'capture') results in the possession of a marble from the ring.

Unscrupulous players use an assortment of tricks like 'chinksing', or 'bringsing' as they attempt to shorten the distance between their marble and the ring or another player. The term 'fen', called by a player to gain an advantage, prefixes many phases such as 'fen-hikes' (you cannot raise your marble above the ground to enable a clearer shot), 'fen-brush' (you cannot dust the dirt in front of your marble away), and 'fen in-between'. If a game was not going well, one of the players would yell 'raf' (<Fr. *rafle*: 'raid') and everyone would scramble for the marbles in the ring, hoping to at least recover their own. The skilled players amassed hundreds of marbles, and it was the mark of a good player to show off his marble bank. There is a diversity of marble types, including the big-taw, veiney, glassy, ironese (ball-bearing), cudden, doggle, and the jacks-eye, in a variety of colours and sizes.

MARCH 13 On 13 March 1979, members of the NEW JEWEL MOVEMENT overran the GRENADA DEFENCE FORCE headquarters at True Blue and began what became known as the Grenada REVOLUTION. The NJM would later claim that the hastily planned and executed coup d'état was triggered by intelligence received from within the POLICE FORCE concerning a plan by PM GAIRY to have them detained and subsequently eliminated (as proof eight secret underground cells at the prison were reportedly intended for the detention of the eight-member NJM Political Bureau). It is interesting to note that two NJM members were arrested in the US in February 1979 on charges of illegal arms shipments; they fled the US in late 1979 while on bail. The US government, investigating the case in Grenada, led to the arrest of an NJM member, forcing the remaining leaders underground. It was then that the NJM leadership supposedly made the decision to stage a coup that may or may not have been in the planning stage.

PRG button commomorating the March 13 Revolution

About 'forty-five members' of the NJM ambushed and set fire to the GDF barracks at around 4:15 AM on 13 March, forcing the majority of the soldiers to flee for their lives. Radio Grenada was captured without a shot being fired. At 6:15 AM the NJM announced over the radio station that they had overthrown the government of PM Gairy. They called on police stations across the islands to surrender peacefully. Detained ministers of the GULP government discouraged any resistance to NJM forces. At 10:00 AM Maurice BISHOP broadcast a message to the country and called on all Grenadians to support the armed revolutionary forces under his command. In his message Bishop assured the country that all democratic freedoms would be restored as soon as possible. He outlined the objectives of the revolution as being for 'food, for decent housing and health services, and for a bright future for our children and great grand children.' Bishop also promised that '...all democratic freedoms, including freedom of elections, religious and political opinion, will be restored to the people.'

Throughout the day police stations across the islands surrendered to NJM forces by hoisting a white flag, and little or no gunfire was exchanged by either side. Forces loyal to PM Gairy gathered at the police headquarters at FORT GEORGE in an attempt to mount armed resistance, but realised that their attempt would be futile since most of the island was under the control of NJM forces. By 5:00 PM all police stations across the islands had surrendered, and most government officials, top military and police officers were detained. Two people died in the course of the takeover on March 13, and one indirectly. Throughout the day activities were subdued, yet some businesses were open and a Russian cruise liner was docked on the CARENAGE, its passengers going about their business of sightseeing.

The NJM had taken power by means of a coup d'état, the first in the English-speaking Caribbean (Castro described the coup as 'a successful Moncada', referring to his 1953 failed attempt to topple the Batista regime in Cuba). Though taken by surprise, the majority of Grenadians expressed their support for the coup and the NJM. Many saw the revolution as a new beginning for Grenada following the economic and political turmoil of the 1970s.[165, 363]

MARCH OF THE 10,000 On 28 October 1931 a massive demonstration took place in St. George's to protest against the passage of the Customs Amendment Order of 1931-32; it was the first ever mass protest of its kind, though a group of FREE COLOUREDS had staged a demonstration as early as 1831. The downturn in the local economy, as a result of the world-wide economic depression, caused the government to propose increased taxation. A committee, comprising a majority of unofficial members, opposed any taxation measure and suggested instead reductions in public expenditure. The governor rejected the committee's proposal and pushed through the tax measure. The bill, an amendment to the Customs Duties Ordinance raising duties on basic commodities like (brown) sugar and raw tobacco, was passed by the Legislative Council despite the protest of the minority elected and unofficial nominated members who absented themselves from the final vote. With the urging of T A MARRYSHOW and others, the Grenada Workingman's Association (GWA) decided to organise a protest to 'impress the government... that unless there is full co-operation between government and governed [in Grenada] in tackling acute problems, these problems cannot be solved harmoniously.' The WEST INDIAN newspaper reported that '10,000 persons including merchants, planters, clerks, small peasants and workers participated.' They converged on the MARKET SQUARE in St. George's from across the country and then began a march that took them to the governor's residence at GOVERNMENT HOUSE. A delegation headed by George B Otway presented the GOVERNOR with a petition calling for the revocation of the law and the implementation of the committee's recommendations, which the governor had earlier rejected.

The next day, in an emergency meeting of the Legislative Council, the act was repealed. It was one of the first times that organised mass protest had demonstrated its power, but as Emmanuel states, 'the political leaders [of the GWA] failed to institutionalise the organization as a durable instrument of mobilization and representation, i.e., as a political party.' Mass mobilisation had to wait another two decades for Eric GAIRY, the GMMIWU and the GULP.[98, 179, 310, 333]

MARK, Michael Zephyrine (1905-1978) was an educator, public speaker and social activist. He was born in Mamma Cannes, St. Andrew to Louisa and Philip Mark and attended the Crochu RC (Primary) School. In 1919 he became a pupil teacher in the primary school system. After a number of examinations and teacher training courses, Mark, like a number of prominent educators including J W FLETCHER and T J GIBBS, worked his way through the system to its highest levels. He spent 42 years in the field of education as a teacher, head teacher, and inspector of schools, before his retirement in 1961. Though Mark was proud of his achievements in the field of education, it was his life as a public speaker and lecturer that meant a great deal to him. His public speaking began when as a young boy he participated in tea-meetings where children, by reading prepared speeches, poetry, dialogues and singing songs, learned presentation and public speaking skills. These tea-meetings were quite popular, and provided entertainment as well as education. In 1929 he embarked on lecturing at literary leagues and to any interested audience.

His success led him, in the 1950s, to organise a one-man community education programme by lecturing across the islands on various community issues. At the climax of his lecture career, Administrator Lloyd banned his public speaking, only to rescind the ban a year later. He was a prominent member of the GRENADA LITERARY LEAGUE, forming literary leagues and debating societies around the islands. He also wrote for both The WEST INDIAN and *Grenada Guardian* newspapers. He entered politics in 1961 as a candidate for the People's Progressive Party, and in 1962 as a GULP candidate for St. George's, but was unsuccessful on both occasions. He migrated in 1965 to the US where he died in January 1979, the same year his autobiography, *The Struggle to Construct and Disseminate a Philosophy of Life*, was published.[213]

MARKET SQUARE was laid out by the French in the early 1700s and functioned as the Place d'Armes as well as a central arena for commercial activities and hangings. In 1791 the British officially established the Market (from the Public Parade) by legislative act. It has functioned as a place for political meetings, a midday church for religious

Market Square, St. George's

gatherings, the daily market for fresh produce and spices, and the transport depot for many destinations across Grenada. Because of its central location, the Market Square has played an important role in the islands' history.

Until the middle of the nineteenth century the square was used as a public place for executions, like those of the rebels who took part in FÉDON'S REBELLION. It also housed a public cage for the incarceration of captured MAROONS or unruly slaves. Sunday markets, established from 1773, became the primary social event for the slaves who, on their only rest day, gathered at the public square to enjoy food, song, dance and music. In 1827 the slaves were deprived of Sunday markets following their abolition in favour of the observation of the Sabbath. This abolition was part of the government's efforts to Christianise the slaves in order to prepare them for freedom.

Political rallies and demonstrations have begun and ended here, with speeches by many prominent Grenadians, among them T A MARRYSHOW, Eric GAIRY and Maurice BISHOP. The shops/townhouses surrounding the square were once home to many of Grenada's influential and entrepreneurial families who used the top floors as their residences while the ground floors functioned as businesses. Today, most of the buildings are devoted solely to retail businesses. STREET VENDORS, the majority of whom are women, can be found under umbrellas selling a variety of fresh agricultural produce and spices. The market's two central structures, dating to the 1800s, house vendors under their large corrugated iron (galvanise) canopies, creating an inviting amalgam of spices, local foods and crafts. Occupying the central position is a CENOTAPH or war memorial to the Grenadians who died during World War I, replacing the Wallace Fountain that had occupied that site.

Years ago, the closing of the market on Saturdays was signalled by the ringing of a bell at 8:55 PM. This event either dates to the late 1700s as a reminder to slaves to return to their estates, or most likely as a reminder to FREE COLOUREDS to carry a lighted lantern between 9:00 PM and 5:00 AM. Since free coloureds were believed responsible for the ST. GEORGE'S FIRE of 1775, the legislature passed a law requiring them to carry lighted lanterns so that they were visible to all.

In April 1882 the Market Square was illuminated with 'kerosene lamps attached to the tops of cast-iron lampposts', beginning the lighting of the town. At the back of the Market Square, in the downstairs of the Town Hall, is the Minor Spices Co-operative Society where all of the islands' spices can be found. Over the years the Market Square has changed dramatically, with many unsightly buildings encroaching on the open area. Gone are the trees that once towered over the square in the 1800s, and the openness that gave the market its traditionally welcoming and picturesque atmosphere. The present Market Hill, also known as Constitution Hill, was once surfaced with cobblestones, but paved by the 1950s to allow vehicular traffic.

MAROON The word maroon has a number of meanings, including a group organised for community activities as in the harvesting of crops or the building of a house. In C&PM this co-operative or community work is known as a 'jamboni' since the term maroon has a number of other meanings: an annual celebration to honour the ancestors and the 'interpretation of a dream'. Throughout the islands the traditional maroon involves co-operative or community work. It was utilised predominantly during the farming season when a villager would 'call a maroon' or work party to prepare a farm and plant or harvest a crop. The workers, mainly relatives and friends, would be given a meal and drink (rum) in lieu of wages. This self-help system, common to many African cultures like the AKAN, became widespread after SLAVERY when a farmer needed help but lacked the financial resources to hire workers.

A number of annual maroon festivals are held in different communities across C&PM, either 'to pray for rain,' as community celebrations, or to honour the ancestors. Some of these, like the traditional Corn Maroon in the village of

Bogles, Carriacou, began over 100 years ago. The 'dream message maroon' is a celebration of thanksgiving held by a family or individual to alter a 'bad omen'. The feast or thanksgiving to one's ancestors, once common in both Grenada and Carriacou, is found predominantly in the latter island. This saraca/salacca (<Hausa *sadaka*: 'charity or alms', but 'associated with honouring the dead') is a celebration of life and the things one has to be thankful for, i.e. honouring one's ancestors who have been helpful in financial or other successes.[153]

MAROONS in its common plural sense first applied to escaped AMERINDIAN slaves, and by the 1530s to escaped African slaves. Runaway slaves were thence referred to as maroons (<Am.Sp. *cimarrón* <Sp. *cimarra*: 'wild place', with reference to domesticated animals taking to the wild). These maroons presented the authorities with numerous problems because they attacked ESTATES, raided animals, provisions and women slaves, and by their example encouraged others to escape. They represented the most successful form of resistance to SLAVERY. Slaves, for reasons ranging from inadequate food supply and overwork, harsh treatment or punishment, or the simple desire to be free, ran away. Overseers/owners usually tolerated *petit marronage* or the temporary absence of slaves, but extended absence was severely punished. Though relatively small, maroon communities (or *grand marronage*) developed in the interior of Grenada. In 1691 the French negotiated a deal with the Island CARIBS in the Cabesterre to return runaway slaves to their owners.

By the early 1700s small bands, like that of PETIT-JEAN in 1716, began threatening remote estates. In 1721 more than 10 per cent of adult slaves deserted, stealing small boats and heading south, which caused the government to grant an amnesty to the maroons and complain against the Spanish at Margarita who provided refuge to over 120 escaped slaves. In 1724 some 24 slaves were hunted down, with 14, icluding one woman, killed. In 1725 the maroons, numbering about sixty, created extensive disturbances, forcing the French to establish the Royal Chamber so that captured maroons could be tried and executed promptly as opposed to sending them to Martinique for trial. The maroon threat remained in 1749 when the census recorded 62, with 70 per cent in the districts of SAUTEURS and Megrin. The maroon problem grew in the 1760s because the departure of many French residents gave some slaves the opportunity to escape without much difficulty, creating serious trouble for the new British administration. Raids against the maroons, who numbered in the hundreds, commenced immediately, and POMPEY, a reputed leader, was killed in 1764. Their dauntless activities forced Gov. Melville to offer a general amnesty in 1765, though none accepted.

One of the first acts of the legislature, its hasty establishment in 1766 directly due to the growing maroon problem, was 'an act for the better Government of the slaves and for the speedy and effectual suppression of runaway slaves.' The maroons survived by 'Depredations on the cattle and ground provisions', especially in St. Andrew and St. John. In 1770 the situation in St. Andrew was so critical that a MILITIA company was stationed there to suppress these 'internal enemies'. In 1777 many believed that 'the Inconveniences of Grenada planters sustained by the fugitive Negroes has long been a subject of Complaint and considered as a material obstruction to the progress of cultivation.' In 1790 'the Inhabitants have found it necessary to keep regular Night Guards on the Sea Side, and to support heavy expense of two armed vessels constantly cruising round the Coast, as the only effectual means of preventing a ruinous Emigration of their slaves.'

In 1793 slaves under the command of white militiamen were dispatched to St. Andrew to control the maroon community, which in 1795 most probably joined the rebels during FÉDON'S REBELLION. By 1800 they had difficulty surviving due to the accessibility to the interior and protracted efforts at their recapture, especially by the LOYAL BLACK RANGERS. This body captured 16 maroons in 1815, and in 1821 captured 17, the latter figure stemming from large numbers of escaped slaves in that year and the previous one. By 1823 'there were no longer gangs of maroons in the woods and their tendency to desert had decreased since 1807.' This was related to the ending of the SLAVE TRADE. The term MAROON survives today in the many ceremonies and folk traditions that developed directly from the community activities of the maroon groups and their descendants.[35, 333]

MARQUIS A small village on the eastern coast about 3 miles (5 km) south of GRENVILLE. It was established by the French as Grand Marquis sometime in the late 1600s and derived its name from a Galibi 'chief' whom the French referred to as Grand Marquis and lived in the area. The small town, huddled around the St. Andrew's Bay, was renamed Grenville by the British. On the night of 2-3 March 1795 Julien FÉDON and his rebels attacked the town, beginning FÉDON'S REBELLION. The wooden houses and stores were burned and eleven of the British inhabitants killed. Following the rebellion it was abandoned, losing prominence to LaBaye (itself later called Grenville), to the north.

The site of Grand Marquis is still identified by its ruins, its historic character complimented by the cultural landmark of the religious site at BATTLE HILL and the remains of its former protective fort at Post Royal. In 1888 a government official commented that 'the huts, which are situated on either side of a street running along the shore, were the poorest and dirtiest and most overcrowded of any I saw in Grenada.' The present village, known as Marquis, is typical of most rural villages on the island except that it has a traditional handicraft industry. Termed the 'straw-work capital' of Grenada, the village's inhabitants, mainly women, use the screw pine (*Pandanus utilis*) that grows profusely along the roadsides to manufacture handicrafts. Though locally referred to as a pine, the screw pine or wild pine is not a true pine. The leaves are cut and boiled before sun drying, thorn removal (a variegated variety is thornless), and stripping. The plant is then used to make a variety of crafts. The skill dates back generations when the screw pine was first introduced to the Caribbean in the 1700s. Its beauty is evident when the straw is woven into hats, bags, table mats, purses and other useful crafts for the TOURISM industry. As part of its NATIONAL PARK SYSTEM, the GOG has designated Marquis village a cultural landmark.

MARRYAT A British family that became established in Grenada in the 1780s and had a long association with the islands. Joseph Marryat, Sr. (1757-1824), a merchant, resided in Grenville in the 1780s and served in the Grenada Assembly. He became the islands' colonial agent between 1815 and 1824, representing the islands' colonial interests. As a member of the British Parliament and a banker in the London-based firm Marryat, Kaye, Price and Co., he was an influential member of the West India lobby in England; he was also chairman of the Committee of Lloyds, the insurance company. Upon his death in 1824 he was acknowledged by the Grenada Legislature in a memorial at the ST. GEORGE'S ANGLICAN CHURCH for 'zealously and ably' defending the cause of the 'West India colonists' in a number of pamphlets and books defending SLAVERY and campaigning against its abolition'. His first son, Joseph Marryat, who was born in Grenada, served as the islands' colonial agent between 1831 and 1849. Captain Frederick Marryat, the second son of Joseph Marryat, Sr. was a prolific writer who served as a naval officer in the region in the early 1800s. In *A Diary in America* he commented on the inequality of the black intellect with that of whites, which infuriated FREE COLOUREDS and blacks in Grenada who responded with critical letters in the *St. George's Chronicle* in 1840. The family owned a number of estates in Grenada in the 1700s and 1800s, and suffered financially when the collapse of the sugar industry ruined production in Grenada.

TA Marryshow

MARRYSHOW, Theophilus Albert (1887-1958) was the first Grenadian political leader to achieve Caribbean-wide acclaim and remains Grenada's most revered national hero. He was, among other things, a journalist ('The Prince of West Indian Journalism'), a poet, orator, singer, dramatist and statesman. He began his career as a paper delivery boy at a local newspaper and went on to become a vocal advocate for Caribbean self-government and FEDERATION.

Marryshow was born in St. George's on 7 November 1887 to Eugenia 'Azule' DeSouza and Prosper Isaac Maricheau. He grew up with his godmother and her Madeira-born husband, Antonio Franco, and was apprenticed to a carpenter after leaving primary school. At 17 years he joined the staff of *The Grenada People*, an anti-colonial newspaper edited by William DONOVAN which advocated the rights of the West Indian and regional federation. Marryshow worked his way up from paper-boy and compositor to writer and sub-editor, and developed what would become his life's twin struggle for West Indian self-determination and federation. Around 1907 he changed the spelling of his family name to Marryshow. Aged 22, he became a writer for the *Chronicle and Gazette*, then one of the oldest newspapers in the West Indies.

In 1915 Marryshow became cofounder with 'CFP' RENWICK of the WEST INDIAN, a newspaper he eventually owned and edited until 1934, and which presented his often controversial political views. Marryshow was a founding member of the Grenada REPRESENTATIVE GOVERNMENT ASSOCIATION, which campaigned for a return to representative government in Grenada. His one-man mission to the British government in 1921 aided the establishment of a partially elective body throughout the English-speaking Caribbean in 1925 (and as a result of the recommendations of the Wood Commission). In that same year he was elected to the legislature to represent the town of ST. GEORGE'S, a position he held for 33 years. Between 1925 and 1958 Marryshow served in both the Executive and Legislative Councils, the St. George's District Board and numerous other councils and committees. He was a founder of the GRENADA LITERARY LEAGUE and a role model for many of its members. In 1917 he wrote a pamphlet, *Cycles of Civilization*, now considered his most important literary contribution. The essay was a response to South African President Smuts' 'distortions' concerning African civilisations and peoples.

In 1931, on the advice of British Labour leaders, Marryshow founded the Grenada Workingman's Association (GWA) to work for improved working conditions for labourers throughout the islands. An astute politician and legislator, he recognised the need for representation among the dispossessed rural poor and urban workers. Despite his strong support for them in the LEGISLATURE, he was unable to organise the masses into a viable trade union or political party to lobby for increased wages, better working conditions and adult suffrage. In 1944 he received the CBE and a year later was elected the leader of the Caribbean Labour Congress. Having been instrumental in the struggle for federation, Marryshow was elected to that body as a senator at its inception in 1958. He later commented that 'this is a dream come true. Today I am a member of an august body which I dreamed into existence.' He died that same year.

His undying dedication to the struggle for West Indian representative government and independence earned him the title 'Father of Federation'. Yet, if Gordon Lewis, in *The Growth of the Modern West Indies*, recognises Marryshow's 'noble gifts', he also adds that Marryshow's 'staunch Whig constitutionalism never permitted him to fight the colonial power except on its own polite terms.' His residence, MARRYSHOW HOUSE, has been made a national treasure. Considered an advocate of black pride, Marryshow was hailed as a national hero by the PEOPLE'S REVOLUTIONARY GOVERNMENT.[81, 98, 310]

MARRYSHOW COMMUNITY COLLEGE The MCC was first established as the Grenada National College in 1988 and renamed T A Marryshow Community College in 1994. A number of institutes were integrated to form one tertiary educational institution, a state college of sorts that merged academic, technical and vocational education. These included the Teachers' Training College (f. 1963), the Grenada Technical and Vocational Institute (f. 1972), the Commercial and Domestic Arts Institute (f. 1968), the Institute of Further Education (IFE) or Sixth Form (f. 1979), the Mirabeau Agricultural Training School (f. 1968), the Grenada National Institute of Handicrafts, the Continuing Education Programme, and the School of Pharmacy. Except for the Mirabeau facilities located in Mirabeau, ST. ANDREW, the college is situated in TANTEEN, St. George's. The Teachers' Training College is the oldest of the institutes, training teachers for both the primary and secondary school levels.

The Technical and Vocational Institute developed from the 'Technical Wing' of the GBSS, which dates to 1961. It provides training in technical fields like refrigeration, air-conditioning, and auto-mechanics. The college provides a pre-university education for those with an academic emphasis by pursuing a two-year programme in A(dvanced) Level courses. The combining of these various bodies under one administration within the Ministry of Education, but administered as a statutory body since 1995, has enabled the consolidation of scarce resources and the reduction in duplication of training and staff. Its stated objective is the harmonisation and co-ordination of 'all existing over sixteen education in Grenada, to expand and enrich educational opportunities for all citizens, and to enhance the overall development of the nation.' In 2001 ST. GEORGE'S UNIVERSITY and MCC began collaborations whereby students registered at SGU could take classes offered by MCC. Enrolment averages just over 2,000 pupils, with 600-800 part time.

MARRYSHOW HOUSE is the former residence of T A MARRYSHOW and presently houses the School of Continuing Studies of the UWI. The Rosery, as it was known, was built in 1917; its original architectural style is best characterised as 'eclectic', like most Caribbean architecture. Located on H A BLAIZE Street (formerly Tyrrel Street), the building became Marryshow House in 1965 after its purchase and renovation by the UWI. It replaced the Extra-Mural Department (f. 1950) housed on Granby Street as part of the University College of the West Indies (f.1948) at Mona, Jamaica.

Marryshow House represents a fitting homage to Grenada's national hero. The original two-storey

Marryshow House, now part of the UWI School of Continuing Studies

wooden building has seen a number of renovations and additions since 1965. The most noticeable features of the original structure are the vertical bay windows at the front that occupy both floors, the tiled roof, and the many louvered windows, including the demerara windows. At the front of the building, since 1990, sits a bronze plaque of Marryshow, a gift from West Indians in Curaçao originally placed on the ESPLANADE. In 1982 the outdoor folk theatre on the grounds was enclosed; the theatre promotes local culture and the performing ARTS through FOLK DANCES, plays, poetry and concerts.[330]

MAUBY A drink made from the bark of the tree *Colubrina elliptica*, which is indigenous to the Caribbean and grows to 65 ft (20 m). A local drink is made from the bitter bark, small pieces of which are boiled with spices to produce a brown liquid; sweetened, it is the bittersweet drink called mauby (<Is.Car. *mobi*: 'potato whose root is good to eat'). Its unusual bitter taste can feel harsh to the throat and is not readily liked by everyone. FOLK MEDICINE recommends the unsweetened drink as a treatment for a number of stomach ailments. Mauby, made and sold locally, is predominantly a cottage industry, except the de LA GRENADE Mauby Syrup.

M'DONALD, John (b. c.1787–d. aft. 1838) He was born a slave on the estate of Francis Clozier, a participant in FÉDON'S REBELLION, whose property was forfeited and himself hanged by the British following the revolt. Thus M'Donald gained his freedom. Being orphaned, he was taken by Colonel John M'Donald (of the 3rd Foot/Buff) as his servant and from whom he evidently took his name. While in Colonel M'Donald's service, he accompanied him in his military travels to other Caribbean islands as well as to Egypt, Holland, Prussia, Portugal and India. In the early 1830s he returned home to Grenada to see if any of his family was still alive. After only three months on the island he was jailed as a runaway, spending three months in jail while the authorities awaited his master to claim him. Since there was no master he was sold to 'recover jail expenses' to a trader who took him to Trinidad. There he was sold again following his master's death. He enjoyed three years of freedom when another master died, but was later claimed and subsequently sold to 'a Guinea negress, called Zabet'. In his tale to Captain Studholme Hodgson, M'Donald lamented his situation: 'And here I am, free by rights so many times, who have often conversed with, and waited on, the lamented Mr. Wilberforce, at Greenwich, the servant to Colonel M'Donald. I, a British officer, and was wounded in the service of England. Here am I, the slave of a French African!' He subsequently won his freedom after petitioning the government and being assisted by the Colonial Secretary of the island. His life story was published in 1838 by Captain Hodgson who wrote M'Donald's story as 'The Narrative of John M'Donald or the Curious History of a Black man' in *Truths from the West Indies* and used it, along with others, to illustrate the cruelty of SLAVERY. The story also illustrates how difficult it was to maintain one's free status without extensive documentation.

MEALYBUG, PINK (*Maconellicoccus hirsutus*) was first observed in St. George's on hibiscus plants (hence another of its names hibiscus mealybug) as a white, wax-like substance. It possibly arrived in Grenada in 1994 or earlier, and in 1995 this sap-sucking insect made its presence felt. Its devastation of many of the island's cash crops awoke the memory of the SUGAR ANT, which destroyed many crops in the 1770s, but its closest comparison is to HURRICANES which have devastated the islands' natural environment and economy in 1955 and 2004. Previously absent from the Western Hemisphere, the pink mealybug was accidentally introduced from Asia and has attacked over a hundred species of plants, among them cash crops, fruits, vegetables and ornamentals: COCOA, PIGEON PEAS, HIBISCUS, ANONNA, MANGO, GUAVA, BREADFRUIT, PLUMS, citrus, curcubits and a number of important forest trees. The devastation has been described as 'a natural disaster', with the fear of 'the whole island being defoliated'. The damage to the islands' agricultural economy was estimated at over US$22m for 1995 alone. The TRAFFICKING trade in fruits and vegetables was suspended and exports to Caribbean countries, North America and Europe curtailed. Most affected was the trade with TRINIDAD (where the disease soon spread).

The mealybug, described 'as the single greatest threat to agriculture in the Caribbean during the past 50 years', soon spread to other islands. Chemical control proved inadequate, and in 1995 two of its natural predators were released in Grenada and the Caribbean as biological controls. The Chinese parasitic wasp (*Anagyrus kamali*) and the coccinellid beetle (*Cryptolaemus montrouzieri*) proved successful, and further releases brought the situation under control, though the mealybug is still present. A positive consequence of the mealybug infestation has been the emphasis on biological control and the dethronement of pesticides as the panacea of plant protection.

MELODY (LORD) The sobriquet of Wilfred Baptiste (1929-1990) who, along with the Mighty PAPITETTE, is probably the most recognised name in the history of Grenada's CALYPSO development. A pioneer in the field of calypso, Lord Melody (initially Young Melody), together with Quo Vadis, is credited with the establishment of the first commercial 'calypso tent' in 1958. In that same year he won the calypso monarch for the first time; he went on to win it three more times. Though he never won a major title in the 1970s he remained a seminal part of the art form and made continuous contributions. He was the organiser of the Calypso Revue, Calypso All Stars and Old Fire Stick tents.

Another important contribution is his role in the introduction of written scores in the mid-1970s that aided the musical accompaniment so vital to calypso. Some of Melody's more popular compositions includes 'Jook Me', his patriotic rendition 'Sweet Grenada', 'Neighbour', 'Pussy Cat', 'Black and White', and 'Obeah Wedding Ring'. The annual calypso monarch qualifier has been styled the Melody/Papitette National Calypso Semi-Finals, in memory and recognition of the two most legendary calypsonians. He was a founding member of the Grenada Progressive Calypso Association and cultural officer in the Ministry of Culture.

Calypsonian Lord Melody

MELVILLE STREET is a major road in St. George's Town for traffic going into and out of the city. It derives its name from General Robert Melville, the controversial British governor (1764-1771) of the GOVERNMENT OF GRENADA. The name dates to 1765, running from the ESPLANADE to River Road, linking BAY TOWN to the CARENAGE via the SENDALL TUNNEL. The French did not use it as a primary road, utilising CHURCH STREET, which connected FORT GEORGE to the main road along the western coast.

Along Melville Street can be found examples of the historic and interesting ARCHITECTURAL HERITAGE of the islands. These include a number of Caribbean Georgian brick buildings like the Police Barracks that has housed the GBSS and Wesley Hall schools, the Government Dispensary, businesses, and private residences overlooking the outer harbour. The recent construction of the Cruise Ship Port, Vendor Boots, Fish Market and Bust Terminal, together with the Abattoir and other businesses along Melville Street makes it one of the busiest streets in St. George's. It is also known as Back Street because it faces the sea.

MÉTAYER was a French sharecropping system introduced into the Caribbean, which gained prominence after the 1840s. Local farming systems had been experimented with following the abolition of slavery, as is illustrated by the publication in 1842 of a pamphlet by Henry James Ross, proprietor of Plaisance estate, describing a tenant farming system he had tried on his estate. The métayer's initial adoption, seen as a temporary measure by the PLANTOCRACY in view of the worsening SUGAR industry, was intended 'to solve the dual problems of labour and capital shortage.' This system was one of a number in a series of labour regimes meant to coerce the former slaves to continue working on the estates since many had opted for the cultivation of provision gardens that were either leased, rented, or just squatted on; others chose to work on the estates as and when they needed money.

Though contracts, both written and verbal, were agreed upon, the métayers inevitably bore the burdens of the agreement and often found themselves at the mercy of their employer/landlord, or worse, taken advantage of. The sugar planters had generally opposed the system, yet a

Melville Street from the sea

number of estates employed it by providing métayers with a plot of land, and sometimes planting material, equipment, transport and tools. Though agreements varied, the usual understanding was that a portion of the sugar produced, depending on the ownership of the inputs, went to the estate owner, and the remainder was usually bought by the estate at an agreed upon price. Though it was meant to resuscitate sugar production, many of the encumbered sugar estates turned to COCOA cultivation and by 1854 many of them were cultivated using this regime. By the 1860s cocoa had replaced sugar as the primary plantation crop and export. Cocoa cultivation and métayer helped to increase the holdings of Grenada's peasantry whose numbers by 1881 had grown to 3,000, owning on average less than 5 acres (2 ha). The métayer system continued in various forms into the mid-1900s.[217]

METHODISM came to Grenada in the early 1790s on the wave of Methodism sweeping through the region with Thomas Coke, the pioneer of the Methodist missions in the Caribbean. In 1790, and again in 1793, Coke visited Grenada to encourage the small mission that was formed in 1789 by Samuel Painter, a FREE COLOURED mechanic from Antigua. Abraham Bishop, an American, was the first Methodist missionary in Grenada who, because of his knowledge of French, was recruited by Coke. With support from Rev. Dent and the Church of England, Bishop established a chapel in 1793 from which he began to spread the evangelistic teachings of John and Charles Wesley. By 1797 the Methodist community had attracted some 115 individuals to the faith, the majority of whom were free coloureds, even though its mission objective was the conversion of the slaves.

The French-British conflict in the 1790s and the restrictions imposed on religious denominations other than ANGLICANISM slowed the faith's acceptance. Yet by the early 1800s Methodism was established, and in 1820 it had a congregation of no fewer than 300. The FRENCH CREOLE spoken by the majority of the slaves initially restricted its growth beyond St. George, but that soon changed. In 1835 the Methodists opened a school-chapel at Constantine, St. George, and in 1838 one at Woburn, St. George. Chapels were founded at GRENVILLE, St. Andrew, and CARRIACOU by the 1850s, but the latter, begun in 1823, 'suffered through the lack of any consistent pastoral care.'

The Methodist population stands at just above two per cent of the total population (in 1851 it recorded five per cent). The Methodist Church is part of the South Caribbean District Conference and has seven churches across the islands. One of its oldest churches is the Bethel Methodist Church, St. Paul's, dating to 1899. The Wesley House, the three-storey brick Methodist Mission House at the top of Market Hill, St. George's, was purchased in 1841, but the building probably dates to the late 1700s. This historic building was sold in 1998 and made into offices. The Methodist Church administers four primary schools and one secondary school.

In 1823 the Wesleyans constructed a permanent church in the town of St. George's, replacing the old Wesleyan Chapel on Lucas Street dating to 1793 (and later housing the Wesley Hall School). Though the terra-cotta building is the 'oldest' original church on the island, its design is rather simple, 'resembling a meeting hall rather than a cathedral.' This structure, combining a variety of architectural features, signalled the break with traditional classical architectural designs. Yet its massive medieval-like stone buttresses are its most distinguishing features, built to support the south wall. It is the central place of worship for the Methodists. Church records, including baptisms, marriages and deaths, date to around 1818.[61, 249]

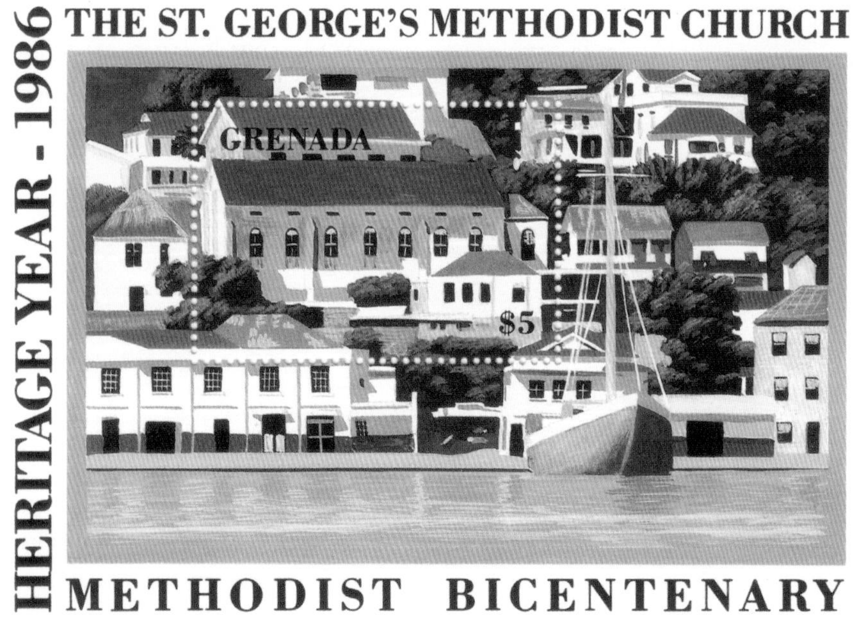

Postage stamp celebrating the Methodist Bicentenary in Grenada

MIGRATION It is often joked that there are more Grenadians in New York than in Grenada, stemming from the fact that many Grenadians have migrated to that US state since the beginning of the twentieth century. According to census records over the past century, more than 160,000 Grenadians have left the islands to take up residence abroad, making Grenadians a major export from the islands. As PM Blaize commented, 'The question is not whether to migrate, but when. It is the normal pattern of behaviour; you don't have to teach it.' Grenadians have left mainly for TRINIDAD, the US, the UK and Canada. As Tobias asserts, Grenada is a 'migration oriented society'. Grenadians have migrated and continue to do so for a number of reasons, including the search for a 'better life', a temporary job in order to procure capital for purchasing property, building a house, or the pursuit of higher EDUCATION. There were steady outflows of Grenadians to Trinidad beginning in the 1780s (as a result of Grenada coming under the control of the British), to Central America between 1906 and 1915 to work on the PANAMA CANAL, to Cuba and the Dominican Republic in the 1910s to 1920s to work as seasonal sugar cane workers, to Venezuela in the early 1900s to work in the oil and gold fields, to ARUBA & CURAÇAO in the 1920s and again in the 1940s to work in the oil refinery industry, and to Canada, the US and UK for a variety of unskilled jobs beginning in the early 1900s.

Born in 1886, Gregory 'Pa-Glen' Joseph, a native of Carriacou, was a prime example of the small-island migrant: 'Back in 1914 it's de Panama Canal. Colonel Goethals, he pay ten cents an hour fo' ten hour day. In Brazil I he'p make de railroad. Then I go minin' coal in Canada, an' hoe (cultivate) cane in Cuba. Mos' from here den go to Brooklyn, makin' tunnels fo' de subway.' The continuous out-migration from Grenada has resulted in a migration rate of two per cent per year, among the highest in the Caribbean. Governments accept that emigration is a reality of small islands like Grenada and Carriacou, with their limited resources, but high migration rates like Grenada's, though reducing domestic unemployment, also drain the country of its skilled and trained workers. The political and economic conditions that force individuals and families to migrate will continue to influence the demographics of these small islands which have never been able to keep their citizens home, or lure them back permanently in large numbers once they have left. Many migrants have left with intentions of returning 'home'; even after spending twenty or more years abroad, they still dream of making that final trip to retirement in the sun. But as with migrants everywhere, the return trip is far more difficult.[35, 153, 262, 286, 348]

MILITIA A paramilitary force that has played a somewhat dubious role in the defence of Grenada throughout its history. The first militia company, comprising all able-bodied white men, was formed in 1649 for the defence of the French colonists against the Island CARIBS. But it was the wars between Europeans for supremacy of the region, intensifying in the late 1600s, which really tested the limited abilities of the militia. By 1718 FREE COLOUREDS and free blacks were obliged to serve in the militia due to the growing slave population which presented a threat to the white minority-dominated society. The initial militia comprised one company, increasing to six in 1741, one in each district. The present MARKET SQUARE in St. George's was established as a Place d'Armes where the militia practised its drills every Sunday.

Following the ceding of the islands to the British, the colonists established a militia in 1764, comprising all able-bodied white men, and in 1767 free coloureds and free blacks were required to serve, but could not become commissioned officers due to discrimination. The militia served a number of purposes, primarily the subjugation of the slaves and the recapture of MAROONS. On a few occasions it was called upon to defend the island, specifically during the French capture of Grenada in 1779 and FÉDON'S REBELLION in 1795. In both instances the militia proved inadequate to the task. Following the establishment of the POLICE FORCE in 1833, the militia lost its primary function and slowly declined.

In 1854, with the withdrawal of the military garrison, a Volunteer Force was formed. It too soon fell into disuse only to be revived in 1878 under the name of the Victoria Rifle Corps, but disbanded in 1881. In 1910 a Volunteer Force was re-established as the St. George's Corps, and the Drill Yard and miniature Rifle Range were established on the site of the old prison for training in 1911. In 1928 a Volunteer Force was again re-established and became a point of debate in the legislature over its continued funding when T A MARRYSHOW ridiculed it as a 'Volunteer Farce'. During World War II the Grenada Volunteer Reserve combined with the Police Force to form the Grenada Defence Force, which disbanded in 1945.

In 1979, following the Grenada REVOLUTION, a rudimentary volunteer militia was formed. In 1980 the People's Revolutionary Militia (PRM) was expanded and strengthened to five battalions, divided into four regions, and comprised over 2,500 men and women at its peak. During the revolution many Grenadians participated in the PRM, with the PEOPLE'S REVOLUTIONARY GOVERNMENT claiming that 35 per cent of the population were members. A constant scene in the last two years of the revolution was the parading through the streets of an armed PRM in what became known as 'manoeuvres' to illustrate Grenadians' willingness to 'die for the Revo.' By mid-1983 the PRM was plagued with problems, including poor training, inadequate leadership and growing disaffection among its recruits. Only a few hundred turned out in October 1983 after desperate appeals by the REVOLUTIONARY MILITARY COUNCIL to 'stand up and fight back, you have nothing to lose.' In less than two days the combined PEOPLE'S REVOLUTIONARY ARMY-PRM force of about 700 had all but surrendered to the invading US military. After the INTERVENTION it was disbanded.

MISS WORLD In 1970 Jennifer Hosten (b. 1948) was selected to represent Grenada at the Miss World beauty competition in London. Coincidentally, Grenada's Premier GAIRY was one of the judges. The competition was embroiled in controversy when a British feminist group, the Young Liberals, decided to disrupt the proceedings because they felt that the show was degrading to women. Also, for the first time, South Africa had two representatives, one black and one white. After 'flour bombs' and other efforts to derail the competition failed, Hosten was crowned queen from among 57 contestants,

Jennifer Hosten, 1970 Miss World

with the coveted title, 'Most beautiful woman in the world'. She became the first black woman to win the contest, with Pearl Jansen, the black Miss South Africa, the first runner-up. The outcome provoked protests from some; others questioned Gairy's role as an impartial judge. The anti-pageant demonstrations created more than the usual publicity and brought Hosten and Grenada much international celebrity. Hosten later served as Grenada's high commissioner to Canada (1978-1981). In 2005 Hosten opened Jenny's Place, rental suites, on Grande Anse Beach.

MITCHELL, Dr Keith Claudius (b. 1946) is a former mathematics professor, politician and Prime Minister of Grenada. The son of Catherine and Albert Mitchell, he graduated from the PBC, and went on to earn degrees in mathematics and statistics from the UWI, Howard

Dr Keith Mitchell

University and the American University, US. As a member of the exiled-based Grenada Democratic Movement, Mitchell returned to Grenada in 1983 following the US-led military INTERVENTION to continue his political career begun some ten years earlier when he unsuccessfully ran as a GRENADA NATIONAL PARTY candidate in 1972. As a member of the NEW NATIONAL PARTY coalition he was elected to PARLIAMENT, and appointed a minister of government. He served as general secretary of the NNP between 1984 and 1989, and was elected the chairman in 1989, defeating PM Blaize. Six months later Blaize relieved him of his cabinet post. In 1990 elections Mitchell was re-elected, but his party won only two seats.

In the 1995 ELECTIONS Mitchell led his party to victory, and was sworn in as the tri-island state's seventh PM. After only three-and-a-half years, he was forced to dissolve his government following the loss of a parliamentary majority. In the 1999 elections he led the NNP to an unprecedented 15-0 victory, and an 8-7 victory in 2003. PM Mitchell became the first incumbent PM since Sir Eric GAIRY to be re-elected twice. His most memorable events as PM to date may have been his state visit to Cuba in 1997, President Castro's visit to Grenada in 1998, and his handling of the relief efforts following HURRICANE IVAN. He has received a number of honours and awards including the José Martí Order, Cuba's highest honour. PM Mitchell is a cricketer and played for the Grenada national cricket team.

MOKO/MOCKA JUMBIE is a masked figure, usually a man, walking on tall stilts and dancing in the streets during CARNIVAL. Like many other characters in Caribbean FOLK CULTURE, the moko jumbie has its origins in West African folk expression. It is related to the infamous JUMBIE spirit, which can be encountered at night with its towering legs spread across the road to block your path and supposedly break your neck if you pass through its legs. The moko jumbie hovers, upon his towering legs, some 10-15 ft (3-4.5 m) in the air, above the heads of spectators. The moko (<Hausa *mugu* 'bad, evil, ugly'; or <Krio *muku*: 'backward') jumbie traditionally dressed in a brightly coloured satin or velvet jacket and long stripped pants disguising its wooden stilts and legs. It was also seen wearing straw clothing, a direct descendant of its possible African ancestor. Disguised in a mask and a hat, the moko jumbie danced through the streets to the music of drums, triangle and flute. It was often accompanied by a dwarf to exaggerate its own enormousness. This mythical figure is rarely seen today. Walking on stilts was associated with the ability to foresee evil sooner than ordinary people.

MONA MONKEY (*Cercopithecus mona*) is one of two species of monkeys brought to the Caribbean either as pets or game animals by slave traders. The other, the green monkey (*C. aethips*), was brought to St. Kitts and later Barbados. The mona monkey is a member of one of the most common West African genera distributed along the Guinea Coast. It was brought to Grenada during the

Lone male Mona Monkey scavenging for food outside the Grand Étang NP

SLAVE TRADE, maybe as early as the eighteenth century. DNA analysis by Glenn indicates that the Grenada population developed from a small group, 'perhaps a single pregnant female' brought to the island from Sâo Tomé. Though the population is highly inbred and lacks genetic diversity, Glenn's studies show that it is healthy, more so than its African cousins. Also known as macaque (<Fr. for a type of monkey), it is found in the Grand Étang Forest Reserve and Mt. St. Catherine where it has lived for possibly as long as 250 years, subsisting on leaves, insects and fruits. Its mountainous hideout may have kept it out of sight for many years, known only to residents of the area. The earliest known written reference to the monkey population is by naturalist Frederick Ober, who in the 1870s went 'monkey hunting in the mountains'. Weighing up to 55 lb (25 kg), the mona monkey is one of a few game species on the island hunted for its meat.

Though HURRICANE JANET in 1955 temporarily destroyed much of its habitat and probably killed a large number, the population recovered over the years, less as a result of the restrictions on hunting than through its ability to avoid capture in the dense forest. HURRICANE IVAN in 2004 killed some of the estimated 6,000 monkeys and decimated their habitat. The mona monkeys gather in familial groups of 8-30 individuals, headed by a single adult male. Its introduction has been blamed for the possible disappearance of an indigenous parrot (*Amazon* sp.), the destruction of wild BIRDS and the raiding of COCOA estates. Research into the CONSERVATION needs and behaviour of the mona monkey have revealed some interesting divergence from its African ancestor:

'a unique copulation call', all-male bands that 'groom each other, sit in contact, engage in homosexual sex, even share food', and are healthy despite inbreeding. A monkey-jug was an earthenware jar used to keep water or other beverages cool. There are numerous PROVERBS & SAYINGS about monkeys, the most common being 'Monkey see, monkey do'.[124, 125, 200]

MONGOOSE (*Herpestes auropunctatus*) was brought to Grenada from Jamaica in the 1870s as a means of controlling rodents in the sugar cane fields. Its impact was probably negligible, considering that the mongoose hunts during the day while rats scavenge at night. The original seven pairs of Burmese mongoose thrived, and as is common with introduced species, they outlived their usefulness. It is popularly held that the mongoose preys on a number of animal species, including BIRDS, SNAKES and LIZARDS (as well as domestic poultry and crops). Corke, however, cautions against the obvious conclusions concerning the 'mongoose hypothesis', since other factors, such as human actions, may have greater impact.

By the 1950s a number of studies confirmed that the mongoose, not BATS, was the main vector of paralytic rabies in Grenada. Between 1956 and the 1970s control programmes, which included trapping mongoose and the island-wide vaccination of dogs and removal of strays, were instituted to reduce the mongoose population following the deaths of a number of people and domestic animals from rabies. Now regarded as a pest, its control and eradication have proved extremely difficult since poisoning also leads to the death of domestic animals. At present rabies is not a serious problem in Grenada though the mongoose is ever present. The proverb 'sly mongoose, dog know your ways' is a reference to those who might believe that their illicit or secretive activity is hidden, but is in fact known.[55, 73, 105]

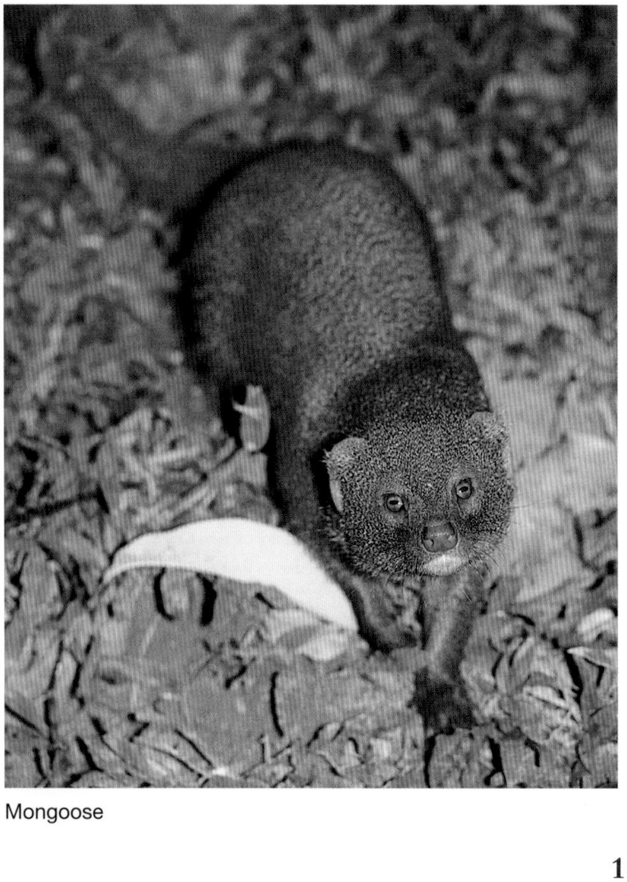

Mongoose

MONGOOSE GANG A notorious group of men who were associated with Premier GAIRY from 1970 and operated as a secret police force (as far back as 1967). The gang's origin nonetheless dates to the 1950s and Gairy's strong-arm tactics during SKYRED. It has been claimed that the Mongoose Gang derived its name from some of its members' participation in the MONGOOSE eradication schemes of the 1950s, similar to the Rat Gangs of the 1930s; a number of these men later developed a loyalty to Eric Gairy because he granted them employment. Maybe the derivation of their name was due more to the mongoose's predatory behaviour. The main aim of Gairy was to use this band of thugs, many of whom had criminal records, to terrorise the NEW JEWEL MOVEMENT and to combat a growing and intimidating opposition. In May 1970 Premier Gairy commented that 'Indeed, hundreds have come and some of the toughest, roughest roughnecks have been recruited.' Noted members of this group included Moslyn 'Pram' and Willie Bishop, Raphael 'Buck' Brizan, Alister 'Thorn' Hood and Albert 'Heads' Clarke.

As political discontent erupted in the early 1970s, the criminal activities of the gang became legendary. In the latter part of 1973 the Mongoose Gang terrorised selected citizens, using clubs to beat suspected supporters of the NJM. BLOODY SUNDAY and BLOODY MONDAY became associated with the Mongoose Gang and its terror, and the 1974 DUFFUS COMMISSION recommended that it be disbanded and its criminal activities investigated.

After the REVOLUTION in 1979, some of the former members of the gang were arrested and held in prison, some remaining there until the US-led military INTERVENTION in 1983. The Mongoose Gang has been likened to Haiti's Tontons Macoutes, the Duvaliers' secret police that terrorised the Haitian people for decades. Though the comparison may be valid on a superficial level, the Mongoose Gang failed to inflict the levels of violence and death for which the Tontons

Macoutes became infamous. Sir Eric, when asked in 1984 to comment on the group's alleged criminal activities, referred to their notoriety as 'a myth created by Communist propaganda'.[94]

MOROCOY (*Geochelone carbonaria*) is a small, slow-moving terrestrial reptile, the only one of its kind in the Caribbean. The morocoy (<S.Am.Sp. *morrocoyo*: 'turtle') was originally from Venezuela, its presence throughout the Caribbean believed due to the AMERINDIANS who travelled with it as a source of 'live meat' hundreds of years ago. Not totally defenceless as might be expected because of its slow movement, the morocoy can recoil its legs and head into its armour-like shell and outwait a predator. The black and gold shell is prized as a decorative artefact. The sexes are differentiable by the paler shell colour and the longer tail of the male. The tortoise lives in leafy burrows where it hibernates for lengthy periods. Hunted for its meat and shell, it became extinct in Grenada. Since its reintroduction from captive populations, little is known of its present status in Grenada though native populations exist in the GRENADA GRENADINES, specifically on Frigate Island, where the wild population is estimated at between 500 and 2,000. It is also known as the red-footed/legged tortoise and turtle.

Morocoy/tortoise

Morne Fendue Great House, St. Patrick

MORNE FENDUE GREAT HOUSE, St. Patrick is all that remains of the former COCOA estate. The 316 acre (128 ha) estate derived its name from French Creole, meaning 'cracked mountain'. The 1912 great house was built of hand-cut stone and mortar reportedly made from lime and molasses, as was the age-old custom. The small two-storey house is beautifully adorned with string-courses and brick quoins along the windows and outer walls. The building's outer walls are covered with the blooms of creeping flowers twining their way to the roof. Morne Fendue has for many years served as a guest house and restaurant specialising in a number of popular Grenadian dishes, including 'a forty-year-old pepper pot'. It was owned and run by Betty Mascoll, the daughter of George Kent, member of the proprietary Kent family who had the house built. Upon the death of Mascoll, the house was sold and continues to be run as a restaurant/ guest house.

MOTOR VEHICLES On 13 March 1906 the first automobile arrived in Grenada. Two years earlier though, Leonard Kent, of the proprietary Kent family, supposedly brought the first motor vehicle to Grenada when he imported a 'Triumph' motor cycle. The first car in Grenada was owned by James Bennett, publisher of the *New York Herald*, who stopped off in Grenada while on a cruise of the Caribbean. A year or so later George Kent, the brother of Leonard, imported a Stanley Steamer.

Thus began the motorisation of Grenada, though there were no paved roads at the time; 'oiled' roads were constructed starting in the 1910s, but especially in the 1920s following the passage of the Main Road and Byway Ordinance in 1916 which prohibited building close to roads. It was a number of years before motor vehicles became common sights on Grenadian roads, but a few wealthy Grenadians sported some of the fashionable models. The government also imported an ambulance and at least three larger cars to aid its rural mail service, which also provided for a small passenger service; it replaced the 'horse and mule' service. In 1914 the legislature passed the first motor vehicles ordinance, setting the speed limit at 16 mph (26 kph), with only five vehicles registered. By 1919 there were 200 motor vehicles on the island and a number of garages, for repairs, rental and sale, had sprung up across the island. In 1934 there were 478 vehicles, increasing to 628 in 1939.

After World War II vehicle importation increased and by 1951 there were 928 vehicles. In 1977 there were 6,880 vehicles, and by 1994 there were over 9,999 vehicles in the country, requiring the GOG to expand its four-letter numbering system to accommodate over 10,000 vehicles. The large number of vehicles on the roads has resulted in traffic jams and other related problems, forcing the GOG to institute traffic policies and build infrastructure like traffic lights and parking garages to accommodate this vehicular increase. There are 650 miles (1,050 km) of roads in Grenada, of which two-thirds are paved. Motor vehicles drive on the left side of the road.[169]

MOUNTAINS The volcanic eruptions that produced the islands have shaped the rugged landscape of their interiors. Grenada's central range, running almost vertically throughout the island, is traversed by a number of mountainous peaks and steep ridges. Grenada's most prominent mountain is MT. ST. CATHERINE. Other prominent mountains are FÉDON'S CAMP, Mt. Qua Qua, Mt. Sinai (2,308 ft/703 m), and the South East Mountains (2,309 ft/704 m). The leeward side of the island rises precipitously from the sea, with winding roads cut out of the hills. Carriacou's central ridge is dominated in the north by High North, which rises to 964 ft (294 m), and Chapeau Carré in the SW, which rises to 938 ft (286 m). Petite Martinique's highest point, Piton (<Fr. 'peak'), rises to 741 ft (226 m).

MT. CARMEL FALLS Located at Mt. Carmel, St. Andrew, along the Marquis River, the falls are also known as the Marquis Falls (from the river/village) and the Post Royal Falls (from the nearby village of Post Royal).

Mountain landscape

These waterfalls, hidden from most visitors until the early 1990s, hold the distinction of being the islands' highest waterfalls. Following the construction of a trail in 1995 by local groups, the falls became an immediate attraction and bathing venue. The 15-minute hike to the more spectacular of the two waterfalls is through beautifully

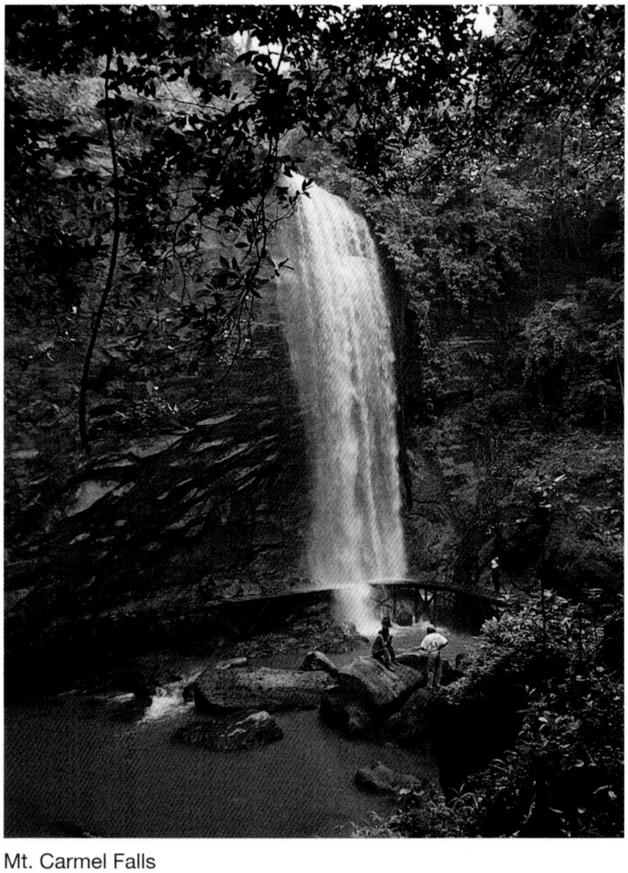

Mt. Carmel Falls

landscaped scenery overgrown with tropical vegetation. The final descent is through a grove of NUTMEG trees opening up to the spray of the river 30 ft (9 m) wide, cascading down a sheer cliff of 65 ft (21 m). The powerful stream flows between huge rocks into a crystal clear basin or pool, which attracts bathers. The lower two-tier fall, located some 60-100 ft (20-30.5 m) down river, is not very high, about 12 ft (3.7 m). The seclusion of the falls makes them a treat for adventure enthusiasts and hikers.

MT. HORNE ESTATE, St. Andrew A former sugar estate presently producing cocoa, nutmeg and banana. The 320 acre (130 ha) estate dates to the mid-1700s, and has been owned by the Berkley family since the 1800s. A water wheel and its discarded machinery (stamped 1847), once used in the manufacture of SUGAR, tell the rusted tale of a forgotten past. In its abandoned graveyard behind the mill headstones recall forgotten lives. One of these stories is preserved on the headstone of Harriet Rose that reads, 'To the Memory of Harriet Rose Wife of George Rose Esquire and the justly lamented Daughter of Isaac and Mary Ann Horsford...' Her husband George Rose, magistrate of St. Andrew in 1795, was taken hostage during FÉDON'S REBELLION and was among the 47 British captives executed in April 1795. The great house is beautifully preserved. In 1971 the GULP government confiscated Mt. Horne estate, but it was subsequently returned.

MT. MORITZ is a small village tucked away on a hill about 1.25 miles (2 km) inland from Molinière Point and about 3 miles (5 km) from the town of St. George's. The village derives its name from Moritz Hardman, a member of the proprietary Hardman family who owned the estate in the 1790s (another member of the family owned what is today called Mt. Hartman estate). In the early to mid-1800s it functioned as a 130 acre (52 ha) sugar estate. Beginning in the late 1800s Mt. Moritz estate produced COCOA. In 1859 Gov. Hicks of Barbados, hoping to resettle some of the poor whites of that island, outlined a scheme for their resettlement to other islands in the Caribbean. The Grenada government welcomed the scheme, acknowledging that it 'might prove advantageous to the island' by increasing the white population. It added that an area in Grand Étang was ideal for the community because it was more 'suitable to the European constitution'. The scheme was not officially followed up—hence there are no records of the eventual settlement of the 'Mt. Moritz Bajans'.

In the late 1870s, though, a small number of whites migrated to Grenada along with hundreds of others from Barbados. The poor whites settled predominantly in the Hermitage and Grand Mal area and worked on the cocoa estate in Mt. Moritz. Probably a few dozen families arrived during that period, but by the 1880s a sizeable community, made up almost exclusively of white Barbadian immigrants, was inhabiting the villages surrounding Mt. Moritz. In the early 1900s many began to work and live on the estate as tenant farmers. The community became practically self-sufficient agriculturally and self-contained socially, interacting with the outside community mainly through the exchange of agricultural produce at Saturday markets. The Mt. Moritz Bajans were either disregarded by the white elite or scorned by the blacks because of their defiant pride and independence. They were taunted and called derogatory names like 'poor BACKRA', 'poor Johnny' and 'Mong Mongs', the latter derived from the village's name. For over 100 years Mt. Moritz was semi-isolated from the larger Grenadian society, with only a small number of blacks and mixed-race individuals gaining access to the closed community.

Willie Weeks, a first generation 'Mt. Moritz Bajan'

In the early 1970s, Grenadian society witnessed political and social upheavals that brought about profound changes. The predominantly white/mixed community of Mt. Moritz began to disintegrate under the pressures of the surrounding society. Many migrated to the US, UK, Canada and Australia, especially the latter which has a sizeable Grenadian community. Some long-time residents moved into the wider Grenadian community, and slowly the surrounding black population migrated into Mt. Moritz. By the end of the 1970s the community was virtually integrated and today it would be difficult for someone without a knowledge of the area's history to account for the present racial mixture which the recent census recorded as 52 per cent mixed, 10 per cent white, and 36 per cent black. Notable members of the community have included Chandler, a popular chantwèl in the early CALYPSO movement; E R L Hinds (1915-2002), former headmaster of the St. George's Anglican School or more popularly 'Hindsy School'; 'Papa Seato', businessman; and Jerry Searles, lawyer and politician. Family names of the original settlers of Mt. Moritz include Searles, Seals, Chandler, Hinds, Gatt, Edghill, Edwards, Gill, Greaves, Medford, Elms and Dowden.

MT. RICH PETROGLYPHS, St. Patrick The most prominent and well-studied PETROGLYPHS in Grenada. The Mt. Rich boulder, covered with many figures and representations of faces, now sits on the St. Patrick's riverbed, having slid down from its original position above the river. The boulder is huge and covered with numerous designs, many of which fit into Cody's petroglyph classification: abstract geometric designs, simple faces, elaborate faces and elaborate figures. Cody suggests the added category of zoomorph to explain some of the petroglyphs that do not easily fit into the other four. The petroglyphs or rock art are the creation of AMERINDIANS, most likely the Island Arawaks from the Troumassan Troumassoid period (c.500-1000 CE) despite the fact that they are popularly called CARIB stones.[59, 162]

Mt. Rich petroglyphs

MT. ST. CATHERINE NATIONAL PARK occupies an area of 1,430 acres (580 ha). This region represents the most undisturbed ecosystem in Grenada because of the ruggedness of the terrain. Since the steep slopes were unsuitable for AGRICULTURE the area was left virtually undisturbed, and has provided protection to some FAUNA and FLORA. This ecosystem of elfin and montane forests consists of natural vegetation covering slopes above 1,600 ft (488 m). As a major water catchment-area, its protection is essential to the island's water supply. Located within the park is Mt. St. Catherine, the islands' highest peak rising to 2,757 ft (840 m). It is believed to be the island's 'youngest major volcanic structure' which, according to the UWI Seismic Research Unit, is very much active. Situated in ST. MARK, it is one of a number of hills that rise above 1,500 ft (460 m) along the central ridge running north-south on the island. Mt. St. Catherine is itself surrounded by a range of hills that obscure its own magnificence. The area also has a number of small crater lakes and HOT SPRINGS. The climb to the summit can take at least three hours up steep hills through thick forest, much of which is old vegetation. Steep ridges make the ascent in the rainy season difficult, but not impossible. At the summit can be seen, on a clear day, much of the east of the island and the Grenadines. Its name dates to the French. The GOG plans to create a forest reserve surrounding Mt. St. Catherine in order to protect the water-catchment areas.[50, 140]

MUNICH, St. Andrew A large rural village which, like the majority of villages, was established after 1838. The origin of its name is unclear, but it dates to at least the early 1820s when James Hay owned the 240 acre (98 ha) estate. Like many of the 'free villages' established after EMANCIPATION, Munich developed on the margins of large estates through plots bought, squatted on, or received in lieu of wages by peasant labourers. Of the first wave of Africans who entered Grenada in 1849 under INDENTURED IMMIGRATION, a large number reportedly settled in Munich following their indenture. Believed to have originated in Ijesha, Nigeria, these African immigrants created a semi-exclusive community where they continued to practise their African religion and customs, including SHANGO. Munich was once well known as a 'Shango village', where the faithful journeyed from across the islands to consult its respected Shango priests. Today, Munich is much like many of the other rural villages, having lost much of its African influences due to social and economic developments.

Munich is located in the southeast of the island not too far inland from Grand Bacolet Point.

NATIONAL DEMOCRATIC CONGRESS The NDC began as a centrist political party in 1987 launched by former members of the NEW NATIONAL PARTY. The original membership included George BRIZAN, Francis Alexis, Tillman Thomas, Jerome Joseph, Kenny Lalsingh, Phinsley St. Louis and Marcel Peters (former GULP/Independent). The inability of PM BLAIZE to manage the diversity within the NNP coalition government led to its almost total collapse when five of its top members resigned. The NDC brought together some of the islands' most prominent politicians and became a viable alternative to the ruling NNP. Brizan was at first elected leader, but in the run-up to the 1990 general elections Nicholas BRATHWAITE was elected leader because of his 'cleaner political image' and his former chairmanship of the ADVISORY COUNCIL. The NDC won only seven seats, but gained a majority when two members of The National Party (TNP) and a dissident GULP member, joined the party. By 1994 the NDC had gained a parliamentary majority of 12 due to further defections from the GULP.

During its term in office, the NDC was confronted with high fiscal deficits and vocal political opposition to its structural adjustment programme, but it did achieve the converted credit worthiness from international lending organisations. Its policy of divestment of a number of public enterprises, including utilities and BANKS, also drew protest from the political opposition. In 1994 PM Brathwaite resigned as head of the party and was replaced by Brizan who became PM in February 1995 after Brathwaite's voluntary departure. In the 1995 general elections the NDC lost to the NNP. Alexis left to form his own party. Following the dissolution of Parliament in December 1998, the NDC attempted to form various coalitions with other opposition parties, but failed. Its devastating defeat at the polls in 1999 left it in disarray. After Brizan resigned, political infighting resulted in the departure of a number of the party's top leadership. By 2002 it had restructured by incorporating former NEW JEWEL MOVEMENT members in hopes of presenting an effective challenge to the NNP government. In parliamentary elections in 2003 it successfully won seven of the 15 seats, presenting the NNP government with a noticeable opposition for the first time since 1998. (See www.ndcgrenada.org)

NATIONAL FOLK GROUP The NFG was founded in 1986, the successor to a number of groups that have over the years attempted to represent the FOLK CULTURE of the islands (under the GULP government there were a number of Lancers groups, and the PEOPLE'S REVOLUTIONARY GOVERNMENT established the National Performing Company). The members of the NFG are drawn from four existing performing ARTS groups: the Veni-Vwai La Grenada Dance Co. (est. 1975 in St. George's by Gloria Payne and Albert Charles from the BEE WEE BALLET); Spice Island Youth Quake (f. 1980 in St. John, specialising in religious songs and drama); Cariawa Folk Group (from St. Patrick, specialising in folk singing); and Impulse Dance Company (est. 1986 in St. George's by Cheryl Joseph-Bernabe, specialising in modern dance). The NFG comprises older and young amateur artists who enjoy learning and performing the islands' traditional folk culture and emerging national culture. Many of them have toured internationally as members of their respective groups and the NFG, entertaining Grenadian and foreign audiences in the UK, North America and the Caribbean. They perform, in traditional costumes, a repertoire of folk songs, many in FRENCH CREOLE, modern Caribbean dance, FOLK DANCES like the bélé, and dramatic skits.

National Folk Group performing

NATIONAL PARK SYSTEM Following a number of attempts by previous governments, the NEW NATIONAL PARTY government, in collaboration with the OAS, undertook a comprehensive study of the islands' natural and cultural resources in 1987. The final document, *A Plan and Policy for a System of National Parks*

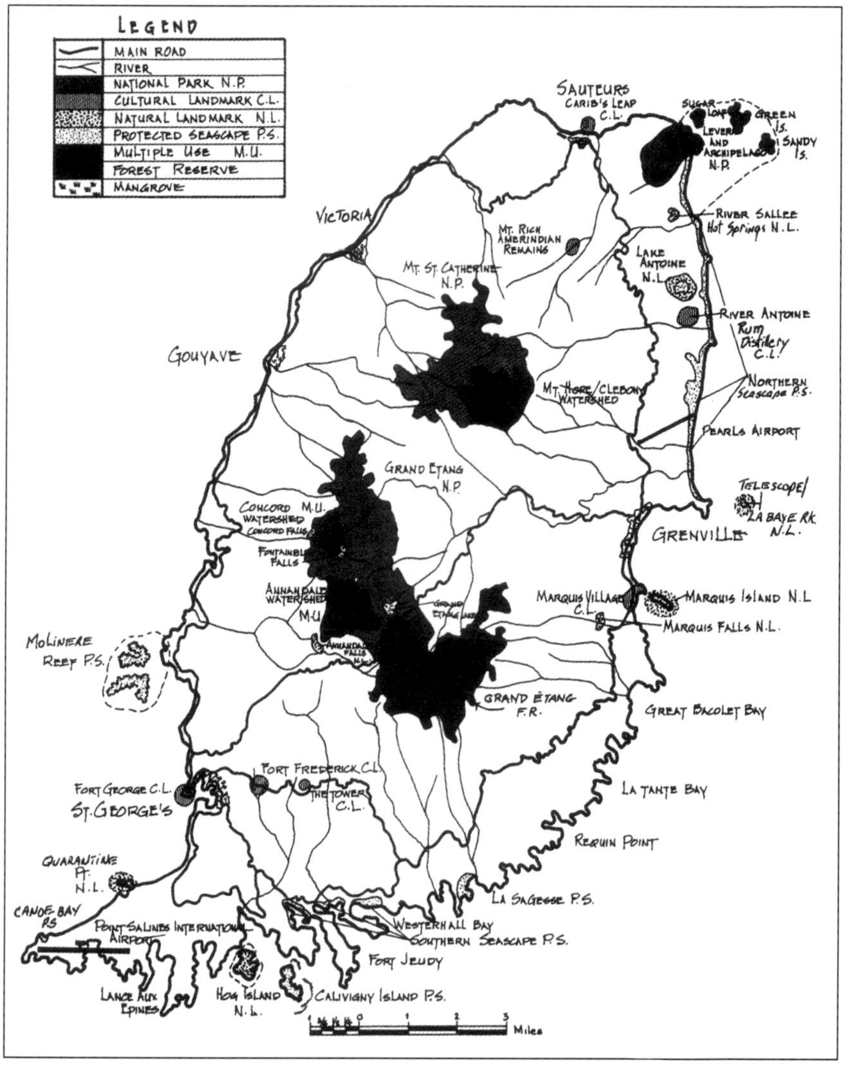

National Park System and cultural sites of Grenada

and Protected Areas in Grenada and Carriacou, described proposed natural and cultural sites and management criteria for their CONSERVATION. The plan outlined the five categories to be managed: national parks, natural landmarks, cultural landmarks, protected seascapes and multiple-use management areas. In 1990 PARLIAMENT passed the National Parks and Protected Areas Act providing for the establishment of a park system for the state of Grenada as outlined in the 1988 study. Since then the GRAND ÉTANG NATIONAL PARK and the LEVERA NATIONAL PARK have been established, their management undertaken by the National Parks Advisory Council.

The planned national parks system, including HIGH NORTH NATIONAL PARK in Carriacou and MT. ST. CATHERINE NATIONAL PARK, will cover approximately six per cent of the total land area of the islands. Grenada's national parks system is foremost among the islands of the Eastern Caribbean, and the continued managed development of its natural resources will contribute to a sustainable environment for its inhabitants and the many visitors who find the islands beautiful and inviting. A major aspect of the plan is the protection of valuable water catchment-areas.[50, 106, 140]

NATIONAL STADIUM

Construction of a national sporting complex began in 1997 following the demolition of the pavilion at the QUEEN'S PARK. Plans for a national stadium date back to the PEOPLE'S REVOLUTIONARY GOVERNMENT, but the unexpected end to the Grenada REVOLUTION in 1983 terminated those plans. The NEW NATIONAL PARTY government, fulfilling a campaign promise, initiated the stadium project as per the Grenada National Stadium Development and Financing Act of 1997. The facilities, completed in 2000, comprised 'two proximal sporting facilities' at a cost of about US$23m. The passage of HURRICANE IVAN in 2004 destroyed the stadiums, necessitating total reconstruction before further

National Stadium with Dabeau Hill in the background (pre-Ivan)

use. In November 2005 the People's Republic of China began reconstruction, completing the cricket stadium in time for the 2007 Cricket World Cup. The 15,000-seat stadium was built at a cost of US$30m; the smaller athletics stadium will be completed later on. The state-of-the-art facilities will serve a number of constituencies, particularly youth, and will generate revenue from international sporting activities, cultural events, musical concerts and conferences. It is managed by an independent National Sports Foundation under the Ministry of Sports. The new facilities are expected to enhance sporting activities in the islands, especially athletics, cricket and football.

NATIONAL SYMBOLS For most of its modern history Grenada has either been a French or British colony, and as such did not fly its own flag until the ASSOCIATED STATEHOOD flag in 1967 and the INDEPENDENCE flag in 1974. Its predecessors had been the French *Fleur de Lys* and the British Union Jack. The present flag has a red border surrounding four triangles with the colours red, green and yellow (the Pan-African colours), representing the fervour of the people, the vegetation and sunshine, respectively. The nutmeg depicts the islands' valued agricultural export and the seven gold stars represent the original PARISHES or districts. Under the PEOPLE'S REVOLUTIONARY GOVERNMENT the revolutionary flag, a red circle on a white background, was flown along with the national flag.

Since 1763 Grenada has had three coats of arms. The first is depicted on the MACE of the House of Representatives and the second, adopted in 1903, is depicted on the Mace of the Senate. The third coat of arms came into effect on Grenada's independence and depicts a number of symbols. The scroll at the base bears the motto: 'For ever conscious of God, we aspire, build and advance as one people.' The BOUGAINVILLEA is the national flower. Grenadians continue to receive traditional British honours (OBE, MBE, CBE, etc.) as part of the annual Queen's New Year Honours List. The National Anthem, with lyrics by Irva Blackette and music by Louis Masanto, replaced the Associated Statehood anthem of 1967.[179]

The Grenada Anthem: 'Hail Grenada/Land of ours/We pledge ourselves to thee/Head, hearts, and hands in unity/ to reach our destiny/Ever conscious of God,/Being proud of our heritage/May we with faith and courage/aspire, build and advance/as one people, one family/God bless our nation.'

The Pledge of Allegiance: 'I pledge allegiance unto the flag/and to the country for which it stands/With liberty, justice and equality for all/I pledge also to defend and uphold the honour/the dignity, the laws and institutions of my country.'

NEDD, Sir Archibald Robert (1916-1991) was a lawyer, magistrate, judge of the High Court, and chief justice of the controversial GRENADA SUPREME COURT (GSC) between 1979 and 1986. He was the son of Robert and Ruth Nedd. A student who distinguished himself academically, he was awarded an ISLAND SCHOLARSHIP in 1934 and pursued law studies at King's College, London, UK. In 1938 he was admitted to the British Bar. He served in the law profession in Nigeria and the Caribbean before being appointed a judge on the Windward Islands Associated States Supreme Court. Following the Grenada REVOLUTION and the suspension of the constitution, he was appointed the chief justice of the newly created GSC under the PEOPLE'S REVOLUTIONARY GOVERNMENT. As chief justice, he presided over the initial trial of the GRENADA 17, but retired in 1986 while the trial was delayed. In 1996 the Grenada Bar Association inaugurated the annual Sir Archibald Nedd Memorial Lecture.[3]

NETBALL is a popular game played predominantly by women throughout the English-speaking Caribbean. An American sport based on basketball, it was brought to the Caribbean by English teachers in the early part of the twentieth century and became popular among school-age girls in Grenada after its introduction in 1922 at the ANGLICAN HIGH SCHOOL. Over the years it has become a national sport, but it was the early efforts of

Grenada's national flag

Louise ROWLEY and the Girls' Physical Cultural Group in the 1930s that have been credited with the success of the sport in Grenada, which is considered the nursery of West Indian netball. It is a very popular sport with annual competitions among secondary schools, government departments and businesses throughout the island (the Inter-sectoral Netball Tournament was begun in 1980). There are also regional competitions between the various islands.

Two teams of seven players engage each other, with the objective of shooting at opposing goal hoops (no backboard). Unlike basketball, the ball is passed across the court and not dribbled, since players are restricted to prescribed regions of the court. Only the two attackers are allowed to shoot while the two defenders guard against the opposing attackers' scoring. Before the advent of women's CRICKET and FOOTBALL, netball was the only team sport in which women participated due to its non-contact nature. Janice Celestine, former captain of the Grenada national and West Indies netball teams, is one of the most celebrated players in the sport's history.

NEW JEWEL MOVEMENT At its formation in March 1973, the NJM represented a national opposition to the GULP government and the ineffective GRENADA NATIONAL PARTY opposition. It was the product of a merger between two groups, the Movement for Assemblies of the People under Maurice BISHOP, and the Joint Endeavour for Welfare, Education and Liberation (JEWEL) under Unison Whiteman. Many believed that the merger of these two groups would produce the political force to successfully challenge the GULP government of Premier Gairy. Its popular slogans like 'Let's Join Hands to Build a Better Land,' 'Not Just Another Society, But a Just Society,' and 'Let Those Who Labour Hold the Reins' appealed to many. Its newsletter, *The New Jewel*, became the popular voice of the organisation. Bishop, seen as the new charismatic leader, became the adored leader.

Throughout its history the NJM saw a number of changes, beginning with its new status as a vanguard party in 1974 and the formation of its Political Bureau. In 1975 the NJM 'secretly' became a Marxist-Leninist party and in 1978 established the Organizing Committee under Bernard COARD, a body responsible for overseeing everyday decisions of the party. The orchestrated actions of the NJM in opposition to the Gairy government propelled it onto the political scene as a party of the left. Its associated mass organisations, the NYO and NWO, and a widely read newsletter captured the hearts and minds of many Grenadians. Gairy's violent attacks against the leadership and members also endeared them to the masses.

A direct outgrowth of the BLACK POWER movement in the early 1970s and modelled on the Cuban Revolution, the NJM, in its manifesto 'Power to the People', called for a comprehensive approach to government and economic development. This approach appealed to many, and with a well orchestrated verbal (some argue subversive and violent) attack on Gairy's haphazard leadership, the NJM gained support across the political spectrum, despite its brand of left-leaning ideology and its stated distaste for the traditional Westminster-style democracy.

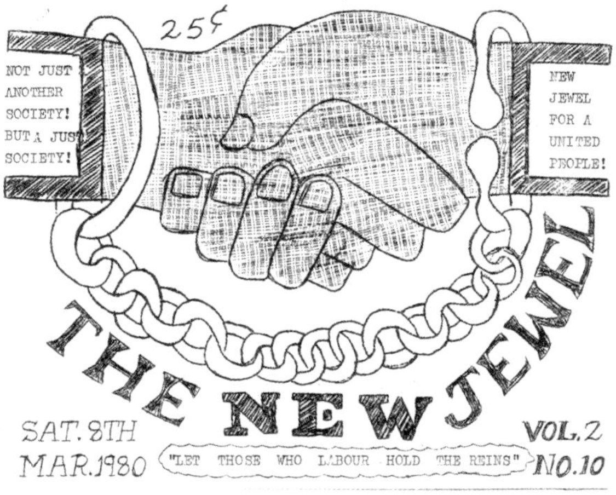

Masthead of *The New Jewel*

With its failed attempt to forestall Grenadian INDEPENDENCE and depose the Gairy government by mass action, the NJM decided to participate in the election process even though it saw it as 'narrow in its ability to create change'. Its association with the PEOPLE'S ALLIANCE extended its appeal to every segment of Grenadian society, even those who had once expressed reservations about its political ideology. Capturing only three of the 15 seats in an election it charged was rigged, the NJM, within the People's Alliance (which won six seats), assumed the role of the opposition in PARLIAMENT. Dissatisfied with its secondary and benign role within an abused parliamentary system, the NJM decided to remove the Gairy government by force of arms, and on MARCH 13, 1979 overthrew the GULP government. In September 1979 the Central Committee was formed and became the general decision-making body of the party and government.

The suspension of the constitution and the establishment of People's Laws quickly consolidated the power of the PEOPLE'S REVOLUTIONARY GOVERNMENT and created the conditions for the path it took the country along for the next four-and-a-half years. During the revolution, the NJM was the sole political party with

70 full members and another 280 in differing stages of recruitment. It was discontinued as a result of the US INTERVENTION.[101, 176, 210, 267]

NEW NATIONAL PARTY Through pressure from the US and conservative Caribbean governments with a desire to forestall either the GULP or the Maurice Bishop Patriotic Movement (MBPM) from gaining political power, the NNP was formed in August 1984. It was the second attempt to form a merger of diverse parties to create an alternative to dictatorship or socialism; the first attempt failed with the collapse of the Team for National Togetherness a few months earlier. The merger had brought together the GRENADA NATIONAL PARTY (under Herbert BLAIZE), the Grenada Democratic Movement (under Francis Alexis) and the National Democratic Party (under George BRIZAN); Winston Whyte's Christian Democratic Labour Party left the NNP coalition before the ELECTIONS.

With conservative and pro-business members, the NNP was readily supported by the US government, which funnelled funds and support through a number of conservative US organisations. Shaky though the alliance was, it held until the December elections and won 14 of the 15 contested constituencies.

The NNP became a moderate party, balancing conservatives against liberals as it promoted the virtues of free-market capitalism. A host of political and economic problems—PM Blaize's style of leadership, supposed favouritism towards former GNP members and retrenchment of government workers—soon dominated internal party politics. By early 1987 factional discord overwhelmed the coalition, resulting in defections that almost brought down the NNP government and created the NATIONAL DEMOCRATIC CONGRESS. The final blow to the shaky NNP government came in 1989 when Dr. Keith MITCHELL replaced PM Blaize as party leader, with Blaize leaving to form The National Party.

In the 1990 elections the NNP won only two seats, but in 1995 it won a majority and formed the government. The NNP has continued with the privatisation of public enterprises, and extensive island-wide infrastructure enhancement. The NNP lost its parliamentary majority due to defections from the party, forcing PM Mitchell to dissolve Parliament in December 1998 and call early elections. The NNP then won a remarkable victory at the polls in 1999, winning all 15 seats and about 62 per cent of the total votes. It became the first incumbent party since 1976 to be re-elected. Grenadian voters gave an unprecedented mandate to the NNP and PM Mitchell to continue its policies. In 2003 it was returned to power, but with a slim margin of one (8 to 7). It became, however, the first incumbent party since the GULP to be re-elected twice.[243] (See www.nnp.com)

NEWSPAPERS The first newspaper published in Grenada was the ROYAL GRENADA GAZETTE, which appeared in 1765, 47 years after the first English-language Caribbean newspaper was published in Jamaica. Together with an earlier established press, these two presses signalled the advent of printing and publishing in the islands, utilising the common wooden letterpresses of the period. Until the early 1800s newspapers and almanacs remained the principal business of printers, but a number of books and pamphlets, primarily government documents like laws, legislative proceedings and notices, were also published. Earlier attempts to publish newspapers in the French Caribbean, of which Grenada was a colony until 1763, proved futile until the 1760s. The only French newspaper published in Grenada was the *Gazette Royale de la Grenade* (1779-1783) by French printer Jean Cassan, 'Printer to the King', but Alexander Middleton also published the *Courrier de la Grenade* (1779-83). In 1787 the islands' longest-running newspaper, *Chronicle and Gazette*, began publication as the *St. George's Chronicle and New Grenada Gazette* to 1798, then as the *St. George's Chronicle and New Gazette* to 1840; it ended in 1915.

The islands have known over thirty newspapers that have provided almost continuous media coverage and recorded local events. With a very limited reading public, it was a struggle to keep even weekly newspapers alive due to low circulation. Subscription was the main form of newspaper purchase for many years, and a successful newspaper often attracted only a few hundred subscribers. Thus many newspapers, begun for various political and social reasons, were short-lived. Some like *The New Era* (1878-1880) established to protest against the CROWN COLONY system, ended once the political stimulus lessened. Other

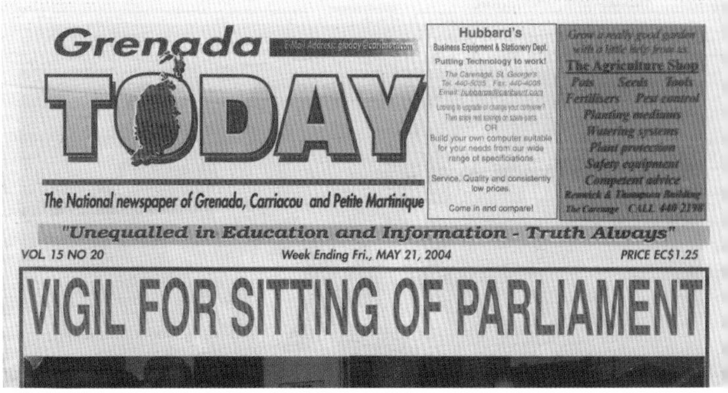

Grenada Today masthead

early printers and publishers included Alexander Murray who established two weeklies, the *Carriacou Observer and Grenadines Journal* (c. 1846) and the *Grenada Observer* (1853-1854/55); Matthew Gallager published the *Weekly Courant and Caribbean Advertiser* in St. George's c. 1794; and George Burnett published an almanac in Grenada in 1787. Newspaper publishing was restricted to the central town of ST. GEORGE'S, and short-lived attempts like the *St. Andrew's Journal and La-Baye/Colonial Miscellany* (1828-1829?) printed by Alexander M'Combie at the *Free Press* office and the *Carriacou Observer* illustrated that fact.

Other newspapers published since the 1800s include the *Grenada Free Press and Weekly Gazette*, later the *Grenada Free Press and St. George's Gazette* (1826-1842), *The Grenada Phoenix* (1863-1865), *The Grenada Reporter* (1867), *Excelsior* (1876), *The Equilibrium* (1882-1887), *Daily Tidings* (1885-1887), and *The Star* (1959-1961?). Religious newspapers have included the *Grenada Magazine* or *Monthly Miscellany of Religious and General Information* (1833), the *Weekly Record* (1853-1864?), and the *Grenada Guardian* (1923-1935) by the RC Church.

Two of the most important newspaper editors/political activists in the islands' history were W G DONOVAN and T A MARRYSHOW (of The WEST INDIAN). The issue of a free press and censorship has confronted governments in the past decades, particularly the GULP, PEOPLE'S REVOLUTIONARY GOVERNMENT and NEW NATIONAL PARTY. The popularity of the NEW JEWEL MOVEMENT and its newsletter, *The New Jewel*, became a political liability for PM Gairy. The Gairy-dominated legislature passed the Newspaper Amendment Act (1975), which required an exorbitant EC$20,000 deposit by the publisher of existing newspapers. As opposed to the outright banning of newspapers, which would have resulted in negative international press coverage, PM Gairy chose to exert his power within the law. Under the PRG the issue of press freedoms became paramount following the closures of the TORCHLIGHT, the only independent newspaper, in 1979, and the *Grenadian Voice* in 1981. The free press issue played an important role in the decline in public support for the REVOLUTION. Between 1984 and 1988 the NNP government openly banned 'objectionable' publications in its attempt to destroy what it considered the remnants of socialism.

There are at present about four weekly newspapers, most presenting the news in tabloid fashion, including the *Grenadian Voice* (f.1981), *Grenada Today* (f.1990), and *The (Grenada) Informer* (f.1985). The bi-monthly *Government Gazette* (est.1883 as the *Grenada Gazette*, succeeding the *Grenada Official Gazette*, est.1862) is the official publication of the GOG. Political party newspapers like *The National* (f.1985 by the NNP), *The Indies Times* (f.1984 by the MBPM), and the *Grenada Guardian* (f.1984 by the GULP) became common in the 1984 election campaign and a number have survived in some form. There is a Press Association of Grenada (f.1986), which has remained under-utilised. There is also the Media Workers' Association of Grenada, the more active of the media organisations. Newspapers are very important to the study of the islands' history, as books like Devas' *Conception Island*, Brizan's *Island of Conflict* and Clyde's *Health in Grenada* illustrate, despite the fact that the earlier newspapers neglected the majority black population and their culture.

NOEL, Dr Walter Clement (1884-1916) had the unfortunate distinction of being the first reported sickle cell anaemia patient in western medical literature. A member of the proprietary Noel family in Grenada, he went to the US in 1904 to study dentistry at the Chicago College of Dental Surgery. On arriving in New York he had to be treated for 'severe skin lesions, pains throughout his limbs and joints, and shortness of breath', symptoms that would become signs of sickle cell anaemia. Noel's symptoms continued throughout his studies (1904-1907), and he received treatment for an unknown anaemia at the Presbyterian Hospital where Dr Ernest Irons, a medical resident, observed him and took regular blood and urine examinations. Three years after Noel returned to Grenada and began a dental practice, Dr Herrick published an article in the *Archives of Internal Medicine* detailing the mysterious illness, especially the presence of irregularly shaped sickle red blood cells in his system.

While it was the beginning of the diagnosis and treatment of this disease afflicting thousands around the world, but particularly people of African/Mediterranean descent, Noel would learn nothing of his disease or the historicity of the finding, and would die in 1916 of pneumonia. Sickle cell anaemia was brought by SLAVES from West Africa, and though the possession of the trait, which both of Noel's parents likely had, appears to protect against the deadly MALARIA parasite, the disease can lead to death in childhood, or early adulthood, as was the case with Noel and possibly other members of his family.

NOGUES, Charles (d. 1796) was one of the leaders of FÉDON'S REBELLION following his appointment as 'Officer of the Republic commanding at Grenada' and captain in the French Republican Army. In official correspondence Julien FÉDON referred to him as 'my aide-de-camp'. He was a FREE COLOURED, probably the son of the French planter Nogues who prior to 1763 owned a 430 acre (175 ha) sugar estate near RIVER SALLEE, St. Patrick. Charles Nogues had worked as a tailor in St. George's, but in 1794 was renting 'cotton land' at Levera, St. Patrick. In 1790 he had sold to Julien Fédon, his brother-in-law, 'some land and tenements' in GOUYAVE, the same year he signed the 'Declaration of Loyalty' to the British.

Early in 1795, together with Jean-Pierre LA VALETTE, he secretly travelled to Guadeloupe to meet with Victor Hugues, the leader of the French Republican forces in the Windward Islands. He most likely received some training and Republican revolutionary indoctrination. He developed a close relationship with Hugues, who may have held him in higher esteem than Fédon, especially after Fédon's failure to destroy the British. As captain he commanded a company of soldiers during the rebellion and played a pivotal role in the revolt. In the final assault on the rebel stronghold of FÉDON'S CAMP Nogues was captured. He was tried and later executed in the MARKET SQUARE on 11 August 1796, the highest-ranking rebel officer captured. It was rumoured that his head was severed from his body in a final act of revenge. In a note to his wife and sons he bade them 'farewell and brotherhood, I die French'.[12, 174]

NOUAILLY, Philibert de (fl. 1640s) was the first French GOVERNOR of Grenada, though he never took up residence there. He travelled to the West Indies in 1643 with de Bretigny's failed expedition to the Guianas, and may have seen or heard of Grenada, developing an interest in the island. On 10 July 1645 he was granted a commission as governor of Grenada for five years by the Compagnie des Isles de l'Amérique, which had claimed much of the Lesser Antilles since 1635. The contract stipulated that he 'occupy and populate' the island, and 'take there, during the first year, 200 persons of all sexes and three members of the clergy to instruct the Savages and administer the sacraments to the settlers.'

Almost a year later he had not reached Grenada, but instead arranged for a representative to take over the contract, but he too was unsuccessful. In 1647, following his re-negotiation of the contract, he made an agreement with his deputy-lieutenant general to recruit twenty armed soldiers and equipment for SETTLEMENT. De Nouailly had even made arrangement for his daughter Catherine to travel to the West Indies, but still the expedition did not leave France. In 1648 he again re-negotiated the contract, receiving a continuance, but de Nouailly's expedition never left due to political problems in France stemming from the Fronde. While de Nouailly hesitated, DU PARQUET set in motion his plans to settle Grenada in 1649.[8]

NOW-NOW was probably the best known of the many eccentric 'characters' who have been a part of the life of St. George's Town for generations. He has been described as 'the best one-man walking advertising agency in Grenada'. He was a sort of town crier who made his living advertising anything and everything, for a price, including RUM. With his bell he attracted attention, and a billboard hung about his body carried his message, encouraging sales for many of the local stores. Known for his rum drinking, Now-Now, dressed in a jacket and tie, made an unofficial bid for political office; his campaign promise was that, if he was elected, 'every man, woman, and child would always have a drink.' He, like many of the individuals who

Now-Now

eked out a living with their talents and sometimes their physical and mental weaknesses, provided comic relief to some, and evoked pity and charity in others.

Now-Now is representative of the many well-known characters who made a living on the periphery of society across the islands. They included street performer Bonzo (who is remembered as the 'Don Rickles of St. George's'), Red Ants ('the educated drunkard on Tyrrel Street'), stammering Mitt, Stone Bruise, Cecil ('everybody's errand boy'), Monica Caway, Strongman or Spanner Toe (who went about collecting kitchen scraps or 'pickin' for his pigs), Vung the LIGAROU, Carriacou Sparrow/Field Marshall (who roamed around singing calypsoes) and Walter Levin alias Walter Doone who was rumoured to have lots of money which he supposedly stole from SA FRANCIS. They were homeless, handicapped, retarded, or just down on their luck. Many made their homes in the MARKET SQUARE, and it was a common practice for children to tease them, making them angry and often creating public disturbances. Many are remembered in song like 'Monica Caway' by PAPITETTE, and poetry like 'Who Remembers' by Chris DeRiggs.[214]

NUTMEG (*Myristica fragrans*) Every Grenadian child knows that the answer to the riddle 'Lady in a boat with a red petticoat' is nutmeg, a reference to the split pear-shaped pericarp housing the mace-laced covered seed, and one of the islands' primary agricultural exports. The nutmeg is an evergreen tree, growing to over 60 ft (18 m), and produces two spices: nutmeg and mace. When ripe, the pale yellow fruit splits open, exposing a scarlet net-like membrane that encloses a glossy brittle shell. The nutmeg of commerce is the small brown seed within the brown shell, and the net-like membrane is mace. The yellow fleshy apricot-like pericarp is used to make jelly, jam, syrup and confectionery. Grated nutmeg is used to flavour rum punch, eggnog, cakes and pastries. Myristicin, a substance in the essential oil of nutmeg and mace, has a powerful narcotic effect when taken in large doses, but is very toxic.

Though a number of 'tales of arrival' are commonly told, the first nutmeg plants probably arrived by the early 1800s, but were not successful. The British brought nutmeg plants to St. Vincent in 1806, and if they were not already present in Grenada, the island may have received plants then. Two popular tales of arrival deserve mention nonetheless. The first involves Louis LA GRENADE, Sr., who in 1773 reportedly received some nutmeg seeds and the secret recipe for an exotic liqueur from a Dutch missionary who was given free passage aboard his schooner *La Louise*. The second tale, the most popular and 'officially' accepted, contradicts the first and claims that nutmegs were first brought to Grenada in 1843 from Banda, Indonesia by Frank Gurney, a Grenadian agriculturist who had worked there.

Whatever its origins, around 1860 the nutmeg became an economic crop, expanding in the early 1900s. Percentages of world exports have ranged between 20 and 33 per cent, the latter recorded for 1918. Grenada's share of world nutmeg and mace exports was 19 per cent in 1995, falling from a high of 43 per cent in 1990 due to the end of the cartel arrangement with Indonesia (from 1987). Nutmeg production employs a large number of workers, especially in the rural areas where the cultivation and processing take place. Nutmeg oil/butter, used in the manufacture of soap and perfumes, has been extracted from the nuts since a nutmeg oil processing plant came on-line in 1994. FOLK MEDICINE prescribes nutmeg oil for the treatment of arthritis. The saying 'one, one nutmeg fill basket' means that no matter how long it may take, success lies ahead, or it is persistence that leads to success. HURRICANE IVAN in 2004 destoyed as much as 70 per cent of fruit-bearing nutmeg trees.[34, 35, 92, 223]

Nutmeg and mace

O

OBEAH is a medico-religious folk practice once common in Grenada (and the Caribbean). It is a fusion of a number of African practices that remained essential to the slaves' lives. Obeah combines folk medicine, SUPERSTITION, divination and magic into a potent belief system. Though it originated in West African culture (Twi *o-bayi-fo*: 'sorcerer', <*bayi*: 'witchcraft'), it was transformed by SLAVERY and colonialism. The practice was widespread as BELL records: 'Before the emancipation, the practice of Obeah was rampant in all the West Indian colonies, and laws and ordinances had to be framed to put it down, and combat its baneful influences.' The mysterious rituals of obeah often involved the sacrifice of animals, particularly chickens and goats, and combined with an assortment of objects—feathers, egg shells, teeth of various animals, hair, graveyard soil, holy water, herbs, and broken glass—to produce 'powerful' remedies used for cures or curses. Obeah was a secret practice that the Churches and state characterised as 'evil' and 'uncivilised', making every effort to eradicate it. Any slave caught with obeah paraphernalia could be severely punished, which included flogging, 'transportation', and even death. The punishment was so severe because many slaves died due to poisoning, either intentionally or through the administering of FOLK MEDICINES. As Bell observed in the late 1800s, 'The darker and more dangerous side of Obeah is that portion under cover of which poison is used to a fearful extent, and the dangerous and often fatal effects of many of the magic draught are simply set down, by the superstitious black, to the workings of the spells of Obeah, and never to the more simple effects of the scores of poisonous herbs growing in every pasture, and which may have formed the ingredients of the Obeah mixture.' The practice also caused whites to fear for their own lives since poisons could be as easily administered to them as to the slaves. They probably feared most the power of the obeah practitioners and the mortal fear of them by the majority of slaves. There was always the fear that these practices could lead to subversive slave activities, and there were instances of 'obeahmen' and 'obeahwomen' leading slaves in rebellion in a number of territories.

Obeah is steeped in sorcery, making use of fear, suspicion, and revenge to achieve its goals. The expertise of an obeahman/woman ('papa-do-good' or 'mama-do-good'), knowledgeable in folk remedies and charms, is hired to execute one's desires. Concerning obeahmen, Bell states that 'They were usually the oldest and most crafty of the blacks, those whose hoary heads and somewhat forbidding aspect, together with some skill in plants of the medicinal and poisonous species, qualified them for successful imposition on the weak and credulous.' The obeahman/woman uses a variety of concoctions, amulets and chants to 'passhand' or 'do' the intended victim who, after believing that s/he has been preyed upon by enemies, will seek the advice of a friendly obeahman/woman to pronounce a curse on the suspected evil doer. Customers from across the islands call upon the more renowned of the obeah practitioners and pay whatever the fee to have their fears allayed. Former PM GAIRY was accused by his political opponents of practising obeah and was rumoured to have employed a powerful obeahwoman to give advice and protection from political enemies. Once widely practised throughout Grenada, obeah has lost a great deal of its importance in the lives of Grenadians as a result of widespread formal education, condemnation by the Christian Churches and the conversion of the majority of the slaves and later peasants to Christianity, and the improving standard of living of most of the population. Yet obeah is still a part of the belief system of some individuals, and there are always rumours of someone engaging in witchcraft. Only rarely is anybody arrested and charged with a crime, as was the case in November 2003 when a woman was held by the police for engaging in the practice. Obeah, like vodum or voodoo, owes elements of its practice to the AKAN people of West Africa. Also known as wanga (<UMbundu *wanga*: 'witchcraft').[18]

OECS The acronym for the Organization of Eastern Caribbean States, a regional grouping of seven Eastern Caribbean countries founded in June 1981 to facilitate closer co-operation between themselves in areas of economic development, foreign relations and defence, and the integration of its members into the global economy. Its members are Antigua-Barbuda, Dominica, Grenada, Montserrat (Br.), St. Kitts-Nevis, St. Lucia, and St. Vincent and the Grenadines; Anguilla and the British Virgin Islands are associate members. The OECS replaced and extended the work begun in 1967 by the West Indies Associated States as the umbrella grouping of the six states granted ASSOCIATED STATEHOOD with the UK.

With headquarters in St. Lucia, the OECS functions through ministerial committees responsible for specific areas and reports to the highest body, the Heads of Government. All territories use the East Caribbean

States Currency issued by the Eastern Caribbean Central Bank (ECCB) in St. Kitts, which was established in 1983 and replaced the East Caribbean Currency Authority. The ECCB, as the monetary authority, is responsible for regional monetary stability, the development of the economies and the financial systems of its member states, thus creating the vital link to other banking and developmental institutions operating in the Caribbean. Member states also belong to the OECS Supreme Court.

In October 1983 the OECS, chaired by Dominican PM Eugenia Charles, invoked the OECS Charter providing for the defence of the signatories and 'invited' the US military to intervene into the political turmoil in Grenada (see INTERVENTION). The East Caribbean Common Market (ECCM) was formed in 1968 to forge greater economic ties between the smaller, least developed states in the English-speaking Caribbean. Its goals are the elimination of custom duties between the islands, the creation of a common agricultural policy, free movement of citizens, services and capital, and the harmonisation of tax policies. In 1981 the ECCM became a part of the OECS, and in 1997 became a division of the OECS Secretariat.[203]

OIL-DOWN Though pelau, calalu soup, fried and stuffed jacks, rice and peas, peas soup, and COU-COU are popular local dishes, oil down comes closest to being Grenada's national dish. Its main ingredients are BREADFRUIT, provisions like YAMS, green BANANAS, TANNIA, bluggoe and DASHEEN, calalu leaves, salt beef, salt pork and/or pig tails. This combination is cooked in COCONUT milk and spices to add flavour. The dish probably owes its name to the fact that the ingredients are allowed to 'boil down', leaving a tasty oily residue over the vegetables. This 'one pot' originated in the countryside where its simplicity made it popular and was once regarded as 'poor people food'. Though it is not a common dish among the traditional middle class, many Grenadians relish it. A taste of oil-down can be had at some of the HOTELS and restaurants that serve local dishes. In Jamaica a similar dish is called run-down.

OLD REPRESENTATIVE SYSTEM (ORS) of government was granted by Royal Proclamation in 1763, and established in 1766 with the election of the islands' first House of Assembly. The first General Council for the four-island grouping GOVERNMENT OF GRENADA was appointed in 1767, but soon dissolved into individual Councils. Grenada's first constitution was modelled on that of the Leeward Islands and Barbados, even though as a ceded territory it could have automatically been made a Crown Colony. Representative government was granted 'to aid the speedy settlement of Grenada by the British who think their liberties and properties more secure when they have a legislative assembly.' The ORS comprised an appointed governor who was responsible to the Colonial Office, a General Council appointed by the governor, and an elected House of Assembly. The governor exercised executive authority, while the appointed Council acted as his advisors. The Council was expected to work in collaboration with the elected Assembly to pass necessary legislation, but the two often failed to work together, and with the high absenteeism and low educational qualifications of members of both councils, the ORS often disintegrated into a farce.

By the mid-1800s political, economic and social changes in Grenada and the BWI had exposed its ineffectiveness and revealed its inherent anachronism. Paramount among these changes were the granting of equal political status to FREE COLOUREDS and free blacks in 1832, and the EMANCIPATION of the slaves in 1834, which brought to the fore the inherent problems with a so-called representative system that failed to represent the majority of the free population. Yet the ORS dragged on until the 1870s when the weight of its own inefficiency brought protests from the Colonial Office and prominent local residents. It has been suggested that the dissolution of the ORS was due to either the desire of the British government to create a federation of the Windward and Leeward Islands, or to control government expenditure given that Grenada would require financial assistance due to its decreasing revenues. In 1875 the legislature voted to establish a 17-member Single Chamber, comprising appointed members who held a majority over the elected members. At its first sitting, the Single Chamber voted to dissolve the ORS Constitution, opening the way for the introduction of CROWN COLONY rule in 1877.[35, 98, 333]

ORINOCO This ill-fated ship was destined for ST. GEORGE'S HARBOUR, but crashed upon the treacherous rocks on the SE coast on 2 November 1900. The SS *Orinoco*, built in 1880, was one of a number of ships of the Pickford & Black's Line of steamers connecting the Caribbean islands with Europe and North America. The ship, on a voyage from Demerara to Halifax, Nova Scotia, had mistakenly thought the immense illumination of the cemetery at LASAGESSE Point, St. David, on All Souls' Night (see ALL SAINTS') to be the lights of the town of St. George's and crashed upon the rugged SE coast. A subsequent investigation censured the master, and the certificate of the first mate was suspended. Over the years its broken hull has become a man-made reef, supporting many marine organisms. Washed by the rough waters of the Atlantic Ocean, this wreck has recently been attracting experienced divers who find the dive challenging. Its sinking led to the erection of a light in 1904 and a LIGHTHOUSE in 1934.

PALMER, Sir Reginald Oswald (b. 1923) served as the GG of Grenada between 1992 and 1996, replacing GOVERNOR GENERAL Paul SCOON. Beginning in 1939, Sir Reginald became involved in EDUCATION as a pupil teacher. He later earned a bachelor's degree in education from the University of Calgary, Canada. He served as assistant teacher and principal of the J W FLETCHER Memorial School, tutor and principal of the Grenada Teachers' College, assistant education officer, and chief education officer in the Ministry of Education. He was an active member of the GRENADA UNION OF TEACHERS and served as its president. He was also a founding member of the Catholic Teachers' Association. Sir Reginald retired in 1980 from the field of education and became involved in a number of private organisations. Both Sir Reginald and Lady Palmer, having spent many years in the teaching profession, gained the respect of Grenadians, many of whom they taught at the J W Fletcher Memorial School, which was popularly known as 'Palmer School' because of their long and dedicated service to that institution. In 1973 he was awarded the MBE, and the GCMG in 1992 following his appointment as GG. Sir Reginald demitted office in 1996 and was replaced by Daniel WILLIAMS.

PALMS are synonymous with tropical islands, and several species can be seen throughout Grenada. They furnish oil, building materials, food and a number of other useful by-products. They are readily identifiable because of their generally tall, unbranched columnar trunks and crown of tufted, fan-like leaves. The most common and useful is the COCONUT palm. The islands are home to four native species: GROU-GROU, mountain palm (*Prestoea montana*), palmiste or cabbage palm (*Roystonea oleracea*), and mountain cabbage or Hagley's palm (*Euterpe hagleyi/dominicana*). The palmiste derives its name cabbage palm (*chou de palmiste*) from the French who consumed the 'whitish, marrow or pith'. The mountain palm is a tall slender tree growing to 30 ft (9 m). A number of introduced palms, including the betel nut (*Areca catechu*), fishtail (*Caryota arens*), bamboo (*Chrysalidocarpus lutescens*), and date (*Phoenix dactylifera*) palms can be seen throughout the islands. The mountain cabbage is dominant in the rain forests of the GRAND ÉTANG NATIONAL PARK. Palms, long considered majestic in the tropics, have draped the entrances to sugar estates, especially the path to the GREAT HOUSE. The BOTANICAL GARDENS is home to a number of species of palms.[160]

Palm tree with fruits, Botanical Gardens

PANAMA CANAL The resumption of the building of the Panama Canal by the US in 1904 (it was first begun by the French in 1879 but ended prematurely in 1889 when the company went bankrupt) meant the availability of work for unskilled and skilled labourers from the Caribbean. West Indians comprised over half of the labour force, with Jamaicans and Barbadians constituting by far the majority. Workers from many of the smaller islands in the Eastern Caribbean migrated there in search of jobs, among them thousands of Grenadians. In 1906 a recruiting agent of the Isthmian Canal Commission visited, resulting in just over 1,500 Grenadians migrating that same year. A report described the MIGRATION as 'an exodus of labourers', especially from the districts of St. Andrew, St. Patrick and St. David.

The work on the Canal was difficult and in most cases dangerous, resulting in the deaths of many labourers from accidents and DISEASES like MALARIA and YELLOW FEVER. Of those who left in 1906 over 800 returned that same year: 'many of these labourers returned absolutely ruined in health.' They were 'suffering from Panama fever, [a] virulent form of malarial fever' which spread throughout the islands beginning in 1906. Over the next eight years of the construction of the Canal hundreds of Grenadians migrated there. Between 1911 and 1913 some 405 labourers were reported to have left for Panama, but their numbers had already begun to decrease, ending by 1914 when the Canal was completed.

Grenadians began returning in large numbers between 1912 and 1915, with smaller numbers continuing into the 1920s. Many labourers were forced to return and even deported by the Panamanian authorities once the Canal was completed. Some returned with 'Panama money' and became involved in politics and business. One of the early MOTOR VEHICLES to arrive in Grenada, a US-made Overland, was brought by a Grenadian returning from the Canal in 1914, and became the islands' 'first taxi'. Quite a number of Grenadians who went to work on the Canal never returned, choosing instead to go to the US or stay in Panama where they married and raised families, becoming part of the vibrant West Indian community. A number of Spanish words in the Grenadian vocabulary were probably brought by Grenadians returning from Panama, including bacalao (<Pg. *bacallao*: 'codfish'/'saltfish'), calaboose (<Sp. *calabozo*: 'dungeon', or 'jail'), and hefe (<Sp. *jefe*: 'boss').

PAPA-BWA A folk character whose job is guardian/protector of the forest and its animals. It can be envisioned as the islands' first environmentalist, as its name suggests. It bears much resemblance to the AKAN *sasabonsam*, 'a monster which is said to inhabit parts of the dense virgin forests. It is covered with long hair, has large blood-shot eyes, long legs, and feet pointing both ways. It sits on high branches of an *odum* or *onyina* tree and dangles its legs, with which at times it hooks up the unwary hunter.' The papa-bwa/bois (<Fr. 'wood') is considered a 'wise old man', usually found in deserted woods where he accosts passers-by, especially hunters, by blocking their path. As a shape-shifter, he supposedly changes into animal form to lead hunters astray, or into hanging branches and lianas that entangle them. He is also said to warn animals of approaching hunters, and cares for sick animals.

The papa-bwa has been described in various forms, from a faun to a hairy old man with cloven hoofs. But the spirit is commonly personified as a tree trunk, with branches for hands and eyes of fire. The bwa-bwa, on the other hand, is a scarecrow meant to scare off animals from KITCHEN GARDENS. With reference to the scarecrow, bwa-bwa also means ugly and foolish. In Carriacou the bwa-bwa refers to the MOKO JUMBIE. The papa-bwa is often portrayed as the lover of MAMA-GLO.

PAPITETTE The byname of Theophilus Augustus 'Theo' Redhead (1930-1993), who during the 1960s and 1970s was one of Grenada's great calypsonians as well as a celebrated all-round cricketer. He was born in St. George's on 8 August 1930. His singing career began in the 1950s in the Pygmalian Glee Club under Pansy ROWLEY, and through creating promotional songs for the Credit Union Movement. In 1960 and 1964 Papitette won the CALYPSO monarch contest. Throughout the 1960s he produced a number of popular songs like 'Monica Kaway' (the 1966 road-march about a popular character), and 'Theresa' (1967 road-match). In 1971 he produced 'Don't Bite It', followed three years later by his patriotic rendition of 'Grenada: Isle of Spice', a tribute to Grenada's achievement of INDEPENDENCE. Other popular songs include 'Way Janice Gone', 'Priests and Lawyers', and 'Every Bitch and He Brother Hypocrite'. After over thirty years in the development of the art form, Papitette retired in 1987.

As great a cricketer as he was a calypsonian, he represented Grenada, Combine Islands and the WINDWARD ISLANDS, especially between 1959 and 1962. Though retired from cricket he continued to coach for many years. He will be remembered as a sportsman and one of Grenada's all-time great calypsonians who won the calypso road-march title three times. The annual calypso monarch qualifier has been styled the Melody/Papitette National Calypso Semi-Finals, in memory and recognition of two legendary calypsonians.

The Mighty Papitette

PARANG A traditional Spanish musical form, popular in the southern Caribbean during the Christmas season. It arrived in Grenada via Trinidad, with origins in Venezuela. Parang (<Am.Sp. *parranda*: 'a spree, binge', or *parar*: literally 'to put up at someone's house') has, however, incorporated African musical instruments and styles over the years. A parang band comprises Spanish string and African rhythm instruments, specifically the drum. Compositions, sometimes impromptu, are usually a combination of Spanish and English. At Christmas time groups travel from house to house and village to village serenading and playing music, stopping occasionally at a 'friend's' house for food and rest. The tradition of parang STRING BANDS celebrating in the streets at Christmas has become rarer as musicians have either died or emigrated. A few STEELBANDS still keep the spirit of parang alive when they take to the streets on Christmas morning.

Carriacou parang is different from Trinidad parang in that it is more like the 'ole-time calypso', but shares a similar origin. Though it occurs at Christmas, when groups, usually men, go from house to house serenading, the themes are not exclusively about Christmas. They are ad-lib renditions of societal caricature common to CALYPSO. Since 1977 the Mt. Royal Progressive Youth Movement has hosted the Carriacou Parang Festival the week before Christmas.

PARENTS' PLATE is an offering of food specially laid aside for the ancestors or old parents to partake of at ritual ceremonies like a MAROON, TOMBSTONE FEAST, boat launching and wedding in C&PM. The food and drink are taken from the lavish display meant for a *saraca* or sacrifice and placed on a table covered with a white tablecloth and lighted candle. The spirits of the ancestors are expected to come and eat the food. To prevent anyone, especially children, from 'stealing' the food before the old parents can have first choice, a 'gangan' (<Efik *ñ-kam*: 'grandmother', or Ibibio *nkam*: 'my grandmother') will stand watch. Usually after midnight, since it is believed that the old parents have already eaten, the parents' plate is 'broken' as people scramble or grapay (<Fr. Cr.<Fr. *grappin*: 'grab' with hooks) for the food. The parents' plate is meant to please one's ancestors and to encourage their blessing. The practice is derived from the islands' AFRICAN HERITAGE.

PARISHES/DISTRICTS The original six parishes of Grenada were established by the French between 1685 and 1740, with a church or chapel in each. The parish boundaries, delineated by the central ridge of MOUNTAINS and the many RIVERS & STREAMS, came to represent administrative districts. In the first French census of 1669, four districts or quarters were delineated. As the French settlements expanded, the boundaries of the original districts changed. The parishes were St. Jacques and St. Phillippe (est. c.1685) in the BASSETERRE, Notre Dame du Bon Secours in SAUTEURS (est. 1718), Notre Dame de l'Assomption in Grand MARQUIS (est. 1722), St. Pierre in L'Ance à GOUYAVE (est. 1734), and St. Jean-Baptiste in Megrin (est. 1736). Though the parish of St. Rose in Grand Pauvre had been established since the 1650s, a chapel was not erected until the 1740s when the Dominicans returned to the colony.

Parish delineations became important with the establishment of the OLD REPRESENTATIVE SYSTEM and were used as electoral districts. LOCAL GOVERNMENT also relied on parish boundaries. The expansion of the number of electoral districts since the 1960s has reduced the importance of parish boundaries, even though districts are created within established parishes based on the shifts in population. Religiously, the main Churches no longer adhere to the original parishes, having created parishes as needed. As a matter of identity, though, parishes remain important. The residents of each parish voice a strong sense of geographical identity; for instance, the people of St. Andrew refer to themselves as being from the 'Big Parish', while those from St. Mark are from the 'Sunset Parish'.

PARLIAMENT The twenty-third article of the Independence Constitution guarantees the establishment of a Parliament. At the head of Parliament sits the GOVERNOR GENERAL, who is the appointed representative of the HEAD OF STATE, the British monarch Queen Elizabeth II. Completing the Parliament are the appointed Senate and elected House of Representatives. This parliamentary form of government is a representation of the British Westminster model common throughout the Caribbean Commonwealth.

The Senate or upper chamber of the Houses of Parliament was established in 1967 and superseded the Executive Council (1877-1967) and the General Council (1766-1876). The Senate comprises 13 members (increased from nine in 1972) who are appointed by the GG, ten on the advice of the PRIME MINISTER (three 'independents' are designated representatives of special interests as deemed important by the PM), and three by the majority elected opposition party. The Senate is fashioned after the British House of Lords, and presided over by a president who is elected from among the 13 senators. Presidents of the Senate (who rank fifth in order of precedence within

The 1967 Parliament outside York House

the government and acts in the absence of the GG) have been: J T GIBBS (1967-1969), Greaves B James (1969-1979), Lawrence Joseph (1984-1988), Margaret Neckles (1990-1995), Dr John Watts (1967, 1988-1990, 1995-1998, 1999-2003), Leslie-Ann Seon (2004-06) and Kenny Lalsingh (2006-).

General elections are usually held every five years at which time eligible candidates, representing POLITICAL PARTIES or rarely running as independents, contest the 15 constituencies. The GG calls upon the party leader with the support of the majority of the newly elected Members of Parliament to form the next government, usually the leader of the party with the majority or plurality of MPs. The 15 MPs constitute the House of Representatives, which dates to the General Assembly (1766-1876) under the OLD REPRESENTATIVE SYSTEM, and the Legislative Council (1925-1967). The House members' primary duty is the passing of legislation deemed necessary for the governance of the country.

Though the House of Representatives is also known as the Lower House, a title derived from the British House of Commons, it wields more power than the Upper House. The speaker of the House of Representatives presides over that body and commands much authority. S/he is elected from among the elected members by the members of the House, or from without; in the latter case the House will have 16 members (this has been the case since the 1950s). Speakers of the House (ranking sixth in precedence in the government) have been: R C P Moore (1958-1962, 1975-1976), Fisher J Archibald (1962-1967), G E D Clyne (1967-1974), A A Reason (1976-1979), Sir Hudson Scipio (1984-1990), Marcel Peters (1990-1995), Sir Curtis Strachan (1995-98, 1999-2003), and Lawrence Joseph (2004-). Members of Parliament hold the title of 'Honourable'. The Parliament meets at YORK HOUSE when in session.[3, 179]

PASSION FRUIT (*Passiflora* spp.) is native to tropical America, some 400 species known throughout the region. This creeping plant, with long tendrils, can grow to over 8 ft (2.5 m). *P. edulis* var. *edulis* is widely cultivated in backyards or KITCHEN GARDENS for its fruits. The globular green fruit turns yellow or purple when ripe, at which time it can be eaten fresh in fruit salads, but it is more commonly used to make passion fruit juice. The plant derives its name from the arrangement of its floral parts which, Christians assert, symbolises the crucifixion of Jesus Christ. The fruits are available year-round. An infusion of leaves of the water lemon vine (*P. laurifolia*) is prescribed in FOLK MEDICINE for the treatment of intestinal worms.

PAUL, Norman James (1897-1970) was a SPIRITUAL BAPTIST preacher, healer and diviner. In 1948 he founded the African Feast Cult, which 'combines Adventism, Shango, Shakerism, and magical beliefs taken from such books as... [the Bible].' A variety of African-derived religions influenced Paul's upbringing in the countryside of Grenada, and on migrating to TRINIDAD in the 1940s he began staging religious feasts, which he claimed he was instructed to perform by Oshun (St. Philomena), the Yoruban river goddess and one of the wives of SHANGO. Even though he disclaimed any relationship with Shango and the other African-derived religions, his African Feasts exhibited many common characteristics with them. He was also known as a popular healer, with people coming from all over Grenada for his prayers and FOLK MEDICINES. His spiritual popularity aligned him with Eric GAIRY in the early 1950s and he served as Gairy's spiritual advisor, opening political meetings. He also had a following in Carriacou. M G SMITH, in a biographical account of Paul's life, provides an exemplary narrative of a folk leader and 'cult personality'. His followers were known as 'Norman Paul's Children', but popularly called Shango Baptists.[316, 322]

PAULINE (fl. 1780s) was a slave, owned by the proprietary PHILIP family, who in 1786 was freed by the legislature because she revealed the escape plans of a number of slaves in CARRIACOU. Slaves from Grenada and Carriacou frequently made their escape to Spanish TRINIDAD and Margarita and were welcomed by the Spanish because of the scarcity of labour there. (After 1789 a Spanish law openly encouraged their colonies to grant refuge to escaped slaves or MAROONS from British and French colonies who could show 'legitimate claim to freedom'.) In granting Pauline her freedom, the legislature emphasised that 'nothing can tend more to the discovery and detection of such dangerous Conspiracies, than offering every possible Encouragement to those who shall be instrumental in preventing the same.'

PAWPAW/PAPAYA (*Carica papaya*) is native to tropical America and most likely was introduced into the Caribbean by AMERINDIANS. The pawpaw (<Taino *papaya*, for the fruit) is a herbaceous soft-wooded tree with hollow stem and no branches. It can grow to 6-35ft (2-10 m), dominated by large palmate leaves attached directly to the trunk. The round or elongated green fruit, weighing up to 20 lb (9 kg), is borne in the axils of the leaves. The fruit turns yellow upon ripening, its yellowish pink flesh eaten fresh, in salads, or processed into jam and juice.

Pawpaw fruit

Both the leaves and the fruit contain papain, an enzyme that breaks down protein, hence the local use of the green fruit and leaf to tenderise meat; the milky latex is used to make commercial meat tenderisers. Many parts of the tree and fruit are used in FOLK MEDICINES to cure boils, warts, worms, ulcers, and to aid poor blood circulation in the legs. The many small black seeds in the fruit, if eaten raw by pregnant women, are reputed to induce abortion. Fruits are available year-round.

PAYWO/SHAKESPEARE MAS A Carriacouan masquerade quite similar to SHORTKNEE in Grenada, both having originated in the once popular paywo Grenade 'speech mas'. The origin of the traditional paywo is unclear, and is possibly derived from French influences. Carr contends that the name is most probably derived from the FRENCH CREOLE 'country king' (<Fr. *pays roi*) as opposed to 'pierrot' (<Fr. 'clown'). Yet its characteristics—mask, long cape and baggy trousers—resemble a number of African folk characters, especially the *Egungun* of the YORUBA. Its costume consists of colourful trousers and long shirt, a mask to hide the player's identity, a long cape suspended from the head onto the back, and a long stick.

The paywo mas' usually comprises teams that compete against each other in the recitation of verses from William Shakespeare's plays (hence Shakespeare mas'), particularly *Julius Caesar,* and/or passages from the Bible. The object is to outperform your opponent by reciting verses accurately and more quickly. Incorrect renditions are met with a blow about the padded head by the 'bull whip' or stick. Historically, the competitions between the groups or villages were often fierce and violent, which led the authorities to regulate costumes so as to discourage the concealing of weapons in baggy costumes. Though the mas' has been infrequent in recent years, it survives.[85, 107, 108]

PBC The acronym for the Presentation Brothers' College by which the school is popularly known. It was opened in 1947 as a RC secondary school for boys, registering over sixty students in its first term. It was originally housed at the VICARIATE and administered by the Presentation Brothers. Though the Brothers were the original teaching and administrative staff, Grenadian teachers have been primary additions since 1948; since 2002 the position of principal has been held by a Grenadian who is not a Presentation Brother. With property leased from the ST. JOSEPH'S CONVENT, a second, larger building was constructed in 1951, and another block of classrooms was added in 2002. It caters to over 400 students. A strong rivalry developed between it and the GBSS that still exists today and is quite evident in annual inter-collegiate sporting activities as well as academic achievements. Famous 'old boys' include Paul and Ricardo Keens-Douglas and three of the islands' recent PMs, Maurice BISHOP, George BRIZAN and Dr Keith MITCHELL. The PBC remains one of the foremost secondary schools on the islands, achieving both academic and sporting excellence. It is sometimes erroneously referred to as the Presentation Boys' College.

PEARLS AIRPORT was opened on 16 January 1943 as Pearls Air Field at Pearls, St. Andrew, 1.5 miles (2.4 km) from GRENVILLE; the first plane landed there on 2 September 1942, but the first plane to 'land' in Grenada was a US Navy flying boat which took the acting governor on a tour of Grenada, St. Vincent and St. Lucia on 10 March 1924. The small grass airstrip linked Grenada to the rest of the world through air transportation. Before Pearls travel from Grenada was by sea, and due to the high cost of air travel this situation continued into the 1960s. Though Point Salines was the preferred site, the 380 acre (153 ha) Pearls estate, owned by the DeGale family, was purchased for the airport. Part of the site was previously used as a golf course, and the construction of the runway revealed the remnants of the extensive Pearls Amerindian site, which was partially destroyed as a result. The grass airstrip was later paved and extended to a length of 5,000 ft (1,600 m), equipped to handle small aircraft exclusively during the day. The airports of Barbados and Trinidad connected to international destinations.

The physical constraints associated with Pearls Airport, surrounded by high mountains to the east and exposed to dangerous cross winds, made expansion impossible, and were often cited as impediments to the growth of TOURISM. The PEOPLE'S REVOLUTIONARY GOVERNMENT in 1980 began the construction of the POINT SALINES INTERNATIONAL AIRPORT and upon its opening in 1984 Pearls was closed. It is presently used by the GOG as a camp for the Special Services Unit of the POLICE FORCE, and the abandoned airstrip is used for motor sport racing.

PEOPLE'S ALLIANCE In an attempt to end the GULP's seemingly unshakeable electoral monopoly, the three main opposition political parties—the leftist NEW JEWEL MOVEMENT under Maurice BISHOP (nominating seven candidates), the centrist GRENADA NATIONAL PARTY under Herbert BLAIZE (nominating five candidates) and the pro-business United People's Party under Winston Whyte, a former GULP senator (nominating two candidates)—formed a coalition party, the People's Alliance (PA), to contest the 1976 general ELECTIONS. Ideological differences between the parties created some tension, as was evident with the establishment of the PA only a few days prior to the deadline for nomination. The PA brought together three politically diverse groups, with only one thing in common, a strong desire to be rid of PM GAIRY and the GULP.

The failure of the NJM to remove Gairy from power by mass protest in 1974 had forced its leaders to participate in parliamentary elections, even though they believed the electoral process to be 'woefully deficient'. The youth vote, from which the NJM garnered much support, became important, especially since 18-year-olds were eligible to vote for the first time. Though the PA had hoped that its broad-based support would be enough to defeat Gairy, it was confronted with a number of political obstacles. Gairy's supposed abuses and corruption of the electoral process, and the passing of a number of laws like the banning of the use of public address systems by opposition parties, thwarted the opposition's every move. The GULP government had a monopoly of the airwaves, and even controlled the choice of an opposition election symbol.

In the end, the PA won six of the 15 contested constituencies, capturing just under 49 per cent of the popular vote. It later protested that the election was not free and fair. It was one of the most hotly contested elections in many years. Despite the PA's loss, the GULP government was confronted with a noticeable opposition for the first time in a decade. By 1979 many believed that 'the Parliament had degenerated into a theatrical act, with Gairy always the leading actor' and the opposition, under Bishop, a reluctant supporting cast. Some have suggested that 'the Grenada Parliament had become a caricature of the Westminster model and, moreover, reflected the inherent weaknesses of that model,' leading to disillusionment in the process, and ultimately resulting in the REVOLUTION. If there were winners among the PA, it was the NJM, which won over new supporters and gained a national platform for its leftist views.[97, 176, 201]

PEOPLE'S REVOLUTIONARY ARMY The PRA was created following the Grenada REVOLUTION in March 1979 to defend and protect the 'people's revolution' from internal and external threats. On the morning of MARCH 13 the rudiments of that army seized power and installed the PEOPLE'S REVOLUTIONARY GOVERNMENT. At its peak the PRA had a 600-man-and-woman-strong army supported by a 2,500-2,800-

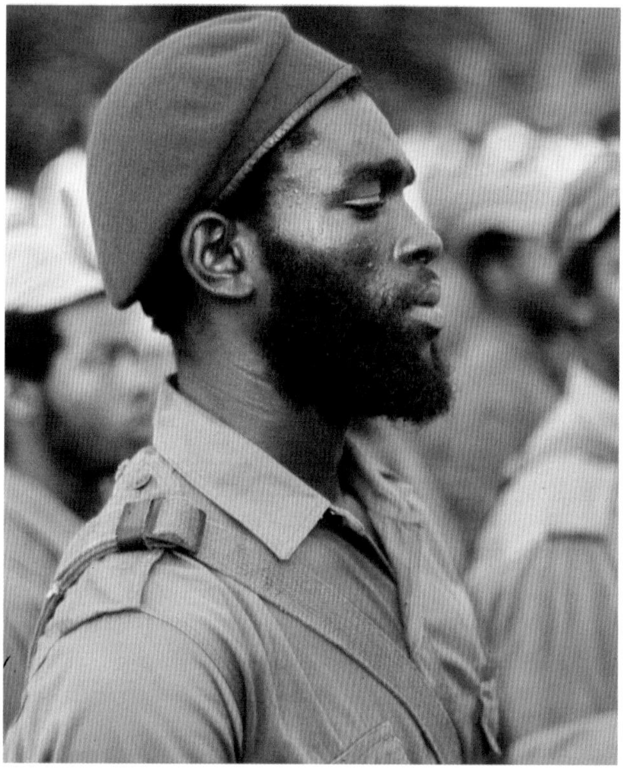

PRA militia man

strong MILITIA, both under the command of General Hudson Austin. There was one regular battalion stationed at Camp Fédon, Calivigny, and five reservist and support units across the islands. Over forty Cuban and Soviet military specialists provided some training, with hardware supplied by the Soviets, Cubans, Eastern Europeans and North Koreans. A total of five secret agreements were believed signed between Grenada and socialist countries concerning arms shipments, military training and the planned expansion of the military.

The establishment of a permanent security force meant employment for young men and women, a group that previously experienced high unemployment rates. In 1981 the PRA became a branch of the People's Revolutionary Armed Forces—together with the People's Revolutionary Militia, Grenada Police Service, Coast Guard and Prison Service. As the perceived US military threat grew, 'manoeuvres' became commonplace, demonstrating the Grenadian people's defiance towards the US and any military threat. Abuses by high-ranking officers brought to the fore the state repression or 'heavy manners' that the PRA had come to represent.

In the wake of the political infighting within the PRG, the PRA supported Deputy PM COARD. The internal coup that led to Bishop's death, along with members of his cabinet and at least 15 others, brought the PRA into full control of the country, with the leadership of the REVOLUTIONARY MILITARY COUNCIL chosen from its highest ranks. On 25 October 1983 the ill-prepared PRA was called upon to fulfil its role as defender of the country when hundreds of US troops invaded. Within two days virtually all resistance by the PRAF had disintegrated as its meagre force of approximately 700 (combined PRA and PRM forces) was overwhelmed by the well-equipped and massive US military presence.

Nineteen military personnel may have lost their lives in the invasion (military and civilian deaths totalled 45). Most of the army regulars and leadership were arrested and detained by the US and Caribbean forces, the leaders later to face trial for their part in the deaths of Bishop and his supporters (see GRENADA 17). The US military, during their occupation of the islands, revealed caches of arms and ammunition across the island, bolstering the popular view that the PRG was creating a police state in Grenada.[2, 146, 299]

PEOPLE'S REVOLUTIONARY GOVERNMENT

The PRG was formed on 16 March 1979 as the Provisional Revolutionary Government following the coup by the NEW JEWEL MOVEMENT on MARCH 13. On 25 March a number of People's Laws suspended the INDEPENDENCE Constitution and established the 'legality' for the non-elected government and its administration. The PRG became a *de facto* government, its core leadership coming from the Central Committee, the decision-making body of the NJM. The PRG had high expectations to live up to, having replaced the demoralising economic and political atmosphere brought about by decades of (mis)rule by PM GAIRY and the GULP. Almost every problem was tackled by the PRG

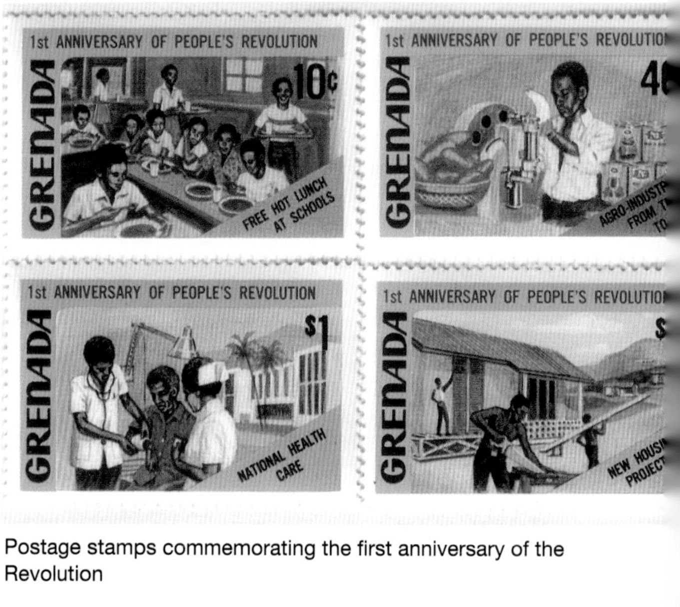

Postage stamps commemorating the first anniversary of the Revolution

with as much enthusiasm as its optimism could muster. With financial and technical assistance from Cuba, the Soviet Union and other socialist and Non-Aligned member countries, Grenada embarked on an impressive development plan, which Pryor termed 'foreign aid socialism'. Its achievements in AGRICULTURE, TOURISM, EDUCATION and social services were many, even in the face of external and internal pressures.

Yet, misdirected policies, lack of an essential management apparatus and haphazard leadership led to conflicts within the PRG. A number of issues like the worsening economy created low morale within the revolution, and support for the PRG declined. This created political pressures that forced a confrontation between PM BISHOP, Deputy PM COARD and the Central Committee. By September 1983, with the political conflict growing, the REVOLUTION began to unravel. In the days preceding 19 October four ministers in the PRG, all Bishop supporters, resigned while Bishop was held under house arrest by his government. On 19 October the PRG was dissolved, following the executions of Bishop and his supporters, and replaced by the 16-member REVOLUTIONARY MILITARY COUNCIL, which took over the running of the country.[101, 253, 267]

PETIT-JEAN (fl. 1715-16) was an escaped slave who achieved fame as a leader of the MAROONS in the early 1700s. In 1716 the maroon population comprised over sixty former slaves and was causing a great deal of problems for the French. Petit-Jean was considered one of the principal leaders, among whom were La Fortune, Samba, Jacob and Bernard. In April 1716 Petit-Jean, at the head of a group of maroons, attacked a hillside estate and burned the dwelling, kitchen and hen-roost. They were reported to have wielded muskets, pistols and cutlasses. Petit-Jean went on to 'calmly sho[o]t every last piece of cattle and all the fowl. The damage inflicted, the band marched frostily away in full panoply of the honours of war.' The daring actions by Petit-Jean and those of the other maroons created such problems for the colonists that they petitioned Martinique to establish a court in Grenada so that they could immediately try and execute captured maroons as a deterrent. The Royal Chamber was not formed until 1726, after the extensive disruptions caused by the maroons in 1725.

PETITE MARTINIQUE 12 31N 61 23W is an island dependency of Grenada situated in the GRENADA GRENADINES, roughly 3 miles (5 km) off WINDWARD, Carriacou; it is 40 miles (64 km) NE of St. George's. It is the last outpost of Grenada, with Petite St.Vincent, a few hundred yards to its north, belonging to St.Vincent and the Grenadines. The island most probably derives its name from the larger island of Martinique whose peak, Mt. Pelée, is said to resemble the island of Petite Martinique (pronounced pitteet mar-ti-neek); it is oftentimes rendered Petit Martinique. Some of the early French settlers to Petite Martinique (PM) most likely came from the larger island as well. The story that PM was named after Martinique because of the presence of the poisonous fer-de-lance snake on the former, as with the latter, has never been substantiated and is probably without foundation. In the late 1700s the island was owned by the PHILIP family and by the early 1800s it was broken up into plots.

Of the islands that constitute the state of GRENADA, Petite Martinique is the fourth largest with an area slightly less than 0.8 sq miles (2 sq km or 196 ha), and a population of 835 (its population was 153 (slaves) in 1833, 193 in 1891, 319 in 1901, 385 in 1911, 500 in 1946 and 586 in 1981). It was probably first settled by the mid-1700s by the French from Carriacou. In 1776 there were eight estates on the island producing some SUGAR, but primarily COTTON. Like Carriacou, Petite Martinique produced cotton into the late 1970s.

The most distinguishing feature of the island is its conical peak Piton (<Fr. *piton*: 'peak'), which rises to 740 ft (225 m) upon an almost round base. Much of the island is relatively steep, its hills barren and rugged, especially the uninhabited windward coast. The gently sloping areas of the leeward coast—the SW and NW facing the island of CARRIACOU—constitute the major areas of human habitation scattered among seven villages. In the village of Paradise on the NW coast is a small jetty used as the primary port. Agriculture and animal husbandry similar to those of Carriacou are practised by many, while the major sources of income are FISHERIES, BOAT BUILDING and maritime trade. Petite Martinique, like Carriacou, experiences water availability problems much of the year. Cisterns are built into every home to collect all available rainwater, and the government in 1927 constructed a large water catchment or cistern. In 1999 a desalination plant was installed to help relieve the water shortage.

Politically, Petite Martinique has been attached to Carriacou. The island received ELECTRICITY by 1983, and has telephone services, a Visiting (Health) Station that the doctor from Carriacou visits weekly, a commercial bank, post office (two weekly mail boats deliver and collect mail), and an RC chapel. The St. Thomas Aquinas RC School (est. 1879) is the only primary school on the island, catering to slightly over 150 students. All of the

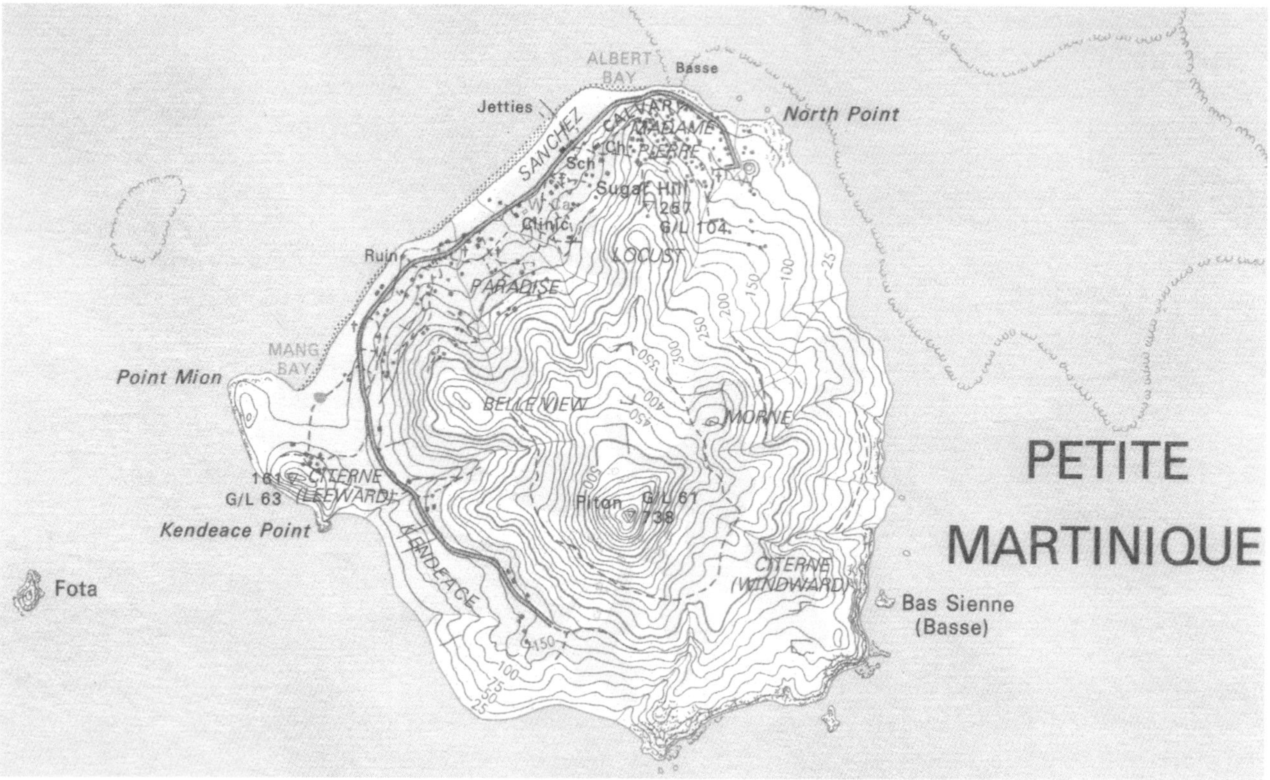

Map of Petite Martinique

above institutions are situated in the north and west of the island in the major villages of MADAME PIERRE, Paradise, Sanchez, Citerne (<Fr. 'tank'), Kendeace and Belleview. Petite Martinique's single major paved road, less than 2 miles (3.2 km), is traversed by few vehicles and extends from the north to the SW.

The island has shared a similar history and culture to that of its sister island, Carriacou, with its only link to Grenada via Carriacou by sea. In 1997 Petite Martinique made international news when protests erupted following the GOG granting the US military permission to build a COAST GUARD BASE there. One of Petite Martinique's most honoured sons is Dr Lamuel Stanisclaus, a retired dentist who has served as Grenada's Permanent Representative to the UN (1985-90, 1997-2004). According to mythology, the present inhabitants of the island are of 'one family' because they descend from twin siblings whose mother was the sole survivor after all Petite Martinicans went over to Carriacou for a wedding or confirmation and were eaten by the devil.[54, 283, 302]

PETROGLYPHS are aboriginal drawings or rock art found on large boulders across Grenada. They have attracted scholarly attention beginning with Huckerby's study in 1921. Within the past few decades, archaeological studies of the AMERINDIANS have produced some order out of the many artefacts that have surfaced over the years. A number of large stones covered with figures of 'faces' and geometric designs have been identified as being of Amerindian origin. The term Carib Stones, first applied to them because the Island CARIBS were the last Amerindian inhabitants of Grenada and the believed artists, turned out to be a misnomer since the artists were most likely Island Arawaks/Tainos. Boulders identified with Amerindian drawings can be found at the Green Bridge, Grand Mal and BEAUSÉJOUR in St. George; Black Bay cave in St. John; Waltham and Victoria in St. Mark; Mt. Rich, Montreuil and Duquesne Bay in St. Patrick; Carrière, Soubise and Telescope in St. Andrew; and Baillies Bacolet in St. David.

The most prominent are the MT. RICH and Victoria petroglyphs. These, according to Cody, 'fit somewhere in the West Indian archaeological record, but currently no one knows exactly how or when.' She adds that 'certain designs worked into the basaltic boulders of Grenada bear stylistic resemblance to pottery traditions originating in Venezuela and the Guianas—the Saladoid (perhaps the controversial, earlier Huecoid), and the Modified (Barrancoid-influenced) Saladoid'. The boulders are covered with the designs of figures and faces, possibly representing gods, myths and/or legends. Cody classifies the petroglyphs into four types: simple faces, which are quite common; elaborate faces with decorations of head-dresses, teeth, ears/earrings and noses; abstract geometric designs are rare, comprising cruciform designs found only at Mt. Rich; and elaborate figures which are not common, but can be seen at Mt. Rich and Duquesne Bay. There has been a recent effort by the GOG and the Grenada Historical Society to protect these petroglyphs as part of the islands' cultural heritage.[59, 162]

PHILIP FAMILY The name of a prominent free-coloured family headed by Jeanette Philip, a 'free Negro' woman and Honoré Philip, a white French landowner who resided in CARRIACOU in the latter part of the eighteenth century. As the common-law wife of Honoré Philip, Jeanette inherited, along with her FREE COLOURED children, his property. She was one of four 'free Mulatto and Negro' persons who owned property, including slaves, as early as 1776.

The Philip family, because of its propertied status, was instrumental in the fight for racial equality among whites and free coloureds in Grenada and TRINIDAD. Judith Philip, daughter of Jeanette and Honoré Philip, was the common-law wife of Edmund Thornton, a white attorney and proprietor, and owned extensive estates. So wealthy was the family that in 1807 Judith travelled to England. Joachim Philip (d. 1803), a carpenter and planter, was one of Julien FÉDON's lieutenants. The unsuccessful revolt resulted in his capture in 1803 in Petite Martinique and subsequent execution. Joachim's brother Louis emigrated to Trinidad in the 1790s. He successfully established extensive sugar plantations at Naparima and his family became one of the leading free-coloured families. Two of his sons, Jean-Baptiste and St. Luce, became European-trained medical doctors. Jean-Baptiste's 1824 publication of *Free Mulatto* was a civil rights appeal on behalf of free coloureds. St. Luce was the first coloured member of the Council of Government in the 1830s. Michael Maxwell Philip, a fourth-generation member of the family, was a Scottish-educated lawyer who was solicitor-general, and later the first coloured member of the Legislative Council, and mayor of Port-of-Spain in 1867; he is the author of *Emmanuel Appadoca or Blighted Life: A Tale of the Boucaneers*. The Philip families in Grenada and Trinidad came to epitomise the changing social and political status of the free-coloured class from marginalisation and discrimination to membership of the social elite throughout the Caribbean.[226]

PIGEON/GREEN PEAS (*Cajanus cajan*) A plant native to Africa and brought to the Caribbean in the 1500s by slaves. A legume, pigeon pea has become an important crop in a number of rotation practices. It is inter-cropped with CORN and may provide some nitrogen to the corn plant. A perennial shrub, it grows to 9 ft (2.7 m) and can be harvested for many seasons, but is replanted annually around July. It produces numerous pods, each containing some 4-6 green or yellow seeds (mottled seeds are called calico) from December through March. Shelling peas is a favourite pastime. The seeds (peas) can be used green in local dishes like 'peas soup' or 'rice and peas', side dishes like 'stew peas' and curries, or are dried in the sun and used similarly. Pigeon peas and corn meal are made into COU-COU pwa, a popular food in C&PM.

Petroglyph on rock at Victoria

PILOT HILL, St. Andrew A small hill overlooking Grenville Bay. It derives its name from the fact that the port's pilot, responsible for guiding ships into the difficult harbour, once lived there. During FÉDON'S REBELLION the strategic site changed hands a number of times in bloody conflicts. It was vital to both the government and the rebels since it commanded the approaches to the Grenville Bay and the movement of incoming supply ships. After sacking the seaside settlement of La Baye (later called GRENVILLE), the rebels took control of Pilot Hill. Fearing a threatened attack by the British the rebels abandoned the site in April 1795. They regained the post in early March 1796 after a two-month siege and a narrow escape by the beleaguered British forces. This was the climax of insurgent control of the island, but a British offensive later that month captured Post Royal Hill to the south, forcing Fédon to order the evacuation of Pilot Hill. The rebels made their final retreat to the fortified interior under the guns of advancing British troops. On the summit of the hill is a signal station.

PITT, Lord David Thomas (1913-1994) was a medical doctor, politician and member of the British House of Lords. He was born at Hampstead, St. David, on 3 October 1913 to Cyril SL Pitt and Gertrude *nee* Redhead. He graduated from the Grammar School (later the GBSS) in 1932 and was awarded the ISLAND SCHOLARSHIP. Between 1933 and 1938 he studied medicine at Edinburgh University, UK, and served as the medical officer in St. Vincent. Between 1939 and 1947 he worked in various positions at the San Fernando Hospital, Trinidad. He became active in borough politics, co-founding the West Indian National Party (f. 1943). Pitt attributed his political awareness to T A MARRYSHOW, who at that time was Grenada's most prominent political figure. Before returning to England in 1947, Pitt served as the deputy mayor of San Fernando.

Back in England, he established a private medical practice and became active in politics. He was elected to the London County Council (1961-1964) and the Greater London Council (1964-1977) as a Labour Party representative. His involvement in a number of political and social organisations, including the Campaign Against Racial Discrimination and the Standing Advisory on Race Relations, made him one of the most popular Caribbean personalities in the UK. He was a member and president (1985-1986) of the British Medical Association. He was an original member of the Community Relations Commission and in 1977 chaired that body. In 1975 he was made a Life Peer, with the title of Lord Pitt of Hampstead, '...the area where he had his first surgery and, by a neat irony, the name of the village in Grenada where he was born'; he became the second black person to enter the House of Lords. In 1984 Lord Pitt was made a member of the Academic Board of ST. GEORGE'S UNIVERSITY, re-establishing ties with his homeland after many years abroad. He died in London on 18 December 1994 and was buried in Grenada. His papers are archived at the SGU.

PLACE NAMES On current maps of Grenada French and British place names are both common, a reflection of the islands' dual colonial heritage. French place names usually suggest the natural features of the area, as illustrated by Grande Anse, Grand Étang and a host of others. The majority of French names attached to villages are either fanciful or euphemistic names, or are derived from French ESTATE owners. Many of Grenada's coastal place names were given by the French prior to 1667 and have remained with only slight modifications other than translations.

After the British captured the islands in 1762 an ordinance provided for the substitution of English for French place names, but they changed only gradually. The British—English and Scots—had a different flair for naming places, preferring instead to honour important British personalities and recreate common British place names. Newly established villages and estates owned by the British also received British/Scottish personal names, many replacing the original French. In her study of Grenadian place names, Wesche investigated over 380 place names, of which 225 were French or English translations of original French names. Over the years only a few French place names were translated into English, like Anse aux Écrevisse—Crayfish Bay and Islet à Cochon—Hog Island. Both French and British place names were repetitive, leaving a number of places with the same name. A few places are known by two names, one French and the other British like GRENVILLE or La Baye and GOUYAVE or Charlotte Town.

Grenada shares many place names with the other islands, particularly the former French islands of Dominica and St. Lucia. Unlike St. Vincent and Dominica, only a few names are believed to have AMERINDIAN, specifically Island Carib, origins—CARRIACOU, Camàhogne, Mabouya, Galby Bay (Anse des Galibis), Mahot (<Is.Car. *maho*: names for blue and red mahoe trees; <Arawakan maho/e), Petit Bacaye Bay (Baye de Bacayo), Les Ances Caouanes (<Is.Car. *caroüanne*: 'sea turtle') and Bacolet; River Antoine and LAKE ANTOINE are named after an Island CARIB known as Chief ANTOINE, and Duquesne Bay and Duquesne Point are named after Chief DUQUESNE. At least three place names are of possible Spanish origin—Sanchez, PETITE MARTINIQUE, and Diego Piece and Tanga Langua, St. Patrick (though Deblando, St. Andrew, appears Spanish, the name is derived from the French 'Deblandeau'). At least two place names originated from Swiss family names, Pécher (Peschier) and Chutz, St. Andrew, as a result of the settlement of a number of Swiss families in Grenada after 1763.

The absence of African names may have less to do with the status, or rather lack of status, of that group and more with the fact that the total land area of the island was occupied and already named prior to EMANCIPATION. A number of small villages established after 1839 and rural street names, however, were named by the former slaves and their descendants, as well as places like Mt. Qua Qua. EAST INDIANS have had little impact on place names such as Cumar, St. John.

The majority of streets are named after British royalty, governors, administrators, military personnel and prominent long-time residents of the islands like Hughes Street (<A Norris Hughes) and Archibald Avenue (<Fisher J Archibald). In celebration of the twentieth anniversary of INDEPENDENCE in 1994, streets were named after Grenadians, including Maurice BISHOP, Herbert BLAIZE, Ben JONES and E A 'Doc' Mitchell. This post-INDEPENDENCE trend, though politically motivated, appears likely to continue.[170, 361]

PLANTOCRACY A term referring to the sugar planters in the BWI around the turn of the eighteenth century, who constituted a distinct economic and social class. They owned the many prosperous sugar estates in the BWI and as a result of the high price of sugar throughout the eighteenth century became wealthy, acquiring political influence in the Caribbean and England. The West Indian sugar lobby in the British Parliament used its wealth to influence many policies that subsequently guaranteed its continued dominance of the economic life of the colonies. Grenadian absentee proprietors were well represented within the West India lobby even as early as 1787 when they, as 'a very active and influential group', convinced the secretary of state for the colonies not to reduce British troops promised to Grenada. (Among them were Joseph MARRYAT, James BAILLIE, Joseph Spooner (colonial agent), William Lushington, Sir George Amyand and his son Sir George Cornewall, Lord Dundas, Sir Thomas Charles Bunbury and the HANKEY family.) The Grenadian plantocracy, developing after 1762, never amassed the same wealth as that of Barbados or Jamaica because of its late start, not having established prosperous sugar estates until the late 1760s. Ragatz characterised the Grenadian plantocracy as 'mere stewards' of their creditors 'rather than actual owners of properties they exploited'. Gov. MACARTNEY commented that the 'planters are not yet opulent,' but with their wealth they built GREAT HOUSES on their plantations and lived a comfortable life in Grenada or England, spending ostentatiously.

The ending of the SLAVE TRADE in 1807 and SLAVERY in 1834 brought changes to the economic system that had made many proprietors wealthy. Worsening sugar prices and labour and capital shortages brought their reign to an end. By 1848 absentee planters accounted for roughly sixty per cent of estate owners. Many eventually left the islands, sold their estates or allowed them to become encumbered. The remaining elements of the plantocracy tried to keep the peasant labour force dependent on the estates through a number of schemes, but ultimately failed. Yet the planter class, by the late 1800s was predominantly local, and along with the appointed British governor controlled the political/economic life of the islands even after the imposition of CROWN COLONY rule.

Though the planter class had changed from predominantly white to incorporate prominent coloured and black families, its dominance of the economic, political and social life of the islands continued until the March 1951 riots known as SKYRED. In Carriacou, the plantocracy abandoned the island following the collapse of the sugar and cotton industries by the late 1800s, leaving a predominantly peasant population, without the estate owner-labourer dependency common to Grenada.[35, 144, 273, 309, 319, 333]

PLUMS There are a number of fruits which go by the general name plum, including the red mombin or Jamaica plum (*Spondias purpurea*), Chinese plum (*S. purpurea* var. *lutea*), hog plum (*S. mombin*), governor plum (*Flacourtia jangomas*), and coco plum or fat pork (*Chrysobalanus icaco*). The red mombin is native to tropical America and the Caribbean and is the most widely consumed plum. A deciduous tree in the dry season, it grows to 25 ft (8 m). Flowers and fruits are produced before leaves re-emerge in the rainy season. The tree is low and spreading, producing purplish red fruits singly or in bunches. Many of the fruits are oblong but some have appendages called nipples or 'teté' (<Fr. *téter*: 'to suck'). The fruit has a glossy skin covering yellow sweet flesh and is eaten fresh, or cooked when ripe to make a preserve called 'plum stew'. The fruits are available from May to June. Fresh cut leaves are used to keep house flies away.

Sir Thomas Charles Bunbury, estate owner and member of the Grenada plantocracy

The Chinese plum is closely related to the red mombin. It is a tall spreading tree that grows to over 60 ft (18 m), with prickles covering its bark. The soft fruit is oval and green, yellow when ripe, with a pungent flavour. It can be eaten fresh or made into preserves. The hog plum, quite similar to the Chinese plum in colour and size, is acidic and not consumed except as a wine. An infusion of hog plum leaves is gargled for hoarseness. Its name dates to the 1600s.

The governor plum bears no taxonomic relationship to the other plums. The tree grows to 20 ft (6 m) and produces small purple-black fruits that are palatable only after being rubbed between the palms of the hands, a process that converts its starch to sugar. Left to ferment, it makes a 'tasty' wine. The bark, root and leaf have been used as FOLK MEDICINE in its native Madagascar. The coco plum (<Is.Car. female 'language' *icaco*; <Taino *hicaco*; <Is. Car./Guajiro *kaako*, for the fruit), of no relation to any of the above plums, is an evergreen shrub native to tropical America and the Caribbean which grows to 10-14 ft (3-4 m). The large fruit, a drupe, is edible. When mature the fruits take on a brownish purple to black colour and are slightly rose-scented. The fruit, with a white, spongy flesh, is mainly eaten fresh by children or made into preserves. An infusion of the root is a local treatment for dysentery. 146b

POINSETTIA/CHRISTMAS PLANT (*Euphorbia pulcherrima*) is native to tropical America and can grow to a height of 15 ft (4.5 m). The plant derives its name from Joel Poinsett, US ambassador to Mexico, who in 1828 brought back a specimen to Charleston, South Carolina. This quick-growing shrub is prized as an ornamental because of its scarlet, white and yellow flower bracts (its white flowers are inconspicuous) which bloom especially at Christmas time (due to the change in day-length). The plant produces a poisonous sap that is highly irritating when in contact with the skin. Its relative, the Christmas bush (*E. leucocephala*), produces 'flowers' that look like small white poinsettias. Other members of the genus prized as FLOWER GARDEN additions include monkey-puzzle (*E. lactea*), crown-of-thorns (*E. sptenders*), and pencil bush (*E. tirucalli*).

POINT SALINES INTERNATIONAL AIRPORT Construction of the PSIA was begun in January 1980 by the PEOPLE'S REVOLUTIONARY GOVERNMENT, with financial and technical assistance from Cuba and a number of other countries, and it became the PRG's most lasting monument. The idea of siting an airport at Point

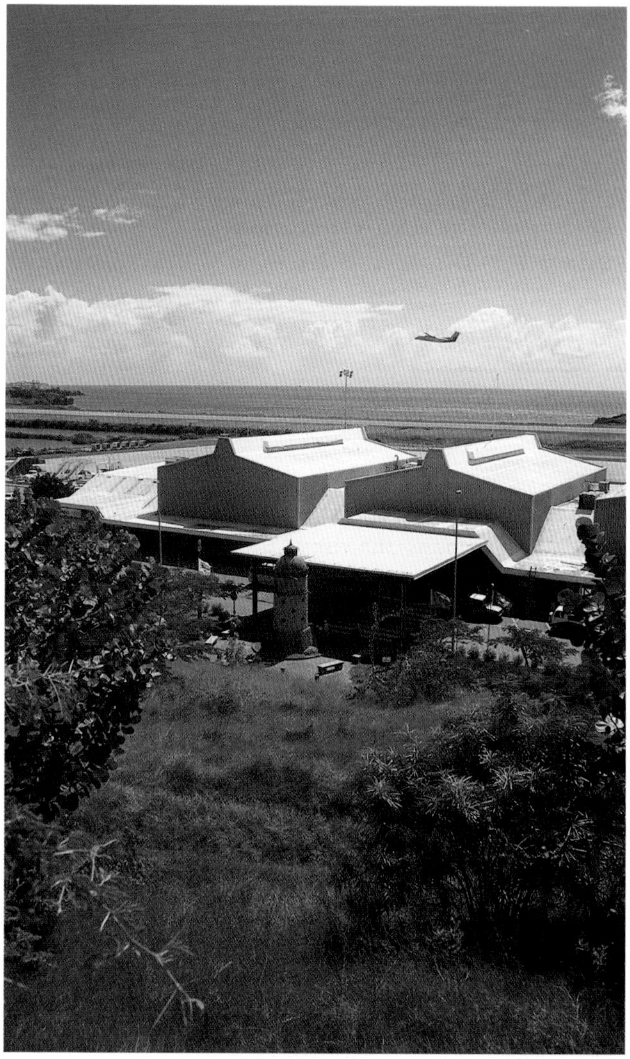

Point Salines International Airport

Salines dates to the 1920s, though it was not until the 1940s that it received serious attention. Either political pressure or a number of technical problems led instead to the construction of PEARLS AIRPORT. Since physical constraints at Pearls made extension and upgrading impossible, Point Salines (pronounced sa-lean) was again viewed as the site for a new airport; the fact that Pearls was over 30 minutes from both St. George's Town, and the HOTELS and BEACHES in the Grand Anse area was a more compelling cause for the move. In 1954 a feasibility study recommended it as the most appropriate site. Eric GAIRY had supported the idea of an airport at Point Salines, and as one NEW JEWEL MOVEMENT news release put it, 'the international airport had become the "opening prayer" in Gairy's annual budget.'

Yet no construction took place under the GULP government, and the NJM had expressed their opposition to Gairy's plan. But by the end of 1979 the airport had become their primary development project. In March

1980 US President Reagan showed satellite images on US television of the 10,000 ft (3,000 m) landing strip being built at Point Salines, charging that its length was excessive for a civilian airport. President Reagan's insistence that this facility would be used as a base for Cuban and Soviet military activities in the hemisphere brought the island of Grenada into the cold war and branded it as a threat to democracy in the region. The PRG insisted that the airport was purely an economic necessity to make the islands more accessible to international overnight tourists.

Before the airport was completed, the US invaded, using the airstrip to land their military aircraft. With further help from the US government the airport was completed and opened on 18 October 1984, making the islands accessible to direct flights from North America and Europe. In August 1998, during the visit of President Castro, a plaque was erected acknowledging Cuba's contribution to the building of the airport. Bishop's supporters agitate for the airport to be renamed in his memory. The total cost was about US$71m, with major contributions from Cuba and the US.[163, 267]

POISONOUS PLANTS Among the many wild plants and ornamentals in the islands are some that contain toxins, making them very harmful to humans and animals either through ingestion or contact. The manchineel tree (*Hippomane mancinella*), common on BEACHES throughout the islands, is poisonous. The bark, leaves and fruits of this native Caribbean tree contain a poisonous sap, which when in contact with the skin can cause blistering; wash with soap and water or sea water within thirty minutes to remove irritant. The small apple-like fruits, if ingested, can lead to poisoning, and the Island CARIBS used the trees' sap to tip their arrows with a substance reputed to cause blisters and temporary blindness.

Angel's trumpet (*Brugmansia suavelens*) is a shrub native to Central America and grows to a height of 16 ft (5 m). It is seen predominantly in the moist interior of Grenada where it flowers frequently throughout the year. The drooping flowers create the effect of hanging bells or trumpets. In the evening the flowers fill the air with a fragrance that has been reported to case nausea, headaches and even dizziness to some. Angel's trumpet belongs to the Solanaceae family, known for its toxic, hypnotic and narcotic genera Devil's trumpet (*D. metel*, syn. *D. alba*) exhibits similar toxic properties. It has been used as a narcotic for centuries, but large doses can result in death. Beneficial uses in medicine include motion sickness prevention, analgesics and poison antidotes.

The red and black JUMBIE BEAD is used to decorate local crafts, but is very poisonous. The castor oil plant (*Ricinus communis*) has star-shaped, deeply lobed leaves and produces yellow prickled capsules inside which are small poisonous seeds. Yet the pressed seeds yield oil used in the

Manchineel fruits

manufacture of soaps, lubricants and candles. The plant is also used in FOLK MEDICINE to relieve fevers and cure worm infections. French cotton (*Calotropis procera*), purple allamanda. (*Cryptostegia grandiflora*), oleander (*Nerium oleander*) and yellow oleander (*Thevetia peruviana*) are some of the other plants that can cause some form of poisoning if ingested, or blistering when in contact with the skin.

Caution should be used when dealing with unfamiliar local plants unless advised by someone who knows about them. A number of common fruits like the MANGO and flowers like the POINSETTIA can produce allergic reactions in some. During SLAVERY and even after, OBEAH practitioners used many plants as cures or curses, some causing the deaths of unsuspecting individuals.[146b, 241]

POLICE AIDES The name given to part of a private 'army' known variously as the Special Reserve Police, Secret Police and the Night Ambush Squad. It comprised men, some of whom had criminal records, recruited for the sole purpose of terrorising the political opponents of Premier GAIRY. Established in 1970, the Police Aides comprised approximately 300 to 500 men who were recruited by the premier. The formation of this supplementary police force was a result of the BLACK POWER movement gaining momentum in Grenada and its possible threats to national security. Premier Gairy described his aides as 'a large number of special Secret Police ranging from business men to the man in the street... [and] there will be no uniforms to betray the secrecy of these persons.' They were first called the Voluntary Intelligence Unit for Property Protection and aimed at protecting wealthy Grenadians from 'Black Power' youths who, according to Premier Gairy, if found 'guilty of molestation of any form should be told, "Good Morning" by the Cat-O-Nine as they start their prison term.'

Since the aides were not recruited under the 1966 Police Ordinance, which would have given them a legal status, they were not to make arrests or searches, or carry firearms. Contrary to this official restriction, it was known that they did carry arms and made frequent illegal searches and arrests. They were also known to 'beat up' members of Gairy's opposition. Though they were meant to be under the direct control of uniformed policemen, the Police Aides functioned as a band of ill-disciplined vigilantes for the premier. The Police Aides further discredited the authority and respect of the POLICE FORCE, creating a rift between the law and the people. Following their part in the civil unrest between 1973 and 1974 (BLOODY SUNDAY and BLOODY MONDAY), the DUFFUS COMMISSION recommended their immediate disbandment, since their creation had violated the country's laws.[94]

POLICE FORCE The modern police force has its origins in 'An Act to Create a Local Police Force' of 1836 (the local Emancipation Act of 1834 had created a police force in each district to administer the gaols and cages). Previously, the Justices of the Peace and the MILITIA performed the task of controlling the population. The police force, comprising 43 constables and officers in its first year, was made up exclusively of free coloureds, free blacks and whites, and acted as a supplement to the militia and the military garrison. Its objective was to create a law enforcement body to provide control of the majority free black population following EMANCIPATION and APPRENTICESHIP, and to enforce the many new laws created to regulate their conduct. After 1854 and the withdrawal of the military garrison, it expanded to assume its permanent role in the maintenance of law and order in the country, under the authority of police magistrates. In 1866 the post of inspector of police was created, along with a rural constabulary that was to supplement the force in the event of civil unrest.

The police force has been quartered at FORT GEORGE since 1854, except during the REVOLUTION when it was housed on the ESPLANADE. The Royal Grenada Police Force (RGPF), as it has been styled since 1966, did not attain its present structure until 1911 when it was reorganised with the position of chief of police created (changed to commissioner in 1960). In 1923, following further reorganisation and expansion, the force numbered 92 enlisted officers. Under the GULP government, the RGPF's authority was continuously undermined, especially with the establishment of PM Gairy's personal POLICE AIDES and MONGOOSE GANG. At INDEPENDENCE in 1974 the RGPF numbered 467, inclusive of the fire service. The 1975 DUFFUS COMMISSION Report charged members of the RGPF with police brutality and civil rights abuses, recommending the dismissal of certain officers and the restructuring of the entire force.

Under the PEOPLE'S REVOLUTIONARY GOVERNMENT, the RGPF lost virtually all of its historical authority, and was relegated to the control of domestic crimes and traffic supervision. The PEOPLE'S REVOLUTIONARY ARMY and other forces within the PRAF maintained law and order and placed the country under 'heavy manners'. In 1980, the PRG changed the name from 'Force' to 'Service' to de-emphasise its military

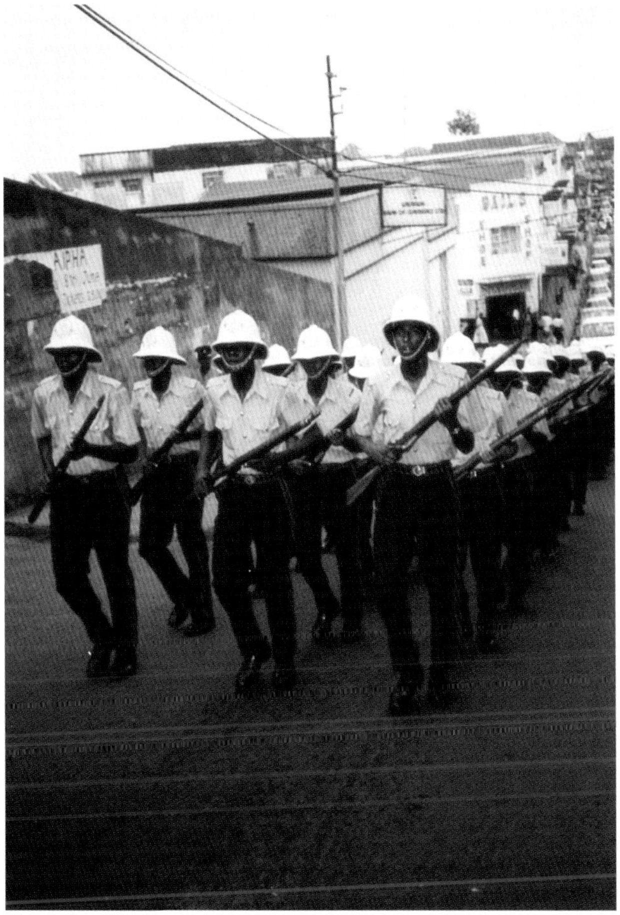

Police officers on parade

association, by now undertaken by the PRA. The RGPF drifted into mediocrity as the people lost all confidence in it as a law enforcement entity.

After regaining its authority in mid-1985 following the US-led military INTERVENTION in 1983, the RGPF was once again responsible for internal and external security. The present police force personnel stands at 520, with an additional 30 attached to the Coast Guard and 80 paramilitary staff, the Special Service Unit, which is part of the Regional Security Services organised by the US since 1984.

Since 1867 the islands have been separated into police districts; there are presently four: Central, including St. George's, with four police stations, Eastern with four, Western with five, and Northern, including C&PM, with two (including the COAST GUARD BASE on Petite Martinique). The RGPF is responsible for the Grenada Fire Service dating to 1843 (in April 1843 a legislative act created a company of firemen to operate a fire engine 'lately imported'; a Fire Brigade was established in 1895 and the present Fire Station completed in 1953; fire plugs were installed in the town since 1886). Immigration and traffic control are also under the RGPF. The Police Band, formerly known as the Government Band (also as 'Bugles and Drums'), was established in the late 1800s, making it one of the oldest government-sponsored bands in the Caribbean. In the late 1960s the Government Band became the Police Band, its members becoming part of the RGPF, though their duties are restricted to band functions unless they also become trained officers.

POLITICAL PARTIES The turbulent 1950s ushered in party politics in Grenada with the formation of the Grenada People's Party (later the GULP) in 1950 by Eric GAIRY. Though T A MARRYSHOW had attempted to organise political candidates under the Grenada Workingman's Association (GWA) in the 1930s and the Action Committee in 1951, he was largely unsuccessful. Until the formation of the GRENADA NATIONAL PARTY in 1956, the GULP had been without a rival, its competition coming exclusively from independent candidates. Party politics until the early 1970s centred on the GNP and GULP, which won the majority of ELECTIONS. There were also a number of minor political parties which participated in elections between 1955 and 1962: the People's Democratic Movement (1957) under L C J Thomas (a former member of the GULP); the West Indian Federal Labour Movement (1957) under John and Joseph Felix; and the People's Progressive Movement (1961) under Derek Knight (who later became affiliated with the GULP).

The 1970s ushered in a new era in party politics with the emergence of the NEW JEWEL MOVEMENT and a cadre of young political activists, many having returned from the US and UK with new and revolutionary ideas of government. To present a serious challenge to the GULP, the opposition parties (GNP, NJM and United People's Party) formed a coalition in 1976 under the PEOPLE'S ALLIANCE and presented the GULP with its strongest challenge to date. Party politics were interrupted between 1979 and 1983 following the NJM coup and its suspension of parliamentary government. Party politics resumed in 1984, with five political groups and 52 candidates participating in the elections, many possessing little or no political base, but relishing the open political atmosphere. In 1990 six parties and 76 candidates participated in elections, in 1995 seven parties and 82 candidates, in 1999 five parties and 48 candidates took part, and in 2003 six parties and 65 candidates contested elections.

Some have argued that the large numbers of both political parties and candidates affirm Grenada's vibrant democracy, while others view the increased participation as unnecessary and wasteful in this small island, and as the root cause of political chaos. Other minor political parties include(d) the Christian Democratic Labour Party (1984) under Winston Whyte, the Grenada Federated Labour Party (1984) under Fenderson Felix, The National Party (1990, 1995) under Ben JONES, United Republican Party (1995), MBPM (1984, 1990, 1995, 1999), the Democratic Labour Party (1995) under Dr. Francis Alexis, the People's Labour Movement (2003) under Dr. Francis Alexis, and the Good Old Democracy (1990, 1995, 1999, 2003) under Justine McBurnie.[97, 98, 99, 100, 111, 233, 243, 254, 318]

POMPEY (d. 1764) was an escaped slave and a reputed leader of the MAROONS. Following the capture of the islands by the British in 1762, a few hundred slaves took the opportunity occasioned by the change in colonial administration to run away from the ESTATES into the hills of ST. ANDREW, ST. DAVID and ST. JOHN. As the alleged leader of the maroons, Pompey was accused of committing 'many murders and other desperate outrages'. In 1764 he was captured and killed by two slaves, L'autriment and Vincent. As a reward and an example to other slaves who would turn in or capture runaways, the two were granted their freedom by the legislature.

POPULATION Grenada's population was 100,900 in 2001, scattered throughout the country's 300 towns and villages on three primary islands. With a population density of roughly 732 per sq mile (293 per sq km), Grenada is one of the most densely populated countries in the Caribbean. This has created tremendous pressures on the limited natural resources and fragile island environment, not to mention the demands on social and economic services.

On the eve of the French landing on Grenada in 1649, the population was probably under 1,000 Island CARIBS. In 1656 the white population was estimated at 300. The first census in 1669 reported a population of 506 persons (284 whites, 222 slaves) which by 1700 had grown to 835 (557 slaves, 257 whites, 53 FREE COLOUREDS); there was no mention of Island Caribs even though J-B LABAT observed some living in the Cabesterre in 1700. It had taken fifty years for the population to increase by roughly 300, the majority African slaves.

By 1763 the population had grown sharply to 13,439, comprising 12,000 slaves. Soon after EMANCIPATION the population was 25,000, with blacks constituting the majority. The slave to white ratio went from 1:1.3 (1669), 2:1 (1700) to a high of 60:1 (1806), but gradually dropped as the slave population decreased after a high of 32,131 in 1779. As was common with all the islands in the BWI, the white population was 'dangerously' low and the legislature made every effort to increase the numbers of whites in the colonies by passing deficiency laws forcing estate owners to employ whites as managers, etc., or pay stiff fines. Not only was the white population low but the male-female ratio so skewed (on average above 60 per cent male) that the prevalence of 'concubine' relationships with slaves, free coloured and black women was common, hence the growth of the mixed-race population.

The white population fluctuated throughout the eighteenth century and showed marked decreases in the early to mid-nineteenth century due to out-migration. The free non-white population showed continuous increases from 53 in 1700 to 4,003 in 1830 (the last year separate figures were recorded; since resumed). Grenada's population, like that of many of the Caribbean islands, has always been affected by MIGRATION. The present population comprises mainly the descendants of Africans (82 per cent), mixed or descendants of whites and blacks (12 per cent), Indo-Grenadians or the descendants of EAST INDIANS (3 per cent), the descendants of the LEBANESE/SYRIAN COMMUNITY (0.1 per cent), and whites (0.6 per cent). Analyses of the 2001 census reveal that 50 per cent of the population are under 30 years, the urban to rural distribution is 38 to 62 per cent, 60 per cent live in the parishes of St. George and St. Andrew, life expectancy is 71.6 for women and 64.5 for men, infant mortality is 16.2 for every 1,000 births, there are 1.12 females for every male, and 32 per cent live in poverty.[35, 267, 333]

PORT LOUIS The site of the first successful European settlement in Grenada, founded by the French in March 1649. Until 1664/65 the struggling settlement was referred to as the 'Grand fort', the site of Fort l'Annunciation, the islands' first fortification. The settlement, in the reign of Louis XIV (hence the name Port Louis), was partially situated on The Spout and Ballast Ground, connected by a sandbar, at the entrance to the LAGOON. It was a suitable site because of the surrounding hills that provided a sheltered harbour. In a letter to FAUDOAS DE CÉRILLAC in 1657 J-B DU TERTRE provides one of the earliest descriptions of the settlement: 'The fort, which is located between the Pond [Étang d'Eau Salée] and the Haven, is a square frame dwelling... it is surrounded at a distance of eight to ten feet from the building with a strong fence made of trees encircling it, at the two corners which face the sea are two small frame lodges, in one is living the Commandant. The house of du Parquet is a large area which enclose the whole mountain near the Haven, at the bottom of which are the warehouses, which are of one hundred or 120 feet of a building made of

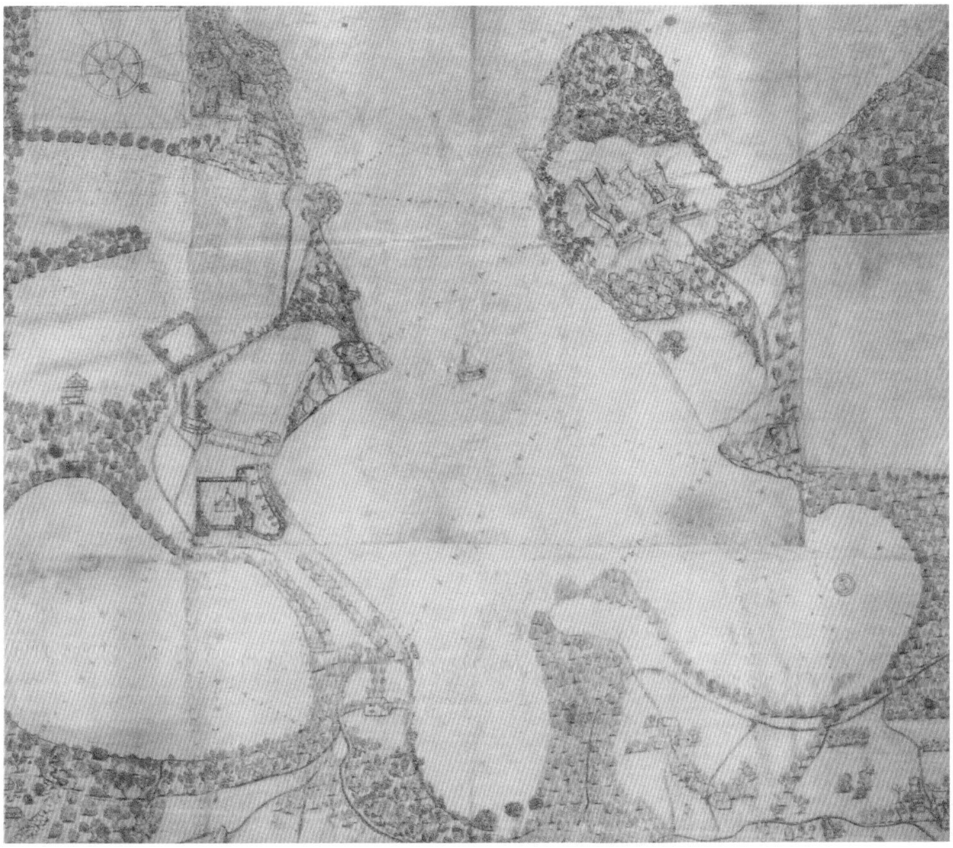

Port Louis, c. 1660s

bricks and framework. The church is located on this place at a distance of about 300 steps from the Fort; but it is made of only pitchforks and reeds and is in very poor condition; the whole place is planted in manioc, potatoes and peas and set with orange-trees and other fruits.' A 1660s drawing graphically shows the buildings mentioned above by du Tertre plus houses scattered around the area.

The colonists experienced a number of problems, including attacks from the Island CARIBS, flooding of the settlement, and 'fevers' or MALARIA. The Lagoon, then a lake of brackish water, supported the breeding of mosquitoes that made the area unhealthy. The elimination of the Island Carib threat and the constant flooding of the sandbar on which the settlement was housed resulted in the move to higher ground by 1705, though the settlement had begun to move since the late 1600s. By 1710 Port Louis was abandoned, the residents removed to the Ville du FORT ROYAL.

In 1988 the Foundation for Field Research carried out an archaeological study of the submerged sandbar but this revealed nothing of the settlement. The only surviving record of the early settlement of Port Louis is *Histoire de l'isle de Grenade en Amérique, 1649-59*, believed written by Father BRESSON. Dredging of the sandbar at the entrance to the Lagoon to expand the port facilities in 1999 completely neglected the historical significance of the area, no one bothering to at least carry out a survey before destroying all evidence of the oldest European settlement in Grenada.[8, 95, 197]

POSTAL SERVICE

Before 1860 the British government administered the postal service in the colony, as it did for all the territories under its control. The local government, given control of the post, failed to provide permanent finances for its maintenance until 1885, with the passage of 'The Post Office Ordinance'. In 1861, following the issuance of its first adhesive postage stamp featuring a portrait of Queen Victoria, Grenada established an internal letter mailing system. It ended in 1863 due to its high cost; it was re-established in 1872 and continues today, but is restricted to St. George's Town. In 1881 Grenada was admitted to the Universal Postal Union. In 1888 the Royal Mail Steam Packet Company (operating in Grenada since 1842) began a weekly steamer service along the leeward coast of the island and to Carriacou, providing passenger and mail services. In 1892, with the addition of a third boat, the

Souvenir sheets of postage stamps from Grenada

service was extended to GRENVILLE. The development of the internal road network enabled more efficient transportation of mail, and by the 1920s 'motor-car mail and passenger services' operated along the eastern coast, while a mail boat carried mail and passengers along the western coast. Post offices were established in rural towns; approximately 52 presently exist.

The General Post Office was housed for much of its existence at the government complex on the CARENAGE, which was destroyed by a fire in 1990, and moved to a former warehouse on the pier (it was briefly housed in the former St. James Hotel while repairs were being made to the GPO). In 1996 the GPO was given statutory status, becoming the Grenada Postal Corporation and managed by a seven-member board appointed by the GOG. During much of the islands' modern history as a British colony, its postage stamps represented foreign themes. In 1898 Grenada was one of the first islands in the Caribbean to issue a stamp, commemorating the 'discovery' of GRENADA. The first local themes appeared on postage stamps in the 1930s with issues showing GRANDE ANSE BEACH, Grand Étang Lake, and ST. GEORGE'S TOWN. In 1969 Grenada issued two sets of stamps commemorating EXPO '69 and Human Right Year, with portraits of Gov. BYNOE, the first Grenadian woman to appear on a postage stamp. To

celebrate Grenada's INDEPENDENCE in 1974 a set was issued featuring PM GAIRY, the national flag and other NATIONAL SYMBOLS. During the REVOLUTION, the PEOPLE'S REVOLUTIONARY GOVERNMENT issued a number of stamps commemorating the MARCH 13 coup d'état, PM BISHOP and subsequent anniversaries.

Grenada is known throughout the philatelic world as a prolific stamp producer for collectors. Almost any theme can be found on Grenadian stamps because the industry is an important economic asset. Yet it is sad that many dimensions of the islands' people, history and culture have been neglected in place of foreign themes like Walt Disney and the American and British personalities who dominate the stamps of Grenada and the GRENADA GRENADINES.[52]

PRESBYTERIAN CHURCH The Scots were an old and fairly large community, among the first British subjects to arrive in Grenada beginning in 1763, and exhibited a large influence on the political and economic institutions (see SCOTISH HERITAGE). In 1830 the LEGISLATURE passed an act granting the 'Old Court House Lot', in the shadow of FORT GEORGE, 'for the purpose of erecting a church, for the performance of divine service, according to the Presbyterian form of worship.' The 'Old Courthouse' had burned in the ST. GEORGE'S FIRE of 1775. In 1831, with the help of the Freemasons, the Presbyterians erected a church, which was established as the Church of Scotland in Grenada in 1833. In 1945 the Church of Scotland withdrew its support, but suggested that it unite with the Methodist Church, a proposal which the Grenada church rejected, instead becoming associated with the Presbyterian Church in Trinidad. In 1986 it became autonomous at the Presbyterian Church in Grenada.

It was a small yet beautiful church, with a tall square-spire tower. It was constructed in the Gothic Revival style common in the post-1830 period. Its construction signalled the beginning of the rise of medieval features over the traditional Caribbean Georgian architecture prevalent during the eighteenth century. The tower, with its pointed corner pinnacles and clock, is a dominant feature of the St. George's skyline. A number of memorial plaques once lined the inner walls, and graves, dating to the 1800s, occupy the churchyard. The passage of HURRICANE IVAN in 2004 destroyed the church, leaving only the steeple and posterior wall standing. Knox House is the presbytery, sitting on the site of the former governor's residence which was destroyed by fire in 1772.

Presbyterian Church (pre-Hurricane Ivan)

In 1860 the government withheld its annual grant to the Presbyterians, forcing them to close the church for the next 15 years. The Presbyterians, unlike the Anglicans, made little effort to convert the slaves and the rural poor, with the congregation remaining dominated by the islands' elite until the twentieth century. Their population has always been small (in 1851 just over half a per cent; presently about one per cent of the population).

Beginning in 1880 the Presbyterian Church established a number of chapel-schools among the East Indian indentured labourers, especially at Bellair, St. Andrew, and SAMARITAN, St. Patrick. These chapel-schools helped convert many of the EAST INDIANS to Christianity. The Presbyterian Church administers a primary school in Samaritan and a secondary school, Macdonald College, St. Patrick. The church building in St. George's is also known as the Scots' Kirk and Presbyterian Kirk.[329]

PRIME MINISTER The title and position of the leader of the government who is selected by the GOVERNOR GENERAL from among the members of the House of Representatives whom s/he feels is the most likely to gain the support of the majority of the House. That individual is usually the leader of the POLITICAL PARTY with the majority of the elected representatives, or the leader of a coalition. Even though the constitution grants executive authority to the GG, it is the PM, as head of the cabinet, who exercises that authority. The PM can designate a deputy PM even though this position is not outlined in the constitution.

The PM usually serves for five years, but may be forced to call early ELECTIONS if s/he loses the majority in the House due to defections or a 'no-confidence' vote. The dissolution of Parliament and the calling of elections are done by the GG in consultation with the PM. Though Maurice Bishop was not elected in parliamentary elections, he held the position of PM, following the enactment of People's Law No.11. The title of PM replaced that of premier following INDEPENDENCE. PMs to date have been Sir Eric Matthew GAIRY, Maurice BISHOP, Herbert BLAIZE, Ben JONES, Sir Nicholas BRATHWAITE, George BRIZAN, and Dr Keith MITCHELL. The official residence of the PM is at Mt. Royal, St. George.[3, 179]

PRINCESS ALICE HOSPITAL was opened in 1949 at Mirabeau, St. Andrew. It replaced the dilapidated St. Andrew's District Hospital (1878-1948), GRENVILLE, which was established along with the St. John's District Hospital (1878-1891) predominantly to treat YAWS patients. The new hospital was located 2 miles (3 km) 'away from the swamps of Grenville' and the dreaded MALARIA which bred there. It has a capacity of 45 beds (increased from its initial 32, and some years later 40), and is part of the larger General HOSPITAL system. It derives its name from Princess Alice, Countess of Athlone, who visited in 1950.

PRINCESS ROYAL HOSPITAL was built in 1957 as the primary health facility for C&PM. It replaced the Belle Vue Hospital (1907-1955), destroyed by HURRICANE JANET, and the Carriacou District Hospital (1886-1907), which a doctor described as 'deficient, dismal, decayed and totally unsuited for the housing of the sick.' The present hospital is located on Hospital Hill, overlooking HILLSBOROUGH, with its two cannons, relics from the lower fort, aiming at a spectacular view. It has a capacity of 45 beds (increased from its initial 30 to 40 in 1963), and is part of the larger General HOSPITAL system. It derives its name from Princess Mary, daughter of King George V and then Princess Royal.

PROVERBS/SAYINGS encompass the philosophies and witticisms of Grenada's FOLK CULTURE. They are pervasive, often subtle utterances disguised in the everyday expressions of most Grenadians. Like other folk traditions, these aphorisms gained much from various West African cultures, but underwent profound alterations to suit the local environment, i.e. slavery, exploitation and racial discrimination, and incorporated French and British cultural expressions and languages. For many individuals (and the folk in particular), these clichés represent a weapon, usually against more powerful physical, political and economic forces, and are a way to remedy one's perceived impotence. They are often veiled threats, or more so curses like in the saying 'ninety-nine days for the thief, one day for watchman'. They are also used by parents or older family members to warn children of the consequences of disobeying their elders as in the forewarning, 'chil', is come you coming.'

Aphorisms, giving voice to the poor and downtrodden, object to injustices and deprivations caused by physical, social or political bullies. They echo the everyday experiences of the poor, with their objective of gaining dignity, retribution and hope in the face of hardships.

QUADRILLE A folk dance that dates to the early nineteenth century and survives in both Grenada and Carriacou but under different names; in Grenada it is called lancers, while in Carriacou it is called quadrille. It derives from the British lancers or lancers quadrille which was introduced in the 1830s (its namesake, the French quadrille, is a similar square dance introduced in the 1730s but has since died out). Quadrille and lancers are often used interchangeably. The quadrille was popular among the British and was subsequently learned by the slaves and altered to suit African music and rhythm, yet retaining European characteristics. It comprises a set of dances, usually six, and is danced by four couples. It was popular at subscription dances and fêtes until the 1960s. Thereafter, it survived in Grenada as an exhibition when the GULP government sponsored the National Group of Lancers Dancers who performed at national festivals and celebrations. Though it is no longer common, it survives in a few rural communities. In Carriacou, especially in the village of L'Esterre, it remained quite popular until recently. Musical accompaniment is by quadrille or STRING BANDS, which comprise violin/fiddle, triangle, bass drum and tambourine.[51, 85, 234]

QUARANTINE STATION This facility was built in 1892 to isolate the victims of smallpox, YELLOW FEVER and other communicable DISEASES common in the region. It was located on an isolated promontory on the SW coast at Goat/Long Point. As the observation centre for the port of St. George's, anyone arriving in Grenada and suspected of being infected with a communicable disease, was immediately brought to the station for observation. Quarantine Station was used as an isolation centre until the mid-twentieth century, by which time most of the dreaded diseases were eradicated or under control.

Beginning in the early 1900s it was frequently used as a government rest house and a holiday resort when not in official use. During the Grenada REVOLUTION the PRG established a military camp there. After falling into disuse, the buildings were finally torn down; the area is now overgrown and occupied by communication antennas. The government plans to protect the area as a natural landmark to preserve its unique geological features. During World War I it housed the Grenadian detachment of the BRITISH WEST INDIES REGIMENT. Situated on the promontory just south of Quarantine Point at Petit Cabrits Point was a Leper Settlement that operated between 1928 and 1957.[55]

QUEEN'S PARK Oral history has it that the Queen's Park was given by Lucy D'Arbeau to the people of Grenada in 1887 to mark the 50th anniversary of the ascension of Queen Victoria to the throne, hence its name. Officially though, it was the Grenada Government that granted to the Parochial Board in 1887 'a large area of level ground to the north of the town to be styled "The Queen's Park," and converted to a place of recreation'. The exact relationship between Lucy D'Arbeau and the property is unclear, but the fact that the surrounding area is called D'Arbeau Hill suggests a link. The area occupied a former explosion crater located just outside the town of St. George's, bounded by the St. John's River and D'Arbeau Hill. It is one of the few flat areas on the island, and beginning in 1887 it became the home of CRICKET. It was quite evident then that 'Sport and recreation probably had a greater influence, but sanitation will also benefit' when in 1915 the permanently flooded areas around the

Queen's Park, c. 1927

park were drained and filled in to destroy the breeding places of mosquitoes and eliminate MALARIA (debris for reclamation was taken from the incinerator installed at Cherry Hill). The house served as a pavilion from around 1908 when HORSERACING activities were transferred from Grande Anse.

The central government took over the administration of the park from the St. George's District Board in 1926, and a pavilion was constructed in 1928. On 7 April 1927 four amphibious planes, part of a 20-nation Pan-American goodwill flight from the US, landed on the beach and were displayed at the Queen's Park. The racecourse defined the park for many years, as did the zinc/galvanise fence that later enclosed the field. Because it could accommodate large numbers of people it was used for military parades, sporting activities like FOOTBALL, CRICKET and athletics, cultural festivals like CARNIVAL and musical concerts, and political rallies. It was also used as a golf course, police shooting range, and prisoner detention centre. On JUNE 19, 1981 it was the site of a bomb explosion that killed three young women. In 1997, after seventy years, the pavilion was dismantled to make way for a NATIONAL STADIUM.[367]

RASTAFARIANISM is a religious movement which holds that former Ethiopian Emperor Haile Selassie I (reigned 1930-1974) is the living god. The movement began in the 1930s in the ghettos of Kingston, Jamaica, where a number of individuals viewed the ascendance of Ras (Prince) Tafari, the claimed descendant of King Solomon and Queen Makeda of Sheba, to the throne as a heavenly sign that 'Africa shall stretch forth its hands unto God.' Marcus Garvey, an early Pan-Africanist from Jamaica, is revered as a prophet, and Ethiopia, the only African country not 'colonised' by Europeans, is regarded as the homeland.

In the late 1960s and early 1970s the Rastafarian faith began to spread throughout the Caribbean and even beyond. It arrived in Grenada on the heels of BLACK POWER and became another element in the growing dissatisfaction with the country's social and political situation. Rastafarianism began to appeal to a small group of individuals, particularly men. Through reggae music and the use of marijuana ('transcendental herb'), the faith spread throughout the islands, especially in the larger towns. As the Rasta population grew so did the fear that they would disrupt the status quo. As unemployment increased, especially among the young, Rasta became more appealing to that segment of society.

Rasta man

Rastas never became involved in the political chaos of the early and mid-1970s because they had yet to attract a large following. After the 1979 REVOLUTION many (Campbell estimates 400) became involved because the NEW JEWEL MOVEMENT's promise of a 'new, just and equal society' appealed to their sense of justice and community. Many probably also believed that the revolutionary government would legalise or at least allow them the free use of marijuana for religious purposes. This actually became a contentious issue between some Rastas and the PRG. The relationship soon disintegrated and by October 1979 there were demonstrations against a segment of the Rastas as illegal drug dealers and 'counters'. A number of them were detained at the Hopevale Rehabilitation Centre for 're-education' because of their rumoured involvement in counter-revolutionary activities. Many lost their prized locks or dreadlock hairstyle, which were shaved while they were detained.

Today, the movement has lost much of its appeal to the young. Though Rastafarianism began as a religious philosophy, that aspect has lost its attractiveness, with many finding the social doctrine more palatable. The hairstyle, 'dreads', has become commonplace, even as a popular fashion statement outside of the region. There is a very small group of Rastas who 'live up in the hills,' shunning society and its material underpinnings. While in the bushes they do not wear clothes, but will wear clothing made from straw when coming to town to sell their fruits and vegetables. The Rastafarian community numbers approximately 1,000 children, women and men.[48]

REDHEAD, Andrew Wilfred 'Willie' (1909-1993) was a playwright, author, community activist and civil servant. He was born in St. George's, the son of Emma *nee* Sweeny and Albert George Redhead. Like many young ambitious individuals at the time, Redhead was a member of the GRENADA LITERARY LEAGUE after leaving the Grammar School (later the GBSS). Between 1928 and 1967 he served in the colonial civil service in Grenada and Barbados as assistant social welfare officer, superintendent of prisons in Grenada and Barbados, and as district officer for C&PM. Redhead loved the Boy SCOUTS, serving as the chief commissioner for Grenada and Barbados. In an article titled 'Truth, Fact and Tradition in Carriacou', he criticised noted sociologist M G SMITH and his study of Carriacouan society. Redhead called into question Smith's 'primitive' depiction of Carriacouan society and referred to his so-called ancestor worship as 'fiction'.

In 1977, in recognition of his community service, Redhead was awarded the CBE. Grenada's cultural and historical heritage were important to Redhead and he was instrumental in the establishment of the Grenada Historical Society; he served as the organisation's first president. A writer, Redhead authored a number of plays, which were the basis of the islands' burgeoning dramatic and performing ARTS in the 1960s. In 1985 he published his autobiography, *A City on the Hill*. A newspaper writer, he wrote for the WEST INDIAN, TORCHLIGHT, *Grenadian Voice* and the *Greeting Tourist Guide*. In December 1994 the Willie Redhead Foundation for the Preservation and Urban Renewal of St. George's was inaugurated to preserve his beautiful Caribbean Georgian 'city on the hill'.[277, 278, 279, 280, 281, 282, 283]

RELIGIONS The strong influence of religion in the lives of Grenadians dates to the early days of colonialism. The tenets of the Code Noir established CATHOLICISM in Grenada. This, together with the expansion of religious indoctrination in the 1820s as a precondition to EMANCIPATION, laid the foundations of a very religious society, especially among the slaves and their descendants. The majority of Grenadians belong to the many Christian denominations brought to the island by Europeans, though some retain membership in, or have affiliations with, African-derived beliefs like SHANGO and OBEAH. As a result of impending emancipation the British relaxed their religious restrictions in the 1820s since EDUCATION, and particularly religious instruction, was seen as essential to the smooth transition from SLAVERY to freedom. This made possible the spread of a number of Protestant denominations that established missions and proselytised among the peasantry.

Today, there are at least thirty religious denominations in Grenada. The Roman Catholics (est. by 1685) form the majority of those who practise the Christian faith. They are followed by the Anglicans (est. 1783), Seventh-Day Adventists (est. 1903), Methodists (est. 1789), Presbyterians (est. 1800), Pentecostals (est. 1927), Bereans (est. 1957) and Jehovah's Witnesses (est. 1931). There are small groups of SPIRITUAL BAPTISTS (est. c.1900), Rastafarians (est. 1970s), Muslims (est. 1970s), and (Plymouth) Brethren (est. early 1900s). Within the past three decades newer Protestant denominations have been growing at the expense of the established Churches.

The pervasive presence of religion has inevitably resulted in the involvement of Churches in politics, as occurred in the 1970s and 1980s. The RC and Protestant Churches, through the Conference of Churches in Grenada (CCG, est. 1975), were members of the COMMITTEE OF 22 that became involved in the political protests of the mid-1970s. The CCG, though expressing initial support for the PEOPLE'S REVOLUTIONARY GOVERNMENT, was nonetheless wary of the socialist orientation of the NEW JEWEL MOVEMENT. The PRG viewed the Churches as adversarial, 'the most dangerous sector for the development of internal counter revolution'. Sermons were closely monitored and the activities of the clergy carefully scrutinised as the PRG tried to control the Churches' influence in the lives of most Grenadians. As the revolution progressed, the relationship between the Churches and the state worsened, especially following the closure of the religious newsletter *Catholic Focus*. The Churches of course survived the PRG—as they had the French and British colonial governments—and will no doubt continue to play a major role in politics and the lives of many Grenadians.[35, 101, 136, 260, 261, 316, 333, 370]

RENWICK, Charles Felix Percival 'CFP' (1887-1943) was a prominent lawyer, legislator and businessman. A member of the proprietary Renwick family, CFP was the son of Stella *nee* Hyams and Charles Renwick. CFP graduated from the University of Oxford, England, and was called to the Bar, Middle Temple around 1911. He returned to Grenada and practised law, through which his ability and reputation as an astute lawyer earned him the title Jab Neg (<Fr.Cr. diable negre: 'black devil'). With T A MARRYSHOW and others he co-founded the WEST INDIAN newspaper in 1915. He served on many committees and boards, including the St. George's District Board.

An advocate of representative government, Renwick, like William DONOVAN, was considered a radical member of the REPRESENTATIVE GOVERNMENT ASSOCIATION. Following the granting of limited representative government in 1925 he was elected to the legislature, representing the parish of St. George (1925-1928, 1937-1943); he was also appointed to the Executive Council (1927-1931). Among his accolades were the OBE and KCM. CFP was also a prominent businessman, owning the Antilles Hotel (see HOME HOTEL) and a large number of shares in the GRENADA SUGAR FACTORY. His reputation as a notorious gambler was well known, and is woven into local mythology. At the pinnacle of his career, he died in 1943. In a brief biographical sketch just before his death, he was hailed as 'one of the Island's greatest sons', and 'Grenada's outstanding public man'. Writer Maurice Patterson feels that 'if a single man's life could signalise the closing of an era, CFP's could.' His former residence at TOWER HOUSE is a national landmark.

REPRESENTATIVE GOVERNMENT ASSOCIATION The RGA was formed in 1917 by many of Grenada's leading citizens to lobby for representative government as opposed to CROWN COLONY rule. Members included leading lawyers, planters and other politically active individuals. They represented diverse political and social interests, pitting conservatives, represented predominantly by the PLANTOCRACY, against the liberals, represented by coloured and black middle-class elements like W G DONOVAN and 'CFP' RENWICK. The liberals demanded a totally elected body within the LEGISLATURE and the conservatives advocated a minority elected chamber. The conservatives, led by D S De Freitas and W A Commissong (both successive presidents of the RGA), were concerned that they would lose their political voice within an extended electorate.

In 1920 the RGA sent a petition to the British colonial government, requesting an end to Crown Colony rule and a return to representative government. In 1921 the Colonial Office accepted the recommendation, but only for a partially elected Legislative Council, which satisfied conservatives and disappointed the liberals. Marryshow then made a trip to the UK on behalf of the liberals, but failed to get further concessions.

When the reforms were implemented in 1925, five representatives were elected to the Legislative Council. Though they lacked a majority to change policy, they became a force that for the first time in decades challenged the authority of the GOVERNOR. Probably the most radical change to the constitution was the granting to women of the right to vote, though subject to qualifications. T A MARRYSHOW proposed that the RGA be established as a POLITICAL PARTY, but he was unsuccessful, and it came to an end in 1924. The RGA achieved the restoration of representative government, which paved the way for adult suffrage in 1951 and full representative government in 1967.[98]

REVOLUTION/'THE REVO' The coup d'état that brought Maurice BISHOP and the NEW JEWEL MOVEMENT to power on MARCH 13, 1979 established a revolutionary style of government in Grenada for the next four-and-a-half years. During this period the PEOPLE'S REVOLUTIONARY GOVERNMENT represented the hopes of many, both nationally and internationally, as the dream of people's power seemed a reality. Yet, to many others the PRG was nothing more than a dictatorial government, and 'a revolution only of words'.

Button supporting the Grenada Revolution

The PRG had replaced the government of PM Eric GAIRY, which through corruption and mismanagement had brought the country to the brink of political and financial bankruptcy. The PRG implemented a number of social programmes that were to be its legacy, many benefiting the poor. Among these were low-cost housing, extended primary medical and dental care through the technical assistance of Cuban doctors and dentists, free school-lunch programmes, literacy and adult EDUCATION, hundreds of educational scholarships abroad, expanded employment through military service and infrastructural work, especially the POINT SALINES INTERNATIONAL AIRPORT, the advancement of working women with the passage of the Maternity Leave Law, social security benefits through the National Insurance Scheme and the extension of pre-school and day care centres. With political support across most social strata, the PRG was able to establish, albeit initially, an unprecedented and popular participation in mass organisations like the National Youth Organisation and the National Women's Organisation, the LABOUR MOVEMENT and participatory LOCAL GOVERNMENT. Community participation through volunteer work groups contributed to the development of community infrastructure.

Though confronted with economic and political pressures aimed at derailing the revolution, the PRG was able to make significant strides, rivalling the combined achievements of previous governments. Yet, this achievement was not accomplished without sacrifice, one that many felt was too harsh on certain segments of society. Though many Grenadians were willing to forget the promise of parliamentary ELECTIONS, the abuses of human rights, an unprecedented military build-up, restrictions of freedom of expression, and secret agreements with communist regimes eventually cost the PRG both domestic and international support. The violation of human rights following the application of 'heavy manners' and the detention of alleged counter-revolutionaries without formal charges brought contention between the PRG and local groups, especially the Churches. Internationally, the US government, beginning in 1979, began to mount economic and military pressure to derail what it considered a communist threat in its backyard.

In the end, the revolution collapsed upon itself, unable to bear the pressures of its own successes and setbacks. What had begun as an experiment in Grenada's economic development proved a course fraught with political and ideological infighting, the abuse of power by a small group of well-armed individuals, and a shortsightedness that was to be the bane of the revolution.[101, 242, 253, 267, 363]

REVOLUTIONARY MILITARY COUNCIL The RMC was established on 19 October 1983 to replace the dissolved PEOPLE'S REVOLUTIONARY GOVERNMENT following the execution of PM BISHOP. General Hudson Austin chaired the 16-member RMC, with notable members including vice-chairmen Lt. Colonels Liam James and Ewart Layne. Though Bernard COARD was not named to any of the positions on the RMC, it was widely believed that he was in charge of the new government. A 24-hour shoot-on-sight curfew was imposed to quell any opposition to RMC rule because of Bishop's widespread appeal. The RMC, recognising its tenuous political and military position, insisted that it 'has no desire or aspiration to rule the country' and would work towards the return to normalcy and democratic government. In an obvious attempt to dissolve US government fears and deter US military action against Grenada, the RMC communicated to the US ambassador in Barbados that discussions with the business community were in progress in the hope of forming a civilian government. The RMC desperately tried to assure the US that its actions would not endanger the lives of the US citizens on the island, especially the students attending ST. GEORGE'S UNIVERSITY, fearing that the US would use the students' safety as a pretext to invade.

The short-lived RMC was never able to gain the confidence of the majority of Grenadians, even after the US had begun a military offensive against the islands. The defence of the country was half-hearted, and within 24 hours resistance collapsed. The US military detained all of the members of the RMC and nine were eventually placed on trial for the executions of PM Bishop and his supporters. Of the 16-member RMC eight were sentenced to death and are now serving life sentences in jail.[2, 363]

RICHMOND HILL FORTS A series of forts that once constituted the extensive fortifications on Richmond Hill, meant to protect St. George's from attacks originating inland, hence the name Back-to-Front-Forts. In 1778 the British constructed entrenchments on Richmond Hill, but these proved inadequate to repel the invading French in 1779, and revealed the inadequacies of the existing defences. To correct the situation the French appropriated the estate of William Lucas (who later got the legislature, of which he was the president, to compensate him with £20,000 after paying £3,000 a decade earlier) and immediately began the construction of fortified points or redoubts on the 800 ft (244 m) high hill, the future

Richmond Hill Prisons

site of Forts Frederick and Matthew. They constructed more extensive fortifications, especially cisterns and underground storage chambers. They were nonetheless of a temporary nature and in a deplorable state when the British regained the island in 1783. The latter immediately began to strengthen the French defences by building more permanent structures. The forts were completed between 1783 and 1795, with the Grenada Legislature contributing the Mt. George estate, slave labour, and 'refreshments' to the troops.

Of the four forts, Fort Frederick (<the second son of George III) was the primary fort, being situated on the highest point. It was completed in 1794 and located to the east of Fort Matthew, facing Mt. Maitland. It was designed to cover the two smaller forts, Forts Lucas and Adolphus, on the ridge to the east. Built with its own cistern, provisions store and magazine, it was self-sufficient and functioned as the main defensive bastion fort. During the REVOLUTION it served as the headquarters for a division of the PEOPLE'S REVOLUTIONARY ARMY and was the command centre during the 1983 US-led military INTERVENTION. At present it is the only fort in the series to be maintained as a visitor attraction. Fort Matthew (<Gov. Matthew, 1784-1785) is a classic siege fort surrounded by a dry moat and protected by massive gun chambers. It faced inland towards Mt. Parnassus to the east. It contained an officers' mess, commanding officer's quarters, cisterns and a parade ground. Fort Matthew served as the Mental Hospital between 1880 and 1987, but was 'accidentally' bombed by the US military in 1983, killing 16 inmates. The ruins of the smaller Forts Lucas and Adolphus are presently located on private property and are beyond repair.[41, 177]

RICHMOND HILL PRISONS Following the withdrawal of the military garrison in 1854, its facilities were minimally remodelled for civilian uses, with the military hospital at Richmond Hill converted to the male prison in 1880 (the military hospital at Richmond Hill was built in 1805, but was destroyed by fire in 1841 and rebuilt in 1854 on Mt. Cardigan). This prison replaced the Common Gaol on Young Street, St. George's, which had been housed in the former French military barracks and jail since the early 1700s, and had proved inadequate. In 1904 an annex to the buildings at Richmond Hill was added to house female prisoners.

Through expansion over the years the buildings have increased to accommodate the islands' prisoners. It has been euphemistically referred to as 'Her Majesty's Hotel' (<Her Majesty's Prisons) because of the breathtaking hillside view it commands of St. George's. Under PM GAIRY the prison attracted attention following questionable arrests of a number of individuals who were vocal opponents of his government. One of the reasons the NEW JEWEL MOVEMENT gave for ousting Gairy was the discovery of secret cells meant for the NJM leaders.

Approximately 800-900 people were detained as political prisoners during the reign of the PEOPLE'S REVOLUTIONARY GOVERNMENT, many without official charges or due process of the law. As PM Bishop stated in his now famous 'Line of March Speech', 'Consider how people get detained in this country. We don't go and call for no vote. You get detained when I sign an order after discussing with the National Security Committee of the Party or with a higher Party body. Once I sign it—like it or don't like it—it's way up the hill for them.' The PRG's detention policy alienated the public and some in the government itself, specifically Attorney General Lloyd Noel, who was later dismissed from the PRG and himself detained. In an attempt to control vocal opposition from a segment of the Rastafarian movement, the PRG converted a government-owned estate, Hopevale, into a so-called drug rehabilitation and agricultural centre. The conditions of the facilities were unsanitary and many suffered humiliation and physical abuse. Though not all inmates were Rastafarians, around 30-50 were believed detained over the course of the revolution. The detention of political prisoners became a volatile issue between the PRG and its detractors, domestically and internationally, tarnishing the achievements of the REVOLUTION. Following the US-led military INTERVENTION, most of the political prisoners were released, some having spent the entire four-and-a-half years of the revolution imprisoned. The convicted former members of the REVOLUTIONARY MILITARY COUNCIL and PEOPLE'S REVOLUTIONARY ARMY have become the prison's most celebrated inmates. As a result of HURRICANE IVAN in 2004 some of the prisoners escaped when the buildings were damaged; most returned voluntarily, but some had fled the island before being apprehended.[353]

RIVER ANTOINE RUM DISTILLERY is situated about 1.5 miles (2.4 km) SE of LAKE ANTOINE in St. Patrick. It is an ESTATE utilising methods, equipment and technologies to produce RUM that have been a part of the process since the 1700s. The grinding of the SUGAR CANE is performed with machinery powered by a 24-foot high water wheel, a technology that differs very little from the days of SLAVERY. Its surviving water-driven distillery is one of only a few in the Caribbean.

River Antoine Rum Distillery

A date stone on one of the buildings records 1785, and the River Antoine Distillery contends that it is the oldest continuously running rum distillery in the Caribbean. The 450 acre (182 ha) sugar estate derives its name from the Rivière Antoine, which itself was named after 'Captain' ANTOINE, an Island CARIB 'chief'. It produces rum popularly known as 'Rivers', marketed as 'Grenada's purest and oldest white rum'. Between 1890 and 1990 Thomas H DeGale II and his heirs owned the estate. In 1980 the workers appropriated the estate and declared it a 'workers co-op', during which time the GREAT HOUSE was burned. It was subsequently 'officially leased' by the PEOPLE'S REVOLUTIONARY GOVERNMENT in 1983 under its Land Development and Utilisation Law. The estate was returned to the DeGale family in 1984 and in 1988 was sold to the Grenadian-owned RDF Enterprises, which has continued producing rum. The GOG has proposed that the River Antoine Distillery be preserved and managed as an educational and interpretative resource. The distillery offers tours of its facilities.[17, 145]

RIVER SALLEE, St. Patrick is a large rural village with a population of roughly 3,000. The area owes its name to the Salée Rivière (<Fr. *Salée*: 'salty' + *Rivière*: 'river'), most probably due to its close proximity to the sulphur or HOT SPRINGS along its banks. River Sallee (pronounced Sally) powered the huge waterwheel that ground the sugar cane at the sugar estate of the same name, which dates to the mid-1700s. River Sallee was one of the many free villages that developed in the post-Emancipation era through small plots of estate land either leased, bought, squatted on, or 'given' to peasant labourers in lieu of wages. In 1939 the 290 acre (117 ha) estate was acquired by the Grenada government as part of its LAND SETTLEMENT and sold as plots to rural residents. It is most readily associated with the River Sallee Boiling Springs. Worship at the springs by SHANGO and SPIRITUAL BAPTISTS led to the village being known as a centre for Shango until recently. It is one of the few villages in Grenada where elements of the BIG DRUM DANCE can still be observed. The River Sallee Credit Union (est. 1962) has been highly successful, with a membership of over 1,700.

RIVERS & STREAMS What Grenadians generally refer to as rivers can be regarded as large streams. There are some 52 major streams, including the Duquesne River in St. Mark, Black Bay River in St. John, St. Patrick's River in St. Patrick, St. John's River in St. George, and the GREAT RIVER, which is by far the largest river in Grenada. These river systems, separated into some 71 watersheds, are vital to the supply of water throughout the island. They are also sources of fresh-water fish like TITIRI, mullet, and river eel or zangri (<Fr. *(le)s—anguilles*: 'eels'). Historically, rivers were important as a direct source of drinking water up until the mid-1900s because pipe-borne water did not become available in the rural areas until after the 1960s. The use of rivers and streams as laundries and dumps for household waste and sewage led to their pollution and resulted in the spread of water-borne DISEASES. They served as laundries, with women gathered along their

Women doing laundry in stream

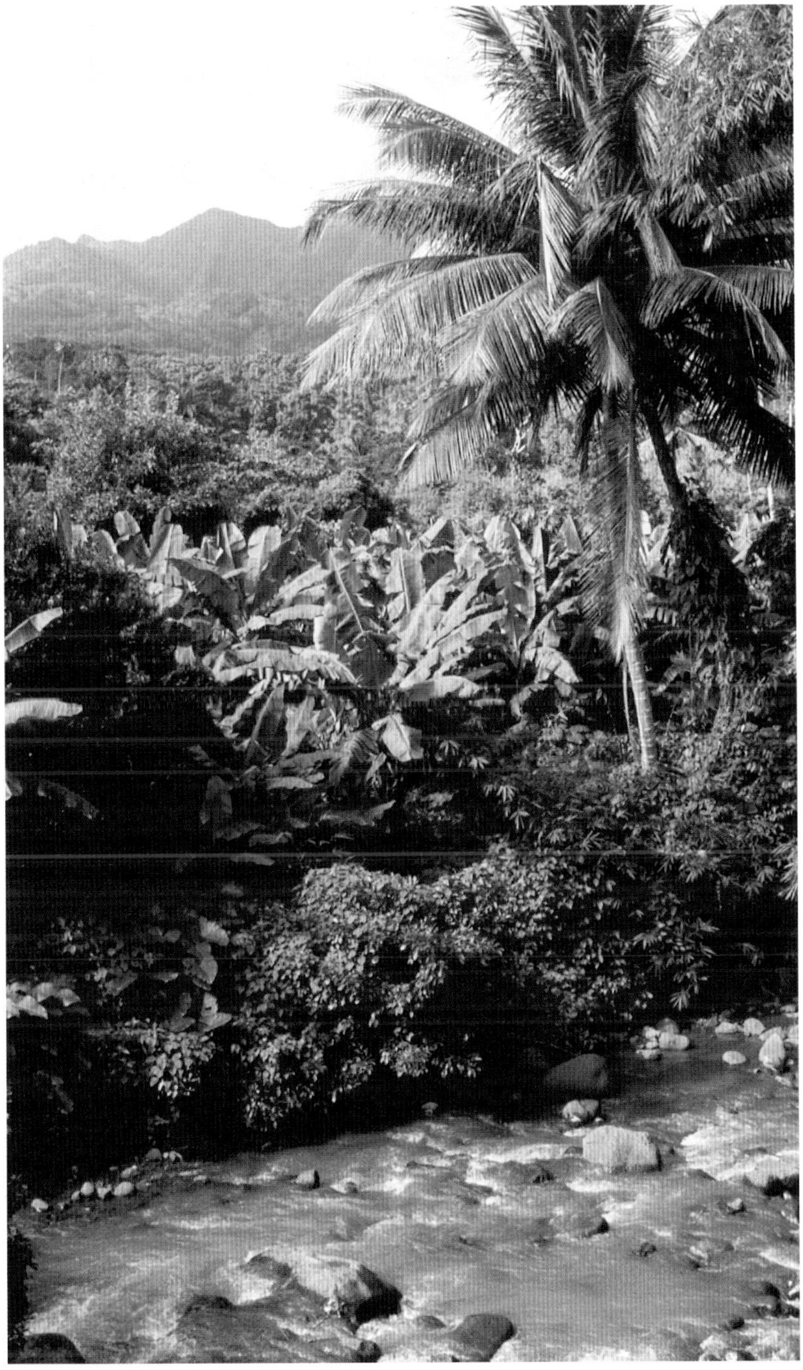
River scenery

banks to 'wash'/launder their clothes, placing them on river stones to 'bleach' and dry; this is rarely practised today except in the most rural areas of the island.

Many streams become flooded during the rainy season and can cause damage to BRIDGES & ROADS, even resulting in the loss of life on occasions. The saying, 'Never bad talk river while sitting on river stone,' is quite illustrative. After a rain storm the people at the mouth of the river often exclaim, 'The river come down!' referring to the muddy water that flows into the sea. During the eighteenth to twentieth centuries many streams were dammed as a source of waterpower on sugar estates, with at least one aqueduct and water mill still utilised at RIVER ANTOINE to produce RUM. The islands of the GRENADA GRENADINES have no streams except during the rainy season, and there exists a great shortage of clean, potable water in those islands.

ROGERS, James (c.1740-1799) was a Bristol slave trader who sold thousands of slaves in Grenada between 1785 and 1792 through slave factors like James BAILLIE; Rogers had, however, invested in slavers to Grenada as early as 1783. His company, James Rogers and Company, outfitted approximately 56 voyages to West Africa, primarily to Sierra Leone, Bonny and Old Calaba (in present day Nigeria), making 'him the twelfth leading British slave trader and the second largest Bristol slave merchant in the decade after 1785'. Twelve of those voyages brought just over 3,000 slaves to Grenada. In April 1792 the abolitionist William Wilberforce, in a speech to Parliament on the horrors of the SLAVE TRADE, mentioned the death of a 15-year-old female slave aboard one of Rogers' ships (*The Recovery*) while on its way to Grenada, at the hands of Captain John Kimber (it led to a prolonged trial, but he was acquitted). In August 1792 there was 'an Insurrection' on one of Rogers' ships (*The Mermaid*) headed to Grenada which 'resulted in the death of 19 men slaves and the scarring of about 11 more through burns caused by attempts to quell the uprising.' In the ongoing debate on the ending of the slave trade Rogers was 'the most vociferous in his denunciations of abolition.' As a result of the financial crisis of 1793 Rogers went bankrupt, but he has left a body of information that sheds light on the infamous slave trade and the role played by British port cities like Bristol and their trade with slave colonies like Grenada. Richardson concludes that 'of all Bristol's leading slave traders in the period 1783-93, Rogers, it seems, was the least efficient or successful.' Other prominent Bristol slave traders who traded in Grenada included Sir James Laroche, James McTaggart and William Tapscott.[237, 289]

RONDE ISLAND 12 18N 61 35W is a small island situated 5 miles (8 km) north of Grenada in the chain of islands known as the Grenadines. It is a dependency of Grenada with an area of 625 acres (253 ha) and a population of a few dozen people. It is the only inhabited island in the GRENADA GRENADINES after C&PM (censuses listed 52 people in 1891, 89 in 1901, and 152 in 1911). It takes its name from the French Île de Ronde/Islet Rond ('Round Island'). It rises to 520 ft (158 m) and exhibits a dry environment much of the year. Goat herding and FISHERIES are the primary economic activities. Ronde Island sits 3 miles (5 km) east of the submarine volcano KICK-EM-JENNY, and any VOLCANIC ACTIVITY may render it uninhabitable.

ROUCOU/ANNATTO (*Bixa orellana*) A native plant of the American tropics that was cultivated in the late 1600s as an export crop. The tree grows to 18 ft (5.6 m), its brownish-red seed pods containing numerous red seeds, used by the Island CARIBS in an application to their bodies believed to protect against insect bites and the sun. Annatto (<Cariban *anondö*, for the plant) created a distinct coloration that possibly led to the term 'Red Indian'. This edible red dye was cultivated for use as a food colouring.

Roucou fruits

Until the availability of other food colourings like curry and 'browning' (burnt sugar), annatto was commonly used as an additive to local foods such as rice, gravy and soup. Roucou (<Guarani *urucú*, for the plant) or oucou, its most common name in Grenada, is still used commercially to colour drugs and cosmetics.

ROUMÉ DE ST. LAURENT, Philippe Rose (1743-1803) was a French Grenadian and estate owner who is credited as the 'real originator of the development of Trinidad'. In 1777, no longer wishing to remain in his native Grenada, which had fallen under 'the British yoke' since 1763, he visited Spanish TRINIDAD and was struck by the economic potential of the island. Trinidad in the 1770s was sparsely populated and experiencing political and economic stagnation. In 1776 the Spanish provided some concessions to French RC immigrants from the ÎLES DU VENT, but St. Laurent suggested that if concessions were enhanced scores of families and their slaves would migrate to Trinidad. During the FRENCH INTERREGNUM St. Laurent served in the Lower and Supreme Courts in Grenada, even though he had acquired property in Trinidad. He went to Trinidad in 1781, and later travelled to Spain to lobby for the opening up of migration to Trinidad. In 1783 the Spanish Crown passed the Cédula of Population that granted RC (white and free coloured) concessions of land, citizenship, and tax credits as incentives to migrate to Trinidad. St. Laurent, however, was not given due recognition. Between 1786 and 1788 he was the administrator of Tobago, and in 1792 served as a member of a commission to Haiti to quell the slave revolt; he was later appointed colonial prefect. He went to France where he died in 1803. By early 1786 Trinidad's population was majority French Caribbean, a direct result of St. Laurent's recruitment efforts. A grant of land in Maraval, supposedly refused by St. Laurent, was later given to his mother who developed it as the Champs Elysees estate.[240, 284]

ROWLEY, Louise (1912-1993) was a social activist and dedicated civil servant who in 1956 became the region's first female permanent secretary. She was born in St. David to Jane and O'Hanley Rowley. She attended the ST. JOSEPH'S CONVENT, and though she was the first female to pass the London Matriculation Examinations she could not receive the ISLAND SCHOLARSHIP, as was the case for men. Instead she joined the male-dominated colonial civil service and worked her way to the top by dedication and perseverance. She struggled against entrenched chauvinism, but in 1956 women were finally admitted into the civil service on the basis of their qualifications and not simply as 'lady clerks'. With the establishment of the Committee System in the BWI, Rowley, with her 26 years of experience, was appointed permanent secretary in the Ministry of Education, Social Services and Labour. In her forty years of service to the government (1930-1969) she worked in various departments. She was deeply involved in the community, participating in many organisations including the Grenada Red Cross, Society of Friends of the Blind (founding member), Home for Handicapped Children (founding member), Soroptimist International (founding member), Girl Guides Association (former president), YWCA, the Grenada Historical Society and the GRENADA NATIONAL TRUST. In 1966 she was awarded the OBE. She will be remembered as a trailblazer for the role she played as a social worker and civil servant.

ROWLEY, Pansy Ouida (1908-1986) is without a doubt one of the most outstanding and unsung Grenadian heroines. She received a degree in social work from the London School of Economics and worked as a social worker in Grenada (she is remembered as the 'first black woman to obtain a university degree'). Rowley's social activism is exemplary. In the 1930s she founded the Girls' Physical Cultural Club, which was instrumental in staging many social events, and has been credited with the hosting of the first CARNIVAL pageant and popularising NETBALL. She also founded the School for the Deaf, the Pygmalion Glee Club and Divi Divi Dance Group (est. 1964), and resuscitated the YWCA.

Rowley was heavily involved in the community, participating in many organisations including the Grenada Red Cross, Society of Friends of the Blind, Grenada Arts Festival, the Grenada Historical Society and the GRENADA NATIONAL TRUST. She was a prominent worker in the ST. GEORGE'S ANGLICAN CHURCH. Rowley is also credited with being the first to 'try to make traditional dances acceptable,' with the Divi Divi Dance Group. In 1940 she was nominated to the St. George's District Board, and elected in 1942, becoming one of the first women in electoral politics. In 1962 she was awarded the MBE.

ROYAL GRENADA GAZETTE The first newspaper published in Grenada, the French having failed to publish one during their occupation. It appeared in 1765, and though published by a British national, was printed in both English and French in order to appeal to the large French population still resident in the islands. Due to the limited reading public, it was published weekly, every Saturday. Only a few copies are known to exist, preserved in US libraries. The *Gazette* continued until at least 1775, though it may have been published as late as 1788 when an extract from an 8 December 1788 issue was printed in the *Bahama Gazette* in February 1789. William Weyland of the 'New Printing Office' printed the *Gazette* for Alexander Middleton. During the FRENCH INTERRGENUM Middleton published the *Courrier de la Grenade* in French.

ROYAL VISITS Over the 200 years of British colonial rule, Grenada has been visited by a queen, many princesses and princes, dukes and duchesses. No fewer than ten high-ranking members of the British royal family have visited. The first royal visitor arrived in 1787. As a naval officer, Prince William Henry, third son of King George III, and later King William IV, visited the island and was extravagantly entertained; the HOSPITAL HILL REDOUBT was re-named in his honour. There is a tale that claims that the Prince, as a joke, approached and kissed a young lady while he was disguised as a midshipman. The lady, unaware of the regal identity of her suitor, responded by boxing the ear of the rude gentleman. In 1880 Princes George (later King George V) and Albert, both naval officers, visited aboard the HMS *Bacchante*. In 1913 Princess Marie Louise visited and the hospital for consumptives was named in her honour. In 1920 the Prince of Wales, later King George VI, visited. In 1955 Princess Margaret visited, and in 1960 Princess Alice visited. Prince Philip visited in 1966 and 1985. The first queen to visit Grenada was Queen Elizabeth II in February 1966 and again in October 1985. In 1992 Princess Alexandra visited and Prince Andrew visited in 2005.

RUM The idea of making rum from sugar cane was most probably invented in the Americas, maybe Brazil, and eventually spread throughout the region. Rum is made either from molasses, a by-product of sugar production, cane syrup or fresh SUGAR CANE juice, which is how it is presently made in Grenada at some factories. Historically, sugar cane was crushed, its juice extracted and boiled in huge iron vats called 'coppers' where the scum or syrup was removed, leaving a non-alcoholic liquid known as 'hot liquor', which was mixed with white lime (see LIMEKILNS) and boiled to remove impurities. After fermentation it was heated and then distilled. Proof rum is produced after the second distillation. Two types of rum, light and heavy, or white and gold are distilled depending on how long they are aged, the type of barrel they are aged in, and the final product desired.

There are two distilleries producing rum from locally grown sugar cane—RIVER ANTOINE and the GRENADA SUGAR FACTORY; WESTERHALL produces blended rum from imported materials. Grenada has only recently begun exporting rum again. In its heyday as a sugar producer in the eighteenth century Grenada exported large quantities of rum to the UK. Rum is an essential ingredient in a number of local dishes and drinks, especially black or fruitcake, sorrel and the famous rum punch. 'Mountain dew' or 'bush rum' is a home-made spirit made from sugar cane.[145]

Grenada rum

RUM SHOPS In almost every village is a rum shop, or an establishment 'licensed to sell spirituous liquors.' These shops may be exclusively for the sale of liquor, but most sell a variety of goods including cigarettes, 'tin (can) goods', and small household necessities. Rum shops have become an institution in many communities as a place for social gatherings. The island of CARRIACOU has been noted for its many rum shops or 'parlours'. The rum shop is a place to 'ole talk' while you 'fire one', either Jack Iron or Clark's Court, 'to keep the blood moving.' Rum shops are frequented predominantly by men. Customers can usually be seen playing dominoes or a game of all fours, surrounded by loud discussions and arguments. In the background can be heard reggae and calypso music. On Saturday nights rum shops take on the vibrant atmosphere of the community as villagers are out LIMING. Many Grenadians have recently called into question alcohol's traditional social acceptance. The prevalence and abuse of alcohol, especially among the young, have resulted in criticisms aimed at curtailing the social approval of this destructive pastime.[145]

ST. ANDREW Nicknamed the 'Big Parish', St. Andrew is the largest of the seven parishes that constitute the State of Grenada. It has a population of over 23,000 and occupies an area of 35 sq miles (91 sq km). Formerly the Paroisse du Grand MARQUIS, it was named St. Andrew by the British about 1764 after the patron saint of Scotland. It is the most easterly of the PARISHES, its entire coastline on the windward side of the island. The relatively level topography of St. Andrew towards the coast has meant the development of extensive ESTATES that produce a large portion of the islands' food crops. GRENVILLE, Grenada's second largest town and port, is the main town in St. Andrew. The pavilion at SEAMOON, now associated with political rallies and the Seamoon Industrial Park, still bears witness to the many horse races held there up until 1976 before HORSE RACING was discontinued. The opening of the POINT SALINES INTERNATIONAL AIRPORT in 1984 replaced PEARLS AIRPORT, which had served as the islands' main airport since 1943. St. Andrew is also home to Grenada's tropical rain forest situated in the GRAND ÉTANG NATIONAL PARK. The district is divided into four political constituencies—St. Andrew's NE, NW, SE and SW. St. Andrew is home to the PRINCESS ALICE HOSPITAL, a Health Centre, four medical stations, 13 primary and three secondary schools: SAASS, St. Joseph's Convent and the Grenville Secondary School.

ST. ANDREW'S ANGLICAN CHURCH The parish church in Grenville is one of many churches built in the 1830s in what was termed 'the church building era'. This handsome church was built between 1829 and 1831 and consecrated in 1833. Its construction combined both Caribbean Georgian and Gothic Revival architectural features of the period. The brick tower, with its corner pinnacles, bell and clock tower, was completed in 1833. The church has a beautiful, newly renovated red tile roof. Located on Victoria Street overlooking the waterfront, this church was the first permanent Anglican church built in the parish. Parish records date to 1798 and include baptisms, marriages, and burials; slave baptisms and marriages date from 1816 to 1833.

ST. ANDREW'S ANGLICAN SECONDARY SCHOOL SAASS holds the distinctions of being the first secondary school outside of the parish of ST. GEORGE, and the first co-educational secondary school in the islands. The GBSS, ST. JOSEPH'S CONVENT and the ANGLICAN HIGH SCHOOL were for many years the only secondary schools in Grenada. It was a burden, both logistical and financial, for parents in the rural districts to send their children to St. George's to school. Due to these hardships, heightened as a result of World War II, SAASS was established in 1945 by its first principal Sir Samuel Graham (1912-99) under the auspices of the Anglican Church. It has grown from 54 boys and girls in its first year to over 600 students to date. SAASS was first housed in the 'Upper Room', a storeroom, before moving to the SEAMOON Pavilion—euphemistically referred to as 'The Stable' because horses were previously housed there. It was moved for the final time in 1978 to its present location at Telescope, following the construction of modern facilities. SAASS has been the centre of secondary education in St. Andrew for many years. Educator and principal Creswell Julien guided its development between 1952 and 1986. Among its graduates are calypsonian Black Wizard, cricketers Rawle Lewis and Dennison Thomas, and athlete Allcyne Francique, the first Grenadian to win an international track and field gold medal.

ST. ANDREW'S RC CHURCH was built between 1915 and 1923, and overlooks the town of Grenville. Its architectural style is Caribbean Gothic Revival, producing a rather medieval facade. Its huge buttresses and rounded posterior walls give it a castle-like appearance. It was the third major RC church in the parish. The first RC chapel built in the parish of Notre Dame de l'Assomption

St. Andrew's RC Church, Grenville

(later St. Andrew) was constructed at Grand MARQUIS sometime after 1664, with the laying of the cornerstone by Capuchin monks that year; it was most likely a temporary structure. The St. Dominique Church, built in 1721, was confiscated by the British (Protestant) government in 1784 and used thereafter as an Anglican place of worship until 1789, when it was abandoned. By 1800 the Marquis chapel had fallen into disrepair and abandoned; its walled ruins are still visible.

In 1840 Father Angelo Leoni re-established the parish at GRENVILLE. The cornerstone of the 'Old Church' was laid in 1841 on property given by Frederick Harford of L'Esterre estate. In 1845 the church ran out of money and the roof remained incomplete until the legislature contributed towards its completion in 1858. In 1915 the 'Old Church' was deemed 'unhealthy for religious worship', but it was not until 1923 that it closed its doors to religious services. The 'Old Church' was used as a junior and combined primary school after 1923, and finally abandoned in 1972. Its decaying remains brought appeals by community organisers to renovate the building to house a cultural centre, museum, art gallery and library following restoration. Church records date to 1840, but are incomplete.[89]

ST. DAVID has an area of 18 sq miles (47 sq km) and is the third largest parish after St. Andrew and St. George. Its population of roughly 11,000 people live in villages scattered through plantations of NUTMEG, COCOA and SUGAR CANE. There is a small central town, St. David's, located inland, where commercial BANKS, police station, post office, and other governmental offices are to be found. Under French rule a small coastal town, the Bourg de Megrin, was established at St. David's Point by 1735; the old French town is now in ruins. Lying towards the SE of the island, its rugged coastline is lined with hidden coves graced with beautiful, unspoiled BEACHES. In the eighteenth to nineteenth centuries Requin Bay was the central port for the SE. Under French occupation St. David was called the Quartier du Megrin, but in 1764 the British changed it to St. David after the patron saint of Wales.

Though close to St. George's, it has not developed as quickly, with vast areas still cultivated as ESTATES or subsistence farms. It is one of the few remaining areas where sugar cane is still grown for the manufacture of RUM. A British architect purchased the peninsula of Westerhall Point in 1959 and transformed the area into an exclusive middle-class neighbourhood, with beautifully built houses overlooking its windswept coast. The Spice Factory at Laura, operated by the Minor Spices Co-operative Marketing Society, processes spices for export and maintains a Herb and Spice Garden and interpretation centre for visitors. The parish constitutes a single political district. It has a Health Centre, six primary schools and two secondary schools: St. David's RC Secondary and Westerhall Secondary Schools. Since 1987 the St. David's Day Planning Committee has organised the St. David's Day Celebration to exhibit the natural beauty and culture of this rural parish.

ST. DAVID'S ANGLICAN CHURCH is a small church begun in 1829 and consecrated by Bishop Coleridge of the Windward Islands upon its completion in 1831. It was the first permanent chapel built by the Anglicans in the parish after the abandonment of the confiscated RC chapel at Megrin. The structure, with a similar design to Anglican churches built in St. Andrew and St. Patrick around the same period, incorporated Caribbean Gothic Revival and Georgian architectural features. It sits on a hill overlooking a cemetery at St. David's Town, the surrounding trees giving it the appearance of an English countryside chapel. In 1915 a

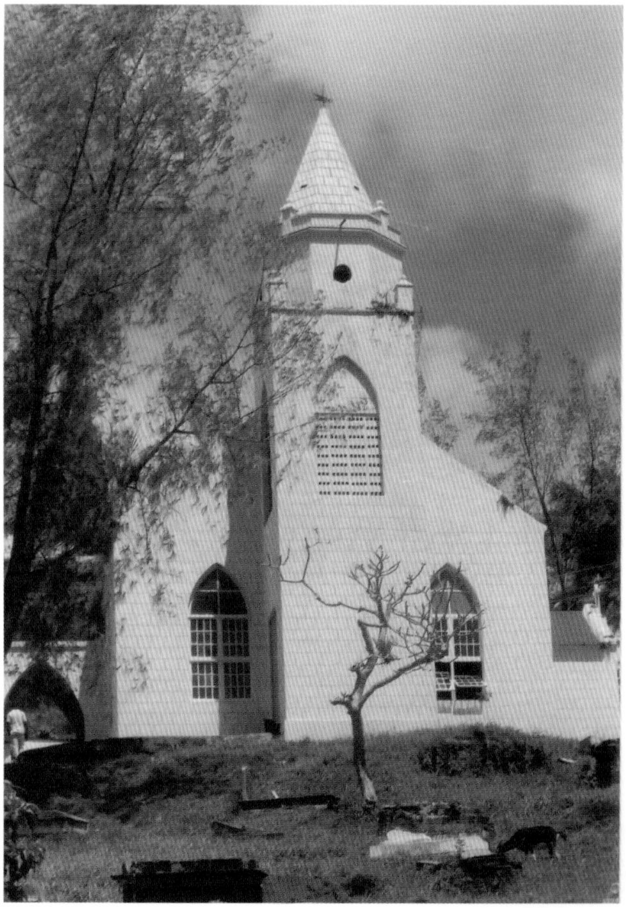

St. David's Anglican Church

fire consumed parts of the church, destroying valuable historical records. Two years later it was expanded to cater to the growing congregation. HURRICANE JANET in 1955 destroyed the top of the tower, which was replaced with the present cupola. For many years it was part of either the St. Andrew/St. Patrick/St. David (1807-1825), or St. Patrick/St. David (after 1825) parish, and records between 1798 and 1975 were included under the united parish of St. Andrew, St. Patrick and St. David; subsequent records under its own parish.

ST. DAVID'S RC CHURCH The Church of the Immaculate Conception and St. Joseph was constructed in two parts between 1852 and 1889. It sits on a hill and commands a view of the countryside. The major structure was begun in 1852 and consecrated in 1859, even though the building lacked doors, windows and a floor. A small tower was added in the 1870s, and in 1889 a sanctuary was built and consecrated to St. Joseph. An earthquake the previous year resulted in minor damage to the structure, especially the tower. This was the second church/chapel built by the Catholics in the parish. The first, St. Jean-Baptiste, was constructed around the 1730s on a hill overlooking L'Anse Père, so named because a priest was said to have drowned there. The Protestants seized the St. Jean-Baptiste chapel in the Quartier de Megrin in 1784 for use as their place of worship, and during FÉDON'S REBELLION it was the scene of fighting between the insurgents and the British, the latter using it as a fortress. Its ruins are still evident in the village. Records date to 1887.[89]

St. David's RC Church

ST. GEORGE The second largest district/parish with an area of 25 sq miles (67 sq km) and a population of approximately 27,400, making it the most populated parish/district. In 1764 it was renamed St. George after the patron saint of England (and King George III), replacing the French name Paroisse de BASSETERRE. St. George is situated predominantly on the sheltered leeward coast and provides superb anchorage at its central port with a deep-water harbour, and along the coast. Continued French and British settlement led to the economic development of St. George far ahead of the other districts. Politically, it is divided into five constituencies—Town of St. George's, St. George's NE, NW, SE and SW. The dry southern coast, dotted with numerous BEACHES, has developed as a tourist recreational area.

ST. GEORGE'S ANGLICAN CHURCH is situated on CHURCH STREET in St. George's, and was reconstructed in 1825 following an earthquake that destroyed the previous structure; it was consecrated in 1826. Its architectural style is Caribbean Georgian, reflecting the dominant style of the period. This brick and pink stucco building was the first church in Grenada

St. George's Anglican Church

constructed by the Anglicans. It sits on the site of the St. James RC Church built in 1690 by the French but confiscated by the Protestant government in 1784 for use as an Anglican church. In 1904 the tower was extended and a crenellated parapet completed, replacing the white spire that dated to at least 1792, possibly earlier. A posterior gallery housed the organ and choir, and stained-glass windows of Christian symbols illuminated the apse. Covering the inner walls were as many as ten marble memorial plaques commemorating Lt. Gov. HOME, soldiers and civilians who died during FÉDON'S

REBELLION, Joseph MARRYAT, and rector Rev. Macmahon. From 1784 to 1874 the church functioned as the official state church, hosting all state functions like national holy days and holidays, with the governor and Grenada's elite in attendance. In 1975 the Anglican community celebrated the one hundred and twenty-fifth anniversary of this the oldest Anglican church in the islands. Parish records, the most complete from Grenada, date to 1784 and include baptisms, marriages and burials, including those of slaves (1817-1834). It suffered extensive damage due to HURRICANE IVAN, neccessitating total reconstruction.

ST. GEORGE'S CEMETERY is situated beneath the ruins of the HOSPITAL HILL REDOUBT and is the main burial ground within the town of St. George's and the most extensive interment site on the island. It may have been used as a burial site since the days of the French Colonial HOSPITAL, established in the vicinity in 1738, but most probably dates to the 1790s when thousands of deaths from YELLOW FEVER and FÉDON'S REBELLION overfilled the churchyards. After the CHOLERA epidemic in 1854 it became the permanent and prominent burial ground in Grenada. Legislation in 1854 and 1881 enforced burials in cemeteries, forbidding the common practice of interring the dead in private places, especially in the towns.

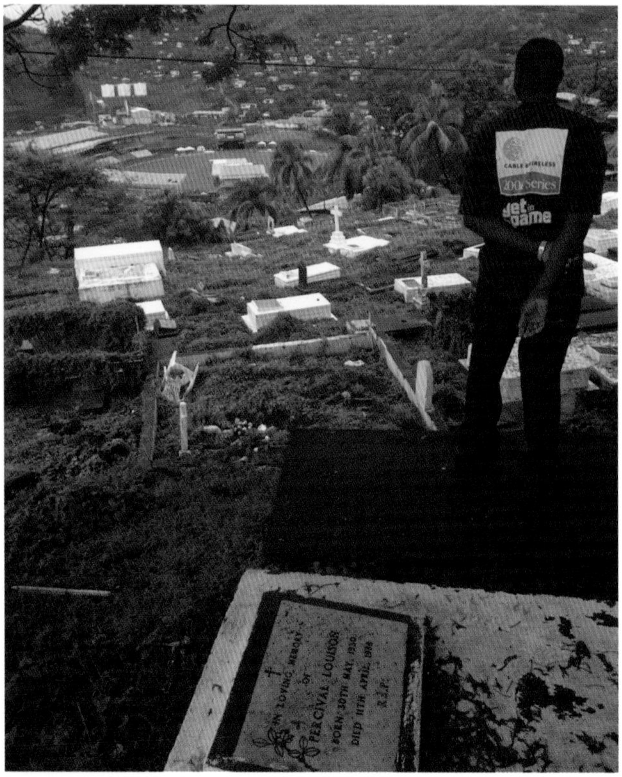

St. George's Cemetery

The cemetery is laid out in three terraced sections along Cemetery Hill or Hospital Hill, the oldest being the middle section (next to the old French Hospital); Wilberforce Cemetery, the lower section, was once the paupers' cemetery. On ALL SAINTS' DAY relatives and friends of the dead light candles on the graves in remembrance. A number of decaying summerhouses add atmosphere to the cemetery. The 'Frenchie Tomb' and the bust of former PM BISHOP are two of the most prominent features of the cemetery when it is not covered with the ubiquitous Mexican creeper or bee vine. There have been no attempts to preserve the old gravestones that are gradually disappearing.

ST. GEORGE'S FIRES On 27 April 1990 a conflagration gutted a complex of government offices on the CARENAGE, destroying a number of primary ministries. Damage was estimated in the millions of dollars. The fire not only destroyed valuable and irreplaceable financial and historical documents, but also ravaged historical buildings. Grenadians, home and abroad, were called upon to contribute to the rebuilding of the office complex, which was completed in 1996 at a cost of EC$11m.

The 1990 fire rekindled memories of fires that have threatened St. George's over the years. On 27 December 1771 a fire that began in a French-owned bakery burned throughout the night, and the town 'being without Fire Engines or even Tools to pull down Houses... was reduced to Ashes.' Damage was estimated at £200,000 currency. Though the governor had wished to influence the new plan of the town by legislating that 'owners of each house

Financial complex fire, 1990

Hubbard's Fire, 2003

to have partition walls of Brick or Stone' built to prevent the spread of future fires, the lack of resources resulted in haphazard reconstruction. Almost three years later another fire destroyed the greater part of the town to the sum of £500,000 currency. FREE COLOUREDS were suspected of starting the fire, though the charges were never substantiated. This fire led to Grenada's first 'building code', which stipulated that all new construction had to be in brick and stone and roofed with tiles.

On 15 May 1792 a fire caused by a burning vessel laden with rum destroyed a 'third' of the CARENAGE. A number of smaller fires have threatened the town, including the 1885 BONFIRE RIOTS, the suspicious fires of January 1920 by the 'TTT Gang', the Hubbard's lumber yard fire of March 1925, the T R Evans fire in 1952, the Kirpalani/Johnson's fire in 1975, political arson in 1979, the Purcell Lumberyard fire in 2000, and Hubbard's Hardware/Courts fire in 2002.

ST. GEORGE'S HARBOUR/THE PIER In 2000 the new facilities at the St. George's Port were completed after a three-year US$11m rehabilitation and expansion project that included extensive dredging along the CARENAGE, land reclamation, repair of the corroded steel piles and cope-wall, and the construction of a new schooner wharf. The old schooner wharf was incorporated into the main dock, which presently measures 1,100 ft (335.3 m), and is capable of berthing as many as three ships at a depth of 30ft (9 m). The secondary dock for schooners and sloops next to The Spout measures 269 ft (82 m) at a depth of 18 ft (5.5 m). Between 1980 and 1983 the port facilities were expanded to accommodate containers, with a container park which incorporated the old 'China Town' of ill repute. A 'Welcome Centre' opened in 1993 and processed the thousands of cruise ship passengers who arrived annually until the opening of the Cruise Ship Port in 2004 on the ESPLANADE. This and other buildings occupy the area formerly known as Burns Point or the Coal Yard, which in the nineteenth century stored coal used to power the steam-powered sugar mills and steamships that frequented the island. Between 1957 and 1958 an 800 ft (245 m) long steel/cement pier, directly connected to the land, was constructed in the inner harbour in ST. GEORGE'S.

The use of the area as a port dates to 1649 when the French settled the island and docked their schooners in the area known today as The Spout. Historically, the natural harbour was always seen as having great potential as a naval station or for trade, especially with Grenada's proximity to South America. In 1778 the legislature passed an act proposing that the site be used as a naval dockyard. Nothing came of the plans, but the natural harbour was to see much economic activity beginning in 1787 when St. George's was made a free port. Within a few years it was 'by far the most important' free port after Jamaica in the BWI. The entrance of Trinidad into the BWI and the absence of warfare in the region after 1814 led to the decline of Grenada's free port.

In 1895 the harbour in St. George's was surveyed with the hope of taking advantage of its 'natural utility', but it was not until 1913 that a plan for the dredging and construction of a wharf, moorings and a coal depot was approved. The outbreak of World War I delayed the project until the late 1930s when the first wharf was constructed (1938-1939) at a cost of £50,000, primarily to aid the BANANA industry. The 850 ft (260 m) long wooden pier stood on piles and connected to the land by a rubble bank. In 1953 its southern end and two of the four warehouses sank after marine worms invaded the wood. The damaged structure was still in use when HURRICANE JANET struck the sheltered harbour in 1955 and sunk what was left of the pier and the two remaining warehouses. A banana boat moored to the pier at the time was almost pulled under.

Before 1939 vessels unloaded their goods along the length of the Carenage. Larger ships laid anchor outside the 'harbour', with small crafts or lighters shuttling the cargo from the ships to the shore. Cranes situated at the sites of the present Fire Station, W E Julien & Co. and the Sheila Buckmire Memorial LIBRARY unloaded the lighters. Smaller ships, anchored in the stream inside the harbour, loaded and unloaded there on jetties located along the Carenage.

ST. GEORGE'S MEN'S CLUB was formed by a group of the islands' most prominent citizens led by A P Short, and opened its doors in June 1888. It soon became a centre of social activity in the islands for many of the elite and middle class. Though it was called the planters' club, the GOVERNOR automatically became the president, and his position and status determined its membership. According to its rules, 'women and dogs' were admitted only as guests. For most of its existence it was housed on the CARENAGE in the upper floor of Jonas Browne & Hubbards Hardware Store. The club provided for the entertainment of its members, all male, housing a bar and billiards room and offering an assortment of activities. There were also rooms for rent, usually occupied by residents from the countryside or foreign visitors. There were strict rules for the admittance of new members, as would be expected. In 1968 it moved to upper LUCAS STREET, and closed in 1985.

ST. GEORGE'S RC CHURCH The Cathedral of the Immaculate Conception took on its present neo-Gothic appearance around 1800 when an apse, a two-storey transept and a chapel were added to the small church. The cornerstone of the original church was laid in August 1840 and construction was completed in 1848. The life-size crucifix dates to 1876 and the Stations of the Cross to 1878. In 1903 the church was enlarged, and in 1930 the tower was completed after the removal of the white spire, and a second chapel added on the southern side. Repairs and extensions have altered the church, which by the mid-1900s was the largest church in the islands. Striking hammer-beam trusses supported and accentuated the interior nave. The Cathedral was rich in RC symbols of worship and faith. The building was dominated by the

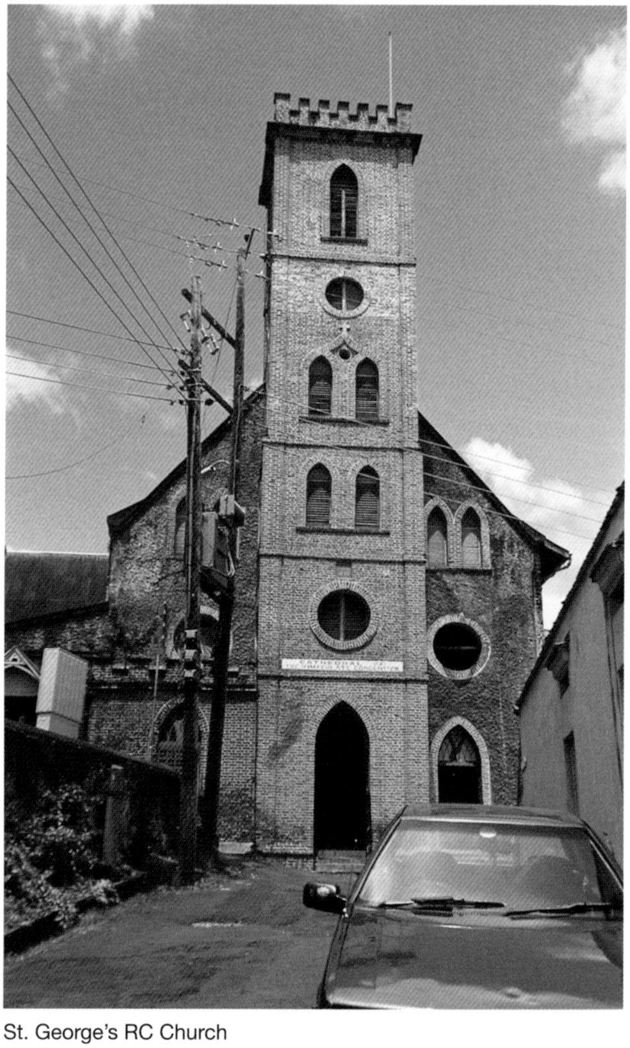

St. George's RC Church

Caribbean Gothic Revival style like most of the churches of the period, exemplified by the pointed-arched windows and crenellated parapet above the tower. It has a number of beautiful stained-glass windows that embellish the apse. A western gallery above the main entrance housed an old pipe organ used by the choir; built in London in 1888, the organ was destroyed by HURRICANE IVAN in 2004.

The Cathedral sits on the site of the St. James Chapel, described as 'a small low building', constructed in 1804 with a grant of £1,000 currency from the legislature. In 1800 the new site was given to the Catholics as replacement for their chapel housed in the old presbytery next to the ST. GEORGE'S ANGLICAN CHURCH since 1784. This was the beginning of the healing of the religious turmoil that had plunged the island into civil war in 1795. The St. Jacques Church was the first Catholic church built in 1690 in the Paroisse de St. Jacques et St. Philippe, but temporary chapels date back to 1649. Parish records between 1784 and 1842 are located in the Grenada Registry since all baptisms, burials and marriages had to be registered with the Anglican Church. Records at the Cathedral date to the 1880s, but are incomplete, some having been destroyed by fire. The Cathedral was demolished by Hurricane Ivan, and will have to be totally rebuilt. Reconstruction plans (costing US$1.4m) call for a new steel frame structure, yet retaining the original foundation and steeple.[89] (See www.stgdiocese.org)

ST. GEORGE'S TOWN 12 02N 61 48W is the capital of Grenada and the major city and port. It was the first area permanently settled and developed by Europeans beginning in 1649. The town, the Ville du FORT ROYAL in the Quartier de BASSETERRE, was established in the 1660s. Though it looked nothing like it does today, it contained Fort Royal, the CARENAGE and a number of estates. The name St. George's was bestowed by the British who renamed the French fort and town of Fort Royal, FORT GEORGE and St. George's after the patron saint of England and the namesake of the then reigning King George III. In the late 1700s it was occasionally referred to as Georgetown.

The city of St. George's, with its deep-water harbour on the Carenage and the remnants of four forts guarding its beauty, encompasses the commercial and administrative

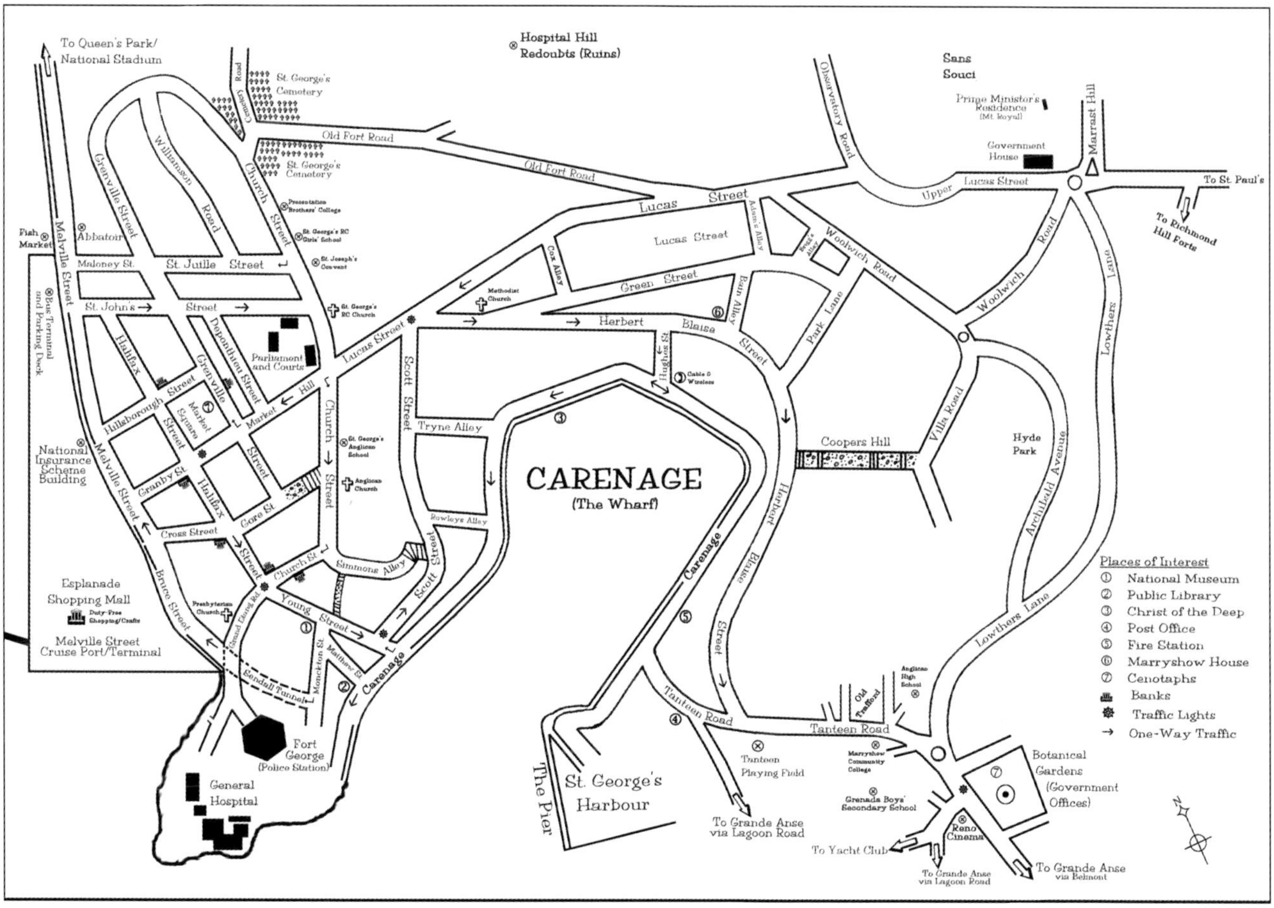

St. George's Town street map

centre of the State of Grenada. The town has grown tremendously from the original settlement of PORT LOUIS to the Carenage, through the SENDALL TUNNEL and across the MARKET SQUARE, reaching as far as the QUEEN'S PARK to the west and the LAGOON to the east. Being the capital, it is the most developed of the towns in terms of infrastructure since it was the domain of the GOVERNOR and many of the wealthy planters. Pipe-borne water arrived in 1837, and by the 1920s most communities in the town had at least communal STREET PIPES; by 1899 there were two waterworks. In 1926 garbage collection was taken over by the centralised Sanitary Authority, installing rubbish bins (old oil drums) along the streets that were collected by lorry and incinerated in TANTEEN. In 1928 the town was electrified and in 1939 a public water carriage sewage disposal system was constructed, eliminating the need for trucks to go house to house to collect solid waste (before the waste disposal trucks sewage was thrown into the sea at night by pail carriers). St. George's Town, with its amalgam of architectural styles, has been proposed as a UNESCO 'Monument of the Caribbean'. The town's population is around 4,500 people.[170, 282]

ST. GEORGE'S UNIVERSITY SGU was opened in January 1977 as a proprietary medical school, the first in the Eastern Caribbean. Its initial reception was guarded, and it faced some opposition locally and regionally. It also had to contend with the generally negative image that most people, especially the American medical community, had of foreign medical schools. To dispel these misconceptions and apprehensions, SGU made a concerted effort to prove its critics wrong, and over the past thirty years it has done just that. It is located in True Blue at its expanding campus (having closed most of its facilities at its Grande Anse campus), and enrols hundreds of students from at least fifty countries, particularly the US and Canada. The students complete two years of medical school (on its campuses in both Grenada and St.Vincent) before going on to hospitals in the US, UK and the Caribbean for clinical training. As both the GOG and the business community had hoped, SGU has benefited Grenadians economically and socially.

In October 1983 SGU came to the notice of the world when the US government used the safety of the students as a pretext to intervene militarily in Grenada following the political chaos that resulted after the execution of PM BISHOP (see INTERVENTION). Though it was founded as a School of Medicine, over the last thirty years its charter has changed and it has undergone tremendous changes. Since 1996 SGU has added Schools of Arts and Sciences, Graduate Studies, and School of Veterinary Medicine, together with a number of affiliated institutes and research centres including the Cricket Institute and the Windward Island Research and Education Foundation. The stated goals of SGU are to train competent medical practitioners, improve health standards and health care delivery systems, promote research in health care-related fields and preventative medicine, and to offer 'enhanced educational opportunities' to students, including those from the Caribbean.

SGU has a teaching staff of over 600 full, assistant and associate professors and instructors from around the world. In its first two decades approximately 58 Grenadians have received scholarships to pursue medical degrees, and many of them have become doctors. A number of Grenadians hold academic and administrative positions at SGU. SGU participates in a number of charities like the Orphans and Elderly Fund and the Heart Fund, and frequently donates medical equipment and personnel to the General HOSPITAL, and its students perform voluntary work through Health Fairs across the islands. Its new multimillion-dollar campus at True Blue, situated on a promontory in the SW of the island, is quickly becoming home to a vibrant centre for higher education in the region. Its present enrolment is over 2,500 students.[293]

St. George's University

ST. JOHN is situated to the north of St. George's parish, and occupies an area of 15 sq miles (39 sq km), with a population of roughly 9,000. The area was settled within the first twenty years of French settlement, and beginning in the 1730s was administered as a church parish and district. Within St. John are Mt. Gregory, FÉDON'S CAMP, CONCORD FALLS and the town of GOUYAVE, its main commercial and administrative centre and port. Formerly the Paroisse de l'Ance Gouyave under the French, it accommodated some of the original French villages, the majority of these settlements situated along the coast due to the mountainous nature of the district. In the 1850s a government official felt that 'The parish of St. John is generally considered to be the most healthy in the Island. It is abundantly supplied with pure wholesome water.'

Throughout the parish can be found ESTATES like DOUGALDSTON planted with COCOA, NUTMEG and BANANA. The Gouyave Nutmeg Pool is the processing centre for nutmeg within the region. BELVIDERE has played an important part in the history of the island, particularly as the rebel headquarters during FÉDON'S REBELLION The annual religious observation of FISHERMAN'S BIRTHDAY becomes a celebration for the entire parish and its people, many of whom depend on the FISHERIES sector for their livelihoods. St. John constitutes a single political district. It has a Health Centre, five primary and two secondary schools: St. John's Christian Secondary and St. Rose Modern Secondary.

ST. JOHN'S RC CHURCH St. John's parish has seen at least four RC churches/chapels from its establishment in the 1730s; two are still standing. The St. Pierre Church, built by 1758 in the Quartier de l'Ance Goyave (in the Paroisse de St. Pierre), was confiscated by the Anglicans but abandoned by 1791. A chapel was erected around 1804 with funds from the legislature, but 'had fallen into decay and gone to ruin' by 1829. The 'Old Church' was constructed on the site of the previous chapel and dates to 1829 when its corner stone was laid, but it was completed many years later due to a lack of funds. The 'Old Church' was built in the Caribbean Gothic Revival style, but Caribbean Georgian features are clearly visible. It stands abandoned today, having been replaced in 1902 by a larger church not too far away. For many years after the construction of the 'New Church' the 'Old Church' housed the RC primary school. Its copper spire, Gouyave's most prominent landmark, is its most striking feature, its open metal belfry unlike any on the island. Parish registers date to the 1830s, but are incomplete.[89]

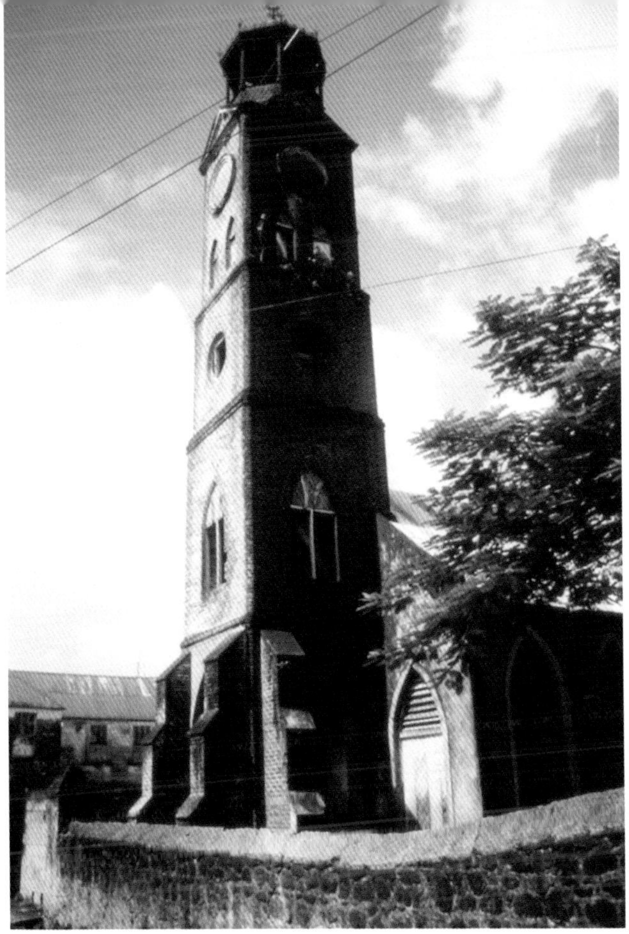

St. John's RC Church

ST. JOHN THE DIVINE was the first permanent Anglican chapel built in the parish of St. John. The original structure was constructed in 1846, but additions were made in 1891 and 1930, completing the present L-shape that is unique among Grenadian churches. The tower has a metal parapet and steep spire dominating the GOUYAVE skyline; a bell was added in 1891. The general architectural style exhibits a number of influences, including Caribbean Gothic Revival and Georgian. Church records—marriage registers, baptismal registers, and minutes of the Vestry and Church Council—date to the early 1800s. On the interior church walls are mural tablets in memory of important figures of the parish, including Dr John HAY and William Smith, owner of Revolution Hall estate in the 1780s. For many years it was part of either the St. George/St. John/St. Mark or St. John/St. Mark parish.

ST. JOSEPH'S CONVENT, St. George's Founded in 1876 as a secondary school for girls, the first of its kind, it began on its present site in the former house of the colonial treasurer. It derives its name from the Sisters of St. Joseph of Cluny who have administered it since its inception. For most of its existence it was a boarding school, and catered predominantly to middle- and upper-class Grenadians in its initial years. With the establishment of secondary schools throughout the islands, the need for boarding accommodation lessened and was discontinued in 1966. This enabled needed expansion to cater to the growing population. It is one of the foremost secondary schools in the islands. Noted graduates include former Dominican PM Eugenia Charles, principal Sister Philomena Fletcher, writer Merle Collins, Gov. BYNOE, Baroness Howells, and Lady Cynthia Gairy, politician. The St. Joseph's Convent, Grenville, was opened in 1953 to accommodate students in the rural PARISHES.

ST. MARK parish is the smallest district with an area of 9 sq miles (23 sq km) and a population of roughly 4,000. Under the French it was called the Quartier du Grand Pauvre. It constitutes a single political district. Within this small rural district can be found Grenada's highest peak, Mt. St. Catherine, Amerindian PETROGLYPHS at La Resource and Waltham, Victoria Falls, a 200 year-old boucan at DIAMOND ESTATE, an old sugar mill at Bonaire estate, and the town and port of VICTORIA. St. Mark is situated in the NW section of the island and in recent years has been referred to as the 'Sunset Parish'. Since 1988 the St. Mark's Fiesta has been celebrated to honour the patron saint of the parish. The festival showcases various features distinctive to the parish and highlights its natural beauty, arts and crafts, agriculture, cultural exhibits, food, dance and music.

ST. MARK'S ANGLICAN CHURCH A stone above the tower entrance dates the present church to 1835. It is a small, austere-looking building with grey-coloured walls and a red corrugated iron roof that detracts from its architectural beauty. The small tower is plastered with cement, giving it a rather severe appearance. There is an old clock in the tower. St. Mark's parish, being small, was either under the united parishes of St. George/St. John/St. Mark (1807-1825), or St. John/St. Mark (aft. 1825), and as such was administered from without for the 1800s and the early 1900s.

ST. MARK'S RC CHURCH The original St. Rose Chapel was one of the first places of worship established on the island on what is today the Diamond estate in the Quartier du Grand Pauvre (or Paroisse de St. Rose). The land was a grant from the governor and proprietor DU PARQUET. A chapel existed in the 1700s, another was built around 1821 'in the vicinity of Bon Air', and the present Catholic church at VICTORIA was constructed sometime after 1844, and renovated and enlarged in 1885. The presbytery was built in the early 1900s. The small church exhibits both Caribbean Georgian and Gothic Revival features. A posterior gallery overlooks the small interior. There are no stained glass windows, as is common with most of the older churches on the island. The historical records, dating to the 1800s, can be found under the combined parish of St. John/St. Patrick/St. Mark.[89]

ST. PATRICK is the most northerly of the districts, occupying an area of 16.5 sq miles (43 sq km) and has a population of just over 10,000. In 1764 the British changed the French name Paroisse des Sauteurs to St. Patrick after the patron saint of Ireland, but the major settlement retained the French PLACE NAME. The parish is divided into two political districts—St. Patrick's West and East. In St. Patrick can be found Levera Beach, LEAPERS' HILL, LEVERA POND, LAKE ANTOINE, BATHWAY BEACH, MT. RICH PETROGLYPHS, River Sallee HOT SPRINGS, 'a slave pen' at Hermitage, and SAUTEURS, the largest town and commercial centre. The St. Patrick's Day Fiesta was begun in 1986 to highlight the district's natural and cultural richness. For one week in March each year the town of Sauteurs comes alive with a variety of activities that showcase the distinctiveness of St. Patrick. Arts and crafts, agricultural and cultural displays, sporting activities and entertainment enliven this small rural town on the northernmost coast.

ST. PATRICK'S ANGLICAN CHURCH is the first and oldest Anglican church constructed in the parish. It sits on the site of a coastal battery and palisade fort, Fort d'Esnambuc, built in 1650 following the French attack on the Island CARIBS at LEAPERS' HILL. The present chapel was begun in 1829 and consecrated in 1831. It is a handsome building tucked away on a picturesque hill overlooking the Caribbean Sea. Its architectural style is Caribbean Georgian, illustrated by the tall tower crowned with pointed quadripartite vaults. Surrounding the church is a cemetery with

St. Patrick's Anglican Chruch

headstones dating back over a hundred years. Historical parish records, including birth and death registers, were included under the combined parishes of St. Andrew/St. Patrick/St. David and St. Patrick/St. David, and later under its own; records date to 1807.

ST. PATRICK'S RC CHURCH The first RC chapel in the parish was built sometime after 1664, following the laying of a corner stone by French Capuchin monks that year on LEAPERS' HILL. The Notre Dame du Bon Secours Chapel in the Paroisse des Sauteurs stood on the site of the present Court House, but was destroyed in 1795 by the insurgents during FÉDON'S REBELLION following its confiscation by the Anglicans in 1784. In 1841 the foundation stone of the present church was laid but it was not completed until 1851.

Like many churches of this period, it was built in the Caribbean Gothic Revival style, with its pointed-arched windows and short octagonal tower, which was completed by 1875. A classical portico was added in the mid-1900s. Within the tower wall is a statue of the Virgin Mary and Child believed to have survived from the RC chapel destroyed during the rebellion. The clock in the tower and the presbytery attached to the church date to the 1880s. The church has a heavy medieval facade, and retains its original fish-scale tile roof. It is situated on Leapers' Hill overlooking Sauteurs Bay. Incomplete parish records date to 1849.[89]

ST. PATRICK'S RC CHURCH, Carriacou Started in 1858 but not completed until after 1874 with help from the Grenada Legislature, this church is located in HILLSBOROUGH, along the waterfront. From 1874 resident priests, as opposed to visiting priests from Grenada, served the parish. It was badly damaged by HURRICANE JANET in 1955. Church records date to 1920, the earlier ones having been destroyed in a fire that same year. Though some form of Catholic worship was present in Carriacou during the initial French occupation, CATHOLICISM was not established until the British period. The ruins of a walled structure at Dover are believed to be that of the 'first permanent RC Church' built in Carriacou. By 1771 Father Maisonneuve had established a mission on the island. Between 1780 and 1802 Father Guy lived on the island and administered to the Catholic faithful. Around 1785 he built a wooden chapel 'situated on the Battery above the town of Hillsborough [which] was formerly the guard-house.' By 1802 it was reported to be in ruins and later became the property of the Anglicans. Father Guy also held chapel in his house at WINDWARD.[89]

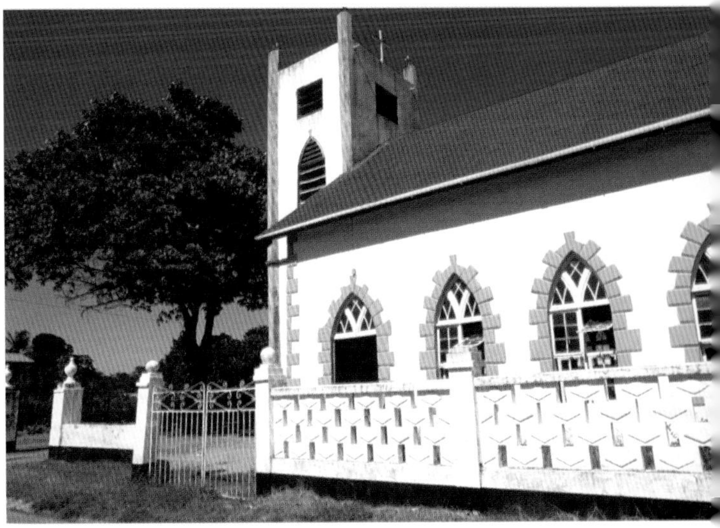

St. Patrick's RC Church, Carriacou

SALTFISH is the cured or salted flesh of the cold-water cod (*Gadus morhua*) and other gadiforms that were once a popular addition to many local dishes. It was imported by the French from the British North American colonies beginning in the seventeenth century because their own fisheries in New France could not meet the demand of the slave colonies; the British imported from Canada following the American War of Independence. Saltfish was an important source of protein for sailors (who called it 'the beef of the sea'), slaves, and the peasant population after EMANCIPATION. It is interesting to note that the slave islands received the lowest quality saltfish which was called 'West India', while the better quality went to other discriminating markets. Throughout the years it has been made into a variety of popular dishes, including 'fish cakes', floaters or akara (<Yor. *akara*: 'an oily cake'), 'salt fish souse', and eaten with rice and ground provisions like YAMS and SWEET POTATOES, and the popular dish OIL DOWN. Saltfish, due to its present high price caused by the depletion of the fishery in the North Atlantic, is euphemistically referred to as a 'delicacy' or 'luxury' food despite its status as a 'poor man' food for most of its history. The popular fish cake or fritters can be eaten as a breakfast dish with bread or biscuits, but tastes best with bake, hence 'bakes and fish cake'. Another legacy of cod fish and British colonialism is the once widespread use of cod liver oil as a health supplement. It is also known as bacallao.[357]

SAMARITAN, St. Patrick One of a number of rural villages with a large EAST INDIAN population. The village developed on the borders of the Samaritan estate, hence its name. The largely East Indian community developed by the 1880s as indentured immigrants completed their indentures and settled into the area. It has been a vibrant East Indian community ever since. The PRESBYTERIAN CHURCH established a mission-school there in the mid-1880s when 'RL Furgerson [of Samaritan estate] gave his liquor loft to hold school and service.' In 1889 the second mission-school was opened to a 'purely Indian congregation' on land donated by George DeGale. The mission was largely responsible for the conversion of the East Indians to Christianity. The school is the only Presbyterian primary school in the islands and caters to about 400 students. In the 1950s Samaritan sponsored one of two East Indian CRICKET teams in Grenada. Among the community's prominent members are/was Prince Lalsie, elder of the Presbyterian Church and cultural activist, and H M Bhola, Anglican priest.[211, 329]

SANDBOX (*Hura crepitans*) A large deciduous tree native to tropical America and the Caribbean, which grows to over 50 ft (15 m). Its thick bark is covered with prickles that were once used by children to make beadwork. The seed capsules are dark brown, ovate and segmented, much like a tiny pumpkin. Upon drying, they explode, making a loud noise as the seeds are discharged with considerable force. Local SUPERSTITION believes that each explosion is a 'JUMBIE wedding', causing many to fear the ominous nature of the sandbox, hence the name jumbie tree. Its name sandbox is derived from the seed capsules' former use as a sand sprinkler for blotting ink. Each seed capsule contains 15 paired lobes that can be used in the making of crafts/jewellery. The finished design, often shaped like a bird with a long beak, or a porpoise or dolphin, is the centrepiece in a bead necklace. All parts of the tree are poisonous, with its milky sap believed capable of causing temporary blindness. The seeds, if consumed, can cause severe bowel movements.

SANDY ISLAND off Carriacou is a small island just west of HILLSBOROUGH Town and situated in the Hillsborough Bay. It takes its name from the ubiquitous white sand that covers its surface. It was long used by Carriacouans for recreation and fisheries, but recently it has become a visitor attraction as well as a rendezvous point for YACHTING and diving. It possesses some of Grenada's most beautiful CORAL REEFS. It has been described as 'nothing but a flawless strip of sand, decorated by a few palms and surrounded by perfect snorkelling reefs.' The island has been undergoing erosion, but local residents have planted coconut trees in the hope of reversing the damage. It is included in the NATIONAL

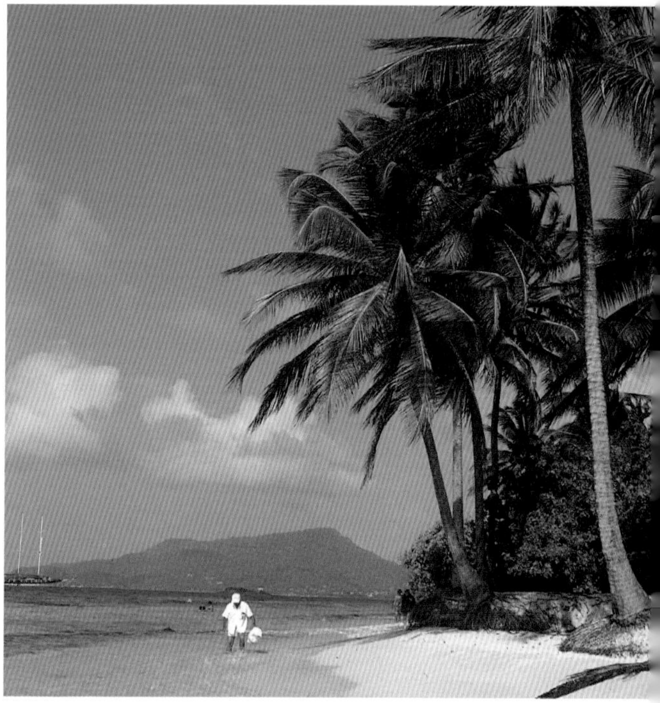

Sandy Island beach

PARK SYSTEM as a protected seascape. Under the French it was paired with Mabouya Island as Les Deux Freres: 'Two Brothers'. Not to be confused with Sandy Island just off Levera Bay, Grenada.

SAPODILLA (*Manilkara zapota*) is native to Central America and the Caribbean, and is grown for its small round brown fruits. The sapodilla (<Am.Sp. *zapot* <Astec *tzapotl* for all soft sweet fruits; + *illa*: 'little', i.e. little zapot) has a yellow to brown flesh that is sweet, smooth in texture and highly flavoured when ripe. It is also used to flavour ice cream and custard. The smooth elongated black seeds, when crushed, are prescribed by FOLK MEDICINE in a drink to treat urinary problems. The latex, chicle, is extracted from the sap of the tree and used in the manufacture of chewing gum. Fruits are available from March to May. Its wood is strong and durable.

SAPOTE/MAMMEE SAPOTE (*Pouteria sapota, syn. Calocarpum sapota*, syn. *C. mammosum*) produces a relatively little known spice outside of the Caribbean that is used to flavour cakes, puddings, confectionery and perfumes. This huge tree, growing to 80 ft (25 m), is native to Central America. It produces a small, brown elliptical fruit. The brown, bitter and oily seed is ground and used as a spice to flavour cakes. The fruit can also be eaten or made into preserve. It is a relative of the SAPODILLA and star apple (*Chrysophyllum cainito*), but should not be confused with MAMMEE-APPLE.

SAUTEURS 12N 61W is the most northerly town and commercial centre in the district of ST. PATRICK. Its name (pronounced so-tez) is derived from the French *sauter*: 'to jump, or leap'. It is a reference to the LEAPERS' HILL massacre of a group of Island CARIBS by the French, who later called the hill Le Morne des Sauteurs: 'The Hill of the Jumpers'. In 1718 the town/hamlet or Bourg des Sauteurs, was established, the second town to be founded in Grenada by the French. Its geography has meant its historical division into 'Lower Town', which houses various markets and the post office, and 'Upper Town' or High Street, with the police station, court house, health centre and other government offices. The town's development is illustrated by its population changes over the last century: 1,052 in 1891; 1,139 in 1901; 960 in 1921; 874 in 1946; and 3,000 in 1991. The majority of the population make their living in AGRICULTURE. The town is situated within Sauteurs Bay and supports a small fishing community that relies on seine and line fishing.

Around 1914 a local official felt that it 'is still the worst kept town in the Colony.' It was not until the early 1900s that social amenities began to be established in Sauteurs: waterworks in 1909, a dispensary in 1913, public pit latrines in the late 1910s, water-carriage latrines in 1954, a health clinic, and ELECTRICITY by 1965. Sauteurs is located in a valley surrounded by verdant mist-covered hills in the distance. Beyond the bay are small islands leading to the GRENADA GRENADINES. There is a quietness and beauty to this rural town only disturbed by the honking horns of BUSES passing to and from other parts of the island.[96]

Sir Paul Scoon

SCOON, Sir Paul (b. 1935) became the GG in October 1978 following the resignation of GOVERNOR GENERAL Leo DEGALE. Sir Paul attended the GBSS, and obtained an external BA from London University. Between 1967 and 1978 he served as chief education officer, permanent secretary and secretary to Cabinet, and the deputy director of the Commonwealth Foundation, London. As GG during the REVOLUTION, his symbolic authority was tenuously maintained by the PEOPLE'S REVOLUTIONARY GOVERNMENT, even though they had suspended the constitution. In the subsequent political vacuum left by the assassination of PM BISHOP in 1983, Sir Paul was recognised by the US and some Caribbean governments as the only 'constitutional authority' in the country. His widely reported request for military INTERVENTION rendered 'legality' to the US-led military action. As the only parliamentary authority in the country, he was instrumental in appointing the ADVISORY COUNCIL and overseeing the islands' return to parliamentary democracy.

After serving as governor general under five PMs and during what was probably the most chaotic political period in the islands' recent history, he demitted office in 1992 and was replaced by R O PALMER. Sir Paul, though heavily criticised by the international community for his role in the US invasion, remains very popular among Grenadians. He has been awarded the OBE, GCMG, and Knight Grand Cross of the Royal Victorian Order. His autobiography, *Survival for Service*, appeared in 2003.[111, 306]

SCOTTISH HERITAGE Though many of the islands' present economic and political institutions are a result of ENGLISH HERITAGE, Scottish immigrants, beginning in the 1760s, arrived in Grenada in large numbers and left lasting influences. They accounted for the majority of British subjects on the islands in the early years and owned many sugar estates and various businesses. According to Gonzalez, 'the Scots came to rival and exceed the English in the accumulation of wealth, property, and political influence.' They also contributed large numbers of estate managers and clerks, and medical doctors from Scotland accounted for over half of all doctors.

The island of CARRIACOU was particularly shaped by their presence, establishing a strong connection with Scottish ports in the late 1700s. It was considered a colony of Scotland rather than England because so much of its trade was geared towards North Britain. The BOAT BUILDING industry on Carriacou owes much to shipwrights who arrived from Scotland in the early 1800s. A number of Scottish customs are common in Carriacou, including sea shanties and BREAKING THE BARREL. The PRESBYTERIAN CHURCH is probably the most visible Scottish legacy, but many PLACE NAMES—Dumfries, CRAIGSTON, Meldrum and Argyle in Carriacou, and DUNFERMLINE and ANNANDALE in Grenada—are only a few examples of their early presence. Among the many influential personalities were Lt. Gov. HOME, Alexander CAMPBELL and James BAILLIE. The islands' LANGUAGE, FOLK CULTURE and SUPERSTITIONS were influenced by Scottish culture, as was the development of printing and publishing, which owes much to the Scots who began some of the early NEWSPAPERS.[126, 319]

SCOUTS/GUIDES/CADETS/PIONEERS The first scout troop of the Grenada Boys Scouts Association was established in 1912. As with the establishment of the earlier Cadet Corps and the later Girl Guides, its organisation was viewed as essential to the advancement of the islands' youth, especially the development of leadership and social skills. It was seen as important in developing the ideal Grenadian citizen. The Boys Scout, with its motto 'Be Prepared', is a world-wide organisation that stresses 'character, citizenship, outdoor life, and service to others'. It comprises Cub, Venture and Sea Scouts, with troops in most of the primary and secondary schools. The chief scout is the governor general, but direct administration is under an island commissioner and district commissioners. The Girl Guides Association was established in 1925 under Lady James, wife of Gov. Seaton James, and the wife of Chief of Police Heidenstein. Thereafter, the wife of the GG automatically becomes the president of the Girl Guides Association. The first company was formed at the ANGLICAN HIGH SCHOOL, a second at ST. JOSEPH'S CONVENT in 1938, and at various other secondary schools thereafter. The Girl Guides comprise Brownies, Rangers and Guides, with companies in most of the primary and secondary schools.

Around 1900 'military training' was started at the Grammar School (later the GBSS), the only male secondary school on the island. Its establishment was due to the view that it would build character and leadership among the nation's youths and prepare them for, among other things, war. In 1921 a 'compulsory' cadet corps was introduced and functioned exclusively at the GBSS thereafter in varying capacities. The mid-1960s brought about the extension of the corps with its introduction in a number of secondary schools throughout the islands among the male students. The GULP government, because of the militancy of the youth and their anti-Gairy involvement, disbanded the cadets in 1975, but the organisation was revived under the PEOPLE'S REVOLUTIONARY GOVERNMENT during the REVOLUTION. It was subsequently disbanded after the demise of the PRG in 1983. In 1980 the PRG formed the Young Pioneers for children five years and over, organised into brigades, units and patrols. It was styled after Cuba's Young Pioneers and became an organ of the revolution, with a strong nationalistic programme. The Rupert Bishop Pioneers, named after the slain father of PM BISHOP, was disbanded after the 1983 US-led military INTERVENTION and replaced by the organisations it had itself superseded only three years earlier. Both Boys Scouts and Girl Guides regularly take part in parades and other national events.

SEA EGG/URCHIN Two types of sea eggs live on CORAL REEFS off Grenada. They are the West Indian or white sea egg (*Tripneustes ventricosus*) and the black sea egg (*Diadema antillarum*). The white sea egg is covered with 1 inch (3 cm) long protective spines. Its eggs or roe are eaten raw, much like oysters, or collected and stuffed into the cleaned brittle shell and then baked to make 'sea egg'. The black sea egg is not edible and its 10 inch (25 cm) long spines can be dangerous as they break on contact with the skin. Their removal is difficult as the brittle spines break easily once imbedded. The body will usually absorb the spine in a few days, but local remedies are often applied, including fresh urine on the affected area, and hot tallow ('soft candle'). Sea eggs are an essential part of the ecology of coral reefs, preserving a delicate balance as a consumer of algae, which if left unchecked can overgrow and destroy coral reefs. In 1983 the black sea egg suffered mass mortality throughout the region due to disease, but its population has seen slow recovery in restricted areas.

SEA GRAPE (*Coccoloba uvifera*) is synonymous with BEACHES where it is found, a ubiquitous presence along the coasts. This low shrub, which is native to the region, grows to 30-35ft (9-11 m) and spreads its broad leaves to create a beautiful shade. It bears an edible reddish-purple velvety fruit, 40-50 clustered in a bunch. The pink

Sea grape

pulp is tart, and can be eaten as a fruit, or used to make a very fine jelly and wine. Fruits are available from August to September. The roots of the seaside grape act as an excellent shore stabiliser, and the removal of trees from beaches has led to erosion along the coast and damage to the scenery.

SEAMAN & WATERFRONT WORKERS' UNION The SWWU was registered as a union in 1953 by G B W Otway and others. It was an outgrowth of the Grenada Workers' Union (f. 1946), having broken off in 1952. It became one of the strongest bargaining bodies in the islands from the late 1950s, representing dock workers (stevedores and longshoremen). In the political chaos of the mid-1970s it played a pivotal role in the protests against the GULP government. The NEW JEWEL MOVEMENT later accused its leadership of abandoning the fight against PM GAIRY due to external pressure when it ordered its members back to work at the time the government was beginning to feel the effects of the three-month long strike in early 1974.

During the reign of the PEOPLE'S REVOLUTIONARY GOVERNMENT the SWWU and the GOG were at odds over labour policies and wages. The union is a primary part of the Grenada Trades Union Council and a major force in Grenada's LABOUR MOVEMENT. Eric Pierre (1925-2000) was a major influence in the SWWU, particularly as its longest serving president in the 1970s and 1980s.[35, 333]

SEAMOON, St. Andrew The Seamoon Cultural Centre is the major recreational and entertainment venue outside St. George and for many years the site of the recreation ground and racecourse in St. Andrew. The name Seamoon dates to the French, but the present spelling is a corruption of Simon (pronounced see-mon), derived from the Rivière Simon and le Mont St. Simon. Prior to the early 1900s the area was not used for recreation due to the prevalence of mosquitoes and MALARIA coming from the surrounding swamps. Its establishment as a recreational park, especially for HORSE RACING by the St. Andrew's Racing Club (est. 1897), eventually led to the replacement of Telescope Race Track as the primary racecourse in the area by the mid-1900s. Seamoon is also associated with the Seamoon Industrial Park, which since the 1980s has been part of the growing industrial landscape in the rural districts.

SEA TURTLES were once common on the beaches of GRENADA and Carriacou, but exploitation for meat to make 'turtle soup', the shell for jewellery and crafts, the skin for leather and the eggs as a delicacy has led to decreased populations. Among sea turtles' characteristics is their habit of returning to traditional breeding grounds year after year to lay their eggs. Egg laying takes place on many of the BEACHES around the islands, especially in the northern seascape and along the SE coast of Grenada, and the GRENADA GRENADINES. Though minimal protection is afforded during their breeding season from May to September and a minimum weight requirement at capture recommended (over 120 lb or 55 kg), their populations continue to decline.

Sea turtles that frequent Grenada's waters include the leatherback (*Dermochelys coriacea*), hawksbill (*Eretmochelys imbricata*), loggerhead (*Caretta caretta*), and green (*Chelone mydas*) turtles. The hawksbill and green turtles are the most common foragers in Grenada and the Grenadines, with the hawksbill and leatherbacks the abundant nesters in Grenada. The predominant nester in the Grenadines is the hawksbill.

Though local laws forbid the removal of their eggs from the beaches at any time, poaching continues. A number of private groups have implemented CONSERVATION programmes to protect unhatched eggs from poachers, and return captured turtles to the sea after purchasing from fishermen. However, populations continue to decline due predominantly to the poaching of eggs, sand mining and

TOURISM development that have made some beaches unsuitable for nesting.[50]

SEDAN PORCHES are attachments to the entrances of at least three nineteenth-century houses in St. George's. They were probably built for protection against rain and sun for people leaving and arriving at these houses. Though their use as such in Grenada is questionable because of the impracticality of sedan chairs as a mode of transportation, they are nonetheless attached to three buildings on CHURCH STREET. They may have been built predominantly as a status symbol among members of the PLANTOCRACY who imitated many architectural embellishments from England to show off their wealth. The examples have only one entrance leading to the doorway of the building, with louvers attached to the closed walls. These unique architectural features are protected.[142]

SENDALL TUNNEL was constructed in 1895 and named after Walter Sendall, the former governor (1885-89) of the Government of the WINDWARD ISLANDS who began the project. An engineering feat for its time, the tunnel provided direct access to the two central parts of the town, the CARENAGE and BAY TOWN, when it broke through the central ridge dividing them. Lady Sendall set off the blast that began the construction on 21 November 1889. Between 1891 and 1893 construction was suspended, but by early 1894 traffic was permitted to use the tunnel. It was closed in late 1894 because the sea washed its western entrance away. The official opening took place almost a year later on 21 October 1895. When completed the 340 ft (104 m) long and 12 ft (4 m) high tunnel, connected to MELVILLE STREET by Bruce St., made it less strenuous for donkey carts and horses, the predominant mode of transportation at the time, to travel through St. George's.

Sendall Tunnel

SETTLEMENT (BRITISH) The first known European attempt to settle Grenada originated in England in 1609. The 'adventure' was organised by a 'London-Dutch syndicate' which was 'intended to found a tobacco producing colony: the 208 Londoners were surely not sent to set up a trading base.' Yet the island's proximity to South America, only 104 miles (167 km) from Venezuela, made it rather attractive as a post from which to engage in contraband trade with the Spanish at TRINIDAD and South America. According to Colonel John Scott, the only known authority on the Grenada expedition, the colonists departed from London in early 1609, and landed in Grenada on 1 April 1609. The ships continued on their journey to Trinidad to trade for TOBACCO. Scott continues that the settlers 'were often Disturbed by the Indians nor Indeed were they Persons, fitt for the settling of Plantacions being the Greater part the People of London, noe way inured to hardship and soe not Capeable of encountring the Difficulty that Attends new Plantations in the West-Indies.'

Informed by the governor of Trinidad that the colony at Grenada was in distress, the ships returned to Grenada, and finding 'their Coloniy the greatest part Destroyed those few that remayned they tooke with them for England.' The survivors of the ill-fated attempt arrived in England in December 1609 'to ye great dissattisfaction of their Employers'. Scott mentions that the colonists arrived 'in the great Bay of this Grenada', which could only be the natural harbour at St. George's where the French colonists settled in 1649. British settlement nonetheless followed the capture of Grenada in 1762, and again in 1783 until 1974.[7, 35, 333]

SETTLEMENT (FRENCH) Between 1638 and 1649 a number of prominent French adventurers cast covetous glances at Grenada, which due to its proximity to South America held promising economic possibilities, especially for trade and/or plunder. The first of these was Phillip de Poincy, French governor of St. Christopher. Around 1639/40 he decided to take possession of the island with the establishment of a settlement, but abandoned his plans because of the hostility of the Island CARIBS in the Windward Islands and the great distance between Grenada and St. Christopher. In 1643, Jean Aubert, governor of Guadeloupe, had an agent sent to the island, but a planned settlement never materialised. In 1645 the French Compagnie des Isles de l'Amérique granted a commission as governor of Grenada for five years to de NOUAILLY, but he never took up residence. DU PARQUET, however, began arrangements to settle Grenada by sending an emissary to build a house at a suitable site where arms and munitions could be stored until a proper fort built. In 1649 du Parquet advertised for volunteers to settle Grenada, offering tax exemptions and land grants.

'Two vessels and two barks with enough rations for several months', building materials, arms and munitions, departed from Fort St. Pierre, Martinique on 14 March 1649 with 45 colonists. On 17 March they dropped anchor off Grenada, and the next day arrived at the ST. GEORGE'S HARBOUR, where they established their settlement. On 20 March du Parquet officially took possession of Grenada in a ceremony after the construction of Fort l'Annunciation, a palisade fort at the settlement site of PORT LOUIS. The arrival of the Island CARIBS created a commotion, but the promise of protection from the British and the exchange of gifts, especially whisky and wine, temporarily resolved the impasse.

Historians, including DU TERTRE, have claimed that Chief KAIROÜANE sold Grenada to the French for beads, knives, mirrors and two bottles of brandy. The fact that the Island Caribs brought animals and fruits to exchange for the French 'gifts' proves that they were merely trading with them, and the exchange could not have been construed otherwise. Also, Chief Kairoüane was in no position to 'sell' the island, a fact made clear when he was banished from the island because he had allowed the French to settle. Jean le Comte, cousin of du Parquet, was appointed the governor.

The French immediately set about the task of clearing land for the cultivation of food crops like cassava and cash crops like TOBACCO. In 1650 du Parquet purchased Grenada, Martinique, St. Lucia and the Grenadines from the bankrupt Compagnie des Isles for a mere 41,000 *livres* (about £1,660), thus 'legalizing his claims' to those islands. Within seven months of the French landing, the Island Caribs began to stage attacks against them in an attempt to dislodge them from the island, but they had already become entrenched. Following a decade of Carib-French conflicts, the French successfully reduced the Island Carib population and eliminated their threat.[8, 95, 197, 221]

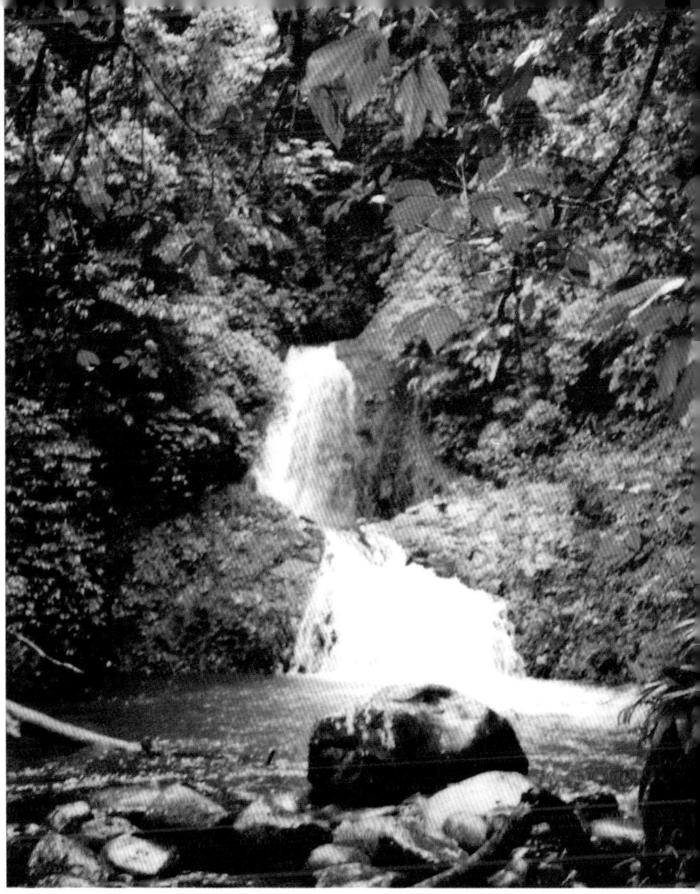

Two of the seven falls making up the Seven Sisters' Falls

SEVEN SISTERS' FALLS A series of waterfalls situated outside St. Margaret (hence another name, Mt. St. Margaret Falls), St. Andrew, just north of the Grand Étang Lake. The series of pristine falls are located along the central ridge at the headwaters of the GREAT RIVER and surrounded by lush tropical forest and plantations. Though of lesser height than either ANNANDALE FALL or CONCORD FALLS, they are nonetheless unique because of their numbers, seven beautiful falls cascading down the mountainside. The last two falls are the most spectacular, with cascades of about 20 ft (6 m) and large basins ideal for swimming. The journey to the falls consists of a hike through a beautiful landscape dotted with tropical ornamentals, trees and plantations.

SHANGO is a religious expression among the peasantry and common throughout the southern Caribbean, particularly Grenada and TRINIDAD. It exhibits significant African influences (variations of Shango or Xango are common in Latin America, particularly Brazil). Its name Shango is derived from one of its most powerful deities, the god of thunder. It is a synergism of traditional Yoruban (Nigeria) religious practices and Christianity, particularly Roman Catholicism. Simpson describes Shango as a neo-African cult/religion because of the incorporation of 'a considerable body of African tradition'. The migration of African INDENTURED IMMIGRANTS from Ijesha,

Nigeria, via Sierra Leone in 1849/50 was instrumental in strengthening and spreading the practice of Shango in Grenada. Its popularity contributed to the disappearance of the BIG DRUM DANCE as it incorporated some ritual aspects of this ancestral belief system.

The synergism of African beliefs and Roman Catholicism was the result of the slave/peasant being forced to renounce his/her African tribal practices and accept Judeo-Christian religious beliefs. The dualism was forged when RC saints merged with Yoruban Orishas (<Yor. 'deity') like St. John the Baptist and Shango (similar to Haitian Voodoo and Cuban Santería). As in Yoruban mythology, water is very important, as illustrated by the baptism of initiates through immersion in water and reverence for rivers, lakes and HOT SPRINGS.

Shango ceremonies feature African drumming, dancing, spirit possession and the sacrifice of animals, similar to the Yoruban practice. Adherents identify with Orishas and every year celebrate an annual feast corresponding to the birthday of the respective saint. These ceremonies are usually led by both men and women, known as 'workers', who, their followers believe, possess unique 'African powers'. Like the Big Drum Dance, a Shango ceremony is staged for celebration, thanksgiving, help from the ancestors, protection from evil, and the blessing of a new house.

A Shango ritual can last many days and entails elaborate rituals. It begins with a procession to a lake, hot spring or river where gods like the 'Mother of the water' or MAMA-GLO are appeased. A *saraka/salaca* or sacrifice of animals and food offerings to the ancestors and the gods is an essential part of the event. During Shango ceremonies adherents 'catch power' and are believed possessed by specific Orishas that manifest themselves through identifiable actions by the possessed. The high priest/priestess of Shango also performs traditional healing with herbs and potions, which has led to a popular association with OBEAH. Small structures or 'stools' in the yard of the Shango priest house altars and other ritual paraphernalia symbolising the power of the leader. The KOLA NUT is used in divination rituals. Coloured flags identify affiliations with specific gods (Shango is red on red) and members will display their Orisha's flag on poles above their homes. Though Shango was not encouraged, it nonetheless survived, and there are a number of groups scattered across Grenada. It has also influenced a number of other religions like the SPIRITUAL BAPTISTS. Also known as 'African work'.[18, 132, 260, 261, 316, 324, 358]

Shango worshippers, 1962

Short knee masqueraders

SHORTKNEE/CHANTIMELLE is a uniquely Grenadian mas'. Masqueraders, dressed in colourful costumes, menacingly stomp through the streets, chanting and dancing to the music of their 'woolos' or foot-bracelets of tinkling bells. The shortknee mas' dates to at least the EMANCIPATION era, and like the PAYWO of Carriacou, has its origins in the pierrot Grenade 'speech mas'' once popular in the southern Caribbean. Each band of masqueraders is identically dressed in colourful knee-length baggy pantaloons (hence the name shortknee), socks reaching to the knees, masked faces, and colourful long-sleeved shirts, over which are draped loose collars adorned with small mirrors. Some groups wear a hat-like headpiece while others wear a loose white piece of cloth to cover the head and neck. The shortknee, in both dress and characteristics, resembles a number of African folk characters, especially the *Egungun* of the YORUBA.

Shortknee groups, coming from the rural villages of Chantimelle, Hermitage, New Hampshire, Willis, VICTORIA and Mt. Reuil, have traditionally fought each other in bloody contests. Even though violent confrontations are rare, they still display their mercurial characteristics. At CARNIVAL the shortknee groups descend on towns like St. George's and Sauteurs, roving and stomping through the streets in their traditional circular pattern. A misty white cloud accompanies the revellers as they sprinkle powder on onlookers and into the air. It remains one of the few traditional masquerades, with groups like the Hermitage Shortknee Band, the Chantimelle Shortknee Band, and the New Hampshire Old Boys participating in the annual carnival festivities.

The name chantimelle is derived from the village of the same name, whose residents are renowned players. The village has another reputation when it comes to playing mas', which Payne describes as 'a history of playing the fiercest mas'', contending that carnival time was 'payback' time as individuals and groups prepared for the confrontations which would settle the quarrels of the previous year. It led to the saying 'you playing chantimelle mas' with yourself', applied to anyone who went over the line of appropriate behaviour.[109, 255]

SILK COTTON (*Ceiba pentandra*) Growing to 200 ft (61 m), this huge deciduous tree takes 60-70 years to achieve maturity. The growth of mosses and bromeliads further contributes to its perceived strangeness, hence names like devil's tree and JUMBIE tree. Native to the West Indies and Africa, this tree is held in awe and feared in both cultures because of the belief that it harbours evil spirits like the SUKUYANT and LAJABLESSE (the Island CARIBS also believed the tree to be the home of a spirit and sacred). The silk cotton tree, of no relation to the COTTON of commerce, produces kapok, a fibre utilised commercially for its durability and buoyancy. An oil, used as a fuel in lamps and soap making, can be extracted from the seeds. Its scientific name, *ceiba*, is derived from the Island Arawak/Taino word for 'canoe', which was constructed from the tree. Other names include kapokier.

Silk Cotton Tree

SKYRED What began as a plea for union recognition and a labour dispute between Eric Gairy's GMMIWU and the Agricultural Employers Association mushroomed into an island-wide strike and protests that left the country in a state of emergency in early 1951. The first strike took place in late January and by mid-February Gairy had called for a general strike among his supporters; those who hesitated were intimidated into striking. On 21 February Gairy's charismatic leadership had rallied agricultural workers from around the island in a massive show of strength at a rally aimed at forcing the colonial government and estate owners to recognise Gairy and negotiate with the GMMIWU.

The ensuing conflict was not merely a wage issue, as most were aware, but a class struggle pitting Eric GAIRY and his peasant supporters against an entrenched urban and propertied class that regarded him as a social and political upstart. To silence Gairy, Acting Governor George Green called in the Royal Navy, and arrested and shipped him off to CARRIACOU aboard a British gunboat. For approximately two weeks following Gairy's arrest (until 15 March), the island was consumed by violence that terrified the middle class and PLANTOCRACY. The striking peasants, in defiance of all authority and with a new-found freedom of political expression that their unity had created, burned schools and ESTATES, destroyed private property and looted crops and animals throughout the island. The governor of the WINDWARD ISLANDS, Sir Robert Arundell, returned to Grenada and immediately rescinded the state of emergency imposed by his acting governor and released Gairy from custody. The embittered planters criticised the governor for not taking more forceful action against what they believed was a communist plot to overthrow the existing society.

Gairy's successful appeals to the peasantry to end their reign of terror elevated him to folk hero status locally, and made him a political leader regionally. The police killed four people, and many others were injured in the uprising that had brought about nothing short of a revolution, in effect the destruction of the historical unequal 'planter-labourer' relationship. Damage to private and public property amounted to as much as £210,000, and some 81 people were convicted for a number of 'petty crimes'.

Gairy received Caribbean-wide support from union organisers including T U BUTLER, Alexander Bustamante of Jamaica, and Robert Bradshaw of St. Kitts.

The planters met Gairy's demand for the recognition of the GMMIWU, and an agreement guaranteed increased wages, retroactive pay and paid holidays for agricultural workers. In the end, Skyred brought about needed social and political changes, and gave a voice to the peasantry, but its profoundest consequence was the emergence of Eric Gairy as a political leader. The name skyred is derived from the incendiary fires set across the island during the unrest.[34, 35, 297, 318, 333]

SLAVE TRADE From around 1520, following the destruction of the indigenous AMERINDIAN populations, slaves from the coastal regions of West Africa were continuously shipped across the Atlantic Ocean to the Americas to supply labour for plantations producing SUGAR CANE, COFFEE, COTTON, INDIGO and TOBACCO. It was a commercial and legal system implemented by many European countries to supply their colonies with slave labour. The Atlantic Slave Trade became part of the larger Triangular Trade involving the exchange of manufactured goods from French and British ports like Nantes, Bordeaux, La Rochelle, Bristol and Liverpool that were exchanged for slaves along the West African coast who were in turn exchanged/sold for agricultural goods from the slave colonies. It has been estimated that as many as 10 million, possibly 15 million people, were abducted from Africa and brought to the Americas as slaves (as many as one million may have died in crossing the Atlantic Ocean, while many others died during African captivity and transportation to the coast). Tropical America received over 90 per cent of the slaves, with South America, predominantly Brazil, receiving upwards of 50 per cent, and the Caribbean the remaining 40 per cent; Grenada received about two percent (124,600) of the total between 1650 and the 1860s. The expansion of AGRICULTURE, especially sugar cane cultivation under the British (who dominated the Slave Trade in the 1700s), led to the drastic increase in the slave population. Noted participants in the trade to Grenada included James ROGERS and James BAILLIE.

In 1807 the British Parliament passed the Abolition Bill that declared its Atlantic Slave Trade illegal, vindicating over 20 years of efforts by a number of anti-slavery organisations and individuals like Quobna CUGOANO to have the trade abolished. It was also hoped that the abolition of the slave trade would gradually lead to the termination of slavery itself, without further political pressure by the British government. Continued resistance by the West Indian PLANTOCRACY to gradual abolition forced the British Parliament to finally outlaw slavery in the BWI in 1833.

The enduring debate over the reasons for ending the Atlantic Slave Trade has continued. Opposing sides have used humanitarian or economic arguments, but both played essential roles in the collapse of slavery. Even though European countries would eventually outlaw the Atlantic Slave Trade, its continuance into the 1860s was guaranteed by the demand for slave labour throughout the Americas, particularly Latin America. The total abolition of slavery in the Americas by 1888 finally brought the dehumanising traffic in Africans to an end. With approximately 30,000 slaves employed on Grenadian ESTATES, the islands were well provided with an adequate labour force even though Grenadian proprietors like Alexander CAMPBELL and James Baillie had defended the trade and predicted the demise of the sugar industry if the slave trade was abolished. In the early 1800s Grenada profitably re-exported thousands of slaves to other islands like TRINIDAD.[231, 237, 289]

SLAVERY Beginning around 1520 captive Africans were brought to the Americas as a chattel labour force, and thus began a system of slavery that continued for the next 350 years. Slavery, using Africans, had developed as a result of the failures of AMERINDIAN forced labour and the inadequate supply of white INDENTURED SERVANTS throughout the Americas. Slaves first arrived in Grenada as early as the 1500s, brought by Island CARIBS who had captured them from the Spanish. The French, following their settlement of the island in 1649, brought in slaves and established the system of chattel slavery that remained a part of the islands' plantation society for the next 185 years.

Captured in Africa, the slaves were shackled into the hold of a ship where they experienced the horrific journey across the Atlantic Ocean on what became known as the Middle Passage. On arriving in Grenada, the slaves who survived the journey (on average 75-80 per cent or higher) were sold to plantation owners using a number of methods, one of which was the 'scramble' system where buyers converged on a pen that housed the slaves and 'grabbed' their choices. These various systems exposed the slaves to numerous indignities that were to continue for the rest of their lives.

The plantation system and slavery became synonymous as the two components of an institution that characterised the social, political and economic life of the islands. On arriving on the plantation, the slave was subjected to the process known as 'breaking in' as the master/overseer sought to destroy all traces of African personality and identity. Cultural displays among slaves were discouraged, fearing that communication and excitement would result in plans to escape or rebel. The 18-hour workday, especially during the harvest months, was filled with strenuous work, little rest, meagre rations, and pain caused by whippings, personal deprivation and DISEASES. Mortality rates among the slaves reached 10 per cent and higher, especially in the first three years, particularly for males. Children were the most vulnerable, which meant that any natural increase in the slave population was minimal until the nineteenth century.

The Grenada Legislature, through pressure from the Colonial Office, reluctantly passed the Comprehensive Slave Acts in 1797, which sought to 'improve' the physical conditions of the slave. Though these laws 'protected' the slaves and 'guaranteed' them minimum rations, clothing, shelter, restrictions on whipping and the provision of religious instruction, they were rarely implemented, and few attempts were made to enforce them because the slave was subject to the arbitrary power of the slave-driver and plantation owners/managers.

The harsh treatment the slaves endured led to their covert resistance to enslavement, especially sabotage, and their continuous attempts to escape. There were many threats of slave uprisings but none materialised. A small MAROON community flourished in Grenada in the late 1700s but did not survive beyond 1820. During FÉDON'S REBELLION the bulk of Fédon's support came from the slaves who heeded his command to rebel under the banner of 'Liberté, égalité ou la mort'.

In the latter quarter of the 1700s the debate over the morality of slavery became intense within many segments of British society. Though there was a popular demand for the immediate ending of the slave trade and the freeing of the slaves, possibly influenced by the French Revolution, a number of issues, like the status of the slave following freedom, created much debate. The British Atlantic SLAVE TRADE was abolished in 1807, with the eventual end to slavery a foregone conclusion. In 1817 the Slave Registry Acts were passed to aid the enforcement of the Abolition Act and believed to encourage the 'better treatment' of the slaves. The British colonial government was concerned that the slave was not aware of the responsibilities of freedom and would 'revert to his former uncivilized self' if left to his own devices. To prepare the slave for eventual freedom the British government in 1824 passed the Amelioration Proposals. These included provisions for moral and religious EDUCATION, the development of economic responsibility among the slave through labouring for wages, the protection of the slave from whippings, the establishment of the family through marriages, and manumissions through self-purchase.

After some ten years of amelioration the British Parliament in 1833 voted to end slavery. In August 1834 the system

Representation of chained Africans taken to Grenada

of slavery was abolished, but the total EMANCIPATION of the slaves did not take place until 1838 after the end of the compulsory APPRENTICESHIP system that had tried to achieve a precarious balance between slavery and freedom, but failed. Some descendants of slaves are presently demanding repatriation and apologies from governments and others who derived benefits from African slavery.[35, 151, 196, 333]

SMITH, Dr Michael Garfield (1921-1993) was a Jamaican anthropologist and professor at a number of prestigious American universities. While at UWI in the 1950s he carried out anthropological fieldwork in Grenada and CARRIACOU in 1952/53 from which he published a number of books and scholarly articles on Grenadian culture, politics and society. Among his publications are *Kinship and Community in Carriacou* (1962), *West Indian Family Structure* (1962), *Dark Puritan* (1963), the story of Norman PAUL, and *Social Stratification in Grenada* (1964). Wilfred REDHEAD criticised Smith's depiction of Carriacouan society as 'primitive'. Smith's studies provided the basis for many later studies on Grenadian society.[321, 322, 323, 324, 325]

SMITH, Thomas Egbert Noble (1885-1977) was a proprietor of estates, 'planter', businessman, legislator, and exemplary member of the PLANTOCRACY in the twentieth century. He was the son of Alice *nee* Goulton and Thomas Smith. He attended the St. George's Methodist School and at the age of 15 became a clerk in his brother's firm. In 1913 he established T E Noble Smith and Co., general and commission merchants. Popularly known as T E Noble Smith, he was an elected member of the St. Andrew's District Board (1913-1940), and chairman for nine years. Between 1933 and 1951 he was an elected member of the Legislative Council. Unlike most of the plantocracy, he was a candidate in general ELECTIONS following the introduction of universal adult suffrage, as an independent in 1951, and again in 1961 for the GRENADA NATIONAL PARTY, but was unsuccessful on both occasions.

Smith had supported 'workers' and peasants' causes', but because he had remained 'socially aloof from the barefooted man', Emmanuel considered him 'hardly qualified for the new role of mass leadership'. Though Smith represented the last of a generation of politically influential merchant/planters, he did show insight into Grenadian society and the need for change. In 1948 he cautioned that the 'time when the capitalist must reap more than his share of the profit at the expense of the worker has come to an end. Conditions during recent times have been so favourable to the planter that some immediate step should be taken to put the matter of labourers' wages right.'

SNAKES Of the six species of snakes that have been recorded in the islands, two are thought to have become extinct, the Grenada ground snake or Shaw's racer (*Liophis melanotus*) and Neuweid's moon snake (*Pseudoboa neuweidi*). Germano *et al.*, however, believe that these two 'extinct' species never existed on the islands, having been recorded in error. The other four species, all native to the islands, are the tree boa or serpent (*Corallus enydris* syn. *C. grenadensis*), Boddaert's tree snake or 'grass snake' (*Mastigodryas bruesi*), the blind worm snake (*Typhlops tasymicris*) and the CRIBO. *T. tasymicris*, known from only two specimens, is considered a single-island endemic. There is little information on its ecology and status, and its rarity is possibly due to its small size and inconspicuous burrowing habit.

The serpent, yellow-brown with olive markings, is very common in Grenada and present in Carriacou. It is found in trees where it lives, feeding on the anole LIZARD, rodents and BIRDS. The MONGOOSE is rumoured to be a prey of most of the snakes and they can often be found engaged in mortal combat. The status of all snake species is either 'uncertain', 'rare' or 'endangered', some possibly 'extinct', except for the serpent. Agricultural pesticides may have had the most detrimental effect on the snake populations, but snakes are readily 'killed on sight' because of the fear surrounding them though none of those present in Grenada is poisonous to humans; a number are caught and killed for use as part of the JAB-JAB revellers' costumes.[122, 148]

SOAP/CHEW-STICK (*Gouania lupuloides*) is a woody vine that was used by the slaves and peasants to clean their teeth before the widespread availability and use of floss, toothbrush and toothpaste. West African slaves brought the practice to Grenada. In 1905 a medical officer commented that 'years ago the teeth of our peasants and their children were beautiful things, though they knew not tooth brush and powders, but the order of things is changing and bad decayed teeth are becoming increasingly common... it is not to be expected that each child can afford a tooth brush but a piece of soap-stick costs nothing and is an excellent substitute.' In Barbados a tea, believed by some to be an APHRODISIAC, is made from the leaves and also used as a treatment for gonorrhoea. Other teeth cleaning materials included baking soda, ashes, and black sage (*Lantana camara*).

The Mighty Sparrow

SPARROW (MIGHTY) A Trinidadian calypsonian, born in Grand Roy, Grenada, in 1925 as Slinger Francisco, the son of Rupert 'Jim' Francisco and Clarissa *nee* Charles. At the age of one he migrated to TRINIDAD with his family, like many Grenadians at that time. At 19 years he made his first public performance, displaying the stage talent that would eventually make him world famous. In 1956, with the calypso 'Jean and Dinah' the Mighty Sparrow won the Trinidad CARNIVAL calypso monarch, a title he would win eight times. He also won the road march title eight times.

For many years Sparrow dominated the calypso scene with the outrageous, satirical and celebratory songs that became his trademark. During his career he has produced over forty albums and is known the world over as a great calypso stage performer. He has made his home both in Trinidad and the US. In 1987 Sparrow was awarded an honorary doctorate degree by the UWI for his contributions to Caribbean culture. Other Grenadian calypsonians who have been successful in Trinidad include the Mighty Bomber (Clifton Ryan), Small Island Pride (Theolophilus Woods) and Valentino (Emrold Phillips).

SPIRITUAL BAPTISTS The development of the Spiritual Baptists in Grenada in the early 1900s was aided by the continual cultural exchanges between Trinidad and Grenada. It is believed that the Spiritual Baptists developed in Trinidad as the Shouter Baptists, who in turn owe their origins to Vincentian Shakers who migrated there. By 1927 they had become so vocal that the legislature passed a law prohibiting public meetings in order to resrtict the practice; the law remains on the books, but is not enforced. Spiritual Baptists take much from Protestantism, but have always incorporated varying elements of African-derived religious beliefs and practices such as drumming and the use of KOLA NUTS in divination rituals. It is the incorporation of African-derived religious practices that creates the diversity among Baptist groups, leading one commentator to conclude that 'no two groups are exactly the same.' Groups are usually small, comprising on average 20-30 members, but popular leaders can attract scores, sometimes hundreds of worshippers. The majority of believers call themselves Spiritual Baptists, but a number of groups are popularly known as Shango and Fire Baptists because of their affiliations with SHANGO.

Christianity and the teachings of the Bible shape Spiritual Baptists' belief system. Initiates are baptised in water, which is viewed as a ritual death and rebirth. Following baptism, they undergo a spiritual renewal known as mourning where they lie blindfolded on the 'mourning ground' for many days in fasting, prayer, meditation and renunciation. While in mourning visions usually appear to them, compelling those deemed 'possessed' or 'mounted' by the Holy Spirit to speak in tongues. They believe in the Holy Trinity, but those who follow the 'African way' incorporate RC Saints and African-derived Orishas or deities, hence another name Orisha Baptist. Folk spirits like the SUKUYANT, LAJABLESS, LOUGAROU and JUMBIE are deemed destructive and cause harm to humans, necessitating elaborate ceremonies to expel them from victims. Each church is led by a 'Pastor', 'Pointer', 'Mother', or 'Brother' around whom many of the activities and the administration of the church revolve. Spiritual Baptists have grown in both numbers and groups, becoming quite conspicuous despite their low overall numbers (2.7 per cent in 1991). These non-traditional religious groups are becoming socially accepted after years of denigration by the established Churches, the elite and middle class because of their 'African' expression. Groups can be found across the islands.[132, 261, 338]

SQUANDERMANIA The 1962 general elections were contested on two major issues, the UNITARY STATE proposal between Grenada and TRINIDAD, and Squandermania, both of which cost Eric GAIRY and the GULP the ELECTIONS. The term squandermania was coined by the WEST INDIAN newspaper reporting on corruption charges against Gairy for using government funds to purchase, among other things, a baby grand piano for his official residence at Mt. Royal. Gairy's term in office, lasting only ten months, was curtailed when the constitution was suspended in June 1962. A Commission of Inquiry Report accused Minister of Finance Gairy of violating a number of financial procedures, leading to questionable and wasteful expenditures. Among the other charges, the most serious was Gairy's subversion of the civil service and its administrative procedures.

Gairy's supporters saw this attack against him as another attempt by the colonial government and its middle-class allies to discredit him and remove a popularly elected figure from political office. He believed that 'the whole thing is a pack of lies. It is a political vendetta, a smear campaign. My government is clean.' At least four civil servants were suspended for their roles in the financial debacle and their association with Gairy. As a consequence of the Commission of Inquiry, a number of changes to the constitution increased the power of the British-appointed administrator, especially in regard to financial procedures. The administrator, James Lloyd, administered the government until general elections were held in September 1962, which brought the GRENADA NATIONAL PARTY to power.[35, 318]

STEELBANDS The most festive celebration in Grenada and Carriacou, carnival would be incomplete without steelband music. Developed to a fine art in Trinidad, the steelband had its roots in the 1930s in the impromptu percussion created by beating almost anything that produced a discernible rhythm to accompany the songs of the revellers. Beginning with the availability of oil drums in the 1940s due to the oil industry, Trinidadians found that indented drums produced a melodic sound, and the process of turning an oil drum into a musical instrument was born, replacing TAMBOO-BAMBOO. The oil drum is burnt to enable easy indentation with a hammer to produce musical notes. It is cut at one end to a specific size that results in a particular pitch. The various instruments in a steelband include the bass pan with its low notes arranged over four (tenor bass), six (six bass) or nine (rocking bass) drums, the three-drum cello, the two-drum high second, the two-drum double tenor, and the one-drum high-pitched tenor, with its finely engraved notes. The collection of these, with varying tones and numbers, creates orchestra-type music synonymous with CALYPSO music and CARNIVAL since the 1940s.

As part of its carnival celebrations, Grenada adopted the steelpan from Trinidad. Willan Dewesbury is credited with the formation of the islands' first steelband, the Hell Cats Steel Orchestra, which he began following his return to Grenada from Trinidad. A 1947 description of that band is illustrative: 'While the Hell Cats favoured the ends of oil drums, cutting off the sides at various lengths and heat tempering for further change of pitch [there was no indentation of the drums], there was another band that used only parts from junked automobiles... The Hell Cats pounded drums with sticks wrapped with heavy black tape. After a while the rhythm seemed to hypnotize the players.' It was not easy for the early bands to gain acceptance and many were literally run out of town because of the 'noise'.

A small band or 'panside' can have from twenty players and large bands over fifty, some being even larger. The pan is played by hitting the notes with a rubber-covered stick in order of the desired arrangement. The Panorama, held annually since 1970, brings together the bands on the islands in competition to determine the best. On

The Hell Cats Steel Orchestra, Grenada's first steel band, 1947 carnival

carnival Monday and Tuesday steelband music fills the air as revellers dance through the streets. Prior to the 1970s steelband players carried their pans around their necks during street celebrations, but over the years motorised vehicles and various wheeled carriers have made steelbands very mobile. The 1970s marked the maturity of steelband music when its popularity was celebrated with frequent events such as classical music contests and weekly 'blockoramas'.

Steelbands frequently made trips aboard cruise liners and perform regularly at HOTELS. Though the outer parishes, especially St. Andrew and even Carriacou, have fielded good steelbands over the years, St. George's parish and particularly St. George's Town continue to hold a monopoly on pan music. The most popular bands at present are ANGEL HARPS, Comancheros, New Dimensions, and Rainbow City Allstars. Though DJs provide some carnival music, it does not appear that steelband music will disappear anytime soon because of its popularity as a local cultural expression and a visitor attraction. The teaching of pan music to secondary school students, as is presently the case in at least six schools, and the organisation of a Junior Panorama competition (est. 1991) will definitely aid the continuance of this truly Caribbean art form. The steelpan is the only original musical instrument developed in the twentieth century. (See nbcangelharps.com.)[167]

STICKY/CLAMMY CHERRY (*Cordia dentata*) was introduced from India to the Caribbean in the eighteenth century and has become a common species in the coastal belt of the dry scrub woodland of Grenada. This medium-size tree grows to over 30 ft (10 m), and produces bunches of marble-sized, cherry-like fruits. The scarlet fruit has a fleshy pulp surrounding a small seed. Children use the edible fruit mainly as glue, though they eat some, but are told that if they consume too many, the glue will 'tie up their navel string' and they will die. The fruits are a favourite of birds. The leaves are used in folk medicine in a tea to induce sleep. The wood from the tree is highly resistant to sea water, hence its use in the construction of 'fish pots' or traps.

STINKING TOE/WEST INDIAN LOCUST (*Hymenaea courbaril*) is a member of the legume family, and native to tropical America where its bark, pod, root and resin are used in FOLK MEDICINES. It is a rather large tree, reaching up to 100 ft (30 m). It produces a fruit enclosed in a hard brown pod 4 by 2 inches (10 cm by 5 cm). Inside the oblong pod is an odorous brown pulp that is eaten mainly by children. Its local name, stinking toe, comes from the foul odour of the pulp surrounding the seed. It produces an excellent wood that is used to make furniture.

STREET/STAN' PIPES Piped water first came to some residents of St. George's in 1836, mainly through street pipes from natural springs at the Springs estate. In 1799 water supply to the shipping at the harbour was established from the same source (piped water referred to water carried by canals specifically constructed for that purpose). In 1841 a reservoir was built, and in 1879, the supply from the natural springs proving insufficient, a new source was found at the Soulier and Morne Repos Rivers. The expanded water supply and reservoir resulted in the establishment of pipe-borne water 'to many of the houses and to provide fire plugs in the streets from which an abundance of water can be projected over the roofs of the highest buildings when necessary.' To increase the water pressure another supply from the Les Avocats River, St. David, was added in 1889, providing water 'for the districts of St. Paul's and Richmond Hill, the Government institutions at the latter place and the Government House being for the first time properly supplied with water.' The towns of GOUYAVE and GRENVILLE received water supplies in 1890 and the other towns thereafter.

Though the water system had been established by 1879, most residents, especially outside St. George's, did not receive pipe-borne water in their communities until the 1920s and 1930s, and in their houses until the 1960s. Stand pipes or street pipes, located centrally in most villages, provided water for many who had to fetch or 'drogue' water in containers, usually buckets. Street pipes became more than just places to procure water, but a venue for social gathering. Women sometimes laundered or washed clothes, while children usually took their baths there. In 1975 all urban residents had access to at least communal water supplies, a large percentage having access to indoor facilities; 75 per cent of rural residents had access to mainly communal supplies. Though street pipes are still common in many villages and along the streets, the availability of pipe-borne water to over 84 per cent of the population has meant their decreasing use.[55]

STREET VENDORS once filled the streets with all manner of foods for sale, but are less common today. They should not be confused with hucksters who sold manufactured merchandise or agricultural produce. The sellers have almost always been women or young girls because most of the foods required preparation and few other business opportunities were open to them. The cries

Market vendors

of the vendors as they informed interested buyers of their foods are rare today, but were quite common years ago. The typical sales pitch began 'Get you boiled corn, hot and sweet!' Foods included CORN, CONKIE, BLOOD PUDDING, sweets, cakes, fried fish, 'bakes and fish-cake', nuts and other confectionery. Women, huddled in street corners over COALPOTS, can still be seen roasting corn, frying JACKS or blood pudding for sale. At holidays and celebrations like CARNIVAL, street vendors can be seen everywhere, hawking their foods. With the availability of processed foods, fast-food restaurants and the convenience of preparing foods readily at home, many people no longer patronise street vendors. Today, street vendors predominantly sell spices and local crafts to visitors.

STRING BANDS were popular up until the 1960s, providing the musical accompaniment for FOLK DANCES like quadrille and lancers, and at wakes, other local celebrations and fêtes, and Christmas carolling and serenading. Even after their demise in the urban areas many continued to entertain in the rural districts. String bands are still very popular in CARRIACOU, especially at the annual PARANG festival. String bands date to at least the 1700s as musical accompaniment at dances and balls. Many of the early musicians were FREE COLOUREDS and blacks, and slaves who entertained for their masters. Creole dances developed among the freedmen, as did the musical accompaniment, comprising groups of predominantly men, with a combination of instruments like the quatro/banjo, fiddle, guitar, bass, flute/fife, 'racker' and tambourine. Many instruments were locally made, copied from foreign instruments that were common. The bands' repertoire consisted of various musical types such as lavwé, cassian, heel-and-toe, reels and meringue, but primarily quadrilles and lancers. They also incorporated calypso, waltzes, and various musical types popular throughout the region. The African drum, as is common among the Carriacou quadrille bands, became part of the band and defined it for many decades. In some of the bands in Grenada a wooden box with a hole replaced the drum. Many villages and communities had their own string bands, but popular bands were in demand across the islands. Though the development of modern CALYPSO music in the late 1950s and its huge acceptance inadvertently displaced string bands, the tradition has survived in Carriacou in the shape of QUADRILLE and parang bands, and there are a few left as well in Grenada. But it was primarily the demise of folk dances like the lancers that ultimately led to the decline of the string bands.[51, 234]

SUGAR The history of the West Indies between 1650 and 1850 is the history of SUGAR CANE and the sugar industry, both of which were synonymous with SLAVERY. It was the demand for sugar in Europe that transformed the West Indies and led to the importation of millions of Africans as chattel labour to work the many sugar plantations. Grenada recorded SUGAR production as early as 1675. By 1687 there were four sugar estates in operation, but Grenadian planters were slow to adopt the monocrop economy sweeping the region. After 1714 sugar manufacture expanded and by the 1750s Grenada had adopted it as its primary crop, with over eighty estates.

Yet, it was not until after the British occupied the islands that agricultural production became overwhelmingly dominated by sugar cane. Between 1763 and 1770, sugar production almost tripled, surpassing the other Ceded Islands. By 1824 there were 124 estates producing sugar, but a number of problems, primarily external, soon led to the total collapse of the industry by the 1860s. Primary among the problems were the high cost of production, increasing quantities of more cheaply produced sugar from Brazil and Cuba, the end to the slave labour regime in the 1830s, and the opening of the protected British sugar market in 1846. Attempts to resuscitate the industry like the Encumbered Estates Act and INDENTURED IMMIGRATION did little to reverse the ailing industry. By the time 'king sugar' was laid to rest, Grenada was able to diversify its agricultural economy with COCOA, but sugar has left intact a cash crop economy that continues to plague the islands and region today. In 1934 local interests established the GRENADA SUGAR FACTORY to produce sugar and RUM.[35, 221, 333]

SUGAR ANTS In 1770 a small red ant 'mysteriously' appeared in St. George's parish and soon spread throughout the island. For the next decade it caused considerable damage to citrus trees and SUGAR CANE, threatening the island's valuable sugar industry. Its appearance at Woodford estate, located near the landing at HALIFAX HARBOUR where smugglers often unloaded their booty, led many to conclude that the ant was accidentally introduced from Martinique, which suffered the scourge in the 1760s. (Gidney Clark, proprietor of Clarks Court estate, was blamed for the sugar ant outbreak in Barbados in 1760 when he imported topsoil from his estate in Tobago.) John Castles, in a May 1790 letter read before the British Royal Society, described the number of ants as 'incredible', adding that he had 'seen the roads coloured by them for miles together; and so crowded were they in many places that the print of the horse's feet would appear for a moment or two, until filled up by the surrounding multitude.' William Hickey, in his memoirs, began his description with the disclaimer that 'had I not myself seen what I am going to describe, I could not have believed it; the earth covered with small red ants heaped in a mass so as themselves to form a body eleven inches in depth.' The sugar ants attacked living animals as well as dead and decaying flesh, devouring anything in their path.

After the failed attempts to eradicate the ants 'by poison, and the application of fire', the General Assembly in 1776 offered a £20,000 bounty to anyone who could 'rid the island of this plague before the sugar industry came to ruin.' Henry Phillips concocted a powder that killed the ants, and though it proved impractical in exterminating them, he was granted a small reward for his 'powder' in 1781. As unexpectedly as the sugar ant had appeared and ravaged the island, the heavy rainfall from the Great Hurricane of 1780 destroyed it. Yet a year later some estates were still devastated by the sugar ants to such an 'extent that it brings in no income whatever.' Brian Edwards lists the species as *Formica omnivore*, but EO Wilson, the eminent myrmecologist, believes it was *Pheidole megacephola*, an African invasive species. Interestingly, these ants do not attack plants directly; the plant damage was caused by a sap-sucking insect living in symbiosis with the ants which protects the insects (*Homoptera*) and feeds off their excrement.[366]

SUGAR CANE (*Saccharum* spp.) Even though this crop is readily associated with the West Indies, it is native to Eastern Asia and was introduced to Hispaniola from the Canary Islands in 1493 by Columbus. Sugar cane reached Grenada in the early 1600s, most probably brought by the Island CARIBS. Serious cultivation did not begin until the 1730s, though economic cultivation dates to the 1660s, and the crop dominated the economy between 1763 and the 1840s, earning it the title 'king sugar'.

A member of the grass family, this perennial reed can grow to a height of 8-12 ft (2.5-3.6 m). Its fibrous stem contains the sweet sap for which it is cultivated. Even though the steep topography was not appropriate for sugar cane cultivation, Grenada nonetheless ranked fifth after Jamaica, Antigua, St. Kitts and Barbados for total sugar exports to Britain between 1773 and 1789. The crop is planted in rows from ratoons, new vegetative shoots, which emerge from the cropped plant. After 15 months in the field, the crop is ready for harvest. This begins the most strenuous work involved in sugar production since the cane has to be processed immediately after cutting to prevent spoilage. The mature cane stalks were cut and loaded onto donkey carts (today trucks) and carried to the SUGAR MILL where the juice from the cane was extracted by a cattle mill, water mill or windmill. The sugar cane juice was then heated in a series of 'coppers', after which the syrup was packed into wooden troughs. At the curing house the 'sugar liquor' stood for several weeks while the molasses drained out or was centrifuged, leaving sugar crystals. The different layers were then separated as to quality grades that were determined by colour. The molasses residue went on to the 'still house' to begin the process of rum manufacture.

The production of rum at RIVER ANTOINE, utilising many of the traditional techniques, sheds some light on the history of this once dehumanising activity. Sugar cane is cultivated on approximately 5,500 acres (2,230 ha) on a few sugar estates purely for rum production, exclusively in the east and south-east of the island. The answer to the riddle, 'water stand up, and water lie down' is sugar cane.

SUGAR MILLS With sugar cane cultivation a major agricultural activity for most of the eighteenth and nineteenth centuries, the machinery used for SUGAR production was prevalent throughout Grenada. Two pieces of construction, water mills and windmills, were the imposing fixtures that defined and dictated the industrial landscape, but cattle mills were the first types of sugar mills employed in Grenada from the 1660s. Cattle mills were the simplest, drawn either by mule, horse, and cattle, or rarely by slaves. They were common throughout

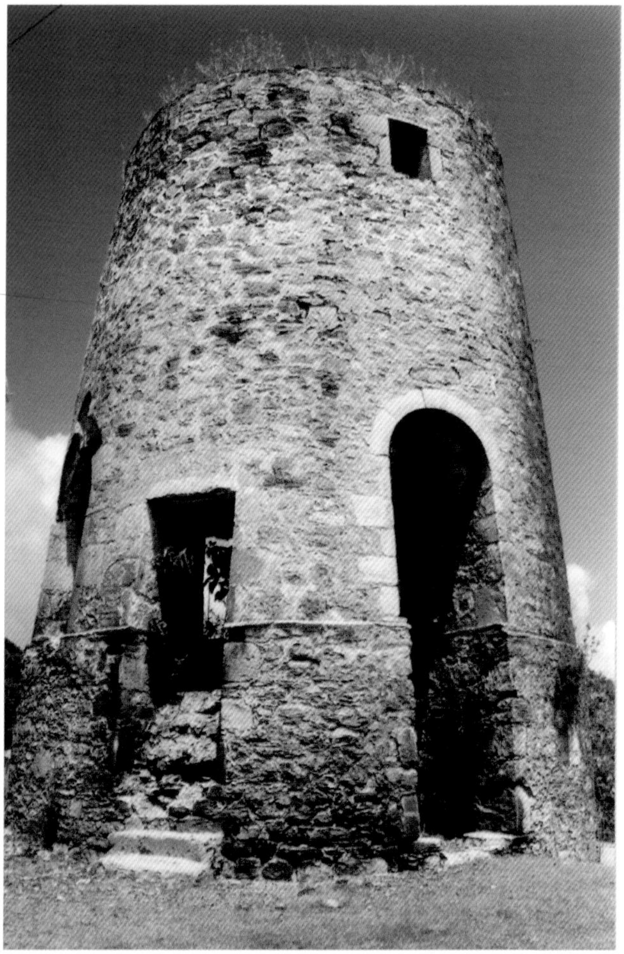

Two-level windmill

the islands on small estates because of cost effectiveness, and though reliable, were slow. They were replaced in the 1700s by faster water mills and windmills on estates suitably located for water and wind power, though some cattle mills survived until the 1960s. A cattle mill is depicted on the MACE of the House of Representatives.

Water mills were the fastest and most reliable of the mills. They were elaborate constructions that required the diversion and damming of a river or stream, and the construction of an extensive elevated stone and brick aqueduct, carrying water hundreds of yards to the mill. From the aqueduct the water flowed into the water wheel's 'buckets', powering the machinery which crushed the SUGAR CANE. By the mid-1700s the French had built 76, and by 1772 there were 95 in operation across Grenada. In 1889 they had dwindled to 34 due to the decline in the sugar industry. In 1905 only 21 were still operating. At RIVER ANTOINE the water mill is still in use, functioning much as it did when constructed by slaves over 200 years ago. Remnants of decaying aqueduct systems can be seen on many ESTATES, and massive rusted water wheels stuck in time.

The regularity and strength of the trade winds during the dry season when sugar cane was usually harvested made windmills more advantageous. Yet, there were no guarantees that wind would always be available when needed. The early post-mills were soon replaced by tower-mills, a number of which can still be seen throughout Grenada and Carriacou in varying stages of decay. Tower-mills were built of brick or stone, a single level with three arched openings. At the bottom of the rollers was a 'liquor box' which collected the sugar cane juice. The British were responsible for those in Grenada and Carriacou, which numbered 12 in 1772 and were restricted to the eastern coast and the Grenadines; in the 1790s CARRIACOU had seven. At least four tower mills in fairly good condition have been selected by the Grenada Historical Society for preservation.

SUKUYANT/SUKUYÂ A folk spirit that has the ability to alter its human form and metamorphose into a ball of fire, enabling it to fly and enter the houses of its victims to suck their blood. The origin of the term sukuyant is confusing, possibly from French (*soupçon/soupçonner/sucer*: 'suspicion/to suspect/to suck'), but more likely Fula/Sonike (*sukunyadyo/ sukunya*: 'a man-eating witch'). Among the AKAN is the *obayifo* that can transform itself into a ball of fire after removing its skin in order to suck people's blood, especially children. The sukuyant's association with witchcraft in general and women in particular bears more similarity to its West African counterpart than the European human-bat vampire.

The supernatural powers of sukuyants, exclusively old women who are described as 'possessing witch-like qualities', are gained by making a pact with the devil. They receive magical powers and the devil gets fresh blood each night, while the victim becomes ill and eventually dies unless an obeahman is called in to catch the sukuyant. Before it can take to the sky it must shed its skin and hide it properly, usually in a 'mortar' or beneath a stone. If its skin is found, it could suffer agonies if someone coats it with salt and pepper, the common remedy for catching a sukuyant. It has been rumoured that this treatment causes it to howl in pain as it utters the comforting words to its skin, '(s)kin ah me kin!' Salt or sand granules placed at the entrances to one's home forces the sukuyant to count each grain before entering. If the rising of the sun catches it counting, its identity will be revealed. The method of repelling a sukuyant while asleep is to place garlic around the neck. In Carriacou the sukuyant is called a coco-mâ (<Fr.Cr.<Fr. *cauchemar*: 'nightmare').

SUPERSTITIONS/BELIEFS The belief in superstitions is common to all cultures, whether materially developed or not. It predominates in the poorer segments of societies where EDUCATION is minimal and the standard of living is low. In Grenada superstitions are a part of most people's lives even though many readily deny that fact since superstition is seen as the belief of 'uneducated' folk. There are entrenched superstitions that influence the everyday decisions of the rural folk and exert subtle influences on many educated members of society. Superstitions envelope all aspects of people's lives, from birth to death and even beyond, incorporating animals, plants, inanimate objects, the weather, supernatural forces and a host of characters employed to explain life's perplexing experiences. It is a belief system that dates back generations, handed down through oral history that often alters the superstition or the explanation as seen fit.

Though Christian theology regards superstitions as pagan and renounces all such practices, folk society has nonetheless adapted many of these beliefs into rituals of Christianity and other RELIGIONS. The islands' occupation by French, British and African peoples, through SLAVERY and colonialism, have created a rich and diverse legacy of superstitions, many of which have been preserved in the countryside, but may no longer be taken seriously. Others, like the LIGAROO and the LAJABLESS, have found resting places in folk tales which entertain and scare children. Superstitions rarely ever disappear but find new meaning as each generation of believers searches for answers to explain their 'bad luck', 'good luck', or just the everyday 'signs and symbols' along the journey of life.

SUSU A system of saving money brought to the islands by YORUBA slaves and still practised among Grenadians. It involves the co-operation of a group of people who pool a set amount of their weekly or monthly earnings and make the total sum available to each member in turn; a sort of rotating fund. Each month a new member 'draws a hand', which allows him/her to save a large amount of money. The susu (<Yor. *esusu*: 'rotating fund') becomes obligatory once one decides to become a member, and so an individual is responsible for the continuation of monthly contributions even after 'drawing a hand'. This system of saving is common among women, but is also practised by men. Before the availability of FRIENDLY SOCIETIES, commercial BANKS and credit unions, this form of saving was common throughout the country and contributed tremendously to the economic livelihood of families. In Jamaica it is called partner hand.[224]

SWEET POTATO (*Ipomoea batatas*) has become a staple in the tropics, especially Africa where its leaves are eaten as a spinach, but is native to South America. In Grenada, the sweet potato is known as a 'ground provision' (root or tuber). It is propagated vegetatively and planted in heaps where its vine-like growth spreads along the ground. There is a diversity of varieties based upon colour, taste and cooking characteristics. The flesh, usually white or yellowish, is rich in carbohydrates, particularly starch, but upon cooking or roasting some of the starch is converted to sugar, giving it its characteristic sweet taste. The sweet potato as a cooked vegetable is a part of many meals, but can also be grated and made into 'potato pudding' or pone. The tubers are available year-round. A number of species in the sweet potato genus produce attractive trumpet-shaped flowers, including the morning glory (*I. purpurea*) with its bright blue flowers; goat's foot (*I. pes-caprea*) which grows on BEACHES and controls sand erosion; and the morning glory bush (*I. fistulosa*), a shrub that produces light-mauve bell-shaped flowers.

SWIZZLESTICK is made from the swizzlestick tree (*Quararibea turbinata*) and is used to blend drinks, beat eggs, 'mash calalu', and for a variety of other tasks that require blending or mixing. The swizzlestick tree is ideal for this culinary tool because of its whirled branches. It is cut about 4.5 inches (12 cm) long with 5-6 smaller branches attached, each about 1-1.5 inches (3-4 cm). A second type of swizzlestick is made from a long stick to which are attached two rows of curled metal at one end. It is held between the palms of the hand and twirled back and forth, creating a circular motion. The swizzlestick is rarely found today, having been replaced by imported beaters, blenders and the like.

TAMARIND/TAMBRAN (*Tamarindus indica*) is a stately evergreen tree that grows to 65 ft (20 m). It is indigenous to eastern Africa and common to Asia. It is found throughout the islands in backyards and roadsides, brought to the Caribbean in 1647. Its compacted crown of leaves produces a comfortable shade. The tamarind (<Arabic *tamr hindi*: 'date of India', which it is not) produces a brown pod 4-5 inches (10-12.7 cm) long, which is mature once the shell surrounding the flesh becomes brittle. The thick brown pulp around the seed has an acidic flavour. It is eaten fresh, or made into a sweetmeat called tamarind balls. These spicy sweets are made from the pressed pulp, mixed with sugar and spices. A drink is also made from the pulp as well as preserves, sauces, chutneys and curries. Locally, a decoction of its leaves is used as a FOLK MEDICINE to treat measles and sore throat. Tamarind is also an ingredient in the Trinidadian-made Angostura Bitters. Fruits are usually available from December through June. The sight or mere mention of a 'tambran branch' in the hands of a parent was enough to elicit co-operation from a disobedient child.

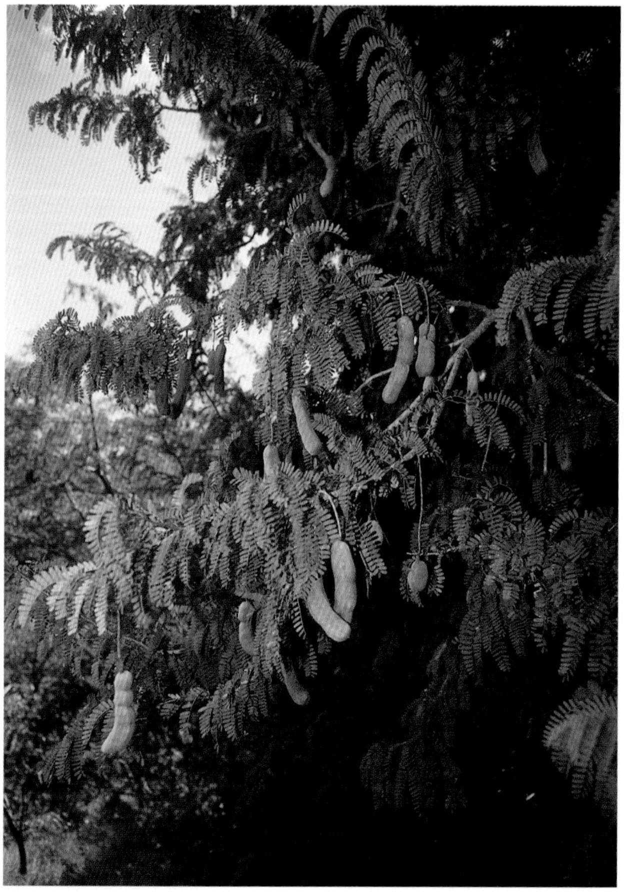

Tamarind tree with fruits

TAMBOO-BAMBOO Before the advent of the STEELBAND as the musical accompaniment for CARNIVAL revellers, it was the versatile BAMBOO that provided the tempo. Beginning in the early 1900s tamboo-bamboo bands became popular in street carnival, replacing the (animal) skin drums. The continuous cultural exchanges between Grenada and TRINIDAD influenced its local development. Tamboo-bamboo (<Fr. Cr.<Fr. *tambour* + *bamboo*: 'bamboo drum', even though it does not possess a skin as in a traditional drum) is an idiophone that is struck with a stick to create a rhythm, and simultaneously bounced on the ground to produce an additional thumping sound. A band comprises groups of players each with a different length and thickness of bamboo: 'cutters' (soprano), 'fillers' (tenor), 'chandles' (alto) and 'bass boom' (bass), hence possessing the ability to create a diversity of tones. In turn, these various tones—together with the 'bottle and spoon', metal scrapers and chac-chac (maracas)—create a tempo that is rhythmic, loud and suitable for the fast-moving 'jump up' of street carnival. By the mid-1940s tamboo-bamboo bands were quickly replaced by a more melodic (though not immediately so) and versatile instrument, the steelpan, which was adopted from Trinidad. The LaPoterie Tambu Bambu, a local group, attempts to keep the almost lost musical art form alive through its performances.

TANNIA (*Xanthosoma sagittifolium*) A ground provision or tuber native to tropical America and the Caribbean. Its cultivation most probably dates to the AMERINDIANS who may have brought it with them from South America. A relative of the eddoe and DASHEEN, tannia (<Tupi-Guarani *taya*, for the plant) is more robust and can withstand harsher climatic conditions. The plant produces a starchy central corm or underground stem, surrounded by smaller cormels. As a vegetable, tannia is boiled, baked or fried. 'Tannia log', a drink, is made from grated corms and coconut milk, and used by some as an APHRODISIAC. Tannia was once used to make fufu (<Twi *fufuu*, for the food), a popular West African dish. Unlike dasheen, the leaves are not consumed.

TANTEEN Much of the area known today as the Tanteen, St. George's, sits on land reclaimed from MANGROVES and swamps. Its reclamation was carried out as part of a nation-wide project to rid the islands of mosquito breeding places and MALARIA. Drainage work in Tanteen began in 1909, but to control the mosquito population small fish known as millions or guppies (*Lebistes reticulatus*) were introduced from Barbados (native to Trinidad and Venezuela) into the large drains to consume the mosquito larvae. (The drains of Tanteen still contain these fish, which also grace many boys' aquariums.) Beginning in 1926 the area was used as a rubbish-processing facility where refuse was incinerated and used to reclaim the surrounding wetlands. By 1933 the Tanteen, CARENAGE and LAGOON wetlands had been filled in and 'a fine recreational park created', today occupied by the Tanteen Recreation Grounds and the MARRYSHOW COMMUNITY COLLEGE.

In the 1930s the small incline upon which the GBSS presently stands was degraded and buildings erected in 1939 by the British Royal Engineers to house the CARIBBEAN REGIMENT. Until the advent of GRANDE ANSE BEACH as the preferred bathing locale after the 1930s, The Spout was the favourite swimming and outdoor bathing place in St. George's. Once the area was filled in around 1943, the surrounding areas like Tanteen Terrace and Archibald Avenue (The Lane) became desirable residential neighbourhoods; some of the houses were built in the 1940s and 1950s by the Grenada government as housing for civil servants.

TECHNICAL & ALLIED WORKERS' UNION The TAWU registered as a labour union in 1958, founded by E A 'Doc' Mitchell who had been involved with the LABOUR MOVEMENT since the 1920s and the founding of the Grenada Workingman's Association. Since the 1950s TAWU has played a major role in the trade union movement, especially during the political turmoil of the 1970s. It is one of the largest unions, representing thousands of workers. Under the leadership of Chester Humphrey (a former NEW JEWEL MOVEMENT member) since 1990, it has been regarded as a militant union in its dealings with both the GOG and private businesses over labour issues.

TELECOMMUNICATIONS Telegraphic services were established in Grenada in 1871 by the West Indian and Panama Telegraph Company (aft. 1938 became Cable & Wireless), linking the island directly to the rest of the world for the first time. In 1887, just 12 years after the invention of the telephone, Grenada received a limited telephone service, linking the police stations throughout the island, except St. David. Private messages were allowed for a small fee. In 1891 the government established a telephone exchange in St. George's, with a limited public service made available in 1893; exchanges were subsequently established across the island. In 1900 there were 164 telephone subscribers, and 201 in 1905. In 1925 a wireless station was installed at Old Fort, St. George's, by the Pacific Cable Board, resulting in direct external communication with Barbados; it was extended in May 1946 to include St. Vincent, St. Lucia, Antigua, St. Kitts and British Guiana under the management of Cable and Wireless (C&W).

In 1926 CARRIACOU received a wireless station, establishing direct communication with Grenada for the first time. By the mid-1900s the telephone had become established in the islands as a means of communication, but subscribers were few and services remained expensive and beyond the reach of the majority of Grenadians (in 1940 there were 541 subscribers, and 763 in 1946, of whom 62 per cent were in St. George's). By 1946 Carriacou had a small internal telephone service run by the Grenada government and linked to the Grenada telephone system via VHF radiotelephone.

HURRICANE JANET in 1955 destroyed much of the telephone system, but in 1957 a new dial system became operative. In the next three decades telephone services slowly expanded. In 1969 the Grenada Telephone Company Ltd. (GTC) was established as a public liability company, with responsibility for domestic telephone services (with 2,368 connections); C&W retained responsibility for external telecommunications. By 1974 telephone subscribers increased to 4,481. In 1982 Grenada Telecommunications (GRENTEL) became government-owned, the PEOPLE'S REVOLUTIONARY GOVERNMENT 'purchasing' the 50 per cent shares of the (US) Continental Telephone Company.

It was not until 1989 (with the privatisation of GRENTEL and majority shares owned by C&W) that the telephone system was totally revamped and upgraded. A fully digital system, with underground fibre optic transmission, provides countrywide service. Prior to 1989 telephone services were restricted to the major towns and of poor quality, but is now available throughout the islands. Other communication services include mobile cellular phones, and Internet services. The telephone exchange building on the Carenage (having moved from its original building on Market Hill) has been beautifully restored and improved.

TITIRI The juvenile stage of the gobiid fish or goby (*Sicydium plumieri*, ?syn. *S. punctatum/ antillarum*), which can be seen in swarms at the boucheré (<Fr. *embouchure*: '(river) mouth') as they prepare to migrate upriver between September and December each year. Hatched from eggs spawned and fertilised upriver, the larvae float down river and enter the sea. The post-larval stage develops in the sea for about a month before beginning the migration upriver. The titiri is regarded as a delicacy and is used

as the main ingredient in 'titiri fish cakes', a fritter. The adults are called suckstone because of their feeding habit of sucking algae from rocks. The once large numbers have been greatly reduced in recent years due to a number of factors, including the damming of and decrease in the water levels of many rivers, and over-fishing which may have a deleterious effect on other fresh-water species like the crayfish which feed on them. Titiri are important 'as a biological indicator of the ecological health of streams', and their decreasing numbers may be directly related to growing pollution in many streams. The titiri (<Is.Car. 'small fish', for the juvenile goby) is also known by a number of other names, tri-tri and tiri-tiri, variations of titiri.

TOBACCO (*Nicotiana tabacum*) was the first crop produced commercially in Grenada in the seventeenth and early eighteenth centuries. Native to tropical America, the tobacco plant was sacred to the Island Arawaks and Island CARIBS who used it in various rituals and as medicine. By the mid-1500s Europeans had developed a taste for the smoked leaves and growing demand was partly responsible for the colonisation of the Lesser Antilles by the French and British at the beginning of the 1600s. The attempt to settle Grenada by a 'London-Dutch syndicate' in 1609 was 'intended to found a tobacco producing colony.' The first harvest by the French colonists in 1649 'was found so good, that a pound was worth three of that of other islands.' Tobacco production continued into the first decade of the 1700s, cultivated by white peasant farmers. As an estate crop it was surpassed by the commercial production of more valuable crops like INDIGO and SUGAR CANE, and was eventually abandoned. Tobacco grows 'wild' throughout the island and is used in FOLK MEDICINE to induce vomiting, and to treat or 'smoke a restless child.' Crushed tobacco leaf and 'soft candle' is a folk remedy for mumps.

TOMBSTONE/STONE FEAST On the island of Carriacou the tombstone feast is an elaborate ceremony and essential part of the folk RELIGION that brings to an end the ritual ceremonies surrounding death. As the name implies, it is the ceremony surrounding the laying of the tombstone or headstone upon the grave of the deceased. It is usually done one year or more after burial, on the anniversary of death, following months of preparation. The elaborate nature of the tombstone feast is a sign of financial success, and relatives will save for years before holding the event. The ceremony begins the day before the feast as the mason prepares the grave to receive the headstone. The feast day opens with a *saraca/salaca* or sacrifice. The PARENTS' PLATE is prepared for the ancestors, as it is believed that they will come to 'eat' of the offering. Before entombment, the headstone is carried to the house of the deceased where family members gather to 'wet the ground' or pour libations and recite prayers. At the grave the headstone is laid in place as libations are poured over it, with the breaking of an egg to symbolise the beginning of prosperity for the family. The following day is filled with celebrations accompanied by the BIG DRUM DANCE. McDaniel believes that the Carriacou stone feast bears much similarity to the Igbo's (Nigerian) ritual of the 'second burial', and 'may be historically linked' to it.[85, 225, 349]

TONKA BEAN (*Dipteryx odorata*) The seed of this rather large South American tree is used as a spice to flavour TOBACCO, perfume, soap, liqueur and confectionery. An evergreen tree that grows to 130 ft (40 m), it produces a pulpy elliptical pod or drupe that becomes yellow-brown when ripe. The single seed is extracted from the pod around March to May. Before use the seed is soaked in alcohol for at least 24 hours, then dried. Soaking in rum releases the main ingredient, coumarin, which gives tonka bean (<Galibi/Tupi *tonka*, for the plant) its sweet and aromatic flavour. It is used as a substitute for vanilla and locally to flavour RUM. The spice, a legume, is not commonly known outside of the Caribbean, especially since coumarin is lethal in large doses because it is an anti-coagulant and possibly carcinogenic.

TORCHLIGHT A conservative bi-weekly newspaper founded in 1955 by L C J Thomas, Reginald Cline and others, and aligned with the GRENADA NATIONAL PARTY. As such, it was considered an anti-Gairy/GULP newspaper. Following the March 1979 overthrow of PM GAIRY by the NEW JEWEL MOVEMENT, *The Torchlight*, though expressing initial support for the new revolutionary government, began to 'criticise' the policies and friends of the PEOPLE'S REVOLUTIONARY GOVERNMENT. It published a number of editorials and features exposing sensitive PRG-Cuban-Soviet Union relationships. The reprint of a German article, 'Soviet in a Holiday Paradise', pictures of Bishop's security force, maps of security installations and its coverage of the Rastafarian protest in October 1979 resulted in the closure of the newspaper by the PRG on the grounds that it was collaborating with the CIA to destabilise the regime.

A cruise ship calls

The ramifications of *The Torchlight* closure were considerable, drawing protest from many, including Caribbean editors, but to no avail. Though it has been claimed that PM BISHOP was against the closure of *The Torchlight*, his views on freedom of the press in his Line of March Speech were totally opposite when he declared that 'When they want to put out [a] newspaper and we don't want that, we close it down.'

The closure of the *Torchlight*, once the sole independent free press on the island, resulted in the press monopoly of the PRG. The PRG, in an attempt to forestall the reopening of *The Torchlight* or the formation of another independent newspaper, prevented individuals in any newspaper publishing company from owning more than four per cent of the shares. Yet the owners of the *Grenadian Voice* successfully manoeuvred around the restrictions when they published the newspaper in May 1981. The PRG nonetheless closed it down and passed the Newspaper Amendment Act banning the publication of any private newspaper until a media code was established.[353]

TOURISM The natural beauty of Grenada was extolled by travellers as early as 1656 when Father DU TERTRE visited and left the first description of the island by a 'tourist'. Later travellers would write glowingly of the small town that developed around FORT GEORGE, the BEACHES along the southern coast, and the friendliness of the people. Travel writer and author of ISLAND IN THE SUN Alec Waugh wrote of Grenada that it was 'the one small island that provides everything a preconceived picture of the tropics has led a visitor to expect.' It was inevitable, then, that with the availability and low cost of travel, many visitors would arrive on our shores.

As in most of the Caribbean islands, tourism has become an economic necessity, contributing significantly to the economies of the smaller islands that have no commercial mineral resources (tourism accounts for 25 per cent of Gross Domestic Product, 40 per cent of export of goods and services, 9 per cent of GOG revenues and about 15 per cent of employment). There were attempts to promote tourism beginning in the later 1800s as with Septimus

Wells' 1890 publication of *Historical and Descriptive Sketch of the Island of Grenada.* Yet it was not until the 1930s that interested groups began to promote Grenada as a tourist locale when day visitors began arriving with the Canadian National Steamship service, which linked Canada, the eastern US and Caribbean countries. After the disruption caused by World War II, the late 1940s witnessed increased local organisation by the Grenada Tourist Board, which began to bear fruit in the 1950s with the arrival of cruise ships beginning in 1956 and steadily increasing thereafter. The visit by Princess Margaret in 1955 and the filming of *Island in the Sun* in 1956 helped promote the islands, but earlier developments like the construction of PEARLS AIRPORT in 1943 and the Santa Maria Hotel in 1948 laid the foundations. By 1959 revenues from tourism had tripled from four years earlier. In that same year Castro's socialist government came to power in Cuba, resulting in the abandonment of the island as the US tourist haven and the spread of tourism to the Eastern Caribbean. The dramatic growth in the sector made it very attractive, and every succeeding government has seen it as a major instrument in the economic development of the islands.

The 1960s witnessed a huge increase in the sector, with more hotel rooms and international promotion. Though tourism continued to grow in the 1970s, due mainly to cruise ship arrivals, a number of problems remained, including the absence of an international airport and adequate accommodation. Yet the most immediate deterrent to growth was the political turmoil in the early to mid-1970s that caused arrival figures to fluctuate. In 1979 the PEOPLE'S REVOLUTIONARY GOVERNMENT embarked on the building of an international airport at Point Salines. The adversarial relationship between the PRG and US government led to negative publicity reported in international newspapers and travel magazines. Grenada earned such titles as 'Police State' and 'Soviet Satellite', discouraging many visitors who were afraid of 'another Cuba'. By the end of 1983 the number of US visitors had declined.

Following the US-led military INTERVENTION and the completion of the POINT SALINES INTERNATIONAL AIRPORT in 1984, there was a marked increase in the number of visitors to the islands, many of them stopover visitors. Yet cruise ship passengers still account for the majority. Of the stopover visitors, Grenadians living abroad and returning for holidays regularly account for about 20 per cent. Next to the civil service and agriculture, the tourism sector employs the largest number of workers in service-related jobs, predominantly in hotels, guest houses, restaurants and local boutiques. Tourism's revenues continue to grow relative to agriculture, but the sector is partly responsible for the growing negative balance of trade caused by its increasing imports, especially food. Grenada, like many of the other countries which find themselves inviting visitors to their shores, is trying to balance the negative social aspects of the industry. Yet tourism has become extremely important to Grenada's economic survival and with the decreasing revenues from traditional agricultural exports, it would appear to be the sector that holds the greatest potential for Grenada's economic development, at least in the short term. Tourism has exhibited positive influences on the economy and the environment, for example the establishment of the NATIONAL PARK SYSTEM and historical/cultural preservation. The tourism industry suffered greatly as a result of HURRICANE IVAN as many hotels and other infrastructure were damaged or destroyed.[50, 267, 320]

TOWER HOUSE was built as a residence in 1917 by prominent lawyer and legislator 'CFP' RENWICK who called it St. Leonards, 'apparently in memory of the English seaside town'. It is a large Caribbean colonial-style building that towers above the landscape in the suburbs of St. Paul's, St. George. It was built of volcanic

Tower House

rock, with a castle-like tower commanding a view above the treetops. It has been described as 'an eclectic mixture of styles, ranging from Queen Anne to Victorian with a measure of British Raj added'.

A popular tale surrounds St. Leonards, with local mythology claiming that this beautiful house was built for CFP's English wife to convince her to stay in Grenada. Another local tale claims that 'CFP', a well-known gambler, lost St. Leonards in a bet with S A FRANCIS, but the latter could not claim the prize because the property on which the house stood was not part of the bet. The property was bought by Dr Leonard A P Slinger in 1943, a member of one of Grenada's prominent families, who changed its name to Tower House. Though it is a private residence now owned by Paul Slinger, tours can be arranged through the beautiful FLOWER GARDENS, halls of prints, paintings and historic family photographs. The estate also produces fruits and spices.

TRAFFICKING At the beginning of each week the CARENAGE is crowded with women and men busily packing agricultural produce, mainly fruits, for export, primarily to TRINIDAD. This also takes place in the port of GRENVILLE where fruits, vegetables and ground provisions are packed into wooden crates, then loaded onto small skiffs and schooners that ply the waters in the southern Caribbean. These agricultural traders are part of an old tradition dating to colonial times, though the trade has expanded since the 1960s as a result of regional integration policies. The business mainly employs women, involved in a little panquai (<Fr. 'a little extra') or 'turn-hand' (buy and sell) to make ends meet. Traffickers should not be confused with hucksters who retail their merchandise locally.

Traffickers purchase green BANANAS, GOLDEN APPLES, ANNONA, MANGOES, citrus and other fruits from farmers for sale in the neighbouring islands. They struggle against high transport and freight costs, and damage and theft of their produce during shipment. Once they have sold their produce, many of them purchase Trinidadian merchandise for resale in Grenada, hoping to make a profit on the reverse trade. They traditionally accounted for a large share of the trade in fresh fruits and vegetables, with their informal trade contributing significantly to the local economy. It also provides work for a section of the community that would not have the resources to enter the established commercial sector. The appearance of the pink MEALYBUG in the mid-1990s caused much disruption in the inter-island trade and left many out of business, as did HURRICANE IVAN in 2004.

TRINIDAD & TOBAGO 10 30N 60 15W is the twin-island republic situated 60-90 miles (97-145 km) to the south of Grenada, which has had close economic, political and cultural ties with its northern neighbour since the 1760s, unofficially earlier. In 1666 French residents from Grenada briefly held Tobago and it was part of the GOVERNMENT OF GRENADA and the Government of the WINDWARD ISLANDS before being united with Trinidad in 1889. To the Grenadian PLANTOCRACY eighteenth-century Spanish Trinidad was 'the common Asylum for Fugitives of every description' and a haven for slaves and MAROONS who were able to make the perilous journey south. Visitors from Trinidad had to pay a bond because of the fear that they might try to encourage slaves to runaway. The Cédula or law of 1776 granted foreign Catholics entry into Trinidad, but the 1783 Cédula of Population, negotiated by French Grenadian ROUMÉ DE ST. LAURENT, went even further in granting French Caribbean residents citizenship and land concessions.

Thus began the migration of Grenadians—planters, free coloureds and their slaves—to Trinidad in the late 1700s. Extensive migration, legal and illegal, continued after FÉDON'S REBELLION and the British capture of Trinidad in the mid-1790s. Thousands of slaves imported into Grenada were resold to Trinidad up until the abolition of the SLAVE TRADE in 1808, but Grenadian planters continued to sell their slaves there illegally. Following emancipation in 1834, numerous Grenadians went to Trinidad in search of lucrative employment on the sugar plantations, as unskilled labourers in the early 1900s, and finally in the oil industry since the mid-1900s. Cheap Grenadian labour helped transform the industry to make it Trinidad's primary economic sector, though on occasions Trinidadians have reacted very negatively to the large numbers of Grenadian migrants settled there. Grenadian workers' most immediate contribution was their participation in the oilfield riots, led by Grenadian T U BUTLER. Michael Anthony believed that the riots altered Trinidad and Tobago's history, being not only directly responsible for many immediate industrial, social and political improvements, but indeed for setting the territory on the road to independence! The enthusiasm for the UNITARY STATE proposal in the 1960s, popularly termed 'Go Trinidad', illustrated the true desire of Grenadians to migrate to Trinidad in search of higher-paying jobs.

With numerous Grenadians settling in Trinidad (the 1980 census listed 21,000 born Grenadians living there), it was inevitable that strong ties would develop, and these have aided continuous exchanges between them in areas of culture like SHANGO, STEELBAND, TAMBOO-

BAMBOO, CARNIVAL, RELIGION and CALYPSO. Probably the strongest ties are economic, as is illustrated by Grenada's high volume of imports from Trinidad. Much of Grenada's TRAFFICKING trade in fruits and vegetables goes to Trinidad. Though there has been a marked decrease in Grenadian migration to Trinidad in recent years, the strong bonds continue to play an important part in the development of relations between the two countries. Notable Grenadians in Trinidad over the years include the Mighty SPARROW, Dame Hilda BYNOE, SPIRITUAL BAPTIST Archbishop Elton George Griffith, Mighty Bomber, Lady Ada Date, Delano DeCoteau and Henry Hudson Phillips. Many Afro-Trinidadians can trace their roots back to Grenada.

TURMERIC (*Curcuma longa*) is locally referred to as saffron, a name from medieval times when it was called 'Indian saffron' because it possessed the characteristic smell and colour of true saffron (*Crocus sativus*). Turmeric, a member of the GINGER family, is a tropical perennial herb native to southern Asia and has spread throughout the tropics. Its use dates back thousands of years to India where it has been used as a yellow dye, condiment and folk medicine. It grows from a rhizome or underground stem, and produces brightly coloured, orange-yellow rhizomes that are dug from the ground, boiled, cleaned and dried in the sun. They are then ground to produce an aromatic yellowish powder used as a condiment and an essential ingredient in curry powder. Planted throughout the year, turmeric is only a minor spice in Grenada, selling mainly for local use and to visitors.

TYRREL BAY 12 27N 61 29.2W is a bay on the southern coast of Carriacou off HARVEY VALE. It is home to the winged tree oysters (*Pedalion* spp.) that attach themselves to the roots of the red (*Rhizophora mangle*) and black (*Avicennia germinans*) mangrove trees and other inshore plants. The oyster beds have been exploited for hundreds of years, first by AMERINDIANS and later by Europeans since the 17th century. DU PARQUET, in setting the selling price of Grenada and the Grenadines to FAUDOAS DE CÉRILLAC in 1656, felt that 100,000 *livres* (later reduced to 90,000) was a good price because Carriacou possessed 'pearle oysters', which was incorrect. In 1893 'The Oyster Fishery Ordinance' was passed to 'control and regulate' the oyster fishery at Tyrrel Bay, but continued commercial utilization in the 1900s has led to the depletion of the shellfish population even with the closed season from May to September.

The 200 acre (81 ha) marine ecosystem, a major breeding ground for fin fishes and other aquatic life forms, is owned by the GOG which has included it in the NATIONAL PARK SYSTEM. It is hoped that management of the bay as a 'recreation, education and tourism' facility will protect the natural ecology, yet still allow for the exploitation of the natural resources to aid the development of the island. The protected bay has also been a traditional anchorage for yachts and schooners, one of the many superb anchorages that make Grenada and the Grenadines the YACHTING centre in the southern Caribbean. Tyrrel Bay derives its name from Rear Admiral Richard Tyrrell, British hero of the Seven Years War who served in Grenada in 1763-64 but is rendered Tyrrel Bay/ Tyrrel Street.

U

UNIA The Universal Negro Improvement Association was a popular black consciousness organisation started in 1914 by Jamaican Marcus Garvey (1887-1940) and spread throughout the Americas and Africa. Though a UNIA chapter did not operate in Grenada until 1927 (to 1940), the organisation's newspaper, *Negro World*, was blamed for the political unrest in 1919 by returned World War I veterans and led to its banning. A number of Grenadians held prominent positions in the organisation, including Innis Abel Horsford (president of the New Haven, Connecticut division of the UNIA in 1920-21), Alphonso Jones (director of the UNIA's trucking and delivery service in 1921), George Tobias (b. 1888) and John Sydney De Bourg (b. 1852). Tobias, who worked on the PANAMA CANAL as a clerk before migrating to the US in 1913, joined the UNIA in 1918 after meeting Garvey. He started as an editorial assistant with the *Negro World*, becoming second vice president of the UNIA (1918-19), director of the Black Star Line (1918), and treasurer of the UNIA, Black Star Line and Negro Factories Ltd. (1919-22). In 1922 he was one of three UNIA members indicted with Garvey for mail fraud, but was acquitted in 1923. De Bourg, a teacher, migrated to TRINIDAD in 1881, and subsequently became a union activist with the Trinidad Workingmen's Association. In 1919 he was deported to Grenada because of his involvement in the 1919 dockworkers strike; the colonial government described him as a 'dangerous radical' and a well-known 'agitator'. He travelled to New York in 1919 as a delegate to the UNIA convention from Trinidad. Garvey encouraged him to serve as an international delegate and he was elected to the position of Leader of the Negroes of the Western Provinces of the West Indies and South and Central America. He also earned the titles of Knight Commander of the Nile and Duke of Nigeria and Uganda, and was awarded the Gold Cross of African Redemption. Even though he was considered Garvey's right-hand man, in 1922 he resigned his position, as the UNIA began to feel the pressures of its own popularity, mismanagement and US Federal government investigations. De Bourg sued the UNIA in 1923, along with a number of others, for back salaries and won. He is, however, remembered by many old Garveyites as 'the Grenadian fella who ratted on Garvey' in the 1922 court trial that led to Garvey's conviction in 1925 on mail fraud, incarceration and subsequent deportation to Jamaica in 1927. Garvey, while living in London, visited Grenada in 1937, and gave a speech, 'Man's Rise to Greatness', at the QUEEN'S PARK.

UNITARY STATE With the dissolution of FEDERATION in 1962, a number of unions were sought among the smaller islands as a means to economic development and political INDEPENDENCE. In May 1962 eight islands, referred to as Little Eight, decided to continue with the objectives of federation; Trinidad and Jamaica had opted for independence. At the same time Trinidad's PM Eric Williams proposed the idea of forming a 'mini-federation' linking his independent twin-island state with other smaller islands into a unitary state. These two alternatives presented to Grenadians—Unitary State and Little Eight—made them the most talked about issues of the ELECTIONS of 1962, with Eric GAIRY and Herbert BLAIZE forced to take sides. The idea that there would be free movement of people between the two neighbouring states proved too enticing for Grenadians. The popular movement became known as 'Go Trinidad', signifying Grenadians' real interest in the proposal, and forced politicians to choose the prospect of a union with TRINIDAD rather than Little Eight. Blaize saw a favourable political issue and quickly come out in favour of the Grenada-Trinidad union, while Gairy wavered. The 'Eight Hater', a poet widely published in the WEST INDIAN newspaper, reflected the sentiments at the time concerning Gairy, Little Eight, Unitary State, and the 1962 elections: 'Come early or come late/Uncle is for 'Little Eight'/But Uncle knows that Trinidad/Is what make Grenada glad/...If you see we put Gairy back/That will be his same attack/Make as if for Unitary State/Then sell us out to Little Eight.' Blaize's support for the issue won him the 1962 elections.

Fact-finding missions from both Grenada and Trinidad visited each other, but by 1965 it had become clear that the proposal was doomed, primarily because of Trinidadian opposition to the already large influx of Grenadians in the island. Sir W Arthur Lewis, commenting on the protracted negotiations and Grenada's high hopes for the union, felt that 'Common decency suggests that this poor deluded island should now be released if Trinidad is not prepared to go ahead [with the Unitary State].' CM Blaize's inability to keep his campaign promise and the fact that Eric Gairy reminded the electorate of that failure proved the main issue in the 1967 elections, which returned Gairy and the GULP to power once again. By 1965 the negotiations for the Little Eight union had also failed.[318]

VECO/VAYCO/VECOUR, like SHORTKNEE, shares a similar origin in the rural towns of GOUYAVE and VICTORIA. The veco (<Fr.Cr. vieux croix: 'cross wake') imitates the dress and demeanour of a priest, with black vestments, tall black hat, studded clogs or 'cebos' (hob-nailed shoes), a cross on the tunic, and carries a coffin. The mass probably derives from the 'wake of the cross', a RC ceremony of 'prayer and praise devoted to a saint or deity' from whom assistance is requested. The masqueraders move in a silent funeral march that seems to depict a fight between good (the church) and evil (the devil), with the latter eventually succumbing to the cross and being forced into the coffin. More colourful costumes have been added over the years, as well as the menacing behaviour of the masqueraders. In 1972 the veco bands from the countryside violently confronted a number of 'town' bands, resulting in a bloody confrontation typical of the traditional CARNIVAL battles between warring communities. The belligerent behaviour of the players led to the banning of the mas' and its subsequent rarity. In recent years however there has been a revival of this traditional mas', as bands like the Angels of Death, Victoria Vaycour Band, and Condemners from Hell compete in the annual carnival.

VICARIATE/PRIORY, St. George's A prominent architectural structure located on upper CHURCH STREET, built between 1914 and 1918 to house the RC clergy (the previous Priory was located on lower Church Street next to the Anglican Church). It was constructed under Father Raphael Moss as the residence of the English Dominican fathers who have administered the RC Church since 1901. Its unique architectural style gives it the appearance of a castle rather than a residence. Though built in the twentieth century, it bears some similarity in architectural style to many of the old churches constructed in the 1800s in the Gothic Revival style.

According to Wilfred REDHEAD, the construction of the edifice would not have been accomplished without the financial and physical contributions made by church members who spent evenings carrying stones needed in the building of the Vicariate. An arcade, featuring huge cement columns, surrounds the ground floor. It has an open roof (its original roof was destroyed during

Vicariate, Church Street, St. George's

HURRICANE JANET) and small tower, crowned with crenellated parapets, which commands the town of ST. GEORGE'S. In 1947 it was granted to the Presentation Brothers for the use as the PBC boys secondary school. Today, this imposing structure houses the Presentation Brothers, who teach at the PBC.

VICTORIA The main town and commercial centre in the parish of ST. MARK. Until the early 1900s it was popularly known as Grand Pauvre (<an Island CARIB whom the French in 1649 referred to as Grand Pauvre: 'Great Poor'). The town and Paroisse du Grand Pauvre, was established in 1741, the last bourg to be created under the French. Though referred to as a town, it was more precisely a hamlet, with a small chapel and port landing facility. Its present name is after Queen Victoria, and was applied around the 1860s but took some time to catch on. Though of lesser importance today, it did achieve some prominence between the 1800s and mid-1900s. This is illustrated by its population changes over the past century: 1,524 in 1891; 1,701 in 1901; 1,514 in 1921; 1,436 in 1946; and 2,000 in 1991.

Located on the NW coast, Victoria supports one of Grenada's well-known fishing communities. The town is situated in the St. Mark's Bay, where numerous fishing vessels can usually be seen on BEACHES, and almost every day fishermen can be found 'hauling nets'. It was not until the early 1900s that social amenities began to be established in Victoria, although it was described as 'a township dame fortune has seldom smiled upon.' In 1914 a waterworks was built, and two years later a dispensary opened. In 1952 the town received its first water-carriage latrines, but public pit latrines date to 1918. ELECTRICITY was installed by 1965. Along Queen Street, its main thoroughfare and part of the Western Main Road, can be found churches, general stores, the Nutmeg Pool, a hotel, and government buildings, including a police station and post office. Surrounding the town are historic and cultural sites, including Amerindian PETROGLYPHS and old ESTATES. Like the other towns on the coast, surrounding steep hills covered with lush vegetation rise abruptly from the sea.

VINCENT (fl. 1664-68) was the French governor of Grenada between 1664 and 1668/69. The captain of the Regiment of Orleans, he accompanied the new lieutenant general of the French West Indies, Prouville de Tracy, to take control of the islands for the French WEST INDIA COMPANY. Vincent arrived in Grenada in November 1664 and was installed as the new governor, replacing de Cérillac's son who was subsequently ordered back to France. Vincent was charged with establishing the administration of the WIC following its take over and eventual purchase of Grenada from FAUDOAS DE CÉRILLAC.

In 1666 France entered the Second Dutch War on the side of the Dutch against England. Fearing attack by the British, 'Governor Vincent considered discretion the better part of valour, for he had only 60 men capable of bearing arms, and he ordered a general retreat into the mountain fastnesses of Grenada.' Governor Vincent, according to du Tertre, 'wanted to gather some of the laurels which our Frenchmen had won in the Antilles,' and in August 1666 sent an officer along with twenty-five volunteers in the ship the *Gilles Gaspert* to Tobago to attempt its capture from the British, who had captured it from the Dutch in 1665. The small British garrison was tricked into surrendering and the French maintained 'a small garrison there which stayed until May 1667 and torched the fort when it returned to Grenada.' Governor Vincent directed the construction of Grenada's first siege fort, Fort Royal (see FORT GEORGE), in 1667 from the plans of François Blondel.[95]

VIOLENCE/TERRORISM Organised violent acts against or by the state did not become social and political concerns until the 1970s with the rise of BLACK POWER and the possible threat it represented. (Yet political intimidation had become ever present since SKYRED in 1951; some might insist that it dates to SLAVERY, or even earlier with the French extermination of the Island CARIBS.) To control what he saw as an unmistakable threat to his government in the 1970s, Premier GAIRY responded with the formation of the MONGOOSE GANG and POLICE AIDES to protect 'law abiding citizens'. He also passed legislation to counter the growing militant political threat.

By the early 1970s the rhetoric between the GULP government and the opposition, led by the NEW JEWEL MOVEMENT, had escalated to incendiary levels. The NJM's manifesto 'We'll Be Free in '73', the 'People's Indictment' of the GULP government on 4 November 1973, and an article 'From Congress to Power', which appeared in the 9 November 1973 issue of *The New Jewel* newsletter, contained veiled threats of subversion, to say the least. Premier Gairy responded that he was going to 'cinderise' the opposition, subsequently resulting in BLOODY SUNDAY and BLOODY MONDAY. The DUFFUS COMMISSION Report concluded that 'instead of tolerance, resort was had to terror and this, by early 1974, became reciprocal.'

What began as isolated acts of terror, primarily in the countryside, mushroomed into civil unrest between 1973 and 1974, with violent repercussions throughout the 1970s and 1980s. A number of violent acts committed by the Police Aides against members of the NJM and supporters led to retaliation against police stations, police officers and staunch supporters of the GULP. By 1979 both the GOG and the opposition claimed that they had suffered political violence at the hands of the other. There were reports of brutality, shootings and 'missing persons' like the acting Commissioner of Police Irie Bishop who disappeared in December 1978. A number of individuals had in fact been killed: Minister of Agriculture BELMAR, Rupert Bishop, Jeremiah Richardson, and Alister Strachan. A number of violent crimes during the reign of the GULP remain unsolved.

The PEOPLE'S REVOLUTIONARY GOVERNMENT, seizing power in 1979, ushered in escalated acts of political violence as dissenters were placed under 'heavy manners'. It is ironic that some of the dissenters were former members of militant (and clandestine) groups that had supported the NJM and its causes during the 1970s. Though no direct evidence was ever presented, the PRG claimed that many of the 'counter-revolutionary' acts were externally financed, pointing the finger at the US's Central Intelligence Agency. To dissuade covert internal opposition to its rule (which had become violent), the PRG in 1979 passed the Terrorism Prevention Act, which made detention of 'counter-revolutionaries' possible without due process of the law. Groups and individuals, predominantly in the countryside, were the most prepared to fight the PRG and its military control.

What resulted were bombings, shoot-outs, arrests, beatings and killings by both sides. Some of the more brutal acts included the JUNE 19, 1980 bombing at the QUEEN'S PARK and the bloody 18 November 1980 incident that left five young militia recruits in St. Patrick dead. A number of individuals opposed to the PRG were killed in shoot-outs with the PEOPLE'S REVOLUTIONARY ARMY and MILITIA, the most notable being Strachan Phillip of St. Paul's, a former member of the PRA, and the Muslims Habib Ali and Ayub of St. Patrick, both former members of PM Bishop's security detail. The desire to silence all vocal opposition by both the GULP and PRG regimes led them inevitably to violent acts against citizens, some of whom were willing to retaliate, thus creating a cycle of violence.[94, 252, 353]

W

WELLS, Dr William (1825-1890) was a prominent medical practitioner, one of a handful of doctors who battled against the CHOLERA epidemic of 1854. In 1858 he became the first government medical practitioner for St. David's parish, where he resided. Wells' appointment led to his resignation from the General Assembly, a position to which he was elected in 1856; he was later nominated to the Legislative Council. In 1862 and again in 1876 he was elected to the Assembly, holding the position of Speaker during that period. When the legislature voted to repeal the OLD REPRESENTATIVE SYSTEM constitution in 1876, Wells was one of three members to cast dissenting votes, protesting that the proposed CROWN COLONY system 'sets aside the undoubted rights of the people to have a voice in the making of the laws by which they are ruled, and particularly in the imposing of taxes.' A portrait of Dr Wells is displayed in the GRENADA NATIONAL MUSEUM.[55]

Dr William Wells

WEST INDIA COMPANY (WIC) administered all French territories in the West Indies between 1664 and 1674. The Compagnie des Indies Occidentales was established by Royal Charter in 1664 under the direction of Jean-Baptiste Colbert (French minister of finance). He believed that the transfer of the French Caribbean territories 'into the hands of a strong company, which would be able to equip a number of vessels in order to colonize and furnish them with all the merchandise of which they had need' would expand French trade in the region and displace the Dutch who had monopolised the trade to date. In 1664 Prouville de Tracy, the representative of the Company, arrived in Grenada. The inhabitants were described as 'abandoned and miserable' due to deprivations caused by the administration of FAUDOAS DE CÉRILLAC and his sons. VINCENT was immediately installed as the new GOVERNOR, and the authority of the Company was established despite de Cérillac's refusal to accept the transfer (in 1665 de Cérillac finally signed a contract handing over control of the islands to the Compagnie for the sum of 100,000 *livres*).

Grenada, since its settlement in 1649, had not fared well under proprietary rule. The struggle to subjugate the Island CARIBS and its own internal political conflicts and mismanagement led to its stagnation. Its 1656 population of 300 was halved by 1664 due to the emigration of many settlers. Under Gov. Vincent there was a renewed effort to develop the island. The island's close proximity to South America added to its attractiveness as a base for establishing contraband trade with the Spanish. New settlers arrived in the colony, but the entry of France into the Second Dutch War (1665-1667) in 1666 on the side of the Dutch against England, placed everything on hold.

At the negotiations for the Treaty of Breda in 1667 the French at St. Christopher proposed to the British that Grenada be exchanged for the British section of that island. Though Gov. Willoughby of Barbados considered it 'no ill bargain', the offer did not appear to be a serious one. Grenada's development became 'Colbert's chief interest' as a result of de Tracy's endorsement, and in 1667 a small fort, Fort Royal, was built to help protect the island. Grenada's prospects were linked to those of the WIC, which experienced a number of problems, not the least of which was financial. Revolts in the larger islands caused by the insufficient supply of needed merchandise, high export taxes, war with England and the United Netherlands, and corrupt administration forced the directors of the WIC to rescind their trade monopoly, allowing private French ships to trade with the islands. Heavily in debt, the WIC never recovered, and Colbert was forced to dissolve it in 1674. Though the French had succeeded in increasing French shipping in the islands; it would be many years before the Dutch would be replaced, especially in Grenada. The islands of the French Caribbean, including Grenada, became French colonies thereafter under the administration of the ÎLES DU VENT.[95, 221]

WEST INDIAN One of Grenada's most popular and significant newspapers of the twentieth century. The WI was established by T A MARRYSHOW, 'CFP' RENWICK and others in 1915, and became the voice of representative government. With the slogan 'The West Indies Must Be West Indian,' Marryshow became an ardent campaigner for FEDERATION. He was the newspaper's first managing editor, wasting no opportunity to attack the governor, administrator or any official of the detested CROWN COLONY government. The newspaper was Marryshow's personal mouthpiece as he criticised the colonial administration with his doggerel, editorials and articles, becoming the biggest thorn in the government's side. In its first year circulation was estimated at 1,600, one hundred of which were foreign sales.

After almost twenty years of single-handedly producing a daily newspaper, Marryshow sold the WI in 1934 due to his deteriorating health and financial difficulties. In 1939 'CFP' purchased the paper and Marryshow was again editor until 1940, when he left. In 1940 the West Indian Printing Co. Ltd. took over the publication of the paper, adding the motto 'The Right Alone Is Right, The Wrong Is Always Wrong.' The WI continued for many years as a major newspaper on the island, though it had lost its former popularity. In 1969 the WI, long critical of Eric Gairy and the GULP, was acquired by the GULP government and became 'the propaganda media machine of the Gairy Government and for the Grenada United Labour Party... and was fully recognized as such at the time of Gairy's overthrow' in 1979. Beginning in 1974 it became a weekly publication, reducing its four issues per week to one.

Following the coup d'état and the installation of the PEOPLE'S REVOLUTIONARY GOVERNMENT in 1979, the WI became the *Free West Indian* (FWI), 'The National Newspaper of Grenada'. The PRG's closure of the independent TORCHLIGHT newspaper in 1979 left the FWI the only newspaper in the islands. Schoenhals described the FWI as 'of such poor quality and appeared so infrequently' that Grenadians depended for their news from foreign sources. By May 1983 the situation had become so acute that the FWI only appeared once in that month due to the breakdown of its printing press. The news content reported was also questionable since 'by mid-1980 the ratio of propaganda to solid news rose to alarming levels.' The *Free West Indian* ceased to appear following the internal coup in October 1983, bringing 'Marryshow's newspaper' to an inglorious end.[303, 310, 353]

WESTERHALL RUM DISTILLERY, St. David, utilises modern technologies and methods for the production, or rather blending, of a variety of RUMS. Westerhall estate, comprising almost 1,000 acres (400 ha),

Westerhall Rum Distillery showing disused waterwheel and aqueduct system

was established around the mid-1700s and developed exclusively as a sugar estate under the French. Like many estates in 1795, it was badly damaged during FÉDON'S REBELLION. In 1911 the government purchased 395 acres (160 ha) as part of its LAND SETTLEMENT and sold plots on the Westerhall Land Settlement. By 1929 the larger estate had been divided into two smaller estates, producing COCOA, COCONUTS and LIMES. The present Westerhall Estate and Rum Distillery has inherited the over 200-year-old legacy. The two broken and crumbling water mills and aqueduct, have not been in use since the late 1800s. The huge dam that supplied the water which powered the waterwheels overflows and runs through a small stream across the estate. A stone dates one of the buildings to 1800, the date the distillery acknowledges it began 'distilling rum the traditional way'. After the decline of sugar in the late 1800s, the estate cultivated coconuts and cocoa, with the remnants of a boucan and cocoa trees illustrative of that change. It presently blends and bottles rum, including the well-known Jack Iron—from imported raw materials.[144, 145]

WILD INDIANS/CLOWNS A historic 'pretty mas" at CARNIVAL that dates to the late 1800s. It is also common in Carriacou. It comprises small groups of men, colourfully dressed and identified by their conspicuous headpieces, or less commonly, roped locks. Their colourful costumes comprise roped or cloth skirts, rope for hair and an assortment of beads, earrings, bracelets and nose rings adorning their bodies. Upon their heads are towering head-dresses of masked ships decorated with colourful streamers waving in the wind (similar to those once worn by maypole dancers). Their bodies are covered with patches of paint to imitate the historical representation of the 'wild' or 'red' South American Indian. Bells, attached to their ankles, tinkle as they stomp around or 'chip' through the streets with the high-pitched sounds of their whistles floating through the air. They carry painted wooden swords or sticks. A once common feature of the band was a queen known as Eloina, but in fact 'she' was a man dressed as a woman. Many groups of wild Indians once ran through the streets in serpentine formation, howling at onlookers with their characteristic mix of wildness and timidity.

Wild Indian masquerade

WILLIAMS A runaway slave from Grenada who sued his employer in a London court to recover wages. Either in 1797 or prior to that date, Williams escaped SLAVERY by leaving the island and taking up employment on a British merchant ship. He was one of many slaves who were able to either leave the island by commandeering small boats and sailing to neighbouring islands, or by signing on aboard merchant ships. In December 1797 Williams arrived back in Grenada aboard the *Holderness* and was claimed by his owner, George Hardtman (owner of Mt. Hardtman, later Mt. Hartman estate), as a runaway. Negotiations between Williams, Hardtman, and Captain Brown of the *Holderness*, resulted in Brown paying the thirty joes manumission fee to have Williams continue as a seaman. Brown and Williams agreed that the latter would work off the manumission fee by working for three years at stipulated wages.

Once the ship returned to London, Williams, with the help of legal counsel, sued Brown for damages in the amount that had been docked from his wages, claiming that the agreement in Grenada was made under duress. In 1802 the court returned a verdict against Williams, but it is the fact that he was able to sue Brown at all that is fascinating. In his ruling, Lord Alvanley opined that 'if such a contract as this is to be sustained, I tremble at the consequences; for if this is allowed the masters of ships may consider themselves at liberty to purchase the freedom of as many Negroes in the West Indies as they may think proper and take engagements from them to serve for life.'

WILLIAMS, Sir Daniel Charles (b. 1935) A lawyer and politician who became the country's fourth GG on 8 August 1996, following the resignation of Sir Reginald PALMER. After attending primary and secondary schools in Grenada and teaching for six years, Sir Daniel migrated to the UK in 1959. He attended London University, earning a LLB degree and was called to the Bar, Lincoln's Inn, in 1968. He returned to Grenada and practised law, and served as a magistrate in St. Lucia. He was elected to the House of Representatives as a candidate for the NEW NATIONAL PARTY in 1984, serving as a minister of government and attorney general under PM BLAIZE. His appointment as GOVERNOR GENERAL was controversial, following the charge by Opposition Leader BRIZAN concerning Sir Daniel's possible political impartiality. Individuals who are apolitical, or at least have a history of no open political alignments, have traditionally held the office of the GG. He received the GCMG in 1996, and is also a Queen's Council. Other activities include his membership and chairmanship of various boards. He is the author of a number of publications.[4]

WINDWARD, Carriacou One of the larger villages on the island. It is situated on the NE coast within Watering Bay or Baye-à-l'eau. It is historically noted for its BOAT BUILDING industry, the oldest on the island. Local history maintains that sometime in the early nineteenth century some shipwrights arrived and settled at Windward where their descendants can still be found. Families with Scottish names like McLawrence, McGillivay, McIntosh, Enoe and McFarlene have persisted among a small group of 'fair-skinned' people who still practise the craft of their ancestors (see SCOTTISH HERITAGE). The importance of trade to Carriacou makes Windward, with its once successful boat building industry, a major contributor to the islands' economy. To the north are Petite Carenage Bay and beach, and mangroves that support many BIRDS. To the south is the village of Dover with its historic ruins. PETITE MARTINIQUE, situated 2.5 miles (4 km) NE of Windward, is connected to Carriacou only by sea. The two islands, especially the region of Windward, have shared similar historical and cultural experiences.

WINDWARD ISLANDS An administrative grouping of islands in the Eastern Caribbean, which was established in 1833 by the British colonial government, with Barbados, Grenada, Tobago and St. Vincent and the Grenadines. A governor was stationed in Barbados and a Lt. Gov. was appointed for each island, with responsibility for the direct administration of the government. St. Lucia and Trinidad were added in 1838, but the latter left in 1842. The Confederation Riots in Barbados in 1876, following an attempt to federate the Eastern Caribbean, resulted in the establishment of that island as a separate territory with its own governor. In 1885 the seat of the Government of the Windward Islands removed to Grenada. In 1889 Tobago was united with Trinidad, forming the present twin-island republic. In 1940 Dominica, a former member of the Colony of the Leeward Islands, was added to complete the final four members. The Government of the Windward Islands was dissolved in 1959 following the islands' integration into the FEDERATION. The four islands are still referred to as the Windward Islands and have developed close economic, cultural and historical ties as a result. Though the term has little geographical applicability today, it is still used to group Dominica, Grenada, St. Lucia and St. Vincent for purposes of aggregation. In the field of sports, especially CRICKET, the members of the Windward Islands team up against the other Caribbean countries.

Y

YACHTING Over the past three decades Grenada, C&PM have come to be known as a 'yachters' paradise'. Grenada and the islands of the GRENADA GRENADINES are dotted with many small coves, sheltered bays and marinas that provide safe anchorage to yachts, especially during the HURRICANE season. The opening of the Grenada Yacht Club (GYC) in 1954 has been instrumental in the promotion of yachting in Grenada over the years. Since the 1960s GYC has promoted sailing through its many yacht races, especially the Easter Regatta Yacht Race (est. 1961). In 1997 GYC opened a new dock (capable of berthing thirty small to medium-sized yachts), with watering and fuelling facilities. Though the LAGOON remains a favourite venue for yachts sailing through the islands, the yachting centre is concentrated along the southern coast, predominantly at Mt. Hartman and Prickly Bay where yachts can be chartered for trips to many of the small islands in the Grenadines, a favourite spot being SANDY ISLAND. Today, almost every month witnesses a sailing competition or festival, attracting yachts from the Caribbean and North America (over 3,000 yachts annually); the islands presently host six major annual sailing events. In an attempt to promote TOURISM and business, there has been a push by HOTELS and marinas to encourage visitors with yachts and others who desire the adventures of sailing. In 2000 the GOG passed a Yachting Act to help promote the sector which has become an important sub-sector of the TOURISM industry.[93]

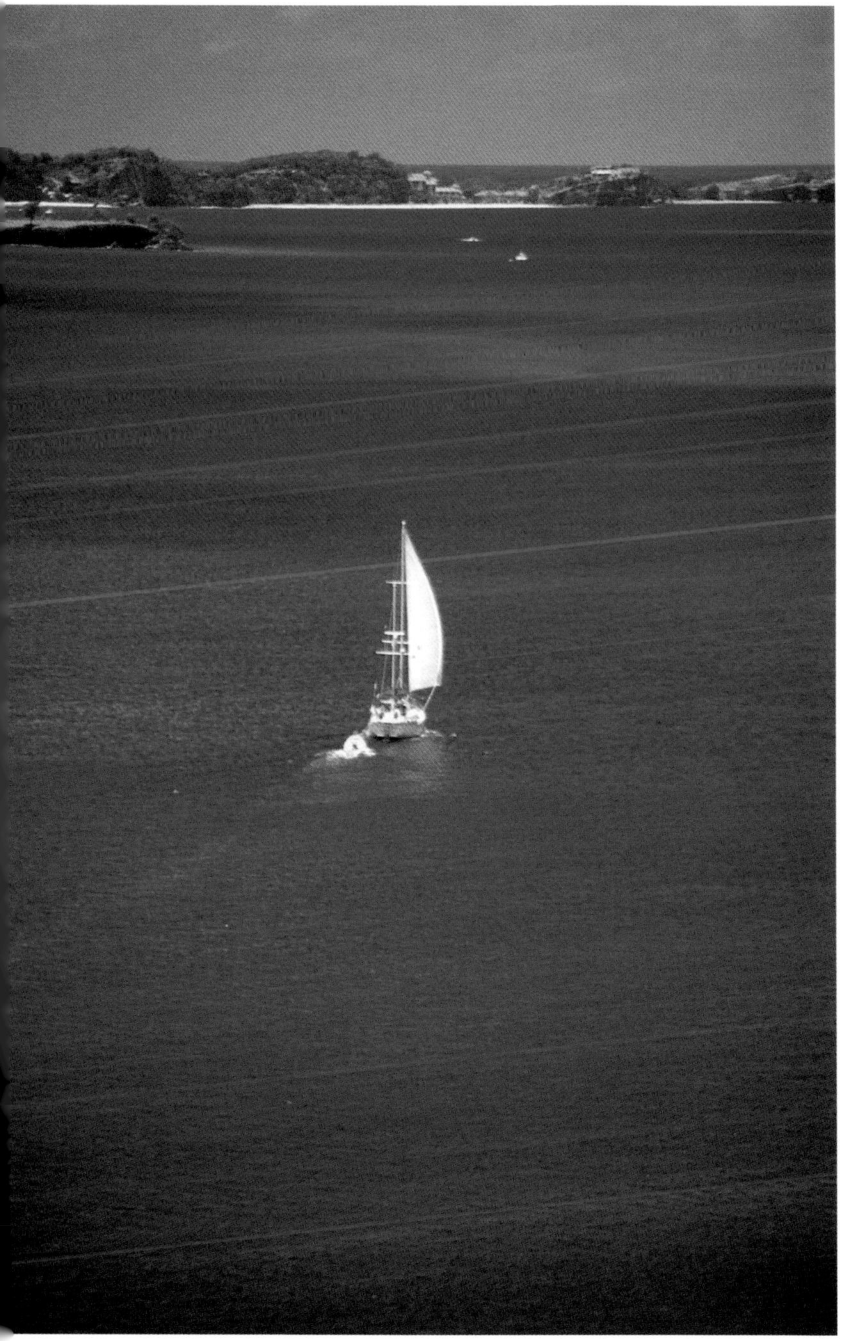

Yachting along Grenada's southern coast

YAMS (*Dioscorea* spp.) are high-fibre tubers that are eaten as vegetables. There are many varieties of yams grown for their starchy root tubers. The yam is a climbing vine, native to the tropics, and grows to about 50 ft (15 m), producing tubers as large as 20 lb (9 kg), with a diversity of textural and colour characteristics. They are grown throughout the year in many backyards and KITCHEN GARDENS. Their rough skin and minimal water content allow them to be stored for months without losing their taste. They are popularly served as cooked vegetables boiled, baked or fried. They can also be pounded and used as a meal.

The species *D. deltoidea* yields the chemical diosgenin, an anti-fertility agent used in the manufacture of oral contraceptives. Common species include the West African white or Guinea yam (*D. rotundata*), the South American cush-cush yam (*D. trifida*), the Southeast Asian water yam (*D. alata*), and atouta (<Fr.Cr. à-tout-temps: 'at all times' because of availability) or yellow yam (*D. cayenensis*). The English word yam (like Fr. *igname*, Sp. *ñame*, and Pg. *inhame*),

according to Allsopp, is derived from a similar African word common to various African groups and frequently used among the slaves 'with the basic meaning "food"'. Mashed yam was a common food for the slaves aboard slave ships as well as during SLAVERY on the estates.[346]

YAWS was one of the most dreaded DISEASES to afflict the slave and peasant populations throughout the eighteenth to twentieth centuries. Together with elephantiasis (filariasis) and Guinea worms (*Dracunculus medinensis*), yaws (?<Is. Car. *yaya*: 'a sore') was most likely brought from Africa during SLAVERY. It is a contagious bacterial infection caused by a spirochete (*Treponema pertenue*) and characterised by 'destructive distemper, ulcers and lesions' that can disfigure the body. In the 1800s it became endemic, forcing the government to take drastic measures to eradicate this seemingly uncontrollable disease. (This probably led to the expression 'bad like yaws': unruly or uncontrollable behaviour; but to 'have cocobay (<Twi *kokobé*: 'leprosy' or skin covered with itchy sores) on top of yaws' is to have more trouble heaped onto an already bad situation.)

Cures included FOLK MEDICINES (like zèb-a-pik or bitter bush), Grainger's castor bulb decoction, and the chemicals antimony and mercury, which in many cases led to the death of yaws sufferers. HOT SPRINGS, believed by many peasants to possess healing powers, provided psychological if not physical relief. Between 1882 and 1927 a Yaws Hospital, occupying the old Ordnance Store at FORT GEORGE and later the Nurses' Hostel site, treated the many patients who were admitted from across the islands; clinics in many towns and villages operated into the 1950s. In 1883 the Yaws Prevention Ordinance practically forced victims of the disease to seek treatment, and ESTATES were compelled by the government to establish yaws houses to isolate victims of the disease.

Though children and the predominant black peasantry were severely afflicted with yaws, the EAST INDIANS proved highly susceptible, most probably due to their poor diets and deplorable living conditions. An island-wide anti-yaws campaign, which began in 1956, along with the improved living conditions of the peasantry and the extension of primary health care facilities, led to the eradication of the disease by 1960. Yaws Bay at Bogles, Carriacou, and Yaws Bay, St. David, were probably so named because they were popular bathing places for yaws sufferers because sea water was believed to cure the disease. Among its advocates was Dr George Patterson who believed that 'it helps with the cure, gives them something to pass the time, and conserves the fresh water.[55]

YELLOW FEVER According to Dr CHISHOLM in the 1780s, yellow fever 'sometimes appears, but observes no season.' While the debate over Chisholm's diagnosis of the epidemic of 1793 as BOULAM FEVER raged in academic journals, by 1794 'yellow fever raged [in Grenada] with dreadful violence. Every house was the abode of death.' Yellow fever is an acute, infectious disease characterised by fever, jaundice and vomiting, and though unknown at the time, was transmitted by the ubiquitous mosquito (*Aädes aegypti*). While the virulence of the disease benefited Toussaint Louverture and his rebellious former slaves in their fight against the British, Spanish and French in Haiti, it wreaked havoc throughout the region and attacked 'men long resident; young and old, temperate and intemperate, were alike affected by it [in Grenada].' The outbreak of FÉDON'S REBELLION in 1795 only compounded the situation, and though the disease threatened the rebels, it also aided them in their fight against the British whose unseasoned troops 'dropped like flies.'

The staggering losses experienced by British troops in the Caribbean as a result of yellow fever forced the British government to organise 'soldiers less susceptible to the climate', and in Grenada the LOYAL BLACK RANGERS were formed in April 1795 (and the West India Regiments throughout the Caribbean). The fever raged throughout the rebellion as the British fought the visible and invisible enemies, not knowing which would eventually overcome them. Among its most celebrated victims were Brigadier-General Lindsay, who after only ten days on the island commanding the British offensive against the rebels, contracted yellow fever and in 'a state of delirium shot himself.' Another was Captain Josias Rogers, captain of the ship *Quebec*, who died in April 1795 and is memorialised in a plaque at the ST. GEORGE'S ANGLICAN CHURCH for coming to the relief of the island.

Even after the British had quashed the rebellion, Dr James McGrigor, who served as a doctor during the uprising, commented that yellow fever still 'presented itself with overwhelming force, and with hideous mortality, being more fatal to the army by far than the enemy. The number that died of yellow fever was four times that of those who fell by the bullet and the bayonet.' He added that the St. George's coffee-house refrain, 'Who died since yesterday?' had become a sort of greeting. Between June 1796 and February 1797 some 1,154 soldiers died from the disease while awaiting orders to leave Grenada. A memorial erected in 1799 by the Grenada Legislature reads 'In remembrance of those brave men... The names of our fellow-Colonists who died at that eventful period, either in the field of battle, or of diseases produced by excessive fatigue, are too numerous to be inscribed within the compass of this stone...'Yellow fever was eradicated from Grenada in 1956 and in Carriacou soon thereafter.[55]

YORK HOUSE is located on CHURCH STREET opposite the ST. GEORGE'S RC CHURCH. As the PARLIAMENT building it is home to both the Houses of Parliament and the Judiciary (see JUDICIAL SYSTEM). The legislature previously met at the Court House, located on the site of the present PREBYTERIAN CHURCH and then next to the present HOSPITAL following the fire of 1772. The present building is one of a few public buildings of the colonial era, since the island's small size precluded the development of extensive government buildings until the mid-1900s. York House was originally a domestic residence owned by Jean de Ponthieu (a French RC who converted to Protestantism and was a member of the General Council), but was purchased for £1,420 currency by the Grenada government in 1801 upon his death; it was remodelled between 1802 and 1807.

York House

It derived its name sometime after 1801 from Frederick Augustus, the Duke of York and the second son of King George III who referred to his residence as York House. The Houses of Parliament, when in session, meet on the upper floor, while the Supreme Court occupies the lower floor. Being one of the largest buildings on the island, York House functioned as a concert, meeting and exhibition hall, hosting balls, dances, church bazaars, fund-raisers and travelling exhibitions from the UK and the US beginning in the mid-1800s. Until the construction of the Anglican Church Hall, Church Street, in 1915 and other large buildings thereafter, it was the primary social centre. It is a plain rectangular brick building, the upper floor dominated by huge arched windows. Brown string-courses and quoins accent the grey bricks. The lower floor has an arcade facing the street. Numerous repairs over the years have altered the original structure, for example the roof, now made of corrugated iron, was once covered with fish-scale tiles. The Grenada Registry, located within the compound, was built in 1780 and is an excellent example of Caribbean Georgian architecture, with its huge windows and high ceiling. The Magistrates' Court is housed in a newer building on the compound. York House was heavily damaged by HURRICANE IVAN which tore off its entire roof. The legislature was forced to find alternate places to convene until York House was repaired.[282]

YORUBA One of Nigeria and Benin's major ethnic groups, which, as a result of SLAVERY and INDENTURED IMMIGRATION, has had a most noticeable and enduring influence on the Grenadian cultural environment. This is due predominantly to the importation of African indentured immigrants between 1849 and 1865, with over 1,000 supposedly coming from Ijesha, Nigeria, via Sierra Leone. Also from the seventeenth to nineteenth centuries, especially in the early 1800s as a result of wars among the Yoruba, the coast of present-day Nigeria became a primary source of slaves. Most conspicuous is the religious expression of SHANGO and its incorporation into a number of folk RELIGIONS and congregations such as Shango Baptists, and the revolving credit system called SUSU. The Yoruba people have passed on, albeit in present altered forms, folklore, FOLK DANCES, PROVERBS & SAYINGS, songs, folk tales and LANGUAGE to Grenadians. But these surviving influences, though connected with a demoralising and brutalised past, have renewed, for some Grenadians, a sense of identity and connection to a prized heritage (see AFRICAN HERITAGE).

A number of words in the Grenadian vocabulary are derived from Yoruba, among them bubu (*buburu*: 'bad or evil'), akara ('an oily cake made from beans ground and fried'), obi seed (KOLA NUT), saraka/salacca ('charity, alms; associated with honouring the dead'), Orisha ('divinity, deity'), chuts ('expression of annoyance or defiance'), and DADA HAIR.[132, 358]

YWCA The Grenada branch of the Young Women's Christian Association was registered in 1889, with Lottie Wells as its first president. It claims to be the oldest YWCA or 'Y' in the Caribbean. Members met in each other's homes for Bible reading until 1908, when they acquired a building on the corner of Scott and Herbert BLAIZE Streets; the building still functions as its office. Among the 'Y's' most noted presidents were Pansy ROWLEY and Phyllis Osbone. For many years Pansy Rowley organised and conducted classes in public speaking, leadership skills, art, sewing, etc. The 'Y' became for women what the GRENADA LITERARY LEAGUE was for men. Branches were established across the island, in towns and villages. Under the presidency of Phyllis Osborne, the 'Y' in 1958 started the YWCA Nutrition Council, which organised a school lunch programme in St. George's and was the forerunner of the Grenada Inter-Church Council for Development (est. 1963). The Council, which brought together individuals of the four major established churches, evolved into the Grenada Council of Churches (est. 1975). The present association focuses on youth, teaching art through its long-established Art Club. The 'Y' is affiliated with the international YWCA and the Grenada National Organization of Women.

References

1 *Acts of the Privy Council* (1966) Colonial Series, vols 4-6, ed. J Munro, Kraus, Nendeln, Liechtenstein.

2 Adkin, M (1981) *Urgent Fury: The Battle for Grenada.* Lexington Books, Lexington, Mass.

3 Alexis, F (1992) *Grenada: The Constitution and You.* UWI/US Agency for International Development Caribbean Justice Improvement Project, Barbados.

4 Alexis, F (1997) 'Confrontation in Grenada: Suspending the Opposition Leader for Criticizing the Queen's Appointment of the Governor General'. *The Parliamentarian: Journal of the Parliaments of the Commonwealth* 78, 2: 137-139.

5 Allsopp, R (1996) *Dictionary of Caribbean English Usage.* Oxford Univ. Press, Oxford.

6 Amnesty International (2003) *The Grenada 17: Last of the Cold War Prisoners.* Retrieved 10 November 2005 from http://web.amnesty.org/library/index/ENGAMR320012003.

7 Andrews, KR (1978) *The Spanish Caribbean: Trade and Plunder, 1530-1630.* Yale Univ. Press, New Haven.

8 Anon (1975) *L'Histoire de l'isle de Grenade en Amérique, 1649-59.* Ed. J Petitjean Roget, Presses de l'Université de Montréal, Montréal.

9 Archives Nationales (1984) *Guide des sources de l'histoire de l'Amérique Latine et des Antilles dans les Archives Françaises.* Archives Nationales, Paris.

10 Archives Nationales (1992) *Voyage aux Îles d'Amérique: Exposition organisée par la direction des Archives de France.* Archives Nationales, Paris.

11 Arculus, R (1976) 'Geology and Geochemistry of the Alkali Basalt-Andesite Association of Grenada, Lesser Antilles Arc'. *Bulletin of the Geological Society of America* 87: 612-624.

12 Ashby, T (1984) 'Fédon's Rebellion'. *Journal of the Society for Army Historical Research* 62, 251: 155-168; 252: 227-235; 63, 256 (1985): 220-235.

13 Aymer, PL (1997) *Uprooted Women: Migrant Domestics in the Caribbean.* Praeger, Westport, Conn.

14 Babb, T, Parks, L, Neese, H, Hughes, D & Berlin, J (1984). *Agriculture in Grenada: A Critical Assessment.* Development Alternatives, Washington, DC.

15 Baker, EC (1968) *A Guide to Records in the Windward Islands.* Published for the Univ. of the West Indies by Blackwell, Oxford.

16 Baptiste, F (2002) 'Gairy and the General Strike of 1951: As Gleaned from British and US Sources'. Grenada Country Conference, UWI. http://www.uwichill.edu.bb/bnccde/grenada/conference/papers/Baptiste.html

17 Barclay, C (1994) *Red Rum Punch: Forging into the First Post-Communist Quagmire with my Partner Uncle Sam.* Cross Cultural Publications, Notre Dame, Indiana.

18 Bell, HJ (1880) *Obeah: Witchcraft in the West Indies.* Negro University Press, Westview, Conn., 1970.

19 Bishop, M (1982) *Forward Ever! Three Years of the Grenada Revolution.* Pathfinder Press, Sydney.

20 Bishop, M (1983a) *Maurice Bishop: Selected Speeches 1979-81.* Casa de las Américas, Havana.

21 Bishop, M (1983b) *Maurice Bishop Speaks: The Grenada Revolution 1979-83.* Pathfinder Press, New York.

22 'The Bishop Killers: Why They Did it and What Happened to Them'. *The Nation*, December 1986, Barbados.

23 Blockstein, DE (1991) 'Population Declines of the Endangered Endemic Birds in Grenada, WI'. *Bird Conservation International* 1: 83-91.

24 Blockstein, DE & Hardy, JW (1989) 'The Grenada Dove is a Distinct Species'. *Auk* 106: 339-340.

25 Boucher, P (1992) *Cannibal Encounters: Europeans and Island Caribs, 1492-1763.* Johns Hopkins Univ. Press, Baltimore.

26 Breese, Charlotte (1999) *Hutch.* Bloomsbury, London.

27 Brierley, JS (1974) *Small Farming in Grenada, W. I.* Univ. of Manitoba, Winnipeg.

28 Brierley, JS (1978) 'Fragmentation of Holdings: A Study of Small Farms in Grenada'. *Tropical Agriculture* 55, 2: 135-140.

29 Brierley, JS (1985) 'West Indian Kitchen Gardens: A Historical Perspective with Current Insights from Grenada'. *Food and Nutrition Bulletin* 7, 3: 52-60.

30 Brierley, JS (1992) 'A Study of Land Distribution and the Demise of Grenada's Estate Farming System, 1940-88'. *Journal of Rural Studies* 8, 1: 67-84.

31 Brinkley, FK (1971a) *This -- is Carriacou.* Carenage Press, St. George's, Grenada.

32 Brinkley, FK (1971b) *This -- is Grenada.* Carenage Press, St. George's, Grenada.

33 Brinkley, FK (1978) 'An Analysis of the 1750 Carriacou Census'. *Caribbean Quarterly* 24, 1/2: 44-60.

34 Brizan, G (1979) *The Grenadian Peasantry and Social Revolution, 1930-51.* Institute of Social and Economic Research, UWI, Kingston, Jamaica.

35 Brizan, G (1998) *Grenada: Island of Conflict.* Macmillan Caribbean, Oxford.

36 Brizan, G (2002) *Brave Young Grenadians - Loyal British Subjects: Our People in the First and Second World Wars*. [The author, St. George's, Grenada].
37 Brizan, G & Brizan, K (2001) *Grenada: Fortitude and the Human Condition*. Paria Publishing, Trinidad.
38 Buffong, J (1992) *Under the Silk Cotton Tree: A Novel*. The Women's Press, London.
39 Buffong, J (1995) *Snowflakes in the Sun*. The Women's Press, London.
40 Buffong, J & Payne, N (1990) *Jump-Up-and-Kiss-Me: Two Stories From Grenada*. The Women's Press, London.
41 Buisseret, D (1980) *Historic Architecture of the Caribbean*. Heinemann, London.
42 Bullen, A (1968) 'Field Comments on the Skull Excavated in 1967 at Calivigny Island, Grenada, West Indies'. In *Proceedings of the 2nd International Congress for the Study of Pre-Colombian Cultures in the Lesser Antilles*. Barbados Museum and Historical Society, St. Ann's Garrison, Barbados.
43 Bullen, A & Bullen, RP (1968) 'Salvage Excavations at Calivigny Island, Grenada: A Problem in Typology'. In *Proceedings of the 2nd International Congress for the Study of Pre-Colombian Cultures in the Lesser Antilles*. Barbados Museum and Historical Society, St. Ann's Garrison, Barbados.
44 Bullen, R (1964) 'Archaeology of Grenada, West Indies'. *Contributions of the Florida State Museum*, 11, Univ. of Florida, Gainesville.
45 Butler, P, Joseph, A & Lazarus, BA (1992) *Promoting Love for the Grenada Dove, Grenada's Conservation Education Campaign*. RARE Centre for Tropical Conservation, Pennsylvania.
46 Bynoe, H (1996) *I Woke at Dawn*. Hanz On Publishers, Port-of-Spain, Trinidad.
47 Caliste, C (1989) *The Mermaid Wakes: Paintings of a Caribbean Isle*. Macmillan Caribbean, London.
48 Campbell, H (1980) 'Rastafarians in the Eastern Caribbean'. *Caribbean Quarterly* 26, 4: 42-61.
49 Carew, J (1994) *Ghosts in Our Blood With Malcolm in Africa, England, and the Caribbean*. Lawrence Hill Books, Chicago.
50 CCA (1991) *Grenada: Country Environmental Profile*. Caribbean Conservation Assoc., Barbados.
51 *Carriacou Calaloo* (1999) Caribbean Voyage Series, The 1962 Field Recordings, Alan Lomax Collection. Rounder Records CD 1722.
52 Charlton, A (1955) *The Postal History and Postage Stamps of Grenada*. Studies in Philately 1, New Series, PL Pemberton & Sons, London.
53 Christine, B (1988) 'Born to Ride: A Trip to Grenada Changed All That for Jockey Karl Korte'. *Los Angeles Times*, 28 April.
54 Clement, PC (1999) *Petite Martinique: Traditions and Social Change*. Clement, New York.
55 Clyde, DF (1985) *Health in Grenada: A Social and Historical Account*. Vade-Mecum Press, London.
56 Clyne, RH (1974) *Against the Currents*. Port-of-Spain, Trinidad and Tobago.
57 Coard, FM (1970) *Bitter Sweet and Spice: These Things I Remember*. Arthur H Stockwell, London.
58 Coard, P (1988) *US War on One Woman: My Conditions of Imprisonment in Grenada*. Karia Press, London.
59 Cody, A (1990) 'Faces and Figures on Grenada: Their Historical and Cultural Relations'. In *Rock Art Papers*, ed. K Hedges, San Diego Museum of Man, San Diego, CA.
60 Cody, A (1991) 'Pre-historic Patterns of Exchange in the Lesser Antilles: Materials, Models and Preliminary Observations'. Master's Thesis, San Diego State Univ.
61 Coke, T (1808) *A History of the West Indies, Containing the Natural, Civil, and Ecclesiastical History of Each Island: With an Account of the Mission*. Frank Cass and Co, London, 1971.
62 Cole, H (1967) *Christophe, King of Haiti*. Viking Press, New York.
63 Collins, MA (1985) *Because the Dawn Breaks: Poems Dedicated to the Grenadian People*. Karia Press, London.
64 Collins, MA (1987) *Angel*. The Women's Press, London.
65 Collins, MA (1990) *Rain Darling: Stories*. The Women's Press, London.
66 Collins, MA (1992) *Rotten Pomerack*. Virago Press, London.
67 Collins, MA (1995) *The Colour of Forgetting*. Virago, London.
68 Collins MA (2003) *Lady in a Boat: Poems*. Peepal Tree, London.
69 Comisiong, LM (1947) *Whither Grenada*. The Author, London.
70 Comisiong, LM (1985) *Poems of Life*. Earth Printing, Barrie, Ontario.
71 Conference on the Implications of Independence for Grenada (1974) *Independence for Grenada: Myth or Reality?* Institute of International Relations, St. Augustine, Trinidad.
72 Constitution Review Commission (1985) *Report on the Grenada Constitution Review Commission Presented to His Excellency the Governor-General of Grenada,*

November 1985. Constitution Review Commission, St. George, Barbados.

73 Corke, D (1992) 'The Status and Conservation Needs of the Terrestrial Herptofauna of the Windward Islands (West Indies)'. *Biological Conservation* 62: 47-58.

74 Cosper, D (1997) 'When Marines Land With no Welcome Mat'. *Christian Science Monitor*, 25 June.

75 Cotman, JW (1993) *The Gorrion Tree: Cuba and the Grenada Revolution*. Peter Lang, New York.

76 Cox, EL (1982a) 'Fédon's Rebellion 1795-96: Causes and Consequences'. *Journal of Negro History* 67, 1: 7-19.

77 Cox, EL (1982b) 'The French Revolution and Blacks in Grenada and St. Kitts, 1790-1800'. *Umoja: A Scholarly Journal of Black Studies* 6, 1: 9-20.

78 Cox, EL (1984) *The Free Coloreds in the Slave Societies of St. Kitts and Grenada, 1763-1833*. Univ. of Tennessee, Knoxville.

79 Cox, EL (1999) 'From Slavery to Freedom: Emancipation and Apprenticeship in Grenada and St. Vincent, 1834-38'. In *Crossing Boundaries: Comparative History of Black People in Diaspora*, ed. D Hine & J McLeod, Indiana Univ. Press, Bloomingdale.

80 Cox, EL (2002a) 'The Grenada Boys' Secondary School and the Debate over Secondary Education in Grenada'. Grenada Country Conference, UWI, http://www.uwichill.edu.bb/bnccde/grenada/conference/papers/cox.html

81 Cox, EL (2002b) '"Race Men": The Pan African Struggles of WG Donovan and TA Marryshow for Political Change in Grenada, 1884-1925,' *Journal of Caribbean History* 36, 1: 69-99.

81b Cox, EL 'Slave Emancipation Celebrations in Grenada, 1888-1938,' *Everybody's Magazine* 29, 5: 32-33, 35-37, 44; 6: 22-23, 26-28.

82 Crain, EE (1994) *Historic Architecture in the Caribbean Islands*. Univ. Press of Florida, Gainesville.

83 Crouse, NM (1977) *French Pioneers in the West Indies, 1624-1664*. Octagon Books, New York.

84 Curtin, PD (1969) *The Atlantic Slave Trade: A Census*. Univ. of Wisconsin Press, Madison.

85 David, C (1985) *Folklore of Carriacou*. Coles Printery, St. Michael, Barbados.

86 De Grauwe, A (1991) 'Education and Political Change: The Case of Grenada, 1979-89'. *Comparative Education* 27, 3: 335-356.

87 DeRiggs, C (1998) *Who Remembers: An Anthology*. Kreol Publications, St. George's, Grenada.

88 Devas, R (1926) *Up Hill and Down Dale in Grenada*. Sands, London.

89 Devas, R (1932) *Conception Island, Or the Troubled Story of the Catholic Church in Grenada, BWI*. Sands, London.

90 Devas, R (1943) *Birds of Grenada, St. Vincent and the Grenadines*. Carenage Press, St. George's, Grenada.

91 Devas, R (1974) *The History of the Island of Grenada, 1650-1796*. Carenage Press, St. George's, Grenada.

92 Douglas, C (2005) *The Battle for Grenada's Black Gold*. Maryzoon Press, Grenada.

93 Doyle, C (2005) *Sailors' Guide to the Windward Islands*. Cruising Guide Publications, Florida.

94 Duffus Commission (1975) *Report of the Duffus Commission of Inquiry into the Breakdown of Law and Order, and Police Brutality in Grenada*. Torchlight Publishing Co., St. George's, Grenada.

95 Du Tertre, J-B (1667-71) *Histoire générale des Antilles habitées par les François*. 6 vols, Éditions des Horizons Caraïbes, Fort-de-France, Martinique, 1973.

96 Dyer, HT & Warr, AD (1968) *Report of a Case Study of Sauteurs, Grenada*. UN Physical Planning Office, Bridgetown, Barbados.

97 Emmanuel, P (1976) 'The Grenada General Elections, 1976'. *Bulletin of Eastern Caribbean Affairs* 2, 11: 1-3.

98 Emmanuel, P (1978) *Crown Colony Politics in Grenada, 1917-1951*. Occasional Papers 7, Institute of Social and Economic Research (EC), UWI, Cave Hill, Barbados.

99 Emmanuel, P (1979) *General Elections in the Eastern Caribbean: A Handbook*. Occasional Papers 11, Institute of Social and Economic Research (EC), UWI, Cave Hill, Barbados.

100 Emmanuel, P, Brathwaite, F & Barriteau E (1986) *Political Change and Public Opinion in Grenada, 1979-84*. Occasional Papers 19, Institute of Social and Economic Research (EC), UWI, Cave Hill, Barbados.

101 EPICA Task Force (1982) *Grenada: The Peaceful Revolution*. Ecumenical Program for Interamerican Communication and Action (EPICA) Task Force, Washington, DC.

102 Epple, G (1977) 'Technological Change in a Grenada, W.I. Fishery, 1950-70.' In *Those Who Live by the Sea: A Study in Maritime Anthropology. American Ethnological Society Monograph no. 62*, ed. ME Smith, West Publishing Co., St. Paul.

103 Euwema, JA (1994) 'The Decline of Sugar Production and the Rise of Cocoa Production in Grenada, 1870-1917: The Changing Fortunes of a Cocoa Peasantry'. Master's Thesis, Virginia Polytechnic Institute and State Univ.

104 Evans, P (1990) *Birds of the Eastern Caribbean.* Macmillan, London.
105 Everard, COR, Murray, D & Gilbert, PK (1972) 'Rabies in Grenada'. *Transactions of the Royal Society of Tropical Medicine and Hygiene* 66, 6: 878-888.
106 Eyre, LA (1989) 'The Changing Caribbean: National Park Development in Grenada'. *Caribbean Geography* 2, 4: 268-79.
107 Fayer, JM & McMurray, JF (1994) 'Shakespcare in Carriacou'. *Caribbean Studies* 27, 3/4: 242-254.
108 Fayer, JM & McMurray, JF (1999) 'The Carriacou Mas' as "Syncretic Artifact"'. *Journal of American Folklore* 112, 443: 58-73.
109 Fenger, FA (1917) 'Black Mardi Gras,' *Harper's Magazine* 134, 803: 723-731.
110 Fenger, FA (1958) *Alone in the Caribbean: Being the Yarn of a Cruise in the Lesser Antilles in the Sailing Canoe 'Yakaboo'.* Wellington Books, Belmont, MA.
111 Ferguson, J (1990) *Grenada: Revolution in Reverse.* London: Latin America Bureau.
112 Fineman, M (2000) 'Grenada's Bank on the Brink'. *Los Angeles Times*, 20 September.
113 Fletcher, LP (1972) 'The Decline of Friendly Societies in Grenada: Some Economic Aspects'. *Caribbean Studies* 12, 2: 99-111.
114 Flowers, HL (1988) *A Classification of the Folktale of the West Indies by Types and Motifs.* Arno Press, New York.
115 Francis, C (1988) 'Kick 'Em Jenny Submarine Volcano'. *Caribbean News*, 14.
116 Franklyn, OD (1992) *Morne Sauteurs (Leapers' Hill): Encounter Between Two Worlds in Grenada, 1650-54.* Talented House Publishers, Guyana.
117 Franklyn, OD (1999) 1999. *Bridging the Two Grenadas: Gairy's and Bishop's.* Talented House Publishers, St. George's, Grenada.
118 Friends of Jamaica (1987) *The Side You Haven't Heard: Maurice Bishop Murder Trial—Testimony by the Defendants and Analysis by the NJM and Other Grenadians.* 2 vols, Friends of Jamaica, New York.
119 Friends of Jamaica (1989) *The Frame-up of Cecil Prime: Five Years of Crimes against a Grenadian Patriot.* Grass Roots, New York.
120 Genoways, HH, Phillips, CJ & Baker, RJ (1998) 'Bats of the Antillean Island of Grenada: A New Zoogeographic Perspective'. *Occasional Papers, Museum of Texas Tech University*, 117.
121 Gentle, E (1999) *Before the Sunset: A Memoir of Grenada.* Shoreline, Ste-Anne-de-Bellevue, Quebec.
122 Germano, JM, Sander, JM, Henderson, RW & Powell, R (2003) 'Herpetofaunal Communities in Grenada: A Comparison of Altered Sites, with an Annotated Checklist of Grenadian Amphibians and Reptiles'. *Caribbean Journal of Science* 39, 1: 68-76.
123 Glean, CA (1981) 'Reaching Beyond the Grasp: A Revolutionary Approach to Education'. *Bulletin of Eastern Caribbean Affairs* 7, 1: 5-11.
124 Glenn, ME (1996) 'Population Density of *Cercopithecus Mona* on the Caribbean Island of Grenada'. *Folia Primatol* 69: 167-171.
125 Glenn, ME (1997) 'Group Size and Group Composition of the Mona Monkey (*Cercopithecus mona*) on the Island of Grenada, West Indies'. *American Journal of Primatology* 43: 167-173.
126 Gonzalez, JA (1994) '"A Strange Discordant Mass of Heterogeneous Animals": The Role of Ethnic Divisions in British Grenada, 1763-1779'. Thesis, Department of History, Harvard Univ.
127 Gosner, P (1982) *Caribbean Georgian: The Great and Small Houses of the Caribbean.* Three Continents Press, Washington, DC.
128 Government of Grenada (1999) *Grenada Silver Jubilee Handbook, 1974-99.* Government of Grenada, St. George's, Grenada.
129 Gravette, A (2000) *Architectural Heritage of the Caribbean: An A-Z of Historic Buildings.* Markus Wiener Publishers, Princeton.
130 Great Britain (1890-1966) *Grenada Reports for the Year.* HM Stationary Office for the Foreign Commonwealth Office, London, serial: annual and biennial reports continued as *Report on Grenada.*
131 Greer, AE (1965) 'A New Subspecies of Clelia Clelia (Serpentes: Colubridae) from the Island of Grenada'. *Breviora: Museum of Comparative Zoology* 223: 1-6.
132 *Grenada: Creole and Yoruba Voices* (2001) Caribbean Voyage Series, The 1962 Field Recordings, Alan Lomax Collection. Rounder Records CD 1728.
133 Grenada Archives. US National Archives, Modern Military Archives Branch, US. Contains 8,000 microfiches (roughly 500,000 pages of documents taken from Grenada by the US military in October 1983).
134 *Grenada, Carriacou, and Petit Martinique: Spice Island of the Caribbean* (1994) Hansib Publishers, London.
135 Grenada Constitutional Conference (1973) *The Grenada Constitutional Conference, 1973.* HM Stationary Office, London.
136 *Grenada Documents: An Overview and Selection* (1984) Ed. M Ledeen & H Romerstein. US Government Printing Office, Washington, DC.
137 *Grenada: Economic Report* (1985). World Bank, Washington, DC.

138 *The Grenada Handbook and Directory 1946* (1946) Compiled by E Gittens Knight, The Advocate Co., Bridgetown, Barbados.

139 *The Grenada Handbook, Directory and Almanac 1896* (1897) Compiled by E Drayton, Colonial Secretary, Sampson, Low, Marston, London. Annual published by the Colonial Office between 1897 and 1927.

140 Grenada National Parks & Wildlife Unit (1988) *Plan and Policy for a System of National Parks and Protected Areas in Grenada and Carriacou.* Department of Regional Development, OAS, Washington, DC.

141 *Grenada: The World Against the Crime* (1983) Editorial de Ciencias Sociales, Havana.

142 Groome, JR (1964) 'Sedan-Chair Porches: A Detail of Georgian Architecture in St. George's'. *Caribbean Quarterly* 10, 3: 31-33.

143 Groome, JR (1970) *A Natural History of the Island of Grenada, W. I.* Caribbean Printers, Trinidad.

144 Hall, D (1961) 'Incalculability as a Feature of Sugar Production During the 18th Century'. *Social and Economic Studies* 10, 3: 340-352.

145 Hamilton, E (1995) *Rums of the Eastern Caribbean.* Tafia Publishing, Puerto Rico.

146 Harding, S (1984) *Air War Grenada.* Pictorial Histories, Missoula, Montana.

146b Hawthorne, WD, D Jules & G Marcelle (2004) *Caribbean Spice Island Plants. Trees, Shrubs and Climbers of Grenada, Carriacou and Petit Martinique: A Picture Gallery with Notes on Identification, Historical and Other Trivia.* Oxford Forestry Institute, Oxford

147 Heine, J ed. (1990) *A Revolution Aborted: The Lessons of Grenada.* Univ. of Pittsburgh Press, Pittsburgh.

148 Henderson, R (1988) 'The Kaleidoscopic Tree Boa: *Corallus Enydirs* in the West Indies'. *LORE Magazine* 38, 4: 25-30.

149 Henige, DP (1970) *Political Governors from the 15th-Century to the Present: A Comprehensive List.* Univ. of Wisconsin Press, Madison.

150 Hickling-Hudson, A (1989) 'Education in the Grenada Revolution, 1979-83'. *Compare* 19, 2: 95-114.

151 Higman, BW (1984) *Slave Populations of the British Caribbean, 1807-34.* Johns Hopkins Univ. Press, Baltimore.

152 Hill, DR (1974) 'More on Truth, Fact, and Tradition in Carriacou'. *Caribbean Quarterly* 20, 1: 45-59.

153 Hill, DR (1977) 'The Impact of Migration on the Metropolitan and Folk Society of Carriacou, Grenada'. *Anthropological Papers of the American Museum of Natural History* 54, 2.

154 Hill, DR (2002) 'From Coromantese to Cromanti: A Folkloric Account of the Spread of Ghanaian Culture to Carriacou, Grenada'. *African Journals OnLine Humanities Review Journal* 2, 1: 1-8.

154b Hill, DR (2005) 'A Carriacouan View of the African Diaspora: "African" Themes in the Paintings of Canute Caliste'. *Calabash: A Journal of Caribbean Arts and Letters 3,* 2: 100-115.

155 Holdren, AC (1998) 'Raiders and Traders: Caraibe Social and Political Networks at the Time of European Contact and Colonization in the Eastern Caribbean (Social Networks)'. Ph.D. Dissertation, Univ. of California, Los Angeles.

156 Honychurch, P (1980) *Caribbean Wild Plants and Their Uses.* Macmillan Publishers, London.

157 Hosten, CD (1974) *An Appraisal of the Prison System in Grenada.* UWI, Cave Hill, Barbados.

158 Hough, SJ & Penelope, RO (1994) *The Beinecke Lesser Antilles Collection at Hamilton College: A Catalogue of Books, Manuscripts, Prints, Maps, and Drawings, 1521-1860.* Univ. Press of Florida, Gainesville.

159 *House of Commons Sessional Papers of the 18th Century* (1975) Minutes of Evidence on the Slave Trade, 1790, Part 1, ed. S Lambert, Scholarly Resources Inc, Wilmington.

160 Howard, RA (1974-89) *Flora of the Lesser Antilles: Leeward and Windward Islands.* 6 vols, Arnold Arboretum of Harvard Univ, Cambridge, Mass.

161 Huber, RM Jr & Meganck, R (1990) 'The Management Challenge of Grand Anse Beach Erosion, Grenada, West Indies'. *Ocean and Coastal Management*, 13, 2: 99-126.

162 Huckerby, T (1921) 'Petroglyphs of Grenada and a Recently Discovered Petroglyph in St. Vincent'. *Indian Notes and Monographs* 1, 3: 143-164.

163 Hudson, BJ (1983) 'The Changing Caribbean: Grenada's New International Airport'. *Caribbean Geography* 1, 1: 51-57.

164 Hughes, A (1966) 'Non-Standard English of Grenada'. *Caribbean Quarterly* 12, 4: 47-57.

165 Hughes, A (1979) 'Reports by Alister Hughes'. *Caribbean Monthly Bulletin* 13, 4: 1-58.

166 Hughes, A (1988) 'Grog: A Relic of the Past; Standard for the Future; and the Controversy Which May Never be Settled'. *The Greeting Tourist Guide* 1, 2: 12-18.

167 Hughes, A (1990) 'How the Steelband was Born'. *The Greeting Tourist Guide* 3, 1: 26-30.

168 Hughes, Alister (1993) 'The Saga of the Bianca C'. *The Greeting Tourist Guide* 6, 2: 20-24.

169 Hughes, A (1994) 'Grenada's Saga of the Horseless Carriage'. *The Greeting Tourist Guide* 7, 1: 16-20.

170 Hughes, A, Mitchell, A, Phillip, T & Whyte, B (n.d.) *The Streets of St. George's; Names of Places and Their Historical Development; History of Selected Business Places; Oral Research on Carriacou's Cultural Heritage.* OAS Multinational Project on Preservation and Use of the Cultural Heritage, St. George's, Grenada.

171 *In the Spirit of Butler: Trade Unionism in Free Grenada* (1982) Fédon Publishers, St. George's, Grenada.

172 International Monetary Fund (1997) *Grenada: Recent Economic Developments.* IMF Staff Country Report No. 97/117, International Monetary Fund, Washington, DC.

173 International Monetary Fund (2005) *Grenada: 2005 Article IV Consultation, Staff Report and Public Information Notice on the Executive Board Discussion.* Country Report no. 05/290. Retrieved 10 November 2005 from http://www.imf.org/external/country/grd/index.htm.

174 Jacobs, C (2002) 'The Fédons of Grenada, 1763-1814'. Grenada Country Conference, UWI, http://www.uwichill.edu.bb/bnccde/grenada/conference/papers/jacobsc.html

175 Jacobs, WR ed. (1976) *Butler Versus the King: Riots and Sedition in 1937.* Key Caribbean Publishers, Port-of-Spain, Trinidad.

176 Jacobs, WR & Jacobs, I (1979) *Grenada: The Route to Revolution.* Casa de las Américas, Havana.

177 Jessamy, M (1998) *Forts and Coastal Batteries of Grenada.* The Author, St. George's, Grenada.

178 Jessie, C (1967) 'Sold for a Song'. *Caribbean Quarterly* 13, 4: 44-52.

179 Julien, CR (1991) *Civic Handbook on Grenada.* Civic Awareness Organisation, St. George's, Grenada.

180 Jung, P (1971) 'Fossil Mollusks from Carriacou, WI'. *Bulletin of American Paleontology* 61, 269.

181 Keens-Douglas, P (1975) *When Moon Shine.* Keensdee Production, Trinidad.

182 Keens-Douglas, P (1976) *Tim Tim.* Keensdee Production, Trinidad.

183 Keens-Douglas, P (1979) *Tell Me Again.* Keensdee Production, Trinidad.

184 Keens-Douglas, R (1992) *The Nutmeg Princess.* Annick Press, Toronto.

185 Keens-Douglas, R (1994) *La Diablesse and the Baby.* Annick Press, Toronto.

186 Keens-Douglas, R (1995) *Freedom Child of the Sea.* Annick Press, Toronto.

187 Keens-Douglas, R (1998) *The Miss Meow Pageant.* Annick Press, Toronto.

188 Kephart, RF (1986a) 'Bilingual Aspects of Language in a Creole Community'. In *Bilingualism: Social Issues and Policy Implications,* ed. AW Miracle, Jr., Univ. of Georgia, Athens, Georgia.

189 Kephart, RF (1986b) 'Verbal Categories in Carriacou Creole English'. *The SECOL Review* 10, 2: 116-130.

190 Kephart, RF (1991) 'Creole French in Carriacou, Grenada: Texts and Commentary'. *The Florida Journal of Anthropology* 16, 7: 81-89.

191 Kephart, RF (1992) 'Ecology of Language in Carriacou'. *SECOLAS Annals* (Journal of the Southeastern Council on Latin American Studies) 23: 110-124.

192 Kephart, RF (2000) *Broken English: The Creole Language of Carriacou.* Studies in Ethnolinguistics, vol. 6, Peter Lang, New York.

193 Kingsbury, RC (1960a) 'Carriacou: An Old World in the New'. *Journal of Geography* 59, 9: 399-409.

194 Kingsbury, RC (1960b) *Commercial Geography of Grenada.* Indiana Univ. Press, Bloomington.

195 Kingsbury, RC (1960c) *Commercial Geography of the Grenadines.* Indiana Univ. Press, Bloomington.

196 Koplan, JP (1983) 'Slave Mortality in 19th-Century Grenada'. *Social Science History* 7, 3: 311-320.

197 Labat, J-B (1742) *Voyages aux Isles de l'Amérique, 1693-1705.* 2 vols. Le Grad, Paris.

198 La Duke, B (1984) 'Women, Art, and Culture in the New Grenada'. *Latin American Perspectives* 11, 3: 37-52.

199 Latron, A (1929) 'Les mésaventures d'un gentilhomme colonial'. *Revue Historique des Antilles,* 3: 1-14.

200 Levy, S (2005) 'Primate Research: Die Hard', *Nature* 434: 268-269.

201 Lewis, DE (1984) *Reform and Revolution in Grenada, 1950-81.* Casa de las Américas, Havana.

202 Lewis, GK (1986) *Roots of Revolution: Gairy and Gairyism in Grenada.* Working Paper No. 24. Universidad Interamericana de Puerto Rico, CISCLA, Puerto Rico.

203 Lewis, GK (1987) *Grenada: The Jewel Despoiled.* Johns Hopkins Univ. Press, Baltimore.

204 Lewis, T (1990) *Caribbean Folk Legends.* Africa World Press, Trenton, New Jersey.

205 Lomax, A (1998) *Caribbean Voyage: Brown Girl in a Ring.* Rounders, Cambridge, MA, compact disk.

206 Lomax, A, Elder, JD & Lomax Hawes, B (1997) *Brown Girl in a Ring: An Anthology of Song Games from the Eastern Caribbean.* Pantheon Books, New York.

207 Macdonald, AC (1978) 'The Big Drum Dance of Carriacou'. *Internamericana* 8, 4: 70-76.

208 Macdonald, J (1973a) 'Cursing and Context in a Grenadian Fishing Community'. *Anthropologica* 15: 89-128.
209 Macdonald, J (1973b) 'Inlaw Terms and Affinal Relations in a Grenadian Fishing Community'. *Caribbean Studies* 12, 4: 44-55.
210 Mahabir, C (1993) 'Heavy Manners and Making Freedom under the People's Revolutionary Government in Grenada, 1979-83'. *International Journal of the Sociology of Law* 21, 3: 219-243.
211 Mahabir, N (1987) 'East Indians in Grenada: A Study in Absorption'. In *Indians in the Caribbean*, ed. I J Bahadur Singh. Sterling, New Delhi.
212 Mains, S (2002) 'The Visual Arts in Grenada: A Sustainable Resource'. Grenada Country Conference, UWI, http://www.uwichill.edu.bb/bnccde/grenada/conference/papers/mains.html
213 Mark, MZ (1978) *The Struggle to Construct and Disseminate a Philosophy of Life: An Autobiography*. Vantage Press, New York.
214 Marryshow, AA (1998) 'Indelible on Our Minds' *The Grenadian Voice*. Part I: 1 August, and Part II: 17 August.
215 Marryshow, TA (1973) *Cycles of Civilization*. Afro-American Institute, New York.
216 Marshall, B (1982) 'Social Stratification and the Free Coloured in the Slave Society of the British West Indies'. *Social and Economic Studies* 31, 1: 1-39.
217 Marshall, WK (1965) 'Métayage in the Sugar Industry of the British Windward Islands, 1838-65'. *Jamaica Historical Review* 5, 1: 28-55.
218 Marshall, WK (1971) 'The Termination of the Apprenticeship in Barbados and the Windward Islands: An Essay in Colonial Administration and Policies'. *Journal of Caribbean History* 2: 1-45.
219 Marshall, WK (1985) 'Apprentice and Labour Relations in Four Windward Islands'. In *Abolition and its Aftermath: The Historical Context, 1790-1916*, ed. D Richardson. Frank Cass, London.
220 Marshall, WK (1993) 'Provision Ground and Plantation Labour in Four Windward Islands: Competition for Resources during Slavery'. In *Cultivation and Culture: Labor and the Shaping of Slave Life in the Americas*, eds. I Berlin & PD Morgan, University Press of Virginia, Charlottesville.
221 Martin, JA (1999) 'L'Isle de la Grenade: French Settlement and Development, 1649-1762'. Master's Thesis, Dept. of History, Clemson Univ.
222 Massing, M (1984) 'Grenada Before and After'. *The Atlantic Monthly* 253, 2: 76-87.
223 Mayers, JM (1974) *The Nutmeg Industry of Grenada*. Working Paper 3. UWI, Mona, Jamaica.
224 Maynard, EL (1996) 'The Translocation of a West African Banking System: The Yoruba Esusu Rotating Credit Association in the Anglophone Caribbean'. *Dialectical Anthropology* 21, 1: 99-107.
225 McDaniel, L (1985) 'The Stone Feast and Big Drum of Carriacou'. *The Black Perspective in Music* 13, 2: 179-194.
226 McDaniel, L (1990) 'The Philips: A "Free Mulatto" Family of Grenada'. *Journal of Caribbean History* 24, 2: 178-194.
227 McDaniel, L (1992) 'The Concept of Nation in the Big Drum Dance of Carriacou, Grenada'. In *Musical Repercussions of 1492*, ed. C Robertson, Smithsonian, Washington, DC.
228 McDaniel, L (1998) *The Big Drum Ritual of Carriacou: Praisesong in Memory of Flight*. Univ. of Florida Press, Gainesville.
229 Mclean, PE (1986) 'Calypso and Revolution in Grenada'. *Popular Music and Society* 10, 4: 87-99.
230 McQuilkin, F & Panchoo, L (1994) *Grenada's Calypso: The Growth of an Art Form*. Print-Rite, Trinidad.
231 Mettas, J (1978) *Répertoire des expéditions négrières françaises au XVIIIe siècle*. 2 vols, ed. S Daget, Société Française d'Histoire d'Outre-Mer, Paris.
232 Middleton, N (1999) 'Shades of Dunkirk: The Story of the Sinking of the Bianca C'. *SportDiver* January: 36-40.
233 Midgett, D (1983) *Eastern Caribbean Elections, 1950-82: Antigua, Dominica, Grenada, St. Kitts-Nevis, St. Lucia, and St. Vincent*. Univ. of Iowa, Iowa City.
234 Miller, R (1998) 'String Band Music and Quadrille Dancing in Carriacou, Grenada'. *CBMB Digest* 11, 2: 11-12.
235 Milstead, H (1940) 'Cocoa Industry of Grenada'. *Economic Geography* 16, 2: 195-203.
236 Mischel, F (1959) 'Faith Healing and Medical Practice in the Southern Caribbean'. *Southeastern Journal of Anthropology* 15, 1: 407-417.
237 Morgan, K (2003) 'James Rogers and the Bristol Slave Trade', *Historical Research* 76, 192: 189-216.
238 Morand, P (1976) *Monsieur Dumoulin a l'Isle de la Grenade: Description Vraie et Pittoresque d'un Voyage... Entre les Annees 1773 et 1782*. Paudex, Éditions Maritimes et d'Outre-Mer, Switzerland.
239 Moreau, J-P (1992) *Les Petites Antilles de Christophe Colomb à Richelieu, 1493-1635*. Éditions Karthala, Paris.
240 Nadin, JC (1965) 'The Old Records of Grenada'. In *Report of the Caribbean Archives Conference*. UWI,

Mona, Jamaica. First published in *Revue française d'histoire d'Outre-Mer* 49 (1962): 117-140.

241 Nellis, DW (1997) *Poisonous Plants and Animals of Florida and the Caribbean*. Pineapple Press, Sarasota, Florida.

242 Naipaul, VS (1984) 'An Island Betrayed'. *Harper's* 268, 1606: 61-72.

243 Norguera, PA (1997) *The Imperatives of Power: Political Change and the Social Basis of Regime Support in Grenada From 1951-1991*. American Univ. Studies, Regional Studies, vol. 15. Peter Lang, New York.

244 OECS Secretariat (2004) *Grenada: Macro-Socio-Economic Assessment of the Damages Caused by Hurricane Ivan, September 7, 2004*. Retrieved 10 November 2005 from http://www.oecs.org/Documents/Grenada%20Report/GRENADAREPORT.pdf

245 OECS Secretariat (2005) *Grenada: Macro-Socio-Economic Assessment of the Damages Caused by Hurricane Emily, July 14, 2005*. Retrieved 10 November 2005 from http://www.oecs.org/Documents/Grenada%20Report/GrenadaAssessment-Emily.pdf

246 O'Neale, E (1998) *De Red Petticoat: A Selection of Caribbean Folklore*. The Author, St. George's, Grenada.

247 Oakes, E (1988) 'Grenada Under Occupation: US Economic Policy, 1983-87'. *Rethinking MARXISM* 1, 3: 131-157.

248 Oliver, VL ed. (1927) *The Monumental Inscriptions of the British West Indies*. F. G. Longman, Friary Press, Dorchester.

249 Parker, JA (1959) *A Church in the Sun: The Story of the Rise of Methodism in the Island of Grenada, West Indies*. Cargate, London.

250 Patterson, M (1994) *So Far So Mad: Four Fictional Stories*. Tri-Story, St. George's, Grenada.

251 Patterson, M (1991) *The Future of the Past*. Tri-story, St. George's, Grenada.

252 Patterson, M (1992) *Big Sky Little Bullet: A Docu-novel*. Tri-story, St. George's, Grenada.

253 Payne, A, Sutton, P & Thorndike, T (1984) *Grenada: Revolution and Invasion*. St. Martin's Press, New York.

254 Payne, DW (1999) *The 1999 Grenada Elections: Post-Election Report*. Western Hemisphere Election Study series, vol 17, CSIS Americas Program, Washington, DC.

255 Payne, N (1990) 'Grenada Mas, 1928-88'. *Caribbean Quarterly* 36, 3-4: 44-63.

256 *Personalities Caribbean: The International Guide to Who's Who in the West Indies, Bahamas, Bermuda* (1952-) The Commonwealth Caribbean Publishing Company, Port-of-Spain, Trinidad.

257 Peters, C & Perry, D (1994) *Caribbean Social Studies: Our Country—Grenada*. Macmillan, London.

258 Platt, O (2003) *One Big Fib: The Incredible Story of the Fraudulent First International Bank of Grenada*. iUniverse, Inc., New York.

259 Poland, BD, Martin Taylor, S & Hayes, MV (1990) 'The Ecology of Health Care Utilization in Grenada, W. I.'. *Social Science Medicine* 30, 1: 13-24.

260 Polk, P (1993) 'African Religion and Christianity in Grenada'. *Caribbean Quarterly* 39, 3/4: 73-81.

261 Pollak-Eltz, A (1993) 'The Shango Cult and Other African Rituals in Trinidad, Grenada, and Carriacou and Other Possible Influences on the Spiritual Baptist Faith'. *Caribbean Quarterly* 39, 3/4: 12-26.

262 Pool, GR (1995) 'Artisanal Fisheries in Grenada: Community Fisheries and Development Policy'. *LABOUR, Capital and Society* 28, 1: 8-43.

263 Pool, GR (1989) 'Shifts in Grenadian Migration'. *International Migration Review* 23, 2: 238-267.

264 Potkay, A & Burr, S eds. (1995) *Black Atlantic Writers of the 18th Century: Living the New Exodus in England and the Americas*. St. Martin's Press, New York.

265 *The Presbyterian Church in Trinidad and Grenada, History of the San Juan/Santa Cruz Pastoral Charge: National Centenary Celebration, 1868-1968* (1969) Presbyterian Church, Trinidad.

266 Procope, B (1955) 'Launching a Schooner in Carriacou'. *Caribbean Quarterly* 4, 2: 122-131.

267 Pryor, FL (1986) *Revolutionary Grenada: A Study in Political Economy*. Praeger, New York.

268 Public Record Office (1963) *List of Colonial Office Records Preserved in the Public Records Office*. Lists and Indexes no. 36. Kraus Reprint Corporation, New York. An online catalogue is available at the National Archives website http://www.nationalarchives.gov.uk/.

269 Purseglove, JW (1972) *Tropical Crops: Monocotyledons*. Longman, London.

270 Purseglove, JW (1974) *Tropical Crops: Dicotyledons*. Wiley, New York.

271 Pyle, DC (1998) *Clean Sweet Wind: Sailing With the Last Boatmakers of the Caribbean*. McGraw Hill, New York.

272 Quintanilla, M (2003) 'The World of Alexander Campbell: An 18th-Century Grenadian Planter', *Albion* 35, 2: 229-256.

273 Ragatz, LJ (1928) *The Fall of the Planter Class in the British Caribbean, 1763-1833: A Study in Social and Economic History*. Octagon Books, New York, 1971.

274 Ragatz, LJ (1929) *Statistics for the Study of British Caribbean History, 1763-1833*. Bryan Edwards Press, London, 1971.

275 Ragatz, LJ (1970) *A Guide For the Study of British Caribbean History, 1763-1834*. Da Capo Press, New York.

276 Reddock, R (1985) 'Popular Movement to "Mass Organization": The National Women's Organization of Grenada (NWO), 1979-83'. In *New Social Movements and the State in Latin America*, ed. D Slater, Centre for Latin American Research and Documentation, Amsterdam.

277 Redhead, W (1965) 'Goose and Gander', in *Caribbean Plays*, vol 2, UWI ESU, St. Augustine, Trinidad.

278 Redhead, W (1966) *Hoist Your Flag*. Extra-Mural Studies, UWI, St. Augustine, Trinidad.

279 Redhead, W (1970) 'Truth, Fact and Tradition in Carriacou'. *Caribbean Quarterly* 16, 3: 61-63.

280 Redhead, W (1978) *Three Comic Sketches: A Collection of One-act Plays*. Extra-Mural Studies, UWI, St. Augustine, Trinidad.

281 Redhead, W (1979) *Canaree and Pot*. Extra-Mural Studies, UWI, St. Augustine, Trinidad.

282 Redhead, W (1985) *A City on the Hill*. Letchworth Press, Barbados.

283 Redhead, W (1992) 'Petite Martinique Ahoy'. *The Greeting Tourist Guide* 5, 1: 58-60.

284 Renault, FP (1920) "L'Odysseé d'un colonial sous l'ancien régime: Philippe-Rose Roume de Saint-Laurent (1776-96)'. *Revue de l'Histoire des Colonies Françaises* 9: 327-348.

285 *Report on the 1995 Grenada Agricultural Census* (1996) Ministry of Agriculture, Planning Unit, St. George's, Grenada.

286 Richardson, BC (1974) 'Labor Migrants From the Island of Carriacou: Workers on the Margins of the Developed World'. *Proceedings of the Association of American Geographers* 6: 149-152.

287 Richardson, BC (1975) 'The Overdevelopment of Carriacou'. *Geographical Review* 65, 3: 390-399.

288 Richardson, BC (1992) 'A "Respectable" Riot: Guy Fawkes Night in St. George's, Grenada 1885'. *Journal of Caribbean History* 27, 1: 21-35.

289 Richardson, D ed. (1966) *Bristol, Africa and the 18th-century Slave Trade to America*. Bristol Record Society, Bristol.

290 Robbins, HH (1908) *Our First Ambassador to China: An Account of the Life of George, Earl of Macartney*. E. P. Dutton, New York.

291 Rodney, P (1998) *The Caribbean State, Health Care and Women: An Analysis of Barbados and Grenada During the 1979-1983 Period*. Africa World Press, Trenton, NJ.

292 Roget, HP (1981) *Archaeology in Grenada: A Report*. Caribbean Conservation Association, St. Michael, Barbados.

293 Rohter, L (1998) 'Stigma of Dr. Do-Little Fades from Grenada University'. *New York Times* 148, 28 October.

294 Romero, A & Hayford, K (2000) 'Past and Present Utilization of Marine Animals in Grenada, WI'. *Journal of Cetacean Research and Management* 2, 3: 223-226.

295 Rosenberg, J & Kosmo, FL (2001) 'Local Participation, International Politics and the Environment: The World Bank and the Grenada Dove'. *Journal of Environmental Management* 62, 2 (July): 283-300.

296 Ross, J, Collins, M, Gebon, R & Hamilton, G (1984) *Callaloo: A Grenadian Anthology*. Young World Books, London.

297 Rottenberg, S (1955) 'Labor Relations in a Small Underdeveloped Economy'. *Caribbean Quarterly* 4: 50-61. First published in *Economic Development and Cultural Change* 1, 14 (1952): 250-260.

298 Sadiq, A (1984) 'Blow by Blow: A Personal Account of the Ravaging of the Revo'. *The Black Scholar* 15, 1: 8-20.

299 Sanchez, ND (1984) 'What was Uncovered in Grenada: The Weapons and Documents'. *Caribbean Review* 12, 4: 20-33.

300 Sandiford, W (2000) *On the Brink of Decline: Bananas in the Windward Islands*. Fedon Books, St. George's, Grenada.

301 Sandrini, D (2003) *High North: A Dream Come Through*. Retrieved from http://kido.optsoftware.com/highnorth/.

302 *Saraca: Funerary Music of Carriacou* (2000) Caribbean Voyage Series, The 1962 Field Recordings, Alan Lomax Collection. Rounder Records CD 1726.

303 Schoenhals, KP (1986) *The Road to Fort Rupert: The Grenadian Revolution's Final Crisis*. Universidad International de Puerto Rico, Puerto Rico.

304 Schoenhals, KP (1990) *Grenada*. World Bibliographical Series, no. 119, CLIO Press, Santa Barbara, CA.

305 Schoenhals, KP & Melanson, RA (1985) *Revolution and Intervention in Grenada*. Westview, Boulder, Colorado.

306 Scoon, P (2003) *Survival for Service: My Experiences as Governor General of Grenada*. Macmillan Caribbean, Oxford.

307 Searle, C (1983) *Grenada: The Struggle Against Destabilization*. Writers and Readers, London.

308 Searle, C (1984) *Words Unchained: Language and Revolution in Grenada*. Zed Books, London.

309 Seymour, S, Daniels, S & Watkins, C (1998) 'Estate and Empire: Sir George Cornewall's Management of Moccass, Herefordshire and La Taste, Grenada, 1771-1819'. *Journal of Historical Geography* 24, 3: 313-351.
310 Sheppard, J (1987) *Marryshow of Grenada: An Introduction*. Letchworth Press, Barbados.
311 Sheridan, RB (1990) 'The Condition of the Slave in the Settlement and Economic Development of the British Windward Islands, 1763-1775'. *Journal of Caribbean History* 24, 2: 121-145.
312 Sheridan, RB (1989) 'Captain Bligh, the Breadfruit, and the Botanic Gardens of Jamaica'. *Journal of Caribbean History* 23, 1: 28-50.
313 Sherlock, P (1983) *West Indian Folktales*. Oxford University Press, Oxford.
314 Showker, K (1989) *Caribbean: Outdoor Traveler's Guide*. Stewart, Tabori & Chang, New York.
315 Sigurdsson, H & Sparks, S (1979) 'An Active Submarine Volcano'. *Natural History* 88, 8: 38-43.
316 Simpson, GE (1975) *Black Religions in the New World*. Columbia Univ. Press, New York.
317 Sinclair, N (2003) *Grenada: Isle of Spice*. Macmillan, London.
318 Singham, AW (1968) *The Hero and the Crowd in a Colonial Polity*. Yale Univ. Press, New Haven.
319 Slade, HG (1984) 'Craigston and Meldrum Estates, Carriacou, 1769-1841'. *Proceedings of the Society of Antiquaries of Scotland* 114: 481-537.
320 Smith, CA (1995) *Socialist Transformation in Peripheral Economies: Lessons from Grenada*. Avebury, Aldershot, UK.
321 Smith, MG (1962) *Kinship and Community in Carriacou*. Yale Univ. Press, New Haven.
322 Smith, MG (1963) *Dark Puritan*. Extra-Mural Dept., UWI, Mona, Jamaica.
323 Smith, MG (1964) *Social Stratification in Grenada*. Univ. of California Press, Berkeley.
324 Smith, MG (1965) *The Plural Society in the British West Indies*. Univ. of California Press, Berkeley.
325 Smith, MG (1974) 'A Note on Truth, Fact, and Tradition'. *Caribbean Quarterly* 17, 3/4: 128-136.
326 Smith, MS & Shepherd, JB (1993) 'Preliminary Investigations of the Tsunami Hazard of Kick'em Jenny Submarine Volcano'. *Natural Hazards* 7, 3: 257-277.
327 Stamps, JA (1990) 'Starter Homes for Young Lizards'. *Natural History*, pp 40-44.
328 Steele, BA (1974) 'Grenada, An Island State, its History and its People'. *Caribbean Quarterly* 20, 1:5-43.
329 Steele, BA (1976) 'East Indian Indenture and the Work of the Presbyterian Church Among the Indians in Grenada'. *Caribbean Quarterly* 22, 1: 28-37.
330 Steele, BA (1995) 'Marryshow House: A Living Legacy'. *Caribbean Quarterly* 41, 3/4: 1-14.
331 Steele, BA (1996) 'Folk Dance in Grenada', *Bulletin of Eastern Caribbean Affairs* 21, 1: 25-45.
332 Steele, BA (2002) 'How Grenada Won World War II'. Grenada Country Conference, UWI, http://www.uwichill.edu.bb/bnccde/grenada/conference/papers/steele.html
333 Steele, BA (2003) *Grenada: A History of its People*. Macmillan Caribbean, Oxford.
334 Steele, BA & St. John, B eds. (1974) *Tim Tim Tales: Children's Stories From Grenada*. Extra Mural Dept., UWI, St. George's.
335 Stoddard, VG (1985) 'Grenada Revisited'. *Américas* 37, 5: 8-15.
336 Sutty, L (1978a) 'A Study of Shells and Shelled Objects from Six Pre-Colombian Sites in the Grenadines of St. Vincent and Grenada'. In *Proceedings of the Seventh International Congress for the Study of Pre-Colombian Cultures in the Lesser Antilles*. Universidad Central de Caracas, Caracas, Venezuela.
337 Sutty, L (1978b). 'Liaison Arawak-Calivigny-Carib Between Grenada and St. Vincent, Lesser Antilles'. In: *Proceedings of the Ninth International Congress for the Study of Pre-Colombian Cultures in the Lesser Antilles*. Santo Domingo, Dominican Republic.
338 Taylor, IA (1993) 'The Rite of Mourning in the Spiritual Baptist Church with Emphasis on the Activity of the Spirit'. *Caribbean Quarterly* 39, 3/4: 27-41.
339 Ternan, JL, Williams, AG & Francis, C (1989) 'Land Capability Classification in Grenada, West Indies'. *Mountain Research and Development* 9, 1: 71-82.
340 Thomson, R (1985) 'Towards Agricultural Self-reliance in Grenada: An Alternative Model'. In *Rural Development in the Caribbean*, ed. PI Gomes. C. Hurst & Co., London.
341 Thomson, R (1987) *Green Gold—Bananas and Dependency in the Eastern Caribbean*. Latin America Bureau, London.
342 Thorndike, T (1974) 'Grenada: Maxi-crisis for a Mini-State'. *The World Today* 30, 100: 436-444.
343 Thorndike, T (1979) 'The Politics of Inadequacy: A Study of the Associated Statehood Negotiations and Constitutional Arrangements for the Eastern Caribbean, 1965-67'. *Social and Economic Studies* 28, 3: 597-617.

344 Thorndike, T (1985) *Grenada: Politics, Economics and Society*. Lynne Rienner Publishers, Boulder, Colorado.

345 Thorstrom, R, Massiah, E & Hall, C (2001) 'Nesting Biology, Distribution, and Population Estimate of the Grenada Hooked-billed Kite, *Chondrohierax uncinatus mirus*'. *Caribbean Journal of Science* 37, 3-4: 278-281.

346 Tindall, HD (1983) *Vegetables in the Tropics*. Macmillan, London.

347 Tobias, PM (1982) 'The Socioeconomic Context of Grenadian Smuggling'. *Journal of Anthropological Research* 38: 383-400.

348 Tobias, PM (1980) 'The Social Context of Grenadian Migration'. *Social and Economic Studies* 29, 1: 40-59.

349 *Tombstone Feast: Funerary Music of Carriacou* (2001) Caribbean Voyage Series, The 1962 Field Recordings, Alan Lomax Collection. Rounder Records CD 1727.

350 Tooley, RV (1970) 'The Printed Maps of Dominica and Grenada'. *Map Collectors' Circle* 7, 62: 7-22.

351 Tremblay, H (1997) *The House That Adna Built: A Family in Grenada*. Portage & Main.

352 Trechmann, CT (1935) 'The Geology and Fossils of Carriacou, West Indies'. *The Geological Magazine* 72, 12: 529-555.

353 Trotman, DA & Friday, KW (1985) *Report on Human Rights in Grenada: A Survey of Political and Civil Rights in Grenada During the Period of 1970-1983*. Bustamante Institute of Public and International Affairs, Jamaica.

354 Tyrrell, Q & Tyrrell, R (1990) *Hummingbirds of the Caribbean*. Crown Publishers, New York.

355 University of the West Indies Seismic Research Unit. *Kick 'em Jenny Submarine Volcano*. Retrieved 10 Nov. 2005 from http://www.uwiseismic.com/KeJ/kejhome.html.

356 Walker, K & DeVooght, J (1989) 'Invasion: A Hospital in Transition Following the 1983 Grenadian Intervention'. *Journal of Psychosocial Nursing and Mental Health Services* 27, 1: 27-30.

357 Walsh, R (1996) 'Untropical Fish: How did the Cold-water Cod Become a Caribbean Staple?' *Natural History* 105, 5: 58-61.

358 Warner-Lewis, M (1991) *Guinea's Other Suns: The African Dynamic in Trinidad Culture*. Majority Press, Dover, Mass.

359 Watts, D (1987) *The West Indies: Patterns of Development, Culture and Environmental Change Since 1492*. Cambridge Univ. Press, Cambridge.

360 Wells, S (1890) *Historical and Descriptive Sketch of the Island of Grenada*. A. W. Gardner, Kingston, Jamaica.

361 Wesche, MB (1961) 'Place Names as a Reflection of Cultural Chance: An Example from the Lesser Antilles'. *Caribbean Studies* 12, 2: 73-98.

362 *West Indies and Caribbean Yearbook* (1929-) Thomas Skinner & Co., London. Annual published until 1979 under various titles.

363 Wilder, AE. *The Grenada Revolution Online*. Retrieved 10 November 2005. from http://www.thegrenadarevolutiononline.com/index.html.

364 Wilkinson, A (1988) *Grenada: A Select Bibliography—A Guide to Material Available in Barbados*. Institute of Social and Economic Research (EC), UWI, Cave Hill, Barbados.

365 Wilson, B (1993) 'An Interview with Merle Collins'. *Callaloo* 16, 1: 94-103.

366 Wilson, EO (2005) 'Early Ant Plagues in the New World', *Nature* 433: 32.

367 Worme, SM (1999) *Spice Island Cricket: The History and Development of Cricket in Grenada, 1830-1999*. Kreol Publications, St. George's, Grenada.

368 Worme, SM (2005) *Ivan the Terrible in Grenada*. The Author, St. George's, Grenada.

369 Zimmerman, JD (1999) *A Short History of Fort George, St. George's, Grenada*. Retrieved 10 November 2005 from www.forts.org/history.htm. Portcullis Ltd.

370 Zwerneman, AL (1986) *In Bloody Terms: The Betrayal of the Church in Marxist Grenada*. Greenlawn, South Bend, Indiana.

Index

A

B

C

D

N

O

P

T

U

V

W

X

Y

Z

Picture Credits

Alvin Clouden pp 160, 171, 183, 218 (r), 155
Art Directors and Tripp pp 47, 86,100(t), 194, 210, 220, 229, 247
Barbara Brown p 71
Jacques Nicholas Bellin pp 85(t), 123
Bibliothèque nationale de France p 152 (7)
Nicolas de Cardona p 100(b)
Centre des archives d'outre-mer, France p 199 (t)
Merle Collins p 144
A 'Colourpicture' Publication p 102
Michael Donelan p 77
Jean-Baptiste DuTertre p 70
Francois Dumolin p 69
Eastern Caribbean Currency Authority p 62
EMPICS p 83
French Crown p 121
Arnold E. Gay (post card) p 96
Ronald Grant p 125
Grenada Government Information Service pp 75, 190, 227
Grenada National Museum pp 30, 67 (t&b), 117, 119 (b), 136 (r), 143 (t), 177, 191, 216, 217 (l), 242, 255, 257
Grenada Postal Service pp 12, 33, 57 (b), 118, 122, 162, 188 (b), 199 (b), 200 (t&b)
Donald Hill pp 21, 34 (r), 79
Hutchison pp 4, 17, 27, 205, 232(r), 235, 240
Thomas Jefferys p 84
Elizabeth Kennedy pp 3, 10, 18, 26, 37, 56 (tl), 63 (r), 98, 109, 136 (b), 142, 143 (b), 170, 182, 195, 208, 223, 252, 256
Jean-Baptiste Labat p 134
Allan Lomax Archives pp 1, 82, 85 (b), 131, 232 (l)
London Daily Express p 91
Lonely Planet pp 8, 16, 65, 96, 127, 135, 172(b), 226, 259
Angus Martin pp 2, 40 (l), 50, 51, 53, 64, 80 (b), 99 (t), 107, 110, 124, 140, 141, 159, 165, 170, 182,197, 203, 230, 231
Liam Martin title page
Mary Evans Picture Library pp 6, 23, 38, 49, 214
National Portrait Gallery pp 97, 148, 193
New Jewel Movement pp 153, 174, 207
Noah's Arkade p 221
Organization of American States pp 42, 172 (t)
O.S.F pp 9, 13, 15, 22, 28, 29, 34(l), 63(l), 80(l), 87, 93, 112(t), 129, 150, 151, 166, 167(b), 178, 233, 244
Nicholas Ponce p89
Popperfoto pp 23, 24, 111, 157, 164, 185, 186, 218(l), 237
Picturesofgrenada.com pp 74, 115, 130, 147, 212, 222
RARE pp 56-7 (t), 103
Carlyle R. Roberts p 75
Science Photo Library pp5, 145
Brian Steele pp 40 (r), 60, 116 (t), 119 (t), 151 (b), 161, 215, 219
Tate Gallery p 14
Tropix pp 44, 46, 48, 73, 99(b), 106, 132, 167(t), 168, 188(t), 201, 211, 217(l), 224, 225, 248, 261
Leslie A Ward p 36

The publishers have made every effort to trace the copyright holders, but if they have inadvertently overlooked any, they will be pleased to make the necessary arrangements at the first opportunity.